# The American Democracy

# The American Democracy

## THOMAS E. PATTERSON

*Professor of Political Science*
*Maxwell School of Citizenship*
*Syracuse University*

McGRAW-HILL PUBLISHING COMPANY

New York    St. Louis    San Francisco    Auckland    Bogotá    Caracas    Hamburg
Lisbon    London    Madrid    Mexico    Milan    Montreal    New Delhi    Oklahoma City
Paris    San Juan    São Paulo    Singapore    Sydney    Tokyo    Toronto

To Ellie, Alex, and Leigh

**THE AMERICAN DEMOCRACY**

2 3 4 5 6 7 8 9 0 DOC DOC   9 4 3 2 1 0

ISBN   0-07-557123-4

This book was set in Palatino by Black Dot, Inc.
The editors were Bertrand W. Lummus, David A. Damstra, and
Cele Gardner; the designer was Joan E. O'Connor;
the production supervisor was Stacey B. Alexander.
R. R. Donnelley & Sons Company was printer and binder.
Cover Photo: *East front of Capitol* (David Fisher/Gamma Liaison)

**Library of Congress Cataloging-in-Publication Data**

Patterson, Thomas E.
The American democracy / Thomas E. Patterson.
        p.        cm.
Includes bibliographical references.
ISBN 0-07-557123-4
1. United States—Politics and government.     I. Title.
    JK274.P358        1990        89-13042
        320.973—dc20

**Part Opener Credits:**

1.  Michael Bryant/Woodfin Camp & Associates
2.  Bob Daemmrich/The Image Works
3.  Michal Heron/Woodfin Camp & Associates
4.  Costa Manos/Magnum
5.  Bohdan Hrynewych/Southern Light
6.  Owen Franken/Stock, Boston
7.  Murray Alcosser/The Image Bank

*Additional permissions appear on page xxii.*

# ABOUT
# THE AUTHOR

Thomas E. Patterson is a professor and past chairman of the department of political science in the Maxwell School of Citizenship at Syracuse University. Raised in a small Minnesota town, he received his Ph.D. from the University of Minnesota in 1971. He began his graduate training four years earlier upon return from Vietnam, where he served as a U.S. Army officer.

Patterson is the author or coauthor of several books and dozens of articles, most of them based on his research on political communication. His most extensive research project culminated in *The Mass Media Election,* which was named an Outstanding Academic Book, 1980-81, by *Choice.* He has lectured at many universities and colleges in the United States and in Europe.

He is married to Ellen Bifano, a pediatrician, and they are raising two young children, Alex and Leigh.

# CONTENTS

THE CONSTITUTIONAL FRAMEWORK

## INDIVIDUAL RIGHTS

## CITIZEN POLITICS

POLITICAL ORGANIZATION

## ELECTED REPRESENTATIVES

## APPOINTED OFFICIALS

## *Part Seven*

### PUBLIC POLICY

# PREFACE

Politics is so alive and immediate that it is hard to imagine why anyone would think it is dull or remote. By the same token, it is also hard to imagine why anyone would think that today's college students, who are otherwise so eager to learn, are unable or unwilling to study politics carefully and systematically. I have taught American government for twenty years and have found that, when politics is expressed in lively and meaningful terms, students invariably take a keen interest in it.

Fortunately, political science has been served through the years by some very good introductory American government texts. These texts have been distinguished, not so much by the raw material they contain, as by their ability to hold the interest of students and help them to integrate the wide array of concepts, facts, and principles that make up the study of American government. My ideal type in some ways is one that I read as an undergraduate, V. O. Key's *Politics, Parties, and Pressure Groups.* Last published in 1964, Professor Key's wonderful book was chock full of ideas, of politics, and of a lucid prose that belied the laborious effort that is required to turn the raw material of American government into a compelling whole.

This book is my version of an introductory text written to inform and motivate today's generation of college students and as such is a fusion of accepted practice and innovation. On the one hand, I have tried my best to respect the way that most instructors approach the introductory course. My text surveys the whole of American national government, beginning with constitutional issues and then moving on to mass politics, governing institutions and officials, and public policy. The text is also conventional in that it uses the several forms of analysis that are common to political science—the philosophical, historical, behavioral, legal, policy-analytic, and institutional. Each form of analysis has its benefits and its place in the study of American government.

On the other hand, the text incorporates some distinguishing features, each of which represents a conscious effort to respond to the instructional needs of those who teach and take the basic course. There are four features that set *The American Democracy* apart:

1.   Although political scientists have developed a deep understanding of American government, this knowledge exists largely as a set of more or less unrelated observations. When presented in this form in a text, fact is piled upon fact and list upon list, which is almost guaranteed to dull student interest and thought. I have tried to follow the cardinal rule of always telling students where they are in the text, why they are there, and where they are going. As part of this effort, several unifying themes appear in the text:

- that American politics from the nation's earliest years has been shaped by a set of governing ideas, which, although subject to dispute in practice, have served as Americans' common bond;
- that the American political system is characterized by an extreme fragmentation of authority that has far-reaching implications for the exercise of power and the making of public policy;
- that the United States has an extraordinary range of interests of all kinds— economic, religious, ethnic, regional, and so on—and that this diversity is fundamental to the nature of political conflict and consensus in America; and
- that Americans tend to draw sharp distinctions between what is political (and therefore to be decided in the public arena) and what is economic (and therefore to be settled through private relations).

These guiding principles are augmented by a listing at the beginning of each chapter of its main points and by an opening example or story in each chapter that illustrates the significance of these points.

My approach permits frequent use of the narrative form of writing, which has been shown by pedagogical research to be a superior method of teaching students a "soft" science such as politics. Each chapter contains plenty of facts, but they are always presented in context. If students soon forget many of the details, as they invariably will, they may at least remember the main points.

2.   This text has twenty-nine shorter chapters rather than the twenty or so longer ones found in other introductory American government texts. The instructional purpose of this innovation is to give each chapter a clearer focus. Rather than a single chapter on political parties, for example, I have written one chapter on U.S. party organizations and another on the American party system. When a text's chapters are few in number—one each on parties, Congress, the Constitution, and so on—they tend to be diffuse. When more chapters are used, they can convey a sharper message and, I would argue, a message that flows more "naturally" from what political scientists have discovered about American politics. My chapter on the party system, for example, looks squarely at two-partyism: why it exists in America and how fully it channels political

competition and choice. These points are stated in the chapter's introduction, developed in the chapter's body, and restated in the conclusion, thus driving home to students their central importance.

I believe that most political science professors will find that a text of shorter chapters is a more flexible teaching tool and provides students a more satisfying way of studying American government. Each chapter of this text can be read in an hour or less, and thus each lecture's reading assignment can reasonably consist of a full chapter. My experience with teaching American government suggests that many students find it unrewarding to be assigned to read just part of a chapter at a time because that approach makes it very difficult for them to see the chapter's argument in its entirety. My text makes it easier for students to see each chapter through from beginning to end in a single reading.

3. This text includes special materials that are designed to encourage students to step back and think about what they have just read, thereby changing a passive form of learning into a more active one. These materials include the following:

- At the end of each of the book's seven parts is a pair of brief original essays. These essays, written by some of America's best political scientists, are intended to direct the student's attention back to a recurring point in the section's chapters. For example, Part Six features one-page essays by Professors Hugh Heclo and Martin Shapiro on the issue: "Is Too Much Public Policy Decided by Nonelected Officials in the Bureaucracy and Judiciary?" The authors of the other original essays are Benjamin R. Barber, George C. Edwards III, Morris Fiorina, Louis Fisher, Richard Flathman, Charles M. Hardin, Stephen D. Krasner, Jane Mansbridge, Bruce Russett, Robert H. Salisbury, Frank Sorauf, and James Sundquist.
- Each chapter has a "How the United States Compares" box that compares the United States with other countries on a subject emphasized in the chapter. American students invariably gain perspective and a deeper understanding of their own politics when they recognize how it resembles and how it differs from politics elsewhere.
- Each chapter contains several "Analyze the Issue" boxes that ask students to relate current issues or personal experiences to material presented in the chapter. These boxes invite students to connect the world outside to the one described in the text—an intellectual exercise that is designed to promote both better scholarship and better citizenship. In addition, throughout the text other boxed discussions profile key historical and contemporary issues.

4. Early in the writing of this text, I concluded that it would be enormously helpful if a way could be found to bring into each chapter the judgment of those political scientists who, like myself, teach the introductory course year in and year out. Any insights that exist for improving the pedogogical value of an introductory text are concentrated among these instructors. This recognition led me to undertake what is, as far as I have been able to determine, the most thorough review process ever undertaken for a new American government text.

We went beyond the normal process of having the draft chapters reviewed by a select number of expert scholars who are recognized experts in the subject matter. After these reviewers had critiqued a chapter, I revised it and we then sent it to as many as ten faculty members at U.S. colleges and universities of all types—public and private, large and small, four-year and two-year. These political scientists, 213 of them in all, have well over a thousand years of combined experience in the teaching of the introductory course. Each of them was asked, in effect, two questions: "How well does this chapter instruct your students in what they need to know about its subject?" and "How can the chapter be changed so that it better serves your students' needs?"

They had a plenty of ideas. For example, after noting that "it is unusual for authors to be interested in the thinking of those of us on the 'frontline' of undergraduate teaching," a professor at a state university suggested three major adjustments in the chapter he had read. I spent the better part of two years rewriting the text in response to such suggestions. My rule of thumb was that if more than one introductory instructor said something was a problem, it likely *was* a problem. I am very thankful for their help.

Since I began work on this book six years ago, I have viewed it as a personal and ongoing commitment to the education of students of American government, who are also about to become active citizens. I hope you will conclude that the text contributes significantly to their development. I invite comments, favorable or otherwise, on the text material. I cannot promise that your ideas will alter the next edition, but I can promise that they will receive my careful attention.

*Thomas E. Patterson*

## ACKNOWLEDGMENTS

A great many people contributed to this book. They include the scholars who gave generously of their professional time and knowledge, the office staff and research assistants who with skill and good humor helped to assemble the many drafts of the manuscript, and the editorial team who guided the book from start to end. I owe a major debt to all those who helped.

Bert Lummus, my editor, deserves a very special thanks. He initiated this book by asking of my interest in writing it, and he stayed with the project throughout its six years. His keen judgment, steady encouragement, and endless patience led, draft by draft, to a book that I am proud to have authored. No editor could have been more helpful, and I am pleased to say that our years of working together produced a friendship as well as a book. Cecilia Gardner also had a major impact on the book; thought by thought and line by line, she spent months sharpening its points and improving its readability. Cele and Bert, like this book, underwent an organizational change in 1988 when the College Division of Random House, of which they were a part, was bought by McGraw-Hill. In addition to Cele and Bert, the following Random House and McGraw-Hill people helped on the project and deserve my thanks: Pat Plunkett, Greg Berge, David Damstra, Joan O'Connor, Safra Nimrod, and Kathy Bendo.

In the typing of the manuscript, I had the able assistance of the political science staff at Syracuse University, where I teach. June Dumas, the office coordinator, spent hundreds of hours at the word processor working on my draft copy. June should have told me at some point to get lost, but she never did and always made sure that my work got quick and close attention. I also wish to thank Judith Jablonski, who was office secretary during most of the period this book was in progress. Like June, Judy spent hundreds of word-processor hours on the manuscript and did so with good grace and great care. For shorter periods, Jacquelyn Meyer and Jennifer Pallone of the political science staff also helped out. Finally, there were a large number of graduate assistants and work-study students who contributed to the manuscript in one way or another at various points in its production. To each and all of them, I extend my thanks.

Lastly, I would like to acknowledge the assistance of the many political scientists who reviewed a portion of the text. Their reviews were thoughtful and constructive. I am deeply grateful for their high standard of professionalism and collegiality. I wish to thank:

John R. Abshire, Tarrant County Junior College
Joseph R. Aicher, Jr., North Carolina Central University
Dennis M. Anderson, Bowling Green State University
Raymond V. Anderson, University of Wisconsin, River Falls
William G. Anderson, Suffolk County Community College
Tom Anton, Brown University
Herrick Arnold, Orange Coast College
David N. Atkinson, University of Missouri, Kansas City
David G. Baker, Hartwick College
Kathleen L. Barber, John Carroll University
Glenn Barkan, Aquinas College
Larry Bartels, University of Rochester
Thomas Barth, University of Wisconsin, Eau Claire
Larry Baum, Ohio State University
Charles S. Bednar, Muhlenberg College
Larry Bennett, DePaul University
Larry Berman, University of California, Davis
Diane Blair, University of Arkansas
Richard Bloss, Chicago State University
John C. Blydenburgh, Clark University
Mary A. Boutilier, Seton Hall University
Gloria J. Braxton, Southern University and A & M College
Jerry Brekke, Northwest Missouri State University
Lynn R. Brink, North Lake College
Roger G. Brown, University of North Carolina, Charlotte
Jere W. Bruner, Oberlin College
Gary Bryner, Brigham Young University
Vincent Buck, California State, Fullerton
Gary J. Buckley, Northern Arizona University
Donald Buzinkai, King's College
Raymond L. Carol, St. John's University
Carol Cassel, University of Alabama
James Cecil, Bemidji State University
Shirley Chapman, East Tennessee University
William L. Chappell, Jr., Columbus College
Ann Charney, Rosary College
Stephen Chen, Lincoln University
Richard Chesteen, University of Tennessee, Martin

Alan Clem, University of South Dakota
Ronald Coan, Canisius College
Robert L. Cord, Northeastern University
Robert J. Courtney, LaSalle University
Jack Crampton, Lewis and Clark College
Mary Paige Cubbison, Miami Dade Community College, South
Everett W. Cunningham, Middle Tennessee State University
David D. Dabelko, Ohio University
Richard J. Dalton, University of Connecticut, Avery Point
Abraham L. Davis, Morehouse College
Paul H. DeForest, Illinois Institute of Technology
Robert DiClerico, West Virginia University
Joel Diemond, Dutchess Community College
John R. Dierst, Eastern Connecticut State University
Robert H. Dixon, Lyndon State College
Lawrence Dodd, University of Colorado
William M. Downer, Thiel College
James W. Dull, University of New Haven
Pat Dunham, Duquesne University
Charles W. Dunn, Clemson University
Gloria S. Durlach, Columbia College
Valerie Earle, Georgetown University
George C. Edwards III, Texas A & M University
Ahmed H. El-Afandi, Winona State University
Larry Elowitz, Georgia College
James Enelow, State University of New York, Stony Brook
Alan S. Engel, Miami University
Joe E. Ericson, Stephen F. Austin State University
Gerald R. Farrington, Fresno City College
Louis Fisher, Congressional Research Service
R. F. Flannery, University of Wisconsin Centers, Sheboygan/Manitowoc
Marvin Folkertsma, Grove City College
Patricia A. Fontaine, Northeast Louisiana University
Richard Foster, Idaho State University
Eugene Fulton, County College of Morris
Anne Freedman, Roosevelt University
Joseph F. Freeman, Lynchburg College

Henry P. French, Jr., State University of New York, Monroe Community College at Rochester
David A. Frolick, North Central College
Arthur L. Galub, Bronx Community College of CUNY
Dan B. German, Appalachian State University
Ernest Giglio, Lycoming College
Terry Gilbreth, Ohio Northern University
Tracey L. Gladstone, University of Wisconsin, River Falls
Robert Golembiewski, University of Georgia
LeRoy Goodwin, Fort Lewis College
Fred Greenstein, Princeton University
Forest Grieves, University of Montana
Gary Griffith, Temple Junior College
Kathryn Griffith, Wichita State University
Joel Grossman, University of Wisconsin
Martin Gruberg, University of Wisconsin, Oshkosh
Mary E. Guy, University of Alabama, Birmingham
William K. Hall, Bradley University
Beth Halteman, Belmont College
Leroy C. Hardy, California State University, Long Beach
Keith Henderson, State University College, Buffalo
Beth Henschen, Loyola University
John Hibbing, University of Nebraska
Arthur C. Hill, Minneapolis Community College
Thomas R. Hills, Black Hills State College
Herbert Hirsch, Virginia Commonwealth University
Richard D. Hirtzel, Western Illinois University
Douglas I. Hodgkin, Bates College
James B. Hogan, Seattle University
Louisa S. Hulett, Knox College
Margaret A. Hunt, University of North Carolina, Greensboro
Jon Hurwitz, University of Pittsburgh
Reverend Emerick J. Hydo, C.M., Niagara University
Malcom Jewell, University of Kentucky
Evan M. Jones, St. Cloud State University
Hugh E. Jones, Shippensburg University
Robert E. Jones, Belmont Abbey College
Thomas A. Kazee, Davidson College
Robert Keele, University of the South
Richard C. Kelley, University of Washington
Henry Kenski, University of Arizona
Elwyn Kernstock, St. Michael's College
Frank Kessler, Missouri Western State College
Hoyt King, Tennessee State University
Michael P. Kirby, Rhodes College
William Kitchin, Loyola College
Louis Koenig, New York University
Melvin Kulbicki, York College of Pennsylvania
Robert Kvavik, University of Minnesota
Stanley Kyriakides, William Paterson College of New Jersey
Walter L. Lackey, Jr., Frostburg State University

Byron G. Lander, Kent State University
Robert Langran, Villanova University
Margaret K. Latimer, Auburn University
James F. Lea, University of Southern Mississippi
Timothy A. Leonard, Siena Heights College
Erwin L. Levine, Skidmore College
Frederick Lewis, University of Lowell
Paul Light, University of Minnesota
James Lindeen, University of Toledo
Connie L. Lobur, State University of New York College at Purchase
Duane Lockard, Princeton University
Burdett Loomis, University of Kansas
Joseph Losco, Ball State University
R. Philip Loy, Taylor University
David C. Maas, University of Alaska, Anchorage
Thomas Mans, Creighton University
Susan H. Marsh, Providence College
John L. Martin, University of Maine
Gerald A. McBeath, University of Alaska, Fairbanks
Charles H. McCall, California State University, Bakersfield
James L. McDowell, Indiana State University
Patrick J. McGeever, Indiana University–Purdue University, Indianapolis
William McLauchlan, Purdue University
Carl E. Meacham, State University of New York, Oneonta
James A. Meader, Augustana College
Daniel R. Minns, American University
Virgil L. Mitchell, Seminole Junior College
James E. Mock, Austin Peay State University
Tommie Sue Montgomery, Agnes Scott College
Margaret V. Moody, Auburn University at Montgomery
Richard E. Morgan, Bowdoin College
Thomas J. Morillaro, Nicholls State University
William Morrow, William and Mary College
Kenneth F. Mott, Gettysburg College
Gordon D. Munro, San Bernardino Valley College
Nelda A. Muns, Wharton County Union College
Robert E. Murphy, St. Louis Community College at Florissant Valley
Walter Murphy, Princeton University
Marie D. Natoli, Emmanuel College
Arturo Nava, Laredo Junior College
Frederick Neikirk, Westminster College
Patricia M. Nelson, New Mexico State University, Carlsbad
David Neubauer, University of New Orleans
Dail Neugaiten, Arizona State University
Stephen L. Newman, York University
G.K. Oddo, University of San Diego
Edwin Allen O'Donnel, Wayne State College
Madelin Olds, Del Mar College

Bruce Oppenheimer, University of Houston

Shirley E. Ostholm-Hinnau, York College of the City University

Roger N. Pajari, Georgia Southern College

Wayne Parent, Louisiana State University

John D. Parker, Western Kentucky University

Ronald W. Perry, Arizona State University

Robert K. Peters, Tyler Junior College

Frank Petrusak, College of Charleston

Doris F. Pierce, Purdue University, Calumet

Monte Piliawsky, Dillard University

J.L. Polinard, Pan American University

Freeman W. Pollard, St. Ambrose College

Larry Pool, Mt. View College

Mary Cornelia Porter, Barat College

Bill Postiglione, Quincy College

Herman Pritchett, University of California, Santa Barbara

David H. Provost, California State University, Fresno

Brian F. Rader, Northeastern Oklahoma State University

Gene Rainey, University of North Carolina, Asheville

Craig Ramsay, Ohio Wesleyan University

Thomas A. Reilly, Trinity College

Pamela R. Rendeiro, Southern Connecticut State University

Delbert J. Ringquist, Central Michigan University

Bradley R. Rice, Clayton College

Linda K. Richter, Kansas State University

George C. Roberts, Indiana University Northwest

David Robinson, University of Houston—Downtown

Ted Robinson, Louisiana State University

Jerel Rosati, University of South Carolina

Gary Rose, Sacred Heart University

Raymond K. Rossiter, Rockland Community College

Annetta St. Clair, Missouri Southern State College

Richard T. Saeger, Valdosta State College

Steven S. Sallie, Boise State University

Frank Schwartz, Beaver College

Lawrence Schwartz, College of Staten Island

Seymour J. Schwartz, Kennedy-King College of the City College

Jeffrey A. Segal, State University of New York, Stony Brook

Martin Shapiro, Law School, University of California, Berkeley

Stewart P. Shapiro, Bentley College

Earl Shaw, Northern Arizona University

John N. Short, University of Arkansas at Monticello

James D. Slack, Cleveland State University

Herbert C. Smith, Western Maryland College

James George Smith, West Chester University

Neil Snortland, University of Arkansas at Little Rock

Robert J. Spitzer, State University of New York, Cortland

Terry Spurlock, Henderson County Junior College

Grover Starling, University of Houston

Henry Steck, State University of New York, Cortland

Ronald Stidham, Lamar University

Barbara S. Stone, California State University, Fullerton

Emily Stoper, California State University, Hayward

Richard P. Strada, Ocean County College

Sue E. Strickler, Eastern New Mexico University

Theodore Sturm, Robert Morris College

John A. Sullivan, Jacksonville University

George Sulzner, University of Massachusetts

Carl Swidorski, College of Saint Rose

Gary Thompson, Abilene Christian University

H. Christian Thorup, Cuesta College

Charles M. Tidmarch, Union College

Joan Tronto, Hunter College

James Chih-yuan Tsao, Houston Baptist University

John R. Vile, Middle Tennessee State University

Stephen Wainscott, Clemson University

Diane E. Wall, Mississippi State University

Hanes Walton, Jr., Savannah State College

Elizabeth C. Warren, Loyola University of Chicago

James D. Weaver, Marymount College

David G. Wegge, St. Norbert College

Herbert Weisberg, Ohio State University

Warren Weston, Metropolitan State College

R. Eric Weise, University of Cincinnati

Charles Weymann, Los Angeles Valley College

Donald Whistler, University of Central Arkansas

Howard R. Whitcomb, Lehigh University

Bob White, Humboldt State University

Larry D. White, University of Wisconsin Center, Fox Valley

John F. Whitney, Jr., Lincoln Land Community College

David H. Wicks, Mississippi Valley State University

Henry Wilkins III, University of Arkansas, Pine Bluff

John F. Wilson, University of Hawaii, Manoa

Edward Woodhouse, Rensselaer Polytechnic Institute

Gerald Wright, Indiana University

James P. Young, State University of New York, Binghamton

Alton C. Zimmerman, Northwestern Oklahoma State University

F. Donald Zucker, Ursinus College

# PERMISSIONS

Figure 5-1: Based on data from the General Social Survey, NORC (National Opinion Research Center) as reported in Howard D. White, "Majorities for Censorship," reprinted from *Library Journal*, copyright © 1989, Reed Publishing, U.S.A.

Figure 6-1: Adapted from Herbert McClosky and John Zaller, *The American Ethos: Public Attitudes toward Capitalism and Democracy* (Cambridge, Mass.: Harvard University Press, 1984). Reprinted by permission.

Table 6-1: From 1985 *Los Angeles Times* survey. Copyright © 1985, *Los Angeles Times*. Reprinted by permission.

Table 7-1: From *Gallup Reports*, 1982. Reprinted by permission of The Gallup Organization.

How the U.S. Compares, page 185: From "Attitudes toward the Soviet Union and the United States" A Four Country Comparison, *Public Opinion*, March/April 1988, pp. 29–30. Reprinted with the permission of the American Enterprise Institute for Policy Research, Washington, D.C.

Figure 8-2: From May and September 1988 polls by The Gallup Organization for the Times Mirror Company. Reprinted by permission of The Gallup Organization.

Table 8-2: Adapted from Herbert McClosky and John Zaller, *The American Ethos: Public Attitudes toward Capitalism and Democracy* (Cambridge, Mass.: Harvard University Press, 1984). Reprinted by permission.

Figure 8-3: From M. Kent Jennings and Richard C. Niemi, *Generations and Politics: A Panel Study of Young Adults and Their Parents.* Copyright © 1981 by Princeton University Press. Figure, p. 91, adapted with permission of Princeton University Press.

Table 8-3: From Benjamin I. Page and Robert Y. Shapiro, "Effects of Public Opinion on Policy," *American Political Science Review*, March 1983 Reprinted by permission of the American Political Science Association.

How the U.S. Compares, page 204: From David Glass, Peverill Squire, and Raymond Wolfinger, "Voter Turnout: An International Comparison," *Public Opinion*, December/January 1984. Reprinted with the permission of the American Enterprise Institute for Public Policy Research, Washington, D.C.

Table 9-1: From Sidney Verba and Norman Nie, *Participation in America: Political Democracy and Social Equality* (New York: Harper & Row, 1972). Reprinted by permission of the authors.

Figure 9-3: Adapted from Raymond E. Wolfinger and Steven J. Rosenstone, *Who Votes?* (New Haven: Conn.: Yale University Press, 1980). Reprinted by permission.

Figure 9-4: Adapted from Sidney Verba and Norman Nie, *Participation in America: Political Democracy and Social Equality* (New York: Harper & Row, 1972). Reprinted by permission of the authors.

Figure 10-1: From *Gallup Reports*, April 1985, Gallup Poll, January 1988. Reprinted by permission of the Gallup Organization.

Table 10-1: From Stanley Kelley, Jr., *Interpreting Elections.* Copyright © 1983 by Princeton University Press. Table, p. 138, adapted with permission of Princeton University Press.

Figure 10-2: From Gallup Polls, July 1986, based on surveys from January to June 1986. Reprinted by permission of The Gallup Organization.

Table 10-2: Supplied by the Survey Research Center/Center for Political Studies, American National Election Studies, University of Michigan.

Figure 11-2: From *Congressional Quarterly Weekly Report*, November 12, 1988. Reprinted by permission of Congressional Quarterly, Inc.

Figure 11-3: From "The Makeup of the Republican and Democratic Party Coalitions," *The New York Times*, July 17, 1988. Copyright © 1988 by The New York Times Company. Reprinted by permission.

Figure 12-1: From Edie N. Goldenberg and Michael W. Traugott, *Campaigning for Congress* (Washington, D.C.: Congressional Quarterly Press, 1984). Reprinted by permission of Congressional Quarterly, Inc.

Table 12-1: Adapted from James L. Gibson, Cornelius P. Cotter, John F. Bibby, and Robert L. Huckshorn, "Wither the Local Parties?" *American Journal of Political Science*, 29, (February 1985): pp. 149–151. Reprinted by permission of The University of Texas Press.

Table 13-1 and Table 13-2: Selections from *Encyclopedia of Associations, 1988.* Edited by Karin E. Koek and Susan Boyles Martin. Gale Research, 1988. Copyright © 1988 by Gale Research, Inc. Reprinted by permission of the publisher.

Table 13-4: From Sidney Verba and Norman Nie, *Participation in America: Political Democracy and Social Equality* (New York: Harper & Row, 1972). Reprinted by permission of the authors.

Figure 17-1: From Roger H. Davidson and Walter J. Oleszek, *Congress and Its Members* (Washington, D.C.: Congressional Quarterly Press, 1981). Reprinted by permission of Congressional Quarterly, Inc.

Table 19-2: Data for 1980–1988 from *The New York Times*, November 10, 1988. Copyright © 1988 by The New York Times Company. Reprinted by permission.

Figure 19-2: From William C. Adams, "As New Hampshire Goes . . . ," in *Media and Momentum: The New Hampshire Primary and Nomination Politics*, ed. Gary R. Orren and Nelson W. Polsby (Chatham, N.J.: Chatham House, 1987). Reprinted by permission.

Figure 19-3: From Gerald M. Pomper with Susan S. Lederman, *Elections in America* (New York: Longman, 1980). Reprinted by permission of the author.

Figure 21-1: From *Congressional Quarterly Weekly Report*, November 19, 1988. Reprinted by permission of Congressional Quarterly, Inc.

Figure 23-1: Adapted from Joel D. Aberbach and Bert A. Rockman, "Clashing Beliefs within the Executive Branch: The Nixon Administration Bureaucracy," *American Political Science Review*, June 1976. Reprinted by permission of American Political Science Association.

How the U.S. Compares, page 551: From *The Politics of Bureaucracy* by B. Guy Peters. Copyright © 1989 by Longman Publishing. Reprinted by permission of Longman Publishing.

Table 28-1: Data from *The Military Balance 1988–1989* (London: International Institute for Strategic Studies, 1988), pp. 18, 25–28. Reprinted by permission.

Table 28-2: Data from *The Military Balance, 1988–1989* (London: International Institute for Strategic Studies, 1988), p. 1237. Reprinted by permission.

Figure 28-1: From "Where Star Wars Fit In," *The New York Times*, November 18, 1985. Copyright © 1985 by The New York Times Company. Reprinted by permission.

## A GUIDED TOUR TO THE AMERICAN DEMOCRACY

*Chapter 11*

### THE TWO-PARTY SYSTEM: DEFINING THE VOTERS' CHOICE

*Political parties created democracy and . . . modern democracy is unthinkable save in terms of the parties.*

E. E. Schattschneider[1]

They were the kind of strange bedfellows that American politics regularly produces. One of them stood for gun control, busing, and an end to the death penalty and proposed that the United States terminate its Star Wars project, MX missile construction, and aid to the Nicaraguan rebels. His running mate held the opposite position on each of these issues. They were the 1988 Democratic ticket, Michael Dukakis of Massachusetts and Lloyd Bentsen of Texas.

The Dukakis–Bentsen partnership was a product of the country's two-party system, which compels candidates and voters with diverse opinions to find common ground. Because the Republican and Democratic parties have dominated U.S. elections for so long and are the only parties with any realistic chance of acquiring political control, Americans nearly take their **two-party system** for granted. However, most democracies have a **multiparty system**, in which three or more parties have the capacity to gain control of government separately or in coalition. Even democracies that have what is essentially a two-party system typically have important smaller parties as well. For example, Great Britain's Labour and Conservative parties have dominated that nation's politics since early in this century, but they have had competition from the Liberal party and, more recently, the Social Democrats. At present all four of these parties have representatives in Parliament. In contrast, the U.S. Congress consists entirely of Democrats and Republicans.

[1]E. E. Schattschneider, *Party Government* (New York: Rinehart, 1942), 1.

247

### OPENING ILLUSTRATION

Intriguing narrations of compelling events introduce the concepts of the chapter to follow.

### DEFINITIONS

The first occurrence of each major concept is signaled by bold type and accompanied by a concise definition. A complete list of these concepts is found at the end of each chapter, as well as in the end of book Glossary.

### FOCUS POINTS

Three or four sentences appearing at the beginning summarize the major ideas of the chapter. These brief statements present its *major themes.*

### ANALYZE THE ISSUE

Over 100 boxes in the margins present searching questions in order to stimulate the students to analyze critically what they are reading.

PART TWO ★ INDIVIDUAL RIGHTS

concentrates on groups because the history of civil rights has been largely one of group claims to equality. The chapter emphasizes the following main points:

★ *Americans have substantial equality under the law.* They have, in legal terms, equal protection of the laws, equal access to accommodations and housing, and an equal right to vote. Discrimination by law against persons because of race, sex, religion, and ethnicity is now largely a thing of the past.

★ *Disadvantaged groups have had to struggle for equal rights.* Blacks, women, Native Americans, Hispanics, and Asian Americans have all had to fight for their rights in order to come closer to equality with white males.

★ *Legal equality for all Americans has not resulted in de facto equality.* Blacks, women, Hispanics, and other traditionally disadvantaged groups have a disproportionately small share of America's opportunities and benefits. Existing inequalities, discriminatory practices, and political pressures are still major barriers to their full equality. Affirmative action and busing are policies designed to help the disadvantaged achieve full equality.

**▸ ANALYZE THE ISSUE**

**The Impact of Federalism on Equality**
Disadvantaged groups have achieved a greater degree of equality primarily through federal laws and federal court rulings, rather than through state and local measures. What do you think are the main reasons for this development? Do James Madison's arguments (in *Federalist* No. 10) about the greater diversity of the nation under a federal system apply to the situation? Do issues of equality affect your opinion about whether a federal system is preferable to a unitary one?

### Equality under the Law

Equality has always been the least completely developed of America's founding ideas. Not even Thomas Jefferson, who had a deep admiration for the common man, believed that broad meaning could be given to the claim of the Declaration of Independence that "all men are created equal." Jefferson rejected any suggestion that people should be equalized in their possessions, interests, positions, or opinions. To Jefferson, "equality" had a restricted, though significant, meaning: people are of equal moral worth and thereby deserving of equal treatment under the law.[4] Even then, Jefferson made a distinction between free men, who were entitled to legal equality, and slaves, who were not.

Since Jefferson's time, Americans' beliefs about equality have changed substantially, but the emphasis on legal equality has not. The catchphrase of nearly any group's claim to a fairer standing in American society has been "equality under the law." The importance that people attach to legal equality is understandable. When made into law, claims to equality assume a power that they do not otherwise have. Once people are secure in their legal rights, they are in a stronger position to seek equality on other fronts, such as in the economic realm. In addition, once encoded in law, a claim to equality can force officials to take positive action on behalf of a disadvantaged group. For example, some communities refused to allow the children of illegal aliens to attend public school until a 1982 Supreme Court ruling required those communities to do so.[5]

Americans' claims to legal equality are contained in a great many laws. Among the most noteworthy are the equal-protection clause of the Fourteenth Amendment, the Civil Rights acts of 1964 and 1968, and the Voting Rights Act of 1965.

[4]Robert Nisbet, "Public Opinion versus Popular Opinion," *Public Interest* 41 (1975): 171.
[5]*Plyler v. Doe*, 457 U.S. 202 (1982).

480     PART FIVE ★ ELECTED REPRESENTATIVES

If presidential appointees are to influence career bureaucrats, they must gain their confidence. However, career bureaucrats are likely to be more committed to their agencies' goals than to the president's.[39] The civil service system protects careerists, so they cannot easily be removed from their positions even if they work against the president's objectives. To gain their cooperation, presidential appointees must achieve a working compromise between the president's goals and those of the bureaucratic organizations. Such delicate maneuvering requires managerial skills that many inexperienced appointees lack. Chapters 22 and 23 examine more closely the relationship between presidential appointees and career bureaucrats.

### ORGANIZING THE EXTENDED PRESIDENCY

Effective use of appointees by the president requires two-way communication. The president cannot possibly meet regularly with all his appointees or personally oversee their activities. Yet if he is to be in control, he must receive essential advice from his subordinates and have means of communicating his views to them.

#### Patterns of Organization

Presidents have relied on a variety of techniques to regulate the flow of information to and from the Oval Office. One arrangement, used by Eisenhower, Nixon, Reagan, and Bush, resembles the way the military and most corporations are organized. It places the president at the top of an organizational pyramid and his closest personal advisers, each of whom is assigned specific responsibilities, at the second level (see Figure 20-2). All information and

[39]Joel D. Aberbach and Bert A. Rockman, "Clashing Beliefs within the Executive Branch," *American Political Science Review* 70 (June 1976): 461.

### • HOW THE UNITED STATES COMPARES

**Heads of State and Heads of Government**

Most democracies divide the executive office between a head of state, who is the ceremonial leader, and a head of government, who is the policy leader. In Great Britain these positions are filled by the queen and the prime minister, respectively. In democracies without a hereditary monarchy, the position of head of state is usually held by an individual chosen by the legislature. West Germany's head of state, for example, is a president, who is elected by the Federal Assembly; the head of government is a chancellor, who is chosen by the majority party in the lower house (Bundestag) of the Federal Assembly. The United States is one of a few countries in which the roles of head of state and head of government are combined in a single office, the presidency. The major disadvantage of this arrangement is that the president must devote considerable time to ceremonial functions, such as dinners for visiting heads of state. The major advantages are that the president alone is the center of national attention and that his power as head of government is enhanced by his prestige as the personification of the American state.

| Country | Head of State | Head of Government |
|---|---|---|
| Canada | Governor general (representative of the British monarch) | Prime minister |
| France | President | Premier |
| Great Britain | Queen | Prime minister |
| Italy | President | Prime minister |
| Japan | Emperor | Prime minister |
| Mexico | President | President |
| Sweden | King | Prime minister |
| United States | President | President |
| West Germany | President | Chancellor |

---

## HOW THE U.S. COMPARES

A series of boxes compares the United States with the other major western democracies with respect to a variety of political characteristics.

---

294     PART FOUR ★ POLITICAL ORGANIZATION

### Summary

America's political parties are relatively weak organizations. They lack control over nominations, elections, and platforms. Candidates can bypass the party organization and win nomination through primary elections. Individual candidates also control most of the organization and money necessary to win elections and run largely on personal platforms.

Primary elections are the major reason for the organizational weakness of America's parties. Once the parties lost their hold on the nominating process, they became subordinate to candidates. More generally, the political parties have been undermined by election reforms, some of which were intended to weaken the party and others of which have unintentionally done so. Recently the state and national party organizations have expanded their capacity to provide candidates with modern campaign services and are again playing a prominent role in election campaigns. But this role is less influential than it once was, because party organizations at all levels have few ways of controlling the candidates who run under their banner. They assist candidates with campaign technology, workers, and funds, but cannot compel candidates' loyalty to organizational goals.

America's parties are decentralized, fragmented organizations. The relationship among local, state, and national party organizations is marked by paths of common interest rather than lines of authority. The national party organization does not control the policies and activities of the state organizations, and they in turn do not control the local organizations. The fragmentation of parties prevents them from acting as cohesive national organizations. Traditionally the local organizations have controlled most of the party's work force because most elections are contested at the local level. Local parties, however, vary markedly in their vitality; today only a few can be described as active, powerful machines, while most are understaffed and underfunded.

America's party organizations are flexible enough to allow diverse interests to coexist within them; they can also accommodate new ideas and leadership, since they are neither rigid nor closed. However, because America's parties cannot control their candidates or coordinate their policies at all levels, they are unable to present the voters with a coherent, detailed platform for governing. The national electorate as a whole is thus denied a clear choice among policy alternatives and has difficulty influencing national policy in a predictable and enduring way through elections.

### Major Concepts

candidate-centered politics
nomination
party-centered politics

party organizations
primary election (direct primary)

### Suggested Readings

Allswang, John. *Bosses, Machines, and Urban Voters.* Baltimore: Johns Hopkins University Press, 1986. A penetrating study of the party machines that once flourished in America's cities.

Broder, David. *The Party's Over.* New York: Harper & Row, 1972. One of America's leading journalists discusses the declining influence of parties on election campaigns.

Crotty, William, ed. *The Party Symbol.* San Francisco: W. H. Freeman, 1980. A series of articles by leading scholars on the activities and influence of contemporary American parties.

Davis, James W. *National Conventions in an Age of Party Reform.* Westport, Conn: Greenwood Press, 1983. An assessment of how the role of national conventions has changed as a result of the changes in the parties and nominating system.

Eldersveld, Samuel J. *Political Parties: A Behavioral Analysis.* Chicago: Rand McNally, 1964. A behavioral study of the activities of the Democratic and Republican organizations in Detroit.

Epstein, Leon D. *Political Parties in Western Democracies.* New Brunswick, N.J.: Transaction Books, 1980. A comparative analysis of political parties, with special emphasis on those of the United States and Great Britain.

Frantzich, Stephen E. *Political Parties in the Technological Age.* New York: Longman, 1989. An insightful analysis of how parties are adapting to the information age.

---

## SUMMARY

A short essay strengthens ties between the chapter's major concepts and those of the rest of the text.

## KEY TERMS

A list of the chapter's boldfaced terms facilitates review.

## SUGGESTED READINGS

Annotated references encourage further pursuit of "real" political science: both classic studies and recent research.

## DIALOGUES

In these *original* essays following each of the text's seven parts, prominent political scientists discuss a major issue of the American system.

DIALOGUE

### Is the United States Past Its Peak as an Economic and Military Power?

**STEPHEN D. KRASNER**

*The United States has not yet adjusted to its new, more vulnerable international position.*

At the end of World War II the United States was the most powerful country in the world. In fact, it was the most powerful state that had ever existed in the 300-year history of the modern international system. It was the only country that possessed nuclear weapons. Its gross national product was three times that of the Soviet Union and six times that of the United Kingdom, the next most economically productive nation in the noncommunist world. American industries held the commanding heights in high-technology industries. The United States was a net exporter of petroleum.

These extraordinary resources made it possible for American leaders to adopt very ambitious foreign policies. The United States created a system of alliances designed to contain the Soviet Union's expansionism. America fought bloody wars in Korea and Vietnam, countries that had few economic resources and were of little strategic importance. Large numbers of American troops were more or less permanently garrisoned in Western Europe and Japan. Defeats, especially the communist victory in China, were attributed to internal betrayal, not to any limitations of American power.

In the past two decades, however, American power has declined, in some areas dramatically. The gross national product of the United States is now only about 40 percent larger than that of Japan, which has half our population and few natural resources. Germany and Japan export more manufactured products than does the United States. The Soviet Union has achieved parity in nuclear weapons. Japan has challenged America's supremacy in high-technology industries. The United States has been a net importer of petroleum since 1970. Even though the United States remains very powerful, it can no longer consider itself able either to control the international environment or to extricate itself from it.

The United States has not yet adjusted to its new, more vulnerable international position. Even crushing setbacks, most notably the loss of the Vietnam war and the quadrupling of oil prices in the 1970s (which could have been prevented if the United States had had surplus productive capacity), have not prompted a fundamental reassessment of American policies. Commitments that were made forty years ago have not been radically changed. Half the American army is still dedicated to the defense of Western Europe, even though Western Europe's gross national product is now higher than that of the United States. American leaders continue to treat trade and financial relations with Japan as purely an economic issue, rather than a matter of national power, except in some rare instances where American defense capabilities are directly affected by Japanese control of specific technologies. The stability of the American economy is now hostage to the public and private foreign-investment decisions made in Japan, because neither the American people nor American leaders have been willing to adopt fiscal policies that would close the budget and trade deficits. Hard choices are ahead for Americans, but our attitudes, our history, and our institutions are not particularly well suited to make them.

*Stephen D. Krasner is Chair of the Department of Political Science at Stanford University. He is the author of* Structural Conflicts: The Third World Against Global Liberalism.

684

---

**BRUCE M. RUSSETT**

*The basic interests of the United States, and the values that Americans cherish, are more secure than ever.*

As an individual nation-state, the United States probably has passed its peak of power. But the Western alliance, which the United States leads and has nurtured, is still rising in power and influence. As a result, the basic interests of the United States, and the values that Americans cherish, are more secure than ever. In November 1988 British Prime Minister Margaret Thatcher declared, "The cold war is over." And the West has won.

Immediately after World War II the United States was the world's dominant military and economic power. Europe and Japan were devastated and economically exhausted; Germany and Japan were also defeated and occupied; the Soviet Union was victorious and had vast new territories under its control, but it too was devastated by the war and remained technologically backward. Against this low point, subsequent American power would necessarily look diminished as the war-torn economies recovered. Just as important, the United States chose to help many of its wartime allies and enemies rebuild, thereby hastening its own relative decline from its temporary solitary splendor.

In so choosing, American leaders acted in the true long-term interests of the country. The United States needed strong allies to help contain the perceived threat from Soviet communism. It also needed a prosperous world economy that could serve as both a market for American goods and a source of competitors to supply American markets and keep American producers on their toes. American policy [sought these] ends, and achieved them.

Communism, by contrast, has been a [major] economic failure—in the Third World, China, Eastern Europe, and the Soviet Union itself. Communist countries of the Third World have stagnated, and some have turned to the West for capital and technology. China's economy has prospered only since it became more open to the West and began to abandon socialist ownership and central planning. Mikhail Gorbachev and many East European leaders have begun to realize that their own stagnant economies cannot prosper unless they adopt many features of capitalism. They also know that in order to grow, their economies need political liberalization and a greater degree of democracy. Even noncommunist Third World countries have moved away from state control of the economy as well as from authoritarian political rule. After decades of military dictatorship, many Asian and Latin American countries have returned to democratic government.

Democracy and free-market capitalism are central American values; they are what the cold war was all about. As these values have become entrenched around the world, American security has increased. American military power is no longer superior to the Soviet Union's, as it was just after World War II, but it has not become inferior, either. The Soviet–American military balance has in fact helped maintain peace between the two countries. Neither that balance nor the military superiority of either superpower over any other state is really now in question.

True, both the United States and the Soviet Union risk losing economic competitiveness if they continue to devote so much of their resources to the military. The United States must raise its rate of saving and investment if it is to maintain its technological edge. In the decades ahead, Japan and other countries may surpass it in important respects. But if that happens, it will do so in a world that is basically the one that the leaders of postwar America hoped would come into being.

*Bruce M. Russett is Dean Acheson Professor of International Relations and Political Science at Yale University. He is the author of* Controlling the Sword: The Democratic Governance of National Security.

685

# Chapter 1

## THE AMERICAN HERITAGE: GOVERNING IDEAS

*One hears people say that it is inherent in the habits and nature of democracies to change feelings and thoughts at every moment . . . . But I have never seen anything like that happening in the great democracy on the other side of the ocean. What struck me most in the United States was the difficulty experienced in getting an idea, once conceived, out of the head of the majority.*

*Alexis de Tocqueville[1]*

At noon on January 20, 1989, George Bush took the oath of office as the forty-first president of the United States. Standing on the steps of the Capitol, Bush spoke plainly but earnestly of his hopes for America. He envisioned prosperity at home and peace abroad, pledging "a kinder nation and a gentler world."

The news media reported Bush's inaugural address as a beginning, the start of a new administration. However, Bush's speech was at least as remarkable for its links to the past. Threaded among its suggestions for the 1990s were repeated references to time-honored American ideas: personal freedom, social justice, civic duty, self-reliance, social diversity, and national unity. The same ideas had permeated the inaugural addresses of Ronald Reagan and John Kennedy, of Franklin Roosevelt and Abraham Lincoln, of Andrew Jackson and Thomas Jefferson. The ideas were also there at the nation's beginning, when they were put into words in the Declaration of Independence and the Constitution.

Of course, the practice of these ideas has changed greatly during the two centuries that the United States has been a nation. When the signers of the Declaration of Independence proclaimed in 1776 that "all men are created equal," they did not have in mind racial minorities or women. They were saying that the rigid inequality and absolutism of European governments had been

[1]Alexis de Tocqueville, *Democracy in America* (1835–1840), ed. J. P. Mayer and A. P. Kerr (Garden City, N.Y.: Doubleday/Anchor), 1969), 640.

U.S. politics is remarkable for its historical continuity—although tributes to that connection sometimes take unusual forms. These portraits of past presidents were carried in George Bush's inaugural parade. (Wally McNamee/Woodfin Camp and Associates)

rejected by Americans and would have no place in their future. Today the American idea of equality is a more active concept, including such policies as busing to achieve racial integration in the schools, welfare programs for the poor, and affirmative action programs.

It could be argued that the idea of equality today is so different in practice from the idea of equality of 200 years ago that it is foolish to see them as sharing the same root. There is in fact no way to show scientifically that American ideas have developed steadily for two centuries. Yet the circumstantial evidence is compelling.[2] The American political experience has been remarkably cohesive. During the same period in which the United States has had one system of government, Germany has been governed as a group of principalities, a monarchy, a parliamentary democracy, a fascist dictatorship, and, today, as a divided state, partly democratic and partly communist. Furthermore, although throughout their history Americans have quarreled over the practice of their principles, they seem never to have questioned the principles themselves. As Clinton Rossiter concluded, "There has been, in a doctrinal sense, only one America."[3]

This is a book about contemporary American government, not U.S. history. Yet American government today cannot be understood apart from the nation's heritage. Government does not begin anew with each generation. It builds on the past. In the American case, the most significant link between past and present has been formed by the nation's founding ideas. This chapter briefly examines the ideas that have shaped American politics since the country's earliest years. The chapter aims to highlight the power and persistence of these ideas and thereby to provide a starting point for an understanding of the United States' governing system.

[2]See, for example, Louis Hartz, *The Liberal Tradition in America* (New York: Harcourt, Brace, 1955).
[3]Clinton Rossiter, *Conservatism in America* (New York: Vintage Books, 1962), 67.

## Political Culture: The Core Ideas of American Government

The people of every nation have a few great ideas that affect their political life, but, as James Bryce has observed, Americans are a special case.[4] Their ideas are the basis of their national identity. Other people take their identity from the common ancestry that led them gradually to gather under one flag. Long before there was a France or a Japan, there were French and Japanese people, each a kinship group united through blood.[5] Even today, it is kinship more than political ideas that link the French or the Japanese. Not so for Americans. The United States is a nation that was founded abruptly in 1776 on a set of ideas that became its people's common bond.[6]

No exact list of these ideas exists. They are not chiseled in stone like the Ten Commandments. Rather, they are habits of mind, a customary way of thinking about the world. They are part of what social scientists call **political culture,** a term that refers to the characteristic and deep-seated beliefs of a particular people.[7]

The first efforts to analyze the American political culture were largely impressionistic. Many of the most astute observers were foreign visitors, such as the Frenchman Alexis de Tocqueville; these visitors' knowledge of other cultures heightened their sense of what was distinctive about America's.[8] The modern study of political culture relies on more systematic methods of identifying people's beliefs, such as public opinion polls.[9] Whatever the method or time, however, most analysts have reached similar conclusions about the American political culture. It is said to include the following beliefs in idealized form:[*]

★ *Liberty* is the belief that individuals should be free to act and think as they choose, provided they do not infringe unreasonably on the freedom and well-being of others.

★ *Self-government* is the belief that the people are the ultimate source of governing authority and that their general welfare is the only legitimate purpose of government.

★ *Equality* holds that all individuals have moral worth and are entitled to fair treatment under the law.

---

[4]James Bryce, *The American Commonwealth,* vol. 2 (New York: Macmillan, 1960), 247–254. First published in 1900.

[5]Theodore H. White, ''The American Idea,'' *New York Times Magazine,* July 6, 1986, 12.

[6]Ralph Barton Perry, *Puritanism and Democracy* (New York: Vanguard Press, 1944), 124–125. See also Seymour Martin Lipset, *The First New Nation* (New York: Basic Books, 1963); Hartz, *Liberal Tradition in America.*

[7]See Gabriel Almond and Sidney Verba, *The Civic Culture* (Boston: Little, Brown, 1963); Donald Devine, *The Political Culture of the United States* (Boston: Little, Brown, 1972); Walter A. Rosenbaum, *Political Culture* (New York: Praeger, 1975); Richard Merelman, *Making Something of Ourselves: On Culture and Politics in the United States* (Berkeley: University of California Press, 1984).

[8]See de Tocqueville, *Democracy in America.*

[9]See, for example, Herbert McClosky and John Zaller, *The American Ethos* (Cambridge, Mass.: Harvard University Press, 1984).

[*] More extensive definitions of these terms will be provided in later chapters.

★ HOW THE UNITED
STATES COMPARES

**Americans as a Political People**

By some standards, Americans are not a very political people. The United States ranks near the bottom, for example, in voter turnout. Barely half of Americans go to the polls in a presidential election, compared with more than 80 percent of eligible voters in most other democratic countries. In Italy, for example, turnout exceeds 90 percent.

In other ways, however, Americans are highly political. In a five-nation study, published as *The Civic Culture*, Gabriel Almond and Sidney Verba asked respondents why they were proud of their country. Of the American respondents, 85 percent identified their political system as the main source of their pride. Respondents in the other four countries—Great Britain, West Germany, Italy, and Mexico—were much less likely to mention government. The extreme case was the Italians, only 3 percent of whom mentioned their system of government. Italians instead took pride in their country's physical beauty and its artistic heritage.

Americans' political orientation is also evident in the degree to which their core beliefs constrain political choices. Political scientists conclude that the range of political debate in the United States is narrower than that in most other democracies. Policy alternatives that do not conform with "the American way," such as the nationalization of key industries, are not seriously debated. These extreme policy measures are dismissed as "un-American," a term that is itself revealing. Other people do not have such a word. There is no "un-Italian" in the vocabulary of Italian politics.

SOURCE: Gabriel Almond and Sidney Verba, *The Civic Culture* (Boston: Little, Brown, 1965), 64.

★ *Individualism* is a commitment to self-reliance, material accumulation, and a private economic system.

★ *Diversity* holds that individual differences should be respected and that these differences are a source of strength and a legitimate basis of self-interest.

★ *Unity* is the belief that Americans are one people and form an indivisible union.

These ideals, taken together, are sometimes called "the American Creed." In practice, they mean different things to different people, so it is not particularly useful to give them elaborate definitions. Yet if their exact meaning is debatable, their promise is unmistakable. They are the vision of a government of high purpose, in which power is widely shared and used for the common good.

## THE LIMITS OF IDEALS

High ideals do not come with a guarantee that a people will live up to them. The clearest proof in the American case is the human tragedy that began nearly four centuries ago and continues today. In 1619 the first black slaves were brought to America. Slavery lasted 250 years and was followed by the Jim Crow era of legal segregation: black people in the South were forbidden by law to use the same schools, hospitals, restaurants, and restrooms as white people. Today black Americans have equal rights under the law, but they are otherwise far from equal. Compared with whites, blacks are three times as likely to live in poverty, twice as likely to be unable to find a job, twice as likely to die in infancy, three times as likely not to receive necessary corrective heart surgery, seven times as

Even as early Americans were expressing their commitment to the principle of equality, they were allowing slavery to persist. This is the only drawing known to have been made aboard a slave ship as it sailed to America. (National Maritime Museum, London)

likely to be sentenced to death if convicted of an interracial murder.[10] There have always been at least two Americas, one for whites and one for blacks.

A nation's realities will never precisely mirror its ideals. To expect otherwise is to misjudge the nature of cultural beliefs and the play of politics. Cultural beliefs have a powerful impact on a nation's politics but not an unlimited one.

## Cultural Beliefs as Myths

Cultural beliefs originate in a country's political and social practices, but they are not perfect representations of these practices. They are mythic ideas—symbolic positions taken by a people to justify and give meaning to their way of life.[11] Despite the claim that "all men are created equal," equality is not an American birthright. As we will see in Chapter 7, no minority—not blacks, Asians, women, Hispanics, Catholics, or Jews—has advanced toward equality without a struggle. In 1892 Congress suspended Chinese immigration on the assumption that the Chinese were an inferior people. Calvin Coolidge in 1923 asked Congress for a permanent ban on the Chinese, saying that people "who do not want to be partakers of the American spirit ought not to settle in America."[12] Not until 1965 was discrimination against the Chinese and other Asian peoples effectively eliminated from U.S. immigration laws.

---

[10]U.S. Census Bureau figures, except for the data on heart surgery (reported on the CBS Evening News of January 16, 1989) and the data on sentencing in interracial murders (*New York Times*, April 23, 1987).

[11]See Claude Lévi-Strauss, *Structural Anthropology* (Chicago: University of Chicago Press, 1983); Clifford Geertz, *Myth, Symbol, and Culture* (New York: Norton, 1974); Albert S. Yee, *Westward to Asia* (in preparation).

[12]Ralph Volney Harlow, *The Growth of the United States*, vol. 2 (New York: Henry Holt, 1943), 497.

★ ANALYZE THE ISSUE

**Cultural Beliefs as Myth and Reality**
Cultural beliefs are mythical in that they are combinations of fact and wishful thinking. This mythical dimension can have far-reaching consequences. Consider the 1988 Harris poll in which two-thirds of white Americans said they believed that black Americans "get equal pay for equal work." The reality is otherwise: statistics indicate that, on average, blacks are paid less than whites in every job category. Does the mythical aspect of belief in equality allow white Americans to deceive themselves about how well-off black Americans are? If not, what else might account for the misperception? To what degree do such misconceptions lessen the concern of white Americans with racial equality? Conversely, how does equality as myth promote progress in racial relations?

The exclusion of the Chinese is not among the stories that we like to tell about ourselves. Such lapses of historical memory can be found among every people, but the tendency to recast history is perhaps exaggerated among Americans because our beliefs are so idealistic. How could a people that professes human equality have barred the Chinese, enslaved the blacks, and stolen the Indians' lands?

Cultural beliefs can even lull a people into a false sense of what they have accomplished. Some Americans think that by saying they believe in equality, they have achieved it. A 1988 Harris poll showed that two-thirds of white people believe that blacks "get equal pay for equal work." In fact, as U.S. Department of Labor statistics show, blacks in every occupational category are paid less than whites.

Nevertheless, the United States would be a very different country today if equality were not among its core values. All minority groups have benefited from the spirit of equality that can be found in American life. The belief that every individual has moral worth and thus deserves respect and fair treatment has given weight to demands for equality. Consider the situation of women. Although American women do not have full equality with men, they fare better than women in most other countries. According to a 1988 study by the Population Crisis Committee, U.S. women rank third in the world in degree of equality with men. The rankings were based on data in five areas: employment, education, social relations, marriage and family, and health. The United States had a score of 82.5 percent, compared with 87 percent for first-ranked Sweden. Women in the United States have substantially lower incomes than men and have slightly lower levels of education, but they live longer than men and have comparable levels of nutrition and health care. In Bangladesh, which ranked

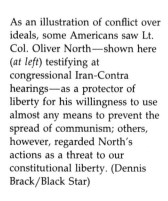

As an illustration of conflict over ideals, some Americans saw Lt. Col. Oliver North—shown here (*at left*) testifying at congressional Iran-Contra hearings—as a protector of liberty for his willingness to use almost any means to prevent the spread of communism; others, however, regarded North's actions as a threat to our constitutional liberty. (Dennis Brack/Black Star)

last in the study and makes no pretense of sexual equality, women fare worse than men on all counts.[13]

## Conflicts over—and between—Principles

America's core ideas are general principles, not fixed rules of conduct. They are subject to dispute in practice, a fact that limits their impact. During the writing of the Declaration of Independence, Thomas Jefferson and John Adams argued over the meaning of liberty, Jefferson contending that its basis was in individual freedom and Adams centering it on a free state. The debate has been restaged countless times in U.S. history. Congressional hearings in 1987 revealed that Lt. Col. Oliver North had broken laws and misused public funds in an effort to assist Nicaragua's anticommunist rebels, the Contras. Representative Lee Hamilton, co-chair of the congressional investigative committee, concluded that North's action violated the Constitution and threatened liberty, a judgment that many Americans shared. However, many other Americans, including committee member Senator Orrin Hatch, concluded that North was a hero for his willingness to guard America at all costs against the threat of communism.

Conflicts also occur because America's principles cannot be fully reconciled with one another. They derive from somewhat different experiences and philosophical traditions, and there are points at which they conflict. Self-government, for instance, emphasizes civic participation and majority rule, whereas liberty emphasizes personal freedom and threats posed to it by unchecked political power. Conflict between the two is inevitable: the ideal of self-government implies that the view of the many should prevail over the opinion of the few, whereas the principle of liberty implies that individuals have rights and interests that are inviolate.

How far should the majority be permitted to go in imposing its will on the individual? To what extent should the individual be allowed to engage in activities that are objectionable to the majority? These are everyday questions of American politics, affecting issues as diverse as school prayer, business regulation, and welfare rights. In the case of school prayer, it once was common for teachers in public schools to lead their students in prayer at the start of the school day, but in 1962 the Supreme Court ruled that school prayer violated the constitutional guarantee of separation of church and state. School prayer still has majority support in opinion polls, and its advocates have repeatedly tried to get around the Supreme Court's ruling. Which position has America's ideals on its side? Each side can say it does, and no resort to logic can settle the difference.

## The Play of Politics

Although government is about ideas, it is also about scarcity and self-interest. Society's resources are not infinite, and people see things in different ways. These facts limit the ability of ideas to contribute to resolutions of conflict. The right of abortion is freedom of choice to some and murder to others. Such disagreements are resolved through politics, not ideals.

---

[13]*Los Angeles Times* wire story, June 27, 1988.

Politics involves the struggle over authority—the legally conferred power to decide public policy. Few controversies of recent years have provoked as much conflict as the issue of abortion. (Dennis Brack/Black Star)

Harold Lasswell once wrote that politics is the struggle over "who gets what, when, and how."[14] Defined more formally, **politics** is the process by which it is determined whose values will prevail in the making of public policy. Those who do prevail are said to have **power,** a term that refers to the ability of persons or institutions to control policy.[15] When power is exercised through the laws and institutions of government, authority is involved. **Authority** can be defined as the recognized right of an official or institution to exercise power. Those who have sufficient power can impose taxes, imprison lawbreakers, permit or prohibit abortions, protect or take private property, provide or refuse welfare benefits, impose or relax trade barriers.

With so much at stake, it is not surprising that people try to exercise power in order to further their selfish interests. Of course, self-interest and principles are not entirely separate. They come together in complex ways, so that, at some level, adherence to principles is in the self-interest of all. The right to a fair trial protects the innocent as well as the guilty. Still, self-interest is a powerful force and does not always coincide with the collective interest.

## THE POWER OF IDEALS

Although their influence has obvious limits, cultural beliefs are a powerful political force. They affect what people will regard as reasonable and desirable. If people believe, as Americans do, that politics exists to promote liberty, self-government, equality, individualism, diversity, and union, then they will attempt to realize these values through their politics.

Why, for example, is the United States the only advanced industrial democra-

[14]Harold D. Lasswell, *Politics: Who Gets What, When, How* (New York: McGraw-Hill, 1938).
[15]Harold D. Lasswell and Abraham Kaplan, *Power and Society* (New Haven, Conn.: Yale University Press, 1950), 75–77.

cy that does not provide government-paid health care for all its people? Are we so much healthier than other people that we have no need of socialized medicine? The answer is no. The United States is not even in the top ten countries in statistical measures of health. Are we, then, so wealthy that all of us can afford to buy private medical insurance? The answer again is no. In 1988, 37 million Americans had little or no health insurance. Part of the real answer is that the United States differs from other countries in the emphasis it places on economic individualism. We have resisted giving government the major responsibility for health care because of our cultural belief that able-bodied individuals should provide for themselves.

In such ways do cultural beliefs lend context to a nation's politics. Ideals serve to define the boundaries of acceptable action. They do not determine exactly what a people will do, but they have a marked influence on where a people will look for answers to their governing problems. For example, whenever Americans have faced a crisis of leadership, their belief in self-government has always inclined them to look first to themselves for a solution. They have sought ways to make democracy work better rather than turning to a military junta or charismatic leader. This was the case, for instance, when Americans' influence on government was threatened by elitism in the 1820s, by bossism and corruption in the early 1900s, and by a presidency gone haywire in the late 1960s and early 1970s. Each time, as with the introduction of the primary election in the early 1900s, Americans found their answer in electoral reforms designed to make their leaders more responsive to them.

A nation's ideals cannot provide all the answers, but they are the source of many solutions. William James noted that human culture is largely "the resettlements of our ideas."[16] Through trial and error, a society—including American society—finds principles that work for it.

## Factors in the Origin and Persistence of America's Core Ideas

In its two centuries as a nation, the United States has changed greatly. The first American settlers lived a rural life near the Atlantic seaboard and were subject to the colonial ambitions of the great European powers. Today's Americans live in an urban society that spans an entire continent and is itself a world power. During its history, the United States has grown from 4 million people to 250 million and from thirteen states to fifty. Yet the political life of the United States has been characterized by remarkable continuity because of the persistence of its founding ideas.

Few observers would argue with the proposition that this continuity of ideas is the most remarkable aspect of the American governing experience. But where did these ideas come from, and why do they persist? Although full answers to these questions would fill volumes, even partial answers are instructive.

[16]William James, *The Principles of Psychology* (New York: Dover Publications, 1950), 638. First published in 1918.

**National Conditions That Foster Democracy**

Democracy appears to flourish when a country is relatively affluent, when its people are in general agreement on the goals of their society, and when its social and economic systems complement its political system (as when all three systems emphasize the importance of individuals). How do these factors help to explain why the United States is a stable, enduring democracy? How do they help to explain why most countries of the world are *not* stable, enduring democracies?

## OPPORTUNITIES FOR LIBERTY IN THE NEW WORLD

Popular history thrives on the illusion that freedom and justice were somehow invented in America in the late eighteenth century. In reality, the outlook of the first white American settlers was shaped by centuries of European life, which, in turn, had been molded by Greco-Roman and Judeo-Christian traditions. As Paul Gagnon has noted, "The first settlers did not sail into view out of a void, their minds as blank as the Atlantic Ocean. . . . Those who sailed west to America came in fact not to build a New World but to bring to life in a new setting what they treasured most from the Old World."[17]

America's special contribution was the enrichment of the freedom and dignity that the first settlers treasured most. The New World's vast wilderness and great distance from the mother country allowed a way of life that was

[17]Paul Gagnon, "Why Study History?" *Atlantic Monthly*, November 1988, 47.

This is a portion of Thomas Jefferson's handwritten draft of the Declaration of Independence, a formal expression of America's governing ideals. (Library of Congress)

unthinkable in the Old World.[18] Although British kings and Parliament tried to stretch their authority across the Atlantic Ocean, the great distance made it possible for the first white settlers to govern themselves more fully than even they had anticipated. They also found in America more liberty, equality, tolerance, and opportunity than they had imagined. Europe's rigid aristocratic system was unenforceable in frontier America. Ordinary people had no reason to accept inferior status when greater freedom was as close as the next area of unsettled wilderness.

It was this natural sense of personal freedom and dignity that Jefferson captured so forcefully in the words of the Declaration of Independence: "We hold these truths to be self-evident, that all men are created equal, that they are endowed by their Creator with certain unalienable rights, that among these are life, liberty, and the pursuit of happiness."

The United States, as the historian Louis Hartz said, was "born free";[19] Americans' freedom enabled them to strengthen their ideals by writing them into their Constitution. Its elaborate system of checks and balances, for example, was designed to foster liberty by placing restraints on the exercise of power. A century after the Constitution was written, Bryce concluded that the United States was still the only nation in which values and institutions were in full harmony. In lands still ruled by princes and kings, he said, people yearned for greater freedom and equality. In countries whose royal governments had

---

[18]White, "American Idea," 12.
[19]Hartz, *Liberal Tradition in America,* 12.

---

# AMERICAN EXCEPTIONALISM

Early in the settlement of the New World, the idea of "American exceptionalism" emerged. According to this belief, Americans are uniquely able to achieve nearly any goal to which they are committed, and their ideals and accomplishments will inspire other peoples. President Ronald Reagan was a strong advocate of American exceptionalism. In his farewell address, as in several other major speeches during his presidency, Reagan quoted John Winthrop's sermon aboard the Puritan ship *Arbella* as it sailed toward America in 1630: "We shall be as a City upon a Hill, the eyes of all people on us."

The reverse side of American exceptionalism is the tendency of Americans to question whether they are living up to their ideals. The Swedish sociologist Gunnar Myrdal claimed that Americans are more self-critical than any other Western people. The nagging worry that the country is not living up to its ideals is a recurrent theme of American politics. In his inaugural address, President George Bush reminded Americans, "We are not the sum of our material possessions," and asked them to rededicate themselves to their civic "stewardship."

The moralistic nature of the American political culture has worked to both the advantage and the disadvantage of the country. The problems have been most evident in foreign policy, as Americans have tried to impress their standards on people who have ideals and goals of their own and who sometimes resent what they perceive as Americans' arrogance. Presented after World War I with President Woodrow Wilson's plan for world peace based on American principles, the French premier Georges Clemenceau exclaimed, "This man Wilson with his Fourteen Points! The good Lord had only ten." The benefits of Americans' moralistic outlook have been felt primarily in domestic politics. Jeffersonian democracy, the abolitionist movement, the Progressive movement, and, most recently, the civil rights and women's rights movements were moral crusades intended to bring American practices more closely into line with American principles.

**Natural Advantages**
In 1940 Senator Kenneth Wherry soberly exclaimed, "With God's help, we will lift Shanghai up and up, ever up, until it is just like Kansas City." Like many Americans before and since, Wherry did not recognize how uniquely favored the United States is. For such ideas as liberty, self-government, equality, individualism, diversity, and unity to be fulfilled, politics must not be primarily a struggle for physical survival. Extreme poverty and insecurity tend to lead countries to restrict personal freedom, initiative, and influence, and contribute to intolerance and divisiveness.

Its geographical isolation from Europe and Asia gives the United States natural protection against potential enemies. The country also has great natural resources. With its vast fertile plains, the United States is often referred to as the breadbasket of the world. It ranks among the top three countries worldwide in production of corn, wheat, potatoes, peanuts, cotton, eggs, cattle, pigs, and horses. As for energy resources, the United States is first in uranium production, third in coal reserves, third in natural gas reserves, and sixth in petroleum resources. In regard to nonfuel minerals, the United States ranks among the top five in copper, lead, sulfur, zinc, gold, iron ore, silver, and magnesium.

SOURCE: *The New Book of World Rankings* (New York: Facts on File, 1984), 479–480.

been replaced by democracies, people had not yet completely grasped the democratic spirit. The United States alone had achieved a joining of purpose and power.[20]

## THE NATURAL ADVANTAGES OF WEALTH AND GEOGRAPHICAL ISOLATION

Although a proper constitution can promote a desired form of government, no constitution in and of itself can ensure such a government. When other nations and peoples achieved independence in the nineteenth century, some of them copied the U.S. Constitution, only to fall eventually under autocratic rule. In most cases, the cultural traditions and natural conditions of these countries were not supportive of limited government.

In truth, the persistence of America's governing ideals owes as much to good fortune as to the enlightenment of its people. Principles such as liberty and self-government tend to flourish only where wealth is reasonably abundant and widespread. In countries where poverty is prevalent, the politics of physical survival is far more compelling than the politics of free speech or open elections. The same can be said of the politics of national insecurity. Living under the threat of conquest by neighboring states does not promote free and open government. In much of Asia, Africa, the Middle East, and Latin America, the ideas that have marked the American governing experience are not yet widely applicable.

With its great wealth and its ocean barriers against potential enemies, the United States has been able to afford its idealized form of government. The Soviet Union is an instructive contrast. The modern Soviet state grew out of an impoverished and absolutist feudal society, whose lands were coveted by its neighbors. Even in modern times the Soviet Union has been a target of conquest. Its invasion by Germany in World War II left 25 million of its people dead, compared to our loss of a half-million combatants in the same war. It is really no great surprise that the American and Soviet systems—one open and democratic, the other closed and authoritarian—developed in vastly different ways.

Americans have never fully appreciated the connection between their politics and their country's natural advantages. "Americans who think about the problem of unifying the world," Lasswell wrote, "tend to follow the precedent set in their own history."[21] The Vietnam war is a case in point. Even as the military situation worsened, U.S. leaders pressed for an American solution to an Asian problem. President Lyndon Johnson compelled the South Vietnamese government, America's ally, to adopt a U.S.-style constitution and to conduct a U.S.-style national election, expecting the people of South Vietnam to rally behind their newly acquired democracy. No such thing happened. They had a feudal legacy, were exhausted by years of internal war, and were alienated from their own government because of its corrupt leadership. The realities of Vietnamese life and culture were far more powerful than the governing ideas that America was offering.

---

[20]Bryce, *American Commonwealth*, 182.
[21]Harold D. Lasswell, *World Politics and Personal Insecurity* (New York: Free Press, 1965), 182.

## POLITICAL SOCIALIZATION: LEARNING THE AMERICAN WAY

As this example illustrates, governing ideas that Americans take to be perfectly natural are not natural at all. They are culturally transmitted, acquired through a learning process that social scientists call **political socialization** (which will be discussed in detail in Chapter 8). For most Americans, the process starts in the

A country's governing ideas are transmitted through political socialization, which begins in childhood. (Michael D. Sullivan/TexaStock)

family with exposure to the political views of one's parents. The schools later contribute to the process, as do the mass media, friends, and other influences.[22]

It is through political socialization that a culture reproduces itself. The new generation learns from the old and thereby perpetuates the society's characteristic beliefs. Change does occur, but the normal effect of political socialization is to preserve existing patterns of thought. In the United States this process is relatively casual. It is not the rigid program of indoctrination that some societies impose on their people. Nevertheless, Americans receive a thorough political education. Their country's core ideas are impressed upon them by every medium: news, public addresses, daily conversations, television, movies, books.[23] The thoroughness of the process is evident in the fact that some of America's political catchphrases are so familiar that just about everyone can complete them:

"Government of, by, and for _____."

"The land of the free and the home of _____."

"Life, liberty, and the pursuit of _____."

"All men are created _____."

"One nation, under God, indivisible, with _____."

Once ingrained, cultural beliefs affect personal behavior. The life of a people consists of experience, not logic. It is the rare individual who can step back and see the world differently from the way in which years of socialization have made him or her perceive it. Steeped in a society that values liberty, self-government, equality, individualism, diversity, and unity, Americans can be expected to think and act along these lines. It has been that way for two centuries and will stay that way in the foreseeable future. Polls show that Americans take great pride in their country and its political system (see Table 1-1). As long as that is so, they have no reason to question their fundamental political beliefs.

**TABLE 1-1  Degree of National Pride Reported by Citizens of Major Democracies**

| DEGREE OF NATIONAL PRIDE | COUNTRY | | | |
| --- | --- | --- | --- | --- |
| | *United States* | *France* | *Great Britain* | *West Germany* |
| Very proud | 87% | 42% | 58% | 20% |
| Quite proud | 10 | 39 | 30 | 42 |
| Not proud | 2 | 15 | 11 | 32 |
| No opinion | 1 | 4 | 1 | 6 |
| | 100% | 100% | 100% | 100% |

SOURCE: New York Times/CBS News polls, 1985.

[22]See Richard E. Dawson, *Political Socialization*, 2d ed. (Boston: Little, Brown, 1977); M. Kent Jennings and Richard G. Niemi, *Generations and Politics* (Princeton, N.J.: Princeton University Press, 1981); Roberta S. Sigel and Marilyn B. Hoskin, *The Political Involvement of Adolescents* (New Brunswick, N.J.: Rutgers University Press, 1981); Stanley W. Moore, *The Child's Political World* (New York: Praeger, 1985).
[23]See James E. Combs, *Polpop: Politics and Popular Culture in America* (Bowling Green, Ohio: Bowling Green University Press, 1984).

## Studying American Government

The chapters that follow describe and explain the main features of the American governing system. The analysis begins with the constitutional framework of the United States, focusing in Part One (Chapters 2–4) on the governmental structure and in Part Two (Chapters 5–7) on individual rights. The analysis then shifts to the relationship between the American people and their government. Part Three (Chapters 8–10) looks at public opinion, political participation, and voting, while Part Four (Chapters 11–15) examines the intermediaries that enable citizens to act together: political parties, interest groups, and the news media. The functioning of governing institutions and officials is the next general topic. Part Five (Chapters 16–21) examines the nation's elective institutions— Congress and the presidency—and Part Six (Chapters 22–25) looks at the appointive institutions—courts and the bureaucracy. Building on all the previous units, Part Seven (Chapters 26–28) examines public policy areas—the economy, social welfare, and foreign affairs. In the Conclusion (Chapter 29) I venture some judgments about the condition of American democracy.

The chapters are collectively designed to convey a reliable body of knowledge that will enable the introductory student to begin to think *systematically* about the nature of American government. Systematic thought rests not on the ability to rattle off unconnected facts but on an understanding of general patterns in American politics.

What are these general patterns? In a sense this whole book is an answer to the question, but a few basic ones can usefully be noted at the outset. The extreme fragmentation of the U.S. governing system is one of these patterns. In most countries final authority is vested in the national government alone, but in the United States it is vested also in state governments. In addition, at both the national and state levels, authority is divided among executive, legislative, and judicial branches. In many other democratic countries, there is no comparable fragmentation of power. Furthermore, there are in the United States many bodies, including bureaucratic agencies and regulatory commissions, that were not established by the Constitution but that, practically speaking, have policy-making authority. America's fragmented system creates competing centers of power and ambition that, as we will see, have enormous implications for how politics is conducted, who wins out, and what policies result.

A second characteristic of American politics is its high degree of differentiation. The United States has a great range of interests of all kinds—economic, religious, ethnic, regional—that are in competition for power. Moreover, they compete through a political process that is itself differentiated. Patterns of action and power vary across the legislative, executive, judicial, and bureaucratic arenas; they also vary across issues and time, with today's losers sometimes becoming tomorrow's winners.

A third broad pattern in American politics is the extraordinary degree to which the scope of governmental action is restricted. Americans tend to draw sharp distinctions between what is political, and therefore to be decided in the public arena, and what is economic, and therefore to be settled through private relations. For all practical purposes, this outlook places many kinds of choices, which in other countries are decided collectively, beyond the reach of political majorities in the United States.

These three patterns and others will be developed in the ensuing chapters. Beneath this book's concern with the patterns in American government is a question that must be asked of any democracy: What is the relationship of the people to their government? Thinking about this question is the foundation not only of reasonable judgments about the state of American democracy but also of good citizenship. Responsible citizenship depends finally on an informed perspective, on a recognition of how difficult it is to govern effectively and yet how important it is to try. It cannot be said too often that the issue of governing is the most difficult issue facing any society. It also cannot be said too often that governing is a quest and a search, not a resolved issue. E. E. Schattschneider said it clearly: "In the course of centuries, there has come a great deal of agreement about what democracy is, but nobody has a monopoly of it and the last word has not been spoken."[24]

[24]E. E. Schattschneider, *Two Hundred Million Americans in Search of a Government* (New York: Holt, Rinehart and Winston, 1969), 42.

## Major Concepts

| | |
|---|---|
| authority | politics |
| political culture | power |
| political socialization | |

## Suggested Readings

Gertz, Clifford. *Myth, Symbol, and Culture.* New York: Norton, 1974. An analysis of the mythic and symbolic nature of cultural beliefs.

Graham, George J., Jr., and Scarlett G. Graham, eds. *Founding Principles of American Government.* Chatham, N.J.: Chatham House, 1984. A collection of insightful essays on traditional themes of American government.

Hartz, Louis. *The Liberal Tradition in America.* New York: Harcourt, Brace, 1955. A historical assessment of the liberal tradition underlying the American political system.

Jennings, M. Kent, and Richard Niemi. *Generations and Politics: A Panel Study of Young Adults and Their Parents.* Princeton, N.J.: Princeton University Press, 1981. A careful study of the relationship over time between the political beliefs of young adults and those of their parents.

Lipset, Seymour Martin. *The First New Nation.* New York: Basic Books, 1963. An analysis of America's origins in political ideas.

Merelman, Richard. *Making Something of Ourselves: On Culture and Politics in the United States.* Berkeley: University of California Press, 1984. An evaluation of culture and politics in the United States.

Rosenbaum, Walter A. *Political Culture.* New York: Praeger, 1975. A comparative study of political culture that helps to place Americans' beliefs in perspective.

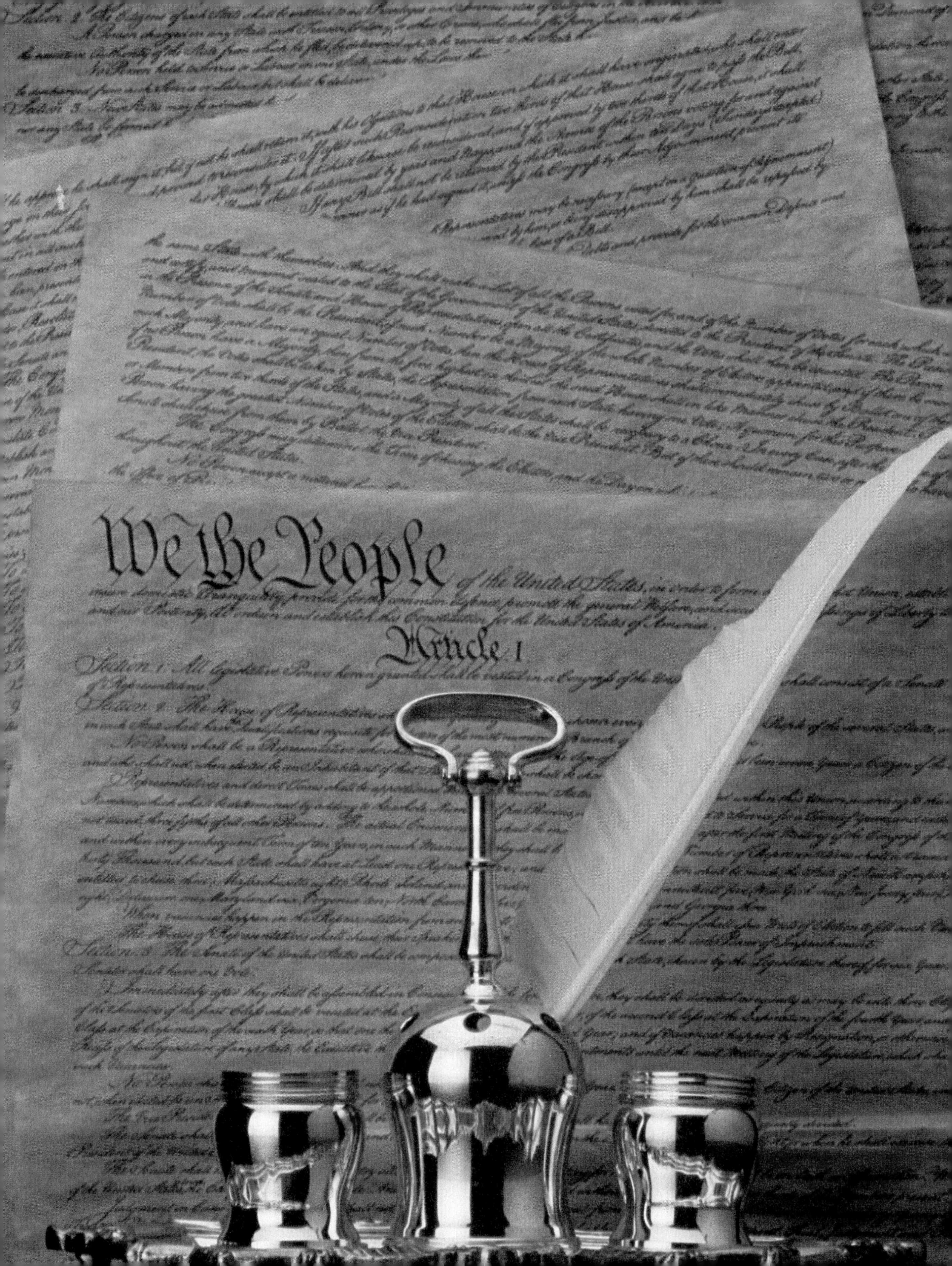
We the People
of the United States

# Part One

---

## THE CONSTITUTIONAL FRAMEWORK

Even though the Declaration of Independence may be a more stirring document, the U.S. Constitution is the greater human achievement. Countries have fought for their independence in every century, often against odds and tyrannies far greater than those which Americans faced in 1776. However, when Americans placed themselves under the Constitution in 1789, they achieved what no people before them had accomplished. They had, during a time of grave crisis and without bloodshed, debated a form of government radically different from any that had gone before and then adopted it without resort to arms.

The U.S. Constitution provided the world with more than a model of peaceful revolution. It became a living symbol of enduring government, a testimony to the idea that a determined people, if given a properly structured political system, can maintain their governing commitment through good times and bad. Today the United States has the world's oldest written constitution still in force. France has had fourteen constitutions during the same period in which the United States has had one.

The task of the writers of the Constitution was particularly challenging because of the need to design a government that could satisfy three different and somewhat competing objectives at the same time. The most pressing goal, which occasioned the writing of the Constitution in 1787, was to establish a government that could serve as the foundation of an American nation. Only a strong and energetic government could bind the separate American states and their diverse interests. The second aim was to keep the nation's government from being so powerful as to threaten liberty. Liberty had inspired the revolution against England and was Americans' highest political aspiration. Thus the power of the U.S. government would have to be balanced carefully by restraints on that power. Finally, the Constitution would have to embody Americans' desire for self-government. This objective was not wholly compatible with the goal of nationhood, which required a transfer of power to a government that was more distant from the people than were the state governments. Nor was the objective of self-government entirely consistent with the goal of individual liberty, which required that there be limits on the power of the majority.

The chapters of this section focus on the U.S. Constitution and are organized so as to address the document's chief objectives— nationhood (Chapter 2), liberty (Chapter 3), and self-government (Chapter 4). Each chapter explores the circumstances that led the first Americans to value a particular ideal, such as liberty, and then indicates how this ideal was embodied in the Constitution's original provisions, such as the elaborate system of checks and balances. Each chapter then evaluates changes in constitutional thought and action during the country's two centuries and closes with a brief commentary on modern practices. The chapters of the section are intended to demonstrate why the British statesman William Gladstone in 1878 declared the U.S. Constitution to be "the most wonderful work ever struck off at a given time by the brain and purpose of man."                                              ★   ★   ★

# *Chapter 2*

## A FEDERAL GOVERNMENT: FORGING A NATION

*The question of the relation of the states to the federal government is the cardinal question of our Constitutional system. It cannot be settled by the opinion of one generation, because it is a question of growth, and each successive stage of our political and economic development gives it a new aspect, makes it a new question.*

*Woodrow Wilson[1]*

The statistics were grim. Over the next year, 45,000 Americans would die in traffic accidents. Nearly 10,000 of those fatalities would be accounted for by persons under age twenty-five involved in alcohol-related accidents. "Raising the drinking age will reduce fatalities among the younger drivers of this country," claimed an official of the National Highway Traffic Safety Administration. A study conducted for the insurance industry estimated that 1,250 lives a year could be saved if a minimum drinking age of twenty-one were established. In July 1984 Congress passed legislation requiring states either to impose a minimum age of twenty-one for the purchase of alcohol or to lose their share of federal funds for highway construction.[2]

Opponents of the law included restaurant and bar owners and college students on some campuses. A common argument advanced by these groups was that if eighteen-year-olds are considered old enough to vote and to be drafted to fight in war, they should be considered old enough to drink. But the most determined opposition came from some of the states. Issues of public safety and health have traditionally been the constitutional responsibility of

[1]Woodrow Wilson, *Constitutional Government in the United States* (New York: Columbia University Press, 1908), 173.
[2]Details in this paragraph and the immediately following ones are from *U.S. News and World Report*, June 25, 1984, 8; July 9, 1984, 14; and June 9, 1986, 21.

state governments rather than the national government. When the drinking-age legislation was passed by Congress, twenty-seven states allowed persons younger than twenty-one to buy alcoholic beverages. These states had two years to raise their legal drinking age or lose their federal highway funds. One governor described the federal legislation as "blackmail." Another called it "Washington arrogance."

South Dakota was one of several states that challenged the law in court on the grounds that it violated powers reserved to the states by the Tenth Amendment to the U.S. Constitution. These legal challenges failed. In the end, all the states that had permitted persons under twenty-one to drink changed their laws. The financial stakes were too high for the states to stand on principle. New York and Texas, for example, would each have lost $60 million annually in highway funds had they not changed their drinking age, and smaller states such as Connecticut, Iowa, and Hawaii would have lost between $10 million and $15 million annually.

The drinking-age issue is one of thousands of controversies during American history that have hinged on whether national or state authority should prevail. Americans possess what amounts to dual citizenship: they are citizens both of the United States and of the state in which they live. The American political system is a **federal system,** one in which constitutional authority is divided between a national government and state governments: each is assumed to derive its powers directly from the people and therefore to have sovereignty (final authority) over the policy responsibilities assigned to it. The federal system consists of nation *and* states, indivisible and yet separate.[3]

This initial chapter on American constitutionalism focuses on federalism. The nature of the relationship between the nation and the states was the question that dominated all others when the Constitution was written in 1787, and this chapter describes how the issue helped form the Constitution. The chapter's closing sections discuss how federalism has changed during the nation's history and conclude with a brief commentary on contemporary federalism. The main points presented in the chapter are the following:

★ *The power of government must be equal to its responsibilities.* The Constitution was needed because the nation's preceding system (under the Articles of Confederation) was too weak to accomplish its expected goals, particularly those of a strong defense and an integrated economy. The Constitution created a stronger national government by granting it significant powers, particularly in the areas of taxation and the regulation of commerce

★ *Federalism—the Constitution's division of governing authority between two levels, nation and states—was the result of political bargaining.* Federalism was not a theoretical principle, but a compromise made necessary in 1787 by the prior existence of the states.

★ *Federalism is not a fixed principle for allocating power between the national and state governments,* but a principle that has changed in response to changing political needs. Federalism has passed through several distinct stages during the nation's history.

---

[3]Richard H. Leach, *American Federalism* (New York: Norton, 1970), 1.

★ *Contemporary American federalism tilts toward national authority.* When national officials choose to act, their efforts are not likely to be blocked by the courts on constitutional grounds. Expanded national authority reflects the increased interdependence of the various segments of American society and the corresponding need for more uniform public policies.

## Before the Constitution: The Articles of Confederation

On June 12, 1776, as the thirteen American colonies braced for full-scale revolutionary war against England, the Continental Congress appointed a committee composed of a member from each colony to decide the form of a central government. The task would be difficult. The colonies had always been governed separately, and their residents considered themselves Virginians, New Yorkers, or Pennsylvanians as much as they thought of themselves as Americans. Moreover, the American Revolution was sparked by grievances against the arbitrary policies of King George III of England, and Americans were in no mood to replace him with a powerful central authority of their own making.

These concerns led to the formation of a very weak national government that was subordinate to the states. Under its constitution, known as the Articles of Confederation, each state kept its "sovereignty, freedom, and independence." There was a national Congress, but its members were appointed and paid by their respective state governments. Each of the thirteen states had one vote in Congress, and the agreement of nine states was required to pass legislation. Moreover, any state could block constitutional change: the Articles of Confederation could be amended only by unanimous approval of the states.

The American union held together during the Revolutionary War out of necessity: the states had either to cooperate or to surrender to the British. But once the war ended, the states felt free to go their separate ways. Several states sent representatives abroad to negotiate trade agreements. Others negotiated directly with the Indian tribes. New Hampshire, with its eighteen-mile coastline, even established its own navy. In a melancholy letter to Thomas Jefferson, George Washington wondered whether the United States deserved to be called a nation.

### A LACK OF NATIONAL POWER

Under the Articles of Confederation, Congress was denied the powers it needed if it was to achieve national goals. Although Congress had responsibility for defense of the states, it was not granted the power to tax, so it had to rely on the states for the money to maintain an army and navy. During the first six years under the Articles, Congress asked the states for $12 million but received only $3 million—not even enough to pay the interest on Revolutionary War debts. Georgia and North Carolina contributed no money at all to the national treasury between 1781 and 1786. By 1786 the national government was so desperate for funds that it sold the navy's ships and had fewer than 1,000 soldiers in uniform—this at a time when England had an army in Canada and Spain occupied Florida.

Congress was also expected to shape a national economy, yet it was powerless to do so because the Articles forbade interference with the states' commerce policies. States imposed trade barriers among themselves. Connecticut placed a higher tariff on finished goods from Massachusetts than it did on the same goods shipped from England. New Jersey imposed a duty on foreign-made goods shipped from other states. New York responded by taxing goods from New Jersey shipped through New York ports.

The Articles of Confederation showed the fallacy of the adage "That government is best which governs least." If England's George III had exposed the dangers of an overly powerful authority, the Articles revealed the consequences of an overly weak authority: public disorder, economic chaos, and inadequate defense.

## A NATION IN DISARRAY

By 1784 the nation was unraveling. Congress was so weak that its members often did not bother to attend its sessions. In November of that year the French ambassador reported to his government, "There is in America no general government, neither Congress, nor president, nor head of any one administrative department."[4] From Europe, Thomas Jefferson reported that European countries refused to negotiate with U.S. representatives. Jefferson found not "the smallest token of respect towards the United States in any part of Europe."[5]

Finally, in late 1786, a revolt in western Massachusetts prompted leading Americans to conclude that the country's government had to be changed. A ragtag army of 2,000 farmers, armed with staves and pitchforks, marched on county courthouses to prevent foreclosures on their land and cattle. Many of the farmers were veterans of the Revolutionary War; their leader, Daniel Shays, had been a captain in the Revolutionary army. They were angered by high taxes on their land and by high interest rates on their mortgages. They had been given assurances during the Revolution that their land, which lay fallow because they were away at war, would not be confiscated for reasons of unpaid debts and taxes. Although the farmers' anger was understandable, Shays' Rebellion scared creditors thoroughly, and they called upon Massachusetts' governor to put down the revolt. As he had no state militia to call upon, he asked Congress for help, but it had no army to send. A disgusted George Washington asked why a country that had won a long and difficult war was not able to maintain public order in time of peace.[6]

Shays' Rebellion demonstrated that the nation's government was nearly worthless and that a breakdown of the country was a real possibility. In response, Congress authorized a constitutional convention to be held in late spring of 1787 in Philadelphia. Congress planned a limited convention: the delegates were to meet for "the sole and express purpose of revising the Articles of Confederation."

[4]Quoted in George Bancroft, *History of the Formation of the Constitution of the United States of America*, 3d ed., vol. 1 (New York: D. Appleton, 1883), 166.
[5]Quoted in Dumas Malone, *Jefferson and the Rights of Man* (Boston: Little, Brown, 1951), 26.
[6]Catherine Drinker Bowen, *Miracle at Philadelphia* (Boston: Little, Brown, 1986), 10.

## *Negotiating toward a Constitution*

The delegates to the Philadelphia constitutional convention ignored the instructions of Congress. Meeting behind closed doors, they drafted a plan for an entirely new form of government. Prominent delegates (among them George Washington, Benjamin Franklin, and James Madison) were determined from the first to establish an American nation built upon a strong central government. Recognizing their goal, Patrick Henry, who preferred a state-centered system, refused appointment as a convention delegate, saying that he "smelt a rat" in the plans for Philadelphia. After the convention had adjourned, he realized that his fears were justified: "Who authorized them," he asked, "to speak the language of 'We, the People,' instead of 'We, the States'?"[7]

That question—"people or states?"—was the most basic one confronting the Philadelphia convention. If the national government was to be made workable, as Pennsylvania's James Wilson argued, it had to be a government of the people, not of the states. The Confederation was inherently feeble because the central government had no sure way short of war to make a state comply with its laws.

### THE GREAT COMPROMISE: A TWO-CHAMBER CONGRESS

Debate at the constitutional convention of 1787 began over a plan put forward by the Virginia delegation, which was dominated by strong nationalists. The Virginia Plan (also called the large-state plan) called for a two-chamber Congress that would have supreme authority in all areas "in which the separate states are incompetent," particularly defense and interstate trade. The Virginia

[7]William Wirt Henry, *Patrick Henry: Life, Correspondence, and Speeches*, vol. 3 (New York: Scribner's, 1891), 431.

Junius Brutus Stearn's painting, *Washington Addressing the Constitutional Convention.* The Constitution of the United States was written during the summer of 1787 in the East Room of the Old Pennsylvania State House, where the Declaration of Independence had been signed a decade earlier. (The Virginia Museum)

Plan also provided that the states would have numerical representation in Congress in proportion to their populations or tax contributions. Either way, the small states would be greatly outvoted. Small states such as Delaware and Rhode Island would be allowed only one representative in the lower chamber, while large states such as Massachusetts and Virginia would have more than a dozen.

Not surprisingly, the Virginia Plan was roundly condemned by delegates from the smaller states. What was the difference, asked Delaware's John Dickinson, between rule by a foreign power and rule by a few powerful states? The small states rallied around a counterproposal made by New Jersey's William Paterson. The New Jersey Plan (also called the small-state plan) called for a stronger national government with the power to tax and to regulate commerce among the states; in most other respects, however, the Articles would remain in effect. Congress would have a single chamber in which each state, large or small, would have a single vote.

The debate over the New Jersey and Virginia plans dragged on for weeks, and it appeared for a time that the convention was hopelessly deadlocked. The small-state delegates even threatened to go home unless their demands were met. Finally a special committee composed of a member from each state reached what is now known as the Great Compromise. The delegates agreed on a bicameral (two-chamber) Congress: the House of Representatives would be apportioned among the states on the basis of population and the Senate on the basis of an equal number of votes (two) for each state.

The small states would never have agreed to join a union in which their vote was always weaker than that of large states, a fact reflected in Article V of the Constitution: "No state, without its consent, shall be deprived of its equal suffrage in the Senate." In retrospect, however, the worries of the small states appear to have been exaggerated. Seldom in U.S. history has a major national issue aligned members of Congress from the large states against those from the small states. Other differences between the states, such as those dividing North and South, have been of far greater significance than differences of size.[8]

## THE NORTH–SOUTH COMPROMISE: THE ISSUE OF SLAVERY

The separate interests of the states were also the basis for a second major compromise: a North–South bargain over economic issues. The South had a slave-based agricultural economy, and its delegates feared that the North, which had a strong commercial sector, would gain a numerical majority in Congress and then proceed to enact unfair tax policies. If Congress levied high import tariffs on finished goods from foreign nations in order to protect domestic manufactures and placed heavy export tariffs on agricultural goods, the burden of financing the new government would fall mainly on the South. Its delegates also worried that northern representatives in Congress might tax or even bar the importation of slaves.

After extended debate, a compromise was reached. Congress was to be prohibited by the Constitution from taxing exports but could tax imports. In addition, Congress would be prohibited from passing laws to end the slave trade until 1808. The South also gained a constitutional provision requiring each state

[8]Alfred H. Kelley and Winfred A. Harbison, *The American Constitution*, 5th ed. (New York: Norton, 1976), 122.

The strong agricultural basis of the South's economy, with its dependence on slave labor, intensified the regional pressure that led to the North–South Compromise. Each slave would be counted as three-fifths of a person in determining taxation and representation in the lower house of the proposed U.S. Congress. (Library of Congress)

to return runaway slaves to their state of origin. A final bargain was the infamous "Three-fifths Compromise": for purposes of both taxation and representation in Congress, five slaves were to be considered the equivalent of three white people; in effect, a slave was to be counted as three-fifths of a human being.

Although the Philadelphia convention has been criticized for the compromise over slavery, the issue of slavery was a powerful argument against a union. Northern states had no economic use for forced labor and had few slaves, whereas southern states had based their economies on large slave populations (see Table 2-1). John Rutledge of South Carolina asked during the convention

**TABLE 2-1  U.S. Population and Percentage of Black Persons, by State, 1790**

| State | Total Population | Blacks (Percent) |
|-------|------------------|------------------|
| Connecticut | 238,000 | 2.5% |
| Delaware | 59,000 | 22.0 |
| Georgia | 83,000 | 36.1 |
| Maryland | 320,000 | 21.3 |
| Massachusetts | 476,000 | 1.3 |
| New Hampshire | 142,000 | 0.7 |
| New Jersey | 184,000 | 7.6 |
| New York | 340,000 | 7.6 |
| North Carolina | 394,000 | 26.9 |
| Pennsylvania | 434,000 | 2.3 |
| Rhode Island | 69,000 | 5.8 |
| South Carolina | 249,000 | 43.8 |
| Virginia | 748,000 | 40.9 |

SOURCE: U.S. Bureau of Census, *Historical Statistics of the United States, Colonial Times to 1970*, Part 1 (Washington D.C.: U.S. Government Printing Office, 1975), 24–36.

**Federal vs. Unitary
Governments**

Federalism involves the
division of sovereignty
between a national
government and subnational
(such as state) governments.
It was invented in 1787 in
order to maintain the
preexisting American states
while establishing an
effective central government.
Since then a number of other
countries have established a
*federal* government, but most
countries have a *unitary*
government, in which all
sovereignty is vested in a
national government. In some
cases, countries have
developed hybrid versions.
Great Britain's government is
formally unitary, but
Parliament has granted some
autonomy to regions.
Mexico's system is formally
federal, but in actuality
nearly all power is
concentrated in the national
government.

| Country | Form of Government |
| --- | --- |
| Canada | Federal |
| France | Unitary |
| Great Britain | Modified unitary |
| Italy | Modified unitary |
| Japan | Unitary |
| Mexico | Modified federal |
| United States | Federal |
| Sweden | Unitary |
| West Germany | Federal |

debate whether some of the delegates thought southerners were "fools." He explained that the southern states would form their own union rather than accept one that prohibited slavery.

## Federalism: National and State Sovereignty

Viewed historically, the most important constitutional decision of the Philadelphia convention was one that underpinned all the deliberations but was not itself debated at great length. This decision was to institute a system of federalism. **Federalism** is the division of **sovereignty,** or ultimate governing authority, between a national government and regional (that is, state) governments.* America's federal system makes its people citizens both of a common nation and of individual states. Because of federalism, the U.S. Congress must act with due regard for the states, which are protected constitutionally from abolition or unwarranted interference by the national government. In contrast to a federal system, a **unitary system** vests sovereignty solely in the national government. Great Britain is an example: the Parliament, its national legislature, can decide policy without regard to the authority of the country's other governments, and the British people are subjects only of the Crown.

Unlike many other features of the U.S. Constitution, the provisions for federalism had no basis in political theory. Indeed, federalism did not exist anywhere in the world before 1787. Other countries had unitary systems of government. The United States had to be different because the states already existed and had the loyalty of their people. Virginia's George Mason spoke for nearly all the delegates in Philadelphia in saying that he would never consent to a union that abolished the states.

Federalism was an accommodation of the ideals of unity and diversity. Americans would be governed as one people through their national government and as separate peoples through their respective state governments. The federal system gave the states the power to address local matters on a separate basis, thus providing for a responsiveness to local values and differences. At the same time, federalism gave the national government the power to decide matters of broad national scope on a uniform basis.[9]

### THE POWERS OF THE NATION AND THE STATES

The Philadelphia convention met to decide the powers of the national government. Accordingly, the U.S. Constitution focuses primarily on the lawful

---

*According to the Constitution, sovereignty is technically held by the people of the United States. In practice, however, their sovereignty is vested in the national and state governments. For convenience we will adhere to the convention of discussing the national and state governments as if they in fact held sovereignty. Local governments in the United States derive their authority from the state governments. Although local units often have considerable autonomy, it is granted at the discretion of the state government, which can overturn local policy and in some circumstances even abolish a local unit. Thus local governments do not have sovereign (ultimate) authority.

[9]"The U.S. Constitution Today," report of the Seventy-third American Assembly, Columbia University, April 23–26, 1987.

authority of the national government, which is provided through *enumerated* and *implied powers*. Authority that is not in this way granted to the national government is left—or "reserved"—to the states. Thus the states have *reserved powers*.

## Enumerated Powers

Article I, section 8, of the Constitution lists, or enumerates, the national government's powers. These seventeen **enumerated powers** are designed primarily to enable the national government to provide for the nation's defense and commerce. Congress is empowered, for instance, to tax, to establish an army and navy, to declare war, to regulate commerce among the states, to create a national currency, and to borrow money. The Constitution also prohibits the states from interfering with the national government's exercise of its lawful powers. Article I, section 10, forbids the states to make treaties with other nations, raise armies, wage war, print money, or make commercial agreements with other states without the approval of Congress.*

Furthermore, acts of the national government, when those acts are within its constitutional powers, prevail over conflicting actions by state governments. Article VI of the Constitution grants this dominance in the so-called **supremacy clause,** which states that "the laws of the United States . . . shall be the supreme law of the land."

## Implied Powers

The enumeration of powers in the Constitution was intended to limit as well as to grant authority to the national government. By listing the national government's powers one by one, the Framers were placing a restraint on its authority: it could not lawfully assume additional powers. A desire for liberty from oppressive government had inspired Americans to revolt against England eleven years earlier, and it was believed that the preservation of liberty required a government of restricted powers. (This subject is discussed at length in Chapter 3.)

The Framers believed, however, that an overly narrow definition of national authority would result in a government incapable of adapting to change. Under the Articles of Confederation, Congress had had authority to exercise only those powers expressly granted it, and partly for that reason it had been unable to respond effectively to the country's changing needs after the Revolutionary War. To ensure that the new national government would be more responsive, the Framers granted it **implied powers** through the **"necessary and proper" clause,** also called the "elastic" clause. Article I, section 8, gives Congress the

**National vs. State Powers**
The Constitution establishes a system in which authority is divided between the nation and the states. What do you regard as the most important powers assigned to national government? (These powers are listed in Article I, section 8.) Are there any important powers—for example, in the areas of law enforcement and education—that you think should have been assigned to the federal government but were not? What would be different if, say, education policy were established largely by Washington rather than by states and localities?

---

*A federal system requires relations not only between the national and state governments but also among the states themselves. The Constitution's provisions in this area need only be mentioned briefly. A first provision is that states are not permitted to enter into commercial arrangements with other states except as approved by Congress. Citizens of the various states also are afforded "all privileges and immunities of citizens in the several states." This vague clause has come to mean that a state cannot unreasonably discriminate against citizens from other states. Finally, each state must guarantee "full faith and credit" to the legal acts and judgments of other states. This means that such things as marriages, wills, and court settlements rendered in one state are to be upheld by other states.

power "to make all laws which shall be necessary and proper for carrying into execution the foregoing [enumerated] powers."

### Reserved Powers

The elastic and supremacy clauses were of deep concern to some leading Americans of 1787, who worried that the Constitution would lead eventually to national domination of the states. Hamilton tried to quiet their fears by arguing (perhaps less than candidly, for he was an ardent nationalist) that these clauses were merely logical devices. Unless legitimate national laws were declared supreme, Hamilton said, the states could break them at will.[10] And, he said, Congress had to be able to pass the laws necessary to exercise its powers or such powers would be meaningless.[11]

Nevertheless, states'-rights advocates insisted on a constitutional amendment to guard against encroachment by the national government. Ratified in 1791 as the Tenth Amendment to the Constitution, it reads: "The powers not delegated to the United States by the Constitution, nor prohibited by it to the States, are reserved to the States. . . ." The states' powers under the U.S. Constitution are thus called **reserved powers.**

## THE RATIFICATION DEBATE

The Tenth Amendment symbolized a controversy that had raged since the Philadelphia convention's adjournment. Many Americans feared a powerful national government. Although Anti-Federalists (as opponents of the Constitution were called) recognized a need to strengthen defense and interstate commerce, they did not see why these goals required the creation of a sovereign national government. To them, the confederacies of ancient Greece and Europe's Hanseatic League were proof that separate governments could work together successfully for defined purposes of common defense and commerce.

To the Anti-Federalists, the sacrifice of states' power to the nation was as unwise as it was unnecessary. They argued that a distant national government could never serve the people's interests as well as the states could. Although Americans had a common language and culture, and thus a reason for union, they also had their differences. The interests of the people of New Hampshire were not identical to those of Georgians or Pennsylvanians, and the Anti-Federalists argued that only state-centered government would protect and preserve this diversity. In support of their contention, Anti-Federalists turned to the French philosopher Montesquieu (1689–1755), who had concluded that small republics were more likely than large ones to respect the people's interests. When government encompasses a small area, he argued, its leaders are in closer touch with the people and are more responsive to their concerns.[12]

The Federalists (supporters of the Constitution) responded that the national government would have no interest in submerging the states.[13] The national and state governments, James Madison wrote, "are but different agents and trustees

Alexander Hamilton (1757–1804) was just thirty-two years old when he served as a delegate to the Constitutional Convention. (Courtesy of the New York Historical Society, NYC)

[10]*Federalist* No. 28.
[11]*Federalist* No. 33.
[12]Montesquieu, *The Spirit of the Laws,* vol. 1 (New York: Hafner, 1979), bk. VIII, ch. 16; bk. IX, ch.1.
[13]*Federalist* No. 2.

of the people, constituted with different powers and designed for different purposes." The national government would take responsibility for establishing a strong defense and for promoting a sound economy, while the states would retain nearly all other governing functions, including oversight of public morals, education, and safety. The national government, Madison said, would neither want these responsibilities nor have the competence to undertake them.[14]

Madison also took issue with the small-republic theory of Montesquieu. In *Federalist* No. 10, Madison argued that whether a government serves the common good is a function not of its size but of the range of interests that share political power. The problem with a small republic, Madison claimed, is that it is likely to have a dominant faction—whether it be large landholders, financiers, an impoverished majority, or some other group—that is strong enough to take full control of government, using this power to advance its selfish interests. A large republic is less likely to have such an all-powerful faction. If financiers are strong in one area of a large republic, they are likely to be weak elsewhere, and the same will be true of other interests. By this reasoning, Madison concluded that political control in a large republic could not be won by a single interest but would require a joining of interests, each of which would be forced to limit its demands and to respect those of others. (*Federalist* No. 10 is widely regarded as the greatest political essay ever written by an American. It is reprinted at the back of this book.)

## A STRATEGY FOR RATIFICATION

In authorizing the Philadelphia convention, Congress had stated that any proposed change in the U.S. government would have to be "agreed to in Congress" and then "confirmed by [all of] the States." Realizing that this procedure would result in defeat for their proposed constitution, the Framers boldly established their own ratifying process. They instructed Congress to submit the document directly to the states, and it would become law when it had been approved by nine states in special ratifying conventions of popularly elected delegates. This was a masterful strategy: there was no hope that all thirteen state legislatures would approve the Constitution, but nine states through conventions might be persuaded to ratify it.

The Philadelphia convention had no authority to override a congressional directive, much less to ignore the amending process required by the Articles of Confederation. The Federalists justified their high-handed switch to popular ratification on the grounds that the people are the only legitimate source of political authority.[15] The Anti-Federalists disputed this notion, claiming that "the basis of legitimate contract was an agreement among sovereign states."[16]

Despite protests by the Anti-Federalists, ratification proceeded in the manner proposed by the Philadelphia convention. The state conventions began in the late fall of 1787. Delaware became the first state to ratify, and Connecticut, Georgia, and New Jersey followed, a sure indication that the Great Compromise had satisfied many of the small states. In the early summer of 1788, New

[14]*Federalist* No. 45.
[15]*Federalist* No. 22.
[16]Quoted in Advisory Commission on Intergovernmental Relations, *The Condition of Contemporary Federalism* (Washington, D.C.: ACIR, 1981), 29.

Hampshire became the ninth state to ratify. The Constitution was law. But neither Virginia nor New York had yet ratified, and a stable union without these two states was inconceivable: they were as large in area as some European countries and conceivably could survive as independent nations.

Virginia and New York nearly did choose an independent course. In Virginia's convention the proposed constitution barely passed, 89–79, and then only after the Federalists agreed to support a series of amendments (a bill of rights) designed to protect individual freedoms. In New York the Anti-Federalists appeared to have a majority. At the last moment, however, a promise of support for a bill of rights, news of Virginia's ratification, and New York City's threat to join the union on its own altered the balance and gave the Federalists in New York State a slim, 30–27 victory.

North Carolina and Rhode Island did not give their support until after the new government had begun its work. Only the fear of isolation finally prompted debtor-controlled Rhode Island to ratify. This smallest state at first had refused even to call a ratifying convention. The shrewdness of the strategy of the men in Philadelphia was thus borne out. Had the ratification procedure rested upon unanimous approval, as Congress had proposed and the Articles required, Rhode Island would surely have cast a veto and killed the new constitution.

## Federalism in Historical Perspective

Since ratification of the Constitution two centuries ago, no aspect of it has provoked more frequent or bitter conflict than federalism. By establishing two levels of sovereign authority, the Constitution created competing centers of power and ambition, each of which was sure to claim disputed areas as belonging within its realm of authority.

Conflict between national and state authority was also ensured by the brevity of the Constitution. The Framers deliberately avoided detailed provisions, recognizing that brief phrases would give flexibility to a government that they hoped, as Madison put it, would last "through the ages." And in no respect is the Constitution more sparing of words than in its provisions for federalism. The document does not define what is meant by the "necessary and proper" clause, does not list any of the states' reserved powers, does not indicate whether the supremacy clause allows the states discretionary authority in areas where state and national responsibilities overlap, and does not indicate how *inter*state commerce (which the national government is empowered to regulate) differs from *intra*state commerce (which presumably is reserved for regulation by the states).

Not surprisingly, federalism has been a dynamic system, its development determined less by constitutional language than by the strength of contending interests and by the country's changing needs. In rough terms, federalism can be viewed as having progressed through three historical eras, each of which has involved a different relationship between nation and states.

*Our Constitution is in actual operation; everything appears to promise that it will last; but in this world nothing is certain but death and taxes.*

Benjamin Franklin, 1789

### ENSURING THE NATION'S SURVIVAL (c. 1789–1865)

The issue during the first era, which lasted through the Civil War, was the nation's survival. The history of America before the Constitution was of government by colonies-turned-states, and it was only to be expected that the states would dispute national policies that they perceived as inimical to their separate interests.

## The Nationalist View: *McCulloch* v. *Maryland*

A first dispute over federalism arose early in George Washington's presidency when his secretary of the treasury, Alexander Hamilton, proposed the creation of a national bank, which would be capitalized jointly by government funds and private investors. Thomas Jefferson, Washington's secretary of state, opposed the bank on the grounds that its activities were calculated to benefit commercial interests only and that its policies would adversely affect small farmers, who in Jefferson's view were the backbone of the new nation. Jefferson rejected Hamilton's claim that because the government had constitutional authority to regulate currency, it had the "implied power" to establish a national bank.

Hamilton's view prevailed when Congress in 1791 established the First Bank of the United States and granted it a twenty-year charter. When the charter lapsed in 1811, Congress did not renew it, but, in 1816, over the objections of state and local bankers, established the Second Bank of the United States. A large number of banks had been chartered by the states after the First Bank of the United States went out of business, and local bankers did not want competition from a national bank. Responding to their complaints, several states, including Maryland, attempted to drive the Second Bank of the United States out of existence by levying taxes on its operations within their borders. Edwin McCulloch, who was head cashier of the U.S. bank in Maryland, refused to pay the Maryland tax, and the resulting dispute reached the Supreme Court.

John Marshall, the chief justice of the Supreme Court, was, like Hamilton, a strong nationalist, and in *McCulloch* v. *Maryland* (1819) the Court ruled decisively in favor of national authority. In his opinion for the Court, Marshall asserted that the "necessary and proper" clause was "a grant of power, not a restriction." Although the Constitution made no mention of a national bank, it was reasonable, Marshall concluded, to infer that a government with powers to tax, borrow money, and regulate commerce could establish a bank in order to exercise those powers properly.

Marshall also addressed the meaning of the Constitution's supremacy clause. Maryland had argued that it had the sovereign authority to tax the national bank even if it was a legal entity. The Supreme Court rejected Maryland's position, concluding that valid national law prevailed over conflicting state law. Because the national government had the power to create the bank, it could also protect the bank from actions by the states, such as taxation, that might destroy it.[17]

John Marshall was a chief architect of national power in the republic's early decades. The *McCulloch* decision provided the basis for a broad interpretation of the supremacy clause and the "necessary and proper" clause, thus serving as precedent for future assertions of national authority. The *McCulloch* decision also reaffirmed a position that the Supreme Court had taken in the case of *Martin* v. *Hunter's Lessee* (1816), in which it rejected Virginia's claim that state courts could decide for themselves the extent of national authority under the

*We admit, as all must admit, that the powers of the government are limited, and that its limits are not to be transcended. But we think the sound construction of the Constitution must allow to the national legislature that discretion, with respect to the means by which the powers it confers are to be carried into execution, which will enable that body to perform the high duties assigned to it, in the manner most beneficial to the people. Let the end be legitimate, let it be within the scope of the Constitution, and all means which are plainly adapted to that end, which are not prohibited, but consistent with the letter and spirit of the Constitution, are constitutional.*

John Marshall, *McCulloch v. Maryland* (1819)

[17]*McCulloch v. Maryland*, 4 Wheaton 316 (1819).

John C. Calhoun (1782–1850), a South Carolinian, was a champion of states' rights. (Library of Congress)

U.S. Constitution.[18] In placing its judgment over that of state courts, the Supreme Court made itself the final arbiter of judicial disputes over federalism.[19] This development was of the utmost significance: as Justice Oliver Wendell Holmes, Jr., noted a century later, the Union could not have survived if each state had been allowed its own interpretation of national law.[20]

### The States'-Rights View: The *Dred Scott* Decision

Although John Marshall's rulings helped to strengthen national authority, the issue of slavery posed a growing threat to the union's survival. A resurgence of cotton farming in the early nineteenth century revived the South's flagging dependence on slaves and heightened southerners' fears that Congress might move to abolish slavery. Southerners consequently did what others have done throughout American history: they devised a constitutional argument to fit their political needs. John C. Calhoun of South Carolina argued that the Constitution had created "a government of states united in a political union, not a government of individuals united by what was usually called a social compact."[21] This line of reasoning led Calhoun to his famed "doctrine of nullification," which declared that each state had the constitutional right to nullify a national law.

In 1832 South Carolina invoked this doctrine, declaring "null and void" a tariff law that favored northern interests. President Andrew Jackson retorted that South Carolina's action was "incompatible with the existence of the Union," a position that was strengthened when Congress authorized Jackson to use military force against South Carolina. The state backed down when Congress agreed to amend the tariff act slightly.

States'-rights advocates gained an ally when Roger B. Taney became chief justice of the Supreme Court in 1836. Taney held a state-centered view of federalism and led the Supreme Court in this direction.[22] In 1857 the Taney Court issued its infamous *Dred Scott* decision, a constitutional debacle that helped propel the nation toward civil war. Dred Scott, a slave, had lived several years with his master in the free territory of Wisconsin, but was living in the slave state of Missouri when his master died. Scott applied for his freedom, citing a federal law—the Missouri Compromise of 1820—that made slavery illegal in a free state or free territory. Six justices, including Taney, concluded that slaves were "beings of an inferior order," who, within the meaning of the Constitution, were "property" rather than "citizens." As property, a slave could never be made free solely by virtue of place of residence.[23]

The *Dred Scott* decision outraged public opinion in the North and contributed to a sectional split in the majority Democratic party that enabled the Republican

Dred Scott (1795?–1858). (Library of Congress)

---

[18]*Martin* v. *Hunter's Lessee*, 1 Wheaton 304 (1816).
[19]Valerie A. Earle, "The Federal Structure," in George J. Graham, Jr., and Scarlett G. Graham, eds., *Founding Principles of American Government*, rev. ed. (Chatham, N.J.: Chatham House, 1984), 160–161.
[20]Oliver Wendell Holmes, Jr., *Collected Legal Papers* (New York: Harcourt, Brace, 1920), 295–296.
[21]John C. Calhoun, *The Works of John C. Calhoun* (New York: Russell & Russell, 1968).
[22]See *Cooley* v. *Board of Wardens of the Port of Philadelphia*, 53 Howard 299 (1851).
[23]*Dred Scott* v. *Sanford*, 19 Howard 393 (1857).

Abraham Lincoln to win the presidency in 1860 with only 40 percent of the popular vote. Lincoln had campaigned for an end to slavery's expansion and for its gradual, compensated abolition. By the time he assumed office, seven southern states had already seceded from the Union. In justifying his decision to wage civil war on these states, Lincoln argued that the United States was founded on its people, not on its states. "The Union," he declared, "is older than the states." In 1865 the superior strength of the Union army settled by force the question of whether national authority would be binding on the states.

*The Union is older than the states.*

Abraham Lincoln

## DUAL FEDERALISM AND LAISSEZ-FAIRE CAPITALISM (c. 1865–1937)

Although the Civil War preserved the Union, new challenges to federalism were surfacing. Constitutional doctrine held that certain policy areas, such as national commerce and defense, were the clear and exclusive province of national authority, while other policy areas, such as public health and morals, belonged clearly and exclusively to the states. This doctrine, known as *dual federalism,* was based on the idea that a precise separation of national and state authority was both possible and desirable. However, American society was undergoing great changes in racial relations and commerce that raised questions about the suitability of dual federalism as a governing concept. Could former slaves gain the full rights of citizenship if they were subject to the discretion of the South's white-dominated state governments? And could the economic problems spawned by the Industrial Revolution be adequately controlled if they were left to the states?

The fact of the matter was that emerging issues of race and commerce required an expansion of national authority. From the 1860s through the 1930s, however, the Supreme Court stood as a major obstacle to national action. This was an era of state supremacy in racial policy and of business supremacy in commerce policy.

### The Fourteenth Amendment and State Discretion

Ratified after the Civil War, the Fourteenth Amendment was intended to protect citizens (mainly black Americans) from discriminatory actions by state governments. A state was prohibited from depriving "any person of life, liberty, or property without due process of law," from denying "any person within its jurisdiction the equal protection of the laws," and from abridging "the privileges or immunities of citizens of the United States." The Fourteenth Amendment appeared to promise that Americans, whatever their state of residence, would be more or less equal in their rights of citizenship.[24]

However, the Supreme Court refused to give the Fourteenth Amendment this interpretation. In the *Slaughter-House Cases* of the 1870s, the Court held that the Fourteenth Amendment did not substantially restrict the authority of states to define the rights of their citizens.[25] A decade later the Court concluded that the

*All persons born or naturalized in the United States, and subject to the jurisdiction thereof, are citizens of the United States and of the State wherein they reside. No State shall make or enforce any law which shall abridge the privileges or immunities of citizens of the United States; nor shall any State deprive any person of life, liberty, or property, without due process of law; nor deny to any person within its jurisdiction the equal protection of the laws.*

U.S. Constitution, Fourteenth Amendment

---

[24]Edward S. Corwin, *The Constitution and What It Means Today,* 12th ed. (Princeton, N.J.: Princeton University Press, 1958), 248.
[25]*Slaughter-House Cases,* 16 Wallace 36 (1873).

Justice John Marshall Harlan was the lone dissenter from the Supreme Court's ruling in *Plessy* v. *Ferguson* (1896) that "separate but equal" accommodations for blacks and whites were constitutional. Harlan wrote: "Our Constitution is color-blind and neither knows nor tolerates classes among citizens. . . . The thin disguise of 'equal' accommodations for passengers in railroad coaches will not mislead anyone nor atone for the wrong this day done." (Library of Congress)

Fourteenth Amendment was not meant to prevent discrimination by owners of private property, who thus could legally exclude black people from hotels, restaurants, and other public accommodations.[26] Then, in *Plessy* v. *Ferguson* (1896), the Court issued its infamous "separate but equal" ruling. A black man, Adolph Plessy, had been convicted of violating a Louisiana law requiring white and black citizens to ride in separate railroad cars. The Supreme Court upheld his conviction, concluding that state governments could require blacks to use separate railroad cars and other accommodations as long as those facilities were "equal" in quality to those reserved for use by whites. "If one race be inferior to the other socially," the Court concluded, "the Constitution of the United States cannot put them on the same plane."[27]

With this decision, the Court in effect repealed the Fourteenth Amendment, allowing southern states to establish a thoroughly racist system of legalized segregation. Black children were forced into separate schools that seldom had libraries and usually had few teachers, most of whom had no formal training. Hospitals for blacks had few doctors and nurses and almost no medical supplies and equipment. In some places in the South, no hospitals were built for black citizens, who could be refused admission to the whites-only facility. Legal challenges to these discriminatory practices were generally unsuccessful. The *Plessy* ruling had become a justification for the separate and *unequal* treatment of black Americans. For the next seven decades, "states' rights" was often invoked by southerners as a guise for the perpetuation of racism.

## Judicial Protection of Business

Through its rulings after the Civil War, the Supreme Court also provided a constitutional basis for uncontrolled private economic power. By the late nineteenth century, the Industrial Revolution had given rise to huge business trusts, which used their monopoly power to gouge consumers and oppress labor. Individual consumers and workers were powerless to combat the trusts. Government was the only possible counterforce. Which level of government— state or national—would regulate the trusts?

In large part, the answer was that neither level of government would be permitted to do so. In 1886 the Supreme Court, which was dominated by adherents of the doctrine of *laissez-faire capitalism* (which holds that business should be "allowed to act" as it pleases), decided that corporations were "persons" within the meaning of the Fourteenth Amendment, and thus their property rights were protected from substantial regulation by the states.[28] The Court also prevented the national government from taking substantial action by narrowly interpreting its commerce power. The Constitution's **commerce clause** says that Congress shall have the power "to regulate commerce" among the states but does not spell out which economic activities are included in the term "commerce." When the federal government invoked the Sherman Anti-trust Act (1890) in an attempt to break up a monopoly on the manufacture of

[26]*Civil Rights Cases*, 109 U.S. 3 (1883).
[27]*Plessy* v. *Ferguson*, 163 U.S. 537 (1896).
[28]*Santa Clara County* v. *Southern Pacific Railroad Co.*, 118 U.S. 394 (1886).

sugar, the Supreme Court blocked the action, claiming that "commerce" included only the "transportation" of goods, not their "manufacture."[29]

Although the national government subsequently made some inroads on business regulation, the Supreme Court remained an obstacle. An example is the case of *Hammer* v. *Dagenhart* (1918), which arose from a 1916 federal act that

[29]*U.S.* v. *E. C. Knight Co.,* 156 U.S. 1 (1895).

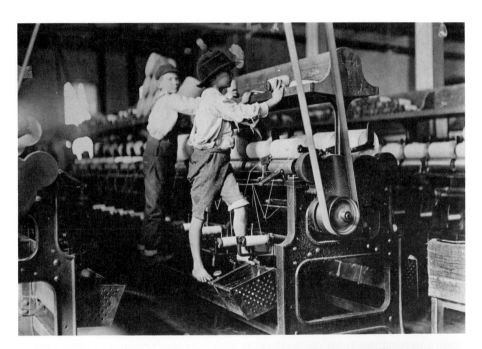

Between 1865 and 1937, the Supreme Court's rulings severely restricted national power. Narrowly interpreting Congress's constitutional power to regulate commerce, the Court forbade Congress to regulate child labor and other aspects of manufacturing. The Court also ruled that the Fourteenth Amendment did not substantially restrict state governments; this allowed state governments to establish racially segregated public schools. (Library of Congress)

prohibited the interstate shipment of goods produced by child labor. The act was popular because factory owners were exploiting children, working them for long hours at low pay. However, the Supreme Court invalidated the law, ruling that Congress's commerce power did not extend to factory practices. Citing the Tenth Amendment, the Court said that these activities could be regulated only by the states.[30] However, in an earlier case, *Lochner* v. *New York* (1905), the Court had prevented a state from regulating labor practices, concluding that such action was a violation of firms' property rights.[31]

In effect, the Supreme Court had denied lawmaking majorities the authority to decide economic issues. Neither Congress nor the state legislatures were permitted to interfere with big business. As the constitutional scholars Alfred Kelly and Winifred Harbison have concluded, "No more complete perversion of the principles of effective federal government can be imagined."[32]

## A NEW DIRECTION: NATIONAL AUTHORITY PREVAILS (SINCE 1937)

Judicial supremacy in the economic sphere ended abruptly in 1937. In the two previous years the Supreme Court had invalidated nearly all the economic-recovery legislation of President Franklin D. Roosevelt's New Deal. The Court then suddenly reversed its position, and American federalism was fundamentally and forever changed.

The stock market crash of 1929, which ushered in the most severe economic depression in the nation's history, served as a catalyst for constitutional change. The economic crisis was so sudden and so profound (at the depths of the Great Depression one-fourth of the nation's work force was unemployed) that government was nearly incapacitated. The states by tradition had responsibility for providing welfare services, but they were nearly penniless because of declining revenues from property taxes and the growing ranks of poor people. The New Deal programs were a way out of the crisis; for example, the National Industrial Recovery Act (NIRA) of 1933 called for a massive public works program to create jobs and for coordinated action by major industries. However, the New Deal was opposed by economic conservatives (who accused Roosevelt of leading the nation down the road to communism) and by justices of the Supreme Court. In *Schechter* v. *United States* (1935) the Court invalidated the Recovery Act, ruling that it usurped powers reserved to the states.[33]

The *Schechter* decision and others like it[34] had disastrous implications for sound governance. The nationwide depression required national solutions, which the states acting separately could not provide. Moreover, when the states did act, the Court was likely to find their policies in violation of the property rights of business, as it did in a 1936 case.[35]

---

[30]*Hammer* v. *Dagenhart*, 247 U.S. 251 (1918).
[31]*Lochner* v. *New York*, 198 U.S. 25 (1905).
[32]Kelly and Harbison, *American Constitution*, 529.
[33]*Schechter Poultry Co.* v. *United States*, 295 U.S. 495 (1935).
[34]See, for example, *Carter* v. *Carter Coal Co.*, 298 U.S. 238 (1936), and *United States* v. *Butler*, 297 U.S. 1 (1936).
[35]*Morehead* v. *New York ex rel. Tipaldo*, 298 U.S. 587 (1936).

Frustrated by the Court, Roosevelt in 1937 proposed his famed "Court-packing" plan. Roosevelt recommended that Congress enact legislation that would permit an additional justice to be appointed to the Court whenever a seated member passed the age of seventy. The number of justices would increase, and Roosevelt's appointees would presumably be more sympathetic to his programs. Roosevelt's scheme was resisted by Congress, but the controversy ended with "the switch in time that saved nine," when, for reasons that have never become fully clear, Justice Owen Roberts abandoned his opposition to Roosevelt's policies and thus gave the president a 5–4 majority on the Court.

Within months the Court upheld the 1935 National Labor Relations Act, which gave the national government broad authority over labor–management relations. As it turned out, this decision signaled the end of the Court's interference in applications of the Constitution's commerce clause. In 1946 the Court openly acknowledged the change when it said that "we have nothing to do" with regulating commerce and asserted that Congress's commerce power is "as broad as the needs of the nation."[36] Thus the constitutional path was open to a substantial increase in the national government's authority. The extent of national power was evident, for example, in the 1964 Civil Rights Act, which forbids racial discrimination by hotels and restaurants on the grounds that they provide lodging and food to travelers engaged in interstate commerce. When the law was challenged, the Supreme Court upheld it, concluding that "commerce" included public accommodations.[37]

**★ ANALYZE THE ISSUE**

**The Supreme Court vs. Congress**
In the late 1930s the Supreme Court ended its interference with congressional application of the Constitution's commerce clause. In your view, is the Supreme Court or Congress better equipped to safeguard America's federal system? Keep in mind that members of the U.S. Senate are elected from states and members of the House of Representatives are elected from districts within states.

## A Perspective on Contemporary Federalism

Since the 1930s, the relation of the nation to the states has changed so fundamentally that some analysts have asked whether it is still appropriate to describe the United States as a federal system. They speak of the "nationalization" of the states and of a "decentralized unitary state."[38] Although these descriptions exaggerate the degree to which national authority has come to define American political life, there is no question that developments of recent decades have diminished state authority in the federal system. Among these developments are the following:

National authority has been used to establish a vast system of social-welfare programs that are funded and defined largely by Washington but are administered primarily through states and localities (see Chapters 6 and 27).

National standards have been developed for policies in traditionally state-dominated areas such as health, safety, education, and transportation (see Chapter 27).

[36]*American Power and Light* v. *Securities and Exchange Commission*, 329 U.S. 90 (1946).
[37]See *Heart of Atlanta Motel* v. *United States*, 379 U.S. 241 (1964).
[38]See Michael Reagan, *The New Federalism* (New York: Oxford University Press, 1972); Jerome Hanns, ed., *The Nationalization of State Government* (Lexington, Mass.: D. C. Heath, 1981); Robert B. Hawkins, ed., *American Federalism: A New Partnership for the Republic* (San Francisco: Institute for Contemporary Studies, 1982); Advisory Commission on Intergovernmental Relations, *The Transformation in American Politics: Implications for Federalism* (Washington, D.C.: ACIR, 1986), 3.

Federal regulation has been extended to cover nearly all aspects of business activity, including labor practices, environmental protection, and consumer affairs (see Chapters 6 and 26).

Federal grants-in-aid have been used to encourage states and localities to adopt policy priorities designated by Washington (see Chapters 18 and 27).

Federal authority (often applied through the judiciary) has compelled states and localities to eliminate government-sponsored discrimination and, in some cases, to create special opportunities for racial minorities and women (see Chapter 7).

Federal authority (usually applied through the judiciary) has required states and localities to broaden individual rights of free expression and fair trial (see Chapter 5).

These developments have been accompanied, and to some extent promoted, by corresponding changes in constitutional doctrine. The extreme expression of this doctrine was a 1985 Supreme Court decision, *Garcia* v. *San Antonio Transit Authority*, which held that state and local governments must apply *federal* minimum wage and hour standards to their own employees. Reasoning that the president and members of Congress are elected by voters in the states, the Court held that states derive their protection from the local ties of these officers, not from judicial interpretations of the Constitution.[39] In other words, national officials may choose not to act in a particular policy area, but when they do, their efforts are not likely to be blocked by the courts on constitutional grounds.

## THE STATES: STILL VITAL, BUT LESS AUTONOMOUS

The expansion of national authority does not deprive the states of all authority. Rather, changes in federalism have served to narrow the areas in which states can operate without encountering federal authority. For example, public schools were once almost entirely controlled by the states (and by local governments, which operate under state authority), but they now must be run within restrictions set by national law, such as prohibitions on racial discrimination and school prayer. Yet public education remains largely a state and local function. About 90 percent of the funding for primary and secondary schools is provided by states and localities, which also decide most policy issues, from teachers' qualifications to course requirements to the length of the school year. Any broad claim that public education in America is "controlled" by Washington overlooks the fact that states actually have wide leeway in educational policy. In terms of public school expenditures, for example, New Hampshire, North Dakota, Arizona, and Kentucky spend less than half as much on each pupil as do New York, Minnesota, California, and Colorado.[40]

As with education, states and localities typically have the larger role in the policy areas that touch Americans' lives most directly—among them public morals, safety, health, and transportation. Most crimes, for example, are defined by state law, most criminal acts are investigated by state and local law-enforcement officials, most trials take place under state law, and most prisoners are held in state penitentiaries and local jails. Or consider government employ-

---

[39]*Garcia* v. *San Antonio Transit Authority*, 469 U.S. 528 (1985).
[40]Advisory Commission on Intergovernmental Relations, *Significant Features of Fiscal Federalism, 1985–86 Edition* (Washington, D.C.: ACIR, 1986), 190.

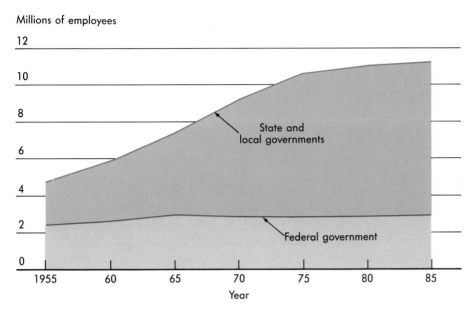

Millions of employees

**FIGURE 2-1 Full-Time Civilian Employees of State and Local Governments and of the Federal Government, 1955–1985** Levels of employment in state and local governments have more than doubled in the past thirty years, while the number of federal government employees has remained fairly constant—evidence that the national government does not completely dominate America's system of federalism. *Source: U.S. Advisory Commission on Intergovernmental Relations. Based on statistics compiled by U.S. Bureau of the Census.*

ment levels (see Figure 2-1). More than 11 million Americans are employees of state and local governments—close to four times as many as the roughly 3 million who work for the federal government.

Nevertheless, federalism is a far different system today than it was in earlier times. What began 200 years ago as a state-centered system has become one in which national officials can, when they choose, intervene in the policy choices of state and local officials. For political and practical reasons, Washington officials do not concern themselves with a wide range of policies, but their potential reach is now very wide. Although members of Congress have not tried to tell localities how to collect their residents' garbage, for instance, localities must comply with federal environmental laws and regulations when they dispose of the garbage they collect.

## INTERDEPENDENCE AS THE CHIEF SOURCE OF NATIONAL ENCROACHMENT

Increased national authority has brought with it a more intrusive government and a concentration of power, much of it in the hands of unelected federal judges and bureaucrats. Not surprisingly, many Americans say they would prefer a smaller and less intrusive national government. This sentiment contributed to the 1980 presidential election of Ronald Reagan, who had campaigned on a promise to return power to the people through a revitalization of the states. In 1982 Reagan proposed a "New Federalism" (discussed in greater detail in Chapter 27), whereby federal programs, regulations, and spending would be curtailed in areas traditionally dominated by the states. Reagan proposed, for example, that Medicaid, a joint federal–state health-care program for the poor, be turned over entirely to the states.

Reagan's New Federalism never materialized. Although the expansion of national authority slowed in the Reagan years, there was no rollback. In fact, federal employment rose by roughly 100,000 during Reagan's presidency, and he acknowledged that state authority was sometimes a better idea in theory than in practice. For example, Reagan's backing was critical to passage of the 1984 legislation that forced states to raise the legal drinking age to twenty-one or lose federal highway funds. Reagan claimed that the high incidence of fatal alcohol-related traffic accidents involving youthful drivers made the issue "bigger than the states."

The major reason national authority has expanded greatly in recent decades and has shown resistance to rollback attempts such as Reagan's is that the states and their citizens have become increasingly interdependent. Governing decisions that in a slower-paced age could be reserved for the states must now be made for the nation as a whole. The economy, for example, is not principally local and state; it is national and international in scope. Such realities have been accepted by most state and local officials. Although they sometimes complain about encroaching federal power, since the 1960s they have eagerly sought federal programs and dollars. States and localities now form one of the largest lobbying interests in Washington, and collectively they receive about $100 billion annually in federal grants for programs that they want but that must be run in accord with federal standards (see Chapter 27).

From the perspective of the full sweep of American history, it might be concluded that the Framers' principle of federalism has been negated. But if federalism is regarded as a pragmatic principle, as the writers of the Constitution actually saw it, then federalism has simply changed with the times. In 1787 circumstances required deference to state authority. Today circumstances often require broad applications of national authority.

## Summary

Perhaps the foremost characteristic of the American political system is its division of authority between a national government and the states. The first U.S. government, established by the Articles of Confederation, was essentially a union of the states. They controlled the national Congress, which had too few powers to fulfill the responsibilities—for defense and commerce—assigned to it.

In establishing the basis for a stronger national government, the U.S. Constitution also made provision for safeguarding state interests. The Great Compromise—whereby each state was equally represented in the Senate, as the smaller states demanded, and membership in the House of Representatives was apportioned by population, as the larger states insisted—was the breakthrough that enabled the delegates to the constitutional convention of 1787 to reach agreement. However, this agreement on the structure of Congress has been less historically significant than the Philadelphia convention's pragmatic decision to create a federal system in which sovereignty was vested in both national and state governments. The Constitution enumerates the general powers of the national government and grants it implied powers through the "necessary and proper" clause. Other powers are reserved to the states by the Tenth Amendment.

From 1790 to 1865, the nation's survival was at issue. The states found it convenient at times to argue that their sovereignty took precedence over national authority. In *McCulloch* v. *Maryland* and other cases, Chief Justice John Marshall argued for the principle that valid national law took precedence over any conflicting state law. Eventually, however, it took the Civil War to establish the idea that the United States was a union of people, not of states.

From 1865 to 1937, federalism reflected the doctrine that certain policy areas were the exclusive responsibility of the national government, while others belonged exclusively to the states. This constitutional position enabled the South, in the name of states' rights, to establish two standards of citizenship, a superior one for whites and an inferior one for blacks. The Supreme Court also promoted the laissez-faire doctrine that private property rights took precedence over the commerce authority of either the national government or the states. As a result, the growing power of big business was placed largely beyond governmental control.

Federalism as we know it today began to emerge in the late 1930s. The Constitution, in the Supreme Court's judgment, could no longer be interpreted to protect the states or private parties against actions by the national government. In the areas of commerce, taxation, spending, civil rights, and civil liberties, among others, the federal government assumed an increasingly larger role, one that was the inevitable consequence of the increasing complexity of American society and the interdependence of its people.

## Major Concepts

commerce clause
enumerated powers
federalism (federal system)
implied powers
"necessary and proper" clause (elastic clause)

reserved powers
sovereignty
supremacy clause
unitary system

## Suggested Readings

*Federalist Papers.* Many editions, including a one-volume paperback version edited by Isaac Kramnick. New York: Penguin, 1987. A series of essays written by Alexander Hamilton, James Madison, and John Jay under the pseudonym "Publius." The essays were published in a New York newspaper in 1787–1788 to explain the Constitution and to generate support for its ratification.

Ferrand, Max. *The Records of the Federal Convention of 1787.* New Haven, Conn.: Yale University Press, 1966. A four-volume work that includes all the important records of the Philadelphia convention.

Glending, Parris N., and Mavis Mann Reeves. *Pragmatic Federalism.* Pacific Palisades, Calif.: Palisades, 1977. An analysis of the relationship among the national, state, and local governments that reveals the pragmatic nature of modern federalism.

Holcombe, Arthur N. *Our More Perfect Union.* Cambridge, Mass.: Harvard University Press, 1967. Traces federalism's development from eighteenth-century principles to twentieth-century practices.

Nice, David C. *Federalism.* New York: St. Martin's Press, 1987. An up-to-date survey of the theory and practice of American federalism.

Riker, William. *Federalism: Origins, Operation, Significance.* Boston: Little, Brown, 1964. A critical assessment which concludes that American federalism's virtues are outweighed by its contribution to slavery and state-sponsored racial segregation.

Rossiter, Clinton. *1787: The Grand Convention.* New York: Macmillan, 1966. An interesting account of the constitutional convention, its members, and the battle over ratification.

Storing, Herbert. *What the Anti-Federalists Were For.* Chicago: University of Chicago Press, 1981. An analysis of Anti-Federalist thought and its origins.

# Chapter 3

## LIMITED GOVERNMENT: PRESERVING LIBERTY

*In framing a government which is to be administered by men over men, the great difficulty lies in this: you must first enable the government to control the governed; and in the next place oblige it to control itself.*

*James Madison*[1]

On the night of June 17, 1972, a security guard at the Watergate apartment-office complex in Washington, D.C., noticed that the latch on a basement door had been taped open. He called the police, who apprehended five burglars inside the National Democratic Party headquarters. As it turned out, the men had links to Republican President Richard Nixon's Committee to Re-elect the President.

Nixon called the incident "bizarre" and denied that anyone on his staff had had anything to do with the break-in. Nixon was lying, but he realized that telling the truth would bring down his presidency. The Watergate break-in was just one incident in an orchestrated campaign of "dirty tricks" designed to ensure Nixon's reelection. Funded by illegal contributions and conducted through the CIA, IRS, FBI, Secret Service, and Nixon's own operatives (called the White House "plumbers"), the dirty-tricks campaign extended to wiretaps, tax audits, and burglaries of Nixon's political opponents (the "enemies list"), who included journalists and antiwar activists in addition to Democrats. Nixon understood that if his abuse of power became known, his impeachment and removal from office by Congress were distinct possibilities. He told his close aides, "I want you all to stonewall it, let them [the Watergate burglary defendants] plead the Fifth Amendment, cover up, or anything else"[2]

---

[1]*Federalist* No. 51.
[2]Tape of White House conversation, March 22, 1973.

Although the Nixon White House managed for a time to obstruct justice (in one ploy, the president's assistants asked the CIA to tell the FBI to stop the Watergate investigation on fictitious "national security" grounds), the facts of Nixon's dirty-tricks campaign gradually became known. Initially two persistent *Washington Post* reporters, Bob Woodward and Carl Bernstein, kept the story alive. Additional revelations materialized during special Senate hearings in 1973. Televised to the nation, they portrayed a broad pattern of official corruption that, according to the unconfirmed testimony of former White House counsel John Dean, extended to the president himself.

In early 1974 the House Judiciary Committee began impeachment proceedings, helped along, ironically, by Nixon's own words. During the earlier Senate hearings, a White House assistant had revealed that all Nixon's telephone and personal conversations in the Oval Office had been tape-recorded. At first Nixon refused to release transcripts of the tapes, but then made public what he claimed were "all the relevant" ones. The House Judiciary Committee demanded additional tapes, as did the special prosecutor who had been appointed to investigate criminal aspects of the Watergate affair. In late July the Supreme Court of the United States unanimously ordered Nixon to supply sixty-four additional tapes. Two weeks later, on August 9, 1974, Richard Nixon, citing a loss of political support, resigned from office, the first president in U.S. history to do so.

Nixon's downfall was owed in no small measure to the handiwork, two centuries earlier, of the writers of the Constitution. They were well aware that power could never be entrusted to the goodwill of leaders. "If angels were to govern men," James Madison wrote in *Federalist* No. 51, "neither external nor internal controls on government would be necessary." Madison's point, of course, was that leaders are not angels and, as mere mortals, are subject to temptation and vice, including a lust for power—hence the Framers' insistence on constitutional checks on power, as when they gave Congress the authority to impeach a president and remove him from office.

The Framers' goal was **limited government**—government that is subject to strict limits on its lawful uses of power, and hence on its ability to deprive people of their liberty. The essential idea of limited government is captured in the phrase "a government of laws, not of men." The authority of officeholders is restricted by grants of lawful power; it is illegal for them to rule by whim or dictate.

This chapter examines the foundations of limited government in the United States. The chapter begins with a review of developments that predisposed Americans in 1787 to favor restrictions on political power and then discusses constitutional provisions for limited government and the related issue of judicial review. The chapter concludes with a brief assessment of the Constitution's historical contribution to limited government. The major ideas that are discussed are these:

★ *America during the colonial period developed a tradition of limited government and individual freedom.*

★ *The Constitution provides for a limited national government mainly by defining its lawful powers and by dividing those powers among competing institutions, each of which acts as a check on the others.* The Constitution, with its Bill of Rights, also prohibits government from infringing on individual rights.

★ *The power to decide whether government is acting within its lawful powers rests mainly with the judiciary.*

★ *Historically, the U.S. government has usually (though not always) acted with restraint.* This record is primarily a result of America's diversity and wealth but also stems from the Constitution's provisions for limited government.

## The Roots of Limited Government

Early Americans' admiration for limited government was based partly on their English heritage. Other European nations of the eighteenth century implicitly acknowledged the divine right of their kings; England was an exception. British courts had developed a system of precedent known as "common law," which guaranteed trial by jury and due process of law as safeguards of life, liberty, and particularly property. These rights were defended by the courts and ordinarily respected by the king and Parliament.

John Locke *(top)* was an English philosopher who contended that every individual has a right to personal liberty. Thomas Jefferson *(bottom)* admired Locke's views and used some of his phrases almost word for word in writing the Declaration of Independence. (National Portrait Gallery, London. The White House Historical Association; photograph by the National Geographic Society.)

The English tradition of limited government was enhanced by the Glorious Revolution of 1688–1689. During the preceding century, England had been racked by religious upheaval and political intrigue. Under the Stuart kings James I and Charles I, Protestants were taxed heavily and persecuted for their religious beliefs, while commercial monopolies and other privileges were granted to Catholics. The Stuarts' reign was interrupted by the dictatorship of Oliver Cromwell, a Puritan whose religious intolerance exceeded even that of the Stuarts. When the Stuarts' restoration to the throne in 1660 did not bring domestic peace, the English nobility in 1688 invited William of Orange, a Protestant Dutchman, to become king. He was offered the monarchy on condition that he accept a bill of rights guaranteeing certain liberties to propertied Englishmen. He was also forced to rule through Parliament, and was made dependent upon it for an annual subsidy. Parliament further insisted that William accept an Act of Toleration, which gave Protestants of all sects the right to worship freely and publicly.

To the English philosopher John Locke (1632–1704), the arbitrary rule of the Stuarts and of Cromwell conveyed a clear lesson: government must be restrained in its powers if it is to serve the common good. Locke's theory of individual rights and limited government became an inspiration to a generation of American leaders. Thomas Jefferson declared that Locke "was one of the three greatest men that ever lived, without exception."[3] In his *Two Treatises of Government* (1690) Locke advanced the liberal principle that people have **inalienable rights** (or **natural rights**), including those of life, liberty, and property. In Locke's view, such rights belonged to people in their natural state before governments were created and thus cannot legitimately be taken from or surrendered by the individual. Locke claimed that people established governments (or, in his term, entered into "social contracts") in order to protect their inalienable rights from lawless rogues. That being the case, Locke concluded, the purpose of government is to protect people's rights; if authorities fail to do so, the people can rightfully rebel against their rulers.[4]

[3]Thomas Jefferson to John Trumball, February 15, 1789, quoted in Dumas Malone, *Jefferson and the Rights of Man* (Boston: Little, Brown, 1951), 211.
[4]John Locke, *The Two Treatises of Government*, ed. Thomas I. Cook (New York: Hafner, 1947), 159–186, 228–247.

## COLONIAL AND STATE CONSTITUTIONS

The English tradition of limited government was reflected in the American colonial governments. In each colony there was a right to trial by jury and some freedom of expression.

The first formal constitution among the colonies, the Fundamental Orders of Connecticut, was written in 1639. It gave "freemen" the right to vote and commanded public officials to use their authority for "the public good." The Massachusetts Body of Liberties, drafted two years later, forbade arbitrary sentences by judges and guaranteed a citizen accused of a crime the right to challenge witnesses. Rhode Island's constitution of 1663 was an even bolder step toward limited government: it granted religious freedom for Christians and placed strict limits on the powers of the governor and the town representatives. In other colonies, however, officeholders had fewer restrictions on their authority and citizens had fewer rights. Religious freedom, for example, was not granted by all colonial governments.

When the American colonies declared their independence from England, they adopted state constitutions that defined the limits of government's scope and authority. The new states preferred written constitutions, since they had been governed by formal charters as colonies. In addition, Americans admired the contract theory of government, which was premised on a defined relationship between the people and those who exercised governing authority. By putting the nature of this relationship in writing, Americans believed they were placing limits on the rightful powers of government. No state chose to adopt the British model of an unwritten constitution.*

## THE DECLARATION OF INDEPENDENCE

The Revolutionary War was partly a rebellion against England's failure to respect its own tradition of limited government in the colonies. Many of the colonial charters had conferred upon Americans "the rights of Englishmen," but English kings and ministers showed less and less respect for this guarantee as time went on. Americans were forced to garrison English soldiers in their homes, and Parliament in 1765 levied a stamp tax on colonial newspapers and business documents, disrupting commerce and public communication. As the colonists were not represented in the British Parliament that had imposed the tax, the colonial pamphleteer James Otis declared that the Stamp Act violated the fundamental rights of the colonists as "British subjects and men." The colonists convened a special congress, which declared that the only laws binding on the colonies were those enacted by a legislature "chosen therein by themselves."

Although Parliament backed down and repealed the Stamp Act, it then passed the Townshend Act, which imposed taxes on all paper, glass, lead, and tea entering the colonies. In *Letters from a Farmer in Pennsylvania* (1767), John Dickinson claimed that the Townshend duties were punitive and destructive of the goodwill between Britain and its colonies. When other colonists joined the protest, King George III sent additional British troops to America and interfered

---

*The British Constitution is unwritten in the sense that no single document defines the precise powers and institutional structure of the British government. Britain's constitution exists in the form of custom, common law, and legislative acts.

with colonial legislatures. These actions served only to arouse the colonists further. England then tried to placate the Americans by repealing the Townshend duties except for a nominal tea tax, which Britain retained in order to display its authority. The colonists viewed the tea tax as a petty insult, and in the "Boston Tea Party" of December 1773 a small band of patriots disguised as Indians boarded an English ship in Boston Harbor and dumped its cargo of tea overboard.

Three years later, sporadic acts of defiance had become a full-scale revolution. In a pamphlet called *Common Sense*, which sold 120,000 copies in its first three months, Thomas Paine had claimed that all of Europe—England, too—was rife with political oppression, and that America was humanity's last hope of liberty. "Freedom has been hunted around the globe. . . . Receive the fugitive, and prepare in time an asylum for mankind." The idea was codified in the Declaration of Independence, which Thomas Jefferson prepared and Congress adopted on July 4, 1776. The Declaration honored the British tradition of specific rights by listing their violations by George III and based its argument for inalienable rights on Locke's philosophy. Even two centuries later, the words of the Declaration of Independence are eloquent testimony to the vision of human liberty:

> We hold these truths to be self-evident, that all men are created equal, that they are endowed by their Creator with certain unalienable rights, that among these are life, liberty and the pursuit of happiness.
>
> That to secure these rights, governments are instituted among men, deriving their just powers from the consent of the governed.
>
> That whenever any form of government becomes destructive of these ends, it is the right of the people to alter or to abolish it, and to institute new government. . . .

## Constitutional Restraints on Political Power

The U.S. Constitution was written eleven years after the Declaration of Independence, with a different purpose. The Declaration was a call to revolution rather than a framework for government and therefore could not be used as a blueprint by the men who gathered in Philadelphia in 1787 to write a constitution. Nevertheless, a concern for liberty was no less fundamental to the thinking of the delegates to the constitutional convention than it had been to leaders of the Revolution.

The challenge facing the Framers of the Constitution was how to control the coercive force of government. Fundamentally, government is based on the use of physical force. The German sociologist Max Weber noted that government is defined by its "monopoly of the legitimate use of physical force within a given territory."[5] Government's unique characteristic is that it alone can *legally* arrest, imprison, and even kill the people who break its rules. Force is not the only basis of effective government, but government must have a last-resort option of coercion if its authority is to prevail. Otherwise, persons could break the law

★ ANALYZE THE ISSUE

**Human Nature as a Factor in Limited Government**
A distinguishing characteristic of government is its authority to compel people to behave in certain ways. The Framers recognized this fact, and also had a cautious view of human nature, regarding people as not entirely trustworthy. Why do these considerations lead inevitably to a belief in limited government?

[5]Max Weber, "Politics as a Vocation," in Hans H. Gerth and C. Wright Mills, eds., *From Max Weber: Essays in Sociology* (New York: Oxford University Press, 1958), 78.

with impunity, and society would degenerate to anarchy. Where there is no rule of law, the strong bully the weak.

The dilemma is that government itself can destroy civilized society by using its monopoly on the legitimate use of force to brutalize and intimidate its opponents. "It is a melancholy reflection," James Madison wrote to Thomas Jefferson shortly after the Constitution's ratification, "that liberty should be equally exposed to danger whether the government has too much or too little power."[6]

The men who wrote the Constitution sought to establish a government strong enough to enforce collective interests, including national commerce and defense, but not so strong as to destroy liberty. In devising a government that was both strong and restrained, the Framers were inclined to err on the side of restraint. Limited government was built into the Constitution through both grants and restrictions of political power.

## GRANTS AND DENIALS OF POWER

The Framers chose to limit the national government in part by confining its scope to constitutional **grants of power.** Authority not granted to it was in theory denied to it. In a period when other governments held broad discretionary powers, this was a remarkable restriction.

Unlike the British Parliament, which had largely unrestricted legislative authority, Congress was limited by an enumeration of its powers. As we saw in Chapter 2, Congress's lawmaking is constitutionally confined to seventeen specified powers and to those actions that are "necessary and proper" to the execution of those powers. The U.S. president was similarly restricted by constitutional grants of authority. Unlike the English king, who could invoke broad extraconstitutional authority in a time of crisis, the president was given no extraordinary powers. As for the judiciary, the Framers contained federal judges' authority by forbidding them to make broad rulings on issues of their own choosing. The judiciary can decide only those issues raised by actual cases brought before it by litigants.

The Framers also used **denials of power** as a means of limiting government, prohibiting certain practices that European rulers had routinely used to intimidate their political opponents. The French king, for example, could order a subject jailed indefinitely without charge or trial. (Among the thousands of French victims of this power were Diderot and Voltaire.) The U.S. Constitution prohibits such action, granting individuals the right to be brought before a court under a writ of *habeas corpus* for a judgment as to the legality of their imprisonment. The Constitution also prohibits bills of attainder (legislative trials) and forbids Congress to enact *ex post facto* laws, under which citizens could be prosecuted for acts that were legal at the time they were committed.*

---

[6]Gaillard Hunt, ed., *The Writings of James Madison* (New York: Putnam, 1904), 274.
*The Constitution contains other prohibitions as well. By declaring that "no title of nobility shall be granted," it protects the nation from the creation of an aristocracy. Moreover, the document prohibits Congress from giving any state preference in taxes or duties in order to prevent a group of states from aligning themselves against the others. The Founders also withdrew powers from the states, forbidding state governments to pass *ex post facto* laws and bills of attainder.

Finally, the Framers made it difficult for those in power to change the Constitution and thereby increase their lawful authority. An amendment can be proposed only by a two-thirds majority of both houses of Congress or in a national constitutional convention called by the legislatures of two-thirds of the states. Such a proposal must then be ratified by three-fourths of the state legislatures or by three-fourths of the states in a special national convention before it can become part of the Constitution.

## USING POWER TO OFFSET POWER

*The accumulation of all powers, legislative, executive, and judiciary, in the same hands . . . may be justly pronounced the very definition of tyranny.*

James Madison, *Federalist* No. 47

The Framers believed that political power could not be controlled if it were concentrated in one institution. "The accumulation of all powers, legislative, executive, and judiciary, in the same hands, whether of one, a few, or many, and whether hereditary, self-appointed, or elective," Madison claimed, "may be justly pronounced the very definition of tyranny."[7] Locke, too, had warned against concentrated political power, arguing that those who make the laws should not also be allowed to enforce them. In 1748 the French theorist Montesquieu enlarged this idea into a concept of separated powers, contending that liberty depended on a precise division of executive and legislative authority.

Montesquieu's principle was widely accepted in America, and when the states drafted new constitutions after the start of the Revolutionary War, they built their governments around a separation of powers. Pennsylvania was an exception, and its experience only seemed to prove the necessity of separated powers. Unrestrained by an independent judiciary or executive, Pennsylvania's all-powerful legislature systematically deprived minority groups of their basic rights and freedoms: Quakers were disenfranchised for their religious beliefs, conscientious objectors to the Revolutionary War were prosecuted, and the right of trial by jury was eliminated.

In *Federalist* No. 10, Madison asked why popular governments often act according to the interests of overbearing majorities rather than according to principles of justice. He found the cause in "the mischiefs of faction." People, he argued, are divided into opposing religious, geographical, ethnic, economic, and other factions. These divisions are not only natural in society but also desirable, in that free people have a right to their personal opinions and interests. Yet factions can themselves be a source of oppressive government. The threat, Madison noted, arises from "a minority or majority, actuated by interest adverse to the rights of others or to the permanent or aggregate interests of the community." If such a majority or minority faction gains full power, it will use government to advance itself at the expense of all others.

Out of concern for this possibility came the Framers' special contribution to the doctrine of the separation of powers. They did not believe that it would be enough, as Montesquieu had suggested, to divide the government's authority strictly along institutional lines, granting all legislative power to the legislature, all judicial power to the courts, and all executive power to the presidency. This *total* separation would make it too easy for a single faction to exploit a particular kind of political power. A faction that controlled the legislature, for example,

[7]*Federalist* No. 47.

could enact laws ruinous to other interests. A better system of divided government is one in which authority is allocated in such a way that no institution can do much on its own. In this situation, political power can be exercised only when institutions cooperate. Since the probability is small that any one faction can gain control over all institutions, factions have to work together, a process that requires each to moderate its demands and thus serves many interests rather than one or a few.[8]

## SEPARATED INSTITUTIONS SHARING POWER: CHECKS AND BALANCES

The Framers' concept of divided powers has been described by Richard Neustadt as the principle of **separated institutions sharing power.**[9] The separate branches are interlocked in such a way that an elaborate system of **checks and balances** is created (see Figure 3-1). No institution can act decisively without the support or acquiescence of the other institutions. Madison explained in *Federalist* No. 48 that "unless these departments be so far connected and blended as to give to each a constitutional control over the others, the degree of separation which the maxim requires, as essential to a free government, can never in practice be duly maintained." Thus legislative, executive, and judicial power in the American system came to be divided in such a way that they overlap; each of the three branches of government checks the others' powers and balances those powers with powers of its own.

### Shared Legislative Powers

Under the Constitution, Congress has legislative authority, but that power is partly shared with the other branches and thus checked by them. The president can veto acts of Congress, recommend legislation, and call special sessions of

---

[8]See *Federalist* Nos. 47 and 48.
[9]Richard Neustadt, *Presidential Power* (New York: Wiley, 1960), 33.

---

**★ HOW THE UNITED STATES COMPARES**

**Checks and Balances**
The U.S. constitutional framework rests on an elaborate system of checks and balances that is designed to limit and control the uses of political power. The system is based on a separation of powers among executive, legislative, and judicial branches, but it also includes judicial review—the power of the courts to invalidate actions of the legislature or executive. These two features are not part of the structure of all democracies.

| Country | Separation of Powers? | Judicial Review? |
|---|---|---|
| Belgium | No | No |
| Canada | No | Yes |
| France | Yes | No |
| Great Britain | No | No |
| Israel | No | Yes |
| Italy | No | Yes |
| Japan | No | Yes |
| Mexico | In theory only | Yes |
| United States | Yes | Yes |
| West Germany | No | Yes |

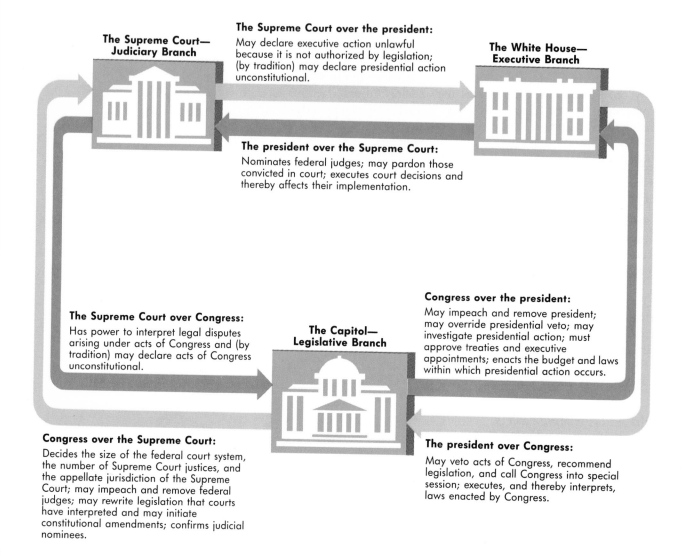

**The Supreme Court— Judiciary Branch**

**The Supreme Court over the president:**
May declare executive action unlawful because it is not authorized by legislation; (by tradition) may declare presidential action unconstitutional.

**The White House— Executive Branch**

**The president over the Supreme Court:**
Nominates federal judges; may pardon those convicted in court; executes court decisions and thereby affects their implementation.

**Congress over the president:**
May impeach and remove president; may override presidential veto; may investigate presidential action; must approve treaties and executive appointments; enacts the budget and laws within which presidential action occurs.

**The Supreme Court over Congress:**
Has power to interpret legal disputes arising under acts of Congress and (by tradition) may declare acts of Congress unconstitutional.

**The Capitol— Legislative Branch**

**Congress over the Supreme Court:**
Decides the size of the federal court system, the number of Supreme Court justices, and the appellate jurisdiction of the Supreme Court; may impeach and remove federal judges; may rewrite legislation that courts have interpreted and may initiate constitutional amendments; confirms judicial nominees.

**The president over Congress:**
May veto acts of Congress, recommend legislation, and call Congress into special session; executes, and thereby interprets, laws enacted by Congress.

**FIGURE 3-1 The System of Checks and Balances**

Congress. The president also has the power to execute—and thereby to interpret—the laws made by Congress. The Supreme Court has the power to interpret acts of Congress that are disputed in legal cases. By tradition, the Court can also decide whether laws of Congress are constitutional and declare them void when it finds that they are not.

Within Congress, there is a further check on legislative power: for legislation to be passed, a majority in each house of Congress is required. Thus the Senate and the House of Representatives have a veto over each other's actions.

### Shared Executive Powers

Executive power is vested in the president, but the Framers meant this power to be constrained by legislative and judicial checks. The president's power to make treaties, conduct war, and appoint high-ranking officials is subject to congressional approval. Congress can also override the president's vetoes of its legislation with a two-thirds majority in both houses and can impeach a president for wrongdoing and remove him from office. Congress's greatest checks on executive action, however, are its lawmaking and appropriations powers. The executive branch cannot act without laws that authorize its activities or without the money that funds these programs. The judiciary's major check on the presidency is its power to declare an action unlawful because it is not authorized by the legislation that the executive claims to be carrying out.

### Shared Judicial Powers

Judicial power rests with the Supreme Court and with lower federal courts, which are subject to checks by the other branches of the federal government. Congress is empowered to establish the size of the federal court system; to restrict the Supreme Court's appellate jurisdiction in some circumstances; and to impeach federal judges and remove them from office. More important, Congress can rewrite legislation that the courts have misinterpreted and can initiate amendments when it disagrees with the courts' rulings on constitutional issues. The president has the power to appoint federal judges with the consent of the Senate and to pardon federal judges convicted in the courts. The president is also responsible for executing court decisions, a function that provides opportunities to influence the way rulings are implemented.

## FEDERALISM AS A FURTHER CHECK ON GOVERNMENT POWER

Theorists such as Locke and Montesquieu had not proposed a division of power between national and local authorities as a further means of protecting liberty. Nevertheless, the Framers came to look upon federalism (discussed in Chapter 2) as part of the system of checks and balances established by the Constitution. Hamilton argued in *Federalist* No. 28 that the American people could shift their loyalties back and forth between the national and state governments in order to keep each under control. "If [the people's] rights are invaded by either," Hamilton wrote, "they can make use of the other as the instrument of redress." Madison wrote in *Federalist* No. 51 that a federal system was a superior form of limited government because power was divided between two distinct governments, as well as among their separate branches. "The different governments will control each other," he said, "at the same time that each will be controlled by itself."

## THE BILL OF RIGHTS

Although the delegates to the Philadelphia convention discussed the possibility of placing a list of individual rights (such as freedom of speech and the right to a fair trial) in the Constitution, they ultimately decided that such a list was unnecessary because of the doctrine of expressed powers: government could not lawfully assume powers, such as the abridgment of human rights, that were not authorized by the Constitution. Moreover, the delegates concluded that a bill of rights was undesirable because government might feel free to disregard any right that was inadvertently left off the list or that emerged at some future time.

# LIMITS ON GOVERNMENT IN THE U.S. CONSTITUTION

*Grants of power:* powers granted to the national government by the Constitution. Powers not granted it are denied it unless they are necessary and proper to the carrying out of granted powers.

*Denials of power:* powers expressly denied to the national and state governments by the Constitution.

*Separated institutions sharing power:* the division of the national government's power among three branches, each of which is to act as a check on the powers of the other two.

*Bill of Rights:* the first ten amendments to the Constitution, which specify rights of citizens that the national government must respect.

*Federalism:* The division of political authority between the national government and the states, enabling the people to appeal to one authority if their rights and interests are not respected by the other authority.

Gilbert Stuart, *Portrait of President James Madison.* Madison is often called "the father of the Constitution" because he was instrumental in its writing and in its ratification (through his contributions to the *Federalist Papers).* (Bowdoin College Museum of Art, Brunswick, Maine)

These considerations did not allay the fears of leading Americans who believed that no possible safeguard against arbitrary government should be omitted. "A bill of rights," Jefferson argued, "is what the people are entitled to against every government on earth, general or particular, and what no just government should refuse or rest on inference." Jefferson had included a bill of rights in the constitution he wrote for Virginia at the outbreak of the Revolutionary War, and all but four states had followed Virginia's example.

Opposition to the absence of a bill of rights in the federal constitution led the Federalists finally to support its addition. Madison himself introduced a series of amendments during the First Congress, which approved twelve of those proposed. Ten of these amendments were subsequently ratified by the states.* These amendments, traditionally called the Bill of Rights, took effect in 1791; they include such rights as free expression, property ownership, and due process for persons accused of crimes. (These rights, termed "civil liberties," are the subject of Chapter 5.)

The Bill of Rights is a precise expression of the concept of limited government. Constitutional safeguards of individual rights rest upon a distinction between lawful and unlawful actions of government. In consenting to be governed, the people agree to accept the authority of government in certain areas but not in others, including the area of individual rights. The people's constitutional rights cannot lawfully be denied by governing officials.

## *The Judiciary as Guardian of Limited Government*

The Framers both empowered and limited government through the Constitution. But who was to decide whether the government was operating within its constitutional powers? Who was to be the official guardian of limited government? The Constitution itself makes no direct mention of such authority.

*The two defeated amendments were about administration and congressional pay.

Whether by oversight or by design, the Framers did not specifically entrust this power to a particular branch of government, although they did charge the Supreme Court with deciding on "all cases arising under this Constitution."

## INTERPRETING THE CONSTITUTION

Many delegates to the Philadelphia convention apparently assumed that the Supreme Court would guard against unlawful uses of political power. The most cogent argument for judicial oversight came from Alexander Hamilton. In *Federalist* No. 78 he argued that there was no reason to fear judicial scrutiny and every reason to favor it. The Court, he wrote, was "beyond comparison the weakest of the three departments of power," since Congress has fiscal power and the president has military authority, while the Court possesses "merely judgment." This judgment could be used to keep the other branches within constitutional bounds. Limits on government, Hamilton said, can be preserved in practice through the courts, whose duty it is to declare void all acts contrary to the Constitution.

Hamilton's position, however, was only an opinion. Not only did the Constitution fail to authorize judicial oversight explicitly, but other nations offered no clear precedent for it. The English courts had the authority to interpret acts of Parliament but not to declare them invalid on constitutional grounds. Not surprisingly, during the nation's first years some Americans believed that the Supreme Court should not be entrusted with final guardianship of the Constitution's meaning. Thomas Jefferson contended that each branch and level of government had the right to decide the meaning of the Constitution for itself. In Jefferson's view, each body was obligated to act within its constitutional powers but could not be told by another institution what its lawful powers were. Jefferson promoted this belief in 1799 in the famous

★ ANALYZE THE ISSUE

**Limited Government as a Contributor to Judicial Power**
Alexis de Tocqueville noted 150 years ago that "scarcely any political question arises in the United States that is not resolved, sooner or later, into a judicial question." Though Tocqueville's observation is an overstatement, it captures an enduring tendency in U.S. politics. Americans turn more readily to the courts to settle disputes than other people do. To what degree do you think this tendency is a result of the concept of limited government, which is embedded in the U.S. constitutional structure? Does the tendency give the courts too much power, especially in view of the fact that judges are appointed to office, not elected?

During the Watergate crisis of the mid-1970s, the American system of checks and balances operated dramatically, as Congress acted to curb the excesses of the Nixon presidency. (David Burnett/ Gamma)

Kentucky Resolutions. Passed by the Kentucky legislature at Jefferson's urging, these resolutions declared that a state could oppose any national law that it deemed contrary to the Constitution.

Jefferson's reason for promoting the Kentucky Resolutions was not to create powerful state governments. In fact, Jefferson opposed concentrated political power of any kind, expressing a preference for government that kept out of individual affairs as much as possible. In advocating the Kentucky Resolutions, Jefferson was reacting to the Sedition Act of 1798, which had been passed by the Federalist-controlled Congress for the stated purpose of stopping subversive activities but was actually applied against Jefferson's followers, the Republicans.

Ironically, if Jefferson's view had prevailed, it would ultimately have led to chronic abuse of political power. If every governmental institution could decide for itself whether its own actions were constitutional, each would be likely to stretch its self-defined constitutional powers to the limit and beyond.

## *MARBURY* v. *MADISON:* **THE PRINCIPLE OF JUDICIAL REVIEW**

The landmark case of *Marbury* v. *Madison* (1803) became the foundation for the principle of **judicial review:** the power of the courts to decide whether a governmental institution has acted within its constitutional powers and, if not, to declare its action void. Judicial review has enabled the U.S. Supreme Court to become one of the most powerful courts in the world. The judiciaries of many other countries lack this authority. The British high court, for example, cannot invalidate an act of Parliament.

The *Marbury* case grew out of the election of 1800, in which John Adams lost his bid for a second presidential term after a bitter campaign against Jefferson. Between November 1800, when Jefferson was elected, and March 1801, when he was inaugurated, the Federalist-controlled Congress created fifty-nine additional lower-court judgeships, thus giving Adams an opportunity to appoint loyal Federalists to those positions before he left office. However, Adams's term expired before the secretary of state's office could deliver seventeen of the judicial commissions. When Jefferson took office, he ordered his secretary of state, James Madison, to withhold them. William Marbury was one of the seventeen Federalists who was denied a commission, and he asked the Supreme Court to issue a writ of *mandamus* that would compel Madison to provide it.

Marbury's petition posed a dilemma for the Supreme Court. On the one hand, if it ordered Madison to deliver the commissions, he might refuse to do so; and as the Court could not force him to act, it would be branded as feeble and inconsequential. On the other hand, a decision in Madison's favor might suggest that a president could do anything he wanted, possibly loosening the restraints on government intended by the Constitution.

Chief Justice John Marshall wrote the Court's unanimous opinion. His decision was ingenious, asserting the power of judicial review without forcing the Court into a showdown with the executive branch. The Court ruled that Marbury had a legal right to his commission, thus implicitly criticizing the president for failing in his duty to execute the law faithfully. However, the Court said it could not issue Marbury a writ because its authority to issue such writs was provided by the Judiciary Act of 1789 rather than by a constitutional

John Marshall forcefully expressed his nationalist views in important Supreme Court decisions during his thirty-four years as chief justice. (Boston Athenaeum Collection)

amendment. Only through amendment could the Court's original jurisdiction be altered. That being the case, Marshall stated, the provision of the Judiciary Act was unconstitutional.[10]

This decision established the Court's authority without placing it in jeopardy. There was no writ of *mandamus* for Madison to ignore, only a Court opinion critical of his actions. Furthermore, the Court had invalidated an act of Congress, thereby asserting its power to interpret the Constitution. Congress could not retaliate, for it had no way to force the Court to issue a writ if the Court refused to do so. John Marshall served as chief justice for more than thirty years after *Marbury*, and his Court did not again invalidate an act of Congress. Nevertheless, *Marbury* had asserted the principle that the lawful powers of government were subject to judicial check. *Marbury* became a precedent for later Court rulings that clearly established the Supreme Court's position as the authoritative voice on the Constitution's grants of power and thus a critical actor in the preservation of limited government.

## Limited Government in Perspective

In the course of their history Americans have not always honored the principle of limited government. The greatest test of the nation's commitment to liberty came shortly after Reconstruction, when the question was whether former slaves would be granted a full measure of freedom. The answer was no. The North turned its back as the South's white majority systematically stripped black people of their constitutional rights, an injustice in which even the Supreme Court of the United States participated by its ruling in *Plessy* v. *Ferguson* (discussed in Chapter 2).

Yet by the standards of a world in which brutal government is all too common, the United States has been relatively successful in restraining political power. Periods of severe repression have been rare in American politics and have seldom lasted very long.[11] When Eldridge Cleaver, a founder of the Black Panther party in the 1960s, returned to the United States from a decade-long voluntary exile brought about by his disillusionment with the country's racial progress, he admonished Americans for not living up to their nation's creed, but added, "With all its faults, the American political system is the freest in the world."[12]

### WEALTH, DIVERSITY, AND GEOGRAPHY: CONDITIONS FAVORABLE TO LIMITED GOVERNMENT

The freedom that Americans enjoy cannot be attributed solely, or even primarily, to the Constitution. No document alone can ensure a limited government. During the early nineteenth century, for example, most of the

---

[10]*Marbury* v. *Madison*, 1 Cranch 137 (1803).
[11]Robert A. Dahl, *Pluralist Democracy in the United States* (Chicago: Rand McNally, 1967), 370.
[12]Quoted in Thomas J. Maroney, "Supreme Law Checks Powers of Government," *Syracuse Herald American*, May 24, 1987, T5.

newly independent Latin American countries adopted U.S.-style constitutions, only to fall under authoritarian rule. Even today some Latin American countries are governed by harsh military dictatorships that use intimidation, torture, and murderous "death squads" to suppress political opposition. In those countries, as in some African and Asian countries, politics is a deadly struggle for survival between the many who are poor and the very few who are rich.

The fact that the United States is a relatively wealthy country has served to moderate its politics. In *Federalist* No. 10 James Madison anticipated that America's economic riches and opportunities would protect it from political extremism. Because property ownership was widespread, Madison foresaw that conflict would not degenerate into a war between those with property and those without it. Economic divisions would occur instead among differing property interests—landed, industrial, and commercial—each of which would be further divided, as in the case of small and large landholders. The net effect of this economic and social diversity, Madison concluded, would be a moderate level of political conflict that could be settled peacefully within a framework of limited government. The exercise of political power in all cases would depend on a joining of factions, so that each of them would be compelled to respect the rights and interests of the others.

Madison's prediction was reasonably accurate. In 1893 Friedrich Engels, the collaborator of Karl Marx, said that he saw no real chance of a wrenching class struggle in America because of its economic diversity and abundance.[13] And Engels was writing *before* the full fruits of the Industrial Revolution had produced for Americans a standard of living that was the envy of the world.

America's ethnic and religious diversity has also contributed to its tradition of limited government. With the major and tragic exception of racial antagonisms,

[13]Daniel Bell, *The End of Ideology* (New York: Collier, 1961), 67.

The United States, with its great social and economic diversity, is less subject to the extreme polarization between two groups that is found in some other societies. In South Africa, for example, conflict between the governing white minority and the oppressed black majority is common. (David Turnley/Black Star)

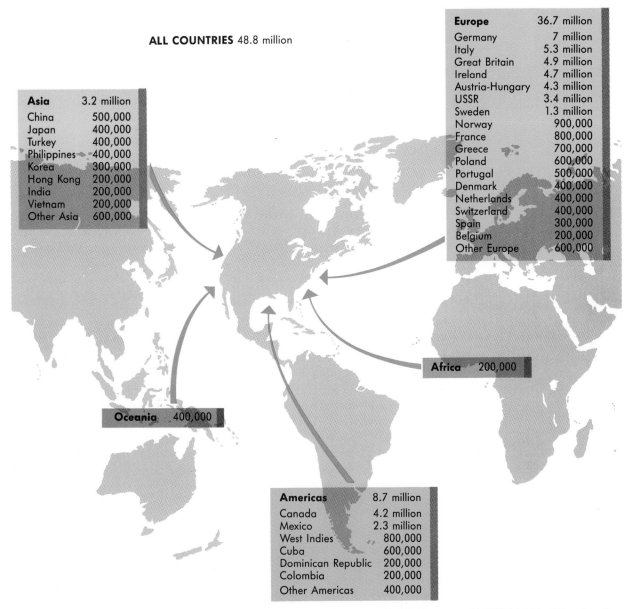

**ALL COUNTRIES** 48.8 million

| Asia | 3.2 million |
| --- | --- |
| China | 500,000 |
| Japan | 400,000 |
| Turkey | 400,000 |
| Philippines | 400,000 |
| Korea | 300,000 |
| Hong Kong | 200,000 |
| India | 200,000 |
| Vietnam | 200,000 |
| Other Asia | 600,000 |

| Europe | 36.7 million |
| --- | --- |
| Germany | 7 million |
| Italy | 5.3 million |
| Great Britain | 4.9 million |
| Ireland | 4.7 million |
| Austria-Hungary | 4.3 million |
| USSR | 3.4 million |
| Sweden | 1.3 million |
| Norway | 900,000 |
| France | 800,000 |
| Greece | 700,000 |
| Poland | 600,000 |
| Portugal | 500,000 |
| Denmark | 400,000 |
| Netherlands | 400,000 |
| Switzerland | 400,000 |
| Spain | 300,000 |
| Belgium | 200,000 |
| Other Europe | 600,000 |

| Africa | 200,000 |
| --- | --- |

| Oceania | 400,000 |
| --- | --- |

| Americas | 8.7 million |
| --- | --- |
| Canada | 4.2 million |
| Mexico | 2.3 million |
| West Indies | 800,000 |
| Cuba | 600,000 |
| Dominican Republic | 200,000 |
| Colombia | 200,000 |
| Other Americas | 400,000 |

**FIGURE 3-2 Total Immigration to United States, 1820–1980, by Continent and Country of Origin** *Source: U.S. Immigration and Naturalization Service.*

American political life has not tended toward extreme polarization of one group against another. A nation of immigrants (see Figure 3-2), the United States is home to a population so varied in its national origins and religions that a general struggle between two readily identified and entrenched sides would not easily be sparked. We can perhaps best understand the significance of this diversity by thinking about the dismal situation in countries where two dominant groups are constantly at each other's throats, such as Protestants and Catholics in Northern Ireland, Greeks and Turks in Cyprus, Jews and Palestinians in Israel, and whites and blacks in South Africa.

Finally, the United States has had the benefit of a favorable geography: the nation's size and the two huge oceans that separate it from Europe and Asia have given it unrivaled protection against possible enemies. The immediate threat of a large-scale invasion by foreign armies has never served as an excuse to entrust power to a repressive regime. As the "Red scares" of the 1920s and 1950s showed, Americans have no special immunity to the political intolerance that can flow from fear of another nation. We can only imagine how much worse these anticommunist witch hunts might have been had the Soviet Union been situated just across the border from the United States rather than in far-off Eurasia.

## THE CONSTITUTION'S CONTRIBUTION TO LIMITED GOVERNMENT

Although no constitutional arrangement could have checked political power had the United States lacked these favorable conditions, the American experience indicates that constitutional provisions also contribute to limited government.

### Allocation of Power

★ ANALYZE THE ISSUE

**The Power of Limited Government**
The use of power to offset power is traditionally American. Is the approach as viable today as it was 200 years ago? Consider the following: First, Americans today are a relatively well-educated and affluent people with a long tradition of self-government. Could they be expected to uphold limited government even if it were not deeply embedded in their political system? Second, American society today requires a government far more powerful than the one that met its needs in the past. Can modern government be sufficiently powerful when it must operate within the constraints of strong checks and balances? Do these constraints result in a stalemated government rather than an energetic one? Think of examples of policies that support your view.

Of all features of the U.S. constitutional system, none has been more important to the control of power than its allocation among separate branches. Throughout most of the country's history, each branch has jealously guarded its authority from the others, a system that has served to check the power of all three branches. For example, when it became known in late 1986 that officials in the Reagan administration had attempted illegally and covertly to trade weapons for hostages held by the extremist regime in Iran and had then used profits from the weapons sales to sneak arms to Contra rebels fighting against the Sandinista government in Nicaragua, Congress launched an immediate investigation. The inquiry brought the unlawful practices to an abrupt halt, produced administrative changes within the White House designed to prevent such abuses of executive authority, and subjected President Ronald Reagan to sharp criticism.

Those in the Reagan administration who devised and executed the Iran-Contra policy justified their actions by saying (rather illogically) that they had merely done what Congress had refused to do. This claim to authority by unelected officials of a single branch of government illustrates vividly why the Framers placed so much emphasis on the sharing of power by separate institutions: they recognized that political power had to be exercised openly and by multiple institutions if it was to be applied accountably and with restraint.

In the American experience, determined opposition from one branch of government has ordinarily constrained another branch's attempts to overreach its authority. Even during times of grave national crisis, this system of checks and balances has usually held up remarkably well. During the depths of the Great Depression of the 1930s, when the Supreme Court was voiding New Deal programs intended to relieve the nation's suffering, President Franklin D. Roosevelt's plan to undermine the Supreme Court by packing it with additional justices (see Chapter 2) was opposed by Congress even though its majority was solidly behind the New Deal.

Of course, each branch of the national government has significantly broadened its authority since the Constitution was written 200 years ago. Congress's taxing and commerce powers, the president's executive and national security powers, and the judiciary's power over civil rights and social policy are far greater than anything the Framers could have anticipated in 1787. Such developments might be interpreted as contrary to the Framers' plan to limit government by enumerating the powers granted to it. Yet the writers of the Constitution were well aware that government would necessarily evolve in response to social change. The Framers used broad language when they listed the constitutional powers of the national government and added the "necessary and proper" clause so that their concept of a government of elastic powers would not be misunderstood. In the final analysis, however, the Framers recognized that restraints on government rest not with grants and denials of power but with competition for power. As Justice Antonin Scalia noted in a 1988 Supreme Court case: "In the dictatorships of the world, bills of rights are a dime a dozen. It is the structure of government, the separation of powers and the balancing of powers, that best ensures preservation of rights."[14]

## Provision for Judicial Review

Judicial review has been an important element in our system of limited government, for two major reasons. First, judicial review was essential if the Court was to be the constitutional equal of the two other branches and thus to have legitimate authority to act against them when necessary. Neither elected branch has much to gain and might have much to lose by being rebuffed by the Supreme Court. Congress and the president have sometimes refrained from initiating policies of questionable constitutionality simply because they knew that the Supreme Court could invalidate their actions, thereby damaging their prestige and calling into question the legitimacy of their actions.[15]

Second, judicial review has proven to be a powerful instrument for protecting individual rights, particularly when they are infringed by state and local governments. Although the Supreme Court has invalidated national laws on constitutional grounds only about a hundred times, it has struck down more than a thousand local and state laws. In the past half century particularly, these rulings have tended to involve issues of individual rights and liberties, such as state and local infringements of free expression, fair trial, and equal protection under the laws. The authors of the Bill of Rights might be amazed by the range of protections it now encompasses, but they probably would not be surprised that the judiciary has become the prime guardian of individual rights. The Bill of Rights was added to the Constitution to transform what were regarded as inalienable rights into legal rights and thereby, as Justice Robert Jackson noted, "to place them beyond the reach of majorities and officials and to establish them as legal principles to be applied by the courts."[16]

[14]*Morrison* v. *Olson,* 108 S.Ct. 2597 (1988).
[15]Richard M. Johnson, *The Dynamics of Compliance* (Evanston, Ill.: Northwestern University Press, 1967), 10, 11.
[16]Quoted in ibid., 3.

## THE RULE OF LAW

Of America's contributions to the practice of government, James Bryce ranked its written constitution first, noting that the United States in 1787 gave the world a model of government in which the word of authorities was subordinate to the words of a written document.[17] Bryce did not claim that the Constitution was perfect or free of bias; no human work is. But Bryce noted that a proper constitution, backed by a people's determination to live within it, can contribute mightily to rule by law. What else but the U.S. Constitution and the American tradition of limited government gave Congress the moral authority to pursue, without threat of military coup or popular insurrection, the possibility of impeaching President Nixon? The Watergate scandal was a remarkable chapter in American history and proof enough that not even the most powerful officer in the U.S. political system stands higher than the Constitution.

## Summary

The Constitution was designed to provide for a limited government in which political power would be confined to its proper uses. Liberty was a basic value of America's political tradition and a reason for its revolt against British rule. The Framers wanted to ensure that the government they were creating would not itself be a threat to freedom. To this end, they confined the national government to expressly granted powers. The federal government also was forbidden certain acts (such as *ex post facto* laws) that could be used to intimidate political opponents. Other prohibitions on government were later added to the Constitution in the form of stated guarantees of individual liberties—the Bill of Rights. The most significant constitutional provision for limited government, however, was a separation of powers among the three branches. The powers given to each branch enable it to act as a check on the exercise of power by the others.

The Constitution, however, made no mention of how the powers and limits of government were to be judged in practice. In its historic ruling in *Marbury* v. *Madison*, the Supreme Court assumed the authority to review the constitutionality of legislative and executive actions and to declare them unconstitutional and thus invalid.

The history of the United States, though blemished by episodes of repressive government, has been relatively free of the political oppression that has so often characterized other governments. Limits on government in the United States have apparently been made possible primarily by the nation's abundant wealth, diversity of interests, and geographical situation, which together have had the effect of reducing and moderating applications of political power. But the Constitution has also contributed to limited government, particularly through its provisions for the separation of powers and its stated guarantees of individual rights.

## Major Concepts

checks and balances
denials of power
grants of power
inalienable (natural) rights

judicial review
limited government
separated institutions sharing power

---

[17]James Bryce, *The American Commonwealth*, 2 vols., 2d ed. (New York: Macmillan, 1891).

## Suggested Readings

Becker, Carl L. *The Declaration of Independence.* New York: Knopf, 1966. An analysis of the Declaration of Independence and the events that inspired it.

Burns, James MacGregor. *The Vineyard of Liberty.* New York: Knopf, 1982. A well-written historical study of the political, social, and theoretical influences on Americans' conceptions of liberty.

Fisher, Louis. *The Constitution between Friends.* New York: St. Martin's Press, 1978. An analysis of the constitutional relationship of the executive and legislative branches both in the Founders' conception and in subsequent developments.

Locke, John. *The Two Treatises of Government.* New York: Hafner, 1947. Published originally in 1690, Locke's work is a broad statement of the fundamental principles of limited government.

Schwartz, Bernard. *The Great Rights of Mankind: A History of the American Bill of Rights.* New York: Oxford University Press, 1977. A historical overview of the Bill of Rights and its importance to limited government in the United States.

Wood, Gordon S. *The Creation of the American Republic.* Chapel Hill: University of North Carolina Press, 1969. An examination of American political thought before the Philadelphia convention.

# Chapter 4

## REPRESENTATIVE GOVERNMENT: PROVIDING POPULAR SOVEREIGNTY

*The people must be governed by a majority, with whom all power resides. But how is the sense of this majority to be obtained?*

*Fisher Ames (1788)[1]*

The Iran-Contra arms-trading scandal of 1986 had been public knowledge for about a month when the Reagan administration fought back on the issue of Central American policy. President Ronald Reagan's communications director, Patrick Buchanan, accused congressional Democrats of exploiting the scandal in order to achieve a cutoff of all assistance to the Nicaraguan rebels and thereby to undo a decision made by the American people two years earlier, when they had resoundingly reelected Reagan. In Buchanan's view, Reagan's landslide reelection victory proved that the American people desired a continuation of Republican leadership and policies, including support for the Contras. But was that really the case? After all, the Democrats had won a landslide of their own in 1984, gaining a 253–182 seat advantage in the House of Representatives.

Americans are accustomed to thinking of their country as the most democratic on earth. However, if democracy is defined by the directness with which an electoral majority leads to a governing majority, the American system is less democratic than many others. As the 1984 campaign illustrates, U.S. elections do not always produce a clear-cut governing majority. Since World War II, control of the presidency and of one or both houses of Congress has been split between the Republican and Democratic parties for more years than it has

[1]Quoted in Charles S. Hyneman, "Republican Government in America," in George J. Graham, Jr., and Scarlett G. Graham, eds., *Founding Principles of American Government*, rev. ed. (Chatham, N.J.: Chatham House, 1984), 19.

rested with a single party. The situation is different elsewhere. In Great Britian, West Germany, Japan, and many other democracies, when the voters go to the polls, one party is almost certain to capture full control of legislative *and* executive power, leaving no doubt that its policy agenda should prevail.

The roots of the American situation lie two centuries deep, in the Framers' distrust of popular majorities. The delegates to the Philadelphia convention built significant antimajoritarian devices into the Constitution. In the Framers' judgment, the great risk of popular government was **tyranny of the majority.** Inflamed by a personality or issue of the moment, the majority could become an irrational mob with no regard for others. There would be times, James Madison wrote in *Federalist* No. 10, when "[the] passions . . . , not the reason of the public, would sit in judgment." Moreover, an unreasoning majority was hard to contain because it would arrogantly believe that its view should prevail over any view held by a minority of citizens. Yet the minority also had its rights and interests, including property, personal freedom, and a fair chance to persuade the majority of the merits of its viewpoint.

The challenge for the Framers was to devise a government that allowed for majority rule but also protected minority interests and individual rights. No form of self-government could eliminate the threat of majority tyranny, but the Framers believed that this danger would be greatly diminished by properly structured institutions. The United States would have, not a democracy, but a republic. Today the terms **democracy** and **republic** are used interchangeably to refer to a system of government in which ultimate political power rests with the people through their capacity to choose representatives in free and open elections. In 1787, however, "democracy" and "republic" referred to quite different governing systems. When the people gathered in a large assembly to decide public issues directly, that was democratic government. When elected officials met in representative institutions to decide policy, that was republican, or representative, government.[2]

The United States was much too large to be governed directly by the people through popular assemblies, so the Framers also had another distinction in mind when they called their plan republican rather than democratic in its form. In the Framers' conception of representative government, representatives were placed at a considerable distance from the people. The public would elect directly only the members of the U.S. House of Representatives. U.S. senators, the president, and federal judges would be chosen by indirect forms of popular election. The purpose was to make it difficult for a popular majority to gain and exploit the full power of government.

Although the Framers maintained that these arrangements would result in a government that served the public's "true interest,"[3] opponents of the Constitution charged that the people had been denied self-government. Officials would be free to pursue policies of their choosing, and even if they were committed to serving the public's interest, they would be so distant from the people as to have no real understanding of their needs. For its critics, the Constitution was a blueprint not for popular sovereignty but for rule by the upper classes.

[2]Ibid.,6.
[3]*Federalist* No. 10.

The debate over the power of the majority which began with the writing of the Constitution has continued in one form or another throughout the country's history. This chapter traces that debate, concentrating on the theory and practice of representative government as originally expressed by the Constitution and as modified by subsequent developments, such as the change to direct election of U.S. senators. The major ideas presented in the chapter are these:

★ *The structure of government provided by the Constitution is based on the idea that political power must be separated from immediate popular influences if sound policies are to result.* This idea was central to the Framers' theory of government and still has its advocates today.

★ *The idea of popular government—in which the majority's desires have a relatively direct and immediate impact on public policy—has gained strength since the nation's beginning.* Political parties and primary elections have increased the public's direct influence on the national government. The impulse for these developments has come largely from the American people themselves and from leaders acting on the majority's behalf.

★ *At the root of the debate over the proper form of representative government is an irreconcilable difference of opinion about worst consequences.* Those who fear a concentration of power in the hands of the majority believe that it leads to a government that does not respect the legitimate rights and interests of the minority. Those who fear a lack of power in the hands of the majority claim that it leads to a government that serves primarily the rights and interests of a small upper-class elite.

## Representation in the Constitution

To the Framers, a representative government that worked effectively only in good times was undeserving of respect. The true test of a governing system was its ability to withstand the stress of a period of desperation and fear. And in this regard, the record of democracies left much to be desired. In 1786, for example, debtors had gained control of Rhode Island's legislature and made paper money a legal means of paying debts, even though existing contracts called for payment in gold. Creditors were then hunted down and held captive in public places so that debtors could come and pay them in full with worthless paper money. A Boston newspaper wrote that Rhode Island should be renamed *Rogue* Island. James Madison offered a broader indictment: "It may be concluded . . . that such [uncontrolled] democracies have ever been spectacles of turbulence and contention; have ever been found incompatible with personal security, or the rights of property; and have in general been as short in their lives, as they have been violent in their deaths."[4]

To guard against chaos and incivility, the Framers devised a government that incorporated the principle of majority rule along with built-in protections against majority power. The objective was a government that would be sensitive to the majority's immediate concerns yet deliberative enough to promote society's broader and more enduring interests.

[4]*Federalist* No. 10.

The Framers' concept of **representative democracy** was similar to an idea put forth by the English theorist Edmund Burke (1729–1797). In his *Letter to the Sheriffs of Bristol*, Burke argued that representatives should act as public **trustees:** they are obliged to promote the interest of those who elected them, but the nature of this interest is for them, not the voters, to decide. Burke was concerned about the ease with which society could degenerate into selfishness, and he thought it imperative for representatives not to surrender their judgment to popular whim.

## INDIRECT POPULAR RULE

Under the Constitution, all power is one or two steps removed from the people. The Constitution has no provision for any form of direct popular participation in the making of public policy.

Edmund Burke, English political theorist. (The Bettmann Archive)

The House of Representatives was the institution placed closest to the people, who would directly elect its members to two-year terms of office. Frequent and direct election of House members was intended to make government sensitive to the concerns of popular majorities. The Constitution specified, however, that the House could have no more than one representative for every 30,000 inhabitants; this provision was designed to ensure that each representative would represent a large area and population and thus not be bound too closely to local concerns.[5]

U.S. senators would be appointed by the legislatures of the states they represented. Because state legislators were popularly elected, the people would be choosing their senators indirectly. Every two years, a third of the senators would be appointed to six-year terms. The Senate was expected to check and balance the House, which, by virtue of the more frequent and direct election of its members, would presumably be more responsive to popular opinion.

Presidential selection was an issue of considerable debate at the Philadelphia convention. Hamilton favored a life-term president, but others feared that life tenure would turn the office into a monarchy. Another proposal was to have the president chosen by Congress, but this suggestion was defeated on the argument that it would upset the balance between the legislative and executive branches, since one would be appointing the chief of the other. Direct election of the president was twice proposed and twice rejected because the delegates were uneasy about linking executive power directly to popular majorities.

The Framers finally chose to have the president selected by the votes of electors (the so-called Electoral College; see Chapter 19). Each state would have as many electors as it had members in Congress and could select them by any method it chose. Each elector would vote for two candidates for president. The candidate who received the largest number of electoral votes, if that number constituted a majority (that is, more than 50 percent), would be selected as president; the runner-up would become vice-president. If no candidate won a majority, the election would go to the House of Representatives, which would choose the president from among the top five finishers. The president would serve a four-year term and be eligible for reelection.

With regard to the Supreme Court justices, the Philadelphia convention was

[5]*Federalist* No. 10.

# CHOOSING NATIONAL LEADERS

Because the Framers feared the concentration of political power, they devised alternative methods of selection and terms of service for national officials.

| OFFICE | METHOD OF SELECTION | TERM OF SERVICE |
|---|---|---|
| President | Electoral College | 4 years |
| U.S. senator | State legislature | 6 years (1/3 of senators' terms expire every 2 years) |
| U.S. representative | Popular election | 2 years |
| Federal judge | Nominated by president, approved by Senate | Indefinite (subject to "good behavior") |

in general agreement that they should be appointed rather than elected. At first the delegates decided that the Senate should make the appointments, but they finally chose to have judges nominated by the president and confirmed through approval by the Senate. Once confirmed, the Constitution declared, judges "shall hold their offices during good behavior." Although the selection procedure tied the judiciary to the other branches, the Framers intended to ensure an independent judiciary by allowing judges, in effect, to hold office for life unless they committed a crime.

These differing methods of selecting national officers would not prevent a determined majority from achieving full power if it had sufficient strength and longevity, but control could not be attained easily or quickly. The House of Representatives might surrender to an impassioned majority in a single election, but the Senate, presidency, and judiciary were unlikely to yield so quickly. The delay would reduce the probability that government would degenerate into mob rule. The Framers believed that majority tyranny would be impulsive. Given time, the people would presumably come to their senses.

## ANTI-FEDERALIST DISSENT

The Anti-Federalists viewed the Constitution's scheme of representation as at best a severe restriction on majority rule and at worst an elaborate conspiracy by the Federalists to secure power for the wealthy. As the Anti-Federalists saw it, the Constitution was not a bulwark against mob rule, but a barrier to rule by the people. The Senate and presidency in particular were seen as elite institutions.

Richard Henry Lee of Virginia criticized even the House of Representatives, which he said had "very little democracy in it" because each of its members would represent a large population and area. Madison had claimed that this

A Peep into the Antifederal Club

This 1793 cartoon depicts the Anti-Federalists as a "club" gathering to condemn federal government. Jefferson is shown standing with an auctioneer's gavel, wondering "whether 'tis nobler in the mind to knock down [that is, auction off] dry goods with this hammer or with this head to introduce[?] some means of knocking down a Government and on its ruins raise myself to Eminence and Fortune." (Historical Picture Service)

arrangement was necessary because otherwise representatives would be "unduly attached" to local interests and "too little fit to comprehend and pursue great and national objects." To Lee and others, such arguments were a mask for elitism—rule by a few who claimed to know the people's interest better than the people knew it themselves.[6]

## Modifying the Framers' Work: Toward a More Democratic System

The Framers denied that the Constitution was intended to thwart popular government. They claimed that it was formulated instead to correct flaws that had ruined previous attempts at rule by the people. Madison declared in *Federalist* No. 10 that the Constitution was "a republican remedy" for the defects inherent in democratic government.

Nevertheless, the Framers' conception of self-government was somewhat at odds with prevailing theory and practice. From Aristotle on, it had been held that majority rule was the defining characteristic of a government of the people. The majority might not be any wiser than the minority, but the view of the greater number ought to prevail over that of the smaller number. Furthermore, the promise that they would govern themselves was what had lured ordinary Americans by the thousands to make great sacrifices in the war against England. The spirit of 1776 was democratic in its nature, a fact that was reflected in the constitutions of the states. Every state but South Carolina held an annual

[6]Richard Henry Lee, *Letters from the Federal Farmer*, in Forrest McDonald, ed., *Empire and Nation* (Englewood Cliffs, N.J.: Prentice-Hall, 1962), 103–117.

legislative election, and several states also chose their governors through annual election by the people.[7]

In this context, the Constitution's provisions for popular rule were paltry, and it was not long after the Constitution was ratified that Americans sought a stronger voice in their own governing. The process has continued throughout the country's history: in no other constitutional area have Americans shown such a willingness to experiment.

## THE ERA OF JEFFERSONIAN DEMOCRACY

Thomas Jefferson, who otherwise admired the Constitution, was among the prominent Americans who questioned its provisions for self-government. To Jefferson, America was the hope of ordinary people everywhere for liberation from rule by the elite few, and he reasoned that the American people might someday rebel against the small governing role assigned them by the Constitution.[8]

Ironically, it was Jefferson who may have spared the nation a bloody revolution over the issue of popular sovereignty. Under John Adams, the nation's second president and a thoroughgoing elitist, the national government increasingly favored the nation's wealthy interests. Adams publicly suggested that the Constitution was designed for a governing elite, while Alexander Hamilton urged him to use force if necessary to suppress popular dissent.[9] Jefferson asked whether Adams, with the aid of a strong army, planned soon to deprive ordinary Americans of their freedoms altogether. Jefferson challenged Adams in the next presidential election and, upon defeating him, hailed the victory as the "Revolution of 1800."

Although Jefferson was a champion of the common people, he had no clear

[7]Rosemarie Zagarri, "Two Revolutions," *New Republic*, May 28, 1984, 10.
[8]Hannah Arendt, *On Revolution* (New York: Viking, 1963), ch.6.
[9]Benjamin Ginsberg, *The Consequences of Consent* (New York: Random House, 1982), 22.

This painting of Monticello, the home Jefferson designed for himself in Virginia, portrays the agrarian way of life that Jefferson regarded as the wellspring of an independent and self-governing society. (Thomas Jefferson Memorial Foundation, H. Andrew Johnson)

vision of how a popular government might work in practice. He believed that legislative majorities were the proper expression of the public's interest and accordingly was reluctant to use his presidency for this purpose.[10] Jefferson also had no illusions about a largely illiterate population's readiness for a significant governing role and feared the consequences of inciting the public to pursue their resentment of the moneyed class. An assault on the wealthy, in Jefferson's opinion, would be not only wrong but also destructive of the nation's general prosperity, and therefore ruinous to all. Jeffersonian democracy was thus mainly a revolution of the spirit; Jefferson taught Americans to look upon the national government as belonging to all, not just to the privileged few.[11]

## THE ERA OF JACKSONIAN DEMOCRACY

Not until Andrew Jackson became president in 1828 did the country have a powerful leader who was willing and able to involve the public more fully in government. Jackson carried out the constitutional revolution that Jefferson had foreshadowed.

### The President as a Popular Leader

Jackson recognized that the president was the only official who could easily claim to represent all the people. Unlike the president, members of Congress were elected from separate states and districts rather than from the whole of the country. Yet the president's claim to popular leadership was diminished by the existence of the Electoral College. If the president and the people were to be brought closer together, so that each could draw power from the other, the office would have to rest on popular election. Jackson first tried to persuade Congress to initiate an amendment that would abolish the electoral voting system. Failing in this effort, Jackson persuaded the states to make popular voting the basis for choosing their presidential electors. By 1832, all states except South Carolina had done so.

Jackson's reform is still in effect today and basically places the choice of a president in the voters' hands. The winner of the popular vote in each state is awarded its electoral votes, and the probability is strong that the candidate who wins the popular-vote contest will also receive a majority of electoral votes. Since Jackson's time, only once has the loser of the popular vote won the presidency (Rutherford B. Hayes in 1876).

### The "Spoils System"

Andrew Jackson also sought to put an end to the aristocracy of wealth that had been governing the country through control of public offices. He urged the states to abolish property ownership as a condition for voting, promoted rotation of office as a means of keeping officials in close touch with the people, and appointed common people to high administrative posts. Politically out-

---

[10]Robert Dahl, *Pluralist Democracy* (Chicago: Rand McNally, 1967), 92.
[11]This interpretation is taken from Walter Lippmann, *Public Opinion* (New York: Free Press, 1965), 178–179.

Andrew Jackson used his presidency to institute rotation in public office, but the result of this civil service "reform" was the spoils system, whereby offices became available every four years for the victorious party to hand out to loyal followers. (New York Public Library)

**CIVIL SERVICE REFORM.**
OFFICE-SEEKER. "St. Jackson, can't you save us? Can't *you* give us something?"

numbered, the nation's upper classes could only deride Jackson's policies as a mere "spoils system." Believing that "to the victor belong the spoils," Jackson had appointed his campaign workers to government posts of all kinds (see Chapter 12).

### The "Party Constitution"

Jacksonian democracy's greatest contribution to majority government was the grass-roots political party. America's first parties, the Federalists and the Republicans, had developed in the 1790s out of disputes between Hamilton and Jefferson over national policy. These parties were thoroughly dominated by political and community leaders. Ordinary citizens had no large role in them.[12]

Andrew Jackson had a different kind of political party in mind.[13] He wanted a party built from the "grass roots"—that is, based on participation at the local level by ordinary citizens. Its strength would be its popular base, not its ties to the elite. By the election of 1832, Jackson's Democratic party had enlisted the

[12]See Joseph Charles, *The Origins of the American Party System* (New York: Harper & Row, 1961).
[13]See Richard P. McCormick, *The Second American Party System* (Chapel Hill: University of North Carolina Press, 1966).

participation of thousands of citizens. The election of 1832 also marked the appearance of the party nominating convention in presidential politics.

Jackson's protégé and successor as president, Martin Van Buren, shared Jackson's admiration of political parties. Van Buren was connected with New York City's Tammany Hall, one of the country's first party "machines," and he realized that parties could revolutionize government. In the absence of strong parties, Van Buren concluded, government naturally serves the interests of the rich and powerful. When ordinary citizens are not organized in parties, they lack power; individually they cannot hope to compete against people of wealth and status. Through party organization, however, ordinary citizens can act together as a voting majority that is capable of gaining political control by electing leaders committed to their interests.[14]

Alexis de Tocqueville, astute French observer of the young American democracy. (The Bettmann Archive)

This vision of strong national parties was never fully realized in the United States, partly because federalism and the separation of powers have enabled party organizations and leaders in various states and institutions to hold differing views of their party's principles (see Chapter 12). Nevertheless, the development of grass-roots political parties in the 1830s gave the people a powerful means of collective influence. Until then, each voter had a say only in the selection of his single representative. With the advent of grass-roots parties, a majority of individuals throughout the nation, united by affiliation with a political party, could choose a majority of representatives who shared the same policy goals. Majority opinion could thereby be more readily translated into public policy. So fundamental was the emergence of the grass-roots party to the influence of the people that the historian James MacGregor Burns has called it America's "second constitution."[15]

When the Frenchman Alexis de Tocqueville visited America in the early 1830s—at the peak of Jacksonian democracy—he felt compelled to say that "in the United States, the majority governs." But Tocqueville's evaluation was not altogether favorable. "I know of no country," Tocqueville said, "in which there is so little independence of thought and real freedom of discussion as in America." In Tocqueville's judgment, Americans were too inclined to defer to what they perceived to be majority opinion. They feared the isolation that can come to those who hold unpopular views. Tocqueville mistrusted majorities created in this way; opinions that were not fully considered and debated were to him, as to the Framers, an improper basis for governing.[16]

*I know of no country in which there is so little independence of thought and real freedom of discussion as in America.*
Alexis de Tocqueville

## THE PROGRESSIVE ERA

After the 1840s, the parties gradually drifted toward localism, corruption, and favoritism. In the cities especially, they were taken over by powerful party bosses whose arrogance was matched only by their appetite for patronage. By the 1880s, many party bosses were in league with the robber barons to block government from regulating business trusts (see Chapter 2).[17]

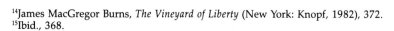

[14]James MacGregor Burns, *The Vineyard of Liberty* (New York: Knopf, 1982), 372.
[15]Ibid., 368.
[16]Alexis de Tocqueville, *Democracy in America* (1835–1840), ed. J. P. Mayer (Garden City, N.Y.: Doubleday/Anchor, 1969), bk. I, chs. 15, 16.
[17]See William Allen White, "The Boss System," in Richard Hofstadter, ed., *The Progressive Movement, 1900–1915* (Englewood Cliffs, N.J.: Prentice-Hall, 1963), 104–107.

FOUR CYLINDER ROTARY TYPE-REVOLVING PRESS

The high-speed rotary printing press made newspapers cheaper to produce and brought their price within the reach of the ordinary American. (Brown Brothers)

Progressive reformers looked for ways to weaken the power of corporations and party bosses and to give the public a greater voice in politics. In its Declaration of Principles of 1911, the National Progressive League defined its goal as "the promotion of popular government." The Progressives rejected the Burkean idea (discussed earlier in this chapter) of representatives as trustees; they embraced instead the idea of representatives as **delegates**—officeholders who are obligated to respond directly to the expressed opinions of the people whom they represent.

The Progressive movement was made possible by changes in education and communication during the nation's first century. In 1787 the vast majority of Americans were illiterate, and many of those who could read could not afford the hand-printed newspapers of the time. During the nineteenth century, however, a broad-based public school system was created, and the invention of the high-speed printing press led to the "penny" newspaper. By the time of the Progressive movement, literacy was widespread in America, as was newspaper readership. Ordinary Americans believed themselves to be politically informed and wanted the greater influence that the Progressives promised. The strongest force behind the Progressives' call for a more direct democracy was the persistent American belief that government should be subject to popular control—the more, the better.

### Progressive Reforms

Two of the Progressives' reforms gave voting majorities the direct power to decide policy at the state and local levels. One device was the *initiative*, which allows citizens through petition to place legislative measures on the ballot. A related measure was the *referendum*, which permits legislative bodies to submit proposals to the voters for approval or rejection. The Progressives also sought to give the public recourse against wayward state and local officials through the *recall*, in which citizens petition for the removal of an elected official before the scheduled completion of his or her term of office.

In terms of national politics, a more significant Progressive reform was the direct election of U.S. senators, who, before the Seventeenth Amendment was

# PROGRESSIVE REFORMS

The Progressive movement's major goal was to curb the power of party bosses and big business. Led by such men as Wisconsin's Robert La Follette, it influenced nearly every aspect of American political life, local and state as well as national. No other reform movement before or since has had such a broad and lasting effect on American politics. Among the Progressive reforms are the following:

*Municipal government:* Utilities converted from private to public ownership; government contracts awarded through public bids rather than political deals; administration of government through city managers or commission plan instead of elected mayors; nonpartisan elections substituted for partisan ones.

*State government:* Nomination of candidates by direct primary rather than party caucuses; use of initiative and referendum as means of allowing the public to enact legislation; dependence on experts and proven administrators instead of party workers to staff executive branch.

*National government:* Use of primaries rather than caucuses as method of choosing delegates to presidential nominating conventions; election of U.S. senators directly rather than through state legislatures.

These newer ways of governing were not adopted everywhere. Cities and states of the East and South were much more likely than those of the Midwest and West to retain the older systems. Party bosses and big business remained strong in many (perhaps most) locations, but their power would never again be what it was before the Progressive era.

ratified in 1913, had been chosen by state legislatures and were widely perceived as agents of the rich (the Senate was nicknamed the "millionaires' club"). Earlier attempts to amend the Senate election procedure were blocked by the senators, who stood to lose their seats if they had to submit to direct vote by the people. At length, however, the Senate was finally persuaded to support an amendment by pressure from the Progressives and by revelations that corporate bribes had influenced the selection of several senators.

Of the many Progressive reforms, the most significant was the *primary election,* which gave rank-and-file voters a voice in the selection of party nominees. Party bosses would no longer have absolute control of nominations, which had been a chief source of their power. No greater blow to political parties can be imagined. When a party does not have the power to select its candidates, it cannot command their loyalty to its organizational and policy goals. Candidates will embrace or reject their party as it suits their needs. In other democracies, which have no primary elections, parties have retained control of the nominating process and therefore have remained strong. (Chapter 12 discusses party organization in detail.)

Political parties in America were further undercut in the early twentieth century by the extension of merit-based civil service, which cost the parties thousands of patronage jobs. By 1916, elections were becoming "advertising-style" campaigns in which candidates appealed to the voters directly rather than through party organizations.[18] The time was coming when no institution of any strength would stand between the voters and their representatives.

★ ANALYZE THE ISSUE

**Reform of Government**
The Progressive era was a major period of reform. What does it suggest about the ability of self-government to renew itself? In your judgment, were the reforms themselves, such as the initiation of primary elections, consistent with the spirit of Progressivism? Do you see a need for reform today? Is the United States sufficiently democratic? If you believe that it is not, what reforms might reasonably be introduced?

[18]Richard Jensen, "American Election Campaigns," paper delivered at Midwest Political Science Association meetings, Chicago, May 1968.

The Progressives gained the support of two strong presidents, Theodore Roosevelt and Woodrow Wilson, who shared the Progressives' opposition to business monopolies but also recognized the power inherent in a popular presidency. Roosevelt described the office as a "bully pulpit." Wilson, writing about the president's potential for national leadership, said: "His is the only national voice in public affairs. Let him once win the admiration and confidence of the country, and no other single voice will easily overpower him."[19] Roosevelt and Wilson's conception of the president as national leader, legitimized through election by a majority of voters, helped to change the president's image. In the view of the public, the president was replacing Congress as the chief instrument of democracy (see Chapter 19).

Ironically, as the American system was being opened to greater popular participation early in this century, the power of government was increasing.[20] This parallel development was no coincidence. Although open elections are a means to popular influence, they are also a means by which government accumulates power. Official actions gain legitimacy when they are pursued in the name of a public that has freely chosen a leadership to act on its behalf. Although George Bernard Shaw was overgeneralizing, he was not completely off the mark when he concluded, "The more democratic a government is the more authoritative it is. . . ."[21]

## Beard's Economic Theory of the Constitution

In the Progressives' view, the Framers had erred in giving the majority too little power. Not surprisingly, the Progressive movement spawned attacks on the Framers. A notable work in this vein is the historian Charles S. Beard's *Economic Interpretation of the Constitution.*[22] Arguing that the Constitution grew out of wealthy Americans' fear of debtor rebellions, Beard claimed that its elaborate systems of power and representation were devices for keeping power in the hands of the rich. As evidence, Beard cited the Constitution's protections of property (see Chapter 6) and referred to James Madison's secret notes on the Philadelphia convention, which showed that property interests were high on the delegates' list of priorities.

Beard further noted that not one of the delegates was a workingman or small farmer. Most of the Framers had large landholdings, controlled substantial interests, or were major bank creditholders. A few had large debts, but their debts merely reflected the scope of their ambitions. This dominance of the Philadelphia convention by wealthy men reflected the fact that the delegates had been chosen by the state legislatures, which were controlled by the propertied classes. Only Rhode Island's legislature was in nonpropertied hands—and, as Beard noted, only Rhode Island refused to send a delegation to Philadelphia.

Beard's thesis was challenged by other historians, and he later acknowledged that he had not taken the Framers' full array of motives into account. Their

[19]Woodrow Wilson, *Constitutional Government in the United States* (New York: Columbia University Press, 1908), 67.
[20]Ginsberg, *Consequences of Consent*, ch.1.
[21]George Bernard Shaw to editor of *New Republic*, 1936, reprinted in ibid., August 8 and 15, 1988, 32.
[22]Charles S. Beard, *An Economic Interpretation of the Constitution* (1913; New York: Macmillan, 1941).

concept of separation of powers, for example, was a time-honored governing principle that had previously been incorporated in state constitutions. Nevertheless, the Framers clearly did not have a high opinion of popular government. Their system of representation was premised on a mistrust of popular majorities, and they did not establish voting as a basic right of citizens. The Constitution required only that a state impose no stricter suffrage qualifications in elections for the U.S. House of Representatives than it applied to elections for the larger house of its own legislature. The states allowed only propertied white males to vote, and it would seem likely that a majority of the Framers believed that suffrage should be limited to this class. But it would be inaccurate to conclude that the Framers were blatantly antidemocratic by the standards of their time. Property ownership was relatively widespread in America in the late eighteenth century, and in some states half or more of adult white males were eligible to vote.[23]

## RECENT DEVELOPMENTS: POLLS, TELEVISION, AND PRESIDENTIAL NOMINATIONS

The Progressive movement declined in the 1920s, after most of its institutional reforms had been achieved. If it had not subsided then, it would surely have done so in the 1930s, when the Western world's trust in majority government was shaken by developments in Europe, particularly in Germany. In 1933 the German people in a national election freely turned power over to Adolf Hitler. Germany's Weimar Republic had been founded on popular institutions; it was about as close as any modern nation had come to establishing a pure democracy. When the Weimar Republic degenerated first into chaos and then into Hitler's Third Reich, its demise seemed only to confirm Madison's assertion, quoted earlier in this chapter, that direct democracies are "spectacles of turbulence and contention . . . as short in their lives as they have been violent in their deaths."[24]

Nevertheless, the idea of popular government regained strength in the United States after World War II, when changes in communications, technology, and political organization brought the American people and their representatives into an increasingly close relationship. The new mass medium of television began to enable political leaders to reach the public more easily. And as televised politics became routine, more Americans came to believe that leaders *should* deal with the public directly rather than through political parties.[25]

This perspective was evident during the late 1960s, when reform Democrats sought a change in the presidential nominating system. In 1968 the leaders of the Democratic party nominated Hubert H. Humphrey, who, as Lyndon Johnson's vice-president, was associated with the unpopular Vietnam war. Antiwar Democrats challenged the legitimacy of Humphrey's nomination because he had not participated in a single primary election. When Humphrey then lost the general election to Richard Nixon, reform-minded Democrats demanded a change from a nominating system dominated by party leaders to one controlled by the party's rank-and-file voters through primaries and open caucuses. Their position easily prevailed (see Chapter 19).

[23]Bruce A. Campbell, *The American Electorate* (New York: Holt, Rinehart and Winston, 1979), 12–13.
[24]*Federalist* No. 10.
[25]See Richard L. Rubin, *Press, Party, and Presidency* (New York: Norton, 1981), 191–196.

Senator Robert Kasten (R-Wis.) holds a press conference. Politicians today rely heavily on television as a means of communicating with the public. (Photri)

Advances in public opinion polling have also promoted popular influence. Until scientific polling was developed several decades ago, representatives could always argue that their views were shared by a majority of the people. Now it is largely polls that identify majority opinion. While officeholders do not always follow the polls in deciding what to do, they are at least mindful of what polls indicate the public is thinking and are especially wary of taking a stand on issues about which majority opinion is intense. (Public opinion polling is discussed in detail in Chapter 8.)

# HOW THE NATIONAL POLITICAL SYSTEM WAS MADE MORE RESPONSIVE TO POPULAR MAJORITIES

| CONSTITUTION OF 1787 | SUBSEQUENT DEVELOPMENTS |
| --- | --- |
| Separation of powers, as a means of dividing authority and blunting passionate majorities. | Political parties, as a means of uniting authorities and linking them with popular majorities. |
| Indirect election of all national officials except House members, as a means of buffering officials from popular influence. | Primary elections, direct election of U.S. senators, and popular voting for president (linked to electoral votes), as means of increasing popular control of officials |

## *The Continuing Debate over the Majority's Role*

The United States today has a hybrid system of representation which combines original countermajoritarian elements with newer majoritarian aspects. Popular majorities still encounter barriers to influence in the elaborate system of divided powers, staggered terms of office, and separate constituencies devised by the Framers. Although Americans take these devices for granted, most democracies do not have them. In Great Britain, for example, executive and legislative authority are combined in a single institution, the House of Commons, whose members are all chosen at the same time and for terms of the same length. A British national election normally produces a clear-cut majority: the victorious party gains control of government. As we noted at the beginning of this chapter, the U.S. experience is different: in the past four decades, control of the presidency and of one or both houses of Congress has been split between the Republican and Democratic parties for more years than it has been in a single party's hands. In other words, it has been common in recent years for the United States to have no governing majority party.

However, the U.S. political system also has its majoritarian features.. Holders of all national offices—representatives, senators, and president—are now chosen by popular vote.* Moreover, no democracy conducts elections for its

*Technically, the president is still chosen by the votes of electors rather than by those of the American people. Consequently, it is still possible for the winner of the popular vote to lose the electoral vote; however, this has not occurred since 1876.

---

### ★ HOW THE UNITED STATES COMPARES

**Electing and Governing**

All democracies are characterized by free and open elections, but not all democracies have the same electoral systems. The United States has a separation of powers and elects its chief executive separately from its legislators. The result in five of the last six presidential elections has been a divided government, with the presidency held by one party and one or both houses of Congress held by the other. When such a division occurs, the people's influence is diluted. By electing a Republican president and a Democratic-controlled Congress in 1988, for example, Americans in a sense denied themselves a majority government.

Parliamentary systems, such as Great Britain's, provide a stronger and more direct opportunity for majority influence through elections. Voters choose the legislators, who then choose one of their members to be the prime minister, who serves as the chief executive. Legislative and executive power are thus combined in one institution, the control of which is determined in each national election. In the United States, control of government is not necessarily at stake in a national election. House elections take place every two years, a presidential election is held every four years, and senators are elected at two-year intervals to six-year terms.

Although the U.S. system complicates and can frustrate the translation of electoral majorities into governing majorities, popular influence can be looked at in other ways. One way is to ask whether control of government shifts completely or partially from one party to another as a result of elections. If government remains constantly in the hands of one party, either the party is running things very well or, more likely, barriers to competition are keeping elections from being decisive events. From this perspective, the U.S. system is responsive to electoral majorities. In roughly three-fourths of the world's democracies, including the United States, elections frequently result in a change in party control of government.

larger legislative chamber more frequently than does the United States, and no democracy requires more frequent election of its chief executive. Moreover, the United States is the only country that relies extensively on primary elections for the selection of party nominees; elsewhere, they are selected by party organizations. The electoral principle, which the writers of the Constitution regarded as a prerequisite of popular sovereignty but also one to be used sparingly, has been extended further in the United States than anywhere else.

The present system of representative government in the United States, as we have seen, has been created piecemeal. New elements have been added to old ones, which in turn have been variously kept, modified, or superseded. In no other area of their constitutional system have Americans had so great a penchant for experimentation. Presidential electors and primary elections, for example, are American inventions, which other countries have chosen not to copy. At present Americans are not clamoring for additional changes in their representational system. Nevertheless, the theoretical debate over representation that began in 1787 is far from settled.

## ADVOCATES OF THE CLASSICAL VIEW

The public's role in national government is obviously far more substantial than the Framers had planned or thought desirable. Their philosophy continues to have its proponents, who argue that the issue is not how directly the people exercise influence but whether government serves the people's interests.

In this view, the public is likened to a community formed on the basis of its members' shared and deeply held values. The public is not synonymous with a temporary majority, for if it were, then a mob could also be the public—a possibility that modern holders of the classical view reject. One such proponent, Robert Nisbet, says the idea that majority opinion should always prevail is the "great heresy . . . of modern democracies." If government is to work properly, Nisbet concludes, political leaders must exercise true leadership, using their informed judgment to decide issues of public policy.[26]

The claim that representatives must look inward to their own understanding of the public interest, rather than outward to get the pulse of the people, is as characteristic of modern critics of popular government as it was of Edmund Burke and the Framers. Ironically, the argument finds support in public opinion polls, which show that the policy views of most citizens are seldom backed by an awareness of relevant facts (see Chapter 8). In the early 1980s, for example, polls indicated that most Americans did not know which side the U.S. government was supporting in Nicaragua's civil war.

Reasoning from such evidence, proponents of the classical model of representation claim that the public is not equipped to tell its leaders which policies to pursue. They argue further that policy made in response to public pressure is nearly always bad policy. Consider the five separate inflation-fighting programs that President Jimmy Carter proposed in the late 1970s in response to public discontent with rising inflation. Each program was hastily prepared and all failed in one way or another. In the classical view, a government that is not designed to formulate effective policies is not an adequate government, whatever other virtues it may have.

[26]Robert Nisbet, "Public Opinion versus Popular Opinion," *Public Interest* 41 (1975): 169.

In the classical scheme, the principle of majority rule is satisfactorily met when the people have the opportunity through periodic elections to pass judgment on what government has been doing. It is not required that citizens take a direct part in government or that representatives do what they think the people want. The vote is the sanction that encourages officials to serve the public rather than themselves.[27]

## ADVOCATES OF POPULAR GOVERNMENT

The idea that distant leaders understand the people's interests better than the people themselves has always struck some analysts either as fanciful speculation or as a pretext for self-serving rule by an elite. According to this view, the possibility of tyranny by the majority, although a frightening prospect, is far more remote than the likelihood of tyranny by a self-interested elite. To deny majority control, the argument goes, is to invite representatives to serve the narrow purposes of the rich and powerful. If the people's interests are to prevail, there must be institutional arrangements that promote popular influence.

One such arrangement has been proposed by the historian and political scientist James MacGregor Burns, who favors modifying the Constitution to provide concurrent four-year terms for the president and members of the House of Representatives and staggered eight-year terms for senators. This arrangement would help to overcome the countermajoritarian possibilities inherent in the separation of executive and legislative elections and powers. The change would enhance the president's ability to lead a national majority and bring cohesion to a Congress fragmented by its members' diverse local ties.[28]

Other proposals to grant the public greater influence are more radical.[29] They typically involve a shifting of governing decisions from the national level to the local level, where the opportunities for direct citizen influence are greater, and from the private sector to the public sector, which would expand the range of policies decided by popular participation. The objective is to achieve "a participatory democracy in all respects," in Carole Pateman's phrase.[30] Some reformers would even apply new communication technologies, such as interactive cable television, to enable the American people to participate directly in *national* policymaking (see box).

Most political scientists would prefer an older solution to the problem of strengthening the majority's power: the development of stronger political parties. They argue, much as Martin Van Buren did 150 years ago, that competition between strong opposing parties provides a voting majority with its best opportunity to have broad and predictable influence on public policy. In this view, the problem of U.S. political parties is that they lack the strength to bind candidates to a common platform. As things stand, candidates for

---

[27]See, for example, Karl Mannheim, *Freedom, Power, and Democratic Planning* (New York: Oxford University Press, 1950), 156–161.
[28]"James MacGregor Burns Delivers 1987 Rothbaum Lecture," *Extensions* (Winter 1988): 8. A publication of the Carl Albert Center, University of Oklahoma.
[29]See, for example, Benjamin Barber, *Strong Democracy* (Berkeley: University of California Press, 1984).
[30]Carole Pateman, *Democratic Theory* (New York: Cambridge University Press, 1970), 3.

## NATIONAL "TOWN MEETINGS": NEW COMMUNICATION TECHNOLOGIES AND AMERICAN DEMOCRACY

New communication technologies—including video-conferencing and interactive cable television—may soon bring changes to the practice of popular government. The possibilities are suggested by two pilot projects.

One project enables constituents in five congressional districts to use their home computers to communicate directly with their representative's office in Washington. The number of these messages has been found to peak just before votes are taken during House debates televised on C-SPAN, Congress's cable television network.

The other project, "QUBE," began in the late 1970s in Columbus, Ohio. QUBE used two-way cable to enable viewers to express their opinions on policy issues simply by pressing buttons on a console connected to their TV sets. Some observers predict enthusiastically that national "town meetings" through two-way cable are in America's future. Other observers are not convinced that teledemocracy is such a good idea. They point out that the agenda would be set not by the viewers but by the people who controlled the content of the program, and that the opinions expressed by viewers would not necessarily be representative of the views of the general public.

Congress run on individual platforms, so that the vote in one state or district is not necessarily linked to the vote in other states or districts. In Great Britain, which has strong parties, each party develops a national platform that its candidates support. British voters thus have a common choice regardless of the legislative district in which they live. By electing a legislative majority of one party, they essentially are choosing the national platform put forth by that party's candidates.

Whatever their particular position, advocates of popular government share a central principle: that the people are far and away the most appropriate judges of their own interests. Although proponents of majoritarianism recognize a need for effective leadership, they claim that a democratic society must give priority to the expressed wishes of the people, not the presumed wisdom of the leaders.

### IS THE AMERICAN SYSTEM DEMOCRATIC ENOUGH?

In this chapter's introduction, we suggested that Americans may be mistaken when they claim that their country is the most democratic in the world. The point, of course, was that the U.S. political system poses obstacles to governing majorities, which are a defining characteristic of democracy.

The issue today, as it has always been, is not whether the U.S. political system is democratic but whether it is democratic enough. The issue centers on the balance between the influence of popular majorities and the influence of representative institutions. If greater weight is given to popular majorities, can they be trusted to respect the interests of society as a whole? If the majority is outweighed by representative institutions, can those institutions be trusted to serve the majority's interests, and not those of a powerful minority? These are difficult questions, and we have no final or single answers to them. That is why they will continue to be debated and why they deserve consideration by any student of American government. Later chapters will explore further the issue of popular influence in America.

## Summary

Since 1787, a major issue of American politics has been the public's role in governing. The Framers of the Constitution respected the idea of self-government but distrusted popular majorities. They designed a government that they felt would temper popular opinion and slow its momentum, so that the public's "true interest" (which includes a regard for the rights and interests of the minority) would guide public policy. Different methods were established to select members of the House of Representatives and of the Senate, the president, and federal judges as a means of separating political power from momentary and unreflecting majorities. This philosophy of representative democracy was suggested in the writings of Burke, Locke, and Montesquieu and still has strong advocates today.

Since the adoption of the Constitution, however, the public has gradually assumed more direct control of its representatives, particularly through measures affecting the way in which officeholders are chosen. Political parties, presidential voting (linked to the Electoral College), and primary elections are among the devices aimed at strengthening the majority's influence. These developments are rooted in the idea, deeply held by ordinary Americans, that the people must have substantial direct control of their government if it is to serve their real interests. For advocates of majority rule, the alternative is government by privileged interests.

## Major Concepts

| | |
|---|---|
| delegates | republic |
| democracy | trustees |
| representative democracy | tyranny of the majority |

## Suggested Readings

Beard, Charles S. *An Economic Interpretation of the Constitution.* New York: Macmillan, 1941. Argues that the Founders had selfish economic interests uppermost in mind when they wrote the Constitution.

Goldwin, Robert S., and William A. Schambra, eds. *How Democratic Is the Constitution?* Washington, D.C.: American Enterprise Institute, 1980. Essays on various interpretations of the Constitution.

Lippmann, Walter. *The Phantom Public.* New York: Harcourt, Brace, 1925. Argues that the public's capacity to govern directly is extremely limited and that a democracy must take this into account in developing its institutions.

MacDonald, Forrest. *We the People: The Economic Origins of the Constitution.* Chicago: University of Chicago Press,

1958. Argues against Beard's thesis that the Framers wrote the Constitution to suit their own economic needs.

Schattschneider, E. E. *The Semisovereign People: A Realist's View of Democracy in America.* New York: Holt, Rinehart and Winston, 1960. Contends that the public's influence depends mainly on fair, open, and partisan competition among elites for power.

Spitz, Elaine. *Majority Rule.* Chatham, N.J.: Chatham House, 1987. An analysis of majority rule which goes beyond the mechanical issue of vote counting.

Tocqueville, Alexis de. *Democracy in America*, vols. 1 and 2. Ed. J. P. Mayer. New York: Doubleday/Anchor, 1969. A classic analysis (originally published 1835–1840) of American democracy by an insightful French observer.

# Is Our Fragmented System of Government Adequate to Today's Needs?

### JAMES L. SUNDQUIST

*The risk of governmental impotence is far greater now than in most periods of our history.*

The fragmented system of government designed for the United States two centuries ago brings both good news and bad news for us today.

The good news is that the dispersion of powers among the executive, legislative, and judicial branches —and, within the legislature, between the Senate and the House—has accomplished the Framers' purpose: it has forestalled tyranny. No individual or political clique has ever been able to gain enough control over the separated institutions to endanger the country with either of the specters that haunted the delegates to the constitutional convention—an absolute ruler disguised as a democratically elected president, or a rampant congressional majority trampling on the rights of the minority.

But the bad news is that a system that makes it difficult for evil or misguided leaders to assemble the powers of government for wicked or imprudent purposes also, inevitably, hinders the most public-spirited of leaders when they must assemble those powers to achieve proper and even noble ends.

As we enter the third century of our national life, the question is which represents the greater danger: the menace of a government that is too powerful and thus too capable of tyranny, or the threat that a government confronted with enormous challenges at home and abroad will prove too weak to discharge its responsibilities? I am among those who find the latter to be the greater danger. And the risk of governmental impo-

tence is far greater now than in most periods of our history, for two reasons.

First, the advance of technology has enmeshed the United States in an intricately interdependent world economy and an equally intertwined set of global political and security relationships that require the government to act promptly and decisively in concert with other governments to protect and advance the country's interests. When the president, the Senate, and the House pursue independent and contradictory policies, as they often do, the United States cannot cope effectively with the forces and events that weigh in upon it all around the globe.

Second, the difficulty of concerting the powers of government has been greatly increased by a disturbing recent political development: the tendency of the voters to entrust the executive and legislative branches to opposing political parties. In six of the last nine presidential elections, beginning in 1956, the people have chosen a Republican president but have returned Democratic majorities to the House of Representatives and, in four of those elections, to the Senate also. In these circumstances, the conflict between parties that is normal and healthy in a democracy becomes a debilitating struggle within the government itself, between a president and a Congress that simply must get together if they are to accomplish anything constructive.

To deplore a governmental system that fosters disunity where unity is needed, that inhibits the formation and execution of consistent and decisive policies, is of course far easier than to devise acceptable remedies. Perhaps President Bush can find the road to bipartisan harmony that eluded his Republican predecessors Eisenhower, Nixon, Ford, and Reagan, but history and political realism tell us that that is hardly likely. Constitutional reform is not an undertaking for the fainthearted, but it is high time to think seriously about this possible avenue to governmental unity.

*James L. Sundquist is Senior Fellow Emeritus at The Brookings Institution. He is the author of* Constitutional Reform and Effective Government.

**CHARLES M. HARDIN**

*The separation of powers between President and Congress threatens constitutional government itself.*

Is our system of government adequate? Maybe. Is it threatening? More likely. We may well continue to enjoy our easygoing, widespread affluence for years, even decades. But danger signs persistently appear, brought on and aggravated by our fragmented system of government.

Fragmentation is the product of our famous separation of powers between the president and the Congress, which are empowered separately and sometimes in ways that overlap, and which are chosen separately for terms of different lengths, in elections whose timing is rigidly bound to the calendar. The result is an unremitting struggle between president and Congress for control. The president tries to govern by budgeting, managing, coordinating, and playing rival forces against each other. Congress tries to govern by dividing governmental activities into policies with their own agencies and programs that are parceled out among committees and subcommittees. The result is often the emergence and flourishing of "iron triangles," consisting of strategically positioned legislators, bureaucratic heads of programs, and organized interests. These iron triangles often elude much control by either the president or Congress as a whole. Such independence cannot be complete, but it does not have to be: it only needs to be strong enough to make effective control of a program very costly politically.

The result is that Congress becomes "a body without a head" (Roland Young), devoted to "taking care of the home folks first" (James MacGregor Burns). As such, Congress is subject to nearly continuous derision and vilification. This denigration is laughed off with the remark that although people may despise Congress, they obviously love their own representatives (as shown by the recent victories of 96 percent of congressional incumbents who ran for reelection).

But the joke ignores the menace of an overblown presidency whose incumbent is more and more encouraged to feel that he embodies the American people. The danger is intensified by the persistent dominance of foreign and military affairs. Since World War II we have repeatedly witnessed what James Madison warned the constitutional convention against: "In time of actual war, great discretionary powers are constantly given to the Executive. . . . Constant apprehension of War [also tends] to render the head too large for the body. A standing military force, with an overgrown Executive will not long be a safe companion to liberty. . . ." If demurrers object that we have been blessed with a conscientious military leadership (and we often have), one may recall that Madison made his remarks with General George Washington in the chair.

Thus, *the separation of powers between president and Congress threatens constitutional government itself.* A fragmented and despised Congress does not constitute a reliable check on a rampant president/commander in chief, supported (or maybe surrounded) by an aggressive and ubiquitous military with the habit of operating under a thick cloak of secrecy and with a disturbing cult of covert action. How to control the executive? Madison and George Mason's reliance on "a good militia" essentially based in and controlled by the states is now absurd. If there is a cure, it would seem to require a fundamental rethinking of our constitutional principles. A different kind of separation of powers may hold promise: a separation between the government and the opposition, with both sides having identifiable leadership, both sides having a legislative component, and both sides supported by a popular base.

*Charles M. Hardin is Professor Emeritus at the University of California, Davis. He is the author of* Constitutional Reform in America.

# *Part Two*

## INDIVIDUAL RIGHTS

Constitutional government, as we have just seen in Part One, is partly a matter of the structure of government. However, it is also a matter of individual freedom. As Alfred H. Kelly wrote, "A system of constitutional government worthy of the name embodies . . . a 'system of ordered liberty,' in which the people are guaranteed certain fundamental rights and immunities against the exercise of arbitrary power by the state."[1]

The concept of individual rights holds that each person should be free to pursue a life of his or her own choosing, as long as this freedom does not unduly restrict that of other people. This idea came to America from England. The early settlers enjoyed "the rights of Englishmen," which included trial by jury and some freedom of expression. These rights had developed over centuries and gained strength when John Locke declared (in *Two Treatises of Government,* 1690) that the purpose of the state is to protect the natural rights of individuals. The Declaration of Independence (1776) proclaimed that "all men . . . are endowed by their Creator with certain unalienable rights," but when the Constitution was written in 1787, no list of protected rights was included. The Bill of Rights (1791) provided such a list and has been the constitutional focus of individual rights in the United States.

Although individual rights are rooted in principle, they are achieved through politics. The fact that the rights of individuals often conflict with the desires of majorities is the reason for both the constitutional protection of these rights and the reluctance of majorities to grant them. Moreover, rights must be constantly redefined in the light of social, economic, and political change. No matter how "unalienable" Americans' rights have been said to be in theory, they have hardly been so in practice. No group has achieved a greater measure of equality without a struggle, and no significant extension of any right has been won without a fight.

In the nineteenth century, issues of individual rights were almost entirely issues of freedom *from* government. Modern life has made individual rights also an issue of freedom *through* government. Guarantees of rights can be nothing more than empty promises unless government intervenes to correct or compensate for conditions that keep individuals from enjoying genuine freedom. Chapter 5 discusses how civil liberties—specifically, the rights of free expression and fair trial—are protected both from and through government. Chapter 6 extends the analysis into the realm of economic rights. Chapter 7 examines the degree to which Americans' equality of rights and opportunities is affected by considerations of race, sex, color, and creed. ★ ★ ★

# Chapter 5

## CIVIL LIBERTIES: PROTECTING INDIVIDUAL RIGHTS

*A bill of rights is what the people are entitled to against every government on earth, general or particular, and what no just government should refuse, or rest on inference.*

*Thomas Jefferson[1]*

On the night of November 11, 1983, Robert and Sarisse Creighton and their three children were asleep when FBI agents and local police broke into their home. Brandishing guns, they searched the house for a relative of the Creightons who was suspected of bank robbery. When asked to show a search warrant, they said, "You watch too much TV." Failing to find the suspect, they departed, leaving behind three screaming children and two angry parents. The Creightons sued the FBI agent in charge, Russell Anderson, for violating their Fourth Amendment right against unlawful search.

The Creightons won a temporary victory when the Eighth U.S. Court of Appeals, noting that individuals are constitutionally protected against warrantless searches unless officers have good reason ("probable cause") for a search and unless they have good reason ("exigent circumstances") for conducting that search without a warrant, concluded that Anderson had been derelict in his duty. In the judgment of the appellate court, Anderson should have sought a warrant from a judge, who, on the basis of Anderson's information about the suspect's whereabouts, could have decided whether a search of the Creightons' home was justified.

On June 25, 1987, the Supreme Court of the United States overturned the lower court's ruling. In a 6–3 decision written by Justice Antonin Scalia, the Court stated: "We have recognized that it is inevitable that law enforcement

---

[1]Julian P. Boyd, ed., *The Papers of Thomas Jefferson*, vol. 12 (Princeton, N.J.: Princeton University Press, 1955), 440.

officials will in some cases reasonably but mistakenly conclude that probable cause is present, and we have indicated that in such cases those officials . . . should not be held personally liable." Justice John Paul Stevens sharply dissented. He accused the Court's majority of absolving the police of their "constitutional accountability" and of showing "remarkably little fidelity" to the Fourth Amendment.[2] Civil liberties groups endorsed Justice Stevens' view, claiming that the Court's decision gave police an open invitation to invade people's homes on the slightest pretext, thereby diminishing personal liberty. However, the Court's decision was praised by law-enforcement officials and conservatives, who contended that a ruling in the Creightons' favor would have made police hesitant to pursue suspects for fear of a lawsuit if a search failed to produce the person sought.

As this case illustrates, issues of individual rights are contentious and complex. No right is absolute. For example, the Fourth Amendment protects Americans, not from *all* searches, but from *"unreasonable* searches." The public would be unsafe if law officials could never search for evidence of a crime or pursue a suspect into a home. Yet the public would also be unsafe if police could frisk people at will or invade their homes with impunity. Such acts are characteristic of a police state, not of a free society. The challenge to a civil society is to establish a level of police authority that balances the demands of public safety with those of individual freedom. The balance point, however, is always subject to dispute. Did FBI agent Anderson have sufficient cause for a warrantless search of the Creightons' home? Or was his evidence so weak that his forcible entry constituted an "unreasonable" search? Not even the justices of the Supreme Court could form a unanimous opinion on these questions.

The idea of a **compelling governmental interest** is the abstract standard by which all claims of constitutional rights are evaluated. In theory, government protects or prohibits activities according to whether they serve an overriding goal of society. The right of people to be secure in their homes and persons, for example, is considered a basic condition of a civil society, and thus deserving of judicial protection. On this basis federal courts have rejected mandatory drug testing of all government employees. In a 1986 New Jersey case, a lower federal court concluded that "mass roundup urinalysis" of city employees violates constitutional prohibitions; the court stated that fear of drug abuse was no excuse for trampling on "fundamental principles and protections."[3] Yet the courts have upheld regulations requiring mandatory drug tests for some federal employees in certain jobs, concluding that a compelling national interest is served by a law designed to ensure that drugs will not undermine performance in jobs affecting the nation's defense.

This chapter examines issues of **civil liberties:** specific individual rights, such as freedom of speech and protection against self-incrimination, which are constitutionally protected against infringement by government. As we saw in Chapter 3, the Constitution's failure to enumerate individual freedoms led to demands for the **Bill of Rights.** Enacted in 1791, these first ten amendments to the Constitution specify certain rights of life, liberty, and property which the national government is obliged to respect. A later amendment, the Fourteenth,

---

[2]*Anderson* v. *Creighton,* 483 U.S. 635 (1987).
[3]Tom Morganthau, "A Question of Privacy," *Newsweek,* September 29, 1986, 18.

became the basis for extending these protections of individual rights to actions by state and local governments.

Issues of individual rights have become increasingly complex and important. The writers of the Constitution could not possibly have foreseen the United States of the late twentieth century, with its huge national government, enormous corporations, pervasive mass media of communication, urban crowding, nuclear weapons, and the rest. These developments are potential threats to personal freedom, and the judiciary in recent decades has seen fit to expand the rights to which individuals are entitled. However, these rights are constantly being balanced against competing individual rights and society's collective interests. The Bill of Rights operates in an untidy world where people's highest aspirations collide with their worst passions, and it is at this juncture that issues of civil liberties arise. Should an admitted murderer be entitled to recant a confession? Should the press be allowed to print military secrets whose publication might jeopardize national security? Should prayer be allowed in the public schools? Should neo-Nazis be allowed to take their anti-Semitic message into predominantly Jewish neighborhoods? Such questions are among the subjects of this chapter, which focuses on the following major points:

★ *Freedom of expression is the most basic of democratic rights, but, like all rights, it is not unlimited.* Free expression recently has been strongly supported by the Supreme Court.

★ *"Due process of law" refers to legal protections (primarily procedural safeguards) that are designed to ensure that individual rights are respected by government.*

★ *During the last half century particularly, the civil liberties of individual Americans have been substantially broadened in law and given greater judicial protection from action by all levels of government.* Of special significance has been the Supreme Court's use of the Fourteenth Amendment to protect these individual rights from action by state and local governments.

★ *Individual rights are constantly being weighed against the demands of majorities and the collective needs of society.* All political institutions are involved in this process, as is public opinion, but the judiciary plays the central role in it and is the institution that is most partial to the protection of civil liberties.

## Freedom of Expression

Freedom of political expression is the most basic of democratic rights. Unless citizens can openly express their political opinions, they cannot properly influence their government or act to protect their other rights. They also cannot hear what others have to say, and thus cannot judge the merits of alternative views. And without free expression, elections are a sham, a mere showcase for those who control what is on people's lips and in their minds. As the Supreme Court concluded in 1984, "The freedom to speak one's mind is not only an aspect of individual liberty—and thus a good unto itself—but also is essential to the common quest for truth and the vitality of society as a whole."[4]

[4]*Bose Corp.* v. *Consumers Union of the United States,* 466 U.S. 485 (1984).

*Congress shall make no law respecting an establishment of religion, or prohibiting the free exercise thereof; or abridging the freedom of speech, or of the press; or the right of the people peaceably to assemble, and to petition the Government for a redress of grievances.*

U.S. Constitution,
First Amendment

It is for such reasons that the First Amendment provides a guarantee of **freedom of expression**—the right of individual Americans to hold and communicate views of their choosing. For many reasons, such as a psychological need to conform to social pressure or a fear of harassment, Americans do not always choose to express themselves freely. Nevertheless, the First Amendment provides that the individual shall have freedom of conscience, speech, press, assembly, and petition.

Freedom of expression, like other rights, is not absolute. It does not entitle individuals to say or do whatever they want, to whomever they want, whenever they want. Free expression can be denied, for example, if it endangers national security, wrongly damages the reputations of others, or deprives others of their basic freedoms. An individual's private thoughts are completely free, but words and actions may not be. For example, in 1983 when a group of demonstrators gathered outside an Air Force base in upstate New York to protest against the deployment of bomber-launched nuclear missiles at the site, they were acting within their constitutional right of free expression. When they proceeded to scale a fence and attack the bombers with sledgehammers, however, they were no longer within their legal rights. They were arrested and convicted of trespassing and destruction of government property.

In recent decades, free expression has received broad protection from the courts. Today, under most circumstances, Americans can freely verbalize their political views without fear of governmental interference or reprisal. In earlier times, however, Americans were less free to express their political views.

## THE EARLY PERIOD: THE UNCERTAIN STATUS OF THE RIGHT OF FREE EXPRESSION

The first legislative attempt by the U.S. government to restrict free expression was the Sedition Act of 1798, which made it a crime to print false or malicious newspaper stories about the president or other national officials. The act was passed by Congress when fear of treason by French sympathizers was high, but its purpose was to muzzle Republican opponents of the Federalist president

---

### ★ HOW THE UNITED STATES COMPARES

**Civil Liberties**
Individual rights are a cornerstone of the American governing system and receive strong protection from the courts. The government's ability to restrict free expression is severely limited, and the individual's right to a fair trial is protected through elaborate due-process guarantees.

According to Raymond Gastil, the United States is one of only twenty countries that deserve a top rating for

their protection of civil liberties. Also in this group are Canada, Japan, and all Western European democracies except Finland, France, Germany, and Spain, which are in the second rank. Their constitutional protections are not so well developed as those of the countries in the top group. Most Latin American countries are in either this second category or the third one, at which some censorship and political

imprisonments occur. Gastil's rankings bottom out at seven, a level that includes some Communist, African, and Middle East countries. In these nations, the state is oppressive, granting individuals almost no freedom of expression and routinely using brutal methods to suppress political opposition.

SOURCE: Raymond D. Gastil, *Freedom in the World: Political Rights and Civil Liberties* (Westport, Conn.: Greenwood Press, 1985).

John Adams. The Sedition Act expired in 1801, but not before lower federal courts, presided over by Federalist judges who did not pretend to be objective, had imposed fines and jail sentences on ten Republican newspaper editors. Thomas Jefferson called the Sedition Act an "alarming infraction" of the Constitution and, upon replacing Adams as president in 1801, pardoned the convicted newspapermen and had their fines returned with interest. As the Supreme Court did not review the sedition cases, however, the judiciary's position on the lengths to which the government could legally go in restricting free expression remained an open question.

Supreme Court justice Oliver Wendell Holmes, Jr. (1841–1935). (UPI/Bettmann Newsphotos)

The Court also did not rule on free speech during the Civil War era, when the government severely restricted individual rights. In one instance during Reconstruction, Congress actually prevented the Court from issuing a judgment. The case involved a Mississippi newspaper editor who had sought to arouse citizens against the Union occupation and had been jailed without charge by military authorities. He appealed his imprisonment to the Supreme Court on a writ of *habeas corpus* (discussed in Chapter 3). Fearful that his release would encourage other Confederate diehards to resist Reconstruction policies, Congress passed a law that prohibited the Supreme Court to hear appeals involving those policies. In 1869 the Court accepted this congressional "court-stripping" and declined to rule on the editor's appeal.[5]

Not until 1919 did the Court rule on a case that challenged the national government's authority to restrict free expression. Two years earlier, Congress had passed the Espionage Act, which prohibited forms of dissent deemed to be harmful to the nation's effort in World War I. Nearly 2,000 Americans were convicted for such activities as interfering with draft registration and distributing antiwar leaflets. The Supreme Court upheld one of these convictions in *Schenck* v. *United States* (1919), ruling unanimously that the Espionage Act of 1917 was constitutional. In the opinion written by Justice Oliver Wendell Holmes, the Court said that Congress could restrict speech that was "of such a nature as to create a clear and present danger" to the nation's security. This **clear-and-present-danger test** implied the converse: government could *not* restrict political speech that presented no such danger.[6]

The Supreme Court did not adhere to its own standard, however. Less than a year after *Schenck,* the Court upheld the conviction of six anarchists for writing a pamphlet protesting the U.S. government's attempts to overthrow the newly formed Bolshevik regime in Russia.[7] Holmes dissented, writing that the anarchists' "silly leaflet" posed no substantial threat to the United States. Along with Justice Louis D. Brandeis, Holmes subsequently argued that government should not be allowed to limit expression unless it posed an "imminent" danger to national security.[8]

## THE MODERN PERIOD: PROTECTING FREE EXPRESSION

Until the twentieth century, the tension between national security interests and free expression was not a pressing dilemma for the United States. The country's

[5]*Ex parte McCardle,* 7 Wallace 506 (1869).
[6]*Schenck* v. *United States,* 249 U.S. 47 (1919).
[7]*Abrams* v. *United States,* 250 U.S. 616 (1919).
[8]*Whitney* v. *California,* 274 U.S. 357 (1927).

great size and ocean barriers provided such protection from potential enemies that it had little to fear from internal subversion. World War I, however, intruded upon America's isolation, and World War II brought it to an abrupt end. Since then, Americans' rights of free expression have been defined largely in the context of national security concerns.

## The Communist Threat and Limits on Free Expression

During the cold war that followed World War II, many Americans perceived the Soviet Union as bent on destroying the United States through internal subversion and global expansion. Senator Joseph McCarthy's sensational allegations that communists had infiltrated key positions in the U.S. government intensified public anxiety. In this climate of fear, the Supreme Court allowed government to put substantial limits on free expression. In *Dennis* v. *United States* (1951) the Court upheld the convictions of eleven members of the U.S. Communist party who had been prosecuted under the Smith Act of 1940, which made it illegal to advocate the forceful overthrow of the U.S. government.[9]

Fears of communist subversion began to subside in the mid-1950s, and the Court modified its *Dennis* position. In *Yates* v. *United States* (1957), the lower-court convictions of fourteen Communist party members were overturned because evidence indicated that they had not directly advocated lawless action. The Court said that their advocacy was "theoretical" and therefore protected by the First Amendment.[10] In subsequent rulings the Court stated that only active, high-ranking communists with a "specific intent" to destroy the U.S. government are subject to conviction.[11]

## The "Preferred Position" Doctrine

Since the late 1950s, court decisions involving *political* expression (other types of expression, such as obscenity, are a different matter, as we shall see) have generally followed a legal doctrine outlined by Justice Harlan Fiske Stone in 1938. Stone argued that although government had broad discretion in certain areas, such as economic policy, the Court should carefully scrutinize legislative attempts to restrict First Amendment rights. These rights, Stone said, should have a "preferred position" in a democratic society. If those in power can limit free expression, they can control what people will come to know and think. For this reason, Stone contended, laws that restrict free expression require "more exacting [judicial] scrutiny . . . than most other types of legislation."[12]

Although the Supreme Court has not explicitly endorsed Stone's position, its decisions since the late 1950s have been consistent with the **preferred position** doctrine regarding First Amendment rights. The judiciary has held that government officials must show that national security is directly and substantially imperiled before they can lawfully prohibit citizens from voicing their

---

★ ANALYZE THE ISSUE

**Personal Freedom vs. National Security**
During the writing of the Declaration of Independence, Thomas Jefferson and John Adams disagreed over the meaning of liberty. For Jefferson, it meant personal freedom. For Adams, it had to do with establishing a state powerful enough to protect an American way of life, of which personal freedom was only a part. Since the dawn of the atomic age, the tensions between personal freedom and national security have increased beyond anything Adams and Jefferson could have imagined. How far would you go in allowing government to restrict personal freedom for reasons of national security?

---

[9]*Dennis* v. *United States,* 341 U.S. 494 (1951).
[10]*Yates* v. *United States,* 354 U.S. 298 (1957).
[11]*Noto* v. *United States,* 367 U.S. 290 (1961); *Scales* v. *United States,* 367 U.S. 203 (1961).
[12]*United States* v. *Carolene Products Co.,* 304 U.S. 144 (1938).

The right to free expression of political views was widely evident during the Vietnam war, when many Americans demonstrated against U.S. involvement. (UPI/Bettmann Newsphotos)

political views. This demanding criterion was widely applied during the Vietnam war, when, despite the largest sustained protest movement in the country's history, not a single American was convicted solely because of spoken objections to the government's Vietnam policy. (Some dissenters were found guilty on other grounds, such as inciting to riot and disturbing the peace.)

The Supreme Court distinguished, however, between verbal speech and "symbolic speech." During the Vietnam period the Court upheld the conviction of David O'Brien for burning his draft registration card on the steps of the South Boston Courthouse. The Supreme Court acknowledged that O'Brien's act had a "communicative element"—that in a way it *was* political expression—but ruled against him all the same, saying that the government can prohibit action that threatens a legitimate public interest as long as the main purpose in doing so is not to inhibit free expression. The Court held that the federal law prohibiting the destruction of draft cards was designed primarily to provide for the military's manpower needs.[13] Yet the Court in 1989 held that burning of the American flag was a protected form of expression, a ruling that led to widespread demand for a constitutional amendment to ban desecration of the flag.[14]

## Press Freedom and Prior Restraint

Freedom of the press received strong judicial support during the Vietnam period. In *New York Times Co.* v. *United States* (1971) the Court ruled that the *Times*'s publication of the "Pentagon papers" (secret government documents revealing official deception about the success of the United States' conduct of

[13]*United States* v. *O'Brien,* 391 U.S. 367 (1968).
[14]*Texas* v. *Johnson,* 88-155 (1989).

**Rights in Conflict**
In *Nebraska Press Association v. Stuart* (1976), the Supreme Court overruled a Nebraska judge who had issued a "gag order" forbidding the press to report the lurid details of a crime. The judge reasoned that the accused's right to a fair trial would be jeopardized if the press sensationalized the crime. How would you have ruled in this case? Can you think of other situations in which rights come into conflict? What criteria would you use in resolving such conflicts? Do you believe that any right or rights should take precedence over all others? If so, why?

the war) could not be blocked by the Department of Justice, which claimed that publication would hurt the war effort. The documents had been illegally obtained by antiwar activists, who had turned them over to the *Times* and other news organizations for publication. The Court ruled that "any system of prior restraints" on the press is unconstitutional unless the government can clearly justify the restriction. "The press was protected [by the First Amendment] so that it would bare the secrets of government and inform the people," wrote Justice Hugo Black in a concurring opinion. "Only a free and unrestrained press can effectively expose deception in government."[15]

The unacceptability of **prior restraint**—government prohibition of speech or publication before the fact—is basic to the current doctrine of free expression. The Supreme Court has said that any attempt by government to prevent expression carries "a 'heavy presumption' against its constitutionality."[16] News organizations and individuals are legally responsible after the fact for what they report or say (for example, they can be sued by an individual whose reputation is wrongly damaged by their words), but generally government cannot stop them in advance from expressing their views.

Nevertheless, the role of the United States in a world of nuclear weapons and communist insurgencies creates tension between the demands of national security and freedom of individual expression. In an exception to the doctrine of prior restraint, for example, the courts have upheld the government's authority to ban uncensored publications by certain past and present government employees, such as CIA agents, who have taken part in classified national security activities.

## FREE EXPRESSION AND STATE GOVERNMENTS

In 1790 Congress rejected a proposed amendment to the Constitution which would have applied the Bill of Rights to the states. They had their own bills of rights, and anyway, early Americans were more worried about the power of the national government than about the power of the states. Thus the freedoms guaranteed in the Bill of Rights were initially protected only from action by the national government, a constitutional arrangement that the Supreme Court upheld in 1833.[17] A century later, however, the Court began to protect individual rights from infringement by state governments. The vehicle for this change was the Fourteenth Amendment to the Constitution.

### The Fourteenth Amendment and the States

*No State shall . . . deprive any person of life, liberty, or property, without due process of law. . . .*

U.S. Constitution,
Fourteenth Amendment

Ratified in 1868, the Fourteenth Amendment forbids a state to deprive any person of life, liberty, or property without due process of law. It was not until *Gitlow* v. *New York* (1925), however, that the Supreme Court decided that the Fourteenth Amendment applied to state action in the area of freedom of expression. Although the Court upheld Benjamin Gitlow's conviction for violating a New York law that prohibited advocacy of the violent overthrow of

---

[15]*New York Times Co. v. United States*, 403 U.S. 713 (1971).
[16]*Nebraska Press Assn. v. Stuart*, 427 U.S. 539 (1976).
[17]*Barron v. Baltimore*, 7 Peters 243 (1833).

the U.S. system of government, the Court indicated that the states were not completely free to limit expression:

> For present purposes we may and do assume that freedom of speech and of the press—which are protected by the First Amendment from abridgement by Congress —are among the fundamental personal rights and "liberties" protected by the due process clause of the Fourteenth Amendment from impairment by the states.[18]

Having developed this new interpretation of the Fourteenth Amendment, the Supreme Court proceeded during the next decade to overturn state laws that restricted expression in the areas of speech, press, religion, and assembly and petition.[19] The most famous of these judgments came in the case of *Near* v. *Minnesota* (1931). Jay Near was the publisher of a Minneapolis weekly newspaper that regularly made scurrilous attacks on blacks, Jews, Catholics, and labor union leaders. His paper was closed down on authority of a state law that banned "malicious, scandalous, or defamatory" publications. Near appealed the shutdown, and the Supreme Court ruled in his favor, saying that the Minnesota law was "the essence of censorship." Chief Justice Charles Evans Hughes wrote the Court's opinion: "The fact that the liberty of the press may be abused by miscreant purveyors of scandal does not make any the less necessary the immunity of the press from previous restraint.[20]

When the Fourteenth Amendment was debated in Congress after the Civil War, there was no indication that its framers meant it to protect First Amendment rights from state action. Seventy years later the Supreme Court justified the change by reference to **selective incorporation**—the absorption of certain provisions of the Bill of Rights, particularly freedom of expression, into the Fourteenth Amendment so that these rights would be protected from infringement by the states. The Court asserted that such rights are an indispensable condition of American life because "neither liberty nor justice would exist if they were sacrificed."[21]

### Limiting the Authority of States to Restrict Expression

Since the 1930s, the Supreme Court has broadly protected freedom of expression from action by the states and by local governments, which derive their authority from the states. A leading free-speech case was *Brandenburg* v. *Ohio* (1969). The appellant was a Ku Klux Klan member who, in a speech at a Klan rally, had been recorded as saying, "If our president, our Congress, our Supreme Court, continues to suppress the white Caucasian race, it's possible that there might have to be some revenge taken." He was arrested and convicted of advocating force under an Ohio law prohibiting "criminal syndicalism," but the Supreme Court reversed the conviction, saying that

---

[18]*Gitlow* v. *New York*, 268 U.S. 652 (1925).
[19]*Fiske* v. *Kansas*, 274 U.S. 30 (1927) (speech); *Near* v. *Minnesota*, 283 U.S. 697 (1931) (press); *Cantwell* v. *Connecticut*, 310 U.S. 296 (1940) (religion); and *De Jonge* v. *Oregon*, 299 U.S. 253 (1937) (assembly and petition).
[20]*Near* v. *Minnesota*, 283 U.S. 697 (1931).
[21]*Palko* v. *Connecticut*, 302 U.S. 319 (1937).

the constitutional guarantees of free speech and free press do not permit a state to forbid or proscribe advocacy of the use of force or of law violation except where such advocacy is directed to inciting or producing imminent lawless action, and is likely to produce such action.[22]

In a key case involving the right to assemble peaceably, the U.S. Supreme Court in 1977 upheld a lower-court ruling against local ordinances of Skokie, Illinois, which had been invoked to prevent a parade there by the American Nazi Party. The Nazis had chosen Skokie for their assembly in order to dramatize their message of hate: the town had a large Jewish population, including many survivors of Nazi Germany's concentration camps. The American Nazis ultimately called off the parade, but not because they were compelled by law to do so. The Supreme Court has held that the right of free expression takes precedence over the mere *possibility* that a riot or some other evil might result from what is said. Before government can lawfully prevent a speech or rally, it must show persuasively that an evil is almost certain to result from the event and must also demonstrate that there is no alternative way (such as assigning police officers to control the crowd) to keep the evil from happening.

The Supreme Court has recognized, however, that freedom of assembly may conflict with the routines of daily life. Accordingly, individuals do not have the right to hold a public rally in the middle of a busy intersection during rush hour, nor do they have the right to command immediate access to a public auditorium. The Court has held that public officials can regulate the time, place, and conditions of public assembly, provided that these regulations are reasonable and do not discriminate on the basis of what is likely to be said at these gatherings. Officials have an obligation to accommodate public gatherings and

[22]*Brandenburg* v. *Ohio*, 395 U.S. 444 (1969).

The Constitution guarantees the right of assembly, even for neo-Nazis and other fringe groups with unpopular views. (Arnold Zann/Black Star)

to treat all groups—including those that espouse unpopular views—in accordance with reasonable standards.

In sum, the Supreme Court's position on the power of state and local governments to limit free political expression is relatively straightforward: they cannot lawfully impose substantial infringements on what people may say or write. If anything, the Court has been less tolerant of restrictions imposed by states and localities because, unlike the national government, they are not responsible for national security and thus cannot justify limiting free expression on that basis.

## LIBEL AND SLANDER

The constitutional right of free expression is not a legal license to avoid responsibility for the consequences of what is said or written. If information that is known to be false and that greatly harms a person's reputation is published (libel) or spoken (slander), the injured party can sue for damages. The ease or difficulty of winning such suits has obvious implications for free expression. Individuals and organizations are less likely to express themselves openly if they stand a good chance of subsequently losing a libel or slander suit.

A leading decision in this area is *New York Times Co.* v. *Sullivan* (1964), in which the Court overruled an Alabama state court that had found the *Times* guilty of libel for printing an advertisement that accused Alabama officials of physically abusing black citizens during civil rights demonstrations. The Court ruled that libel of a public official requires proof of "actual malice," which was defined as a knowing or reckless disregard for the truth with intent to damage the official's reputation.[23] Although later decisions refined the Court's position, this imposing standard of proof remains essentially intact today. It is very difficult to prove that a publication was intentionally malicious in its reporting on a public figure.

A widely publicized lower federal court decision in 1985 revealed how nearly complete is the protection of the news media against libel cases brought by public figures. During Israel's invasion of Lebanon in 1983, *Time* magazine had reported that Israeli defense minister Ariel Sharon had tacitly consented in advance to a massacre of Palestinian refugees by Lebanese Christian forces. Sharon sued *Time* in a U.S. court, charging that the story was false, careless, and deliberately malicious. The jury agreed with Sharon that *Time* had been wrong in its allegation and had been careless about trying to ascertain the facts. But the jury concluded that *Time* had not acted with actual malice; its basic motivation in reporting the story, the jury believed, was not to harm Sharon's reputation. Sharon therefore lost the case.

The courts have made it more difficult to sue successfully for libel than for slander. Because the press acts as a surrogate for the public, the courts have reasoned that plaintiffs seeking judgments against the press for libel must meet a tougher standard of evidence than plaintiffs seeking judgments against ordinary citizens for slander. The press's range of discretion is very broad, as evidenced by a 1988 Supreme Court ruling that *Hustler* magazine did not have to pay damages to the Reverend Jerry Falwell, who had claimed emotional

---

[23]*New York Times Co.* v. *Sullivan*, 376 U.S. 259 (1964).

Former Israeli defense minister Ariel Sharon speaks to reporters during his libel trial against *Time* magazine. (UPI/Bettmann Newsphotos)

distress as a result of a *Hustler* parody that portrayed him as having an incestuous relationship with his mother in an outhouse. The Court held that parody was a centuries-old form of political expression that deserved judicial protection, even when it was in bad taste.[24]

The press has less protection when its target is a "private" person rather than a "public" figure such as Falwell. The courts have reasoned that information about private individuals is less basic to the democratic process than information about public figures and that the press accordingly must take greater care in ascertaining the validity of claims about a private citizen.

## OBSCENITY

Obscenity is a form of expression that—over objections by some justices, such as Hugo Black—is not protected by the First Amendment. However, the Supreme Court has had difficulty in defining which publicly disseminated sexual materials are obscene and which are not. The Court has struggled to develop a standard that gives predictability to the law without endangering First Amendment rights.

Declaring that because "what would offend the people of Maine or Mississippi might be found tolerable in Las Vegas or New York City," Chief Justice Warren Burger wrote in *Miller* v. *California* (1973) that obscenity must be judged by "contemporary community standards."[25] The Court has also reasoned, however, that local standards cannot be the sole criterion of obscenity. In *Jenkins* v. *Georgia* (1974), for example, the Court overturned a local court's conviction of a theater owner who had shown a film (*Carnal Knowledge,* starring Jack

[24]*Hustler Magazine* v. *Jerry Falwell,* 108 S.Ct. 876 (1988).
[25]*Miller* v. *California,* 413 U.S. 15 (1973).

Nicholson) that included scenes of a partially nude woman. The scenes were regarded by the Court as neither "patently offensive" nor aimed at people's "prurient interest"—two criteria the Court has used in judging obscenity. In 1987 the Court ruled that sexual material could not be judged obscene simply because local residents objected to its content. Apparently "community standards" must be reasonable in the broader context of society; sexual content is not in itself evidence that a book, magazine, or film is obscene. Obscenity requires sexual content of a particularly offensive type—still a rather vague criterion.

## Freedom of Religion

Free religious expression is the precursor of free political expression, at least within the English tradition of limited government. England's Glorious, or Bloodless, Revolution of 1689 centered on the religious issue and resulted in the Act of Toleration, which gave members of all Protestant sects the right to worship freely and publicly. The English philosopher John Locke (1632–1704) extended this principle, arguing that legitimate government could not inhibit free expression, religious or otherwise. The First Amendment reflects this tradition, providing for freedom of religion along with freedom of speech, press, assembly, and petition. In regard to religion, the First Amendment reads: "Congress shall make no law respecting an establishment of religion, or prohibiting the free exercise thereof. . . ." The prohibition on laws aimed at "establishment of religion" (the establishment clause) and its "free exercise" (the free-exercise clause) applies to states and localities through the Fourteenth Amendment.

### THE ESTABLISHMENT CLAUSE

The **establishment clause** has been interpreted by the courts to mean that government may not favor one religion over another or support religion over no religion. (This position contrasts with that of a country such as England, where Anglicanism is the official, or "established," state religion, though no religion is prohibited.) The Supreme Court's interpretation of the establishment clause has been described as maintaining a "wall of separation" between church and state, which includes a prohibition on nondenominational support for religion.[26] The Court has taken a pragmatic approach, however, permitting some establishment activities but disallowing others. The Court has permitted states to provide secular textbooks for use by church-affiliated schools,[27] for instance, but has forbidden states to pay part of the salaries of teachers in church-affiliated schools.[28] Such distinctions follow no strict logic but are based on judgments of whether government action involves "*excessive* entanglement with religion."[29]

---

[26]See Frank J. Sorauf, *Wall of Separation: The Constitutional Politics of Church and State* (Princeton, N.J.: Princeton University Press, 1976).
[27]*Board of Regents* v. *Allen,* 392 U.S. 236 (1968).
[28]*Lemon* v. *Kurtzman,* 403 U.S. 602 (1971).
[29]Ibid.

Under the First Amendment, Americans are free to practice any religion, or no religion. (Bill Stanton/Magnum)

In allowing public funds to be used by religious schools for secular textbooks but not for teachers' salaries, the courts have indicated that, whereas it is relatively easy to ascertain whether the content of a particular textbook promotes religion, it would be much harder to determine whether a particular teacher was promoting religion in the classroom.

The Court has developed a three-point test that a law providing aid to religion must pass to be considered constitutional: First, the main purpose of the aid must be secular and not religious; second, the main effect of the assistance must not be to promote one religion or religion per se; and third, the aid must not excessively involve the government in religion.[30] These restrictions do not, for example, allow substantial government grants to religious schools but do permit lesser contributions under some circumstances, such as the provision of secular textbooks and copies of standardized examinations. Some of the Court's applications of the three-point test have been controversial. The Court in 1983, for instance, upheld a Minnesota law allowing parents a tax deduction for certain school expenses, including tuition, incurred by their children. The Court reasoned that, because the tax deduction was available to parents with children in either public or private (including nonreligious) schools, the law's purpose was not to support religion.[31] Opponents claimed that the law promoted religion because the parents of public school children, who pay no tuition, were entitled to smaller tax deductions than parents who paid tuition to send their children to private schools, most of which were affiliated with a church.

Since the early 1960s, the Court has held that the establishment clause prohibits the saying of prayers in public schools. In the *Engel* (1962) case, the Court ruled against the Board of Regents of New York State, which had written

[30]Ibid.
[31]*Mueller* v. *Allen*, 463 U.S. 388 (1983).

a nondenominational prayer to be recited in the public schools at the start of each day. Even though no particular religion was favored in the prayer, the Court concluded that the prayer promoted religion over nonreligion.[32] A year later the Court struck down Bible readings in public schools.[33]

Religion is a strong force in American life, and the Supreme Court's position on school prayers has had strong opposition, particularly from Protestant fundamentalists. A recent attempt to circumvent the prayer ruling was an Alabama law permitting the public schools to set aside one minute each day for silent prayer or meditation. In 1985 the Court voted 6–3 to declare Alabama's minute of silence unconstitutional, ruling that "government must pursue a course of complete neutrality toward religion."[34] Whether the Supreme Court would invalidate a silent-meditation law that was less clearly religious in its intent than Alabama's is an open question that is sure to be tested in future cases.

*Government must pursue a course of complete neutrality toward religion.*
U.S. Supreme Court,
*Wallace v. Jaffree* (1985)

Advocates of school prayer have pressured Congress to propose a constitutional amendment permitting some form of prayer in the public schools. In 1984 the U.S. Senate rejected by eleven votes a school-prayer amendment that had the support of President Ronald Reagan. A change in the constitutional status of religion might also come about through changes in the Supreme Court's membership. Chief Justice William Rehnquist and three other current justices (Byron R. White, Sandra Day O'Connor, and Antonin Scalia) have indicated a willingness to lower some of the barriers between church and state, although not one advocates that they be eliminated completely.

## THE FREE-EXERCISE CLAUSE

The First and Fourteenth amendments also prohibit governmental interference with the "free exercise" of religion. The idea behind the **free-exercise clause** is clear: Americans are free to hold any religious belief they choose.

Although people are free to *believe* what they want, they are not always free to *act* on their beliefs. The courts have tolerated government interference with the exercise of religious beliefs when such interference is the secondary result of a compelling and overriding social goal. An example is the legal protection of children with life-threatening illnesses whose parents refuse on religious grounds to permit medical treatment. A court may order that such children be given medical assistance because the social good of saving their lives overrides their parents' free-exercise rights. And in 1986 the Supreme Court concluded that military regulations requiring standard headgear took precedence over an Orthodox Jewish serviceman's practice of wearing a yarmulke.[35]

In some circumstances exceptions to certain laws have been permitted on free-exercise grounds. The Supreme Court ruled in 1972 that Wisconsin could not compel Amish parents to send their children to school beyond the eighth grade because this policy violated a centuries-old Amish religious practice of having children leave school and begin work at an early age.[36] The Court has

[32]*Engel v. Vitale,* 370 U.S. 421 (1962).
[33]*Abington School District v. Schempp,* 374 U.S. 203 (1963).
[34]*Wallace v. Jaffree,* 472 U.S. 38 (1985).
[35]*Goldman v. Weinberger,* 475 U.S. 503 (1986).
[36]*Wisconsin v. Yoder,* 406 U.S. 295 (1972).

also held that Quakers, unlike adherents of most other religions, cannot be compelled to serve in the military because their religious doctrine encompasses a conscientious objection to war. In upholding free exercise in such cases, the Court may be said to have violated the establishment clause by granting preferred treatment to people who hold a particular religious belief. The Court has recognized the potential conflict between the free-exercise and establishment clauses and, as in other such situations, has tried to strike a reasonable balance between the competing claims.

When the free-exercise and establishment clauses cannot be balanced, the Supreme Court has been forced to make a choice. In 1987 the Court ruled unconstitutional a Louisiana law requiring that creationism (the Bible's account of how the world was created) be taught along with the theory of evolution in public school science courses. Creationism, the Court concluded, is a religious doctrine, not a scientific theory; thus its inclusion in public school curricula violates the establishment clause by promoting a religious belief. Creationists viewed the Court's decision as a violation of their right to the free exercise of religion; they claimed that their children were being forced to study a theory, evolution, that contradicts the Bible's account of the origins of the human race.

## Rights of Persons Accused of Crimes

Every society must protect itself against wrongdoers, but not all societies have concerned themselves with protecting the innocent. All too many societies have not been above using force to liquidate political opposition. To cite just one recent example: in the early 1980s more than 10,000 people, many of them college students whose "offense" had been merely to question the legitimacy of Argentina's military dictatorship, simply "disappeared." They were seized by the police or military authorities and, without even a pretext of being formally charged with any crime, were summarily tortured and killed. It is no wonder that Justice Felix Frankfurter once wrote: "The history of liberty has largely been the history of the observance of procedural guarantees."[37]

*The history of liberty has largely been the history of the observance of procedural guarantees.*
Justice Felix Frankfurter

### PROCEDURAL DUE PROCESS

Due process of law is rooted in the idea of ensuring justice for all, with special emphasis on persons accused of crimes. "Due process" refers to legal protections that have been established to preserve the rights of individuals. The most significant form of these protections is **procedural due process;** the term refers primarily to procedures that authorities must follow before a person can legitimately be punished for an offense. (A second form, *substantive due process,* is discussed in the next section.)

The U.S. Constitution provides for several procedures designed to protect a person from wrongful arrest, conviction, and punishment (see box). A person has, according to Article I, section 9, "the privilege of the writ of *habeas corpus.*" Any person taken into police custody is entitled to seek such a writ, which requires law-enforcement officials to bring him or her into court and state the

---

[37]*McNabb* v. *United States,* 318 U.S. 332 (1943).

legal reason for the detention. If the reason is inadequate, the court must order the prisoner's immediate release. The Fifth and Fourteenth amendments provide generally that no person can be deprived of life, liberty, or property without due process of law. And specific procedural protections for the accused are spelled out in the Fourth, Fifth, Sixth, and Eighth amendments:

The *Fourth Amendment* forbids the police to conduct searches and seizures unless they have probable cause to believe that a crime has been committed.

The *Fifth Amendment* protects against double jeopardy (being prosecuted twice for the same offense) and self-incrimination (being compelled to testify against oneself).

The *Sixth Amendment* provides the right to have legal counsel, to confront witnesses, to receive a speedy trial, and to have a trial by jury in criminal proceedings.

The *Eighth Amendment* protects against excessive bail or fines, and prohibits the infliction of cruel and unusual punishment on those convicted of crimes.

## Defining Procedural Protections

These procedural protections have always been subject to interpretation. The Fourth Amendment, for example, protects people against "unreasonable searches" of their persons, homes, and belongings. In a 1968 decision, the Supreme Court said that a determination of whether a search was "reasonable" could be based only on the concrete facts of the individual case.[38] The admissibility in court of evidence obtained in an unreasonable search has also varied. In *Weeks* v. *United States* (1914), the Court formulated the **exclusionary rule,** which prohibits the use in federal trials of evidence obtained by illegal search and seizure.[39] In subsequent decades, the Supreme Court expanded the application of the exclusionary rule, but, in the 1980s, restricted the rule's application, concluding that in some circumstances illegally obtained evidence can be admitted in trials if the procedural errors are small, inadvertent, or ultimately inconsequential.

*Allowing the States to Differ.* At first, the exclusionary rule applied only to federal cases. States in their criminal proceedings were not bound by the rule. Nor were states compelled, as was the federal government,[40] to provide attorneys for felony defendants who could not afford to pay for legal counsel. There were limited exceptions, such as a 1932 ruling that a defendant charged in a state court with a crime carrying the death penalty had to be provided with an attorney.[41] The Court's general position, however, was that the states themselves could decide what procedural rights their residents would have.

A noteworthy case was *Palko* v. *Connecticut* (1937). A Connecticut court had convicted Frank Palko of killing two policemen, and he was sentenced to life imprisonment. But Connecticut had a statute that permitted law-enforcement

★ ANALYZE THE ISSUE

**The Rights of the Accused**
On January 24, 1989, Ted Bundy, a serial killer convicted of murdering three young women and suspected in the deaths of as many as 100 more, died in Florida's electric chair. He had been on death row for nearly ten years, and his incarceration and legal appeals had cost the state of Florida several million dollars. Is America's lengthy and elaborate appeals process too costly? Does it encourage lawbreakers to believe that they can get away with crime? These questions are often asked, but are they the most important ones? Should protection of the innocent be the paramount consideration? It is sometimes said that it is better to let 100 guilty persons go free than to convict one innocent person. If the price of justice really is 100 to 1, do you think it is too high or too low?

---

[38]*Sibron* v. *New York*, 392 U.S. 59 (1968).
[39]*Weeks* v. *United States*, 232 U.S. 383 (1914).
[40]*Johnson* v. *Zerbst*, 304 U.S. 458 (1938).
[41]*Powell* v. *Alabama*, 287 U.S. 45 (1932).

# PROCEDURAL DUE-PROCESS RIGHTS IN ACTION: A HYPOTHETICAL CASE

Perhaps the best way to illustrate how procedural due-process rights protect the individual is to present a hypothetical case. Let us say that John Q. Student has been selling illegal drugs on campus. In order for the police to arrest Mr. Student legally, they must have "probable cause" to do so—some indication that a crime has been or is about to be committed, such as evidence linking Mr. Student to drug sales. If the police apprehend Mr. Student merely because they wonder how he got the money to pay for the new sports car he is driving and then happen to discover evidence of drug trafficking, he may avoid conviction on the grounds that his Fourth Amendment protection against illegal search and seizure has been violated.

When Mr. Student is arrested, the police may search for evidence, although the extent of this search is subject to Fourth Amendment limitations. In general, the Supreme Court has held that the area that can be searched without a warrant is limited to the suspect's person and the immediate area, and then only to preserve the evidence and to protect the arresting officers from harm. Ordinarily, police should have a search warrant to look for evidence in a suspect's house or place of business; to obtain such a warrant, police must go to a judge and show probable cause.

After Mr. Student has been arrested, police interrogation should not begin until he has been informed of his rights, including the right to remain silent (Fifth Amendment) and the right to have an attorney present (Sixth Amendment). Mr. Student also has the right to be brought before a judge without undue delay and informed of the charge against him. If he is not, Mr. Student can apply for a writ of *habeas corpus* to secure his release. At his hearing, Mr. Student also has the right to seek reasonable bail (Eighth Amendment), an amount normally based on the severity of the alleged crime and the likelihood that the accused person will return for trial if he or she is released on bail.

If Mr. Student is charged with a federal crime, an indictment must be handed down by a grand jury, which hears evidence from the prosecution and determines whether this evidence is strong enough to suggest that Mr. Student has indeed violated the law and should be indicted to stand trial. Most states do not make extensive use of the grand jury; rather, they let prosecutors directly file a bill of information with a court, detailing the charge and the evidence. After an indictment, the bail decision is reviewed by the court. In more serious cases, bail can be revoked if it has not already been denied. In federal cases, the Bail Reform Act of 1966 requires that accused persons be released on their own recognizance if they are unable to make bail, unless the judge has adequate evidence to believe that they will not appear for trial or are dangerous to others.

Under the Sixth Amendment, Mr. Student is entitled to a "speedy trial." But court backlogs and assorted other delays can push a criminal trial back as much as a year after an arrest. Jury trials are required (Sixth Amendment) for serious crimes unless that right is waived by the defendant. Most juries consist of twelve persons. On the federal level and in most states, a unanimous jury verdict is needed for a conviction. At his trial, Mr. Student cannot be forced to give testimony against himself (Fifth Amendment) and has the right to confront witnesses against him (Sixth Amendment). There are also prohibitions on the introduction by the prosecution of illegally obtained evidence (Fourth Amendment), although the Supreme Court has relaxed this ban in certain instances, such as when the evidence would eventually have been discovered anyway.

If Mr. Student is convicted, he may appeal the verdict to a higher court. While the Constitution does not guarantee an appeal after conviction, the federal government and all states permit at least one appeal. The Supreme Court has ruled that the appeal process cannot discriminate against poor defendants. At a minimum, government must provide convicted persons unable to pay the costs of an appeal with free legal counsel and transcripts of the original trial.

The Constitution limits the punishment that Mr. Student can be given for his crime. The Eighth Amendment forbids "cruel and unusual punishment," a provision that the Supreme Court cited in 1972 when it temporarily halted the death penalty because the states were imposing it arbitrarily. A few years later, the Court declared that the death penalty as such was constitutionally permissible.

Our discussion of Mr. Student's case presumes that all his rights were respected by the police and the courts. However, there is often a marked difference between procedural rights and actual practices. For example, police sometimes conduct sweep searches, frisking people on the street without having any reason to believe they have committed a specific crime. A person found to be carrying a concealed weapon, stolen property, or drugs is likely to be arrested, tried, and convicted, for it is very difficult to prove in court that the police had no reasonable basis for the search that led to the arrest.

SOURCE: Much of the material on arrest, search, interrogation, formal charge, trial, appeal, and punishment which informs this example is derived from Walter F. Murphy and Michael N. Danielson, *Robert K. Carr and Marver H. Bernstein's American Democracy* (Hinsdale, Ill.: Dryden Press, 1977), 465–474.

legal errors had been made at the trial. The authorities had wanted Palko to receive the death penalty, so they appealed the decision. Palko was tried again on the same charges, and this time was sentenced to death. He appealed to the U.S. Supreme Court, claiming that Connecticut's second trial violated his right not to be tried twice for the same crime. The Fifth Amendment to the U.S. Constitution prohibits double jeopardy, and so do many state constitutions, but at the time Connecticut's did not. The Supreme Court refused to overturn Palko's second conviction, and he was executed.[42]

Justice Benjamin Cardozo wrote the Court's *Palko* opinion, which stated that the Fourteenth Amendment protects rights "fundamental" to liberty but not other rights provided in the Bill of Rights. Free expression is a "fundamental" right, since it is "the indispensable condition of nearly every other form of freedom." Some procedural due-process rights, such as protection against double jeopardy, are not in the same category, Cardozo claimed.

*Freedom of expression is the matrix, the indispensable condition, of nearly every other form of freedom.*
Benjamin Cardozo, *Palko* v. *Connecticut* (1937)

*Selective Incorporation of Procedural Rights.*   Not until the 1960s did the Court broadly require states to safeguard procedural rights. The Court "incorporated" Bill of Rights protections for the accused in state courts by ruling that these protections are covered by the Fourteenth Amendment's guarantee of due process of law (see Table 5-1). This incorporation process began with *Mapp* v. *Ohio* (1961). Dollree Mapp's home had been entered by Cleveland police, who, though they failed to find the drugs they were looking for, did discover some pornographic material. Mapp's conviction for its possession was overturned by the Supreme Court on the grounds that she had been subjected to unreasonable search and seizure.[43] With this decision, the Court extended the exclusionary rule to state trial proceedings.

[42]*Palko* v. *Connecticut*, 302 U.S. 319 (1937).
[43]*Mapp* v. *Ohio*, 367 U.S. 643 (1961).

**TABLE 5-1   The Supreme Court's Application of the Bill of Rights to the States: Leading Cases**

| Case | Year | Constitutional Right at Issue |
| --- | --- | --- |
| Gitlow v. New York | 1925 | First Amendment's applicability to free speech |
| Fiske v. Kansas | 1927 | Free speech |
| Near v. Minnesota | 1931 | Free press |
| DeJonge v. Oregon | 1937 | Freedom of assembly and of petition |
| Cantwell v. Connecticut | 1940 | Religious freedom |
| Mapp v. Ohio | 1961 | Unreasonable search and seizure |
| Gideon v. Wainwright | 1963 | Right to counsel |
| Malloy v. Hogan | 1964 | Self-incrimination |
| Pointer v. Texas | 1965 | Right to confront witnesses |
| Miranda v. Arizona | 1966 | Self-incrimination |
| Klopfer v. North Carolina | 1967 | Speedy trial |
| Duncan v. Louisiana | 1968 | Jury trial in criminal cases |
| Benton v. Maryland | 1969 | Double jeopardy |

In incorporating constitutional rights, the Supreme Court has ruled that, like the federal government, the states must safeguard criminal suspects' due-process rights—including the right to be told of their other legal rights when arrested. (Seth H. Goltzer/The Stock Market)

Two years later, the Court's decision in *Gideon* v. *Wainwright* (1963) required the states to furnish attorneys for poor defendants in all felony cases. Clarence Gideon, an indigent drifter, had been convicted and sentenced to prison in Florida for breaking into a poolroom. He had no lawyer, nor was he entitled to one under the Florida constitution. He appealed on the grounds that he had been denied due process because he could not afford to pay an attorney. The Supreme Court agreed, thus extending the right to free legal counsel to defendants in state felony trials.[44]

During the 1960s the Court also ruled that defendants in state criminal proceedings cannot be compelled to testify against themselves;[45] have the rights to remain silent and to have legal counsel when they are arrested;[46] have the right to confront witnesses who testify against them;[47] must be granted a speedy trial;[48] have the right to a jury trial;[49] and cannot be subjected to double jeopardy.[50] The most famous of these cases is *Miranda* v. *Arizona* (1966), as a result of which police are required to tell suspects about their rights at the time of arrest. Ernesto Miranda had confessed during police interrogation to kidnapping and raping a young woman. His confession led to his conviction, which he successfully appealed to the Supreme Court on the grounds that he had not been informed of his rights to remain silent and to have legal counsel present during interrogation. Using other evidence of Miranda's crime, the state of

[44]*Gideon* v. *Wainwright*, 372 U.S. 335 (1963).
[45]*Malloy* v. *Hogan*, 378 U.S. 1 (1964).
[46]*Miranda* v. *Arizona*, 384 U.S. 436 (1966). See also *Escobedo* v. *Illinois*, 378 U.S. 478 (1964).
[47]*Pointer* v. *Texas*, 380 U.S. 400 (1965).
[48]*Klopfer* v. *North Carolina*, 386 U.S. 213 (1967).
[49]*Duncan* v. *Louisiana*, 391 U.S. 145 (1968).
[50]*Benton* v. *Maryland*, 395 U.S. 784 (1969).

Arizona then retried and again convicted him. He was paroled from prison in 1972 and four years later was stabbed to death in a bar fight. Ironically, Miranda's assailant was read his "Miranda rights" when police arrested him. By now the wording has become familiar: "You have the right to remain silent. . . . Anything you say can and will be used against you in a court of law. . . . You have the right to an attorney. . . ."

By 1969, when Chief Justice Earl Warren retired, nearly all of the rights guaranteed by the Fourth through the Eighth Amendment had been extended to defendants in state trial proceedings. Evidence indicates that local and state law-enforcement and judicial officials do not always uphold these rights fully,[51] but legal protections have been greatly expanded in the course of the century.

### Weakening the Exclusionary Rule

As the Warren Court expanded defendants' rights during the 1960s, many law-enforcement officials, politicians, and private citizens accused the Court of "coddling criminals" to such an extent that law-abiding people were not safe on the streets and in their homes. When Richard Nixon won the presidency after promising to restore "law and order" in the country, expectations were widespread that government would pursue a tougher line on issues of crime. In 1969 Nixon named Warren Burger to succeed the retiring Earl Warren as chief justice and within two years had named three other justices (including William Rehnquist, who became chief justice in 1986).

Warren Burger *(top)*, chief justice of the Supreme Court from 1969 to 1986, and William Rehnquist *(bottom)*, the current chief justice. (top, Yoichi R. Okamoto/Photo Researchers; bottom, UPI/Bettmann Newsphotos)

All of the Nixon appointees were said to have conservative views on the rights of the accused, but not all of the Court's decisions during Burger's tenure (1969–1986) confirmed this belief. The Burger Court decided, for example, that defendants cannot be prosecuted if they have been denied their Sixth Amendment right to a speedy trial.[52] The Burger Court also extended the right to legal representation beyond felonies to all cases in which imprisonment is a possible outcome. In 1986 the Court ruled (with Burger dissenting) that black defendants are denied their rights when prosecuting attorneys use peremptory challenges (that is, challenges without explanation) to exclude black potential jurors, so that the trial is conducted with an all-white jury.[53]

In recent years, however, the Court has substantially weakened defendants' rights in some areas. The greatest change has been to the exclusionary rule barring the use of illegally obtained evidence in criminal cases. A 1974 decision held that evidence that would be inadmissible during a trial can be presented at the grand jury hearing that precedes the trial.[54] In 1983 the Court allowed the use of evidence obtained without a properly issued search warrant when the "totality of circumstance" suggests that the police are justified in their action.[55] Then in 1984 the Court ruled that evidence discovered under a faulty warrant can be used in a trial if the police acted in "good faith."[56] In another 1984 case,

[51]See Richard L. Medalic, Leonard Zeitz, and Paul Alexander, "Custodial Police Interrogation in Our Nation's Capital: The Attempt to Implement *Miranda*," *Michigan Law Review* 66 (1968): 1347.
[52]*Strunk* v. *United States*, 412 U.S. 434 (1973).
[53]*Batson* v. *Kentucky*, 476 U.S. 79 (1986).
[54]*United States* v. *Calendra*, 414 U.S. 338 (1974).
[55]*Illinois* v. *Gates*, 462 U.S. 213 (1983).
[56]*United States* v. *Leon*, 468 U.S. 897 (1984).

# *NIX* v. *WILLIAMS:* WEAKENING THE EXCLUSIONARY RULE

The exclusionary rule, which bars the use in courts of evidence obtained by police through illegal means, was weakened in the celebrated case of Robert Anthony Williams, who killed a ten-year-old girl in Iowa. Apprehended by police, Williams refused to discuss the crime, and his lawyer obtained a promise from police that they would not interrogate him. Despite this promise, a detective who was transporting Williams across the state asked him whether he felt that "this little girl should be entitled to a Christian burial." Williams then told the detective where he had hidden the body.

Williams's subsequent conviction was overturned by the Supreme Court in 1977. The Court held that by inducing Williams to incriminate himself in the absence of his lawyer, the detective had violated his constitutional right to counsel. But the Court did say that the body's discovery would be admissible evidence in a retrial if the state could show that the body would have been found even if Williams had not confessed. Williams was again convicted in an Iowa court when the prosecution showed that 200 volunteers were searching for the girl when Williams arrived at the scene with police and would inevitably have found her body. When Williams appealed, the Court in 1984 upheld his conviction, affirming the "inevitable discovery" rule, which had been in use in lower federal courts.

SOURCE: Linda Greenhouse, "Top Court Allows Illegal Evidence in Trial if Finding Was Inevitable," *New York Times,* June 12, 1984, A21.

*Nix* v. *Williams* (see box), the Court said that illegally obtained evidence can be used against a defendant if the prosecution can prove that it would have discovered the evidence anyway. "Exclusion of physical evidence that would have inevitably been discovered adds nothing to either the integrity or fairness of a criminal trial," Burger wrote in his opinion for the majority.[57]

These and other decisions have weakened the legal position of the accused, but analysts disagree about broader implications of the rulings. Proponents say that the Court's recent direction has primarily eliminated loopholes that in the past have allowed guilty persons to go free on minor technicalities. Detractors see a darker consequence, noting that police can always claim to have acted in good faith in violating an individual's person or property, whatever their true motives at the time. One of the Supreme Court's own justices, John Paul Stevens, has even suggested on several occasions that the Bill of Rights is being downgraded into an "honor code" for police. However, no one claims that recent decisions have returned the standard of justice to the low level that prevailed before the 1960s. Most of the Warren Court's precedents remain in effect, including the most important one of all: the principle that procedural protections guaranteed to the accused by the Bill of Rights apply to the states as well as to the federal government.

## SUBSTANTIVE DUE PROCESS

Most issues of criminal justice have centered on procedural due process. However, beyond the question of whether proper legal procedures have been followed is the more general question of **substantive due process**—the

[57]*Nix* v. *Williams,* 467 U.S. 431 (1984).

requirement that the government and its laws be reasonable in their purposes and consequences. Adherence to proper legal procedures (procedural due process) does not necessarily produce reasonable outcomes (substantive due process). In recent years, for example, courts have addressed the issue of whether properly convicted persons are treated justly when they are confined in overcrowded, filthy, or outmoded jails and prisons. Courts have ordered officials in some cases to relieve inmate overcrowding and to improve prison facilities.

In general, the legal standard for assessing substantive due process is whether the policy in question appears reasonable and fair by current standards. Convicts are not entitled to suites at seaside resorts, but neither do they deserve to be housed in unclean and unsafe jails. The difficulty with judgments about substantive due process is that they are usually highly subjective. At what point between the extremes of dungeons and country clubs do jail conditions become unjust? The courts have often shied away from such decisions, preferring to leave them in the hands of legislative bodies. For example, judges have generally been reluctant to rule on whether the penalties defined by law for particular crimes constitute unreasonable punishment for those crimes. In 1989, for instance, the Supreme Court upheld the legality of capital punishment in cases where the accused was a juvenile or was mentally impaired.

## The Right of Privacy

Until the 1960s, Americans' constitutional rights were confined largely to those enumerated in the Bill of Rights. This situation prevailed despite the Ninth Amendment, which reads: "The enumeration in the Constitution, of certain rights, shall not be construed to deny or disparage others retained by the people."

In 1965, however, the Supreme Court added to the list of individual rights, declaring that Americans have "a right of privacy." This judgment arose from the case of *Griswold* v. *Connecticut*, which challenged a state law prohibiting the use of birth-control devices, even by married couples. The Supreme Court invalidated the statute, concluding that a state had no business interfering with a married couple's decision in regard to the use of contraceptives. The Court did not base its decision on the Ninth Amendment, but reasoned instead that an underlying right of privacy gave rise to such individual protections as the freedom from unreasonable search and seizure. "We deal with a right of privacy older than the Bill of Rights," concluded Justice William O. Douglas.[58]

The right of privacy was the basis for the Supreme Court's ruling in *Roe* v. *Wade* (1973), which gave women full freedom to choose abortion during the first three months of pregnancy.[59] (During the second three months of pregnancy, the Court said, a state could regulate abortions, but only to safeguard the health of the woman. In the final three months, a state could ban abortion except when the woman's life was endangered by her pregnancy.) In a 7–2 decision that overturned a Texas law prohibiting abortion except to save the life of the mother,

---

[58]*Griswold* v. *Connecticut*, 381 U.S. 479 (1965).
[59]*Roe* v. *Wade*, 401 U.S. 113 (1973).

Despite the Supreme Court's ruling in *Roe* v. *Wade*, the controversy over the right to abortion remains heated. (Donna Binder/Impact Visuals)

the Supreme Court said that the right of privacy is "broad enough to encompass a woman's decision whether or not to terminate her pregnancy."

After *Roe*, antiabortion activists sought to reverse or weaken the Court's ruling. Attempts to pass a constitutional amendment that would ban abortions were unsuccessful, but abortion foes succeeded in some of their efforts, such as their campaign to establish laws that prohibit the use of government funds to pay for abortions for poor women. Then, in 1989, the Supreme Court upheld a Missouri law that prohibits abortions in public hospitals and by public employees.[60] The ruling was in part a consequence of the efforts of antiabortion groups to influence Supreme Court appointments during the Reagan presidency. The Missouri law was upheld by a 5-4 majority and all three Reagan appointees on the Court (Justices O'Connor, Scalia, and Kennedy) voted with the majority.

The Missouri ruling brought swift denunciations from proabortion advocates, and abortion will certainly be a leading controversy for years to come. The issue today is not the right of privacy itself but how far that right extends and whom it protects.[61] At present, the issue is focused on women's control of their reproductive capacity.

## The Courts and a Free Society

A free and democratic nation has a vital stake in maintaining individual freedoms. The United States was founded on the belief that individuals have an

---

[60]*Webster* v. *Reproductive Health Services*, 88-605 (1989).
[61]See, for example, *Bowers* v. *Hardwick*, 478 U.S. 186 (1986).

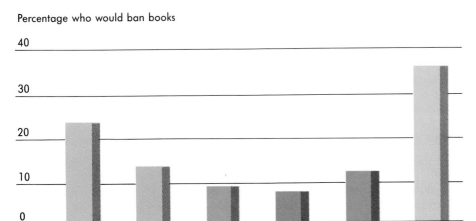

Percentage who would ban books

Number of categories of authors whose books would be banned

**FIGURE 5-1 Percentage of Respondents Who Would Remove from Public Libraries a Book by Controversial Author in from One to Five Categories** Despite their general belief in the principle of free expression, a majority of Americans surveyed said that they would ban from public libraries a book by an author in from one to five categories: an atheist, a communist, a homosexual, a militarist, and a racist. A minority—37 percent—would allow books by authors in all of those categories. *Source: Based on National Opinion Research Center data reported in Howard D. White, "Majorities for Censorship,"* Library Journal, *July 1986, 33 (Figure 2).*

innate right to personal liberty—to speak their minds, to worship as they choose, to be free of police intimidation. The greatest threat to individual rights in a democratic society is a popular majority backed by elected leaders determined to carry out its will. Majorities have frequently preferred policies that would diminish the freedom of those who hold minority views, have unconventional lifestyles, or simply "look different" from the majority.

Opinion surveys have repeatedly shown that many Americans, while they may support individual rights in the abstract, have only moderate respect for those rights in practice.[62] Although nearly all Americans say that they favor free expression as a general principle, for example, a significant proportion oppose the expression of certain viewpoints. Surveys conducted by the National Opinion Research Center between 1976 and 1982 found that *most* Americans would ban from public libraries a book by an atheist, communist, homosexual, militarist, or racist (see Figure 5-1). Only 37 percent of those interviewed said they would ban books by none of the authors, and 22 percent were willing to remove the books of all the authors.

The rights of the accused receive even less support from Americans, who apparently fear crime more than they value due-process rights that they themselves expect never to need. A 1985 Gallup poll indicated that a majority of Americans believed that police are sometimes justified in ignoring procedural rights if their actions lead to the conviction of guilty individuals. When conditions are favorable, many politicians have been willing to play on the public's fear of crime and insensitivity to civil liberties issues—as when scores of politicians rode the "law and order" issue to election victory during the 1960s.

Nor is the Supreme Court entirely insulated from these popular moods. During the communist scare of the early 1950s, for example, the Court upheld convictions of communists who spoke in favor of the overthrow of the U.S.

[62]See Herbert McClosky and Alda Brill, *Dimensions of Tolerance* (New York: Russell Sage Foundation, 1983); David C. Lawrence, "Procedural Norms and Tolerance: A Reassessment," *American Political Science Review* 70 (1976): 80–100; Michael Corbett, *Political Tolerance in America* (New York: Longman, 1982).

★ ANALYZE THE ISSUE

**The Necessity of the Bill of Rights**

The Bill of Rights was added to the Constitution despite the Framers' objection that it was unnecessary. Whose position—the Framers' or those who advocated the Bill of Rights—do you think history supports? Can you think of additional rights that you might have today if the Framers' position had prevailed? Can you think of rights that you might *not* have today if their view had prevailed?

government. Nevertheless, the judicial branch can normally be expected to grant more consideration to the individual citizen, however unpopular his or her views or actions, than will the elected branches, which are more responsive to majority and established interests. How far the Supreme Court will go in protecting a person's rights depends on the facts of the case, the political leanings of the justices, the existing status of the law, and prevailing social needs. But the Court's protection of individual rights is one of its most significant responsibilities, a development that is owed in no small measure to the Bill of Rights. It transformed the inalienable rights of life, liberty, and property into legal rights, thus putting them under judicial protection.[63]

Civil liberties are not blessings that government kindly bestows on the individual. Because of their constitutional nature, these rights are above government: in fact, it can be said that government exists to protect these rights. True, government does not always act lawfully; the temptations of power and the pressures of the majority can at times lead governmental institutions to usurp individual rights. The courts are not immune to these influences and have the additional pressure of the obligation to seek an accommodation between the claims of individuals and the collective interests of society (which, of course, include respect for civil liberties). However, while the courts have not always sided with individuals in their claims to rights, it is at least as noteworthy that they have not always sided with government in its claims against the individual.

The judiciary's importance to the preservation of civil liberties has increased as society has grown in complexity. Large, impersonal bureaucracies—public and private—are a defining characteristic of the modern age, and their power can easily dwarf the individual. Courts of law are an exception. The isolated citizen, who standing alone carries no weight with huge bureaucracies, is the center of attention in legal proceedings. Not surprisingly, then, individuals have increasingly turned to the courts for protection. In the Supreme Court's 1929 session, issues of civil liberties accounted for less than 10 percent of its case load. Today, such cases amount to roughly half of the Court's docket.[64]

Nonetheless, courts alone cannot provide adequate protection for individual rights. A civil society rests also on enlightened representatives and a tolerant citizenry. If, for example, politicians and the public encourage police to infringe the rights of vaguely threatening minorities or nonconformists, the judiciary's protection of persons accused of crimes will not ensure justice. It may be said that the test of a truly civil society is not its treatment of popular ideas and of its best citizens but its willingness to tolerate ideas that the majority detests and to treat even its unpopular citizens with respect.

[63]Alpheus Thomas Mason, *The Supreme Court: Palladium of Freedom* (Ann Arbor: University of Michigan Press, 1962), 58.
[64]Lawrence Baum, *The Supreme Court* (Washington, D.C.: Congressional Quarterly Press, 1981), 151.

## Summary

In their search for personal liberty, Americans added the Bill of Rights to the Constitution shortly after its ratification. These amendments guarantee certain political, procedural, and property rights against infringement by the national government. Freedom of expression is the most basic of democratic rights. People are not free unless they can freely express their views. Nevertheless, free expression may conflict with the nation's security needs during times of war and insurrection. The courts at times have allowed government to limit expression substantially for purposes of national security. For the past twenty-five years, however, the courts have protected a very wide range of free expression in the areas of speech, press, and religion.

The guarantees embodied in the Bill of Rights originally applied only to the national government. Under the principle of selective incorporation of these guarantees into the Fourteenth Amendment, the courts extended them to state governments, though slowly and unevenly. In the 1920s and 1930s, First Amendment guarantees of freedom of expression were given protection from infringement by the states. The states, however, continued to have wide discretion in criminal proceedings until the early 1960s, when most of the fair-trial rights in the Fourth through Eighth amendments were given broad federal protection.

"Due process of law" refers to legal protections that have been established to preserve individual rights. Due process is of two kinds: procedural and substantive. The former consists of procedures or methods (for example, the opportunity of an accused person to have an attorney present during police interrogation) designed to ensure that an individual's rights are respected; the latter consists of legal proceedings that lead to reasonable and fair results (for example, the conditions of imprisonment of an individual convicted of a crime).

Civil liberties are not absolute but must be balanced against other considerations (such as national security or public safety) and against one another when rights come into conflict. The judicial branch of government, particularly the Supreme Court, has taken on much of the responsibility for protecting and interpreting individual rights. The Court's positions have changed with time and conditions, but the Court has generally been more protective of and sensitive to civil liberties than have elected officials or popular majorities.

## Major Concepts

Bill of Rights
civil liberties
clear-and-present-danger test
compelling governmental interest
establishment clause
exclusionary rule
freedom of expression

free-exercise clause
preferred position (of First Amendment rights)
prior restraint (of the press)
procedural due process
selective incorporation
substantive due process

## Suggested Readings

Abraham, Henry. *Freedom and the Court*, 4th ed. New York: Oxford University Press, 1982. A general survey of judicial interpretations of civil liberties.

Haiman, Franklyn S. *Speech and Law in a Free Society*. Chicago: University of Chicago Press, 1981. An assessment of the primacy of speech in a free society.

Halpern, Stephen C., ed. *The Future of Our Liberties*. Westport, Conn.: Greenwood Press, 1982. A collection of essays that consider how the freedoms enumerated in the Bill of Rights may be affected by developing conditions in American society.

Krislov, Samuel. *The Supreme Court and Political Freedom*. New York: Free Press, 1968. An account of the Supreme Court's political-freedom decisions.

Lewis, Anthony. *Gideon's Trumpet*. New York: Random House, 1964. A summary of the case of Clarence Gideon and its effects on the right of persons accused of crime to legal counsel.

Mason, Alpheus T. *The Supreme Court: Palladium of Freedom*. Ann Arbor: University of Michigan Press, 1962. An assessment of the Supreme Court's role in protecting individual rights.

Mendelson, Wallace. *The American Constitution and Civil Liberties.* Homewood, Ill.: Dorsey Press, 1981. A text that examines U.S. civil liberties in constitutional theory and practice.

O'Brien, David M. *The Public's Right to Know.* New York: Praeger, 1981. A penetrating analysis of the Supreme Court and the First Amendment.

Rutland, Robert A. *The Birth of the Bill of Rights, 1776–1791.* New York: Macmillan, 1962. A description of the historical developments leading to the addition of the Bill of Rights to the U.S. Constitution.

Sorauf, Frank J. *Wall of Separation: The Constitutional Politics of Church and State.* Princeton, N.J.: Princeton University Press, 1976. A well-written account of religious freedom as a constitutional issue.

# Chapter 6

## ECONOMIC RIGHTS AND OPPORTUNITIES: EXPRESSING INDIVIDUALISM

*The true foundation of republican government is the equal right of every citizen, in his person and in his property.*

*Thomas Jefferson*[1]

In 1974 Allied Structural Steel closed down its operations in Minnesota. The closing triggered the implementation of a Minnesota law requiring companies that go out of business in the state to secure the pension benefits of their laid-off employees. The law was enacted to prevent companies from absconding with pension funds that had been set aside for workers.

Allied Steel sued the state of Minnesota, arguing that it was protected by the **contract clause** (in Article I, section 10) of the U.S. Constitution, which forbids a state to pass laws that impair "the obligation of contracts." Allied's contract with its workers stated that the company had sole discretion to determine the status of pension benefits. Allied contended that it could not be forced to provide pension benefits to its former employees. In *Allied Structural Steel* v. *Spannaus*, the Supreme Court of the United States ruled in Allied Steel's favor. Minnesota's law was judged to impair severely, not incidentally, on Allied's pension contract with employees and thus was concluded to violate the contract clause of the Constitution.[2]

The *Allied* case is an example of the stakes that can be involved in a dispute over property rights. **Property rights** are rights of ownership, use, and contract.

[1]Quoted in Catherine Drinker Bowen, *Miracle at Philadelphia* (Boston: Atlantic–Little, Brown, 1966), 71–72.
[2]*Allied Structural Steel Co.* v. *Spannaus*, 438 U.S. 234 (1978).

Property rights are defined mainly through common law (judge-made law arising out of legal disputes between private parties). Common law dictates, for example, that individuals have a right to establish a home of their own.

The U.S. Constitution also provides property protections. In addition to the contract clause, the Constitution's Fifth Amendment prohibits the national government from depriving individuals of their property rights except through due process of law and from taking private property for public use without just compensation to the owner. The Fourteenth Amendment extends due-process protection of property to include actions by state governments.

These constitutional provisions are intended to keep government from unreasonably infringing on the rights of individuals who already hold property or are parties to contracts. The Constitution does *not* grant each citizen a right to economic security: the document is silent on the issue of whether a citizen is entitled to a minimum standard of living. However, legal protections of property are not designed simply to allow individuals to do whatever they want with the property they have accumulated.[3] In theory, property rights are granted to promote both individual interests *and* the common good. For example, corporations are protected in their property rights not only because such protection is beneficial to individual stockholders but also because it can benefit workers (through, for example, income security and stable employment) and consumers (through, for example, a dependable supply of goods).

This chapter discusses individual rights and opportunities in the economic realm, focusing particularly on how these rights and opportunities reflect basic cultural values and affect Americans' everyday lives. Related economic issues are covered in later chapters, notably in Chapters 26 ("Economic Policy") and 27 ("Social-Welfare Policy"). The main points of this chapter are the following:

★ *Property rights are protected through due process from infringement by government.* This protection is consistent with the concept of *negative government,* which holds that personal liberty is enhanced when the power of government is strictly constrained.

★ *Government intervention can promote economic fairness and security.* The concept of *positive government* holds that government intervention to promote liberty is necessary when individuals are subject to social and economic forces beyond their control.

★ *A prevailing principle in the United States is equality of opportunity.* Unlike many other democracies, the United States has not established an individual right to economic security.

★ *In its idealistic form, economic individualism fosters human growth and accomplishment; in its perverse form, it culminates in selfishness and elitism.*

## Property and Liberty

In a classic study, the political scientist Robert Lane asked workingmen to talk about freedom. They made scant mention of the right to a fair trial or free expression. They spoke instead of the freedom that extends from property. One worker said, "I work where I want to work, I spend my money where I want to

[3]Richard A. Posner, "What Am I? A Potted Plant?: The Case against Strict Constructionism," *New Republic,* September 28, 1987, 23.

For many Americans, home ownership epitomizes the right of property and the personal freedom associated with it. (Gabe Palmer/Stock Market)

spend it . . . . What else—what else could you want?'' Another worker stated, ''When the day is over, I come home to my family and [then] if we want to go somewhere in the car, we can go . . . . I just like the system we have.''[4]

Americans place a very high value on the freedom that property can provide. The sociologist Herbert Gans found that ''middle Americans''—that majority of the population who are neither rich nor poor—are oriented primarily toward family and are distrustful of large institutions. Gans discovered that homeownership is particularly valued by middle Americans, who seek in a house the privacy and freedom of action that is otherwise elusive. They place much less emphasis on political expression or collective goods than on their personal well-being, a tendency that Gans labels ''middle American individualism.''[5]

Opinion polls reveal how firmly attached Americans are to private property and to the country's economic system (see Figure 6-1). By 87 percent to 4 percent, for example, Americans agree that ''private ownership of property is as important to a good society as freedom.''

## NEGATIVE GOVERNMENT

Personal property and liberty have always been closely linked in Americans' minds. In the Europe left behind by the first American immigrants, ordinary persons had no significant opportunity to own property. Nearly all land was vested in the church and a small aristocracy. A growing commercial class existed, but its profits were subject to confiscatory taxation. The effect was that

[4]Quoted in Robert E. Lane, *Political Ideology* (New York: Free Press, 1962), 21, 24.
[5]Herbert J. Gans, *Middle American Individualism: The Future of Liberal Democracy* (New York: Free Press, 1988); Michael Schudson, ''Pumping Polyester,'' *The Nation,* June 4, 1988, 794.

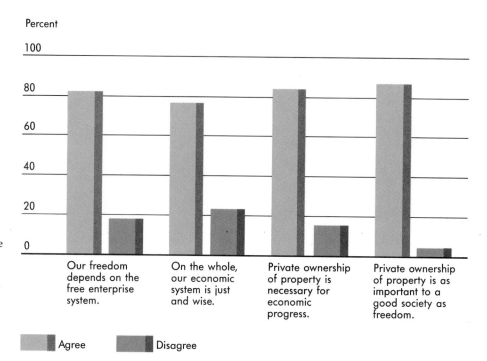

Percent

**FIGURE 6-1 Opinions on Property and Capitalism**
Americans strongly believe in the value of property rights and free enterprise. *Source: Adapted from Herbert McClosky and John Zaller,* The American Ethos: Public Attitudes toward Capitalism and Democracy *(Cambridge, Mass.: Harvard University Press, 1984), 133, 140 (Tables 5-1 and 5-3).*

most people had no sphere of privacy: even the most intimate aspects of their lives were subject to the prying eyes of the ruling class.

America offered an alternative. Its open land and vast wilderness made it relatively easy for individuals to acquire property and establish an independent life. The situation appealed to the new immigrants, most of whom were

In America's colonial times, work was hard but opportunities were abundant; as a result, people's commitment to self-reliance was heightened. (The Bettmann Archive)

Protestants from the British Isles and northern Europe whose religious values made virtues of hard work and thrift. Rather quickly, these early Americans came to believe that their liberty included the freedom to establish themselves economically and that their rights included those of property.[6]

To the writers of the U.S. Constitution, protection of property was primarily an issue of restraints on government. Of course, government had to have economic resources of its own, so it had to have the power to tax property. But, in the Framers' view, government's chief economic duty was *not* to interfere in property relations. Their guiding philosophy was that of **negative government,** which holds that government governs best by staying out of people's lives, thus giving individuals as much freedom as possible to determine their own pursuits. Liberty is enhanced when government refrains from acting. As Thomas Jefferson said in his first inaugural address in 1801,

> a wise and frugal government, which shall restrain men from injuring one another, which shall leave them otherwise free to regulate their own pursuits of industry and improvement, and shall not take from the mouth of labor the bread it has earned. This is the sum of good government.

The concept of negative government is embodied in the contract clause and the Fifth and Fourteenth amendments of the Constitution. These provisions are barriers to government usurpation of property. The Constitution protects property chiefly through due process of law, which, as we noted in Chapter 5, can take either substantive or procedural form.

## SUBSTANTIVE DUE-PROCESS PROTECTION OF PROPERTY

For a lengthy period in American history, substantive due process, which is concerned with the reasonableness of a law (see Chapter 5), was a major protection of propertied interests, particularly big business. Through its substantive due-process rulings, the Supreme Court blocked legislation affecting such areas as workers' wages, hours, and unions. In *Lockner* v. *New York* (1905), for example, the Court invalidated a New York statute that forbade bakery firms to require employees to work more than sixty hours a week. The Court said: "There is no reasonable ground for interfering with the . . . right of free contract. . . . They [bakers] are in no sense wards of the state."[7] The right of contract was presumed to protect business from governmental regulation of employer–employee relations. Sir Henry Maine wrote that the Constitution's contract clause "is the bulwark of American individualism against democratic impatience and socialist fantasy."[8]

The Supreme Court's support of business interests had begun long before *Lockner.* The Court concluded in 1810 that the Constitution's contract clause, which was originally designed to govern the relationship between individual

*"No State shall . . . make anything but gold and silver coin a tender in payment of debts; [nor] pass any . . . law impairing the obligation of contracts. . . ."*
　U.S. Constitution, Article I, section 10 (the contract clause)

*"No person shall . . . be deprived of life, liberty, or property, without due process of law; nor shall private property be taken for public use without just compensation."*
　U.S. Constitution, Fifth Amendment

*"No State shall . . . deprive any person of life, liberty, or property, without due process of law. . . ."*
　U.S. Constitution, Fourteenth Amendment

---

[6]Seymour Martin Lipset, *The First New Nation* (New York: Basic Books, 1963), ch.3.
[7]*Lockner* v. *New York*, 198 U.S. 25 (1905).
[8]Quoted in Geoffrey R. Stone, Louis M. Seidman, Cass R. Sunstein, and Mark V. Tushnet, *Constitutional Law* (Boston: Little, Brown, 1986), 1428.

Until the 1930s the Supreme Court tended to protect the property interests of businesses, even at the expense of workers' safety and health. At the turn of the century most factories were dark, dirty, and hazardous. (The Bettman Archive)

creditors and debtors, also barred states from impairing contracts involving corporate parties.[9] A few years earlier, in a precedent-setting Philadelphia jury trial, union organizers were found guilty of conspiracy, a verdict that effectively gave business an overwhelming advantage in its relations with labor.

By the late nineteenth century, business reigned supreme in the United States (see Chapter 2). As President Calvin Coolidge was later to say, "The business of America is business." The idea of individualism at the personal level had, at the level of the economic system, become the doctrine of *laissez-faire capitalism*. As we saw in Chapter 1, **individualism** stresses the values of hard work and self-reliance and holds that the individual should be left to succeed or fail on his or her own. Individualism and a capitalist economic system complement each other. Capitalism's principles of competition, profit, and private enterprise parallel individualism's emphasis on striving, achievement, and self-reliance.[10]

In the era of laissez-faire capitalism, government left business alone on the assumption that the free market is largely self-regulating and will ultimately produce for society the greatest possible social and economic benefits. As it turned out, though, unbridled capitalism became destructive of individualism. Large trusts dominated nearly every sector of the economy and virtually controlled the lives of their workers, most of whom labored sixty hours a week or more for meager wages under conditions so unsafe that more than a thousand were killed or critically injured every week. James Madison had recognized that private economic power could jeopardize personal liberty, but he had concluded that the threat was small in comparison with the dangers posed by powerful government. A century later, economic change had rendered Madison's analysis obsolete. The iron grip that the business trusts had on

[9]*Fletcher* v. *Peck*, 6 Cranch 87 (1810).
[10]Herbert McClosky and John Zaller, *The American Ethos: Public Attitudes toward Capitalism and Democracy* (Cambridge, Mass.: Harvard University Press, 1984), 113.

# THE CONSTITUTIONAL PRIORITY GIVEN TO PROPERTY RIGHTS

Analyses of individual rights by scholars have typically focused on the guarantees of freedom of religion, freedom of expression, and fair trial. Rights of property are typically neglected. Most American government textbooks, for example, do not have even a major section, much less a full chapter, on property rights.

By some constitutional indicators, however, property rights have priority over other rights. Consider the following facts:

The U.S. Constitution was written largely in response to the threats to property posed by Shays' Rebellion and by other actions taken by debtors.

The contract clause (which prohibits the states from passing laws that greatly harm creditors) is one of the few individual protections in the original Constitution of 1787 and one of the few protections that applied to the states from the nation's earliest years.

John Locke, whose philosophy of limited government underlies the U.S. Constitution, maintained that "the preservation of their property is the reason why men enter into society."

The Supreme Court initially applied the Fourteenth Amendment's due-process clause only to the protection of property from state action; decades elapsed before the clause was used to protect the rights of free expression and fair trial.

workers and consumers was every bit as oppressive as any governmental power Americans had known.

The destructive force of the Great Depression in the 1930s finally awakened Americans to the folly of laissez-faire capitalism. As we saw in Chapter 2, it took the Supreme Court longer than other government institutions to recognize the need for change. In 1937, however, the Supreme Court reversed its opposition to government regulation of the marketplace and largely abandoned its use of substantive due process to protect business interests. In so doing the Court, in effect, accepted a dissenting argument that Justice Oliver Wendell Holmes had made thirty years earlier in *Lockner*: "A constitution is not intended to embody a particular economic theory, whether of paternalism or . . . laissez-faire."[11]

Although today's Supreme Court has indicated that it might resurrect on a limited basis the doctrine of substantive due process as applied to property issues, its basic position is that broad economic policy is largely the responsibility of legislatures, not courts. Although the Supreme Court has never said so directly, this reversal of precedent was based on a belated recognition that individual property rights—although a good unto themselves—must also be judged on their contribution to the common good. They are a means to desirable social and economic goals, and it is largely up to the majority, not to the courts or powerful corporations, to decide the nature of these goals.

## MODERN DUE-PROCESS PROTECTION OF PROPERTY

Today due-process protection of property is largely procedural rather than substantive. In general, procedural due process requires that government follow proper procedures when it takes action that is potentially harmful to an individual (see Chapter 5). For example, the Fifth and Fourteenth amendments

[11]*Lockner* v. *New York*, 198 U.S. 25 (1905).

prohibit government from taking private property without giving the owner adequate compensation. Government can legally take private property for public purposes (a power known as *eminent domain*)—to build a road, for example—but it must pay the owner a fair price. If the owner contends that the proposed public purpose is not a valid one or that the offered price is too low, he or she can take the government agency to court to resolve the difference.

Property rights are less straightforward today than they were in the past. As American society has become increasingly complex, it has also become increasingly "public." Actions by individuals are more likely now to affect other individuals—that is, to have a public impact. The judiciary has recognized this fact in upholding, for example, zoning and antipollution laws that place substantial restraints on the uses that people can make of their own property.

Government's power of eminent domain provides another example. Years ago, the courts held that the Fifth Amendment's reference to "public use" meant that property taken by government had to become public property, as in the case of private land that is taken in order to construct a public park. Today the courts hold that "public use" can mean merely a public benefit. In 1954, for example, the Supreme Court upheld the action of a District of Columbia planning commission when it took over a department store in a blighted neighborhood for the purpose of letting a private developer make the area more attractive. The Court ruled that this use of eminent domain was justified "once the public purpose [that is, beautification of the area] had been established."[12]

On the whole, however, Americans are still substantially protected in their property from detrimental government action. A noteworthy recent example is the *Nollan* case. The California Coastal Commission granted the Nollan family a permit to build a beach house on their ocean-front property, subject to the condition that the public be allowed to walk along the beach. Such permit conditions are a means by which state and local governments have forced private developers to take public and environmental considerations into account. The Nollans believed that the California Coastal Commission had exceeded its authority, and they challenged the public-access condition of their permit. In 1987 the Supreme Court ruled in the Nollans' favor, concluding that, although government had the authority to protect the public's view of the ocean, the requirement concerning public access to the beach was a "taking" that could not be imposed on the Nollans without compensation.[13]

The *Nollan* decision reaffirmed a position taken decades earlier by Justice Oliver Wendell Holmes, who argued that a taking occurs when governmental action greatly diminishes the value of private property, even if that property remains in the hands of its private owners.[14] Holmes foresaw that private property would increasingly be subject to public encroachment as population density increased and that owners ought to be compensated when such encroachment substantially affects their property and privacy.

## Property and Equality

Individualism and strong property rights encourage people to become economically unequal. They are urged to achieve, and, if they are successful, their

---

[12]*Berman* v. *Parker*, 348 U.S. 26 (1954).
[13]*Nollan* v. *California Coastal Commission*, 107 U.S. 314 (1987).
[14]David A. Farber, "'Taking' Liberties," *New Republic*, July 27, 1988, 200.

accumulated property is protected by law. In a sense, property rights are the modern equivalent of the feudal order. Instead of status defined by ancestry, as was the case under feudalism, status is defined by property relationships: employer-employee, creditor-debtor, capital-labor, landowner-tenant.

In the early nineteenth century economic inequality was not a critical issue in America, for two major reasons. First, Americans were economically more equal than other peoples. There was no aristocratic class in America. Second, as long as economic opportunities were relatively open and abundant, Americans could claim an equality of opportunity. Alexis de Tocqueville noted both sides of the American character—its egalitarian spirit and its individualistic competitiveness. He said: "America thus exhibits in her social state an extraordinary phenomenon. Men are there seen on a greater equality . . . than in any other country of the world, or in any age." But Tocqueville also noted that "in no other country in the world is the love of property keener or more alert than in America."[15]

*In no other country in the world is the love of property keener or more alert than in America.*

Alexis de Tocqueville

By the late nineteenth century, however, liberty and equality in the economic sphere had come into conflict. In the industrial age, the power of capital and labor were vastly unequal, and most factory workers had no real hope of advancement. As Franklin D. Roosevelt was later to say, "Equality of opportunity as we have known it no longer exists."[16]

## POSITIVE GOVERNMENT

Constitutional doctrine until the 1930s essentially held that governmental inaction in the economic realm meant neutrality toward the contending parties. This doctrine made some sense in the preindustrial age, but made no sense in the industrial age. Nonintervention during the era of the business trusts left workers at the mercy of private interests much more powerful than they. The reformer Henry George said that the argument for a hands-off policy by the government was like insisting that each individual "should sink or swim for himself in crossing a river, ignoring the fact that some had been artificially supplied with corks and others artificially loaded with lead."[17]

This recognition that gross economic inequality undermines human freedom and dignity became the justification for **positive government**—the idea that government intervention is necessary in order to enhance personal liberty when individuals are buffeted by economic and social forces beyond their control. Whereas the concept of negative government had regarded government as the enemy of liberty, the concept of positive government holds that government action can give individuals greater control over their lives. This objective can be met when government acts to offset repressive social and economic forces or provides individuals with the means to resist those forces.

The concept of positive government found its first and fullest expression in the United States in Franklin Roosevelt's New Deal, which rested on the twin ideas that government must act to correct inequities in the free market and that it must protect individuals from severe economic hardship. Because the marketplace is driven by an uncompromising commitment to profit, govern-

[15]Alexis de Tocqueville, *Democracy in America* (1835–1840), ed. J. P. Mayer (Garden City, N. Y.: Doubleday/Anchor, 1969), 55.
[16]Advisory Commission on Intergovernmental Relations, *Conditions of Contemporary Federalism* (Washington, D.C.: ACIR, 1985), 115.
[17]Quoted in McClosky and Zaller, *American Ethos*, 87.

★ ANALYZE THE ISSUE

**Events That Force
Political Change**
In their concern with patterns
and processes, political
scientists sometimes fail to
acknowledge that great
events have the power to
change government. The
Great Depression of the
1930s, for example,
challenged Americans to
harness the power of a
modern economy and a mass
society without destroying
what they treasured from
their past. Franklin
Roosevelt's New Deal was
designed to do exactly that.
How did its policies (such as
public works programs, social
security, and bank depositors'
insurance) hark back to old
ways and yet reach toward
new ones?

ment is obligated to intervene in order to promote human values, including
freedom from want and freedom from market exploitation. This "new public
philosophy," as Samuel Beer and others have labeled it, found expression in a
great many New Deal policies and programs.[18] Among them were child-labor
laws, a minimum wage, the right of labor to bargain collectively, business
regulation of varying types, public works projects, unemployment compensation, and social security for the elderly, infirm, handicapped, and widowed.

Since the 1930s, the concept of positive government has extended beyond
what even the most ardent New Dealer might have imagined. Government now
has ongoing responsibilities for regulating, promoting, and monitoring economic relationships and for protecting individuals from the vagaries of the
marketplace. Nevertheless, the idea of positive government has not replaced
that of negative government. The two ideas coexist, sometimes uneasily, in
American public opinion and public policy. As James David Barber notes,
Americans want "security *and* opportunity, money *and* liberty, fairness *and*
variety."[19] They want freedom from government and yet they want government
to protect them from personal deprivation and loss of control.

## ECONOMIC PRIVILEGES: ENTITLEMENT PROGRAMS

Modern life has led to a weakening of the traditional distinction between a right
and a privilege. A **right** is an individual claim that has unquestioned legal status
and protection. A **privilege** is a claim that does not have clearly defined legal
status and protection. Thus an individual does not have a right to own a home;
homeownership is a privilege. Yet once an individual owns a home, his or her
ownership is protected by rights of property.

In recent years, however, certain privileges have almost attained the status of
rights. Most of these involve government *entitlement programs*. The benefits
provided by such programs cannot be denied to individuals who meet the
criteria for eligibility and are thus "entitled" to the benefits. For example, a
retired person who meets the lawful conditions for social security income but
whose claim is denied by government can resort to due-process proceedings.
Due process has also been a means by which individuals have sometimes forced
government to expand entitlement programs. In cases involving public housing
and other forms of assistance, courts at times have ordered government to
expand eligibility to include categories of citizens who appear to have been
arbitrarily excluded by a government agency.

Today the range of entitlement programs is quite extensive, and these
programs have become every bit as significant to some Americans' lives as
traditional rights of property and contract. Some leading entitlement programs
are:

Social security benefits for eligible retirees

Medical benefits for the poor (Medicaid) and eligible retirees (Medicare)

Aid to Families with Dependent Children (AFDC)

---

[18]Samuel Beer, "In Search of a New Public Philosophy," in Anthony King, ed., *The New American
Political System* (Washington, D.C.: American Enterprise Institute, 1978), 6–13.
[19]James David Barber, *The Pulse of Politics* (New York: Norton, 1980), 317; emphasis added.

In the food stamp program, as in all other government entitlement programs, eligibility criteria determine who is "entitled" to receive the benefits. (Kevin Horan/Picture Group)

Food stamps for low-income individuals and families

School lunch subsidies for poor children

Public housing for low-income families

## Equality of Opportunity: The American Way

All democratic societies promote both economic liberty and economic security, but they do so in varying ways and to different degrees. Economic security has a higher priority in European democracies than in the United States. European democracies have instituted such programs as government-paid health care for *all* citizens; compensation for *all* unemployed workers; and retirement benefits for *all* elderly citizens. By comparison, the United States provides these benefits only to *some* citizens in each category. For example, not all elderly Americans receive social security benefits. Eligibility is confined to those persons (including their spouses) who contributed special payroll taxes during their working years. If they paid social security taxes for a long enough period when they were employed, they get the benefits. Otherwise, they do not, even if they are in dire economic need.

Such policy differences between Europe and the United States stem from cultural and historical differences. Democracy developed in Europe in reaction to centuries of aristocratic rule, the inequities of which brought the issue of human equality to the forefront. When strong labor and socialist parties then emerged as a consequence of industrialization, European democracies initiated sweeping social-welfare programs that brought about greater economic equality. In contrast, American democracy emerged out of a tradition of limited government that emphasized personal freedom. Equality was a lesser issue, and class consciousness was weak. No major labor or socialist party emerged in America during industrialization to represent the working class, and there was no persistent and strong demand for welfare policies that would bring about an economic leveling.

These differing legacies are evident today in the opinions of Americans and Europeans toward liberty and equality. When asked in a Gallup study whether they placed a higher value on freedom or on equality, Americans chose freedom

In the United States a high value is placed on free public education as an avenue to equal opportunity. (Paul Conklin)

TABLE 6-1   What Americans Believe Should Be Done to Help the Poor

| Form of Assistance | Percent Favoring |
|---|:---:|
| Give money to the poor | 1% |
| Do nothing and wait for a strong economy to lift up the poor | 2 |
| Provide government services for the poor | 5 |
| Create government jobs for the poor | 20 |
| Give poor people education and training for jobs in the private sector | 72 |
| | 100% |

SOURCE: 1985 *Los Angeles Times* survey.

by 72 percent to 20 percent. Among Europeans, the margin was only 49 percent to 35 percent.[20]

With their strong commitment to individualism, Americans tend to look upon equality less as an issue of economic sharing than as one of economic opportunity. Americans are disinclined to help the poor through welfare payments; they prefer that the poor be given training and education so that they can learn to help themselves (see Table 6-1). This attitude is consistent with Americans' preference for **equality of opportunity,** which is the idea that individuals should have an equal chance to succeed on their own. The concept embodies equality in its emphasis on giving everyone a fair chance to get ahead. Yet equality of opportunity also embodies liberty because it allows people to succeed or fail on their own as a result of what they do with their opportunities. The presumption is that people will end up differently—some rich, some poor. It is sometimes said that equality of opportunity offers individuals an equal chance to become unequal.

In practice, equality of opportunity works itself out primarily in the private sector, where Americans compete for jobs, promotions, and other advantages. However, a few public policies have the purpose of enhancing equality of opportunity. Two of these policies are public education and affirmative action.

## PUBLIC EDUCATION: LEVELING THROUGH THE SCHOOLS

Widespread public education was established in America in the nineteenth century. Public schools sprang up in nearly every community and were open free of charge to children who could attend. The contrast with Europe was stark. There, schooling was a privilege that was reserved largely for the upper classes. Leon Sampson, a nineteenth-century American socialist, commented on the difference: "The European ruling classes . . . were open in their contempt for the proletariat. But in the United States equality, and even classlessness, the creation of wealth for all and political liberty were extolled in the public schools." Sampson concluded that Americans had a unique conception of equality: everyone was primed to become a capitalist. "It is," he said, "a socialist conception of capitalism."[21]

Of course, public education has never been a uniform experience for

[20]McClosky and Zaller, *American Ethos,* 18.
[21]Quoted in Michael Harrington, *Socialism* (New York: Bantam, 1973), 142.

American children. Cities in the late nineteenth century neglected the education of many immigrant children, who were thereby placed at a permanent disadvantage. And of course, southern schools for black children in the segregationist era were designed to subjugate them, not to educate them.

Today, whether an American child gets a good education depends to a significant extent on the wealth of the community in which he or she resides. In 1973 the Supreme Court ruled that education of high quality is not a right to which all children are entitled. This ruling came in response to a suit initiated on behalf of students in a poor and largely Hispanic school district in San Antonio, which had an annual budget of $356 per pupil. By comparison, a school district in a nearby wealthy suburb spent $594 per pupil per year. In deciding that Texas was not obliged to equalize per-pupil spending in its schools, the Supreme Court concluded that education "is not among the rights afforded explicit protection under [the] Constitution. Nor . . . [is it] implicitly so protected." A state is obliged only to provide "an 'adequate' education for all children," not "equal quality of education."[22]

Nevertheless, the United States through its public schools has educated a broad segment of the population. Arguably, no country in the world has made an equivalent effort to give children, whatever their parents' backgrounds, an equal opportunity in life through education. The United States ranks first in the world in per capita spending on education and first in the proportion of adults receiving a college education.[23] In the United States, about 40 percent of young people eventually go on to college, compared with 10 percent in Britain, for example.

## AFFIRMATIVE ACTION: PROVIDING GENUINE OPPORTUNITY

Opportunity in America has never been as equal in practice as it is in theory. When women and members of minority groups seek a job or a promotion, they are more likely than white males to find that an employer wants someone else. Few employers today are likely to say outright that they prefer a white male to a woman or a black person, but the statistics speak for themselves. White males get more jobs, better pay, and more promotions than do members of other groups (see Chapter 7).

Affirmative action programs are a response to this chronic discrimination in the marketplace. **Affirmative action** is a deliberate effort to provide full and equal opportunities in employment, education, and other situations for women, minorities, and individuals belonging to other traditionally disadvantaged groups. Affirmative action requires corporations, universities, and other organizations to establish programs designed to ensure that all applicants are treated fairly. Affirmative action also places the burden of proof on the providers of opportunities; to some extent, they must be able to demonstrate that any disproportionate granting of opportunities to white males is not the result of discriminatory practices.

In the abstract, affirmative action is not a controversial idea. Most Americans say that minorities and women deserve a truly equal chance at jobs and other opportunities. Yet affirmative action programs are controversial in practice

---

[22]*San Antonio Independent School District* v. *Rodriguez*, 411 U.S. 1 (1973).
[23]Sidney Verba and Gary Orren, *Equality in America* (Cambridge, Mass.: Harvard University Press, 1985), ch.1.

because they can end up favoring women and minorities over white males, an outcome that is called "reverse discrimination." Although there is no evidence that reverse discrimination is rampant (and plenty of evidence that white males still have an edge in educational and marketplace opportunities), the idea that minorities and women may receive preferential treatment in some instances has resulted in attacks on affirmative action.

## The *Bakke* Case: Clouding the Issue

Affirmative action was first tested before the Supreme Court in *University of California Regents* v. *Bakke* (1978).[24] Alan Bakke, a white man, had twice been denied admission to the medical school of the University of California at Davis, even though his admission test scores were higher than those of several minority-group students who had been accepted. Bakke sued, claiming that the medical school had admitted less qualified minority students through an affirmative action program that set aside sixteen places for such students. In a 5–4 decision with six separate opinions, the Court ruled in Bakke's favor and ordered the university to admit him.

Although the *Bakke* case was a setback for advocates of affirmative action, the Supreme Court did not invalidate the policy. The Court said that race could be one consideration in admission policy, along with such other considerations as test scores and extracurricular activities, as long as no rigid racial quotas were imposed. Writing for four justices on the majority side, Justice William Brennan concluded that race could—and should—be taken into account in opportunity decisions: "We cannot and . . . need not under our Constitution . . . let color blindness become myopia which masks the reality that many 'created equal' have been treated within their lifetimes as inferior both by law and by their fellow citizens."[25]

## Subsequent Cases: Clarifying the Issue

*Bakke* was followed by two rulings in favor of affirmative action programs, one of which—*Fullilove* v. *Klutznick* (1980)—upheld a quota system that required 10 percent of federal public works funds to be awarded to minority-owned firms.[26] These initial decisions created uncertainty about the precise criteria for determining the legality of a particular affirmative action program. Not until halfway through the 1980s did the Supreme Court begin to define the permissible remedies more exactly. The rules were spelled out in a series of decisions that are described in Chapter 7. Here it is necessary only to summarize the Court's position.

According to the Supreme Court, affirmative action remedies that give preference to minorities and women are lawful when they are narrowly tailored to a particular situation and when they are designed to correct clear-cut cases of past discrimination. In other words, when an organization is guilty of unlawful and substantial discrimination, it can be compelled to rectify the situation through a program that benefits individuals who belong to groups victimized

[24]See Allan P. Sindler, *Bakke, DeFunis, and Minority Admissions: The Quest for Equal Opportunity* (New York: Longmans, 1978).
[25]*University of California Regents* v. *Bakke*, 438 U.S. 265 (1978).
[26]*Steelworkers* v. *Weber*, 443 U.S. 193 (1979); *Fullilove* v. *Klutznick*, 448 U.S. 448 (1980).

Alan Bakke was the focus of the first Supreme Court ruling on affirmative action. (AP/Wide World Photos)

by this discrimination. In one case, the Supreme Court upheld an admissions quota for minorities that a federal judge had imposed on an all-white labor union. The union had ignored two previous court orders to admit minority members, so the federal judge devised a specific timetable and quota for their admission. The Supreme Court concluded that the judge's plan was appropriate, given the union's long history of blatant racial discrimination.[27]

Although affirmative action is now an established policy, it is certain to remain a source of controversy. Most Americans have no real enthusiasm for a policy that is designed in part to make up for past wrongs. For example, 76 percent of the respondents in a national survey said that programs giving preference to minorities in hiring and promotion are "unfair to qualified people who are not members of a minority," whereas only 10 percent said that such preference is "necessary to make up for a long history of discrimination."[28]

## Individualism: A Mixed Blessing

*Thus not only does democracy make every man forget his ancestors, but it hides his descendants and separates his contemporaries from him; it throws him back forever upon himself alone and threatens in the end to confine him entirely within the solitude of his own heart.*

Alexis de Tocqueville, *Democracy in America*

Americans' beliefs about economic rights and opportunities have, it is clear, been molded primarily by a commitment to individualism. The first observer to evaluate this relationship was Alexis de Tocqueville, who in the 1830s questioned whether individualism was altogether a good thing. He acknowledged that individualism had contributed to America's economic progress but was

[27]*Local No. 28, Sheet Metal Workers* v. *Equal Employment Opportunity Commission*, 478 U.S. 421 (1986).
[28]McClosky and Zaller, *American Ethos*, 93.

concerned that individualism led Americans to value their private lives over citizenship and their self-interest over the public interest. Others have since reached the same judgment, concluding that individualism is the source of much that is undesirable—as well as much that is admirable—in American society.

## A SELF-CENTERED PUBLIC

Individualism can degenerate into crass materialism, fostering a society in which human needs become marketplace commodities. The United States is the only advanced industrial democracy that has no comprehensive system of government-paid health care for all citizens. Health care is not a recognized right of each citizen, so the quality of the health care Americans receive depends to a considerable degree on their ability to pay. In some democracies this policy would be thought unconscionable, but in the United States it is not even particularly controversial. On the basis of his study of political values, Karl Lamb concluded that most Americans "cannot really imagine a society that would provide substantial material equality."[29]

Individualism also diminishes Americans' inclination toward collective action. Only 50 percent of America's adult citizens went to the polls to elect a president in 1988. In contrast, turnout levels of 70 to 90 percent are common in other democracies. One reason for the difference is that Americans are more inclined to believe that they can get what they want through the private sector. Americans have an interest in politics, but they are immersed in their economic pursuits.[30] In fact, when they are highly active politically, it is often for the purpose of advancing their economic interests. The United States ranks first in the number of its lobbying groups, most of which have the goal of promoting a special economic interest, not the common interest.

## AN ECONOMIC ELITE

A critical perspective on American politics, **elite theory** (see box), holds that the people and their elected representatives have less to say about how the United

[29]Karl A. Lamb, *As Orange Goes: Twelve California Families and the Future of American Politics* (New York: Norton, 1974), 178.
[30]See Gans, *Middle American Individualism*.

> **★ ANALYZE THE ISSUE**
>
> **Individualism vs. the Common Good**
> For many early Americans, the sum of good government was the sum of individual satisfaction, a view that many of today's Americans accept. Alexis de Tocqueville could not accept it, and his view, too, has its modern adherents. Tocqueville argued that individualism leads people to judge everything by its material value and to place their self-interest above the common good. Which of these views reflects your own opinion?

# "WORKFARE": ENCOURAGING SELF-RELIANCE

Individualism exalts self-reliance, and many Americans believe that self-reliance is within the capacity of nearly everyone. When Gallup pollsters asked in 1985 whether a lack of effort or circumstances beyond control are more often to blame if a person is poor, only 34 percent of the respondents attributed poverty mainly to uncontrollable circumstances. Such opinions account for the persistence of the idea of "workfare"—the requirement that able-bodied welfare recipients either work in unpaid jobs or receive training for employment. In the early 1980s Con-gress rejected workfare as national policy. Opponents said that as workfare forces welfare recipients to do any job that officials assign, it amounts to involuntary servitude. In 1988, however, Congress enacted a national workfare law. Proponents claim that workfare can break the pattern of welfare dependency that can envelop entire families for several generations. When a welfare recipient is trained or employed, in this view, the probability increases that he or she will eventually find gainful, permanent employment.

Workfare—the performance of public services, such as maintaining the grounds of a housing project, in exchange for government-paid financial assistance—is gaining in popularity as an alternative to welfare "handouts." (Kevin Horan/Picture Group)

States is run than does an economic elite composed of wealthy individuals and corporate managers. This elite controls the country's agenda by dominating its financial resources.[31] The richest 1 percent of Americans own 33 percent of the nation's total wealth, and the top 100 corporations (out of a total of 200,000) control half of all industrial assets.

[31]See G. William Domhoff, *Who Rules America Now?* (Englewood Cliffs, N.J.: Prentice-Hall, 1983).

# THE PROCESS OF ELITE INFLUENCE

Elite theory holds that America is essentially run by a tiny economic elite that controls public policy through both direct and indirect means. Members of the economic elite occupy all high positions in leading corporations and hold a disproportionate number of positions in the federal executive and Congress, particularly the Senate. In addition, members of this elite are said to have inside influence over political officials because they contribute a disproportionate share of the campaign funds that candidates receive and because they underwrite many foundations, "think tanks" (research institutes), and policy groups. The Council on Foreign Relations (CFR), for instance, receives much of its funding from corporations and wealthy contributors, who, along with governmental officials, aca-

demic experts, and journalists, constitute the large majority of its 1,800 members. The CFR publishes the influential journal *Foreign Affairs*; sponsors speeches by world leaders; and organizes study groups of top governmental officials, military officers, corporate managers, and academics who meet periodically to discuss foreign policy issues. Finally, the economic elite is connected to powerful interest groups, particularly the corporations and trade associations that account for more than half of all Washington lobbying groups.

SOURCE: G. William Domhoff, *Who Rules America Now?* (Englewood Cliffs, N.J.: Prentice-Hall, 1983), ch.1.

Individualism is a powerful component of elite influence. In comparison with European democracies, the United States has very low effective tax rates, particularly on high incomes and accumulated capital, supposedly because such low rates constitute incentives and rewards for individual efforts. Even more important to moneyed interests is Americans' mistrust of big government, an attitude that stems from individualism and results in a tendency to leave to the private sector many of the decisions that in other democracies are made by government. Banking, natural resources, health care, and air transportation are among the economic sectors that are controlled by private firms in America but by government agencies elsewhere.

Individualism results in a sharp distinction between that which is properly public (political) and that which is properly private (economic). The public component is subject to partisan debate and action. The private component, which includes most economic relationships, is not. The result is that most of the power and resources of the country's wealthiest interests are effectively beyond the reach of a political majority. Although ordinary people are profoundly affected by the decisions of moneyed interests, they continue to believe that these decisions belong not to themselves but to the holders of property. Thus, although (as we saw in Chapter 2) the Supreme Court decided in 1937 that the Constitution was no longer a powerful protector of business interests, these interests are still protected in significant ways by Americans' persistent belief that politics and economics are largely different realms.

The power of America's economic elite is often exaggerated; it is a mistake to assume that because the nation's politics serves the interests of this elite, it serves *only* those interests. Elite analysis also breaks down when it is ahistorical; some analysts attribute the power of moneyed interests to a grand conspiracy rather than to a cultural bias in favor of economic accumulation and power. But in any case the extraordinary power of wealthy interests in America is both a consequence and a cause of the country's individualistic culture.

## HUMAN ENERGY AND PROGRESS

Individualism as a fundamental value cannot be judged by its costs alone. It has the capacity to liberate human energy and imagination, thereby contributing to societal progress and individual growth.

An individualistic society is open and fluid rather than closed and stratified. By law and custom, there are few formal distinctions—no titles, no fixed class lines—that sharply separate Americans from one another. To a considerable degree, each American must create his or her own place in society. Although material striving is one consequence, another and more salutary effect is that Americans are not locked into inferior social positions. There are fewer barriers to social mobility in the United States than in nearly any other society. Race is the dramatic exception: nonwhites confront formidable obstacles to advancement. For whites, at any rate, American society is remarkably open, a condition that is owed largely to individualism. As Tocqueville noted more than a century and a half ago, there is a natural social equality in a country in which a person's achievement is admired more than his or her family background.[32]

The bias that individualism produces against governmental power also has its positive side. For one thing, personal privacy is strengthened when people

★ ANALYZE THE ISSUE

**Class Consciousness**
Wealth is distributed very unequally in the United States. The richest 1 percent of the population control more than 30 percent of the nation's wealth; the poorest 20 percent control less than 5 percent of the wealth. Yet Americans are not highly class conscious. Why is this? Is America's individualistic culture part of the explanation? Do racial divisions among poorer Americans interfere with the development of class awareness?

★ ANALYZE THE ISSUE

**The Question of a Ruling Elite**
Elite-theory and Marxist sociologists claim that ordinary Americans are duped by elites into supporting a society that does not foster their best interests. One supposed strategy is pervasive advertising, which creates a blind demand for products, enriches the elite, and pacifies the masses with material possessions. Can you think of other examples that seem to support elite theory? Are there examples that disprove it? Do you think America is indeed run by a ruling elite?

[32]Tocqueville, *Democracy in America*, 550.

believe strongly in limited government. Governmental invasion of property and, to a lesser degree, of person is naturally resisted. Government is more intrusive and repressive in most other societies than it is in the United States.

In addition, big government by its nature is less flexible government. Countries that have a larger public sector than the United States have special difficulties, including bureaucratic rigidity, economic inflexibility, and welfare dependency. Such societies suffer an incalculable loss of human initiative; this is a large part of the reason that several European democracies, as well as the Soviet Union and China, have recently placed more emphasis on economic individualism. It has a proven power to unleash human energy and imagination and thereby to stimulate human development.

## Summary

Liberty for the first American immigrants included the right to better themselves economically and to be protected through law in their property holdings. The Constitution codified this idea in the contract clause; property rights are also included within the due-process protections of the Fifth and Fourteenth amendments. The idea behind the granting of individual economic rights is that they are worthwhile in themselves and contribute to the collective good through the social and economic benefits that result from them.

The historic conception of liberty in the United States was freedom from government (negative government). This conception and the nation's open frontier fostered a belief in rugged individualism. Economic self-reliance complemented Americans' commitment to equality; as long as personal liberty and opportunity were provided, Americans could seek individual economic gain without encountering insurmountable barriers and without imposing great costs on others. The Industrial Revolution altered these conditions: concentrated corporate power enabled business monopolists to restrict the freedom and institutionalize the inequality of workers. This pattern was reinforced by the Supreme Court, which, through substantive due process, protected corporations from governmental regulation of employment practices.

In contrast, the premise of the New Deal was that government must act affirmatively to help individuals control their lives and achieve their full human potential (positive government). Acceptance of the New Deal by the American people tempered their commitment to individualism and allowed government to begin to play a signifi-cant role in providing economic security. In the United States, however, the balance between economic equality and individualism is still tilted more toward individualism than it is in other advanced industrialized democracies. Entitlement to social security, for example, is not a universal right of elderly Americans but instead depends on whether the individual has contributed special payroll taxes during his or her working years. Unlike some democracies, however, the United States attempts to provide all children with an education that will give them equality of opportunity.

Idealistically, individualism is a commitment to human potential and accomplishment, but it can devolve into selfishness and elitism. Untempered materialism diminishes public life and creates a selfish reluctance to share society's resources with the less privileged. Elite power stems from the concentration of wealth and the tendency to separate political issues from economic ones, thus leaving large areas of American life subject to control by powerful private interests. Although materialism and an economic elite are undeniably elements of American society, the significant question is whether these elements are as pervasive and decisive as critics claim them to be. No simple answer is possible. To ordinary Americans, political and economic life in the United States is not a stark choice between economic security and opportunity or between public power and private power. A blend of values—individual security and opportunity, public choice and private discretion—constitutes Americans' conception of the good society.

## Major Concepts

| | |
|---|---|
| affirmative action | negative government |
| contract clause | positive government |
| elite theory | privilege |
| equality of opportunity | property rights |
| individualism | right |

## Suggested Readings

Domhoff, G. William. *Who Rules America Now?* Englewood Cliffs, N.J.: Prentice-Hall, 1983. An assessment of wealth and power which concludes that the United States is run largely by and for an economic elite.

Goldwin, Robert A., and William A. Schambra, eds. *How Capitalistic Is the Constitution?* Washington, D.C.: American Enterprise Institute, 1982. A series of essays on the relationship of a liberal democratic society to a capitalist economic system.

Lamb, Karl A. *As Orange Goes: Twelve California Families and the Future of American Politics.* New York: Norton, 1974. A portrayal of Americans' political values and economic aspirations through the words of a selected group of families.

McClosky, Herbert, and John Zaller. *The American Ethos: Public Attitudes toward Capitalism and Democracy.* Cambridge, Mass.: Harvard University Press, 1984. A survey-based analysis of Americans' attitudes toward economic and political issues.

Mintz, Beth, and Michael Schwartz. *The Power Structure of American Business.* Chicago: University of Chicago Press, 1985. An examination of intercorporate connections, with some references to relationships between corporate and political entities.

O'Brien, David M. *Privacy, Law, and Public Policy.* New York: Praeger, 1979. An assessment of privacy and its status in law and policy.

Paul, Ellen Frankel. *Property Rights and Eminent Domain.* New Brunswick, N.J.: Transaction Books, 1986. An examination of the right of property in the United States.

Sundquist, James. *Politics and Policy.* Washington, D.C.: Brookings Institution, 1968. A sweeping analysis of U.S. politics and policy which contains insightful observations on the New Deal philosophy and its consequences.

# Chapter 7

## EQUAL RIGHTS: STRUGGLING TOWARD FAIRNESS

*I have a dream that one day this nation will rise up and live out the true meaning of its creed: "We hold these truths to be self-evident: that all men are created equal."*[1]
—*Martin Luther King, Jr.*

For almost a month in 1977 an unlikely group of protesters staged a sit-in at the San Francisco offices of the U.S. Department of Health, Education, and Welfare.[2] All the protesters were blind, deaf, wheelchair-bound, or otherwise disabled. They were demanding that the federal government carry out its responsibility to implement Section 504 of the Rehabilitation Act of 1973, which outlawed discrimination against disabled persons by organizations that receive federal assistance. In response, Health, Education, and Welfare Secretary Joseph Califano agreed to implement the law; among other accommodations, buildings constructed with the help of federal funds would have access ramps and toilet stalls accessible to the disabled.

The San Francisco sit-in was a struggle for equal rights. In theory, Americans are equal in their rights, but in reality, they are not now equal, nor have they ever been. Blacks, women, Hispanics, the disabled, Jews, American Indians, Catholics, Asians, homosexuals, and members of nearly every other minority group have been victims of discrimination in fact and in law. The nation's creed—"all men are created equal"—has encouraged minorities to believe that they are deserving of equal justice and has given weight to their claims for fair treatment. But full equality is far from being a condition of American life.

Black Americans are the most obviously disadvantaged group. The ancestors of most black Americans came to this country as slaves, after having been

[1]Speech of Martin Luther King, Jr., in Washington, D.C., August 2, 1963.
[2]Example from Mary Johnson, "Overcoming the Social Barriers," *The Nation*, April 9, 1988, 489.

Through protest demonstrations in 1988, students at Gallaudet College, which was founded to provide higher education for the hearing-impaired, succeeded in obtaining the appointment of the college's first hearing-impaired president. The students argued that the appointment of a president with normal hearing would be a severe setback in the effort of handicapped people to achieve equal rights. (Paul Conklin)

captured in Africa, shipped in chains across the Atlantic, and sold in open markets in Charleston and other southern seaports. When the Constitution was being written in 1787, the question was not whether black people would become free citizens, but whether they would even be counted as human beings. It was finally decided, and written into Article I of the Constitution, that each slave would be counted as three-fifths of a person for purposes of taxation and representation. The Civil War freed the slaves, but they were soon subjected to legal discrimination, such as laws that prohibited black children from attending school with white children. It was not until the 1950s and 1960s—not so long ago—that black Americans gained nearly equal standing in law with white Americans. And even today, it requires monumental insensitivity or naiveté to say that America treats its black citizens as well as it does its white ones. To take but one example: blacks with a correctable heart problem are three times less likely to receive the necessary surgery than are whites with the same problem.[3]

This chapter focuses on **equal rights,** or **civil rights**—terms that refer to the right of every person to equal protection under the laws and equal access to society's opportunities and public facilities. We saw in Chapter 5 that "civil liberties" refers to specific *individual* rights, including freedom of speech and protection against self-incrimination. "Equal rights" or "civil rights" has to do with whether individual members of differing *groups*—racial, sexual, and the like—are treated equally. Although the law refers to the rights of individuals first and to those of groups in a secondary and derivative way, this chapter

[3]Reported on CBS Evening News of January 16, 1989.

concentrates on groups because the history of civil rights has been largely one of group claims to equality. The chapter emphasizes the following main points:

★ *Americans have substantial equality under the law.* They have, in legal terms, equal protection of the laws, equal access to accommodations and housing, and an equal right to vote. Discrimination by law against persons because of race, sex, religion, and ethnicity is now largely a thing of the past.

★ *Disadvantaged groups have had to struggle for equal rights.* Blacks, women, Native Americans, Hispanics, and Asian Americans have all had to fight for their rights in order to come closer to equality with white males.

★ *Legal equality for all Americans has not resulted in de facto equality.* Blacks, women, Hispanics, and other traditionally disadvantaged groups have a disproportionately small share of America's opportunities and benefits. Existing inequalities, discriminatory practices, and political pressures are still major barriers to their full equality. Affirmative action and busing are policies designed to help the disadvantaged achieve full equality.

★ ANALYZE THE ISSUE

**The Impact of Federalism on Equality**
Disadvantaged groups have achieved a greater degree of equality primarily through federal laws and federal court rulings, rather than through state and local measures. What do you think are the main reasons for this development? Do James Madison's arguments (in *Federalist* No. 10) about the greater diversity of the nation under a federal system apply to the situation? Do issues of equality affect your opinion about whether a federal system is preferable to a unitary one?

## Equality under the Law

Equality has always been the least completely developed of America's founding ideas. Not even Thomas Jefferson, who had a deep admiration for the common man, believed that broad meaning could be given to the claim of the Declaration of Independence that "all men are created equal." Jefferson rejected any suggestion that people should be equalized in their possessions, interests, positions, or opinions. To Jefferson, "equality" had a restricted, though significant, meaning: people are of equal moral worth and thereby deserving of equal treatment under the law.[4] Even then, Jefferson made a distinction between free men, who were entitled to legal equality, and slaves, who were not.

Since Jefferson's time, Americans' beliefs about equality have changed substantially, but the emphasis on legal equality has not. The catchphrase of nearly any group's claim to a fairer standing in American society has been "equality under the law." The importance that people attach to legal equality is understandable. When made into law, claims to equality assume a power that they do not otherwise have. Once people are secure in their legal rights, they are in a stronger position to seek equality on other fronts, such as in the economic realm. In addition, once encoded in law, a claim to equality can force officials to take positive action on behalf of a disadvantaged group. For example, some communities refused to allow the children of illegal aliens to attend public school until a 1982 Supreme Court ruling required those communities to do so.[5]

Americans' claims to legal equality are contained in a great many laws. Among the most noteworthy are the equal-protection clause of the Fourteenth Amendment, the Civil Rights acts of 1964 and 1968, and the Voting Rights Act of 1965.

[4]Robert Nisbet, "Public Opinion versus Popular Opinion," *Public Interest* 41 (1975): 171.
[5]*Plyler* v. *Doe*, 457 U.S. 202 (1982).

# EQUALITY AND THE DUE-PROCESS CLAUSE OF THE FOURTEENTH AMENDMENT

Although the Fourteenth Amendment's equal-protection clause is more closely associated with issues of equality, its due-process clause is also important in this area. Since the Supreme Court extended the federal Constitution's Bill of Rights to the states, basing its reasoning on the due-process clause of the Fourteenth Amendment, Americans in the various states have become more equal in their rights to free expression and fair trial. On issues of political expression and criminal justice, it still matters whether a person is a Texan, an Oregonian, or a New Yorker, but much less than it did in the past. Americans were once unequal, for example, in their constitutional protection against self-incrimination: they enjoyed this protection in state courts only if it was guaranteed by their state's constitution. But today, because of the Supreme Court's interpretation of the due-process clause, all Americans are entitled to constitutional protection against self-incrimination during criminal proceedings.

## EQUAL PROTECTION: THE FOURTEENTH AMENDMENT

The Fourteenth Amendment, which was ratified in 1868, declares in part that no state shall "deny to any person within its jurisdiction the equal protection of the laws." Through this **equal-protection clause,** the courts have protected such groups as black people and women from discrimination by state and local governments.

*No State shall . . . deny to any person within its jurisdiction the equal protection of the laws.*
U.S. Constitution,
Fourteenth Amendment
(equal-protection clause)

As we noted in Chapter 2, the Supreme Court initially interpreted the Fourteenth Amendment so narrowly that the South's white-dominated governments found it easy to relegate black people to second-class status. By law, they

Federal troops protect black students desegregating Little Rock Central High School after the Supreme Court's *Brown* ruling in 1954 that segregated public schools were unconstitutional. The ruling set off a wave of protests throughout the South. *(Burt Glinn/Magnum)*

were not allowed to attend the same schools, use the same public restrooms, or go to the same hospitals as white people. In 1954, however, the Supreme Court issued its historic decision in *Brown* v. *Board of Education of Topeka*, which declared that racial segregation of public schools violates the equal-protection clause of the Fourteenth Amendment.[6]

### The Reasonable-Basis Test

The equal-protection clause does not require government to treat all groups or classes of people the same way in all circumstances. In fact, laws routinely treat people unequally. For example, age restrictions have been placed on voting participation, the driving of automobiles, and the drinking of alcoholic beverages. By law, twenty-one-year-olds can drink alcohol but twenty-year-olds cannot. Inequality is also written into the tax code: people who make more money pay taxes at a higher marginal rate than people who make less money.

The judiciary allows such inequalities because they are held to be "reasonably" related to a legitimate government interest. In applying this **reasonable-basis test,** the courts give the benefit of the doubt to government. It need only show that a particular law has a sensible basis. For example, the courts have held that the goal of reducing fatalities from alcohol-related accidents involving young drivers is a valid reason for imposing a twenty-one-year minimum age requirement for the purchase of alcohol.

### The Strict-Scrutiny Test

Although the reasonable-basis test applies to most social classifications, it does not apply to racial or ethnic classifications, particularly when these categories serve to discriminate against minority-group members. Any law that attempts a racial or ethnic classification is subject to the **strict-scrutiny test,** under which such a law is unconstitutional in the absence of an overwhelming argument on the need for it. Such an argument is nearly impossible to construct; after all, what could justify a law that treated people less favorably merely because their skin is not white?

The strict-scrutiny test has virtually eliminated race and ethnicity as permissible classifications when the effect is to put members of a minority group at a disadvantage. The Supreme Court's position is that race and national origin are **suspect classifications**—that such classifications have invidious discrimination as their purpose and therefore any law containing such a classification is unconstitutional.

### The "Intermediate"-Scrutiny Test

The strict-scrutiny test emerged after the 1954 *Brown* ruling and became a basis for invalidating laws that discriminated against black people. As other groups, especially women, began to organize and press for their rights in the late 1960s and early 1970s, the Supreme Court gave early signs that it might expand the scope of suspect classifications to include gender. In the end, however, the Court

[6]*Brown* v. *Board of Education of Topeka*, 347 U.S. 483 (1954).

announced in *Craig* v. *Boren* (1976) that sex classifications were permissible if they served "important governmental objectives" and were "substantially" related to the achievement of those objectives.[7] The Court thus placed sex distinctions in an "intermediate" (or "almost suspect") category, to be scrutinized more closely than some other classifications (for example, income levels) but, unlike racial classifications, justified in some instances.

The intermediate-scrutiny test is so inexact that some scholars question its validity as a legal principle. Nevertheless, when evaluating claims of sex discrimination, the judiciary applies a stricter level of scrutiny than is required by the rational-basis test. Rather than allowing government broad leeway to treat men and women differently, the Supreme Court has recently invalidated most of the laws it has reviewed that contain sex classifications. In 1983, for example, the Court disallowed lower monthly pension payments to women merely because they tend to live longer than men. The Court concluded that women were entitled to monthly payments comparable to those of men.[8]

Yet the Supreme Court has upheld some sexually discriminatory laws. In *Rostker* v. *Goldberg* (1980), for example, the male-only registration for the military draft was upheld on grounds that the exclusion of women from combat duty serves a legitimate and important purpose.[9] It is safe to say that the Supreme Court would never have upheld a draft system that required registration of black men but not of white men. That is, the level of scrutiny that the judiciary applies to sexual classifications is less strict than the level of scrutiny applied to racial classifications.

## EQUAL ACCESS: THE CIVIL RIGHTS ACTS OF 1964 AND 1968

The Fourteenth Amendment applies only to action by government. As we saw in Chapter 2, the Supreme Court ruled after the Civil War that the language of the Fourteenth Amendment could not be construed as forbidding discrimination by private parties. Owners could legally bar black people from restaurants, hotels, and other accommodations, and employers could freely discriminate in their job practices.

### Accommodations and Jobs

Since the 1960s private firms have had much less freedom to discriminate for reasons of race, sex, ethnicity, or religion. The Civil Rights Act of 1964, which is based on the commerce power of Congress under the Constitution, entitles all persons to equal access to restaurants, bars, theaters, hotels, gasoline stations, and similar establishments serving the general public. The legislation also bars discrimination in the hiring, promotion, and wages of employees of medium-sized and large firms. The Civil Rights Act of 1964 does not regulate people's beliefs, friendships, or use of their own homes—no legislation could put an end to prejudice and discrimination in these realms—but the act does prohibit discriminatory conduct in public places, such as restaurants and motels, and in employment situations involving interstate commerce. A few forms of job

[7]*Craig* v. *Boren,* 429 U.S. 190 (1976).
[8]*Arizona* v. *Norris,* 459 U.S. 904 (1983).
[9]*Rostker* v. *Goldberg* 453 U.S. 57 (1980).

discrimination are still lawful under the Civil Rights Act of 1964. For example, an owner-operator of a small business can discriminate in hiring his or her co-workers, and a religious school can take the religion of a prospective teacher into account.

The Civil Rights Act of 1964 has nearly eliminated the most overt forms of discrimination in the area of public accommodations. Some restaurants and hotels may provide better service to white customers, but outright refusal to serve blacks or other minority-group members is rare. Such a refusal is a violation of the law and could easily be proven in many instances. It is harder to prove discrimination in job decisions; accordingly, the act has been less effective in rooting out employment discrimination—a subject that will be discussed in detail later in the chapter.

### Housing

The Civil Rights Act of 1968 prohibits discrimination in housing. A building owner cannot ordinarily refuse to sell or rent housing because of a person's race, religion, ethnicity, or sex. More than three-fourths of all housing transactions—sales and rentals—are covered by the antidiscrimination provisions of the 1968 Civil Rights Act. Exceptions are allowed for owners of small multifamily dwellings who reside on the premises and for owners of three or fewer houses who sell or rent without using an agent and who do not indicate a discriminatory preference when advertising the property.

Despite legal prohibitions on discrimination, housing in America remains highly segregated. One reason is the legacy of discriminatory practices that were common in the past. Until 1948, when the Supreme Court outlawed them, [10] "restrictive covenants" in the deeds to many properties barred their sale to blacks, Jews, Catholics, or members of other designated "undesirable" groups. Banks contributed to housing segregation by "redlining"—refusing to grant mortgage loans in certain neighborhoods. This practice drove down the selling prices of homes in these neighborhoods, which led to an influx of blacks and an exodus of whites. "Blockbusting" was a tactic used by some unscrupulous real estate firms: they frightened white homeowners into selling at low prices by moving a black family into a previously all-white neighborhood. Redlining and blockbusting are prohibited by the 1968 Civil Rights Act, but many of the segregated neighborhoods that they helped to create still exist.

Another reason for the persistence of segregated housing patterns is the fact that the economic condition of most black families is greatly inferior to that of many white families (see Figure 7-1). Low income tends to limit the areas in which black families can afford to live. Today less than a third of black Americans live in a neighborhood that is mostly white.

### EQUAL BALLOTS: THE VOTING RIGHTS ACT OF 1965

Free elections are perhaps the foremost symbol of American democracy, yet the right to vote has only recently become a reality for many Americans, particularly those of the black race.

---

**★ ANALYZE THE ISSUE**

**White Americans' Acceptance of Racial Integration**
Comparisons of opinion polls taken in the 1960s and in the 1980s indicate that white Americans have become more accepting of integration in schools, housing, and other aspects of American life. Yet such comparisons also show that Americans are less supportive of federal intervention to promote racial integration. Are these opinions contradictory? From the poll results, what conclusions would you draw about what most white Americans *really* think about racial progress?

---

[10]*Shelley* v. *Kraemer*, 334 U.S. 1 (1948).

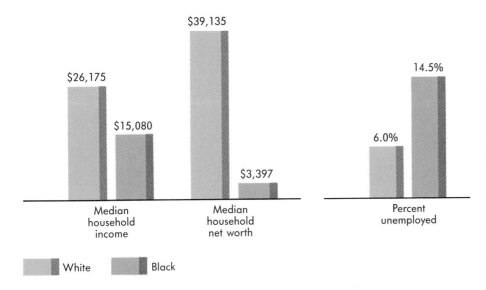

**FIGURE 7-1 Indicators of the Economic Status of Whites and Blacks in the United States** White Americans tend to be better off financially than black Americans. The prevalence of poverty among blacks is both a cause and an effect of persistent racial discrimination. *Source: U.S. Bureau of the Census,* Statistical Abstract of the United States, 1988 *(Washington, D.C.: U.S. Government Printing Office, 1988), 423, 441. Data for median household income are from 1986; data for median household net worth are from 1984; data for percent unemployed are from 1986.*

The Nineteenth Amendment, which in 1920 gave women the right to vote, effectively ended resistance to women's suffrage; paradoxically, resistance to black suffrage was intensified by the Fifteenth Amendment, which in 1870 gave black persons the right to vote. Southern whites invented a series of devices that were designed to keep blacks from voting and thus to prevent them from having an electoral weapon with which to fight discrimination.[11] Through poll taxes, whites-only primary elections, and rigged literacy tests as a qualification for registration to vote, blacks in many areas of the South were effectively disenfranchised. For example, almost no votes were cast by blacks during the years 1920–1946 in North Carolina.[12]

Barriers to black participation in elections began to crumble in the mid-1940s, when the Supreme Court declared that whites-only primary elections were unconstitutional.[13] Two decades later, through the Twenty-fourth Amendment, poll taxes were outlawed.

The major step toward equal voting rights for blacks was passage of the Voting Rights Act of 1965, which forbids discrimination in voting and registration. This legislation empowers federal agents to register voters and to oversee participation in elections. The threat of federal agents descending on county courthouses was enough to persuade officials in most southern communities to allow blacks to register and vote, but agents had to intervene actively in some locations. The Voting Rights Act, as interpreted by the courts, also eliminated literacy tests: local officials can no longer deny registration and voting for reasons of illiteracy. In fact, officials in communities where a language other than English is widely spoken are now required by law to provide ballot materials in that other language.

[11]See J. Morgan Kousser, *The Shaping of Southern Politics: Suffrage Restriction and the Establishment of the One-Party South, 1880–1910* (New Haven, Conn.: Yale University Press, 1974).
[12]V. O. Key, Jr., *Southern Politics* (New York: Knopf, 1949), 495.
[13]*Smith* v. *Allwright,* 321 U.S. 649 (1944).

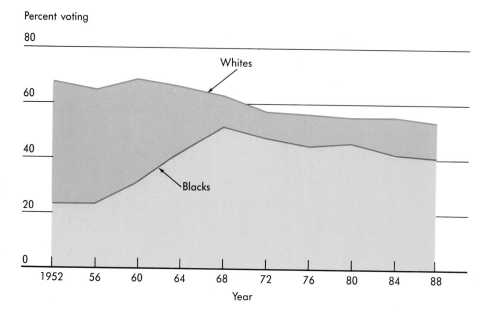

**FIGURE 7-2 Voter Turnout in Presidential Campaigns among Black and White Americans, 1952–1988**
Voter turnout among black Americans rose dramatically during the 1960s as legal obstacles to their voting were removed. *Source: National Election Studies, 1952–1988.*

From the late 1950s to 1968, black registration and voting rose sharply (see Figure 7-2); the increase was especially pronounced in the South. In Mississippi, black registration rose by 900 percent in just the five years from 1965 to 1970. The influx of black voters into the southern electorate does not mean that race is no longer an issue in the region's politics, but its impact has been diminished and candidates who might previously have run blatantly racist campaigns have been forced to moderate their appeals to bigotry.[14]

Blacks have had some success in winning election to public office. Although the percentage of black elected officials nationwide is still far below the proportion of blacks in the population, it has risen sharply since the early 1960s.[15] As of 1989, there were more than twenty black members of Congress and 200 black mayors—including the mayors of Los Angeles, Philadelphia, Atlanta, and Detroit.

Congress renewed the Voting Rights Act in 1970, 1975, and 1982. The 1982 extension is noteworthy because it renews the act for twenty years and requires states and localities to clear with federal officials any electoral change that has the effect, intended or not, of reducing the voting power of a minority group. This provision has the potential to enable minorities to increase their electoral influence. When congressional-district boundaries are redrawn after the 1990 census, a state may find it difficult to gain federal approval of district boundaries that appear designed to keep blacks or Hispanics from having a majority.

## The Struggle for Equality

The history of America shows that disadvantaged groups have rarely achieved an additional degree of legal equality without a struggle. Equality is seldom

[14]See Richard Scher and James Button, "Voting Rights Act: Implementation and Impact," in Charles S. Bullock III and Charles M. Lamb, eds., *Implementation of Civil Rights Policy* (Monterey, Calif.: Brooks/Cole, 1983), ch. 2; Jack Bass and Walter DeVries, *The Transformation of Southern Politics* (New York: Basic Books, 1976), 47.
[15]See Michael B. Preston, Lenneal J. Henderson, Jr., and Paul Puryear, eds., *The New Black Politics* (New York: Longman, 1982).

bestowed by the more powerful upon the less powerful. And, as the effort of black Americans to acquire voting rights illustrates, efforts to achieve legal equality may require decades of struggle before they succeed.

Resistance to granting disadvantaged groups a greater degree of equality is rooted in prejudice and privilege. Certain groups have always claimed superiority over other groups on the basis of superficial differences such as skin color. Even today, more than a fourth of white Americans claim that the black race is "less able" than their own race.[16] Legal discrimination serves the material interests as well as the status needs of a dominant group. The classic case was the white southern plantation owner, for whom slavery was an issue not of human freedom and dignity but of a lavish lifestyle built on the sweat and blood of the black race.

Equality is a subject that loses urgency when it is considered apart from its historical context. The compelling need for the 1964 Civil Rights Act and other such laws, and the great triumph their passage represents, cannot be understood without an awareness of the long struggle that led up to them. We can establish this context by looking briefly at the efforts of American blacks, women, Native Americans, Hispanics, and Asians to achieve fuller equality.

## BLACK AMERICANS

Of all America's problems, none has been so persistent as the white race's unwillingness to yield a full share of society's benefits to members of the black race. It took a civil war to bring slavery to an end, but the conflict did not stop institutionalized racism. When Reconstruction ended in 1877 with the withdrawal of federal troops from the South, southern whites regained power and gradually reestablished racial segregation by enacting laws that prohibited black citizens from using the same public facilities as whites.[17] The Supreme Court accepted this arrangement in *Plessy* v. *Ferguson* (1896), ruling that "separate" facilities for the two races did not violate the equal-protection clause of the Fourteenth Amendment as long as the facilities were "equal."[18]

The Court proceeded to ignore its own standard, allowing southern states and communities to maintain inferior facilities for their black residents. Public schools for blacks nearly always had fewer teachers and books and less classroom space than did those for whites. In some cases, no facilities at all were established for the black community; for example, in the whole of the Deep South, there were no state medical or dental colleges for blacks. Black leaders challenged these discriminatory state and local policies through legal action, but not until the late 1930s and 1940s did the Supreme Court begin to modify its *Plessy* position.[19] The Court began modestly by ruling that where no public facilities existed for blacks, they must be allowed to use those reserved for whites.[20]

[16]Paul M. Sniderman with Michael Gray Hagen, *Race and Inequality* (Chatham, N.J.: Chatham House, 1985), 30.
[17]The classic analysis of this system of legalized segregation is C. Vann Woodward, *The Strange Career of Jim Crow*, 3d rev. ed. (New York: Oxford University Press, 1974).
[18]*Plessy* v. *Ferguson*, 163 U.S. 537 (1896).
[19]See Loren Miller, *The Petitioners* (New York: Meridian Books, 1967).
[20]*Missouri ex rel. Gaines* v. *Canada*, 305 U.S. 57 (1938).

★ ANALYZE THE ISSUE

**Homosexual Rights**
In 1986 the Supreme Court ruled that the Constitution does not give consenting adults the right to have private homosexual relations. Do you approve or disapprove of this ruling? When asked this question in a Gallup poll, 51 percent of the respondents said that they approved and 41 percent said that they disapproved (8 percent had no opinion). With its ruling, the Supreme Court said, in effect, that homosexuals are not a legally protected category, unlike certain other groups, including racial minorities, women, and the elderly. What legal, political, or other considerations might justify society in treating homosexuals differently from these other groups?

In 1989 Tom Bradley was elected to a fifth term as mayor of Los Angeles. He is one of the increasing number of minority-group members who hold public office. (Rick Browne/Stock, Boston)

### The *Brown* Decision

Substantial relief for black Americans was finally achieved in 1954 with *Brown* v. *Board of Education of Topeka*, arguably the most significant ruling in Supreme Court history. The case began when Linda Carol Brown, a black child in Topeka, Kansas, was denied admission to an all-white elementary school that she passed every day on her way to her all-black school, which was twelve blocks farther away. The case was initiated on her behalf by the National Association for the Advancement of Colored People (NAACP) and was argued before the Supreme Court by Thurgood Marshall, who later became the Court's first black justice.[21] In its decision, the Court fully reversed its *Plessy* doctrine by declaring that racial segregation of public schools "generates [among black children] a feeling of inferiority as to their status in the community that may affect their hearts and minds in a way unlikely ever to be undone. . . . Separate educational facilities are inherently unequal."[22]

*Separate educational facilities are inherently unequal.*
*Brown* v. *Board of Education of Topeka* (1954)

A 1954 Gallup poll indicated that a sizable majority of southern whites opposed the *Brown* decision, and billboards were quickly erected along southern roadways that called for the impeachment of Chief Justice Earl Warren. In the so-called Southern Manifesto, southern congressmen urged their state governments to "resist forced integration by any lawful means." In 1957 rioting broke out when Governor Orval Faubus called out the Arkansas National Guard to block the entry of black children to the Little Rock public schools. To restore order and carry out the desegregation of the Little Rock schools, President Dwight D. Eisenhower used his power as the nation's commander in chief to place the Arkansas National Guard under federal control. For their part, northern whites were neither strongly for nor strongly against school desegregation. A Gallup poll taken shortly after the *Brown* decision indicated that a slim majority of whites outside the South agreed with it.

### The Black Civil Rights Movement

After *Brown*, the struggle of black Americans for their rights became a political movement. Perhaps no single event turned national public opinion so dramatically against segregation as a 1963 march led by the Reverend Martin Luther King, Jr., in Birmingham, Alabama. An advocate of nonviolent protest, King had been leading peaceful demonstrations and marches for nearly eight years before that fateful day in Birmingham.[23] As the nation watched in disbelief on television, police officers led by Birmingham's sheriff, Eugene "Bull" Connor, attacked King and his followers with dogs, cattle prods, and firehoses.

The modern civil rights movement peaked with the triumphant March on Washington for Jobs and Freedom of August 2, 1963. Organized by King and other civil rights leaders, it attracted 250,000 marchers, one of the largest gatherings in the history of the nation's capital. "I have a dream," King told the gathering, "that my four little children will one day live in a nation where they will not be judged by the color of their skin but by the content of their character."

A year later, after a months-long fight in Congress that was marked by every

---

[21]See Richard Kugler, *Simple Justice: The History of Brown* v. *Board of Education and Black America's Struggle for Equality* (New York: Knopf, 1976).
[22]*Brown* v. *Board of Education of Topeka*, 347 U.S. 483 (1954).
[23]See Francis M. Wilhoit, *The Politics of Massive Resistance* (New York: George Braziller, 1973).

parliamentary obstacle that racial conservatives could muster, the Civil Rights Act of 1964 was enacted. Even then, southern states resorted to legal maneuvering and other delaying tactics to blunt the legislation's impact. The state of Virginia, for example, established a commission to pay the legal expenses of white citizens who were brought to court for violations of the federal act. Nevertheless, momentum was on the side of racial equality. The murder of two civil rights workers during a voter registration drive in Selma, Alabama, helped to sustain the momentum.[24] President Lyndon Johnson called for new legislation that would end racial barriers to voting. Congress's answer was the 1965 Voting Rights Act.

## The Aftermath of the Civil Rights Movement

After 1965 the civil rights movement went awry. The rising expectations of black Americans were not met in terms of jobs and other benefits, and rioting occurred in Detroit, Newark, Los Angeles, and other cities between 1966 and 1968. In addition, the attention of Washington policymakers had been distracted from the civil rights movement by the escalating war in Vietnam, which was also siphoning away federal funds that might have been used for education, training, and jobs programs for poor blacks (see Chapter 27). When King was murdered in 1968, the most active phase of the modern civil rights movement came to an end.

The most significant progress in history toward the legal equality of all Americans occurred during the 1960s. Yet King's dream of a color-blind society has remained elusive.[25] By some indicators, the status of black Americans has actually deteriorated since the modern civil rights movement began. According

[24]See David J. Garrow, *Protest at Selma: Martin Luther King and the Voting Rights Act of 1965* (New Haven, Conn.: Yale University Press, 1978).
[25]See Sar Levitan, William Johnson, and Robert Taggert, *Still a Dream* (Cambridge, Mass.: Harvard University Press, 1975).

★ ANALYZE THE ISSUE

**Why Are Black Americans Losing Ground?**
Although the lives of black Americans have improved in absolute terms since the mid-sixties, their lives have not improved much in comparison with those of whites. The job and income gaps have grown; the education gap, which had been closing, is now widening; and the life expectancy of blacks has started to drop while that of whites continues to increase. Why are blacks going backward in these important respects? Is it mainly because no major new policy initiatives have been made in their behalf in recent years and some existing programs have been cut back? Or is it mainly because of the destructive impact of drug abuse, violence, and family disintegration within the black community? If both these reasons apply, are they connected? Can anything but racism, historical and contemporary, be at the bottom of the whole problem?

The Rev. Martin Luther King, Jr., became the nation's conscience as he led the black civil rights movement from the Montgomery, Alabama, bus boycott in 1955 until he was murdered in 1968. Here he delivers his famous "I have a dream" speech at the Lincoln Memorial in Washington, D.C., to a crowd of 250,000 people in 1963. (UPI/Bettmann Newsphotos)

to U.S. Department of Labor statistics, the unemployment rate for blacks in 1955 was 1.2 times higher than that for whites, but by 1985 it was 2.3 times higher. Black Americans' income also declined in proportion to white Americans' income during the same period. In the mid-1980s, reversing a previous trend, the proportion of young blacks going to college began to decline.

## WOMEN

*In view of this entire disfranchisement of one-half the people of this country, . . . and because women do feel themselves aggrieved, oppressed, and fraudulently deprived of their most sacred rights, we insist that they have immediate admission to all the rights and privileges which belong to them as citizens of the United States.*
Elizabeth Cady Stanton et al.,
*Declaration of Seneca Falls Convention*

The United States carried over from English common law a political disregard for women, forbidding them to vote, hold public office, and serve on juries. Upon marriage, a woman essentially lost her identity as an individual and usually surrendered her right to own and dispose of property without her husband's consent.

The first women's rights convention in America was held in 1848 in Seneca Falls, New York, after Lucretia Mott and Elizabeth Cady Stanton had been barred from the main floor of an antislavery convention.[26] Thereafter, however, the movement for women's rights became closely aligned with the abolitionist movement, and women had some expectation that black emancipation would also bring them their civil rights. However, the passage of the post–Civil War constitutional amendments proved to be a setback for the women's movement. The Thirteenth, Fourteenth, and Fifteenth amendments barred discrimination by color but not by sex.[27] Finally, in 1920, the Nineteenth Amendment was adopted, forbidding denial of the right to vote "by the United States or by any state on account of sex."

### The Equal Rights Amendment

*Equality of rights under the law shall not be denied or abridged by the United States or by any state on account of sex.*
Proposed Equal Rights Amendment

In 1923 women's leaders proposed another constitutional amendment, one that would guarantee equal rights for women. The amendment failed to gain congressional approval then and on several subsequent attempts. Finally, in 1973, the Equal Rights Amendment (ERA) received congressional approval and went to the state legislatures for ratification. The proposed amendment stated: "Equality of rights under the law shall not be denied or abridged by the United States or by any state on account of sex."

Congressional support for the ERA was an outgrowth of the 1960s civil rights movement and of the changing demands of women. Families were smaller, and more women were entering the labor force.[28] Proponents of the ERA argued that women cannot truly be equal and sexism—discrimination on the basis of sex—cannot be eliminated as long as legal distinctions between men and women are maintained. Ratification of the ERA was opposed by traditionalists, who argued that there is a need to retain special legal protections for women, mainly in the areas of the draft, working conditions, and family life.[29] A 1982 Gallup survey indicated that 55 percent of Americans (including 53 percent of

[26]For a history of the women's rights movement, see Eleanor Flexner, *Century of Struggle*, rev. ed. (Cambridge, Mass.: Harvard University Press, 1975).
[27]See Ellen Carol DuBois, *Feminism and Suffrage: The Emergence of an Independent Women's Movement in America, 1848–1869* (Ithaca, N.Y.: Cornell University Press, 1978); Susan Cary Nicholas, *Rights and Wrongs* (Old Westbury, N.Y.: Feminist Press, 1979).
[28]See Suzanne M. Bianchi and Daphne Spain, *American Women in Transition* (New York: Russell Sage Foundation, 1986).
[29]See Janet K. Boles, *The Politics of the Equal Rights Amendment* (New York: Longman, 1977).

The Equal Rights Amendment fell three states short of ratification in 1982. (Paul Conklin)

men) favored the ERA, 36 percent were opposed, and 9 percent had no opinion. Nevertheless, the ERA failed to gain the support of a majority of state legislators in the thirty-eight states needed for ratification. The proposed amendment was three states short when the deadline for ratification came and went in 1982.

## Women's Legal Gains

Although the ERA did not become part of the Constitution, it helped bring women's rights to the forefront at a time when developments in Congress and the courts were contributing significantly to the legal equality of the sexes.[30] Among the congressional initiatives that have helped women are the Equal Pay Act of 1963, which prohibits sex discrimination in salary and wages by some categories of employers; the Civil Rights Act of 1964, which prohibits sex discrimination in programs that receive federal funding; Title IX of the Education Amendment of 1972, which prohibits sex discrimination in education; and the Equal Credit Act of 1974, as amended in 1976, which prohibits sex discrimination in the granting of financial credit.

The Fourteenth Amendment's equal-protection clause has also become an instrument of women's equality. The *Brown* decision encouraged women's rights activists to believe that the equal-protection clause could be the basis for sex-discrimination rulings. In *Reed* v. *Reed* (1971) the Supreme Court invoked equal protection for the first time in a case involving women's rights, declaring unconstitutional an Idaho statute that gave preference to men in appointments as administrators of the estates of dead children.[31]

The 1984 *Grove City* case, which involved alleged sex discrimination, was a setback: the Supreme Court concluded that the antidiscrimination requirements

### ★ HOW THE UNITED STATES COMPARES

**Women's Equality**
Although conflict between groups is universal, the nature of the conflict is often particularized. Racial conflict in the United States cannot readily be compared with, say, religious conflict in Northern Ireland. The one form of inequality common to all nations is that of gender: women everywhere are not equal to men in law or in fact. But there are large differences between countries. A 1988 study by the Population Crisis Committee placed the United States third overall in women's equality, behind only Sweden and Finland (see Chapter 1).

---

[30]See Joyce Gelb and Marian Lief Palley, *Women and Public Policies* (Princeton, N.J.: Princeton University Press, 1982).
[31]*Reed* v. *Reed*, 404 U.S. 71 (1971).

### ★ ANALYZE THE ISSUE

**Comparable Worth**
Should women receive the same pay as men if their jobs, though different from those held by men, require similar levels of education and experience? Establishment of the doctrine of comparable worth is a major goal of some women's groups. Can it be accomplished on a large scale without disrupting the nation's economy? Can women achieve full equality without achieving income parity with men? Which of these considerations do you think is more important? Which is more likely to win out?

of federal grants to educational institutions applied only to activities funded directly, in whole or in part, with federal money.[32] However, in 1988 Congress altered this policy through legislation that prohibits discriminatory practices in any activity of organizations that receive federal funding.

## Comparable Worth

In the past two decades, increasing numbers of women have found employment in traditionally male-dominated fields. For example, about a third of law school graduates now are women. Women have also attained more and higher political positions than ever before. In 1981 President Ronald Reagan appointed the first woman to serve on the Supreme Court, Sandra Day O'Connor. The Democratic party in 1984 chose Geraldine Ferraro as its vice-presidential nominee, the first time a woman has run on the national ticket of a major political party. In Nebraska in 1986, both the Republican and Democratic parties nominated women to run for governor—another political first.

Despite such signs of progress, women are still a long way from political, social, and economic equality with men. Women occupy less than 5 percent of the nation's gubernatorial and congressional offices. Women also hold a disproportionately small number of the better-paying jobs. On average, women earn only about two-thirds as much as men. This situation has led to demands by women for equal pay for work that is of similar difficulty and responsibility and that requires similar levels of education and training—a concept called **comparable worth.** A comparable-worth policy would eliminate salary inequities resulting from the fact that some occupations are female-dominated while others are male-dominated. This view was the basis for a legal suit against the state of Washington brought by a group of female state employees, who won in

[32]*Grove City College* v. *Bell,* 465 U.S. 555 (1984).

Employees in certain job categories dominated by women—day-care workers, secretaries, and so on—are paid less than those in male-dominated jobs with similar educational requirements and levels of responsibility. The concept of comparable worth is proposed as a remedy for such inequities. (Richard Kalvar/Magnum)

a lower court but were reversed by a U.S. court of appeals. Advocates of comparable worth did persuade the Minnesota and Iowa legislatures to enact new salary structures that will eventually provide employees of those states with equal pay, regardless of sex, for jobs requiring comparable training and skills. On the national level, though, the Reagan and Bush administrations have opposed the concept of comparable worth, contending that market forces alone should dictate salaries in the private sector.

## NATIVE AMERICANS

When white settlers began arriving in America in large numbers during the seventeenth century, 8 to 10 million Native Americans were living in the territory that would become the United States. By 1900, the Native American population had plummeted to less than 1 million. Diseases brought by white settlers had taken a toll on the various Indian tribes, but so had wars and massacres. "The only good Indian is a dead Indian" is not simply a hackneyed expression from cowboy movies. It was part of the strategy of westward expansion, as settlers and U.S. troops alike mercilessly drove the eastern Indians from their ancestral lands to the Great Plains, then took those lands too.

Today Native Americans number more than 1 million in population, of whom about half live on or close to reservations set aside for them. Those who retain ties to a reservation are among America's most impoverished, illiterate, and jobless citizens. Native Americans are less than half as likely to attend college as other Americans, their life expectancy is more than ten years less than the national average, and their infant mortality rate is more than three times higher than that of white Americans.

The civil rights movement of the 1960s at first did not include Native Americans. Then, in the early 1970s, militant Native Americans occupied the

As a result of federal government policy, most Native Americans live on reservations, and many aspects of their traditional way of life have been destroyed. (Rene Burri/Magnum)

Bureau of Indian Affairs in Washington, D.C., and later seized control of the village of Wounded Knee on a Sioux reservation in southwestern South Dakota, exchanging gunfire with U.S. marshals. These episodes brought attention to the grievances of Native Americans and perhaps contributed to passage in 1974 of legislation that granted Native Americans on reservations a greater measure of control over federal programs affecting them. However, Native Americans had already benefited from the legislative climate created by the civil rights movement of the 1960s. In 1968 Congress had enacted the Indian Bill of Rights, which gives Native Americans on reservations constitutional guarantees that are similar to those held by other Americans.

In recent years Native Americans have filed suit to reclaim lost ancestral lands and have won a few settlements. But they stand no realistic chance of getting back even those lands that had been granted them by federal treaty but were later sold off or simply taken forcibly by federal authorities. Native Americans were not even official citizens of the United States until an act of Congress in 1924. This status came too late to be of much help; their traditional way of life had already been seriously eroded.

## HISPANIC AMERICANS

The son of Mexican immigrants, Cesar Chavez organized the United Farm Workers of America in 1962 to fight for better pay and working conditions for migrant farm laborers and to protest discrimination against Hispanics. Ironically, the effectiveness of his efforts made unionization seem less urgent: the UFWA's membership dropped from 100,000 at its peak in the early 1970s to 20,000 in 1987. (John Chase/Stock, Boston)

The fastest-growing minority in the United States is Hispanic Americans, people with Spanish-speaking backgrounds. The 1980 census counted 15 million Hispanics living in the United States, and it is projected that they will replace black Americans as the nation's largest racial or ethnic minority group by the year 2000. They have emigrated to the United States primarily from Mexico and the Caribbean islands, mainly Cuba and Puerto Rico. About half of all Hispanics in the United States were born in Mexico or trace their ancestry there. Hispanics are concentrated in their states of entry; thus Florida, New York, and New Jersey have large numbers of Caribbean Hispanics, while California, Texas, Arizona, and New Mexico have many immigrants from Mexico. More than half the population of Los Angeles is of Hispanic—mostly Mexican—ancestry.

### Migrant Workers

The most publicized civil rights actions involving Hispanics were the farm workers' strikes of the late 1960s and the 1970s, which aimed at gaining basic labor rights for migrant farm workers. Migrants were working long hours for low pay, traveling from place to place as crops became ready for harvesting. They usually lived near the fields where they worked, in shacks without electricity or plumbing. They were unwelcome in many local schools, and sometimes in local hospitals as well, because few of them had health insurance or the money to pay for their medical care.

Farm owners at first refused to bargain with migrant workers over pay, hours, conditions, or benefits. Only after several years of strikes and a surprisingly effective nationwide boycott of California grapes and lettuce did California in the 1970s pass a law giving migrant workers the right to bargain collectively through their organization, the United Farm Workers. The strikes were led in California by Cesar Chavez, who himself grew up in a Mexican American migrant family.[33] Chavez's tactics in California were copied in other states, particularly Texas, but the results were less successful.

---

[33]See Peter Matthiessen, *Sal si Puedes: Cesar Chavez and the New American Revolution* (New York: Random House, 1969).

## Illegal Aliens

Hispanics have benefited from laws and court rulings aimed primarily at protecting other groups. Thus, although the Civil Rights Act of 1965 was largely a response to the condition of black people, its provisions apply broadly. Just as it is unlawful to deny a hotel room to an individual because he or she is black, so it is unlawful to do so because he or she is a Native American, Asian, or Hispanic.

However, Hispanics face some distinctive problems. The fact that many do not speak English is the main reason for a 1968 amendment to the 1964 Civil Rights Act that funds public school programs offering English instruction in the language of children for whom English is a second language. In addition, many Hispanics are illegal aliens; these individuals do not have the full rights of citizens. In *De Canas* v. *Bica* (1976), for example, the Supreme Court upheld a state law barring illegal aliens from employment.[34]

In 1986 Congress passed landmark immigration and naturalization legislation, the Simpson-Mizzoli Act, which affected Hispanics primarily. The legislation provided that illegal aliens who could prove that they had lived continuously in the United States for five years were eligible to become citizens. The act also mandated fines for employers who knowingly hired aliens without work permits; the resulting lack of job openings would eliminate the main reason for aliens to enter the country illegally. The legislation was intended partly to relieve employment and social-service pressures on states bordering Mexico, which is the country of origin of most illegal aliens. Hispanic leaders had mixed reactions to the legislation, welcoming the provision granting citizenship to aliens of long-standing residence but worrying that the deportation of nonqualified aliens would result in the breakup of families. The number of illegal aliens who applied to become citizens fell short of government projections. Apparently some aliens were suspicious of the program, believing that they would be arrested and deported when they applied for citizenship at the offices of the Immigration and Naturalization Service.

## Growing Political Power

Hispanics are an important political force in some states and communities, and their influence is likely to increase substantially in the next decade or two.[35] In 1974 Arizona and New Mexico elected governors of Spanish-speaking background. New Mexico elected its second Hispanic governor in 1982. The Carter administration included a large number of Hispanics in high positions. President Reagan appointed an even greater number to positions of authority, including several members of the White House staff. The growing political and cultural influence of Hispanics, however, has made them a target for criticism in some cities. For example, some non-Hispanic residents of Miami have become increasingly vocal in their opposition to bilingual education, claiming that Spanish-speaking residents (most of whom are of Cuban background) are making little effort to learn English or adjust to their new culture and are thus turning Miami into a Spanish-speaking city.

---

[34]*De Canas* v. *Bica*, 424 U.S. 351 (1976).
[35]See F. Chris Garcia and Rudolph O. de la Garza, *The Chicano Political Experience* (Duxbury, Mass.: Duxbury Press, 1977).

Hispanic Americans are exerting considerable political, social, and cultural influence in many communities, as here in Brownsville, Texas. (Paul Conklin/Texastock)

## ASIAN AMERICANS

Chinese and Japanese laborers were the first Asians to come to the United States in large numbers. They were brought into western states during the latter nineteenth century to work in mines and to build railroads. When the need for this labor declined, Congress in 1892 ordered a temporary halt to Chinese immigration. Over the next three decades informal agreements kept all but a few Asians out of the country. In 1921 the United States ended its traditional policy of unlimited immigration and established immigration quotas based on country of origin. Western European countries were given large quotas and Asian countries tiny ones. The Japanese were entitled to about 150 arrivals a year until 1930, when Congress excluded the Japanese entirely. Japan had protested a California law that prohibited persons of Japanese descent from buying property in the state. Rather than finessing what was called "the California problem," Congress decided to be blunt with Japan: its people were not wanted in the United States.[36]

This discrimination against Asians did not change substantially until 1965, when Congress enacted legislation that adjusted the immigration quotas to favor those who had previously been disadvantaged. This change in the law was a product of the 1960s civil rights movement, which, as we have indicated, sensitized national leaders to all forms of discrimination. About half a million

[36]James Truslow Adams, *The March of Democracy*, vol. 4 (New York: Scribner's, 1933), 284–285.

# EXTENDING THE STRUGGLE FOR EQUAL RIGHTS: THE DISABLED AND THE ELDERLY

Women and racial and ethnic minorities are not the only groups whose members suffer from discrimination. Almost any group that is vulnerable or has a minority characteristic has experienced discrimination in one form or another. Two such groups that have been receiving increased attention from government are the disabled and the elderly.

For years the disabled were thought of as a tiny proportion of the American population and therefore more of a special-interest group than a civil rights classification. But, according to the U.S. Census Bureau, more than 37 million Americans are physically impaired and between 13 million and 14 million have a disability so severe that they are unable to perform some critical function, such as hearing, seeing, walking, or lifting. They constitute about 5 percent of the population—a sizable minority.

A major goal for the disabled is easier access to the mainstream of society. The 1973 Rehabilitation Act has moved them toward this goal. So has the Education for All Handicapped Children Act of 1975, which mandates that all children, however severe their disability, receive a free, appropriate education. Before the legislation, 1 million handicapped children were receiving no education and another 3 million were receiving an inappropriate one (as in the case of a blind child who is not taught Braille or is not provided with instructional materials in Braille). In 1987 Congress enacted the Employment Opportunities for Disabled Americans Act, which allows disabled individuals to earn a moderate income without losing their Medicaid health coverage.

The government has also been moving to protect elderly Americans from discrimination. The Age Discrimination Act of 1975 and the Age Discrimination in Employment Act of 1967 outlaw discrimination against older workers in hiring for jobs in which age is not clearly a crucial factor in job performance. More recently, mandatory retirement ages for most jobs have been eliminated by law. Retirement at age seventy can no longer be arbitrarily decided by management; it must be justified by the nature of the particular job or the performance of the particular employee.

By the year 2020 there will be an estimated one retired American for every two working Americans. By virtue of their numbers, the elderly will become an even more powerful political constituency. As a consequence, political issues of concern to the elderly—including special housing and continued employment at a reduced level—are certain to be taken seriously by elected officials.

SOURCE: Mary Johnson, "Overcoming the Social Barriers," *The Nation*, April 9, 1988, 489–494.

---

people now emigrate to the United States each year, and a majority come from Asian and Latin American countries. By the year 2000, Asian Americans will number about 12 million, or between 4 and 5 percent of the total U.S. population. Most Asian Americans live on the West Coast, particularly in California.

The rights of Asian Americans have been expanded primarily by court rulings and legislation, such as the Civil Rights Act of 1964, that were responses to the problems of other minorities. In a few instances, however, the rights of minorities have been defined by actions of Asian Americans. For example, in *Lau* v. *Nichols* (1974), a case involving Chinese Americans, the Supreme Court ruled that public schools with a large proportion of children for whom English is a second language must offer English instruction in the children's first language. [37]

Asian Americans are an upwardly mobile group. The values of most Asian families include a commitment to hard work, which, in the American context, has included an emphasis on academic achievement. For example, Asians make

[37]*Lau* v. *Nichols*, 414 U.S. 563 (1974).

The emphasis that Asian Americans place on education has much to do with their upward mobility as a group. (Michael Weisbrot/Stock, Boston)

up a disproportionate share of the students at California's leading public universities, which base admission primarily on high school grades and standardized test scores. However, Asian Americans are still underrepresented in certain areas of the workplace. In 1985 they accounted for 4.3 percent of professionals and technicians, nearly the same as their percentage of the population. Yet they hold less than 1.5 percent of managerial jobs; past and present discrimination has kept them from obtaining their fair share of top business positions.[38]

## Equality of Result

The struggles of America's disadvantaged groups have resulted in significant progress toward equal rights, particularly during the past few decades. Through acts of Congress and rulings of the Supreme Court, most forms of government-sponsored discrimination—from racially segregated public schools to gender-based pension plans—have been banned.

However, civil rights problems involve deeply rooted conditions, habits, and prejudices and affect whole categories of people, not just isolated individuals here and there. For these reasons, a new civil rights policy rarely produces a sudden and dramatic change in society. Despite their greater equality in law, America's traditionally disadvantaged groups are still substantially unequal in their daily lives. Consider the income disparity between white males and other groups in America. As we noted earlier, women's salaries average two-thirds those of men. The average Asian American family's income is three-fourths that of the average white family. For Hispanic American families, the average is two-thirds that of white families. The average falls to three-fifths for black families, and still lower for Native Americans.

[38]"The 'Eastern Capital' of Asia," *Newsweek*, February 22, 1988, 58.

Such figures reflect *de facto* **discrimination,** which is discrimination that is a consequence of social, economic, and cultural biases and conditions. This type of discrimination is different from *de jure* **discrimination,** which is discrimination based on law, as in the case of segregation in southern public schools during the pre-*Brown* period. No law says that other Americans cannot have incomes as high as those of white males, but higher average incomes for white males are a fact of American life. *De facto* discrimination is difficult to root out because it is not in the law but in the very structure of society. **Equality of result** is the aim of policies intended to reduce or eliminate *de facto* discriminatory effects so that members of traditionally disadvantaged groups may obtain the same benefits as members of traditionally advantaged groups. Such policies are inherently more controversial than those that provide equality under the law. Many Americans believe that government's responsibility extends no further than the removal of legal barriers to equality. This attitude conforms with the country's individualistic tradition and is a major reason for the lack of any large-scale governmental effort to reduce the economic and social gaps between Americans of varying racial and ethnic backgrounds. However, a few policies—notably affirmative action and busing—have been designed to achieve equality of result.

## ECONOMIC INTEGRATION: AFFIRMATIVE ACTION

The difficulty of converting newly acquired legal rights into everyday realities is evident in the fact that the 1964 Civil Rights Act, which prohibited discrimination in employment, did not suddenly make it easier for women and minorities to obtain jobs for which they were qualified. Many employers maintained a deliberate though unwritten preference for white male employees, while other employers adhered to established employment procedures that continued to keep women and minorities at a disadvantage; membership in many union locals, for example, was handed down from father to son. Moreover, the Civil Rights Act did not compel employers to show that their hiring practices were not discriminatory. Instead, the burden of proof was on the woman or minority-group member who had been denied a particular job. It was costly and often difficult to prove in court that one's sex or race was the reason that one had not been hired. In addition, a victory in court affected only the individual in question; such case-by-case settlements were no remedy for a situation in which established hiring practices kept millions of women and minority-group members from competing equally for job opportunities.

A broader remedy was obviously required, and the result was the emergence during the late 1960s of affirmative action programs. As we indicated in Chapter 6, **affirmative action** refers to programs that are designed to ensure that women, minorities, and other traditionally disadvantaged groups have full and equal opportunities in employment, education, and similar situations.

### Opposing Views on Affirmative Action

Civil rights groups have argued that affirmative action must be broadly and aggressively applied if the effects of past discrimination and lingering prejudice are to be overcome. A Gallup poll found in 1982 that respondents favored a male boss to a female boss by nearly 4 to 1 (see Table 7-1). In such a climate of opinion, strong government action is said to be imperative. If a union, business,

**TABLE 7-1   Attitudes toward Women Bosses**

IF YOU WERE TAKING A NEW JOB AND HAD YOUR CHOICE OF A NEW BOSS, WOULD YOU PREFER TO WORK FOR A MAN OR A WOMAN?

| *Characteristics of Respondents* | *Prefer Male Boss* | *Prefer Female Boss* | *No Difference* | *No Opinion* |
|---|---|---|---|---|
| All respondents | 46% | 12% | 38% | 4% |
| Sex | | | | |
| Male | 40 | 9 | 46 | 5 |
| Female | 52 | 15 | 30 | 3 |
| Education | | | | |
| College | 41 | 13 | 42 | 4 |
| High school graduate | 47 | 13 | 37 | 3 |
| Less than high school | 51 | 7 | 35 | 7 |
| Age group | | | | |
| 18–24 | 33 | 21 | 40 | 6 |
| 25–29 | 41 | 16 | 38 | 5 |
| 30–45 | 45 | 12 | 39 | 4 |
| 50 plus | 53 | 7 | 37 | 3 |

SOURCE: *Gallup Poll Reports,* 1982, 196–197.

university, fire department, or other organization has no or relatively few female or minority employees or members, then it should be ordered by government to give them preferential treatment in hiring or admission. In such cases, some innocent white males may lose out, but this cost is an unavoidable necessity if discrimination against women and minorities is to be curtailed.[39]

This perspective on affirmative action was held by the administration of President Jimmy Carter. In Carter's view, affirmative action was a tool not only for ensuring that women and minorities received fair treatment in specific cases but for eventually enabling them, as groups, to attain a fair share of society's benefits. Thus the Carter administration initiated exclusive contracts on public projects for minority-owned businesses, imposed heavy "back pay" penalties on businesses with inadequate affirmative action programs, relaxed the testing standards for minority-group members applying for government employment, and developed a long-term plan to hire members of five "designated" minorities—the same five we discussed earlier: blacks, women, Native Americans, Hispanics, and Asians—for government jobs in proportion to their numbers in the U.S. population.

Ronald Reagan brought a different view of affirmative action to the presidency. He fired the chairman and two other members of the Civil Rights Commission who believed that aggressive affirmative action programs were necessary to protect the rights of women and minorities. He replaced them with appointees who thought that remedial action should be limited to women and minority-group members who had *individually* experienced direct discrimination. Moreover, the Reagan administration eased the affirmative action regulations for employers doing business with government, and the Justice Department supported suits brought by white workers who claimed to have been victimized by affirmative action quotas or other preference systems.

[39]See Robert M. O'Neill, *Discrimination against Discrimination* (Bloomington: Indiana University Press, 1975).

The philosophy underlying these policies was that past discrimination is never a justification for current discrimination.[40] If women and minorities are given preference for jobs and other opportunities because of past injustices to others of their background, then they are being advanced by discriminatory practices that are unjust to the white males with whom they are competing.

## The Supreme Court's Position on Affirmative Action

The Reagan administration began in 1981 to press its view that racial preferences were rarely, if ever, justified. It won a legal victory in 1984 when the Supreme Court ruled that the city of Memphis could lay off members of its fire department on a "last hired, first fired" basis and did not have to retain black firefighters who had low seniority. Their jobs, the Court said, could not be saved at the expense of white firefighters who had more seniority.[41] Then, in a 1986 case, the Court invalidated a layoff plan of Jackson, Michigan, which kept some black schoolteachers on the job while white teachers with more seniority were released.[42]

The Reagan administration interpreted the Court's ruling in these cases as invalidating *any* affirmative action program that favored minority-group members who had not been individually victimized by discrimination. However, the Memphis and Jackson cases validated this "victim-specific" concept only in regard to job layoffs, leaving open the question of whether it also applied to job hirings and promotions. In two rulings announced at the close of its 1986 session, the Supreme Court rejected the Reagan administration's contention that civil rights remedies should benefit only specific, identifiable victims of discrimination.

In one case, as we saw in Chapter 6, the Court upheld by a 5–4 vote a lower-court order that required New York City's Sheet Metal Workers Local No. 28 to develop a program that would give 29 percent of its memberships to blacks and Hispanics. The formerly all-white union local had disobeyed two earlier lower-court orders to open its ranks to minorities. In such cases of "longstanding or egregious discrimination," Justice Brennan wrote, "requiring recalcitrant employees in unions to hire and to admit qualified minorities in the work place may be the only effective way to ensure the full enjoyment of the rights protected by Title VII [of the Civil Rights Act of 1964]."[43] In the second case, the Court upheld by a 6–3 vote a consent decree* in which the city of Cleveland agreed to reserve half of all promotions for four years for minority firefighters who were not necessarily themselves the victims of past discrimination. The Court's majority concluded that racial quotas were an appropriate remedy for the Cleveland fire department's history of discriminating against minorities in promotions.[44]

---

*In this context "consent decree" refers to an affirmative action plan developed with the consent of the employer and then approved by a court.

[40]See Allan P. Sindler, *Equal Opportunity* (Washington, D.C.: American Enterprise Institute, 1983); Alan Goldman, *Justice and Reverse Discrimination* (Princeton, N.J.: Princeton University Press, 1978); Nathan Glazer, *Affirmative Discrimination* (New York: Basic Books, 1976).

[41]*Firefighters* v. *Stotts*, 459 U.S. 969 (1984).

[42]*Wygant* v. *Jackson*, 476 U.S. 238 (1986).

[43]*Local No. 28, Sheet Metal Workers* v. *Equal Employment Opportunity Commission*, 478 U.S. 421 (1986).

[44]*Local No. 93, International Association of Firefighters* v. *Cleveland*, 478 U.S. 501 (1986).

# DISCRIMINATION BY PRIVATE ORGANIZATIONS

After decades of progress toward equal rights for all, it is surprising to realize that private organizations are often within their constitutional rights in discriminating against women and members of racial or religious minorities. The Fifth and Fourteenth amendments prohibit only discrimination by government bodies. However, one tactic the government can use to discourage private organizations from discriminating is to deny them tax benefits. Thus in 1971 the Internal Revenue Service revoked the tax-exempt status of private schools that practice racial discrimination. In 1983 the Supreme Court upheld the IRS's decision to withdraw the tax-exempt status of Bob Jones University, a private religious college that prohibits interracial dating and marriage among its students.

Laws and statutes also give the courts some opportunities to limit the discriminatory practices of private organizations. Many country clubs and other private social organizations, such as the Jaycees, the Rotary, and the Elks, have used discriminatory tactics to remain nearly all-white, all-gentile, and all-male, particularly at the leadership level.

Many important business connections are made as a result of membership in such organizations, so excluded groups are put at a competitive disadvantage. Accordingly, a number of successful lawsuits have been filed on the grounds of restraint of trade. And in one noteworthy case the Minneapolis and St. Paul chapters of the Jaycees voted to admit women, whereupon the national Jaycees revoked their charters. In *Roberts* v. *United States Jaycees* (1984), the Supreme Court ruled that the Jaycees must admit women in states, including Minnesota, that have statutes barring sex discrimination in any "place of public accommodation"—such as the restaurants and halls in which the Jaycees hold their meetings.

These cases helped to clarify the legal status of affirmative action. Preferential treatment of women and minorities can be justified in cases where discrimination has been severe, whether or not the minority-group members or women who benefit from this treatment were personally victimized by the past pattern of discrimination. However, preferential treatment cannot be applied in a way that infringes on the rights of white employees to keep their jobs.

In a series of 1989 cases, the Supreme Court limited substantially the job protections available to minorities. The Court concluded that affirmative action programs may be approved only after close scrutiny by a court and that such programs are not free of challenge at a later time by white workers. Then in a decision of potentially far-reaching consequence, the Court held that, in some circumstances, minority employees must prove that racial imbalances in employment have no valid business purpose. Previously, the Court had held that the burden of proof in these situations rested on the employer. Perhaps the most significant of the 1989 rulings was one that excluded racial harassment on the job from statutory protection. A credit union employee in North Carolina had claimed that she was required to do menial tasks because of her race. The Court concluded that the federal law in question protected her at the point of hiring but not on the job.[45]

## SOCIAL INTEGRATION: BUSING

In 1944 the Swedish sociologist Gunnar Myrdal gained fame for his book *An American Dilemma*, whose title referred to deep-rooted racism in a country that

[45]*Time*, June 26, 1989, p. 63.

proclaimed itself to be the epitome of an equal society.[46] Since then, legal obstacles to the mixing of the races have been nearly eliminated. Public opinion has also changed significantly in the past half century. In the early 1940s a majority of white Americans believed that black children should not be allowed to go to school with white children; today only 5 percent of white Americans express this belief. There are also visible signs of black progress. In the past two decades, many black Americans have attended college, received undergraduate and graduate degrees, obtained jobs as professionals and managers, and moved into suburban neighborhoods.

However, the majority of black people still live largely apart from white people. The reality of modern American life is racial segregation. More than two-thirds of blacks live in neighborhoods that are all or mostly black; more than two-thirds of black children go to schools that are mostly black; two-fifths attend schools that are more than 90 percent black.

Racial separation in a country dominated by white people means a continuance of black subordination. Recognition of this fact is the justification for one of the few public policies that forces whites into close, regular contact with blacks: the busing of schoolchildren to achieve racial balance in the schools.

### The *Swann* Decision

In 1971 the Supreme Court took the controversial step of requiring the busing of children in some circumstances. Affirming a lower-court decision, the Supreme Court held in *Swann v. Charlotte–Mecklenburg County Board of Education* that the busing of children from one neighborhood to another was a permissible way for courts to compel the integration of public schools where past years of official segregation had created residential patterns that had the effect of keeping the races in separate schools. Busing, the Court said, was allowed as a tool "in the interim period when remedial adjustments are being made to eliminate the dual school system."[47] After *Swann*, lower-court judges involved themselves deeply in busing decisions, even specifying in some cases the exact proportions of black and white children who had to attend each of a district's schools.

### Reactions to Forced Busing

Few issues of recent times have provoked so much controversy as forced busing.[48] Angry demonstrations lasting weeks took place in Charlotte. When busing was ordered in Detroit and Boston, the protests turned violent. Unlike *Brown*, which affected mainly the South, *Swann* also applied to northern communities in which blacks and whites lived apart as a result of economic and cultural differences as well as discriminatory real estate practices. A 1972 University of Michigan survey indicated that more than 80 percent of white

---

[46]Gunnar Myrdal, *An American Dilemma: The Negro Problem and Modern Democracy* (New York: Harper, 1944).

[47]*Swann v. Charlotte–Mecklenburg County Board of Education,* 402 U.S. 1 (1971).

[48]See Jennifer L. Hochschild, *The New American Dilemma* (New Haven, Conn.: Yale University Press, 1985); Michael W. Giles and Thomas G. Walker, "Judicial Policy-Making and Southern School Segregation," *Journal of Politics* 37 (1975): 936.

Americans disapproved of forced busing, and the proportion has not changed significantly since then.

Public officials have been only slightly less opposed to busing. Congress on several occasions has nearly voted to forbid the use of federal funds to assist busing in any way. Richard Nixon was president when the *Swann* decision was announced, and he ordered the Justice Department to act slowly on busing cases; he hoped that opposition to busing would attract racially conservative whites to the Republican coalition. Under President Reagan a decade later, the Justice Department effectively ceased to pursue pro-busing lawsuits. In fact, the Reagan administration endorsed an antibusing initiative passed by voters in the state of Washington, but the Supreme Court ruled the law unconstitutional because it was based on racial categories and as such did not pass the strict-scrutiny test.[49]

### The Impact of Busing

Despite the controversy surrounding it, busing remains a part of national policy. Thousands of children throughout the nation are bused out of their neighborhoods each schoolday for purposes of school integration. Busing has provided equality of result for some black children but has not been nearly so effective as it would have been if the general public and its leaders had supported the concept more wholeheartedly. In part because of the adverse reactions to busing, the Supreme Court has limited across-district busing to situations where it can be shown that school district boundaries were purposely drawn so as to segregate the races.[50] Since school districts in most states coincide with community boundaries, the effect of this position has been to insulate most suburban schools from integration plans. As a result, the burden of busing has fallen most heavily on poorer whites and blacks in the inner cities.

## PERSISTENT DISCRIMINATION: SUPERFICIAL DIFFERENCES, DEEP DIVISIONS

Busing and affirmative action programs are substantial efforts toward achieving a more just society, but they are not likely to produce truly dramatic results in a relatively short time. The American government is making no full-scale effort to wipe out *de facto* discrimination. This is not surprising, given the country's individualistic tradition. Yet the effect is to give the country's professed commitment to equality for all a decidedly narrow focus—on equality under the law but not on the opportunity to share fully in everything that American society has to offer.

[49]*Washington v. Seattle School District*, 458 U.S. 457 (1982).
[50]*Milliken v. Bradley*, 418 U.S. 717 (1974).

Discrimination has been called America's curse. In a country that is otherwise bountiful and generous, superficial differences—sex, skin color, country of origin—are sources of deep divisions and stark contrasts. To cite but one example: a child born in the United States has more than twice the chance of dying before reaching his or her first birthday if that child is black rather than white. The difference in the infant mortality rates of whites and blacks reflects differences in their nutrition, medical care, and education—in other words, differences in their access to the most basic commodities of a modern society. No greater challenge faces America as it approaches the twenty-first century than the rooting out of discrimination based on sex, race, and ethnicity.

## Summary

During the past few decades, the United States has undergone a revolution in the legal status of its traditionally disadvantaged groups, including blacks, women, Native Americans, Hispanics, and Asian Americans. Such groups are now provided equal protection under the law in such areas as education, employment, and voting. Discrimination by race, sex, and ethnicity has not been eliminated from American life but is no longer substantially backed by the force of law. This advance was achieved against strong resistance from established interests, particularly in the South in regard to school and other forms of desegregation.

Traditionally disadvantaged Americans have achieved fuller equality primarily as a result of their struggle for greater rights. The Supreme Court has been an important instrument of change for minority groups. Its ruling in *Brown* v. *Board of Education* (1954), which declared racial segregation in public schools to be an unconstitutional violation of the Fourteenth Amendment's equal-protection clause, was a major breakthrough in equal rights. Through its busing, affirmative action, and other rulings, the Court has also mandated the active promotion of integration and equal opportunities. However, as civil rights policy involves large issues concerned with social values and the distribution of society's resources, questions of civil rights are politically potent. For this reason, legislatures and executives have been deeply involved in such issues, sometimes siding with established groups and sometimes backing the claims of underprivileged groups. Thus Congress with the backing of President Lyndon Johnson enacted the landmark Civil Rights Act of 1964; but Congress and recent presidents have been ambivalent about or hostile to busing for the purpose of integrating public schools.

In recent years affirmative action programs, designed to achieve equality of result for blacks, women, Hispanics, and other disadvantaged groups, have been a civil rights battleground. Affirmative action has had the strong support of civil rights groups and has won the qualified endorsement of the Supreme Court but has been opposed by those who claim that it unfairly discriminates against white males.

## Major Concepts

| | |
|---|---|
| affirmative action | equal rights (civil rights) |
| comparable worth | equality of result |
| *de facto* discrimination | reasonable-basis test |
| *de jure* discrimination | strict-scrutiny test |
| equal-protection clause | suspect classifications |

## Suggested Readings

Barsh, Russel Lawrence, and James Youngblood Henderson. *The Road: Indian Tribes and Political Liberty.* Berkeley: University of California Press, 1979. An analysis of Native Americans' quest for their civil rights.

Bullock, Charles S., III, and Charles M. Lamb, eds. *Implementation of Civil Rights Policy.* Monterey, Calif.: Brooks/Cole, 1983. A thorough examination of the problems, successes, and failures in the implementation of civil rights cases and laws.

Franklin, John Hope. *From Slavery to Freedom,* 5th ed. New York: Knopf, 1978. A valuable history of black Americans.

Freeman, Jo. *The Politics of Women's Liberation.* New York: David McKay, 1975. A thorough study of the historical and contemporary nature and effects of the women's liberation movement.

Garcia, F. Chris, and Rudolph O. de la Garza. *The Chicano Political Experience.* Duxbury, Mass.: Duxbury Press, 1977. An analysis of the Mexican-American political movement.

Gelb, Joyce, and Marian Leaf Paley. *Women and Public Policies.* Princeton, N.J.: Princeton University Press, 1982. An assessment of women's position and influence in public policy.

Graglia, Lino. *Disaster by Decree.* Ithaca, N.Y.: Cornell University Press, 1976. A critical assessment of Supreme Court decisions on race and the schools.

Key, V. O., Jr. *Southern Politics.* New York: Knopf, 1949. The classic study of one-party politics in the South in the period before the civil rights movement.

Kugler, Richard. *Simple Justice.* New York: Random House, 1977. The best evaluation of the *Brown* case and its impact on school desegregation.

Lukas, J. Anthony. *Common Ground.* New York: Knopf, 1985. A study of three families caught up in the controversy over forced busing to achieve racial integration in Boston's public schools.

Orfield, Gary. *Congressional Power: Congress and Social Change.* New York: Harcourt Brace Jovanovich, 1975. An assessment of the congressional politics of civil rights legislation.

Sindler, Allan P. *Equal Opportunity.* Washington, D.C.: American Enterprise Institute, 1983. A critical assessment of the politics and policy of compensatory minority preferences.

Wilkinson, J. Harvie III. *From "Brown" to "Bakke."* New York: Oxford University Press, 1979. An assessment of the Supreme Court's role in promoting school integration.

# Do Americans Place Too Much Emphasis on Individual Rights?

**JANE MANSBRIDGE**

*I would urge that we voluntarily restrict the frequency with which we invoke "rights" as we talk with one another about the way we ought to live.*

Americans do place too much emphasis on individual rights. While reducing that emphasis, I believe we should keep the concept of rights, work to understand which rights are most important, and fight to prevent the most important rights from being diminished.

Philosophically speaking, we could get rid of the concept of rights while still saving a lot of the aspects of it that we like. We could simply agree that some values are more important than others (that, for example, free speech should in most cases be given greater weight than security). At the same time we could, like some non-Western cultures, respect human dignity without having a concept of rights, defined as legitimate claims that individuals always hold against other people and that others have a duty to respect. On balance, however, I would keep the concept of rights, precisely because it adds to the idea of human dignity the notion that others have a duty to respect claims made in its name.

Yet Americans turn too many issues into questions of absolute rights. For example, each side in the abortion debate frames its argument in the language of rights: "a woman's right to control her body" versus "a fetus's right to life." Each side claims the entire moral territory, ruling out discussion of the degree of legitimacy that each moral stance might have at, say, different stages of pregnancy. Similarly, some propo-nents of the right to free speech cut off debate on substance by asserting that *no* printed matter can be curbed, even those forms of erotica or advertising that all agree cause harm.

In talk about rights, many problems arise from their binary quality—either you have rights or you don't; there is no spectrum of values, no middle ground. In practice, the U.S. Supreme Court introduces balance between one right and another. But the polarizing language of rights discourages balance.

Rights also have the quality of being held "against" other people. This is especially true of the quintessential "right to liberty," which Hobbes defined as "the absence of external impediments." Talk about rights encourages those who engage in it to see others as opponents.

I am not urging that we include in the category of rights only those particularly political claims—to free speech, association, or jury trial—that evolved in the eighteenth century and earlier as important compo-nents of democratic life. I would also include the twentieth-century rights—to a job and to the mini-mum level of goods necessary for belonging to the community. However, I *would* urge that we voluntarily restrict the frequency with which we invoke rights as we talk with one another about the way we ought to live. Several rights, like the right not to be tortured, deserve the position of absolute non-negotiability im-plicit in the word "right." Often, however, we use the word "right" the way a five-year-old uses "need" ("Mommy, I *need* that candy!")—that is, as an indi-cation that we feel strongly about a subject and as a substitute for persuasive arguments. When we talk about an issue, let's ask, "Is it necessary to frame this as a question of rights? Couldn't I think of it as a question of what would be good, or good for people?"

*Jane Mansbridge is Professor of Political Science at Northwestern University. She is the author of* Beyond Adversary Democra-cy.

**RICHARD FLATHMAN**

*In recent years the favorable attitudes that we have taken toward basic rights against government have quite rapidly extended into other arenas of social life.*

The best short answer to this question is twofold: "On the contrary," in that we have not been sufficiently insistent upon and respectful of the rights that we have most properly claimed; "Yes," in that we have a growing tendency to claim too many rights. But how can we know or decide how much emphasis is *too* much?

In many parts of the world, and among a small but often articulate minority in the United States, it is thought that *any* emphasis on individual rights is too much. In this view, concern with individual rights encourages selfishness, breeds competition and conflict, divides and weakens society. Rather than asserting rights against our country and our communities, our fellow citizens, neighbors, and family, we should seek ways to cooperate with and to help them.

As it pertains to government and politics, this attitude toward rights was long ago rejected in the United States. Necessary as they are, all governments are aggregations of power and hence potentially dangerous to their citizens; rewarding as it may be, all politics are struggles for and against power. Division and conflict are engendered not by rights but by government and politics themselves. Convinced of these and related propositions, our founding generations concluded that all citizens should have the protections afforded by a small but basic set of individual rights. Although challenged from time to time, this judgment has remained a prominent feature of the American political culture.

In this view, which I share, the appropriate objection is not to American ideas about rights but to our repeated failure to insist that the rights we regard as basic be extended to all members of our society and be fully respected. For long periods we have denied basic rights to very large groups in our population, and we have regularly committed gross violations of rights that we claim are well established in our law and our morality.

In recent years the favorable attitudes that we have traditionally taken toward basic rights against government have quite rapidly extended into other arenas of social life. The anti-rights view outlined above has clearly become a minority position as regards workplaces and schools, and its proponents may be fighting a losing battle in respect to more private domains such as the church, the club, and even the family. We are now claiming a wide range of rights, we are asserting those rights against one another with remarkable frequency, and we increasingly look to government to enforce respect for those rights.

In many ways this is a welcome development. "Private" institutions such as corporations, unions, and universities have increasingly acquired the characteristics—in particular, great power over their employees, members, and students—that led us to establish rights against governments, while clubs, other private associations, and families perpetrate the very kinds of discrimination from which our basic rights are supposed to protect us. The assumption of a natural cooperativeness and mutuality that usually underlies generalized hostility to individual rights has often proved to be as unwarranted in these private domains as it is in public life.

This expanded emphasis on individual rights nevertheless deserves our watchful concern. Whatever its effects on community and solidarity (and whether or not those are good things), it enhances the authority and power of the single most dangerous institution in any society—namely, government. And by doing that it may insidiously diminish the individuals to whom the new rights are accorded.

*Richard E. Flathman is a member of the Department of Political Science at Johns Hopkins University. He is the author of* Toward a Liberalism.

AFTER VOTING
INSERT BALLOT CARD
WITH STUB EXPOSED
INTO ENVELOPE POCKET
AND CLOSE FLAP

BALLOT BOX

605

# Part Three

## CITIZEN POLITICS

Self-government is a grand idea, resting as it does on the notion that government is obliged to obey the people. An older idea, still in place in much of the world, is that the people are obliged to obey government.

"We, the people" are the opening words of the U.S. Constitution. The American political system asks that its citizenry be a reasoning and participatory public, not an unruly mob or a quiescent mass. This requirement is confounded, however, by the practical need to reduce complex alternatives and diverse opinions to simple choices before the people can act. It is impossible for 250 million people to rule directly. They can govern only through systems of representation, in which their influence does not include control over the day-to-day decisions of government.

The role of citizen is accordingly a difficult one. The individual citizen is asked to take time to participate in public affairs and yet does not have the opportunity to exert great influence over these affairs. Not surprisingly, individuals differ in their willingness to exercise their citizenship. Some people cannot be bothered with public affairs, and others spend considerable time at it. Most Americans fall between the two extremes, giving some time to politics but not immersing themselves in it. Nevertheless, the integrity of the American political system depends on popular influence. As Harold Lasswell once wrote, the "open interplay" of the people and their government is "the distinguishing mark of popular rule."[1]

Part Three probes this open interplay along three dimensions: the people's opinions, their participation, and their votes. Chapter 8 examines the way Americans think politically and the effect of their opinions on the policies of government. Chapter 9 explores the nature and implications of citizens' participation in politics. Chapter 10 considers why Americans vote as they do and how their votes affect representative institutions. These chapters provide important insights about American government, but they necessarily leave many questions unanswered, because the relationship between a self-governing people and their government is far from simple.          ★   ★   ★

[1]Harold D. Lasswell, *Democracy through Public Opinion* (Menasha, Wis.: Banta, 1941), 15.

# Chapter 8

## PUBLIC OPINION: EXPRESSING THE PEOPLE'S VIEWS

*To speak with precision of public opinion is a task not unlike coming to grips with the Holy Ghost.*

*V. O. Key, Jr.*[1]

By the end of 1965, Lyndon Johnson was in position to take his place among the nation's great presidents. After only two years in office, Johnson had succeeded in getting an extraordinary number of his Great Society proposals enacted, including the 1964 Civil Rights Act, the 1965 Voting Rights Act, and such War on Poverty measures as the Head Start and Job Corps programs. No other president except Franklin D. Roosevelt had achieved so many major legislative initiatives in so short a time.

Johnson was riding high, but his downfall had already begun. He had inherited from President John F. Kennedy a commitment of U.S. support for the anticommunist side of a civil war in Vietnam. Although America's ally, South Vietnam, was faring poorly, Johnson initially gave the war a lower priority than his domestic policies, saying that he preferred a negotiated settlement over a military solution to the Vietnam conflict. Johnson changed his stance when it became clear in 1965 that South Vietnam would fall without the assistance of U.S. combat troops. Convinced that the American people would never forgive him if Vietnam and other Southeast Asian countries came under communist control, Johnson announced a major buildup of U.S. forces in Vietnam. A November 1965 Gallup poll indicated that a solid majority of the American public (64–21 percent) supported his decision.

Two years later, however, Americans had soured on Johnson and the commitment of a half-million U.S. soldiers to a war that was not being won.

[1]V. O. Key, Jr., *Public Opinion and American Democracy* (New York: Knopf, 1961), 8.

Whereas 70 percent of Americans had expressed satisfaction with Johnson's presidency in early 1965, the figure fell below 45 percent in 1967. Nevertheless, Johnson was able to get public backing for changes in his war policy. For example, a majority approved of his decision to carry the war to North Vietnam by the aerial bombing of Hanoi, its capital city, and Haiphong, its major seaport. Later a majority also supported his decision to halt the bombing temporarily in the hope that North Vietnam would agree to peace talks. But peace did not come during Johnson's presidency, despite his repeated assurances that it would. In early spring of 1968, with his public approval rating at only 40 percent, Johnson announced that he would not seek reelection.

The story of how the Vietnam issue brought down Lyndon Johnson is a revealing example of the influence of public opinion on government. Public opinion rarely compels officials to take a particular action. Johnson was not *forced* by public opinion to increase U.S. involvement in the Vietnam conflict, but public opinion *supported* the escalation. Since the late 1940s, Americans had believed that communist nations were bent on dominating the world and that only a determined United States could protect the interests of democracy. Thus the public was prepared to support Johnson's Vietnam buildup. Yet the public expected Johnson's efforts to succeed. Having led the country into war, he was held responsible by the public for the course of that war.

Public opinion has an important place in democratic societies because of the concept that government springs from the will of the people. The idea that government should attend to the opinions of ordinary citizens is deeply embedded in democratic thought. However, public opinion is a far more elusive phenomenon than conventional commentary suggests. It is widely assumed that there is a clear-cut public opinion on current issues; in fact, however, public opinion is often difficult to gauge and seldom is one-sided. For example, although it might be concluded that Americans' dissatisfaction in 1968 with Johnson's war policy was a sign that the public wanted an immediate withdrawal of U.S. forces from Vietnam, the reality was otherwise. Americans had at least five categories of opinions on Vietnam in 1968, none of which was held by a majority of the public: some were unsure what to think about Vietnam; some supported Johnson's policy; some wanted an immediate withdrawal of all U.S. troops; some wanted a gradual disengagement that would enable the South Vietnamese to prepare to defend themselves; and some wanted the United States to unleash its full military might to bring North Vietnam to its knees.

This chapter discusses public opinion and its influence on the U.S. political system. A major theme is that public opinion is a powerful and yet inexact force in American politics. The policies of the U.S. government cannot be understood apart from public opinion; at the same time, public opinion is not a precise determinant of public policies. This apparent paradox is explained by the fact that self-government in a large and complex country necessarily entails a division of labor between the public and its representatives, which results in a government that is tied only loosely to its public and in a public that can influence only the general direction of its government. The main points made in this chapter are the following:

★ *Public opinion consists of those opinions held by ordinary citizens which government takes into account in making its decisions.* Public officials have many means of gauging public opinion, such as elections and mass demonstrations, but increasingly have relied on public opinion polls to make this determination.

★ *The process by which individuals acquire their political opinions is called political socialization.* This process begins during childhood, when, through family and school, Americans acquire many of their basic political values and beliefs. Socialization continues into adulthood, during which peers, political leaders, events, and the news media are major influences.

★ *Americans' political opinions are shaped by many influences. Three of the most important are the political culture, liberal–conservative conflict, and such personal circumstances as race and income.* These influences form the basis for political consensus and conflict among the general public.

★ *Public opinion has an important influence on government but ordinarily does not directly determine what officials will do.* Public opinion works primarily to impose limits and directions on the choices made by officials. Public opinion is most powerful when political alternatives are organized in ways that enable citizens to act together effectively.

## *The Nature of Public Opinion*

Public opinion is a relatively new concept in the history of political ideas. Not until democracy began to flourish in the nineteenth century did the need arise to obtain some idea of what the public was thinking on political issues. If democracy is government of and for the people, then the public's political opinions are a central concern. Nevertheless, there has always been considerable disagreement about the impact that public opinion should have on government actions. Of course, there is agreement on basic principles. No democrat, past or present, would reject the idea that a just government rests on popular consent or that the people are in some sense the ultimate source of governing wisdom and strength.[2] Beyond these abstractions, however, the range of viewpoints on the proper role of public opinion is wide.

At one extreme are those who claim that government *by* public opinion is perilous. One such analyst, Robert Nisbet, says the idea that "public opinion must somehow govern, must therefore be incessantly studied, courted, flattered and drawn upon . . . is the great heresy . . . of modern democracies." Nisbet targets opinion polls for special criticism, saying that the opinions expressed through polls are unreflective and largely whimsical public reactions to current events. Nisbet claims that government has an obligation to respond only to the enduring and fundamental beliefs that citizens share as members of an ongoing political community. He labels these beliefs "public opinion" and distinguishes them from "popular opinion," which he defines as the transitory thoughts that citizens have about topical events.[3]

In making this distinction, Nisbet is attempting to locate modern thinking about public opinion within the classical liberal tradition expressed in such writings as the *Federalist Papers*. James Madison had differentiated between the public's momentary passions and its enduring interests, a distinction similar to Nisbet's differentiation between popular opinion and public opinion. For Madison as for Nisbet, governments are obligated to respond only to the public's shared and enduring beliefs.[4]

[2]Robert Nisbet, "Public Opinion versus Popular Opinion," *Public Interest* 41 (1975): 167.
[3]Ibid.
[4]*Federalist* No. 10.

In contrast, other analysts contend that almost any opinion held by ordinary citizens—whether stable or fleeting, reasoned or emotional—should be taken into account by government. George Gallup, who founded the public opinion polling industry in the United States, promoted this view. He wrote: "We are often told that the function of leadership is to lead. . . . This is an attractive and appealing concept of leadership and one which has intrigued mankind from the earliest days. Unfortunately, it fits perfectly such eminent leaders as Adolph Hitler, Benito Mussolini, and Premier [Joseph] Stalin." Gallup questioned whether remote leaders can ever be trusted to serve the public. He believed that leaders should be in tune with the citizenry. "In a democracy," Gallup said, leaders "should have available an accurate appraisal of public opinion and take some account of it in reaching their decision. . . . The task of the leader is to decide how best to achieve the goals set by the people."[5]

Gallup's argument fits into the Jacksonian and Progressive traditions. We noted in Chapter 4 that the Jacksonians and Progressives had a strong faith in the judgment of the ordinary citizen and a suspicion of leaders who were not directly accountable to the people. Modern-day Jacksonians and Progressives see public opinion polls not as ephemeral and unreliable snapshots of the public's mood, but as a strong foundation of popular government. Whereas leaders at any earlier time could always claim to be in step with the public's wishes, today's leaders can do so only if the polls show that the public agrees with them.

The ideas of Robert Nisbet and George Gallup are only two of many views on the proper role of public opinion in a democratic society. There is no consensus on the subject. The various ideas are normative ones; they stem from different values and preferences and hence do not lend themselves to factual analysis. Nisbet represents the view that systems of leadership are at the core of effective democratic government. Gallup represents the view that public sentiment should dominate. Such differences are fundamental and, in America, are at least as old as the dispute between Federalists and Anti-Federalists over the Constitution's provisions for popular influence.

## A WORKING DEFINITION OF PUBLIC OPINION

"Public opinion" is an ordinary term, but it refers to a complex reality. Although the term is typically used in reference to the whole society, it is not very meaningful to lump all citizens together as if they constituted a single coherent public. In fact, Americans form *many* publics.[6] As Harwood Childs has said, "There are organized and unorganized publics, primary and secondary, large and small, powerful and impotent, wise and foolish, important and unimportant."[7]

One dimension along which Americans divide into publics is their level of attention to politics. Only a minority of citizens pay close attention to politics on a regular basis. As a result, the level of knowledge that many people have about public affairs is very low. Fewer than half of adult Americans can name the

---

[5]George Gallup, "Polls and the Political Process—Past, Present, and Future," *Public Opinion Quarterly* 40 (Winter 1965): 547–548.

[6]Jerry L. Yeric and John R. Todd, *Public Opinion* (Itasca, Ill.: F. E. Peacock, 1983), 3. ·

[7]Harwood L. Childs, *Public Opinion* (Princeton, N.J.: Van Nostrand, 1965), 12.

References to "American public opinion" can be misleading, because American society consists of many publics, not just one. Americans may divide into publics on the basis of age, sex, race, occupation, and many other dimensions. (Roy Morsch/Stock Market)

Speaker of the House of Representatives or the two U.S. senators from their state. When a 1987 poll asked Americans to identify the chief justice of the Supreme Court, only 8 percent could recall William Rehnquist's name.[8] When it comes to questions of policy choices, such as the fiscal or monetary actions that might be taken in response to rising inflation, the overall level of public awareness is even lower.

Obviously, in defining "public opinion" we cannot assume that all citizens are equally interested in and informed about all aspects of political life. Accordingly, we shall take **public opinion** to mean those opinions held by ordinary citizens which officials take into account when they choose to act or not to act. So defined, public opinion can be the views of many or a few people. On one question public opinion may be the views held by one set of citizens; on another question, the views of a quite different set. Government does not necessarily have to follow expressed opinion in each case; it can also reject, divert, or try to alter opinion. The central point is that the opinions of private citizens become public opinion when government takes them into account.[9] Whether government *should* take these various opinions into account is a separate question.

## THE MAJOR DIMENSIONS OF PUBLIC OPINION

Our definition of public opinion embraces a wide variety of the views that citizens hold, but it is imprecise in describing public opinion on a particular issue. In such situations, it can be useful to refer to the major dimensions of opinion: *direction, stability, intensity,* and *salience.*

[8]Market Facts Survey, June 1987.
[9]The original formulator of this common view of public opinion is unknown. Its foremost advocate was V. O. Key, Jr. See Key, *Public Opinion and American Democracy,* 14–15.

Forced busing to achieve racial integration in public schools has provoked intense opinions in many communities. (Ira Wyman/Sygma)

Direction is a measure of the degree to which opinion on a particular question is favorable or unfavorable. For example, polls indicate that most Americans have an unfavorable opinion on the use of busing to achieve racial integration of public schools. Stability is an indication of whether an opinion on a question is firmly held or readily changeable. As regards busing, most people have stable opinions: they feel the same way about busing today as they did several years ago. Intensity is the degree of feeling that people have about a particular issue. Individuals who feel very strongly about their position on busing are said to have high intensity; those who are indifferent to the busing issue have low intensity. Salience is the importance that a person or public attaches to a particular issue in comparison with other issues. For example, although busing tends to bring out intense opinions, most Americans consider it less important—that is, less salient—than such issues as peace and prosperity.

These dimensions influence the degree of attention that particular opinions are likely to receive from government. Opinions of high salience or one-sided direction tend to receive more attention from officials than low-salience or divided opinions. Similarly, officials are generally more responsive to intensely held or stable opinions than to weakly held or fleeting ones.

## ESTIMATING PUBLIC OPINION THROUGH POLLS

Public officials have numerous ways of assessing public opinion. Election returns are routinely interpreted as an indicator of the public's mood. Letters to the editor in newspapers and the sizes of crowds at mass demonstrations are other means to judge public opinion. However, the most relied-upon measure of public opinion has come to be the poll or survey. More than 100 organizations are in the business of conducting public opinion polls. Some, like the Gallup Organization, conduct polls that are then released to the news media by

★ ANALYZE THE ISSUE

**The Nature of Public Opinion**
What is public opinion? How might public opinion actually differ from what pollsters refer to as public opinion? How might it differ from what the writers of the Constitution thought of as public opinion (see Chapter 4)?

syndication. Most large news organizations also have their own in-house polls; one of the foremost of these is the CBS News/New York Times poll, which conducts about fifteen surveys annually for use in the *Times* and on CBS's newscasts. Finally, there are polling firms that specialize in conducting surveys for candidates and officeholders.

## The Theory of Opinion Sampling

In a **public opinion poll,** a relatively small number of individuals—the **sample**—are interviewed for the purpose of estimating the opinions of a whole **population,** such as the students of a college, the residents of a city, or the citizens of a country. How is it possible to measure the thinking of a large population on the basis of a small sample? How can interviews with, say, 1,000 Americans provide a reliable estimate of what 250 million are thinking? The answer is found in mathematical probabilities. The general idea of mathematical probabilities can be illustrated by the hypothetical example of a huge jar filled with a million marbles, half of them red and half blue. If a blindfolded person reaches into the jar, the probability of selecting a marble of a given color is 50–50. And if 1,000 marbles were chosen in this random way, red marbles and blue marbles would be selected roughly 500 times apiece.

The probabilities of opinion polling are similar. If individuals are selected at random and if enough of them are chosen, their views will tend to be representative—that is, roughly the same as the views held by the population as a whole. The accuracy of a poll is usually expressed in terms of **sampling error,** which is a function of sample size. The larger the sample, the smaller the

George Gallup (*seated*) and his staff meet on the day after the election of 1948. Gallup's American Institute of Public Opinion had wrongly predicted that Republican Thomas E. Dewey would beat Democrat Harry Truman. The Gallup organization subsequently revised its polling procedures and has correctly predicted the outcome of every election since 1948. (AP/Wide World Photos)

**TABLE 8-1  Approximate Sampling Error by Number of Opinion-Poll Respondents**

| Approximate Number of Respondents | Approximate Sampling Error |
|:---:|:---:|
| 200 | ±7% |
| 275 | ±6 |
| 375 | ±5 |
| 600 | ±4 |
| 1,075 | ±3 |
| 2,400 | ±2 |
| 9,600 | ±1 |

*Note:* Figures are based on a 95 percent confidence level. This means that for a given sample size (e.g., 600), the chances are 19 in 20 (95 percent) that the sample will produce results that are within the sampling error (e.g., ± 4 percent) of the results that would have been obtained if the whole population had been interviewed.

sampling error (see Table 8-1). A properly drawn sample of 1,000 individuals has a sampling error of plus or minus 3 percent, which is to say that the proportions of the various opinions expressed by the people in the sample are likely to be no more than 3 percent larger or smaller than those of the whole population. For example, if 55 percent of a sample of 1,000 respondents say that they intend to vote for the Republican candidate for president, then the chances are high that 52 to 58 percent (55 percent plus or minus 3 percent) of the whole population plan to vote for the Republican.*

The impressive record of the Gallup poll in predicting the outcomes of presidential elections indicates that the theoretical accuracy of polls can be matched in practice. For example, the Gallup poll came within 1 percent of the actual vote in predicting the 1988 Bush–Dukakis race. The Gallup Organization has erred badly only once: it stopped polling several weeks before the 1948 election and missed a late trend that carried Harry Truman to victory over Thomas E. Dewey.

### Methods of Sampling

Mathematical estimations of poll accuracy require a **probability sample**—a sample in which each individual in the population has a known probability of being selected at random for inclusion. In practice, pollsters can only approximate this ideal. Because pollsters rarely have a complete list of all individuals in a population from which to draw a random sample, they usually base their sample on telephones or locations. Random-digit telephone sampling is the most commonly used technique. Pollsters use computers to pick random telephone numbers, which are then dialed by interviewers to reach respondents. Because the computer is as likely to pick one telephone number as any

---

*Opinion polling is a fairly complex process that cannot be explained precisely in the space available here. The interested reader might want to read an introductory book on polling such as Charles H. Backstrom and Gerald D. Hursh-Cesar, *Survey Research*, 2d ed. (New York: Macmillan, 1981).

Interviewers for CBS News conduct a poll of individuals who have just voted. Such "exit polls" are designed to discover why voters chose one candidate over another. (Stuart Cohen/ Comstock)

other and because 95 percent of U.S. homes have a telephone, a sample selected in this way can usually be assumed to be representative of the population.[10]

A major drawback to telephone interviewing is that many people refuse to answer phone questions for more than 10 or 15 minutes. When longer interviews are required, they are often conducted face to face. To achieve randomness in this situation, census data are used to select locations (such as city blocks) at random; interviewers then go to these sites to locate and talk with respondents. Whatever the probability sampling method used, the goal is to obtain a representative sample; only then can the pollster have confidence in the accuracy of the results.

Some polls are not based on probability sampling. For example, reporters sometimes conduct "man-in-the-street" interviews to obtain individuals' responses to political questions. Although a reporter may imply that the views of those interviewed are representative of the general public's, the fallacy of this reasoning should be readily apparent. The sample will be biased by where and when the reporter chooses to conduct the interviews. For example, interviews conducted on a downtown street at the noon hour are likely to include a disproportionate number of business employees who are taking their lunch breaks.

A somewhat more reliable form of nonprobability sample is the "quota sample." When this method is used, respondents are categorized by type and a quota is set for each type. For example, a survey might call for a quota sample consisting of 45 percent white females, 45 percent white males, 5 percent black females, and 5 percent black males. These quotas could have been set on the basis of data indicating that the population being studied is 90 percent white and evenly divided by gender. Once the quotas are set, interviewers then locate respondents who fit the designated descriptions. Quota samples have been known to produce reasonably representative findings, but they do not regularly yield results that are as reliable as those associated with probability samples. Quota samples tend to overrepresent individuals who are highly "visible"— that is, individuals, such as regular shoppers, who are easy for interviewers to

[10]See William R. Klecka and Alfred J. Tuchfarber, "Random Digit Dialing: A Comparison to Personal Surveys," *Public Opinion Quarterly* 42 (Spring 1978): 105–114.

approach. Less visible people, such as those who seldom leave their homes or workplaces, are typically underrepresented in quota samples.

### Sources of Polling Errors

Even when probability sampling is used, there are many potential sources of error beyond that of the sampling error. For example, failure to follow acceptable sampling procedures can result in an unrepresentative sample; thus, if interviewers are unwilling to go into slum neighborhoods, the resulting poll will underreport the opinions of low-income people.

The wording of survey questions can also distort poll results. A poll should not contain questions that lead respondents to give answers that do not reflect their true opinions. During Senate confirmation hearings on the appointment of Robert Bork to the Supreme Court in 1987, national polls differed by almost 20 points in the proportion of respondents who opposed Bork's nomination. When the questions mentioned allegations about Bork's civil rights record, the pollsters found a higher level of opposition than was registered by polls whose questions did not remind respondents of these allegations.

Polls can also be misleading if they include questions on subjects to which people have given little or no thought. For example, most Americans have not thought carefully about whether Puerto Rico, currently a U.S. commonwealth, should be granted statehood. If a polltaker were to ask whether Puerto Rico should become the fifty-first state, most respondents would probably offer a yes or no answer, but it seems highly unlikely that they would have a true opinion on the question.

Finally, polls are less than satisfactory in measuring intensity, or the degree of feeling that people have about a given issue. Unlike mass demonstrations and other active expressions of public opinion, polls do not capture the passion or urgency that some political issues inspire.

In spite of such problems, polls can be a valuable means of discovering what is on people's minds. Polls can dissuade political leaders from thinking that the view of those who are speaking the loudest is also the common view. Less than 1 percent of Americans participate each year in a mass demonstration, and fewer than 10 percent write to the president or a member of Congress. The opinions of these small minorities are unrepresentative; political demonstrators and letter writers tend to hold views that are more intense and extreme than those of other citizens.[11]

## Sources of Opinion Conflict and Consensus

For the sake of simplicity, we have been discussing public opinion as if it were merely a question of what is on the minds of individuals at any given time. Yet the opinions of millions of people would mean almost nothing if these opinions had no common threads. The lone citizen is virtually powerless to influence government. The strength of the people is in their numbers. A basic fact of

[11]Sidney Verba and Norman H. Nie, *Participation in America: Political Democracy and Social Equality* (New York: Harper & Row, 1972), 281–284.

# SHOULD PUBLIC OFFICIALS BASE THEIR POLICY DECISIONS ON OPINION POLLS?

Public officials and candidates for public office routinely use public opinion polls to keep track of what the people are thinking. An important question is the degree to which these polls should guide leaders in their actions. There are arguments for and against the use of polls as the basis for policy decisions.

Polls can contribute to effective government by keeping political leaders from getting too far out of line with the public's thinking. In a democratic society, the effectiveness of a public policy often depends on the extent of its public support. When a policy is contrary to the public's desires, people may choose to disregard or undermine it, thus making it counterproductive or inefficient. Further, when government pursues a course of action with which a large proportion of the public disagrees, it risks a loss of public confidence, which can have a negative effect on its ability to lead. The Reagan administration, flying high from 1981 to 1985, was brought low in 1986 by public reaction to news of its secret sales of weapons to Iran. The administration had not paid sufficient attention to polls that revealed the deep antagonism Americans still felt toward Iran because the Ayatollah Khomeini's regime had held sixty-three Americans hostage in 1979–1981.

However, leaders can also do a disservice to the public they represent by using poll results as a substitute for policy judgment. "Effective government," Walter Lippmann wrote, "cannot be conducted by legislators and officials who, when a question is presented, ask themselves first and last not what is the truth and which is the right and necessary course, but 'What does the Gallup Poll say?'" During his presidential term, Jimmy Carter proposed five consecutive inflation-fighting programs, changing his plans with each shift in public sentiment without having invested the political capital necessary to get Congress and the country behind any of the efforts. The nation—and Carter—would probably have been better served by a steadfast commitment to a single course of action.

SOURCES: James R. Beninger and Robert Giuffra, Jr., "Public Opinion Polling: Command and Control in Presidential Campaigns," in Alexander Heard and Michael Nelson, eds., *Presidential Selection* (Durham, N.C.: Duke University Press, 1987), 214; Larry J. Sabato, *The Rise of Political Consultants* (New York: Basic Books, 1981), 321.

democratic politics is that individuals must be organized to take collective action if they are to have a consistent and substantial impact on government. If enough people who hold the same opinion join forces, they may be able to translate this consensus into political power. And of course, whenever there are sizable numbers on each side of an issue, the likelihood of political conflict rises sharply.

In practice, the task of organizing the public for collective action falls chiefly on political parties and interest groups (see Chapters 11–14). However, parties and groups do not start from scratch. They build their appeals largely on existing opinions. They respond to what is already on people's minds, bringing these opinions into the arena of political debate and action. Of basic concern, then, are the foundations on which Americans' opinions rest. This subject could fill an entire book; here we will explore briefly a few of the major bases of opinion and their influence on conflict and consensus.

## POLITICAL CULTURE

As we indicated in Chapter 1, Americans are unusual in their commitment to a set of ideals that nearly define the nature of the American political experience.

A wounded man is evacuated from Grenada in October 1983. The U.S. invasion of that small island nation was strongly supported by the American people, who saw the demonstration of military might as a strike at Soviet-sponsored communist advances in the Caribbean. (Jean-Louis Atlan/Sygma)

Such principles as individualism, equality, and self-government have always meant somewhat different things to different people, but nonetheless are a source of opinion consensus.[12] For example, because of their belief in individualism, most Americans reject policies aimed at redistributing wealth. Such policies are common in Western Europe but have had little appeal for Americans. When George McGovern, the 1972 Democratic presidential nominee, advocated a government-guaranteed income of $1,000 for each family member, his proposal was so widely criticized that he felt compelled to retract it. The outpouring of public scorn that greeted McGovern's proposal can be explained only in terms of Americans' deep-seated belief in individualism.

The kind of reasoning that stems from Americans' fundamental beliefs fits a pattern that has been called "contextualizing"—evaluating a situation in the context of a particular value or experience.[13] Consider the attitude toward welfare mothers expressed by a respondent in a study of mass beliefs: "Welfare! Those lazy sluts having kids like it was a factory. . . . You don't work, you don't live, right?"[14] This man's opinion, whatever else might be said of it, was formed in the context of his conception of individualism: work, not welfare. A broader example is the widespread support that Americans express for social security because retirees have "earned" these benefits by the payroll taxes they paid during their working years. In the context of individualism, whether or not a benefit has been earned is a standard for judging whether or not it is fully deserved.

[12]See Donald Devine, *The Political Culture of the United States* (Boston: Little, Brown, 1972); Richard Merelman, *Making Something of Ourselves* (Berkeley: University of California Press, 1984); John White, *The New Politics of Old Values* (Hanover, N.H.: University Press of New England, 1988).
[13]W. Lance Bennett, *Public Opinion in American Politics* (New York: Harcourt Brace Jovanovich, 1980), 161–162.
[14]Richard Sennett and Jonathan Cobb, *The Hidden Injuries of Class* (New York: Vintage Books, 1972), 135.

★ HOW THE UNITED
STATES COMPARES

**Public Opinion on U.S.–Soviet Relations**

Although the Western democracies are allies, they are sufficiently different in their histories, geography, trade patterns, and defense forces to have differing perspectives on various foreign policy issues. One study revealed marked differences of opinion among the citizens of four countries about a nuclear arms limitation agreement between the United States and the Soviet Union.

| Question | PERCENT WHO AGREE | | | |
| --- | --- | --- | --- | --- |
| | United States | Great Britain | France | West Germany |
| On balance, do you think an agreement between the United States and the Soviet Union to limit nuclear weapons would make [your] country a safer place to live? | 47% | 19% | 47% | 38% |
| How likely is it in your view that the Soviet Union would honor an agreement with the United States to limit nuclear weapons? | 62 | 32 | 59 | 55 |
| How likely is it that the United States would honor such an agreement with the Soviet Union? | 61 | 41 | 81 | 57 |

SOURCE: "Attitudes toward the Soviet Union and the United States: A Four-Country Comparison," *Public Opinion*, March/April 1988, pp. 29–30.

There are limits, of course, to the degree to which Americans' basic beliefs give direction and uniformity to their policy opinions. For nearly two centuries black Americans were inferior by law to white Americans, despite the American creed that "all men are created equal." Such inconsistencies speak to the all-too-human capacity to voice one idea and live another.

Nevertheless, Americans' cultural beliefs have a powerful influence on their thinking. Consider the hostility and mistrust that Americans have held toward the Soviet Union since communism took root there in 1917. Although the United States and the USSR have never been at war and in fact fought on the same side during World War II, most Americans view the Soviet Union with suspicion. This outlook developed before the USSR became a superpower and stems from irresolvable conflict between Soviet and American principles. Communism is rejected as un-American (see Table 8-2), a view that has affected Americans' response to any number of policy issues. For example, although Americans generally oppose unprovoked attacks on weaker nations by stronger ones, they overwhelmingly supported such an attack by the United States on the tiny Caribbean nation of Grenada in 1983, which resulted in the overthrow of its Marxist government.

## IDEOLOGY: LIBERALISM AND CONSERVATISM

Commentators on public opinion in the United States often use such ideological words as "liberal" and "conservative" in describing how ordinary citizens think about political issues. In the early 1980s, for example, analysts spoke of "a conservative tide" that was supposedly sweeping the country and displacing the liberal trend that had dominated American politics for most of the preceding

TABLE 8-2  Americans' Attitudes toward Communism and Socialism

|  | *Agree* | *Disagree* | *No Opinion* |
|---|---|---|---|
| If adopted here [in the United States] the main features of communism would make things worse for most Americans. | 82% | 3% | 15% |
| Some form of socialism would certainly be better than the system we have now. | 11 | 89 | 0 |
| Communism or socialism may not be perfect, but they certainly would be improvements over the dog-eat-dog systems people have lived under until now. | 11 | 89 | 0 |
| The communist countries will go down in history as dictatorships that crushed human freedom. | 68 | 5 | 27 |
| The sacrifices made by the people in the communist countries are necessary and will benefit the people in the long run. | 8 | 62 | 30 |
| There are a great many things in the Soviet Union that could be copied by this country with much benefit to the common people. | 16 | 84 | 0 |

SOURCE: Adapted from Herbert McClosky and John Zaller, *The American Ethos: Public Attitudes toward Capitalism and Democracy* (Cambridge, Mass.: Harvard University Press, 1984), 135, Table 5-2.

★ ANALYZE THE ISSUE

**Are You a Liberal or a Conservative?**
Do you favor government programs that would give each American economic security? Do you favor a broad conception of individual rights? Do you believe that the United States should place less emphasis on military power in the exercise of its foreign policy? If you answered yes, you are probably a liberal. If you answered no, you are probably a conservative.

fifty years. Liberalism and conservatism are examples of an **ideology,** a consistent pattern of opinion on particular issues that stems from a basic underlying belief or beliefs.[15] As used in contemporary politics, **conservatism** includes beliefs in economic individualism, traditional social values, and a strong defense establishment. **Liberalism** refers to support for social-welfare programs and activist government, tolerance for social change and diversity, and opposition to "excessive" military spending and interference abroad.

Of course, individuals can call themselves liberals or conservatives without subscribing to all or any of the associated beliefs. Yet, as Figure 8-1 illustrates, self-identified liberals and conservatives tend to divide along the expected dimensions.

## The Tendency toward Moderation and Pragmatism

Although liberalism and conservatism are influential forces in American politics, their impact is hardly as universal as news commentary sometimes suggests. The fact is that Americans are more likely to think of themselves as moderates than as either conservatives or liberals. A 1988 Gallup poll indicated

[15]Alternative conceptualizations that are potentially useful have not been widely explored. See, for example, Pamela Johnston Conover and Stanley Feldman, "Belief System Organization in the American Electorate: An Alternative Approach," in John C. Pierce and John L. Sullivan, eds., *The Electorate Reconsidered* (Beverly Hills, Calif.: Sage, 1980; Shawn Rosenberg, Dana Ward, and Stephen Chilton, *Political Reasoning and Cognition* (Durham, N.C.: Duke University Press, 1988).

Percent who agreed

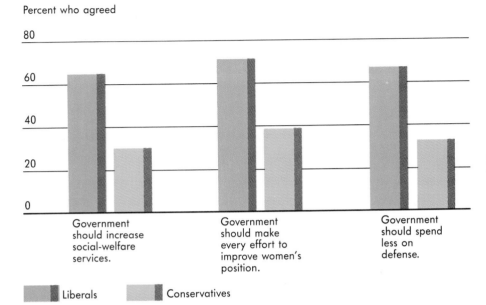

Liberals     Conservatives

**FIGURE 8-1 Correlation between Political Ideology and Opinion on Selected Policy Issues**
Liberals are more likely than conservatives to support social-welfare spending and social change and less likely to support defense spending.
*Source: National Election Studies data, 1984.*

that 46 percent of Americans saw themselves as moderates, 27 percent as conservatives, and 21 percent as liberals. In the 1960s the liberal group was larger than the conservative one, but the largest group then, as now, was the moderates. Americans' opinions on specific issues also support the assertion that the largest proportion of them are moderates. For example, in regard to such social-welfare programs as Medicaid, a majority of Americans take the moderate position that these programs should be continued at current levels— not expanded (the liberal view) or cut back (the conservative objective).

The moderate tendencies of the American people—their reluctance to embrace extreme alternatives—help to explain the durability of the U.S. political system. Within the confines of their cultural beliefs Americans tend to be pragmatic, judging policy choices according to their effectiveness rather than their ideological "correctness." When Ronald Reagan took office in 1981, for example, most Americans, although they had doubts about many of his conservative ideas, were willing to give them a try. The idea of a new approach was less worrisome to most Americans than the fear of the nation's continuing high rates of inflation and unemployment. This type of pragmatism is what the historian Daniel Boorstin labeled "the genius of American politics."[16] Rather than sticking doggedly to fixed solutions, Americans have traditionally been willing to try new approaches when the old ones no longer seem to be working.

The pragmatic and moderate tendencies in American politics are largely a function of the low intensity of class conflict. In contrast to European democracies, where class-based attitudes and organizations have historically been strong (see Chapters 9–11), the United States is a more open society with relatively

[16]See Daniel Boorstin, *The Genius of American Politics* (Chicago: University of Chicago Press, 1953).

muted social and economic conflicts. The result is a greater degree of consensus in the United States. Although the Democratic party tilts toward the lower-income end of society and the Republican party toward the upper-income end, both parties concentrate their attention on the larger middle-class group in the center. Because the Democratic and Republican parties do not consistently and sharply divide along liberal–conservative lines, Americans tend not to perceive their choices as routinely falling along these lines.

Some critics of the U.S. political system complain that the potential influence of public opinion is thwarted by the American parties' tendency not to provide sharply defined political alternatives. This argument, however, reverses cause and effect. In reality, the reason the Democratic and Republican parties are not dramatically different is that public opinion is not deeply divided. The broad consensus that springs from Americans' fundamental beliefs constrains what the parties can reasonably offer. Either party risks a crushing defeat if it places itself outside the mainstream of opinion. Barry Goldwater in 1964 and George McGovern in 1972 were widely perceived as extreme ideologues, and each was defeated in an election landslide of historic proportions.

### The Tendency toward Ideological Activism and Symbolism

Liberalism and conservatism are relatively sophisticated patterns of thought. They require that citizens have general beliefs that they can apply when they respond to an emerging policy alternative. When a new problem or program comes along, a true liberal or conservative judges it by whether or not it calls for activist government or promotes social change.

Given the lack of information that some citizens have about politics, it is perhaps no surprise that about half of adult Americans cannot say what is meant by "liberalism" and "conservatism" and that an additional fourth cannot readily apply these ideas to particular policy issues. Researchers have concluded that only a minority of citizens—between 10 and 25 percent by most estimates—readily understand and can apply ideas of liberalism and conservatism. Philip Converse, a leading scholar of mass opinion, has concluded, "The common citizen fails to develop global views about politics."[17]

Nevertheless, there are at least three reasons for concluding that liberal/conservative ideology is a major factor in American public opinion. First, the proportion of citizens who think ideologically, though a minority, is still sizable. Moreover, the proportion increases whenever the political alternatives are more ideological than normal.[18] For example, when the Democrat Lyndon Johnson, a strong proponent of activist government, campaigned in 1964 against the Republican Barry Goldwater, an equally strong advocate of governmental restraint, the proportion of voters who described their choices in ideological terms doubled from the level in the previous election.[19]

[17]Philip Converse, "The Nature of Belief Systems in Mass Publics," in David Apter, ed., *Ideology and Discontent* (New York: Free Press, 1965), 206.
[18]See John C. Pierce, "Party Identification and the Changing Role of Ideology in American Politics," *Midwest Journal of Political Science* 14 (1970): 25–42; John C. Pierce and Douglas D. Rose, "Non-Attitudes and American Public Opinion," *American Political Science Review* 68 (June 1974), 629–649; Bruce A. Campbell, *The American Electorate* (New York: Holt, Rinehart and Winston, 1979), 148–156.
[19]John Osgood Field and Ronald E. Anderson, "Ideology in the Public's Conceptualization of the 1964 Presidential Election," *Public Opinion Quarterly* 33 (1969): 380–398.

Second, ideology is concentrated among those who are the most politically vocal and visible: the activists. They understand ideological debate, and many of them are strong liberals or conservatives. Studies indicate, for example, that the political activists who serve as delegates to the national presidential nominating conventions are much more ideological than either the voters within their party or the public as a whole (see Chapter 12). Because activists play the most visible and vocal role in politics, ideology has a greater presence and importance in American politics than it would if liberal/conservative ideas were distributed evenly among the population.

Third, liberalism and conservatism are important influences on public opinion because they occasionally take on transcendent symbolic meanings. They become associated with much that is good or bad in American politics. In 1964 conservatism, in addition to its true meanings, was associated with racism, which Johnson was able to exploit in his campaign against Goldwater. During the 1988 campaign, the Republican George Bush repeatedly called his Democratic opponent, Michael Dukakis, "a liberal," knowing that the term has a negative connotation for many Americans. Some people, for example, associate liberalism with wasteful federal spending and others connect it disapprovingly with racial integration. As the proportion of Americans who perceived Dukakis as a liberal increased during the 1988 campaign, his support decreased (see Figure 8-2).

## PERSONAL CIRCUMSTANCES

Although Americans share a political heritage and are connected through modern systems of transportation, public education, and mass communication, the lives they lead vary considerably. Being black in America is not the same as being white. Living in a northeastern city is not the same as living on a southwestern farm. Being a blue-collar worker earning an hourly wage is not the same as being a salaried professional. Such differences in personal circumstances can be sources of both consensus and conflict. Most labor union members, for example, take a self-interested view of labor issues, which unites them but pits them against others who, for their own reasons, oppose the goals

★ ANALYZE THE ISSUE

**Forming Opinions without Information**
The level of the public's knowledge about some policy issues is shockingly low. How does this situation affect the public discussion of policy problems? What circumstances affect whether a citizen is likely to possess much factual information about a policy issue? Can you think of an issue about which a citizen could have a thoughtful opinion without having much information?

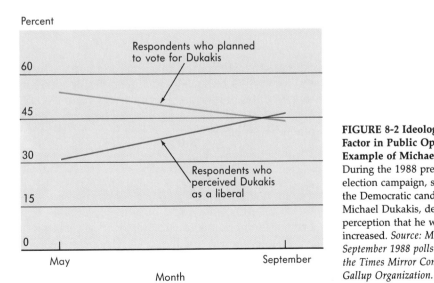

FIGURE 8-2 Ideology as a Factor in Public Opinion: The Example of Michael Dukakis During the 1988 presidential election campaign, support for the Democratic candidate, Michael Dukakis, declined as the perception that he was a liberal increased. *Source: May and September 1988 polls conducted for the Times Mirror Company by the Gallup Organization.*

of unionized labor. Moreover, citizens nearly always pay closer attention to issues that affect their lives directly than to more remote issues. Labor union members can be expected to take an interest in major labor issues but are unlikely to follow, say, farm issues.

Because of the country's great size, settlement by various immigrant groups, and economic pluralism, Americans are a very diverse people. Later chapters will examine some of the differences among Americans more fully, but it is helpful here to mention a few of the major ones.

### Religion

Religious differences have always been a source of solidarity and conflict. Gone, presumably forever, is the virulent anti-Catholicism and anti-Semitism that Protestants directed at immigrants from southern and eastern Europe upon their arrival in America. Today religious differences are evident mainly in the context of specific policy questions, such as school prayer and abortion. For example, fundamentalist Protestants and Roman Catholics oppose legalized abortion more strongly than do other Protestants, Jews, and those who have no religious affiliation.

### Income

Personal income level is less important in the United States than in Europe, but it is nevertheless related to opinions on certain issues. For example, lower-income Americans are more supportive of social-welfare programs, business regulation, and progressive taxation.

### Region

Region has declined as a basis of political differences, but growing up in a particular section of the country is still associated to a degree with opinions on such issues as civil rights and national defense. For example, southern whites are less favorably disposed toward civil rights and more supportive of defense spending than are whites in other geographical areas.

### Race

Race is also a significant source of opinion differences. For example, blacks are more supportive of social-welfare programs and less trustful of government than are whites. Blacks are also more supportive of affirmative action, busing to achieve racial integration in the schools, and other measures designed to promote racial equality.

### Gender

Although male–female differences of opinion are small on most issues, gender does affect opinion on some questions. Perhaps surprisingly, these issues are not primarily those that touch directly on sexual equality. Opinion polls indicate that men and women are about equally supportive of affirmative action and do

Compared with men, women have a less favorable opinion of the use of miltary force as an instrument of foreign policy. During the 1980s, for example, opinion polls consistently indicated that more women than men were opposed to U.S. aid for the Contra rebels who were seeking to overthrow the Sandinista government of Nicaragua. (Rick Reinhard/Impact Visuals)

not hold significantly different opinions on the proposed Equal Rights Amendment to the Constitution. But men and women do divide on issues involving physical coercion by the state. For example, women are less likely than men to favor capital punishment for convicted murderers and less likely to favor military force as a solution to international conflict.

### Partisanship

Party affiliation is the factor that relates most consistently to opinion differences. Republicans and Democrats disagree on a significant range of policy issues. Social welfare is an example: Democrats are much more supportive of government programs for the poor and otherwise disadvantaged than are Republicans. (Such differences will be examined in depth at various points later in this book, particularly in Chapters 10, 11, 26, and 27.)

### Education Level

Educational attainment affects opinions, particularly those relating to basic democratic rights and procedures. As education level increases, so does support for democratic values, such as freedom of expression. The sense of a citizen's obligations—to vote, to be active in community affairs, to take an interest in political news—is also stronger among more highly educated people. These tendencies are due in part to the direct effects of education, particularly college experiences. They also stem from the fact that college-educated people are likely to have more of the skills and contacts that promote political involvement, from which can flow consistent opinions. For example, freedom of expression, like other rights, is prized most highly by those citizens who make active use of it.

In short, then, conflicting opinions among Americans can often be traced to differences in personal circumstances. A white born-again Christian who grew up and lives in a small town in the South can hardly be expected to see politics in precisely the same way as a Hispanic Roman Catholic who lives in Los Angeles. Americans are a people of dozens of religions, scores of nationalities, countless occupations, widely varying incomes, and thousands of communities. In view of their many differences, perhaps the real surprise is the extent to which Americans agree on political questions.

## Political Socialization: Influences on Opinion Formation

Analysts have long been interested in the process by which public opinion is formed. Almost a century ago James Bryce proposed that opinion formation takes place in stages, beginning with the public's first impression of an issue, continuing through a period of public deliberation on the issue, and concluding with a public action—such as the enactment of legislation—that settles the issue.[20] We now know that the process of opinion formation is far more varied and haphazard than Bryce believed. Citizens arrive at their opinions by any number of routes, most of them quite casual and unreflective and many of them involving elaborate psychological defense mechanisms.

We saw in Chapter 1 that the learning process by which people acquire their enduring beliefs and values is called **political socialization.** We also noted that this learning is a lifelong process and that it takes place against the backdrop of a country's political culture, which gives a unique character to the pattern of opinions among its people.

### LONG-TERM INFLUENCES ON OPINION FORMATION

Some influences on opinion formation have a basic and enduring impact. They help to mold core beliefs, and their effect on the individual remains apparent for years.

### The Childhood Years

The family is a powerful agent of political socialization, because children begin with no political attitudes of their own and are likely to accept uncritically those of their parents.[21] Millions of adults are Republicans or Democrats today largely because they accepted their parents' party loyalty (see Figure 8-3). They now can give all sorts of reasons for preferring their party to the other. But the reasons came later in life; the loyalty came first, during childhood. The family also contributes to basic orientations that, while not directly political, have political significance. For example, the American family tends to be more egalitarian than families in other nations, and American children often have a

---

[20]James Bryce, *The American Commonwealth*, vol. 2 (New York: Macmillan, 1900), 247–254.
[21]See M. Kent Jennings and Richard Niemi, "The Transmission of Political Values from Parent to Child," *American Political Science Review* 62 (March 1968): 169–184.

Political socialization during childhood has a profound influence on the individual's basic political views. In school, children are taught love of country and flag as they learn about national heroes and historical events. (Jerry Berndt/Stock, Boston)

voice in family decisions. Such basic American values as equality, individualism, and personal freedom have their roots in patterns of family interaction.[22]

Schools are another major influence on the young, teaching them allegiance to flag and country, steeping them in the exploits of national heroes, and telling them about the superiority of the country's economic and political systems.[23]

[22]See David Easton and Jack Dennis, *Children in the Political System* (New York: McGraw-Hill, 1969); Gabriel Almond and Sidney Verba, *The Civic Culture* (Boston: Little, Brown, 1965), 276.
[23]See Robert D. Hess and Judith V. Torney, *The Development of Political Attitudes in Children* (Chicago: Aldine, 1967), 219.

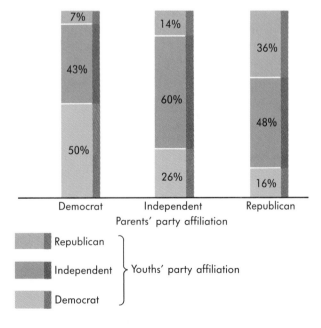

**FIGURE 8-3 Party Identification of Youths Whose Parents Are Democrats, Independents, and Republicans**
Young people usually adopt the party identification of their parents or become independents. These 1973 data are consistent with the general pattern and also show the impact of critical events on partisanship. The leading issue in 1973 was Watergate, which harmed the Republican party's image. Notice that, whereas 50% of youths of with Democratic parents were also Democrats, only 36% with Republican parents were themselves Republicans. *Source: Adapted from M. Kent Jennings and Richard G. Niemi,* Generations and Politics *(Princeton, N.J.: Princeton University Press, 1981), 91 (Table 4-2).*

Americans' sense of social equality is also developed in part through the school. Most American children, regardless of family income, attend public schools, where the curriculum is fairly standard across the nation, at least in the lower grades. By contrast, European children of working-class parents are more likely to be segregated from those of wealthier families, either by financial exclusion from upper-class private schools, as in Britain, or by early placement in vocational programs, as in West Germany.

The family and the school have their major impact on American children's basic political values and beliefs, such as their ideas about equality. Opinions on specific issues of public policy are less substantially influenced by childhood experiences.[24]

### The Adult Years

Basic beliefs acquired in childhood are often carried into adulthood. The same values impressed on American children in the home and at school are emphasized regularly by the mass media and by political leaders.[25] In addition, members of peer groups—friends, neighbors, and co-workers—frequently have similar political views.

Of course, the fact that the United States is a diverse and mobile society increases the possibility of a basic change in a person's political views, especially when childhood and adult experiences are at odds. However, individuals have psychological defenses for their ingrained beliefs: when faced with challenging situations, they can readily muster reasons for clinging to their original views. Republicans of long standing, for example, typically have more favorable opinions of *any* action of an incumbent Republican president than do longtime Democrats, and vice versa. Thus early political attachments often persist despite major changes later in life.

Dramatic political conversion is uncommon and is almost always a consequence of extraordinary changes in national conditions. Without the Great Depression, for example, Americans almost certainly would not have accepted the philosophy of Roosevelt's New Deal, with its emphasis on government intervention in the economy and on regulation of business. Critical events such as the Depression, Vietnam, and Watergate have had their greatest impact on the political thinking of younger people. Young adults are less fixed in their opinions than older people and are therefore more responsive to changing political conditions. During the Depression, for example, most longtime Republicans remained loyal to their party, whereas many younger voters with Republican backgrounds switched their support to Roosevelt's Democratic party.[26]

---

[24]Kent Tedin, "The Influence of Parents on the Political Attitudes of Adolescents," *American Political Science Review* 68 (December 1974): 1579–1592; M. Kent Jennings and Richard G. Niemi, *The Political Character of Adolescence* (Princeton, N.J.: Princeton University Press, 1974).

[25]See Murray Edelman, *Politics as Symbolic Action* (Chicago: Markham, 1971).

[26]See Kristi Andersen, *The Creation of a Democratic Majority, 1928–1936* (Chicago: University of Chicago Press, 1979); Norman H. Nie, Sidney Verba, and John R. Petrocik, *The Changing American Voter*, rev. ed. (Cambridge, Mass.: Harvard University Press, 1979), 60; Stuart Oskamp, *Attitudes and Opinions* (Englewood Cliffs, N.J.: Prentice-Hall, 1977), 131.

## SHORT-TERM INFLUENCES ON OPINION FORMATION

New problems and issues regularly emerge, and the opinions that individuals form about these developments are derived to some degree from their long-term beliefs. However, opinions on current events are also affected by short-term influences, including peers, the news media, political leaders, and new developments.

### Peers

When unsure what to think about an emerging issue, individuals sometimes turn to their peers for advice. Most people trust the views of their friends and associates. They may also be reluctant to deviate too far from what their peers think. An intriguing hypothesis holds that social pressures can prevent deviant opinions from being freely expressed. In her book *The Spiral of Silence*, Elisabeth Noelle-Neumann contends that most individuals want to conform and are afraid to speak out against a dominant opinion, particularly when an issue has a strong moral component. Thus a person who believes that whites are superior to members of other races may be unwilling to express that opinion openly, because belief in racial equality is the dominant and morally acceptable opinion.[27]

### The News Media

The news media are an increasingly important influence on public opinion, particularly in regard to Americans' perceptions of what the country's major issues are.[28] In the early fall of 1986, for example, national polls indicated that drug abuse had become the public's most salient issue. This widespread concern developed in the wake of a string of sensational news reports that drug abuse was becoming an epidemic—even though, in fact, the level of drug abuse had not increased significantly during the preceding six years. (Chapter 15 discusses this agenda-setting role of the media in detail.)

### Political Leaders

People look to political leaders, particularly presidents, as guides to opinion formation. When a leader supports a position, there are always citizens who will agree. Lyndon Johnson's decision to escalate the Vietnam war in 1965, for example, was followed by an immediate increase in public support for a stepped-up war effort. Similarly, public approval of a nuclear arms limitation agreement with the USSR rose in 1987 after President Ronald Reagan endorsed the idea.

### New Developments

Finally, public opinion on current issues is shaped by new developments. Although citizens have a remarkable capacity to believe what they want to

---

[27]See Elisabeth Noelle-Neumann, *The Spiral of Silence* (Chicago: University of Chicago Press, 1984).
[28]See Donald Shaw and Maxwell McCombs, *The Emergence of Political Issues* (St. Paul, Minn.: West, 1977).

believe about political questions, their opinions may yield when reality intrudes. Consider the case of President Gerald Ford, who quickly gained the public's confidence after he succeeded Richard Nixon in 1974. A Gallup poll indicated that 71 percent of Americans initially held a high opinion of Ford's leadership. Two months into his presidency, however, Ford pardoned Nixon for any crimes he might have committed while in office. This development caused a rapid 20-point plunge in Ford's public-approval rating.

## The Influence of Public Opinion on Policy

*Government, in the last analysis, is organized opinion. Where there is little or no public opinion, there is likely to be bad government, which sooner or later becomes autocratic government.*
W. L. Mackenzie King, Prime Minister of Canada (1927)

The question of how people acquire their political opinions is relevant to the question of the influence those opinions should have on government policy. Obviously, opinions that develop out of deeply held values and that are reached after prolonged deliberation or lengthy experience should weigh more heavily in political action than opinions that derive from, for example, a government propaganda campaign. In the latter situation, people are voicing opinions that have been placed in their heads by manipulative officials. When these opinions are then used to justify particular policies, officials are merely adding the veneer of public approval to actions they planned to take anyway. The result is not government of and by the people but government of and by the desires of those in authority.

As it happens, public opinion is not so easily manipulated in most instances. Studies of persuasion through mass communication have found that people's views are relatively resistant to change.[29] The attitudes that people bring to a situation tend to persist and to affect the formation of new opinions. Of course, the likelihood that an individual will be persuaded to change his or her opinion depends on what is at stake. Exposure to televised political advertising is more likely to influence a voter's choice of a candidate for the state legislature than his or her choice of a candidate for the presidency of the United States. But there are limits even to persuasion on less significant political choices. More voters, for example, pick their state legislator on the basis of long-standing party loyalties than on the basis of a recently televised campaign appeal.

The fundamental principle of democracy is that the people's view should prevail on public issues. The difficulty comes in putting this principle into practice. The problem is in part one of realistic expectations. A democracy is typically said to be "rule by the people" and is different from a dictatorship, which is described as "rule by a dictator." These definitions imply that what a dictator does in one system the people do in the other. But the comparison is faulty. Government by the people in a literal sense would mean that 175 million adult Americans were in charge—which is to say that no one would be in charge, because the result would be chaos.[30]

It is simply not possible for the people collectively to formulate public policies and programs. Fortunately, it is not necessary for them to do so in order to exert

[29]See Dan D. Nimmo and Keith R. Sanders, *Handbook of Political Communication* (Beverly Hills, Calif.: Sage, 1981).
[30]E. E. Schattschneider, *The Semisovereign People* (New York: Holt, Rinehart and Winston, 1980), ch.8.

Soviet leader Mikhail Gorbachev and President Ronald Reagan sign a nuclear arms limitation pact in December 1987. After Reagan had announced, two years earlier, that he favored negotiations toward such a treaty, approval of the idea increased significantly among Republicans, who tend to distrust the Soviet Union more than Democrats do. (Gamma Liaison)

a significant influence. Government in a large and complex society requires leaders who are empowered to act on behalf of the people, whose opportunities to participate are limited to voting and similar actions. The principle of democracy is fulfilled by this arrangement if officials are reasonably responsive to the public they represent. By this standard, America's government is democratic, albeit imperfectly so.

The influence of public opinion on government takes several forms (see box). Public opinion is a nearly invincible force when public support for a course of action becomes so overwhelming that the issue ceases to be debatable. Few leaders have understood this aspect of popular influence better than Franklin D. Roosevelt. "No damn politician," he reportedly said, "can ever scrap my social security program."[31] Roosevelt recognized that if social security were funded by payroll taxes, future generations of workers would feel that they had rightfully earned their retirement benefits and therefore would fight to maintain them. Few politicians have dared even to suggest major cutbacks in social security. Barry Goldwater's problems in the 1964 presidential campaign were greatly magnified by the public outcry that followed his tentative suggestion that participation in social security be made voluntary.

Within the limits of what public opinion allows, policymakers have room to maneuver. Here public opinion is a guiding and sanctioning force: it affects what representatives can reasonably consider doing, but less often dictates their precise course of action. When Reagan became president in 1981, he was expected, like all presidents of the nuclear age, to keep tensions between the United States and the Soviet Union under control. But the means by which Reagan would achieve this goal was more or less his to decide. Reagan chose a

[31]Quoted in Arthur M. Schlesinger, Jr., *The Coming of the New Deal* (Boston: Houghton Mifflin, 1958), 309.

# WAYS IN WHICH PUBLIC OPINION CAN AFFECT PUBLIC POLICY

Blocking action | Existing opinion supports an existing policy so strongly that policymakers are prevented from changing the policy significantly. The social security program is an example.

Forcing action | Existing opinion supports a course of action so strongly that officials have little choice but to take that specific course. This form of influence is relatively rare, but includes the declaration of war against Japan following the bombing of Pearl Harbor in 1941.

Defining acceptable boundaries | Existing opinions establish a boundary within which officials can act but beyond which they dare not go. They are not compelled to act but have discretion within the boundary set by opinions. An example is seen in opinions on U.S. involvement in Central America during the 1980s: public opinion precluded the use of U.S. combat troops in the region, but officials had the choice of supporting the Contras.

Response to policy | As a policy develops, opinions about its effectiveness emerge and generate support for or opposition to the policy. Strong opposition forces a change in the policy. An example is the public's response in the late 1960s and early 1970s to the Vietnam conflict.

Response to opinion | Because of their concern with reelection or desire to represent public views, officials actively seek policies that their constituents are likely to favor. An example would be protective trade legislation sought by a representative on behalf of a constituency interest.

defense buildup, arguing that the Soviets would not dare to engage a militarily strong United States.

The power of public opinion is also apparent after policy initiatives are undertaken. To view public opinion simply as a "cause" of what government does is to overlook the public's capacity to pass judgment on the choices its representatives make. President Johnson's Vietnam policy is a prime example. Johnson was not forced by public opinion to increase U.S. involvement in the war, but once he had done so, he had to deal with the public's expectation that the war would be won. In the end, it was the American people, not the generals and politicians, who concluded that Johnson's policy was a failure and a change of leadership was needed. The recognition by elected leaders that they must satisfy public opinion is a powerful constraint on their actions.

Available evidence indicates that U.S. officials are quite responsive to public concerns. In a study covering 1935 to 1979, Benjamin Page and Robert Shapiro found considerable congruence between changes in public opinion and subsequent changes in public policy, particularly on highly visible issues about which opinion change was large and stable. They examined 357 cases of opinion change and then determined what policy change, if any, ensued during the following year.[32] The results of their study are summarized in Table 8-3.

Overall, Page and Shapiro found that policy changed in the same direction as opinion change in 43 percent of the cases and changed in the opposite direction in only 22 percent of the cases. Even in the latter cases, the researchers found that the policy change was nearly always minor in scope. Page and Shapiro concluded, "When Americans' policy preferences shift, it is likely that congruent changes in policy will follow."[33]

[32]Benjamin I. Page and Robert Y. Shapiro, "Effects of Public Opinion on Policy," *American Political Science Review* 77 (March 1983): 175–190.
[33]Ibid., 189.

**TABLE 8-3  Congruence between Changes in Public Opinion and Changes in Policy, 1935–1979**

|  | *All Cases* | *Only Cases Involving a Policy Change* |
|---|---|---|
| Public opinion and policy changed in the same direction | 43% | 66% |
| Public opinion and policy changed in opposite directions | 22 | 34 |
| No policy change | 33 | |
| Unclassified | 2 | |
|  | 100% | 100% |

*Note:* Each case is an instance in which public policy preferences changed significantly, according to repeated administration of identical survey items.

SOURCE: Benjamin I. Page and Robert Y. Shapiro, "Effects of Public Opinion on Policy," *American Political Science Review* 77 (March 1983): 178.

However, Page and Shapiro caution against jumping to the conclusion that the policy process is fully responsive to public opinion.[34] First, the issues they studied were relatively salient. On less visible issues, the general public's views might be much less influential than those expressed by organized lobbying groups. Second, the possibility exists that officials sometimes manipulate opinion in order to make it appear that the public supports actions that these officials intended to take anyway. Finally, officials may respond to public opinion with token measures that are designed merely to appear to reflect what the people want. Later chapters will address these various subjects, and three of the closing chapters will examine directly the impact of public opinion in particular policy areas: the economy (Chapter 26), social welfare (27), and national security (28).

[34]Ibid.

## Summary

Public opinion can be defined as those opinions held by ordinary citizens which government takes into account in making its decisions. Public officials have many ways of assessing public opinion, such as the outcomes of elections, but have increasingly come to rely on public opinion polls. There are many possible sources of error in polls, and surveys sometimes present a misleading portrayal of the public's views. However, a properly conducted poll can provide an accurate indication of what the public is thinking and can dissuade political leaders from thinking that the views of the most vocal citizens (such as demonstrators and letter writers) are also the views of the broader public.

Individual opinions gain power to the degree that others share a similar view. Public opinion thus has the force of numbers. A major source of common opinions among Americans is their cultural beliefs, such as individualism, which result in a range of acceptable and unacceptable policy alternatives. Agreement can also stem from a shared ideology, although most citizens do not have a strong and consistent attachment to liberal or conservative policies. Finally, individuals share opinions as a result of shared personal circumstances, notably religion, income, region, race, gender, partisanship, and education level.

The process by which individuals acquire their political opinions is called political socialization. During childhood the family and schools are important sources of basic political attitudes, such as beliefs about the parties and the nature of the U.S. political and economic systems. Many of the basic orientations that Americans acquire during childhood remain with them in adulthood; but socialization is a continuing process. Major shifts in opinion during adulthood are usually the consequence of changing political conditions; for example, the Great Depression of the 1930s was the catalyst for wholesale changes in Americans' opinions on the government's economic role. There are also short-term fluctuations in opinion that result from new political issues, problems, and events. Individuals' opinions in these cases are affected by prior beliefs, peers, political leaders, and the news media. Events themselves are also a significant short-term influence on opinions.

Public opinion has a significant influence on government but seldom determines exactly what government will do in a particular instance. Public opinion serves to constrain the policy choices of officials. Some policy actions are beyond the range of possibility because the public will not accept change in existing policy or will not seriously consider policy that seems clearly at odds with basic American values. Evidence indicates that officials are reasonably attentive to public opinion on highly visible and controversial issues of public policy.

## Major Concepts

| | |
|---|---|
| conservatism | probability sample |
| ideology | public opinion |
| liberalism | public opinion poll |
| political socialization | sample |
| population | sampling error |

## Suggested Readings

Backstrom, Charles H., and Gerald Hursh-Cesar. *Survey Research*, 2d ed. New York: Macmillan, 1981. A how-to-do-it book on public opinion polling.

Free, Lloyd A., and Hadley Cantril. *The Political Beliefs of Americans*. New Brunswick, N.J.: Rutgers University Press, 1967. A valuable, though somewhat dated, assessment of Americans' political opinions.

Graber, Doris. *Mass Media and American Politics*, 2d ed. Washington, D.C.: Congressional Quarterly Press, 1984. A review of the mass media's role in American politics.

Hess, Robert D., and Judith V. Torney. *The Development of Political Attitudes in Children*. Chicago: Aldine, 1967. A study of how children learn about politics.

Key, V. O., Jr. *Public Opinion and American Democracy*. New York: Knopf, 1961. A thorough examination of public opinion and its relation to the governing process.

Lippmann, Walter. *Public Opinion*. New York: Free Press, 1965. The classic analysis of public opinion (originally published in 1922).

McCloskey, Herbert, and John Zaller. *The American Ethos*. Cambridge, Mass.: Harvard University Press, 1984. A study of how Americans' ideals underpin capitalism and democracy and narrow the range of political choices.

Miller, Warren E., et al. *American National Election Studies Data Sourcebook*. Cambridge, Mass.: Harvard University Press, 1980. A compendium of the results of opinion surveys conducted by the University of Michigan's famed Survey Research Center.

Noelle-Neumann, Elisabeth. *The Spiral of Silence*. Chicago: University of Chicago Press, 1984. An intriguing theory of how public opinion is formed and muted.

Weisberg, Herbert, and Bruce D. Bowen. *An Introduction to Survey Research and Data Analysis*. San Francisco: W. H. Freeman, 1977. A readable account of how public opinion polls are conducted and analyzed.

# Chapter 9

## POLITICAL PARTICIPATION: INVOLVING THE PEOPLE

*We are concerned in public affairs, but immersed in our private ones.*
*Walter Lippmann[1]*

The stakes in the 1986 congressional elections were high. The Republicans had only a narrow 53–47 majority in the U.S. Senate. The party that achieved control of the Senate would be able to decide the direction of national policy during the Reagan presidency's final two years. "I was not elected to be a six-year president," Reagan declared during his frequent campaign appearances on behalf of Republican Senate candidates. As it turned out, however, the voters in 1986 ignored Reagan's pleas and gave control of the Senate to the Democrats, who gained a 55–45 majority. Yet a more compelling fact about the 1986 elections may be that the outcome was determined by the mere 37 percent of adults who bothered to vote. Despite the insistence of political leaders on the importance of the election's outcome, despite a concerted get-out-the-vote campaign by public-service groups and the news media, and despite an unprecedented level of campaign spending (more money was spent per voter than in any previous election in the nation's history), fewer than four out of ten adult citizens voted.

Voting is a form of **political participation**—a sharing in activities designed to influence public policy and leadership. Political participation involves other activities in addition to voting, such as joining political parties and interest groups, writing to elected officials, demonstrating for political causes, and giving money to political candidates.

[1]Walter Lippmann, *Public Opinion* (1922; New York: Free Press, 1965), 36.

Voting is the most common form of political participation, although only about half of eligible Americans vote, even in a presidential election. (Mark Antman/The Image Works)

Democratic societies are distinguished by their emphasis on citizen participation. The concept of self-government rests on the idea that ordinary people have a right, even an obligation, to involve themselves in the affairs of state. A political system that claims to operate in the public's interest is not necessarily a truly democratic system; citizens must also be given meaningful opportunities to participate in the process. From this perspective, the extent of political participation—how much and by whom—is a measure of how fully democratic a society is.[2]

The question of participation also extends to the reasons people are politically involved or not involved. If differences in degree of participation are of a purely individual nature, there is less cause for concern than if the differences have a systemic base. It is one thing if political participation is like attendance at a rock concert, which is mostly a matter of individual taste and proximity, and quite another if participation is like attendance at an elite prep school, which is mostly a matter of social privilege. A democratic political system implies that society will not place substantial barriers in the way of those who want to participate.

As we will see in this chapter, differences in the extent of political participation among Americans are explained by both individual and systemic factors, although the latter are more influential in the United States than in most other Western democracies. One result is that the participation rate in U.S. elections is less than that of other countries, particularly among citizens of lower income and less education. The major points made in this chapter are the following:

★ *Voter turnout in U.S. elections is low in comparison with that of other democratic nations.* The reasons for this difference include the nature of U.S. election laws, particularly those pertaining to registration requirements and the scheduling of elections, but the fundamental reason seems to be Americans' belief that election outcomes are not very important to their lives. This view is especially prevalent among people with lower incomes and less education.

★ *Most citizens do not participate actively in politics in ways other than voting.* Only a small proportion of Americans can be classified as political activists.

[2]Sidney Verba and Norman H. Nie. *Participation in America: Political Democracy and Social Equality* (New York: Harper & Row, 1972), 1.

★ *Most Americans make a sharp distinction between their personal lives and national life.* This attitude reduces their incentive to participate and contributes to a pattern of participation dominated by citizens with higher levels of income and education.

## Voter Participation

At the nation's founding, **suffrage**—the right to vote—was restricted to property-owning males. Tom Paine ridiculed this policy in *Common Sense*. Observing that a man whose only item of property was a jackass would lose his right to vote if the jackass died, Paine asked, "Now tell me, which was the voter, the man or the jackass?" It was not until the 1820s that a majority of states had extended suffrage to propertyless white males, a change made possible by their continued demand for the vote and by the realization on the part of the wealthy that the nation's abundance and openness were natural protections against an assault on property rights by the voting poor.

Women did not secure the vote until 1920, with the ratification of the Nineteenth Amendment. In the 1870s Susan B. Anthony tried to vote in her hometown of Rochester, New York, asserting that she had a right to do so as a U.S. citizen. The men who placed her under arrest charged her with "illegal voting" and insisted that her proper place was in the home. By 1920, men had run out of pretexts for keeping the vote from women. The best argument that the antisuffragists could muster was that women should not vote because they had no voting experience. Senator Wendell Phillips expressed the pro-suffrage view: "One of two things is true: either woman is like man—and if she is, then a ballot based on brains belongs to her as well as to him. Or she is different, and then man does not know how to vote for her as she herself does."[3]

*The right of citizens of the United States to vote shall not be denied or abridged by the United States or by any State on account of sex.*

        U.S. Constitution,
        Nineteenth Amendment

[3]Quoted in Ralph Volney Harlow, *The Growth of the United States* (New York: Henry Holt, 1943), 312.

After a hard-fought, decades-long campaign, American women finally won the right to vote in 1920 (Culver Pictures)

*The right of citizens of the United States to vote shall not be denied or abridged by the United States or by any State on account of race, color, or previous condition of servitude.*

U.S. Constitution,
Fifteenth Amendment

Black Americans had to wait nearly fifty years longer than women to be granted full suffrage. Blacks seemed to have won the right to vote with passage of the Fifteenth Amendment after the Civil War, but as we saw in Chapter 7, they were effectively disenfranchised in the South by a number of electoral tricks, including poll taxes, literacy tests, and whites-only primary elections. The poll tax was a fee of several dollars that had to be paid before one could register to vote. Since most blacks in the South were too poor to pay it, the poll tax barred them from voting. Not until the ratification of the Twenty-fourth Amendment in 1964 was the poll tax outlawed in national elections. Supreme Court decisions and the Voting Rights Act of 1965 swept away other legal barriers to fuller participation by black Americans.

Today virtually any American—rich or poor, man or woman, black or white—who is determined to vote can legally and actually do so. Americans attach great importance to the power of their votes. They claim that voting is their greatest source of influence over political leadership and their strongest protection against an uncaring or corrupt government.[4] In view of this attitude and the historical determination of various groups to gain voting rights, the surprising fact is that Americans are not enthusiastic voters. Millions of them choose not to vote regularly, a habit that sets them apart from citizens of other Western democracies.

## FACTORS IN VOTER TURNOUT: THE UNITED STATES IN COMPARATIVE PERSPECTIVE

**Voter turnout** is the proportion of persons of voting age who actually vote in a given election. Since 1920 the level of turnout in presidential elections has never

[4]See Gerald Pomper with Susan Lederman, *Elections in America,* 2d ed. (New York: Longman, 1980), ch. 1; Jack Dennis, "Support for the Institution of Elections by the Mass Public," *American Political Science Review* 64 (1970): 819–835.

---

**★ HOW THE UNITED STATES COMPARES**

**Voter Turnout**
The United States ranks near the bottom among the world's democracies in the percentage of eligible citizens who vote in national elections. One reason for this low voter turnout is that individual Americans are responsible for registering to vote, whereas in most other democracies, voters are automatically registered by government officials. In addition, unlike some other democracies, the United States does not encourage voting by penalizing citizens who do not participate, as by fining them.

| Country | Voter Turnout | Personal Registration? | Penalty for Not Voting? |
|---------|---------------|------------------------|-------------------------|
| Italy | 94.0% | No | Yes |
| Austria | 89.3 | No | No |
| Belgium | 88.7 | No | Yes |
| Sweden | 86.8 | No | No |
| Greece | 84.9 | No | Yes |
| Netherlands | 84.7 | No | Yes |
| Australia | 83.1 | Yes | Yes |
| Denmark | 82.1 | No | No |
| Norway | 81.8 | No | No |
| West Germany | 81.1 | No | No |
| New Zealand | 78.5 | Yes | No |
| France | 78.0 | Yes | No |
| Great Britain | 76.0 | No | No |
| Canada | 67.4 | No | No |
| United States | 52.6 | Yes | No |

SOURCE: David Glass, Peverill Squire, and Raymond Wolfinger, "Voter Turnout: An International Comparison," *Public Opinion,* December/January 1984, 50.

Percent of voting-age population who voted

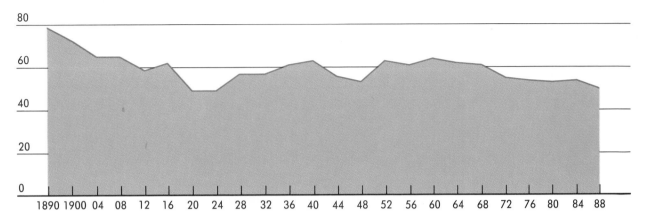

exceeded 63 percent; thus a third or more of voting-age persons stayed away from the polls at each election (see Figure 9-1). Turnout is even lower in nonpresidential elections: at no time since 1920 has it reached 50 percent. When a mere 37 percent of adults voted in the high-stakes congressional elections of 1986, the cartoonist Rigby showed a stray cat wandering into a polling place and an election clerk asking it hopefully, "Are you registered?"[5] The voting rate in U.S. elections is always low enough so that people who do not vote greatly outnumber the voters who provide the winning candidate's margin of victory. In the 1968 presidential election Richard Nixon defeated Hubert Humphrey by just 510,635 votes, while 62 million adult Americans did not participate.

Nonvoting is far more prevalent in the United States than in nearly all other democracies. In recent decades, turnout in major national elections has averaged less than 60 percent in the United States, compared with more than 90 percent in Italy, more than 80 percent in Australia and West Germany, and more than 70 percent in Great Britain and Canada.[6] The major reasons that Americans vote at such a comparatively low rate include registration requirements, the frequency of elections, and the lack of clear-cut differentiation between the major political parties.[*]

**FIGURE 9-1 Voter Turnout in Presidential Elections, 1896–1988**
Voter turnout declined after registration was instituted at the turn of the century and has stayed low for most national elections ever since. *Source: Data for 1896–1968 from U.S. Bureau of Census,* Historical Statistics of the United States, Colonial Times to 1970, Part 2 *(Washington, D.C.: U.S. Government Printing Office, 1975), 1071; data for 1972-1988, Federal Election Commission.*

## Registration Requirements

Before Americans are allowed to vote, they must be registered—that is, their names must appear on an official list of eligible voters. **Registration** began around 1900 as a way of preventing voters from casting more than one ballot during an election. Such fraudulent activities had become a favorite tactic of political party machines in cities where residents were not personally known to poll watchers. However, the extra effort involved in registering placed an added

---

[*]As some analysts have pointed out, the disparity in turnout between the United States and other nations is not so great as these official voting rates indicate. Some nations calculate turnout solely on the basis of eligible voters, while the United States bases its figures on all adults, including ineligibles, such as noncitizens. Nevertheless, even when such statistical disparities are corrected, turnout in U.S. elections remains low in comparison with that of nearly every other Western democracy.

[5]Example from Gus Tyler, "One Cheer for the Democrats," *New Leader*, November 3, 1986, 6.
[6]G. Bingham Powell, "Voting Turnout in Thirty Democracies," in Richard Rose, ed., *Electoral Participation: A Comparative Analysis* (Beverly Hills, Calif.: Sage, 1980), 6.

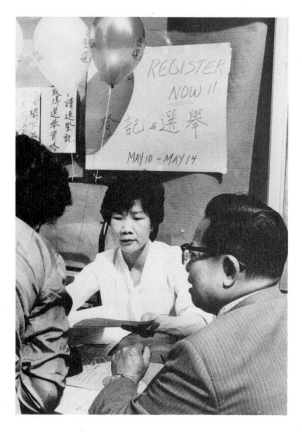

Some states have eased their registration requirements, allowing prospective voters to register at tables set up on street corners, in shopping malls, and at other accessible locations. (Bettye Lane/Photo Researchers)

burden on honest citizens. Turnout in U.S. elections declined steadily after registration was instituted.[7]

Although other democracies also require registration, they place this responsibility on government. In European nations, public officials have the duty to enroll citizens on registration lists. The United States—in keeping with its individualistic culture—is the only democracy in which registration is the individual's responsibility.[8] In addition, registration laws are established by the state governments, and some states make it relatively difficult for citizens to qualify. Registration periods and locations are usually not highly publicized, and many citizens simply do not know when or where to register.[9] Eligibility can also be a problem. In most states, a citizen must establish legal residency by living in the same place for a minimum period, usually thirty days but as long as fifty days, before becoming eligible to register.

States with a tradition of lenient registration laws generally have a higher turnout than other states. Maine, Minnesota, Oregon, and Wisconsin allow

[7]Philip E. Converse, "Change in the American Electorate," in Philip E. Converse and Angus Campbell, eds., *The Human Meaning of Social Change* (New York: Russell Sage Foundation, 1972), 281; see also Stanley Kelley, Jr., Richard E. Ayres, and William G. Bowen, "Registration and Voting: Putting First Things First," *American Political Science Review* 61 (June 1967): 359–379. For insights into the impact on electoral behavior of another reform, the Australian ballot, see Jerrold D. Rusk, "The Effect of the Australian Ballot Reform on Split Ticket Voting: 1876–1908," *American Political Science Review* 64 (December 1970): 1220–1238.
[8]Ivor Crewe, "Electoral Participation," in David Butler, Howard R. Penniman, and Austin Ranney, eds., *Democracy at the Polls* (Washington, D.C.: American Enterprise Institute, 1981), 249.
[9]Philip E. Converse with Richard Niemi, "Non-voting among Young Adults in the United States," in William J. Crotty et al., eds., *Political Parties and Political Behavior* (Boston: Allyn & Bacon, 1971), 456.

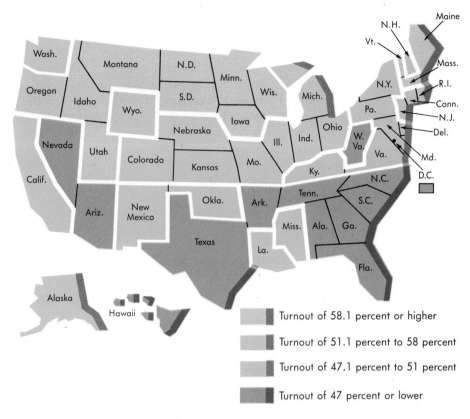

FIGURE 9-2 State-by-State Voter Turnout in the Presidential Election of 1988 Southern states have a tradition of more restrictive registration laws and, even today, they tend to have the lowest rates of voter turnout. *Source: U.S. Bureau of the Census.*

Turnout of 58.1 percent or higher

Turnout of 51.1 percent to 58 percent

Turnout of 47.1 percent to 51 percent

Turnout of 47 percent or lower

people to register at their polling place on election day, and these states are among the leaders in voter turnout. Those states that have erected the most barriers are in the South, where restrictive registration was originally intended to prevent black people from voting. These historical differences continue to be reflected in state voter turnout levels (see Figure 9-2).

It has been estimated that if all states adopted simple registration procedures —for example, lengthening the registration period, allowing weekend and evening registration, and locating registration facilities near workplaces—voter turnout would increase by about 9 percent.[10] In a presidential election, this increase would mean an additional 10 million voters.

Why, then, have not all states simplified their registration procedures? One reason is that many state and local officials, regardless of what they may say publicly, are not very interested in adding lots of new voters to the registration lists. Poor and less-educated citizens are the ones most easily discouraged by restrictive registration laws, and their influx into the electorate could alter the political balance of power in a state, county, or city. The same self-interest prompts officials in many college towns to resist student registration. For example, college students in Syracuse, New York, must complete a lengthy questionnaire to establish their eligibility to register. The procedure discourages most students from trying to register in Syracuse and allows local officials to disqualify other students on the basis of "wrong" responses on the questionnaire. Of 900 students who applied to register in Syracuse in 1986, only 150 were permitted to do so.

[10]Raymond E. Wolfinger and Steven J. Rosenstone, *Who Votes?* (New Haven, Conn.: Yale University Press, 1980), 78–79.

## Frequency of Elections

Another factor that reduces voter turnout is the frequency with which Americans are asked to vote. No other democracy has elections for the lower chamber of its national legislature (the equivalent of the U.S. House of Representatives) as often as every two years, and none schedules elections for chief executive as often as every four years.[11] In addition, elections of state and local officials in the United States are often scheduled separately from national races. Two-thirds of the states elect their governors in nonpresidential election years,[12] and 60 percent of U.S. cities hold elections of municipal officials in odd-numbered years.[13]

This staggered scheduling reflects in some cases a deliberate effort by state and local officials to insulate their election races from the possible effects of other campaigns. During Franklin D. Roosevelt's four terms as president, for example, Republicans in several states, including New York and Connecticut, backed constitutional amendments that required gubernatorial races to be held in nonpresidential years. The purpose was to prevent other Democratic candidates from riding into office on Roosevelt's coattails.

The frequency of U.S. elections reduces turnout by increasing the effort required to participate in all of them.[14] Most European nations have less frequent elections, and the responsibility of voting is thus less burdensome. Many European nations also schedule their elections on Sundays or declare election day to be a national holiday, thus making it more convenient for working people to vote. In the United States, elections are traditionally held on Tuesdays, and most people must vote before or after work.

The contrast with European practice is especially marked in the case of primary elections. The United States is the only democratic nation in which party nominess are commonly chosen by voters through primary elections rather than by party leaders.[15] Consequently, Americans are asked to vote twice to fill a single office. Many voters skip the primaries, preferring to vote just once, in the general election. In contested statewide and presidential primaries, the average voter turnout is about 30 percent, substantially lower than the turnout in general elections.

## Lack of Party Differentiation

An additional explanation for low voter turnout in the United States has to do with voters' perception that there is not much difference between the major political parties. Roughly a third of Americans claim that it is largely irrelevant whether the Republicans or the Democrats gain control of government.[16] This belief is not entirely unfounded. The two major American political parties do not normally differ greatly in their policies. Each party depends on citizens of all

[11]Crewe, "Electoral Participation," 230.
[12]Malcolm Jewell and David Olson, *American State Politics and Elections* (Homewood, Ill.: Irwin Press, 1978), 50.
[13]A. Karnig and B. Walter, "Municipal Elections," in *Municipal Yearbook, 1977* (Washington, D.C.: International City Management Assn., 1977).
[14]Richard Boyd, "Decline of U.S. Voter Turnout," *American Politics Quarterly* 9 (April 1981): 142.
[15]Austin Ranney, "Candidate Selection," in Butler, Penniman, and Ranney, *Democracy at the Polls,* 88.
[16]Angus Campbell, Philip E. Converse, Warren E. Miller, and Donald E. Stokes, *The American Voter* (New York: Wiley, 1960), 104. More recent studies show no significant change in this attitude.

economic interests and social backgrounds for support; consequently, neither party can afford to take an extreme position that would alienate any sizable segment of the electorate. For example, both parties share a commitment to the private enterprise system and to a basic social security system.

Parties in Europe tend to divide more sharply over economic policies. There the choice between a conservative party and a socialist party may mean a choice between private and government ownership of major industries. Studies indicate that turnout is higher in nations whose political parties represent clear-cut alternatives, particularly when religious or class divisions are involved. Conversely, turnout is lower when, as in the United States, a nation's parties compete for the loyalty of voters of all religions and classes.[17] The economist Anthony Downs argues that it is perfectly "rational" for citizens to abstain from voting when the parties do not differ sharply. In this situation, the personal "costs" of voting (that is, the time and effort involved) can exceed the expected personal "benefits" of voting for a particular candidate.[18]

## WHY SOME AMERICANS VOTE AND OTHERS DON'T

Even though turnout is lower in the United States than in other democracies, some Americans do vote in all or nearly all elections. But other Americans seldom or never vote. What accounts for such *individual* differences? The major reasons have to do with citizens' sense of civic duty, age, and socioeconomic status.

### Sense of Civic Duty and Degree of Interest

Regular voters are characterized by a strong sense of **civic duty**—that is, they regard participation in elections as one of the responsibilities of citizenship. On the night of the 1984 presidential election, early returns from the East indicated that Ronald Reagan would win reelection by a landslide, yet regular voters in the West were undeterred. Although they knew that their votes would not affect the outcome, they voted anyway in order to fulfill their duty as citizens.

*Your every voter, as surely as your chief magistrate, exercises a public trust.*

Grover Cleveland

A sense of civic duty is an attitude that most individuals acquire during their political socialization in childhood and adolescence. When parents vote regularly and take an interest in politics, their children are likely to grow up believing that voting is an obligation of citizenship. Schools reinforce this belief by stressing the value of civic involvement. This sense of duty can be thwarted, especially by political disillusionment. Turnout in U.S. presidential elections dropped by 10 percentage points between 1960 and 1980, a time when Americans' trust and confidence in governmental institutions and parties declined under the onslaught of the Vietnam war, the Watergate scandal, economic stagnation, and other national problems. Believing that government was beyond their control, some citizens concluded that participation was pointless.[19]

Citizens who seldom or never vote typically have a weak sense of civic responsibility and believe that government is not interested in the views of

[17]Crewe, "Electoral Participation," 251–253; Powell, "Voting Turnout."
[18]Anthony Downs, *An Economic Theory of Democracy* (New York: Harper & Row, 1957), ch. 14.
[19]Howard L. Reiter, "Why Is Turnout Down?" *Public Opinion Quarterly* 43 (Fall 1979): 297–311; see also Paul R. Abramson, John H. Aldrich, and David W. Rhode, *Change and Continuity in the 1980 Elections* (Washington, D.C.: Congressional Quarterly Press, 1982).

Older Americans have more deeply ingrained political views and are more likely to vote than are younger citizens. (James Kamp/Black Star)

people like themselves.[20] About half of unregistered citizens claim that they would be wasting their time by participating, since public policy would not be affected anyway.[21] More significant, some people do not vote because they have no interest in politics. Just as some people would not attend the Superbowl if it were free and being played across the street, some people would not bother to vote if a ballot were delivered to their door.

## Age

Voter turnout varies with age. Younger people are less likely to have the political concern that can come with homeownership, permanent employment, and a family.[22] In presidential elections, the voting rate among citizens under the age of thirty is 15 percentage points lower than that among older citizens. Failure to vote among the young helps to explain the 10-percentage-point drop in turnout in presidential elections between 1960 and 1980: the postwar "baby boom" resulted in an abnormally large number of young people eligible to vote in the 1960s and 1970s, and the trend was exaggerated when the Twenty-sixth Amendment (ratified in 1971) gave eighteen-year-olds the right to vote.[23]

## Socioeconomic Status

Turnout is also strongly related to socioeconomic status—that is, level of education and income (see Figure 9-3). Americans at the bottom of the

[20]See, for example, Norman H. Nie, G. Bingham Powell, and Kenneth Prewitt, "Social Structure and Political Participation," *American Political Science Review* 63 (September 1969).
[21]U.S. Bureau of the Census, *Current Population Reports,* ser. P-20, no. 344 (Washington, D.C.: U.S. Government Printing Office, 1979).
[22]Verba and Nie, *Participation in America,* 139.
[23]Boyd, "Decline of U.S. Voter Turnout," 136. The trend toward increased turnout between 1920 and 1960 supports Boyd's explanation. The period was marked by a decline in the birth rate, particularly during the Depression of the 1930s.

---

# VOTING AMONG EIGHTEEN- TO TWENTY-YEAR-OLDS

During the Vietnam war, men aged eighteen and over were eligible to be drafted into military service, yet were not eligible to vote in many states if they were under twenty-one. A slogan became familiar: "If someone is old enough to die for his country, he is old enough to vote." Bowing to the pressure for a constitutional amendment to lower the voting age, Congress enacted the Twenty-sixth Amendment in early 1971. Ratified by the states on July 5, 1971, the amendment reads: "The right of citizens of the United States, who are eighteen years of age or older, to vote shall not be denied or abridged by the United States or any state on account of age." The irony is that, despite the hard-fought effort to secure the vote for young adults, most of them do not bother to exercise their right. Less than half of Americans between eighteen and twenty-one voted in the 1988 presidential election.

---

socioeconomic ladder are about one-third less likely to vote in presidential elections than those at the top.[24] The difference is even larger in primaries and in nonpresidential elections.[25]

In European democracies, socioeconomic status does not affect turnout to such a high degree. Europeans of lower income and education levels are encouraged to participate by class-based organizations and traditions—strong socialist parties, politically oriented trade unions, and class-based political ideologies.[26] In Britain, for example, the Labour party emerged with the growth of trade unionism and enrolled many manual laborers. Since 1918 the Labour party's membership card has carried a broad pledge "to secure for the workers by hand or by brain the full fruits of their industry." When the Labour party came to power in 1945, it made good on this promise to the working class by placing key industries under government ownership and adopting new social-welfare programs. A major policy was government-paid medical care for all Britons, which was of particular benefit to lower-income people.

[24]Wolfinger and Rosenstone, *Who Votes?* 17–21.
[25]Nelson W. Polsby, *Consequences of Party Reform* (New York: Oxford University Press, 1983), 158.
[26]Verba and Nie, *Participation in America*, 340.

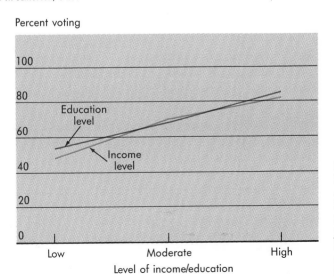

Percent voting

FIGURE 9-3 Voter Turnout and Levels of Income and Education Americans of lower income and less education are much less likely to vote. *Source: Adapted from Raymond E. Wolfinger and Steven J. Rosenstone, Who Votes? (New Haven, Conn.: Yale University Press, 1986), 17, 21.*

★ ANALYZE THE ISSUE

**Changes in Forms of Political Participation**
Elections are the traditional means by which citizens try to exert political influence. Yet as citizens can vote only yes or no on candidates, elections do not give voters much flexibility of choice. Does this fact lessen any concern you may have about low voter turnout? Add another fact: as voting has declined, some other forms of political activity that give citizens more control have increased. These alternatives include going to court over policy issues and informing public officials of opinions on a policy controversy. Some analysts suggest that the United States is shifting from a representative democracy to a participatory one. Does this idea seem plausible to you?

Although social class has declined in importance, European political traditions and institutions continue to encourage lower-class voter participation in ways that the U.S. political system does not.[27] The United States does not have, and never has had, a major socialist or labor party.[28] The Democratic party by and large represents poorer Americans, but their interests tend to be subordinated to the party's concern for the American middle class, which, because of its size and voting regularity, is the key to victory in U.S. elections.

Only during the Great Depression was the Democratic party squarely behind working-class interests. In response to social security, public works projects, and other class-based Democratic programs, turnout rose sharply among lower-income citizens.[29] Their voting rate stayed high throughout the 1950s because the New Deal agenda remained the focus of domestic policy debate. As class-based appeals declined after 1960, turnout among lower-class citizens dropped sharply. By the early 1980s, turnout among those at the bottom of the socioeconomic ladder had dropped by 25 percent from its 1960 level. Turnout at the top declined by only 4 percent. Today barely two-fifths of unemployed and working-class Americans vote even in a presidential election.[30]

## Other Forms of Political Participation

Voting is an unrivaled form of citizen participation. Free and open elections are the defining characteristic of democratic government,[31] and thus voting is

[27]Mark Kesselman and Joel Kreiger, *European Politics in Transition* (Lexington, Mass.: Heath, 1987), 87.
[28]Arthur T. Hadley, *The Empty Polling Booth* (Englewood Cliffs, N.J.: Prentice-Hall, 1978), 40.
[29]Seymour Martin Lipset, *Political Man* (Garden City, N.Y. Doubleday/Anchor, 1963), 194.
[30]Walter Dean Burnham, "The Class Gap," *New Republic*, May 9, 1988, 30, 32.
[31]Richard Rose and Harve Mossawir, "Voting and Elections: A Functional Analysis," *Political Studies Quarterly* 15 (1967): 173.

**TABLE 9-1  Rate of Political Participation in the United States, by Type of Activity**

| Type of Political Activity | Percent |
| --- | --- |
| Report regularly voting in presidential elections | 72% |
| Report always voting in local elections | 47 |
| Active in at least one organization involved in community problems | 32 |
| Have worked with others to solve community problems | 30 |
| Have attempted to persuade others to vote similarly | 28 |
| Have actively worked for a party or candidate | 26 |
| Have contacted a local government official about an issue or problem | 20 |
| Have attended at least one political meeting in last three years | 19 |
| Have contacted a state or national government official about an issue or problem | 18 |
| Have formed a group or organization to solve some community problem | 14 |
| Have contributed money to a party or candidate | 13 |
| Currently a member of a political club or organization | 8 |

SOURCE: Sidney Verba and Norman H. Nie, *Participation in America: Political Democracy and Social Equality* (New York: Harper & Row, 1972), 31.

Taking political participation a step beyond voting, these volunteers are telephoning prospective voters to solicit support for their candidate. (Owen Franken)

regarded as the most basic duty of citizenship. Voting is also the only form of citizen participation engaged in by a majority of adults in every democratic country.[32] Nevertheless, voting is not the only political activity in which citizens engage. They can also contribute money or time to a campaign, lobby public officials, and join political organizations.

## THE EXTENT OF POLITICAL ACTIVISM

In terms other than voter turnout, Americans participate in the political process more than Europeans tend to do.[33] However, other forms of participation are more demanding than voting and less imbued with notions of civic responsibility,[34] and the proportion of Americans who are politically active is still relatively small (see Table 9-1). Verba and Nie have identified six categories of citizens according to level and type of participation:[35]

**1.** *Inactives* (22 percent of population): They take virtually no part in politics; they seldom or never even vote.

[32]Joseph Schumpeter, *Capitalism, Socialism, and Democracy* (New York: Harper Torchbooks, 1950), 269
[33]Samuel H. Barnes and Max Kaase, *Political Action: Mass Participation in Five Western Democracies* (Beverly Hills, Calif.: Sage, 1979), 168–169.
[34]W. Russell Neuman, *The Paradox of Mass Politics* (Cambridge, Mass.: Harvard University Press, 1986), 176.
[35]Verba and Nie, *Participation in America,* 78–81.

2. *Voting specialists* (21 percent): They vote regularly or occasionally but are otherwise politically inactive.
3. *Parochialists* (4 percent): They confine their political activities to occasional contacts with public officials over personal problems.
4. *Communalists* (20 percent): They are active in cooperative community groups (e.g., Lions Club, hospital auxiliary) but dislike the conflict-ridden atmosphere of politics and thus do not participate in politics per se (except for voting).
5. *Campaigners* (15 percent): They participate in political parties or other election-related activities.
6. *Complete activists* (11 percent): They take an active role in both community organizations and political organizations.

Citizens in the first four categories are not highly active in politics. Verba and Nie's final two categories, totaling 26 percent of voting-age adults, include the real political activists. However, that 26 percent figure substantially overestimates the number of true activists. The "campaigner" and "complete activist" categories include citizens who once actively participated in politics but no longer do so and citizens whose involvement is marginal—for example, an individual whose sole participatory act is to serve as a poll watcher on election day. When political activism is defined more rigorously to exclude previously or marginally active participants, the proportion of highly involved citizens drops sharply. W. Russell Neuman concludes: "Roughly speaking, only one in twenty Americans can confidently be described as actively involved. . . . Such activities as attending campaign meetings [and] contributing to political organizations . . . are, all things considered, rare phenomena."[36]

Citizens of higher socioeconomic status are by far the most politically active individuals. They are most likely to possess the financial resources and

[36]Neuman, *Paradox of Mass Politics*, 99.

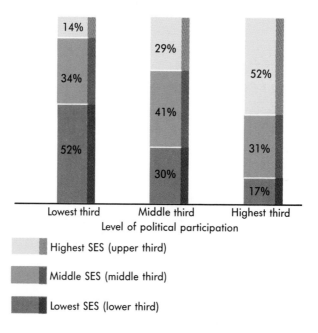

**FIGURE 9-4 Socioeconomic Status (SES) of Americans at Three Levels of Political Participation**
The highest levels of political participation are found among people at the high socioeconomic level. *Source: Adapted from Sidney Verba and Norman H. Nie,* Participation in America: Political Democracy and Social Equality *(New York: Harper & Row, 1972),* 131 (Fig. 8-3).

communication skills that encourage participation and make it personally rewarding.[37] Verba and Nie's study provides a rough indication of the extent to which higher-status individuals fill the ranks of the activists. Among citizens who are *most* active in politics, three times as many are at the top socioeconomic level as are at the bottom level[38] (see Figure 9-4).

## UNCONVENTIONAL ACTIVISM: PROTEST POLITICS

Before mass elections became prevalent, the public often resorted to riots and disorders as a way of expressing dissatisfaction with government. The advent of elections allowed the masses to communicate their views in an institutionalized and less disruptive way. However, elections are double-edged. Although they are commonly viewed as a means by which the people control the government, *elections are also a means by which the government controls the people.*[39] Because they have been freely chosen by the people to rule, representatives can claim that their policies reflect the popular will and must therefore be obeyed by all. Elections provide those in power with a powerful argument for the legitimacy of their policies, and most citizens accept the claim.

Nevertheless, citizens sometimes take to the streets in protest against government. Through demonstrations, picket lines, and marches, protesters dramatize their opposition to official policies. The tactic does not always succeed, but it sometimes assists otherwise politically weak persons to force government to respond to their complaints. For example, the timing and scope of the landmark 1964 Civil Rights Act and 1965 Voting Rights Act can be explained only as a response by Congress to the pressure created by the civil rights movement. American history would be very different had not the abolitionist, labor, suffragist, and other major movements pressed their claims on government.

[37]Verba and Nie, *Participation in America*, 80. See also Lipset, *Political Man*, ch. 3; Clifford W. Brown, Jr., Roman B. Hedges, and Lynda W. Powell, "Modes of Elite Political Participation: Contributors to the 1972 Presidential Candidates," *American Journal of Political Science* 24 (May 1980): 261–262.
[38]Verba and Nie, *Participation in America*, 340.
[39]See Benjamin Ginsberg, *The Consequences of Consent* (New York: Random House, 1982), ch. 2.

★ ANALYZE THE ISSUE

**Riots as Political Behavior**
In early 1989 an off-duty police officer in Miami shot and killed a speeding motorcyclist. The motorcyclist was black, and his death sparked a riot in Miami's black community which lasted several days. Riots are spontaneous outbursts of collective violence, and data show that the incidence of riots (that is, the number of riots in relation to total population) is higher in the United States than in Canada, France, Germany, Great Britain, and nearly all other Western democracies. Does this fact surprise you? What do you think accounts for the relatively high rate of rioting in the United States?

Political participation may take the form of public demonstrations against government policies with which one disagrees. (Hazel Hankin)

Protest can pose a serious threat to established authority, and government at times has responded violently to dissent.[40] In May 1970, during demonstrations against the Vietnam war, several unarmed students at Kent State University and Jackson State College were shot to death and others were wounded by national guardsmen who had been sent onto the campuses to restore order. The majority of the general public sides with authorities in such situations. In a *Newsweek* poll, 58 percent of respondents blamed the Kent State killings on the student demonstrators, while only 11 percent blamed the guardsmen.

Most citizens apparently believe that the proper way to express disagreement over public policy is through voting and not through protesting, despite the First Amendment's guarantee of the right "peaceably to assemble." In a 1972 University of Michigan survey, only 15 percent of those interviewed expressed approval of the civil disobedience that accompanied the civil rights and anti-Vietnam movements (see Chapter 6). Only 1 to 2 percent of the American public took to the streets in protest at any time during the 1960s and 1970s.

## CITIZENS AS SPECTATORS: FOLLOWING POLITICS IN THE NEWS

Voting and demonstrations are active forms of political involvement. There is also a passive form: following politics by reading newspapers and news magazines and by listening to news reports on television or radio. The chief significance of such activities rests on the fact that if people are to participate effectively, they must be aware of political developments.

News about politics is within easy reach of nearly all Americans. More than 95 percent of U.S. homes have a television set, and more than 60 percent receive a newspaper. However, the regular audience for news is smaller than these figures suggest. If the regular audience for politics is defined as those who read a newspaper's political sections almost daily or watch television newscasts almost daily or both, then slightly more than 40 percent of Americans qualify (see box). About 30 percent of the citizenry follow the news intermittently. About 30 percent of all adult Americans pay no appreciable attention to either television news or newspapers.[41]

Even for people who read or watch the news regularly, a question remains as to how much attention they pay to what they are reading or watching. Many people have difficulty remembering news stories they have recently seen. Only about half of those who have been exposed to the news can recall a story they saw twenty-four hours earlier.[42] This pattern is explained by the nature of news exposure. Most newspaper readers skim the headlines and then browse through a story or two. Television news often forms a background to other things people are doing, such as eating dinner. In addition, most news stories, particularly on television, are not very informative. The average television news story is only slightly more than a minute long, provides almost no background information, and focuses on personalities rather than issues.[43]

For many citizens, news exposure is the only significant form of contact with the world of politics. Yet the role of the news audience is akin to that of

### ★ ANALYZE THE ISSUE

**Teledemocracy**

"Teledemocracy" is the use of two-way cable television to allow home viewers, after they have heard arguments on various sides of a political issue, to register their opinions simply by pushing a button on a box wired to the TV set. Some people have hailed teledemocracy as a more immediate form of political participation. Its critics say that no meaningful give-and-take occurs, that viewers act as an audience, not as citizens. What is your opinion? Under what conditions might teledemocracy be a useful way of discovering majority opinion and serving as an instrument of popular influence on government? Under what conditions might it become a tool by which leaders could manipulate public opinion for their own purposes?

[40]See Jerome K. Skolnick, *The Politics of Protest* (New York: Balantine, 1969).
[41]Thomas E. Patterson, *The Mass Media Election* (New York: Praeger, 1980), ch. 6.
[42]Ibid., 63.
[43]Ibid., ch. 13; Jarol B. Manheim, "Can Democracy Survive Television?" *Journal of Communication* 26 (Spring 1976): 84–90.

# WHERE PEOPLE GET THEIR NEWS: TELEVISION VS. NEWSPAPERS

It is commonly believed that television is now the major source of news for Americans. This judgment is based partly on polls, such as those conducted annually by the Roper Organization, which ask Americans where they get most of their news. The 1985 Roper poll, for example, indicated the following pattern: television, 64 percent; newspapers, 40 percent; radio, 14 percent; other, 12 percent. (The total exceeds 100 percent because respondents could name more than one source.) These data suggest that television is far and away the nation's most important information source. However, the data are misleading in that they indicate only where people get "most" of their news, not how much news they actually get. People who say they get "most" of their news from television do not necessarily get a lot of television news. They may watch a television news program every now and then but never read a newspaper. When people's news habits are measured by the frequency with which they read or watch the news, the newspaper emerges as the nation's most important medium. Most readers turn to their newspaper every day. Most viewers do not watch a television news program daily.

In addition, newspaper exposure usually makes a stronger impression on people than does television news exposure. Research has shown that newspaper readers can more readily recall news stories they have seen and acquire more political information from their news exposure. There are several reasons for this finding. Newspaper readers, first, have more control over content. A newspaper can be read and digested as quickly or as slowly as the reader desires. Television viewers, in contrast, must watch their news stories flow one after another, with the time they can spend on each story determined by the time it takes to broadcast it. Viewers also obtain less information, for television stories typically contain only as many words as the first two paragraphs of a newspaper story. Finally, television news receives less attention from its audience than a newspaper does. In its early years, as the communication theorist Marshall McLuhan noted, television was a "high-involvement" medium, but it no longer draws the undivided attention of its viewers. Newspaper readers too can be distracted, but the act of reading requires more concentration than does viewing.

SOURCE: Thomas E. Patterson, *The Mass Media Election* (New York: Praeger, 1980), ch.6.

spectators at a sporting event, not of the players. Marshall McLuhan characterized the modern world of mass communication as a "global village," suggesting that the media, particularly television, have effectively linked citizens everywhere.[44] Benjamin Barber is closer to the truth when he claims that news exposure can never substitute for active participation as the foundation of a true political community.[45]

## *Participation and the Potential for Influence*

Although Americans claim that political participation is important, most of them do not practice what they preach. As we have seen, most citizens take little interest in participation except to vote, and a significant minority cannot even be persuaded that voting is worth their while. Americans are obviously not completely apathetic: many millions of them give their time, effort, and money to political causes, and nearly 90 million go to the polls in presidential elections. Yet sustained political activism does not engage a large proportion of the public.

[44]Marshall McLuhan, *Understanding Media: The Extensions of Man* (New York: McGraw-Hill, 1964).
[45]See Benjamin Barber, *Strong Democracy: Participatory Politics for a New Age* (Berkeley, Calif.: Univerisity of California Press, 1984).

On the local level, political participation may include fundraisers for neighborhood improvement projects. (Mark Antman/The Image Works)

Moreover, many of those who do participate are drawn to politics by a habitual sense of civic duty rather than by an intense concern with current issues.

## INDIVIDUALISM AND COLLECTIVE ACTION

The emphasis that American culture places on individualism tends to discourage a sense of urgency about political participation. "In the United States, the country of individualism *par excellence*," William Watts and Lloyd Free write, "there is a sharp distinction in people's minds between their own personal lives and national life."[46] Although wars and severe recessions can lead the American public to rely on government, most people under most conditions expect to solve their own problems. This is not to say that Americans have a disdain for collective action. In their communities particularly, citizens frequently take part in collective efforts to support a local hospital, improve the neighborhood, and the like. But Americans tend not to see their material well-being as greatly dependent on involvement in politics of the traditional kind.

At times, in fact, Americans appear to be almost oblivious of the swirl of national politics. During the early 1950s, when Senator Joseph McCarthy was claiming that Communists had infiltrated the highest ranks of government and McCarthy's critics were saying that he was trampling on the civil liberties of innocent people, Samuel Stouffer asked a sample of Americans what their major concerns were. Although McCarthy's charges were the subject of front-page headlines and special live television broadcasts seen by millions, only 2 percent of the interviewees mentioned communism or civil liberties as a major concern. The respondents spoke instead of their jobs, the education of their children, their plans to buy a home, and other personal goals.[47]

[46]William Watts and Lloyd A. Free, eds., *The State of the Nation* (New York: University Books, Potomac Associates, 1967), 97
[47]Samuel Stouffer, *Communism, Conformity, and Civil Liberties* (Garden City, N.Y.: Doubleday, 1955), 61.

Of course, Americans' paramount interest in their private lives does not preclude a political commitment. Nevertheless, because Americans are not very class-conscious and because they trust their ability to get ahead on their own, they regard politics as an important activity but hardly a life-or-death proposition. Many people do not even define citizenship in political terms.[48] Their model of the "good citizen" is as likely to be someone who is an economic pillar of the community as someone who is actively involved in politics.

## POLITICAL PARTICIPATION AND SOCIOECONOMIC STATUS

During the 1950s and 1960s, many political scientists argued that low turnout largely reflected an apathetic satisfaction with the status quo. They also argued that low turnout did not matter a great deal because survey data showed that voters and nonvoters had similar preferences in regard to policies and candidates; election outcomes would not change if everyone voted. Such arguments are less persuasive today. As Walter Dean Burnham notes, "It is no longer possible to assume a quiet consensus, a happy apathy. [There are now] significant differences between the preferences of voters and non-voters."[49]

These differences are most pronounced on class-based issues and reflect the difference in turnout between citizens of high and low socioeconomic status. As we have seen, high-status citizens can look after themselves; they have the personal skills and resources to take part in politics on their own. "The rich have the capacity to participate with or without assistance," Benjamin Ginsberg writes. "When assistance is given, it is primarily the poor who benefit."[50] Other democratic countries give the poor such assistance by placing the burden of registering voters on government and by fostering class-based political organizations. By comparison, the poor in the United States must arrange their own registration and have a choice only between major political parties that are attuned primarily to people of higher economic status.

The overall effect, more pronounced in the 1970s and 1980s than at any other time since the 1920s, is to give American politics a decidedly middle-class slant. The relatively high participation rate of the country's middle-class citizens, who constitute the bulk of the population in any case, tends to direct public policies to their benefit. Studies indicate that representatives are more responsive to the demands of participants than to those of nonparticipants,[51] although it must be kept in mind that participants do not always promote only their own interests. It would be a mistake, however, to conclude that large numbers of people regularly support policies that impose great costs on themselves.

In sum, the pattern of *individual* political participation in the United States parallels the distribution of influence that prevails in the private sector. However, the issue of individual participation is only one piece of the larger puzzle of who rules America and for what purposes. Subsequent chapters will provide additional pieces.

> ★ ANALYZE THE ISSUE
>
> **Increasing Political Participation among Low-Income Americans**
> Can you think of any change in U.S. society or politics that would reduce the enormous disparity between social classes in levels of political participation? That is, what would it take to raise significantly the participation level of low-income Americans? How would the change you envision achieve this effect?

[48]Harry Holloway with John George, *Public Opinion*, 2d ed. (New York: St. Martin's Press, 1986), 157.
[49]Burnham, "The Class Gap," 30.
[50]Ginsberg, *Consequences of Consent*, 49.
[51]See Verba and Nie, *Participation in America*, 332; V. O. Key, Jr., *Southern Politics* (New York: Vintage Books, 1949), 527.

# Summary

Political participation is a sharing in activities designed to influence public policy and leadership. A main issue of democratic government is the question of who participates in politics and how fully they participate.

Voting is the most widespread form of active political participation among Americans. Yet voter turnout is significantly lower in the United States than in other democratic nations. The requirement that Americans must personally register in order to establish their eligibility to vote is one reason for lower turnout among Americans; other democracies place the burden of registration on governmental officials rather than on the individual citizen. The fact that the U.S. holds frequent elections also discourages some citizens from voting regularly. Finally, the major American political parties, unlike many of those in Europe, do not clearly represent the interests of opposing economic classes; thus the policy stakes in American elections are correspondingly reduced. Some Americans do not vote because they think that policy will not change greatly regardless of which party gains power.

Only a minority of citizens engage in the more demanding forms of political activity, such as work on behalf of a candidate during a political campaign. About five in every twenty Americans will take an active part in a political organization at some point in their lives, although perhaps no more than one in twenty is highly active in politics at any given time. Most political activists are individuals of higher income and education; they have the skills and material resources to participate effectively and tend to have a greater interest in politics. More than in any other Western democracy, political participation in the United States is related to socioeconomic status.

Overall, Americans are only moderately involved in politics. They are concerned with political affairs but immersed in their private pursuits, a reflection in part on our culture's emphasis on individualism. The lower level of participation among poorer citizens has particular significance in that it works to reduce their influence on public policy and leadership.

# Major Concepts

civic duty

political participation

registration

suffrage

voter turnout

# Suggested Readings

Barber, Benjamin. *Strong Democracy: Participatory, Politics for a New Age.* Berkeley, Calif.: University of California Press, 1984. A provocative assessment of citizenship in the modern age.

Conway, Margaret. *Political Participation in the United States.* Washington, D.C.: Congressional Quarterly Press, 1987. An up-to-date analysis of political participation patterns.

Edelman, Murray. *Politics as Symbolic Action.* Chicago: Markham, 1971. A sweeping analysis of political "participation" defined broadly.

Piven, Frances Fox, and Richard A. Cloward. *Why Americans Don't Vote.* New York: Pantheon, 1988. An analysis of nonvoting which focuses on registration requirements and calls for simplified procedures.

Verba, Sidney, and Norman Nie. *Participation in America: Political Democracy and Social Equality.* New York: Harper & Row, 1972. The most comprehensive study to date of American political participation. Stresses the relationship of social class to political involvement.

Wolfinger, Raymond E., and Steven J. Rosenstone. *Who Votes?* New Haven, Conn.: Yale University Press, 1980. A careful statistical analysis of voters and nonvoters based on a large survey conducted by the U.S. Bureau of the Census.

# Chapter 10

## VOTING: CHOOSING REPRESENTATIVES

*The electoral process is of greatest interest because of its importance in the wider political system. However much voting may tell about the psychology and sociology of human choice, it is important because of the importance of the [policy] decisions to which it leads.*
Angus Campbell et al., The American Voter[1]

The 1964 presidential election was a classic political confrontation. Barry Goldwater, the Republican nominee, was a diehard opponent of federal activism. In his book *The Conscience of a Conservative*, Senator Goldwater had argued for a return to the pre–New Deal free-market economy and for sharp cutbacks in the federal government's social-welfare programs.[2] During his presidential campaign Goldwater gave substance to his philosophy by saying that he would seek to abolish mandatory social security. Goldwater also opposed the use of federal authority to achieve racial desegregation. He was one of the few nonsouthern senators to vote against the 1964 Civil Rights Act.

Lyndon Johnson, the Democratic nominee in 1964, was Goldwater's antithesis in both personality and philosophy. Johnson was committed to an activist federal government. As a young congressman from Texas in the late 1930s, Johnson had nearly worshipped Franklin D. Roosevelt and the New Deal, and upon becoming president in 1963 he had urged the immediate passage of a comprehensive civil rights bill. When he was asked during the 1964 campaign about the extent of his activism, Johnson responded, "We're in favor of a lot of things, and we're against mighty few."[3]

[1]Angus Campbell, Phillip Converse, Warren Miller, and Donald Stokes, *The American Voter* (New York: Wiley, 1960), 4.
[2]Barry Goldwater, *The Conscience of a Conservative* (Shepardsville, Ky.: Victor, 1960).
[3]Quoted in David Broder, *The Party's Over* (New York: Harper & Row, 1971), 45.

The choice available to voters in 1964 could not have seemed clearer, and the outcome could hardly have been more one-sided. Johnson received 60 percent of the popular vote, a landslide nearly unmatched in the history of presidential elections. As the election returns came in, the news media concluded that Johnson's victory signified overwhelming public support for his activist policies. This was a view that Johnson shared. In his State of the Union address the following January, Johnson claimed a solemn responsibility to carry out the voters' will. "Last fall I asked the American people to choose that course," he said. "I will carry forward their command."

The interpretation of the presidential election as a policy mandate was not unusual. Politicians and the press routinely claim that election victory represents the public's approval of the policies espoused by the winner. This view of election returns conforms to Americans' cultural belief in popular sovereignty. The idea of self-government would be meaningless if the sole function of the vote was to give one leader rather than another a position of official authority. The claim that elections are popular mandates amounts to an assertion that the people through their votes choose not just their leaders but the policies by which they will be governed.

But do election returns actually show that voters' preferences are based on the policies they expect candidates to pursue? The fact is that election results do not reveal much of anything about the voters' thinking.[4] As Walter Lippmann noted:

We call an election an expression of the popular will. But is it? We go into a polling booth and mark a cross on a piece of paper for one of two, or perhaps three or four, names. Have we expressed our thoughts on the public policy of the United States? Presumably we have a number of thoughts on this and that with many *buts* and *ifs* and *ors*. Surely the cross on a piece of paper does not express them.[5]

Elections are the primary instrument of self-government in modern democracies, and the question of the relationship of voting to public policy is thus a central concern. Although election returns do not shed much light on this question, election surveys do. Since the 1930s, scholars and pollsters have regularly surveyed voters to discover the reasons for their decisions about candidates, including the part that policy issues have played. Using survey evidence, this chapter argues that citizens exercise an important degree of policy influence through their votes, but they do so in a way that is both less direct and less substantial than is commonly assumed. The main ideas discussed in this chapter are the following:

★ *In most campaigns, most voters do not choose a candidate on the basis of policy promises (a form of choice known as prospective voting). Indeed, voters are as likely to reward or punish the "in-party" for the success or failure of policies it has already pursued (a form of choice known as retrospective voting) as they are to evaluate candidates on promises of future action.*

★ *Realigning elections occur with the emergence of a powerful issue that cuts across existing political divisions. By responding strongly to this issue, the electorate "chooses" a significant and enduring change in national policy. Although rare, a realigning election is the most powerful form of popular influence through voting.*

[4]Stanley Kelley, Jr., *Interpreting Elections* (Princeton, N.J.: Princeton University Press, 1983), 3.
[5]Walter Lippmann, *The Phantom Public* (New York: Harcourt, Brace, 1925), 56–57.

★ *The voters' partisan loyalties are embedded in policy developments, and party-line voting can be a substantial expression of the electorate's policy preferences.* However, the United States is currently in a period of *dealignment*, in which party loyalties have been weakening and the electorate is increasingly responsive to transitory influences.

★ *Although citizens rarely decide through their votes exactly what government will do, the vote is nonetheless a significant constraint on political leaders.*

## Prospective Voting: Looking toward Future Policies

When politicians and journalists claim that election returns reflect a mandate for the policies proposed by the winning candidate, they are assuming that voters engage in what may be called **prospective voting.** This form of voting requires that voters know the positions of the candidates and choose the candidate whose promises match their own preferences. The trouble with this interpretation is that most voters do not behave as it requires. They are not particularly well informed about the candidates' policy positions and often base their decision on other factors. In addition, the mandate interpretation grossly oversimplifies the nature of the vote by assuming that the electorate can be divided into two groups, a majority that supported the winning candidate on every major issue and a minority that unequivocally opposed the winner. In fact, a party constructs an electoral majority by persuading voters with different policy preferences to support its candidate.[6]

### AWARENESS OF THE ISSUES: THE MISSING INGREDIENT

In contrast to the well-informed votes assumed by the prospective-voting model, most voters are only vaguely aware of election issues. In congressional campaigns, less than half of the voters can recall the two major parties' nominees in their district and even fewer know these candidates' stands on the issues.[7] In presidential races, most voters know the candidates by name but often cannot identify their policy positions.[8] During the 1976 campaign, for example, the Democratic candidate, Jimmy Carter, proposed a public-sector jobs program as a way of reducing unemployment. His Republican opponent, Gerald Ford, took a stand against the idea. By the campaign's end, 46 percent of the voters were unaware of Carter's position on public works and 65 percent were unsure of Ford's position.[9]

Several influences combine to limit the electorate's awareness of issues. For one thing, the news media concentrate on the strategic aspects of the candidates' pursuit of office, stressing the day-to-day mechanics of campaigning—the candidates' travels, their organizational efforts, their tactics—as well as voting projections and returns, results of opinion polls, and so on. By covering campaigns as if they were horse races, the media deemphasize substantive questions of policy.[10]

[6]V. O. Key, Jr., *Public Opinion and American Democracy* (New York: Knopf, 1961), 460.
[7]Edie N. Goldenberg and Michael W. Traugott, *Campaigning for Congress* (Washington, D.C.: Congressional Quarterly Press, 1984), ch. 9.
[8]Scott Keeter and Cliff Zukin, *The Uninformed Choice* (New York: Praeger, 1983), chs. 4, 5.
[9]Thomas E. Patterson, *The Mass Media Election* (New York: Praeger, 1980), 155.
[10]Patterson, *Mass Media Election,* ch. 3.

Election campaign reporting tends to focus more on colorful "photo opportunities" and brief "sound bites" than on the candidates' positions on issues. (Mark Richards/The Picture Group)

In addition, candidates do not always make their positions on issues altogether clear. Candidates sometimes are deliberately vague about their intentions, either because they fear that taking a firm stand will lose them votes or because they do not have specific policies in mind. In the 1968 presidential election, Richard Nixon dodged the Vietnam issue by claiming that he had a "secret plan" for ending the war, a plan that he said could not be revealed to the American public because the enemy would also learn of it.

Finally, voters can hardly be aware of issues if they are inattentive to them. If the voters would pay close attention to election campaigns, they could learn about policy issues. But most people do not follow campaigns intently and do not necessarily come to recognize even highly publicized issues.[11] In the 1948 presidential election, for example, the Democratic candidate, Harry S Truman, campaigned vigorously for repeal of the Taft-Hartley Act and for controls on wages and prices to reduce the inflation rate. The Republican nominee, Thomas E. Dewey, strongly opposed these proposals. Yet only 16 percent of the voters could identify the correct stands of both candidates on both issues. Another 21 percent identified correctly three of the four positions. More than 33 percent knew only one stand or none at all.[12] Surveys during more recent elections have produced similar findings.

## ISSUE VOTING THAT YIELDS NO MANDATE

Even when the voters are well informed on election issues, a campaign does not necessarily result in a mandate for the winning candidate.[13] The 1972 presiden-

[11]Ibid., chs. 7–10.
[12]Bernard Berelson, Paul Lazarsfeld, and William McPhee, *Voting* (Chicago: University of Chicago Press, 1954), 227.
[13]See Richard W. Boyd, "Popular Control of Public Policy," *American Political Science Review* 66 (June 1972): 429–449; John L. Sullivan and Robert E. O'Connor, "Electoral Choice and Popular Control of Public Policy," *American Political Science Review* 66 (December 1972): 1256–1268.

tial election is a case in point. The Vietnam war was the leading issue in 1972, and the major parties' nominees held sharply opposing positions on the war. The Democratic challenger, George McGovern, proposed an immediate withdrawal of U.S. forces from Vietnam, while the Republican incumbent, Richard Nixon, promised a continuation of his policy of gradual disengagement. Vietnam had become a national obsession by 1972, and Americans listened to and learned from the candidates. About 80 percent of voters knew of McGovern's proposal for immediate disengagement and nearly 70 percent linked Nixon to a policy of phased withdrawal.[14]

Nevertheless, Nixon's huge victory over McGovern in 1972 was not a mandate for his Vietnam policy. In a careful analysis of Nixon's win, Stanley Kelley found that Nixon's position on Vietnam won him more support than he received from any other issue (see Table 10-1); yet the number of voters who cited his stand on Vietnam as the reason they voted for him was far short of a majority. Moreover, Nixon's supporters who did cite Vietnam had opposing opinions: some thought his policy was the best way to achieve peace, while others saw it as designed to win the war.[15]

Kelley also studied the 1964 Johnson–Goldwater race to discover whether Johnson's landslide victory could be classified as a mandate. He discovered that

[14]Thomas E. Patterson, Robert D. McClure, and Kenneth J. Meier, "Issue Voting," paper presented at the annual meeting of the American Political Science Association, September 1976, Chicago.
[15]Kelley, *Interpreting Elections*, 139.

**TABLE 10-1  Percentage of Voters Who Cited Various Issues As a Reason for Preferring a Candidate in the 1964 and 1972 Presidential Elections**

| Issues | Percent Favoring Winner | Percent Favoring Loser |
|---|---|---|
| *1964* | (Johnson) | (Goldwater) |
| New Deal issues | 49.1% | 24.8% |
|   Economic issues | 14.8 | 12.6 |
|   Liberalism, conservatism | 10.5 | 10.6 |
|   Relation to big business, "common man" | 37.4 | 4.7 |
|   Medical care | 8.9 | 2.3 |
| Peace | 16.1 | 4.2 |
| Poverty program | 5.9 | 2.2 |
| Race-related issues | 16.2 | 11.1 |
| *1972* | (Nixon) | (McGovern) |
| Vietnam war, peace | 33.6 | 18.4 |
| Foreign policy | 20.7 | 6.1 |
|   Détente with USSR | 4.1 | 1.0 |
|   Policy toward China | 7.4 | 1.6 |
| New Deal issues | 28.6 | 39.5 |
|   Monetary and fiscal policy | 6.5 | 8.6 |
|   Welfare | 17.3 | 5.2 |
| Race-related issues | 6.0 | 4.0 |
| Social change issues | 15.2 | 8.1 |

SOURCE: Adapted from Stanley Kelley, Jr., *Interpreting Elections* (Princeton, N.J.: Princeton University Press, 1983), 138.

voters were reasonably well informed about key policy differences between the candidates and that a large proportion of the electorate made their choice on the basis of policy.[16] However, Kelley found that Johnson's majority was composed of voters attracted by a variety of issues (see Table 10-1). Nearly half made reference to a New Deal–style issue, but even these voters responded to different New Deal issues. Some were concerned with social security, others with business regulation, still others with public assistance programs, and so on. Kelley concluded, "American voters are of many minds, and [their] heterogeneity of opinion can be expected to reduce the likelihood of mandates in most elections and to make even rarer [any] highly specific mandates. . . ."[17]

Kelley's conclusion conforms with what Norman Nie, Sidney Verba, and John Petrocik discovered when they studied presidential elections from 1952 to 1976 for evidence of the impact of issues.[18] Early in this period, the candidates' policy proposals had relatively little influence on voters' decisions. The public's degree of concern with issues then increased in the 1960s and early 1970s as a result of Vietnam, the civil rights movement, and urban unrest. Yet the voters who responded strongly to issues of any kind, even during this politically intense period, made up, by generous estimate, only about half of the electorate.[19]

Thus the common idea, heard after every presidential election, that the victorious candidate has received a popular mandate for his policy ideas simply does not conform with the facts. After his landslide reelection victory in 1984, Ronald Reagan claimed that the voters had "voiced their support" for his proposed increase in defense spending. The electorate chose Reagan for a variety of reasons, but a desire for higher defense expenditures was not one of them: polls indicated that most voters favored either maintaining military spending at the current level or reducing it. Like many another victorious candidate, Reagan erred in assuming that because he had won an electoral majority, the people approved of all his ideas. The reality is that electoral majorities are built by successful efforts to persuade voters with different preferences to support the same candidate. Reagan's voters in 1984 included some who were attracted by his defense position, some who admired his economic policies, some who liked his personal style, and on and on. His majority, like nearly all majorities, was in truth a coalition of minorities.

## Retrospective Voting: Judging Past Performance

V. O. Key, Jr., argued that prospective voting is neither the only way nor the best way for the electorate to exercise control over public policy. Key noted that candidates' promises do not always provide a sound basis for voting. A newly elected president, for example, may find that Congress has not the slightest interest in supporting the program that he promised the voters during his campaign. For such reasons, Key suggested that the public is better advised to

---

[16]Ibid. See also John Osgood Field and Ronald E. Anderson, "Ideology in the Public's Conceptualization of the 1964 Presidential Election," *Public Opinion Quarterly* 33 (1969): 380–398; John C. Pierce, "Party Identification and the Changing Role of Ideology in American Politics," *Midwest Journal of Political Science* 14 (1970): 25–42.

[17]Kelley, *Interpreting Elections*, 137–140.

[18]Norman H. Nie, Sidney Verba, and John Petrocik, *The Changing American Voter*, enl. ed. (Cambridge, Mass.: Harvard University Press, 1979).

[19]Ibid., 377.

cast its votes on the basis of government's past performance, which is not only a more tangible basis for decision but also one that is more easily calculated. The voter merely needs to decide whether government has performed well or poorly since the last election.[20]

## REWARD OR PUNISH: EVALUATING THE IN-PARTY

Key used the term **retrospective voting** to describe the situation in which voters support the incumbent party when they judge its policies to have been successful[21] and oppose it when they conclude that its policies have failed. Key found evidence in the presidental elections from 1936 to 1960 that many voters apparently reach their decisions through such backward-looking judgments.[22]

Although Key overstated his evidence,[*] citizens do seem to be at least as likely to exercise the sanctioning power of the vote by looking backward at government performance as by projecting forward on the basis of candidates' campaign promises.[23] The 1980 presidential campaign is a case in point. The electorate in 1980 did not respond enthusiastically to the prospect of Ronald Reagan's election. His conservative economic ideas and belligerent attitude toward the Soviet Union worried many voters, and opinion surveys indicated that Reagan was the least popular presidential winner since polling began in the 1930s.[24] He won because the electorate was even less enthusiastic about the incumbent, Jimmy Carter. High inflation and unemployment in the late 1970s had made the U.S. economy weaker than it had been at any previous time since the Great Depression of the 1930s, and the Iranian hostage crisis, which remained unresolved on the eve of the 1980 election, had severely damaged America's international prestige. Carter's performance in office lost him the support in 1980 of more than one-fourth of the voters who had backed him in 1976.[25]

## ECONOMIC PERFORMANCE AS A KEY TO REELECTION

Reagan's landslide reelection in 1984 indicates how important past governmental performance is to voters. The nation's economy had remained weak during

---

[*]Key undoubtedly overestimated the extent of retrospective voting. Voters who support the incumbent party's presidential candidate are likely to say the "ins" have been doing a good job in office even if this is not their main reason for backing the candidate. They may actually have backed the candidate for reasons of partisanship, personality, or emerging issues rather than past performance. Similarly, those who oppose the in-party's candidate, whatever their actual reasons for doing so, are likely to say the "ins" have been doing a poor job. Moreover, subsequent research by Morris Fiorina has shown that retrospective voting is more prevalent in presidential races than in congressional races. Voters apparently distinguish between the incumbent president's contribution to national conditions and the smaller influence of any individual member of Congress. See Morris Fiorina, *Retrospective Voting in American National Elections* (New Haven, Conn.: Yale University Press, 1981).

[20]V. O. Key, Jr., *The Responsible Electorate* (Cambridge, Mass.: Belknap Press of Harvard University Press, 1966), ch. 1.

[21]Ibid., 61.

[22]Ibid., 7–8.

[23]Gerald Pomper with Susan Lederman, *Elections in America*, 2d ed. (New York: Longman, 1980), 218.

[24]Arthur H. Miller and Martin P. Wattenberg, "Policy and Performance Voting in the 1980 Election," paper presented at the annual meeting of the American Political Science Association, September 1981.

[25]Kathleen A. Frankovic, "Public Opinion Trends," in Gerald Pomper, ed., *The Election of 1980* (New York: Chatham House, 1981), 97.

Ronald Reagan's landslide reelection in 1984 demonstrated that economic prosperity is a key factor in determining a president's chances of being returned to office. (Dennis Brack/Black Star)

the first two years of Reagan's presidency, and opinion polls showed that a majority of Americans disapproved of Reagan's handling of his office. By 1984, however, the economy—and Reagan's approval rating—had rebounded sharply, and this circumstance, more than any promise of future action, led Americans to return Reagan to office. Reagan received the support of more than 90 percent of the voters who had backed him in 1980 and gained additional supporters, particularly among first-time and independent voters.[26]

As Reagan's reelection demonstrated, economic conditions can play a large role in the electorate's response to incumbents. "Voters are disposed," Seymour Martin Lipset concludes, "to credit or blame incumbent administrations for the state of the economy."[27] As voters' confidence in a party's ability to ensure prosperity rises or falls, so does their support for its presidential candidate.[28] Since 1952, the Democratic share of the two-party presidential vote has never fallen below 50 percent when a majority of the public perceived it as the party of prosperity (see Figure 10-1). Conversely, the Democratic vote has never risen above 46 percent when the Republican party was more widely perceived as the party of prosperity.[29] This pattern reflects the essential pragmatism of the American electorate which we noted in Chapter 8. If an incumbent administration presides over an apparently healthy or improving economy, it can expect a good response at the polls.

## ANTICIPATED RESPONSE: A REASON TO SATISFY THE PUBLIC

Retrospective voting is a weaker form of public control than prospective voting.[30] In theory, prospective voting allows the electorate to direct government

[26]*New York Times*, November 8, 1984, A14.
[27]Seymour Martin Lipset, "The Economy, Elections, and Public Opinion," *Tocqueville Review* 5 (Fall 1983): 431.
[28]D. Roderick Kiewiet, *Macro-Economics and Micro-Politics* (Chicago: University of Chicago Press, 1983), 154–158.
[29]*Gallup Reports*, April 1985.
[30]Pomper, *Elections in America*, 212.

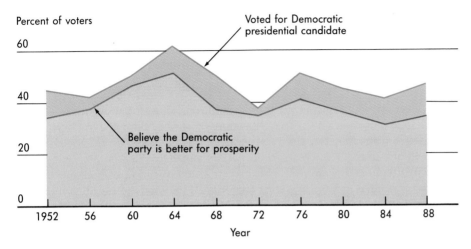

FIGURE 10-1 Democratic Presidential Vote and the Public's Perception of the Democratic Party's Ability to Promote Prosperity, 1952–1988 Voters' support for a party's presidential candidate is related to their opinion of the party's ability to manage the economy. *Source:* Gallup Reports, *April 1985; Gallup poll, January 1988. Respondents were asked whether the Democratic party or the Republican party was "better for prosperity."*

policy in advance. Retrospective voting occurs after the fact: citizens are judging whether they are satisfied with what government has already done. Nonetheless, retrospective voting can be an effective form of popular control over policy because it forces officeholders to anticipate the voters' likely response in the next election. "The fear of loss of popular support," Key concluded, "powerfully disciplines the actions of government."[31]

*The fear of loss of public support powerfully disciplines the actions of government.*
V. O. Key, Jr.

## Realigning Elections: Repudiating the Past

Most national elections result in only moderate changes in public policy. Each newly elected president or Congress has innovative policy ideas, some of which will be enacted into law. But wholesale changes in national policy are rare. During periods of peace and prosperity, elected officials tend to believe that existing policies are working and to avoid tampering with them. Officeholders are more likely to seek alternative policies during difficult periods, but even then they confront significant political obstacles to major changes. Powerful interests that benefit from existing programs will resist radically new approaches. Congress's opposition to the president, or vice versa, can also kill new ideas. The American system of checks and balances generally works to protect the status quo. Unless the executive and legislative branches are united in their determination to forge ahead in a new direction, no significant action is likely.

However, there have been periods in American history when national policy has changed abruptly. These momentous shifts have hinged on what scholars have labeled realigning, or critical, elections.[32] A **realigning election** is one in which the electorate, responding to an extraordinarily powerful issue that disrupts the established political order, literally forces the government to take a new policy direction.

A realigning election involves five basic elements:

1. The disruption of the existing political order because of the emergence of one or more unusually powerful and divisive issues.
2. The widening of divisions between the parties.

---

[31]Key, *Responsible Electorate*, 10.
[32]For the classic analysis of realigning elections, see Walter Dean Burnham, *Critical Elections and the Mainsprings of American Politics* (New York: Norton, 1970).

3. The occurrence of an election contest in which one party has a strong advantage.
4. A major change in policy through the action of the newly dominant party.
5. An enduring change in the party coalitions, which works to the lasting advantage of the newly dominant party.

The election of 1860 met all these conditions. The Republican party was unified in its opposition to the extension of slavery into the new western territories, but the majority Democratic party was divided over this issue along North–South lines. The Democratic party's northern faction nominated for president Stephen A. Douglas, who held that the question of whether a new territory permitted slavery was for a majority of its voters to decide, while the southern faction nominated John C. Breckinridge, who called for the legalization of slavery in all territories. The Democratic vote in the fall election was split sharply along regional lines between these two candidates—with the result that the Republican nominee, Abraham Lincoln, was able to win the presidency with only 40 percent of the popular vote. Lincoln's opposition to the extension of slavery into the new territories prompted southern states to secede from the Union. Determined to preserve the Union, Lincoln declared war on the South. When the Civil War ended four years later, the abolition of slavery was national policy and the Republicans had replaced the Democrats as the nation's majority party. The Republicans were the dominant party in the larger and more populous North; the Democratic party was left with a stronghold in what became known as "the Solid South." During the next three decades the Republicans controlled the presidency except for Grover Cleveland's two terms, and they held a majority in one or both houses of Congress for all but four of those years.

The 1932 presidential election also marked a realignment of American politics. A detailed discussion of that election can serve to illustrate further both the nature of realigning elections and their significance for the electorate's influence on national policy. (The accompanying box briefly discusses other realigning elections.)

## THE REALIGNMENT OF THE 1930S

Until the Wall Street crash of 1929, there was little reason to believe that a major change in U.S. politics was imminent. The pro-business Republican party had been in firm control of national government since the depression of 1893, holding a majority in one or both houses of Congress except for a six-year period (1913–1918) that overlapped the tenure of the period's only Democratic president, Woodrow Wilson. This Republican era was characterized by economic individualism and laissez-faire capitalism. President Calvin Coolidge summed up his party's philosophy when he said, "The business of America is business."

*The fundamental strength of the nation's economy is unimpaired.*
Herbert Hoover (1930)

*The country needs and, unless I mistake its temper, the country demands bold, persistent experimentation.*
Franklin D. Roosevelt (1932)

The Great Depression brought an end to Republican dominance. The Republican Herbert Hoover was president when the stock market crashed, and many Americans blamed Hoover, his party, and its business allies for the economic catastrophe that followed. Millions of Americans lost their jobs, homes, and self-esteem, and Hoover offered only platitudes about patience,

# THE REALIGNING ELECTIONS OF 1800, 1828, AND 1896

In addition to the realignments surrounding the Civil War and the Great Depression, scholars have identified three others. The first was the election of 1800, when Thomas Jefferson's Republican party replaced the Federalists in power. Not only did the election effectively mark the end of the Federalist party as a competitive force in U.S. elections, but it represented an end to the idea that government could properly be more responsive to privileged interests than to the general public interest.

Another realignment took place with Andrew Jackson's election in 1828, which resulted in a broad democratization of politics: rotation of office, political patronage, and grass-roots political parties were among the reforms of Jacksonian democracy. Jackson's election also inspired the formation of a new opposition party, the Whigs.

Finally, the election of 1896 is regarded as a realigning election. Three years earlier, an economic panic following a bank collapse had resulted in a severe depression. Grover Cleveland, a Democrat, was president when the panic occurred, and that circumstance worked to the advantage of the Republicans. They gained strength in the East particularly because of fear of cheap credit, a policy advocated by the Democrats' 1896 presidential nominee, William Jennings Bryan.

In each of these realignments, as in those of the 1860s and 1930s, the party that benefited from events gained an enduring advantage. For example, during the four decades between the 1890s realignment and the next one in the 1930s, the Republicans held the presidency except for Woodrow Wilson's two terms and had a majority in Congress for all but six years.

The new order begins: Franklin D. Roosevelt rides to his inauguration with outgoing president Herbert Hoover after the realigning election of 1932. (UPI/Bettmann Newsphotos)

claiming that the nation's economy would soon rebound without government intervention. In the congressional elections of 1930, the Democrats came within one seat of capturing the U.S. Senate and gained a 220–214 edge in the House of Representatives, which the Republicans had previously controlled by 100 seats. In 1932 the electorate resoundingly rejected Hoover, choosing the Democratic presidential nominee, Franklin D. Roosevelt, by a margin of 58 to 42 percent.

As a candidate, Roosevelt had not promised a sweeping "new deal"; but his first months in office were characterized by unprecedented policies in the areas of business regulation, social welfare, and public works programs. Even though these policies marked an abrupt departure from those of the past, they won support from a public mired in hard times. A 1936 Gallup poll indicated that 61 percent of Americans backed Roosevelt's social security program, while only 27 percent opposed it. If Roosevelt had not provided social security, public works programs, and other innovative policies, his campaign for reelection in 1936 would have fallen as flat as Hoover's had four years earlier. Not all of Roosevelt's policy initiatives were equally popular, but his public support undoubtedly stemmed from a widespread belief that he was leading the country in the right direction.[33]

Realigning elections, then, should be viewed as the most powerful form of popular influence on national policy. Although the electorate does not actually decide the particulars of new programs through its vote in such elections, it does reject an existing policy direction and expresses a demand for new policies appropriate to the crisis. Historically, the peak years in the enactment of innovative national legislation have coincided roughly with periods of realignment.[34]

## PARTY IDENTIFICATION: THE ENDURING INFLUENCE OF REALIGNING ELECTIONS

The sweeping policy changes that follow a realigning election are lasting ones. The Roosevelt years, for example, established a new governing philosophy with broad popular appeal which limited what future political leaders could reasonably propose. When Barry Goldwater, the Republican presidential candidate in 1964, argued for a return to the economic and welfare policies of the 1920s, he was widely branded a reactionary and was soundly defeated at the polls.

The lasting impact of realigning elections is due in part to their effect on **party identification,** an individual's ingrained loyalty to a political party.[35] For most people, partisan loyalty, once acquired, endures throughout their adult lives. Although they may occasionally cross party lines to vote for a candidate of the opposite party, they continue to think of themselves as loyalists of the party they prefer.

No concept has been more central to voting studies than party identification, and no concept has been more frequently misapplied. Many studies have treated partisanship as something completely apart from issues of public policy,

[33]Key, *Responsible Electorate,* 56.
[34]Benjamin Ginsberg, "Elections and Public Policy," *American Political Science Review* 70 (1976): 49.
[35]William H. Flanigan and Nancy Zingale, *Political Behavior of the American Electorate* (Boston: Allyn & Bacon, 1987), 25.

when in fact the two ideas are intertwined. The connection begins with a realignment, which affects party loyalties, particularly those of younger voters.

## Realignment and Partisanship[36]

In the 1930s the Democratic party was widely perceived as the party of the common people and of social security, while the Republican party was seen as the party of business and wealthy interests. The Democratic party's image was more appealing to first-time voters; they came to identify with the Democratic party by a 2-to-1 margin.[37] These new partisans helped establish the Democrats as the nation's majority party. By 1940, according to Gallup polls, Democrats outnumbered Republicans, and their continuing plurality enabled the Democratic party to dominate national politics for decades. Between 1932 and 1968, the Republicans had only one successful presidential candidate, Dwight D. Eisenhower, and held control of Congress only twice, in 1947–1948 and 1953–1954.

As for older voters, the 1930s realignment did not change the party loyalties of most of them. Although Roosevelt won the votes of some long-standing Republicans in 1932 and 1936, he did not convert many of them permanently to his party. Their Republicanism was bolstered by an accumulation of past voting decisions and political beliefs, including a commitment to the economic individualism for which their party still stood. Similarly, older Democrats generally had little reason to rethink their party identification. The strength of the Democratic party in the 1930s and 1940s resided in the nation's working class, which had suffered most deeply from the Depression and benefited most directly from the Democratic administration's New Deal programs.

The effects of the 1930s realignment clearly remained in voters' minds during the 1950s. The following are comments made about the parties by voters in 1956:

> I think of the Republicans as being more conservative and interested in big business. (Woman from Ohio)

> [The Democrats] are more inclined to help the working class of people, and that is the majority in our country. (Man from Ohio)

> I like [the Democratic party's] liberalness over the years. They certainly have passed beneficial legislation like social security and unemployment insurance, which the average man needs today. (Man from upstate New York)

> I don't particularly agree how they [the Democrats] have passed out the money and increased the taxes. (Iowa man)

> I just don't believe [the Republicans] are for the common people. (Texas man)[38]

Of course, the public's images of the parties in the 1950s were not so sharply

---

[36]See James E. Campbell, "Sources of the New Deal Realignment," *Western Political Quarterly* 38 (September 1986): 357; James E. Campbell, "Voter Mobilization and the New Deal Realignment," *Western Political Quarterly* 39 (December 1986): 733.
[37]See Kristi Andersen, *The Creation of a Democratic Majority, 1928–1936* (Chicago: University of Chicago Press, 1979).
[38]Quoted in Campbell et al., *American Voter*, 229–231, 235, 238.

defined as they had been two decades earlier. The economic insecurity of the Depression had given way to the optimism that followed World War II, and young adults of the 1950s had only childhood memories of the hard times of the 1930s.

This blurring of party images was predictable. After a realignment, the losing party must eventually adapt to the new political climate. Because the public had generally accepted the New Deal, most Republican leaders recognized that they had nothing to gain from continued opposition. When the Republicans gained control of the presidency and Congress in 1952, they did not try to return the nation to the policies of the 1920s. The two parties had thus become more alike and less innovative, even while they maintained some opposing positions.[39] For example, the two parties in the 1950s disagreed about labor–management issues but under less compelling circumstances and over less basic principles than in the 1930s, when the question had been whether labor even had a legitimate claim to collective bargaining.

### Party-Line Voting: Blind or Policy-Based?

Some analysts cite party-line voting in the 1950s as evidence that partisan voters do not respond to policy issues. In fact, however, although blind partisanship did exist in the 1950s (as in any other period), party-line voting cannot automatically be assumed to lack a policy component. As long as no new issues arise to change the fundamental basis of party conflict, most voters simply have no good reason to abandon their existing party loyalties. Key noted that, in terms of their policy preferences, most voters are where they ought to be in their loyalty to one party or the other.[40] The fact that blue-collar workers voted strongly Democratic in the 1950s, for example, might be taken as evidence that they acted on blind partisanship, since the majority of them had a Democratic party identification; yet it was also the case that these 1950s blue-collar Democrats believed, and with good reason, that the Democratic party was more likely than the Republican party to serve labor's interests.

The real test of blind partisanship is whether voters stay with their party even when its policies conflict with their interests. The 1960s revealed that most partisans do not behave in this unthinking way. As new issues that arose in the 1960s cut across the partisan divisions created by the New Deal, voters tended to reject their party if they believed it was on the wrong side of an issue that was salient to them.[41] The issue of black civil rights, for example, turned the "Solid South" into a Republican presidential stronghold after nearly a century of staunch support for the Democratic party. In response to northern Democrats' leadership on civil rights, southern Democrats voted overwhelmingly for the conservative Republican Goldwater in 1964. He won only 40 percent of the national vote but carried the states of Alabama, Georgia, Louisiana, Mississippi, and South Carolina. In Mississippi he received fully 87 percent of the votes cast, whereas in 1956, before civil rights became an important partisan issue, Mississippi had cast 72 percent of its votes for the Democratic presidential candidate, Adlai Stevenson.

[39]James L. Sundquist, *Dynamics of the Party System* (Washington, D.C.: Brookings Institution, 1973), 296.
[40]Key, *Responsible Electorate*, ch. 1.
[41]David E. RePass, "Issue Salience and Party Choice," *American Political Science Review* 60 (June 1971): 398–400.

The Democratic "Solid South" more or less ended in 1964, when Barry Goldwater, the Republican presidential candidate, drew the strong support of voters in South Carolina and other states in the Deep South. (Max Scheler/Black Star)

Of course, the argument that party voting is also policy voting can easily be overstated. Some Republicans and Democrats know very little about their party's traditions, policies, or group commitments.[42] For many of these individuals, partisanship is an "inherited" identity. They are Republicans or Democrats primarily because their parents had been, but they have never acquired a clear understanding of the policy support implied by a vote for their inherited party.[43] One study found that party perceptions unrelated to issues characterize 17 percent of voters—a point illustrated by the North Carolina Democrat who said, "I've always been a Democrat just like my daddy."[44] Other partisans have simply closed their minds to the possibility of voting for candidates of the opposing party. Nevertheless, partisans on the whole are not sociological and psychological captives of their party loyalties; their party leanings are intimately connected to the parties' policy traditions.

## IS A NEW REALIGNMENT ON THE WAY?

Party realignments inevitably lose their strength, because the issues that give rise to them cannot remain unresolved indefinitely. The last indisputable realigning election took place in 1932. Does this mean that a new realignment is in the offing? Election analysts have been considering this question for the past

[42]Campbell et al., *American Voter*, ch. 3.
[43]See Herbert Hyman, *Political Socialization* (New York: Free Press, 1959); Fred I. Greenstein, *Children and Politics* (New Haven, Conn.: Yale University Press, 1965); M. Kent Jennings and Richard Niemi, *The Political Character of Adolescence* (Princeton, N.J.: Princeton University Press, 1974), 37–62.
[44]Quoted in Campbell et al., *American Voter*, 246.

two decades.[45] In the late 1960s, when the Democratic party was divided over Vietnam and civil rights, Kevin Phillips claimed that a realignment favorable to the Republicans was under way.[46] When the anticipated Republican majority failed to materialize, Phillips attributed the outcome to the damage done to the Republican party by the Watergate scandal.

The possibility of a new realignment favorable to the Republicans was raised again by Ronald Reagan's victories in 1980 and 1984, which had some features in common with previous realignments. Like Roosevelt's 1932 win, Reagan's first election resulted from widespread dissatisfaction with the incumbent president's handling of the economy. Moreover, like Roosevelt's New Deal, Reagan's policies were a sharp departure from the past. Reagan sought to reverse the growth of national government and in 1981 persuaded Congress to enact the largest cuts in taxes and government spending in the nation's history. Such policies encouraged Americans to believe, as Americans had done in the 1930s, that large and important differences existed between the parties. The Republican party came to be widely regarded as the party of a smaller, less activist national government and the Democrats as the party of a larger, more intrusive government.[47] And, like Roosevelt, Reagan won reelection to a second term by a landslide, largely because the electorate responded favorably to his economic recovery policies. Other parallels between the 1930s and 1980s are also evident. For example, first-time voters identified mainly with the president's party (see Figure 10-2). And, of course, the Republicans retained control of the White House when George Bush, Reagan's vice-president, won the presidential election of 1988.

However, the elections of the 1980s did not represent a true realignment. For one thing, the Republicans did not capture both houses of Congress or sweep

**FIGURE 10-2 Percentage of American Adults Who Identified Themselves as Republicans, Independents, or Democrats in 1986, by Age Group**
Younger voters are the most heavily Republican age group.
*Source: Gallup poll, July 27, 1986. Based on surveys from January though June 1986.*

[45]See, for example, Donald S. Strong, *Issue Voting and Party Realignment* (University: University of Alabama Press, 1977).
[46]See Kevin Phillips, *The Emerging Republican Majority* (New Rochelle, N.Y.: Arlington House, 1969).
[47]Martin P. Wattenberg, *The Decline of American Political Parties* (Cambridge, Mass.: Harvard University Press, 1984), 52–56.

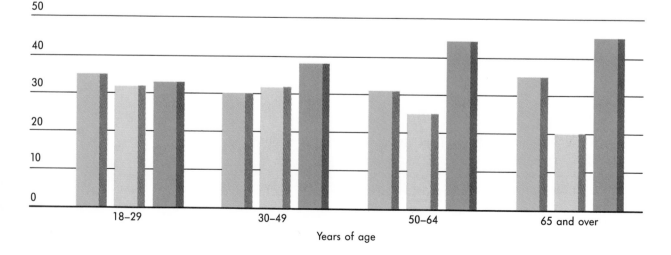

state offices in any of those years. For another, the public was not completely sold on the Reagan–Bush governing philosophy. Although their ideas about lower taxes and a smaller federal government had broad appeal, the majority preferred to retain many of the specific federal programs that Reagan and Bush wanted to cut, including those for the elderly and underprivileged (see Chapter 27). Finally, the Republican party was unable to gain a larger partisan following than its party rival. As of 1988, voters who identified themselves as Democrats still outnumbered Republicans by roughly 10 percent.

## Dealignment: The Decline of Partisanship

Most voting specialists conclude that the United States, rather than experiencing a realignment, has undergone a party **dealignment,** a partial but lasting movement away from party identification. A dealignment is characterized by a greater responsiveness among the electorate to short-term influences, such as the candidates and issues of the moment, than to long-term commitment to a party.

The decline of partisanship began in the 1960s, when cross-cutting issues emerged and started to shake existing loyalties. The civil rights issue, for example, was unsettling not only to many southern Democrats but also to some white northern Democrats, particularly blue-collar workers and members of ethnic groups, who felt that black Americans were making rapid gains at their expense.[48] The lengthy conflict in Vietnam also tested Americans' patience with elected leaders of both parties, and the Watergate scandal of the early 1970s seemed to indicate that incompetence and corruption were widespread in government. Americans' trust in their elected representatives dropped sharply, as did their faith in political parties. By 1976, 55 percent of the public claimed, on balance, to dislike *both* the Democratic and Republican parties. Twenty years earlier, only half as many voters had expressed displeasure with both parties.[49]

Not surprisingly, party identification also declined (see Table 10-2).[50] In the

> ★ ANALYZE THE ISSUE
>
> **Dealignment as the Prelude to Realignment**
> Some analysts believe that a dealignment, rather than a realignment, is taking place among the American electorate. What has not been widely debated is the question of whether a dealignment increases the likelihood that sometime soon a full realignment will occur. Why might a dealignment set the stage for a far-reaching realignment?

[48]Frederick G. Dutton, *Changing Sources of Power* (New York: McGraw-Hill, 1971), ch. 6.
[49]Nie, Verba, and Petrocik, *Changing American Voter,* 364.
[50]Arthur H. Miller, Warren E. Miller, Alden S. Raine, and Thad A. Brown, "A Majority Party in Disarray," *American Political Science Review* 70 (September 1976): 760; Seymour Martin Lipset and William Schneider, *The Confidence Gap* (New York: Free Press, 1983).

**TABLE 10-2  Party Identification, 1952–1988**

| Party Identification | YEAR | | | | | | | | | |
|---|---|---|---|---|---|---|---|---|---|---|
| | 1952 | 1956 | 1960 | 1964 | 1968 | 1972 | 1976 | 1980 | 1984 | 1988 |
| Strong Democrat | 22% | 21% | 21% | 26% | 20% | 15% | 15% | 18% | 18% | 19% |
| Weak Democrat | 25 | 23 | 25 | 25 | 25 | 25 | 25 | 23 | 22 | 20 |
| Independent, leaning Democrat | 10 | 7 | 8 | 9 | 10 | 11 | 12 | 11 | 10 | 12 |
| Independent | 5 | 9 | 8 | 8 | 11 | 13 | 14 | 13 | 7 | 10 |
| Independent, leaning Republican | 7 | 8 | 7 | 6 | 9 | 10 | 10 | 10 | 13 | 9 |
| Weak Republican | 14 | 14 | 13 | 13 | 14 | 13 | 14 | 14 | 15 | 16 |
| Strong Republican | 13 | 15 | 14 | 11 | 10 | 10 | 9 | 8 | 14 | 12 |

SOURCE: Survey Research Center, Center for Political Studies, University of Michigan.

★ ANALYZE THE ISSUE

**The Impact of Ticket Splitting**

Many people believe it is better to vote for the person than for the party. But is it? Ticket splitting can produce a divided government, in which one party controls the presidency and the other controls one or both houses of Congress. This has happened in five of the last six presidential elections. Divided government can result in deadlock and makes it easier for officials to disclaim responsibility for problems: each side can say that the problems are the other party's fault. How important are these considerations? What could be an argument in favor of ticket splitting?

1950s, about 80 percent of adults claimed to identify with the Republican or Democratic party, and nearly half of them professed strong party loyalty. By 1974, the proportion of partisans had dropped to nearly 60 percent, most of whom said they had only a weak attachment to the party of their choice. Correspondingly, the proportion of Americans who described themselves as "independents" nearly doubled between 1960 and 1974—rising to more than 35 percent.

The trend away from party identification in the late 1960s and early 1970s was coupled with widespread **split-ticket voting.**[51] In 1960 more than 60 percent of the electorate cast "straight" ballots (supporting the entire ticket of candidates of one party for all offices), whereas in 1972 about 65 percent cast "split" ballots (dividing their votes among candidates of both parties for various offices). "Perhaps the most dramatic political change in the American public over the past two decades," Nie, Verba, and Petrocik wrote in 1976, "has been the decline of partisanship."[52]

Party-line voting remains at a relatively low level, and some analysts predict that it will not return to previous heights in the foreseeable future. One reason is that the electorate today is better educated and more likely to believe, rightly or wrongly, that partisanship is unnecessary. Many voters are now satisfied to judge the candidates on what they see and hear through the media rather than by the measure of party traditions and performance.

Another, and perhaps the most powerful, factor working against partisanship and a future realignment is the social-welfare programs established in the 1930s and later. Economic downswings no longer produce the extraordinary personal hardships of earlier periods; social security, unemployment compensation, and other government programs protect most Americans from abject poverty, hunger, and hopelessness. Americans become less desperate in times of recession and thus are less likely to see the relevance of party politics to their lives.

A third possible obstacle to unabashed partisanship is the complexity of modern life and public policy. Americans have high expectations for both themselves and their society. They want better jobs, more leisure, and higher incomes, but they also want cleaner air and water, services for the elderly and disadvantaged, and assistance programs for the impoverished. As Americans become increasingly unwilling to choose between public and private progress or to consider the two spheres separable, they are less likely to be persuaded by either the Republican argument for a less active government or the Democratic argument for a more active government. In today's politics, simple choices are becoming scarcer, so the chances are decreasing that either party will gain the full support of an enduring electoral majority. The electoral system may have reached a new equilibrium in which party still matters, but less than it did in the past.[53]

---

[51]Nie, Verba, and Petrocik, *Changing American Voter,* 47, 53. See also Walter Devries and V. Lance Terrance, *The Ticket-Splitter* (Grand Rapids, Mich.: Eerdmans, 1972); David B. Hill and Norman R. Luttbeg, *Trends in American Electoral Behavior* (Itasca, Ill.: F. E. Peacock, 1983), 35; John Ferejohn, "On the Decline of Competition in Congressional Elections," *American Political Science Review* 71 (1977): 166–176.

[52]Nie, Verba, and Petrocik, *Changing American Voter,* 364.

[53]Everett Carll Ladd, "On Mandates, Realignments, and the 1984 Presidential Election," *Political Science Quarterly* (Spring 1985): 1–16.

## Elections and Citizen Influence: Some Conclusions

Cynical observers claim that elections provide only the illusion of popular control of policy. In their view, the electorate chooses leaders who then go their merry way, usually hand in hand with a wealthy elite. This portrayal of the influence, or lack thereof, exerted by voters is overdrawn. The threat of a loss of popular support as a result of failed or unresponsive policies forces officeholders to pay attention to the electorate. The vote is a potentially lethal political weapon: it can end a politician's career.

Candidates are not fools. In a bid for the crucial women's vote in 1988, for example, George Bush proposed a $2.2 billion child-care program, which included a tax credit of up to $1,000 a year to help low-income parents pay for day care. Candidates are also more sincere than they are often said to be. Candidates seldom make such promises as Bush's child-care proposal without intending to fulfill them if they are elected. Candidates do not routinely try to hoodwink the electorate. The best evidence suggests that, once they take office, winning candidates make a genuine effort to keep their promises. Gerald

After years of inaction by the federal government, funding for day care unexpectedly became an issue in the 1988 presidential campaign. (UPI/Bettmann Newsphoto)

★ HOW THE UNITED STATES COMPARES

**Influences on Voting Choices**

The major influences on the vote are party loyalties, class and group attachments, issues, and candidate characteristics. However, the relative influence of these factors can vary significantly from one election to the next and from one country to the next. One study of postwar elections in Western democracies found that the American electorate is somewhat more responsive to issues and somewhat more volatile than are nearly all European electorates. An important reason is that voting choices in the United States are not affected so strongly by group and class attachments, a fact that makes Americans more responsive to short-term influences, such as current issues.

SOURCE: Ian Budge and Dennis J. Farlie, *Explaining and Predicting Elections: Issue Effects and Party Strategies in Twenty-three Democracies* (London: Allen & Unwin, 1983), chs. 3, 5.

Pomper's study of party platforms from 1944 to 1976 revealed that winning candidates and parties fulfilled well over half of their campaign pledges.[54] Indeed, the major obstacle to fulfillment of platform pledges appears to be not bad faith but political roadblocks—as when a Republican president cannot persuade a Democratic Congress to enact his programs.

Arguments that voting does not significantly influence policy also tend to ignore the fact that preferences of the electorate help to define the limits of public policy. Candidates can advance certain policy proposals only at the risk of losing their public support. As we saw at the beginning of this chapter, this is what happened to Barry Goldwater when he proposed that mandatory social security be abolished. Most presidential candidates would have accepted social security as a settled issue that the public did not want reopened. As Angus Campbell and his colleagues noted, "Political leaders develop a strong sense of what the permissible bounds of policy are."[55]

Finally, the importance of voting is underestimated if due attention is not paid to the long-term effects of realigning elections, such as that of 1932, and of other key elections, such as that of 1980. Such elections result in long-term and significant policy changes that are rooted in public dissatisfaction with existing conditions and are shaped in part by public demands stemming from this dissatisfaction. To ignore this type of electoral influence is to ignore perhaps the single most important way in which the voters give direction to national policy.

These observations do not amount to a claim that voting alone drives the American policymaking process. Many important policy issues are not addressed in elections but instead are decided out of the view of the general public. The voters' preferences clearly have more impact on policy at some times than at others, more impact on larger issues than on smaller ones, and more impact on government's general performance than on its specific actions. As Walter Lippmann said, "The popular will does not direct continuously but . . . intervenes occasionally."[56] Thus a complete accounting of how policy is made in America and who benefits from it requires the study not only of elections and voting but also of other institutions and behaviors. Subsequent chapters will undertake these investigations.

*Political leaders develop a strong sense of what the permissible bounds of policy are.*
Angus Campbell et al.,
*The American Voter*

[54]Pomper, *Elections in America*, ch. 8.
[55]Campbell et al., *American Voter*, 547.
[56]Lippmann, *Phantom Public*, 3.

## Summary

Americans view themselves as a self-governing people largely in terms of their right to choose representatives in free elections. Yet voting does not by itself give the public control over policy. When Americans go to the polls, they chose representatives, not policies. A central question, therefore, is the degree to which Americans' choice among candidates for public office is determined by the policies associated with those candidates.

Prospective voting is one way the public can exert influence through elections. It is the most demanding approach to voting: voters must develop their own policy preferences and then must educate themselves about the candidates' positions. The voters must also set aside other considerations, such as the candidates' personalities. Yet most voters do not respond to issues in this way. The degree of prospective voting rises and falls with the importance of the issues of the day, but the electorate as a whole is generally not well informed about the candidates' stands and is only partially inclined to vote for candidates on the basis of the policies they advocate.

Retrospective voting demands less from voters: they need only decide whether the government has been performing well or poorly in terms of the goals and values they hold. The evidence suggests that the electorate is, in fact, reasonably sensitive to past governmental performance, particularly in relation to economic prosperity, and that such judgments affect voting to a significant degree, especially in presidential elections.

Realigning or critical elections offer voters the opportunity to have a large and lasting impact on national policy. Such elections occur when new and powerful issues emerge and disrupt the normal political pattern. In responding to these issues and then by endorsing the action of the party that takes power, the electorate helps to establish a new governing philosophy and its associated policies. A realignment is maintained in part through the development of loyalties among first-time voters to the new governing party and its policies.

Party voting can be habitual, but it is mainly a response to the parties' policy tendencies and traditions. Although party loyalty has declined, over 60 percent of American voters still identify themselves with either the Republican or the Democratic party. For most partisans, particularly during periods when the parties' policies differ clearly and substantially, party-line voting is an important way of expressing a preference for general policy goals. However, the influence of partisanship on election results has declined sharply in the past two decades as we have undergone a dealignment, or decrease in party identification.

The vote is an important influence on public policy. This influence takes the form of general limits on policy debate and action, not of mandates for the specific policies advocated by the winning candidate. The power of the vote rests ultimately on its potential to penalize: elected representatives risk being voted out of office if their policy actions fail to satisfy the electorate.

## Major Concepts

dealignment
party identification
prospective voting

realigning election (critical election)
retrospective voting
split-ticket voting

## Suggested Readings

Andersen, Kristi. *The Creation of a Democratic Majority.* Chicago: University of Chicago Press, 1979. An analysis of the changes in the electorate between 1928 and 1936 which established the Democrats as the nation's majority party.

Berelson, Bernard, Paul Lazarsfeld, and William McPhee. *Voting.* Chicago: University of Chicago Press, 1954. One of the pioneering survey research studies of voting behavior, focusing on the 1948 election.

Burnham, Walter Dean. *Critical Elections and the Mainsprings of American Politics.* New York: Norton, 1970. The classic analysis of how long-term stability in the electoral system is punctuated periodically by major change.

Campbell, Angus, Phillip Converse, Warren Miller, and Donald Stokes. *The American Voter.* New York: Wiley, 1960. The classic study of the influences affecting individual voters, concentrating on the elections of 1952 and 1956.

Clubb, Jerome M., William H. Flanigan, and Nancy Zingale. *Partisan Realignment.* Beverly Hills, Calif.: Sage, 1980. An assessment of the process of party realignment.

Fiorina, Morris. *Retrospective Voting in American National Elections.* New Haven, Conn.: Yale University Press, 1981. A sophisticated study of the nature and prevalence of retrospective voting.

Flanigan, William H., and Nancy H. Zingale. *Political Behavior of the American Electorate.* 6th ed. Boston: Allyn & Bacon, 1987. A concise, up-to-date summary of the literature on voting behavior.

Hill, David B., and Norman R. Luttbeg. *Trends in American Electoral Behavior.* 2d ed. Itasca, Ill.: F. E. Peacock, 1983. A survey of research on America's voters.

Key, V. O., Jr. *The Responsible Electorate.* Cambridge, Mass.: Belknap Press of Harvard University Press, 1966. A provocative analysis of voting as a response to government's performance.

Nie, Norman H., Sidney Verba, and John Petrocik. *The Changing American Voter.* enl. ed. Cambridge, Mass.: Harvard University Press, 1979. A reassessment of the nature of the American electorate in view of the political changes of the 1960s and early 1970s.

Pomper, Gerald, with Susan S. Lederman. *Elections in America.* 2d ed. New York: Longman, 1980. A study of elections which accounts for the actions of parties and candidates as well as the decisions of voters.

# Are Americans Responsible as Citizens?

### BENJAMIN R. BARBER

*Responsibility means that all people take responsibility for at least some public decisions and acts at least some of the time.*

If by "citizens" we mean voters who take themselves to the polls every year or two, about half of the eligible electorate are responsible citizens. (Just 50 percent of Americans voted in the 1988 presidential election.) But if we mean what the ancient Athenians meant—active participants in public office, assembly discussion (every ten days or so), periodic juries and magistracies often chosen by lot from census rolls—then the only people in modern America worthy of the name citizen are professional politicians and public servants. Indeed, although women, slaves, and resident foreigners were excluded from citizenship, about 22 percent of Athenians participated actively in politics, as compared to the 24 percent, on average, of Americans who participate in the far less demanding civic task of voting.

Perhaps the most fundamental question of modern democratic politics, then, is, "What does it mean to be a citizen?" Social scientists often use the language of "elites" and "masses," which suggests not rational individuals engaged in civic activity, but pawns of social forces who simply vote their background or religion or class interests and are stuck in permanent classes defined by their socioeconomic status. And even where the idea of a rational voter is advanced, advocates of representative democracy are satisfied with a minimalist definition of the citizen, associating civic virtue with getting people to the polls. This occasional act by "watchdogs" who otherwise leave governing to the governors is seen as the whole of citizenship.

If, however, by democracy we mean not the selection of accountable representatives to undertake all the real tasks of government, but the burdensome practices of collective self-government, then citizenship becomes a task that, as Oscar Wilde said of socialism, takes up a great many free evenings. To be a competent citizen capable of community self-government requires individuals to deliberate as members of a community—to think "publicly" in a language of civic discourse that does more than merely express sectarian private interests. It also demands that citizens participate—in juries, in referenda, in assembly discussion, and in the rest of the work of democracy. Citizenship in this sense is an acquired art, resting on extended civic education, civic training, and above all civic experience. Responsibility is taught by giving people responsibility—and this includes the right to make mistakes.

Responsibility cannot of course mean that all people take responsibility for all public decisions and acts all of the time; but it can mean that all people take responsibility for at least some public decisions and acts at least some of the time. Responsibility of this kind cannot be ceded to great leaders. As socialist leader Eugene V. Debs once warned his supporters, "Too long have the workers of the world waited for some Moses to lead them out of bondage. He has not come. He will not come. I would not lead you out if I could; for if you could be led out, you could be led back in again."

The language of civic responsibility, like so many other valuable currencies, has been eroded by inflation. We are now urged to believe that voting once every four years constitutes the essence of patriotism. But as Rousseau remarked, "Freedom is a food easy to eat but hard to digest." To digest freedom and transform it into fuel for the sinews of a living democracy is the real challenge of citizenship. Americans have yet to meet it, and until they do, their boast of being responsible citizens of a free country will ring hollow.

*Benjamin R. Barber is Walt Whitman Professor and Director of the Walt Whitman Center for the Culture and Politics of Democracy at Rutgers University. He is the author of* Strong Democracy, The Conquest of Politics, *and (with Patrick Watson) the book and TV series* The Struggle for Democracy.

**MORRIS P. FIORINA**

*It often seems that academic critics of the American citizen are whining simply because more citizens don't share and act on* their *concerns.*

Are Americans responsible citizens? A generation ago political scientists debated a related question: Were Americans sufficiently well informed to merit the term "rational" voters? An exasperated E. E. Schattschneider finally inquired, "Who . . . are these self-appointed censors who assume that they are in a position to flunk the whole human race? . . . Democracy was made for the people, not the people for Democracy." Schattschneider's observation is as appropriate now as then.

Critics of citizen responsibility employ standards of judgment that incorporate assumptions about political life. A number of the assumptions typically made are problematic:

1. Government has some higher purpose—to lead the populace to a more elevated moral plane, to spread democracy throughout the world, and the like.
2. Participation in government is educational and morally uplifting for the citizen. In particular, it fosters an appreciation of the common good.
3. Contemporary citizenship has deteriorated from some past stage of higher development—that of the ancient Greeks, or at least of nineteenth-century Americans.

Each of these assumptions is questionable. As for the first, most Americans are not crusaders. What they want from government is the safety and stability that will enable them to pursue their happiness as they define it. Rather than a crusading government, they want a government that does its job in the background with a minimum of fuss, like the electric company.

Citizens regard politics more as a necessary evil, than as an opportunity for moral development.

The second assumption is faulty on two counts. First, it assumes that communication inevitably produces understanding. On the contrary, getting to know one's neighbors may only reveal that they are more narrowminded and vicious than one had imagined. And, far from producing consensus about the common good, deliberation may only produce the knowledge of particularistic interests necessary to construct a winning logroll that benefits special interests at the expense of the broader community interest. Second, this assumption tends to discount the myriad nongovernmental activities in which citizens engage. All across America, citizens generously volunteer their time for school committees, church groups, youth sports, and a host of community activities. Intellectuals might want citizens to spend their time in meetings discussing the Third World debt problem, but most citizens prefer to stay closer to home.

The third assumption is most likely wrong in fact. High levels of political involvement in the past by no means indicate a more committed, more virtuous citizenry. They may only indicate a lack of alternative forms of entertainment. Crowds of Americans endured four-hour speeches and debates in the nineteenth century primarily because they didn't have TVs. And in an era of seven-day work weeks, election day was a welcome holiday. If an increase in political participation is such a high priority today, we need only resurrect various practices from our glorious past—the spoils system, machine politics, and paying for votes.

Obviously, these comments are overstatements intended to provoke, but the underlying point is serious. On what basis can anyone presume to decide what responsible citizenship is? It often seems that academic critics of the American citizen are whining simply because more citizens don't share and act on *their* concerns. The present era of increasing internationalization of and political arrangements poses new challenges. I am fairly optimistic that the American citizenry will meet these challenges. I am less hopeful that the academic critics, yearning for some glorified version of ancient Athens, will do so.

*Morris P. Fiorina is Professor of Government at Harvard University. He is the author of* Retrospective Voting in American National Elections.

# *Part Four*

## POLITICAL ORGANIZATION

Imagine that all adult Americans were placed heel to toe in a line: the line would stretch across the country, from New York City to Los Angeles and back, five times over. Imagine further that there is a man in the line who seeks to influence others. He shouts out his opinions as loudly as possible, his voice carrying the length of a football field in either direction. Assume now that everyone within earshot is persuaded by the man's arguments and accepts his views. What proportion of the American public has he influenced? The answer is a tiny share: 0.000001. If the proportion seems trivial, then consider the following fact: few flesh-and-blood citizens have influence over as many people as does our imaginary man.

This hypothetical situation suggests why Americans, like any other democratic people, depend on political organization. No citizen acting alone is likely to have a measurable influence on national policies. Some Americans find it difficult to accept the fact of their individual powerlessness, but it is a reality of life in a nation of 250 million people. They acquire power only when they join together in common purpose.

This joining comes through political organization, one form of which is the political party, discussed in Chapters 11 and 12.

Democratic government is almost inseparable from parties, which formed at the grass roots in the 1800s to provide a means by which citizens could act together as an effective majority. Interest groups, the subject of Chapters 13 and 14, are another vehicle of collective action. The interests that they represent tend to be specialized ones, such as soybean farmers or oil companies. Groups have always been a strong force in American politics, and their influence has become even more pronounced in recent decades. The news media, examined in Chapter 15, are a third linking organization. Newspapers, television, radio, and newsmagazines enable citizens to keep in touch with one another and with their leaders. The present era is often described as the age of communications, testimony to the media's current pervasiveness and power.

All democracies depend on parties, groups, and the media to organize their publics, but the United States does so in almost unique ways. America's political parties are among the weakest in the world, while its interest groups and media are among the strongest. The reasons for this state of affairs are many, and the consequences are significant. Organization enables Americans to make their voices heard, and the precise nature of this organization—weak parties, strong groups, and powerful media—determines whose voices will be the loudest.　　　　★　★　★

# Chapter 11

## THE TWO-PARTY SYSTEM: DEFINING THE VOTERS' CHOICE

*Political parties created democracy and . . . modern democracy is unthinkable save in terms of the parties.*

E. E. Schattschneider[1]

They were the kind of strange bedfellows that American politics regularly produces. One of them stood for gun control, busing, and an end to the death penalty and proposed that the United States terminate its Star Wars project, MX missile construction, and aid to the Nicaraguan rebels. His running mate held the opposite position on each of these issues. They were the 1988 Democratic ticket, Michael Dukakis of Massachusetts and Lloyd Bentsen of Texas.

The Dukakis–Bentsen partnership was a product of the country's two-party system, which compels candidates and voters with diverse opinions to find common ground. Because the Republican and Democratic parties have dominated U.S. elections for so long and are the only parties with any realistic chance of acquiring political control, Americans nearly take their **two-party system** for granted. However, most democracies have a **multiparty system,** in which three or more parties have the capacity to gain control of government separately or in coalition. Even democracies that have what is essentially a two-party system typically have important smaller parties as well. For example, Great Britain's Labour and Conservative parties have dominated that nation's politics since early in this century, but they have had competition from the Liberal party and, more recently, the Social Democrats. At present all four of these parties have representatives in Parliament. In contrast, the U.S. Congress consists entirely of Democrats and Republicans.

[1] E. E. Schattschneider, *Party Government* (New York: Rinehart, 1942), 1.

The two-party system has important consequences for American politics. Neither major party can win an election by drawing its votes from only a small sector of the population; as a result, the two parties tend to appeal to many of the same interests. The policy traditions and tendencies of the Republican and Democratic parties do not differ sharply and consistently. For example, each party is committed to social security for the elderly and to substantial expenditures for national defense. Parties in European multiparty systems tend to be more programmatic. Each party has its distinctive platform and voting bloc. Of course, once in power, European parties are forced to adjust their programs to the prevailing realities. France's Socialist party, for example, won power in 1981 by attacking the center-right parties for failing to protect working-class and middle-class citizens from downward economic mobility (déclassement), but the nation's weak economy forced the Socialists to retain many of the pro-business policies of the previous government.[2] Nevertheless, European multiparty systems offer voters a more clear-cut set of choices than does the American two-party system.

To critics, the American parties' failure to take sharply different policy positions means that they offer the public no genuine alternatives. To their admirers, however, America's major parties provide political stability and yet are different enough to give voters a real choice. This chapter investigates America's two-party system and the type of choice it provides the public. It argues that the Republican and Democratic parties do offer a real and significant choice, but only at particular times and on particular issues. The main points discussed in this chapter are the following:

★ *Throughout most of the nation's history, political competition has centered on two parties.* This two-party tendency is explained by the nature of America's electoral system, political institutions, and political culture. Minor parties exist in the United States but have been unable to compete successfully for governing power.

★ *The Republican and Democratic coalitions are very broad.* Each includes a substantial proportion of nearly every economic, racial, religious, and regional grouping in the country.

★ *To win an electoral majority, each of the two major parties must appeal to a diverse set of interests; this necessity normally leads them to advocate moderate and somewhat overlapping policies and to avoid taking detailed positions on controversial issues. Only during national crises are America's parties likely to present the electorate with starkly different policy alternatives.*

## The History of the Two-Party System

Although many Americans distrust political parties and question their role, the fact is that democracy would be nearly meaningless without political parties. The party is the only institution that has the purpose of developing *broad* policy and leadership choices and then presenting them to the voting public for acceptance or rejection. Through the alternatives they offer in elections, parties give the public an opportunity to express its preferences about the direction government should take.

[2]Paul J. Best, Kul B. Rai, and David F. Walsh, *Politics in Three Worlds* (New York: Wiley, 1986), 324.

Congressional Pugilists.

1. Jonathan Dayton, Speaker.    2. Jonathan W. Condy, Clerk.

He in a trice struck Lyon thrice    Who seiz'd the tongs to ease his wrongs,    Congress Hall,
Upon his head, enrag'd sir,    And Griswold thus enjoy'd, sir.    in Philad'a, Feb. 15, 1798.
    S.E. Cor. 6th & Chestnut St.

FIRST FIGHT IN CONGRESS.

Party conflict developed early in the nation's history. The conflict turned violent one day in 1798 on the floor of the House of Representatives, when Roger Griswold (at right), a Federalist, attacked Matthew Lyon, a Republican. (New York Public Library)

Of course, parties are not the only means by which the public can exert influence. Interest groups such as the AFL-CIO and the American Medical Association provide individuals with the opportunity to act collectively. However, most such groups articulate the narrow and specific demands of a *minority* interest in society. In the United States, with its individualistic culture and tradition of freedom of association, group activity is more fragmented than in many other nations. Major political parties function in a different way. The party's goal is to create a *majority* by bringing together individuals with diverse interests. A **political party** is an ongoing coalition of interests joined together to try to get their candidates for public office elected under a common label.[3] Parties serve to pull diverse interests together and in the process offer the public broad policy and leadership alternatives.

Political parties developed spontaneously in the United States. They were not established by the Constitution, and most of America's early leaders were suspicious of parties. George Washington in his Farewell Address warned the nation of the "baneful effects" of parties, and James Madison likened parties to special interests. However, Madison's initial misgivings about parties gradually gave way to a grudging admiration; he recognized that they were a way for like-minded people to work together toward common goals. Gradually parties became the engine of democracy—the instrument by which a mass public could exercise political influence.

*Let me now . . . warn you in the most solemn manner against the baneful effects of party.*
George Washington
Farewell Address, 1796

## THE FIRST PARTIES

Political parties in the United States originated in the rivalry within George Washington's administration between Thomas Jefferson and Alexander Hamil-

[3]Leon D. Epstein, *Political Parties in Western Democracies* (New York: Praeger, 1967), 9.

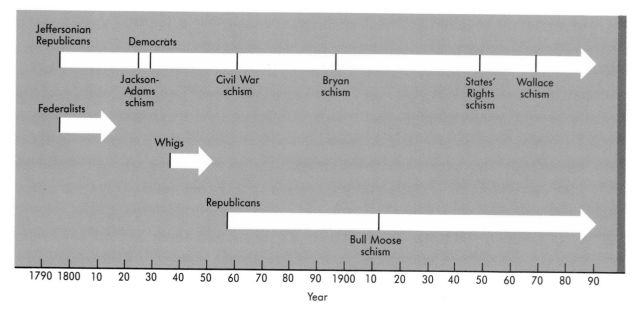

Jeffersonian Republicans

Democrats

Jackson-Adams schism

Civil War schism

Bryan schism

States' Rights schism

Wallace schism

Federalists

Whigs

Republicans

Bull Moose schism

1790 1800 10 20 30 40 50 60 70 80 90 1900 10 20 30 40 50 60 70 80 90

Year

**FIGURE 11-1 A Graphic History of America's Major Parties**

ton: as we saw in Chapter 4, Jefferson defended states' rights and small landholders, while Hamilton promoted a strong national government and wealthy interests. After Hamilton's ideas prevailed in Congress, Jefferson and his followers formed a political party, the Republicans (see Figure 11-1). By adopting this label, which was associated with popular government, the Jeffersonians sought to portray themselves as the rightful heirs to the American Revolution's legacy of self-government and political equality.

Hamilton responded by organizing his supporters into a formal party—the Federalists—and in the process created America's first competitive party system. The Federalists took their name from the faction that had supported ratification of the Constitution, thereby implying that they were the Constitution's true defenders. However, the Federalists' preoccupation with commercial and wealthy interests alienated many people. Under President John Adams, for example, the Federalists tried to intimidate new immigrants—most of whom were poor—by the Alien Acts, which gave government the right through presidential order to deport or imprison political dissenters who had not yet obtained citizenship. These repressive acts fueled Jefferson's claim that the Federalists were bent on establishing a government for the rich and wellborn. After Adams' defeat by Jefferson in the election of 1800, the Federalists and their discredited philosophy never again held sway.

During the so-called Era of Good Feeling, when James Monroe ran unopposed in 1820 for a second presidential term, it appeared as if the nation might exist without parties. Monroe told Andrew Jackson that free government could survive without parties. Yet by the end of Monroe's second term, policy disputes had split the Republican party into the National Republicans, led by John Quincy Adams, and the Democratic Republicans (later shortened to Democrats), led by Andrew Jackson. The National Republicans resembled the earlier Federalists in their support of commercial interests and a larger role for the national government, while the Democrats viewed themselves as Jefferson's rightful successors, since they favored small landholders and states' rights.

The idea of a government without party competition is utopian. The alternative is likely to be, not government for the common good, but government for and by a small elite. In Mexico a single party has dominated government for most of this century and, despite its roots in the popular revolution of 1910, has become the instrument of the nation's wealthiest families. For all its faults, competition between parties is the only system that can regularly mobilize collective influence on behalf of the many who are individually powerless against those few who have extraordinary wealth and prestige.[4] Because they are a vast numerical majority, ordinary citizens have the potential for great power in a democratic system, but that potential cannot become reality unless the people are collectively organized.

It was this realization that led Andrew Jackson during the 1820s to reassert the principle of party. By mobilizing the mass citizenry through party action, Jackson sought to break the hold of the Virginia and Massachusetts aristocracy on the presidency, opening the way to a government that was more directly responsive to ordinary citizens. At the peak of Jacksonian democracy in the 1830s, Alexis de Tocqueville wrote: "The People reign in the American political world as the Deity does in the universe."[5] Tocqueville exaggerated the people's true power but caught the spirit of popular government that was behind the restoration of parties under Andrew Jackson.

## GRASS-ROOTS PARTIES

Jackson's idea of a political party differed from Thomas Jefferson's. Whereas Jefferson's party had been well organized only at the leadership level, Jackson sought a "grass-roots" party, one that was built from the bottom up and was designed to encourage wide participation. Jackson's Democratic party consisted

[4]Walter Dean Burnham, "The End of American Party Politics," in Walter Dean Burnham, ed., *Politics/America: The Cutting Edge of Change* (New York: Van Nostrand, 1973), 132.
[5]Alexis de Tocqueville, *Democracy in America* (Garden City, N.Y.: Doubleday/Anchor, 1969), 60.

★ ANALYZE THE ISSUE

**The Advantages of Political Parties**
The United States has the world's oldest representative government; it also has the world's oldest political parties. Is this just a coincidence? If you believe that it is, then why have political parties emerged in *every* democracy? Can you think of an effective alternative means—such as interest groups or the mass media—by which citizens can acquire collective influence? What are the advantages and disadvantages of parties in comparison with these alternative means of bringing citizens together?

Robert Cruikshank's *All Creation Going to the White House* satirizes the inauguration of Andrew Jackson, who—as a democratic gesture—invited the public to join in the celebration. (Historical Pictures Services)

of committees and clubs at the national, state, and local levels, with membership open to all eligible voters. During the 1828 campaign the Democrats staged public parades, rallies, and barbecues throughout the nation. These popular entertainments, along with more liberal suffrage laws, contributed to a nearly fourfold rise in voter turnout.[6]

In the 1830s the Democrats faced a new opposition party, the Whigs. The Whigs consisted of a diverse set of interests, including states'-rights advocates from the South who felt that the Democrats had abandoned them, former National Republicans who favored a strong central government, and members of the single-issue Anti-Masonic party. About all that these diverse groups had in common initially was their hostility to the strong-willed Jackson, whom they called "King Andrew I." By 1840, however, the Whigs had transformed themselves into an effective opposition party by imitating the Democrats' tactics—grass-roots organization, mobilization of the electorate, and the nomination in 1840 of a national military hero, William Henry Harrison, as their presidential candidate.[7]

This competitive two-party system was short-lived. In the 1850s both parties were torn apart by the slavery issue. Many southern Whigs gravitated to the more pro-slavery Democratic party. Northern Whigs and some antislavery northern Democrats joined a new sectional organization, the Republican party, which opposed the extension of slavery. The Republicans soon eclipsed the Whigs. However, the American party system essentially collapsed in the late 1850s, for the only time in the nation's history.[8] The issues of slavery and union were too basic and serious to be settled through peaceful elections. The presidential victory of the Republican Abraham Lincoln in 1860 marked not the peaceful resolution of these issues but the beginning of a war between the states.

## REPUBLICANS VS. DEMOCRATS: THE ENDURING PARTY SYSTEM

After the Civil War, the nation settled into the pattern of competition between the Republican and Democratic parties that has prevailed ever since. The durability of these two parties is due not to their ideological consistency but to their remarkable capacity for adaptation during periods of crisis. Realigning elections of the kind that occurred during the Great Depression of the 1930s (see Chapter 10) have produced essentially different Democratic and Republican parties—with new bases of support, new policies, and new philosophies. Thus, although the modern Democratic party, as the lineal descendant of the Jeffersonian Republicans, can be labeled the world's oldest political party, today's Democrats, with their emphasis on the national government's power, bear no resemblance to the states'-rights Jeffersonians of the 1790s.

In the course of their history, the Republican and Democratic parties have not always been evenly matched opponents. Following the 1860 election, the Republican "Grand Old Party" (GOP) controlled the White House for more

Abraham Lincoln said that this portrait of him by Mathew Brady, which he used in his campaign literature, contributed to his election to the presidency in 1860. (Library of Congress)

[6]See Richard P. McCormick, *The Second American Party System: Party Formation in the Jacksonian Era* (Chapel Hill: University of North Carolina Press, 1966).
[7]Glyndon G. Van Deusen, "The Whig Party," in Arthur M. Schlesinger, Jr., ed., *History of the U.S. Political Parties*, vol. 1 (New York: Chelsea House, 1973), 344.
[8]William Crotty, "The Party Symbol and Its Changing Meaning," in William Crotty, ed., *The Party Symbol* (San Francisco: W. H. Freeman, 1980), 6.

**FIGURE 11-2 Party Control of State Legislatures, 1989**
Intense party competition is not found in most states. *Source:* Congressional Quarterly Weekly Report, *November 12, 1988, 2893, 3299-3300.*

Legend:
- Democrats control both houses
- Republicans control both houses
- No party controls both houses
- Nonpartisan unicameral

than seventy years, losing it during this period to only two Democrats, Grover Cleveland and Woodrow Wilson, each of whom was assisted by dissension within Republican ranks. Cleveland won in 1884 when the GOP denied nomination to its own incumbent, Chester A. Arthur, and turned instead to James G. Blaine ("the Man from Maine"), who, it appears, had the support neither of progressive Republicans nor of his own running mate, John A. Logan. In 1912 Wilson won when the Republicans were split by the Bull Moose party candidacy of Theodore Roosevelt. Without these internal problems, the Republicans might have held the presidency without interruption from the Civil War to the Depression.

Franklin D. Roosevelt's election in 1932 began a twenty-year period of Democratic presidencies, but since the early 1950s the two parties have divided control of the White House. In 1960, 1968, and 1976, the margin of victory for either party's presidential candidate was a slender 3 percent or less. As for the legislative branch, the Democrats have dominated Congress since 1930, losing control of both House and Senate only in 1947–1948 and 1953–1954, and of the Senate in 1980–1986.

On the state and local levels, intense two-party competition is not the norm. In most states, for example, both houses of the legislature are controlled by the same party (see Figure 11–2). Party dominance tends to follow regional lines. Since the Civil War, Democrats have held sway over southern politics—the South's revenge on the party of Lincoln; only in recent decades has the region begun to see more party competition. The Republican party also has its traditional strongholds, such as New England and the rural Midwest, although Democratic candidates have recently improved their showing in these areas. As political power has shifted toward the government in Washington in the past few decades, states and localities have become less insulated from national influences, and their parties' strengths have become more evenly matched. However, vigorous two-party competition is still the exception rather than the rule in states and localities.

## Minor Parties in America

Although American politics has come to center on two major parties, there have always been minor parties—more than a thousand during the nation's history.[9] Most of them have been short-lived, and only a few have had a lasting impact. A minor party, by definition, has no chance of acquiring a significant share of governing power. Minor parties exist largely to advocate positions that their followers believe are not being adequately represented by either of the two major parties.

### TYPES OF MINOR PARTIES

Minor parties may be formed in response to the emergence of a single controversial issue, out of a commitment to a certain ideology, or as a result of a rift within one of the major parties.

#### Single-Issue Parties

Some minor parties form around a single issue of overriding concern to its supporters. The present-day Right-to-Life party, for example, was formed to oppose the legalization of abortion. Of course, right-to-life interest groups have also formed in opposition to legalized abortion. In fact, single-issue parties are similar to interest groups in that each is preoccupied with a narrow and specific policy area. The difference is that a single-issue party places candidates for public office on the ballot, whereas an interest group, although it may otherwise be active in election campaigns, does not. (Interest groups are discussed in detail in Chapters 13 and 14.)

Some single-issue parties have seen their policy goals enacted into law. The Prohibition party contributed to the ratification in 1919 of the Eighteenth Amendment, which prohibited the manufacture, sale, and transportation of alcoholic beverages (but was repealed in 1933). Single-issue parties usually disband when their issue is favorably resolved or fades in importance.[10]

#### Ideological Parties

Other minor parties are characterized by their ideological commitment, or concern for a broad and radical philosophical position, such as redistribution of economic resources. Modern-day ideological parties include the Citizens party, the Communist party, the Socialist Workers party, and the Libertarian party,

---

[9]See Frank Smallwood, *The Other Candidates: Third Parties in Presidential Elections* (Dartmouth, N.H.: University Press of New England, 1983); Steven J. Rosenstone, *Third Parties in America* (Princeton, N.J.: Princeton University Press, 1984).
[10]Daniel A. Mazmanian, *Third Parties in Presidential Elections* (Washington, D.C.: Brookings Institution, 1984), 143–144.

The Right to Life party is a modern example of a single-issue party. Its sole concern is the reversal of the legalization of abortion. (Paul Conklin)

each of which operates on the fringe of American politics. In fact, their combined popular vote was less than 1 percent of the total in the 1988 presidential election. Ideological parties tend to gain strength during times of social and political upheaval. The Socialist party received 6 percent of the presidential vote in 1912, largely from voters dissatisfied with the monopolistic practices of business trusts.[11]

One of the strongest ideological parties in the nation's history was the Populist party.* Its candidate in the 1892 presidential election, James B. Weaver, gained 8.5 percent of the national vote and won twenty-two electoral votes in six Western states. The party began as a protest movement in response to the economic depression and business monopolies of the 1890s.[12] It had an agrarian base, a result of the anger of small farmers over low commodity prices, tight credit, and the high rates charged by railroad monopolies to transport farm goods. The Populist platform called for government ownership of the railroads, a graduated income tax, low tariffs on imports, and elimination of the gold standard. The Populist party in 1896 endorsed the Democratic presidential nominee, William Jennings Bryan, and its support probably hurt the Democrats

---

*Some classifications of minor parties place the Populists in a category—"economic protest parties"—that is not used here. In this author's judgment, parties that other scholars place in the economic protest category are actually either ideological parties, as in the case of the Populists, or single-issue parties, such as the Greenback party. The Populists' positions on economic power and redistribution constitute a broad and radical philosophy, which is the defining characteristic of an ideological party.

[11]Ibid., 58–59.

[12]Walter Dean Burnham, *Critical Elections and the Mainsprings of American Politics* (New York: Norton, 1970), 27; see also Lawrence Goodwyn, *The Populist Movement* (New York: Oxford University Press, 1978).

In 1896 the Populist party—a strong ideological party—nominated William Jennings Bryan as its presidential candidate. Bryan was also the Democratic nominee in that election. (Brown Brothers)

nationally.[13] Large numbers of "Gold Democrats" left their party in fear of the inflationary consequences of Bryan's advocacy of the free coinage of silver.

Unlike the Populists, most ideological parties do not work directly for election victory; instead they try to publicize their point of view, hoping for a dramatic political or social change that will win the public over to their side. This sense of historic mission has given some ideological parties a long life. The Socialist Labor party, for example, has existed in America since 1888.

### Factional Parties

The Republican and Democratic parties are relatively adept at managing internal conflict. Although each party's support is diverse, the differences among its varying interests can normally be reconciled. However, there have been times when factional conflict within the major parties has led to the formation of minor parties.

The most successful of these factional parties at the polls was Theodore Roosevelt's Bull Moose party. In 1908 Roosevelt, after having served eight years as president, declined to seek a third term despite the GOP's overtures. Roosevelt hand-picked William Howard Taft for the Republican nomination, expecting him to continue the Progressive tradition that he, Roosevelt, had established. When Taft as president showed neither Roosevelt's enthusiasm for a strong presidency nor Roosevelt's commitment to business regulation, relations between the two men soured. In 1912 Roosevelt challenged Taft for the Republican presidential nomination. Progressive Republicans backed Roosevelt, but Taft won the nomination with the backing of conservative Republicans and the Republican National Committee. Roosevelt led a Progressive walkout to form the Bull Moose party (a reference to Roosevelt's claim that he was "as strong as a bull moose"). Roosevelt won 27 percent of the presidential vote to

★ ANALYZE THE ISSUE

**The Role of Minor Parties**
At the end of the nineteenth century, neither the Republican nor the Democratic party was providing substantial leadership in addressing problems spawned by the Industrial Revolution. How does this fact help to explain the rise of the Populists? What does the story of the Populist party suggest about the role and eventual fate of minor parties?

[13]James L. Sundquist, *Dynamics of the Party System* (Washington, D.C.: Brookings Institution, 1973), 140.

Theodore Roosevelt campaigns in Atlantic City, N.J., in 1912 with a symbol of his Bull Moose party. (UPI/Bettmann Newsphotos)

Taft's 25 percent, but the split within Republican ranks enabled the Democratic nominee, Woodrow Wilson, to win the presidency.

The States' Rights party in 1948 and the American Independent party in 1968 are other examples of strong factional parties. Each of these parties was formed by southern Democrats who were angered by northern Democrats' support of racial desegregation. The States' Rights platform asserted that the Truman administration was "totalitarian" in its disregard for states' rights.

Factional parties usually flourish for just one or two elections, and their electoral appeal is typically tied to a powerful issue and a well-known candidate. When Theodore Roosevelt returned to Republican ranks in 1916, the Bull Moose party as such ceased to exist, although Senator Robert La Follette ran a strong campaign as a Progressive in 1924, receiving 16 percent of the national vote. George Wallace was the founder and 1968 presidential nominee of the American Independent party (AIP). Wallace considered making a second presidential run under the AIP's banner in 1972 but decided finally to seek the mainstream Democratic nomination, leaving the AIP without a candidate. In 1976, in what turned out to be its last campaign, the AIP nominated the segregationist Lester Maddox, a former Georgia governor, who received less than 1 percent of the national vote.

Deep divisions within a party give rise to factionalism, and such wounds are not easily healed. Conservative Republicans were never very comfortable with Progressivism, and it eventually came to be represented mainly by the Democratic party, beginning with Wilson and continuing in the New Deal policies of Franklin D. Roosevelt. Similarly, the conflict over civil rights that began within the Democratic party during the Truman years continued for the next quarter century, resulting first in widespread support by many southern whites for Republican presidential candidates and later in their general loyalty to the Republican party. In short, such factional splits usually represent irresolvable conflicts within a major party that eventually help to redefine the divisions between the two major parties.

# THE INDEPENDENT CANDIDATE

Some candidates for public office run not under a party label but as independents. The most prominent such candidate in recent years was John Anderson, a congressman from Illinois who, having failed in a bid for the 1980 Republican nomination for president, continued to campaign as an independent. Anderson attracted support among some liberal Republicans who were dissatisfied with their party's nomination of Ronald Reagan, liberal Democrats seeking an alternative to the incumbent president, Jimmy Carter, and independent voters. Anderson's support in opinion polls reached nearly 25 percent during the summer of 1980 and it appeared that he had an outside chance of winning the presidency if the electorate otherwise divided closely between Carter and Reagan. When it later became evident that Anderson would lose, his support dwindled rapidly. In the end he received only 7 percent of the presidential vote. Anderson tried to counter the slippage by denying that his candidacy was indirectly contributing to the election of either Carter or Reagan. "A vote for Anderson is a vote for Anderson" was his rallying cry. Nevertheless, of voters who had at one time indicated a preference for Anderson, about half cited his inability to win as a reason for their defection.

As Anderson's experience indicates, the problems of an independent candidate can be similar to those of a factional party candidate, such as George Wallace, who ran as the American Independent party's presidential nominee in 1968. In fact, an independent presidential candidate is comparable to a factional party presidential candidate except for the former's lack of a party label and of associated candidates. When Wallace ran in 1968, the American Independent party also fielded candidates in some congressional races, just as, in 1912, Progressive Republicans had slated other candidates in addition to Theodore Roosevelt. Except for his vice-presidential running mate (Patrick Lucey, a former Democratic governor of Wisconsin), Anderson ran alone, and thus ran as a true independent.

## THE DILEMMA OF MINOR PARTIES

Only one minor party, the Republican party, has ever achieved majority status. Minor parties in America have a recurrent dilemma. Their followers are motivated by issue positions that are vital to them but unattractive to other voters. To increase its following, a minor party must broaden its platform; in so doing, however, it risks alienating its original supporters. Yet if it remains small, it cannot win elections and may eventually wither away.

Historically, the influence of minor parties has resided mainly in the response of the major parties to the issues they raise. Strong support for a minor party can encourage one or both major parties to try to capture its backers. For example, George Wallace's strong showing in the South in 1968 apparently prompted the Nixon administration to develop its "southern strategy," which included nomination of a southern conservative to the Supreme Court and opposition to court-ordered busing for purposes of school integration.[14] Richard Nixon reportedly believed that if Wallace's followers could be won over, the GOP would replace the Democrats as the nation's dominant party.

## *Why Only Two Parties?*

Minor parties come and go, but the two major parties go on and on. What accounts for their persistence? The long tradition of the Republicans and

[14]Mazmanian, *Third Parties*, 85–87.

Democrats is obviously a factor in their current strength. Most voters give serious consideration only to the Republican and Democratic nominees, and the news media devote nearly all their coverage to the major parties.[15] These tendencies, however, do not explain why only two parties took firm root in the United States in the first place.

## THE ELECTORAL SYSTEM

One reason for America's two-party system is the fact that the nation chooses its officials through plurality voting in **single-member districts.**[16] Each constituency elects a single candidate to a particular office, such as U.S. senator or representative; only the party that gets the most votes (a plurality) in a district wins the office. This system discourages minor parties. Assume, for example, that a minor party received exactly 20 percent of the vote in each of the nation's 435 congressional races. Even though one in five voters nationwide backed the minor party, it would win *no* seats in Congress because none of its candidates placed first in any of the 435 single-member-district races. The winning candidate in each case would be the major-party candidate who received the larger proportion of the remaining 80 percent of the vote.

By comparison, most European democracies use some form of **proportional representation,** in which seats in the legislature are allocated according to a party's share of the popular vote. West Germany's electoral system, for instance, combines single-member districts and proportional representation. Each party not only nominates candidates to run in single-member local districts but also prepares a ranked list of national candidates. All single-member-district winners receive seats in the Bundestag, the West German legislature. Each party then can select candidates from its list until its legislative seats total roughly its proportion of national votes. Thus in the West German elections of 1983, the Green party won slightly more than 5 percent of the national vote. Although none of its candidates placed first in an election district, the party was able to choose candidates from its list to occupy about 5 percent of the Bundestag's seats. If the Green party had been competing under the rules of the American electoral system, it would not have won any seats.

The adverse effect of electoral laws on U.S. minor parties is evident also in the election of the president. A presidential race is a winner-take-all contest, and only a strong party has any chance of gaining the office. The presidency can be won with less than a majority of the popular vote, as was the case in 1968, when Republican Richard Nixon was elected with only a 43 percent plurality. In that election George Wallace won 13.5 percent of the national vote as the American Independent party candidate, but his relatively strong showing gave him no share of executive power. By comparison, in France there must be a runoff election between the two candidates who receive the most votes if neither receives a majority—50 percent or more—of the vote. Minor parties that fare poorly in the first election can bargain with the final contenders, trading support

[15]Michael Robinson and Margaret Sheehan, *Over the Wire and on TV* (New York: Russell Sage Foundation, 1983), 73.
[16]The classic account of the relationship of electoral and party systems is Maurice Duverger, *Political Parties* (New York: Wiley, 1954), bk. II, ch. 1; see also Giovanni Sartori, *Parties and Party Systems* (Cambridge, England: Cambridge University Press, 1976); Douglas Rae, *The Political Consequences of Electoral Laws* (New Haven, Conn.: Yale University Press, 1967).

West Germany's electoral system allocates legislative seats on the basis both of single-district voting and of the overall proportion of votes a party receives. This system requires that the German voter cast two ballots in legislative races: one to choose among the candidates in the particular district and one to choose among the parties. Shown here is a ballot from a 1987 West German election. The left-hand column lists the candidates for the legislative seat in a district, and the right-hand column lists the parties. (Note the relatively large number of parties on the ballot.)

in the runoff election for policy concessions or cabinet positions in the new government. In this way, the French system—unlike the American one— provides an incentive for smaller parties to compete.

Finally, election laws in some states discourage minor parties by making it difficult for them to get their candidates on the ballot. Unlike the major parties, minor parties cannot easily meet statutory requirements for a place on the ballot—such as having received a certain proportion of the vote in the preceding election. A party that does not meet this requirement must collect the signatures of a large number of registered voters before its candidates can appear on the ballot—another task that is difficult for a minor party. In his 1968 presidential bid, Wallace had to collect 2.7 million signatures in order to get his name on the ballot in every state.[17]

## PARTY PRAGMATISM

The pragmatic nature of America's major parties also contributes to their persistence. Because the Republican and Democratic parties have opened their ranks to people of all views, they have been able to accommodate individuals who might otherwise have allied themselves with minor parties. In Congress, for example, members with sharply different political philosophies find it

★ ANALYZE THE ISSUE

**The Possible Effects of Proportional Representation**
If the United States had an electoral system based on proportional representation, it would probably have more than two competitive parties. What might these other parties be? Do you think one of them would be a socialist party? How about a party representing the fundamentalist Christian right? Blacks? Women? Others? Would proportional representation make a great or only marginal difference in U.S. politics?

[17]Robert J. Huckshorn, *Political Parties in America*, 2d ed. (Pacific Palisades, Calif.: Brooks/Cole, 1983), 70.

possible to coexist in the same party. Consider Claudine Schneider of Rhode Island and Bobbi Fiedler of California, both Republican members of the House of Representatives. In 1982 Schneider, a liberal Republican, voted the same way as Fiedler, a conservative, on less than half of major House bills. In fact, Schneider sided more often with Democrats than with Republicans on legislative issues.[18]

Europe's legislative parties, in contrast, generally insist on the loyalty of their elected representatives. A member of the French National Assembly who votes with the opposition party on a key legislative measure may be denied renomination. Conflicts within French parties have at times forced dissident leaders to leave and form new parties. The broad base of American parties makes this response unlikely: party mavericks in Congress usually find that they gain more power by staying in the party and acquiring the seniority that leads to positions of committee leadership. For example, Senator Robert Packwood of Oregon is less conservative than most of his Republican colleagues, yet his seniority has made him the ranking Republican on the Senate Finance Committee and thus an influential voice in the formulation of Republican positions on tax issues within the Senate.

The fragmentation of power that characterizes the American political system gives the major parties almost no choice but to accept divisions within their ranks. Because members of Congress are highly responsive to the interests of the states and districts they represent, members of the same party can find themselves at odds over national issues. Yet in attending to their constituents' needs and demands, they build an electoral base separate from that of their party nationally. The party is thus not in a position to dictate what its congressional representatives will do once they are in office.[19]

The pragmatism that helps to maintain the two major parties in a dominant position is also dictated by federalism. Because they compete for offices at the national, state, and local levels, where the issues and divisions can differ significantly, the parties cannot realistically demand that their candidates adhere to a common philosophy.[20]

## Policy Formulation and Coalition Formation in the Two-Party System

The overriding goal of a major American political party is to gain control of government by getting its candidates elected to office. This goal can be stated more broadly in terms of the party system's major function: the organization of political conflict.[21] The parties transform conflict over society's goals into electoral competition in which the losers accept the winners' right to make policy decisions. In this **party competition,** which is at the core of the democratic process, the parties form coalitions of interests, articulate policy and leadership positions, and compete for electoral dominance. In the process, parties give individual citizens a choice among leaders and policies.

[18]Michael Barone and Grant Ujifusa, *The Almanac of American Politics, 1984* (Washington, D.C.: National Journal, 1983), 128, 1059.
[19]Frank Sorauf, *Party Politics in America,* 5th ed. (Boston: Little, Brown, 1984), 42–43.
[20]Duverger, *Political Parties,* bk. II, ch. 1.
[21]E. E. Schattschneider, *The Semisovereign People: A Realist's View of Democracy in America* (New York: Holt, Rinehart and Winston, 1961), 86–96.

*The American people are quite competent to judge a political party that works both sides of a street.*

Franklin D. Roosevelt

The choice that parties offer, however, depends significantly on the type of party system in which they operate. Because there are only two major American parties, their policies and bases of support differ from what could be expected if numerous parties were in competition. To gain control of the government, the Republicans or Democrats must attract a majority of the electorate, and so must appeal to a broad and diverse set of interests. The need to gain wide support usually leads both parties to advocate moderate policies and to avoid taking highly specific positions on controversial issues. American parties, Clinton Rossiter said, are "creatures of compromise."[22]

Rossiter's characterization describes American parties with reasonable accuracy during normal times. In periods of national crisis or political realignment, however, the parties have sometimes pursued policies that have sharply divided Americans and offered them a clear choice. To be complete, a description of the alternatives provided by the major American parties must include their actions in periods both of stability and of change, as the following discussion indicates.

## SEEKING THE POLITICAL CENTER

In Europe's multiparty systems, the various parties of the left (liberal), right (conservative), and center (moderate) typically offer voters sharply defined alternatives. A far-left party, for example, may advocate government control of all key industries, while a far-right party may propose the elimination of all but the most essential social-welfare programs. These differences are substantial and reflect the wide spectrum of political opinions in European societies and the need of each party to stake out a clear position along this spectrum.[23] The Communist party of France, for instance, has a core constituency that expects it to advocate Marxist policies, so the party does not try to attract capitalist business interests to its cause.

By comparison, most Americans prefer moderate policies to ideological extremism, so the two major parties tend to stay close to the center of the political spectrum.[24] Any time a party makes a pronounced shift toward either extreme, the middle is left open for the opposing party. Barry Goldwater, the Republican presidential nominee in 1964, proposed the elimination of mandatory social security and said he would consider the tactical use of small nuclear weapons in such wars as the Vietnam conflict—extreme conservative positions that cost him many votes. At the opposite end of the spectrum, George McGovern, nominated by the Democrats in 1972, advocated such extreme liberal policies as sharp cuts in defense spending, an immediate and unconditional withdrawal of U.S. combat troops from Vietnam, and a guaranteed annual income for every American family, and was resoundingly defeated in the general election.

Republican and Democratic candidates usually try to develop stands that will have broad appeal or at least will not alienate significant blocs of voters. Often this strategy results in campaigns in which the candidates avoid committing themselves to unequivocal stands on controversial issues. This tendency has been thoroughly documented in Benjamin Page's study of presidential cam-

---

[22]Clinton Rossiter, *Parties and Politics in America* (Ithaca, N. Y.: Cornell University Press, 1960), 11.
[23]Duverger, *Political Parties*, 372–392.
[24]See Anthony Downs, *An Economic Theory of Democracy* (New York: Harper & Row, 1957), chs. 7 and 8.

The Communist party is much more active and visible in France than in the United States, which focuses on only two major parties. (A. Nogues/Sygma)

paign rhetoric from 1928 to 1976.[25] The main issue of the 1968 campaign, for example, was the United States' involvement in Vietnam, but neither Richard Nixon nor Hubert Humphrey outlined a detailed plan for dealing with that issue (see box).

At times, however, the parties have strayed from the political center and still prevailed. In 1980 Ronald Reagan campaigned on a platform calling for sharp cuts in domestic spending programs and for a confrontational policy toward the Soviet Union (see Chapter 10). These positions were worrisome to most Americans, but they still preferred Reagan to the Democratic incumbent, Jimmy Carter, who most Americans felt had mishandled the presidency.

The lesson of Reagan's victory and some others, such as Franklin D. Roosevelt's in 1932, is that the center of the American political spectrum can be moved. Candidates risk a crushing defeat by straying too far from established ideas during times of general satisfaction with government, but they may do so with some chance for victory when times are turbulent. Then, if conditions improve, the American public may show their support for the new president's initiatives by reelecting him, thereby contributing to the creation of a new political center.

Changes in the presidential nomination system since 1972 have made it more difficult for presidential candidates to avoid taking stands on issues.[26] To win nomination, presidential contenders must appeal directly to primary electorates, which tend to be somewhat ideological. Republican primary voters are more conservative on the whole than other Republicans, and Democratic primary voters tend to be somewhat more liberal than other Democrats.[27] The national convention delegates who choose the presidential nominees are even

[25]Benjamin I. Page, *Choices and Echoes in Presidential Elections* (Chicago: University of Chicago Press, 1978), 132, 153–156.

[26]Dennis C. Sullivan, Jeffrey L. Pressman, and F. Christopher Arterton, *Explorations in Convention Decision Making* (San Francisco: W. H. Freeman, 1976).

[27]See Jeane Kirkpatrick, *The New Presidential Elite* (New York: Russell Sage Foundation, 1976), ch. 10; Norman H. Nie, Sidney Verba, and John Petrocik, *The Changing American Voter* (Cambridge, Mass.: Harvard University Press, 1976), ch. 12.

# HOW CANDIDATES TALK ABOUT ISSUES: EXCERPTS FROM RICHARD NIXON'S 1968 ACCEPTANCE SPEECH

The following excerpts from Richard Nixon's acceptance speech at the 1968 Republican convention illustrate the tendency of major-party candidates to talk in generalities, identifying problems that need the government's attention but avoiding taking clear-cut positions on controversial issues. Nixon's vague statements on Vietnam are particularly revealing. The Vietnam War was the issue uppermost in voters' minds in 1968, but it was also an issue over which Americans were sharply divided, so Nixon was careful to speak about it in broad terms.

As we look at America, we see cities enveloped in smoke and flame. We hear sirens in the night. We see Americans dying on distant battlefields abroad. We see Americans hating each other; fighting each other; killing each other at home. And as we see and hear these things, millions of Americans cry out in anguish: Did we come all this way for this? Did American boys die in Normandy and Korea and in Valley Forge for this?

When the strongest nation in the world can be tied down for four years in a war in Vietnam with no end in sight . . . then it's time for new leadership for the United States of America.

Never has so much military and economic and diplomatic power been used so ineffectively. And if after all of this time and all of this sacrifice and all of this support there is still no end in sight, then I say the time has come for the American people to turn to new leadership—not tied to the mistakes and the policies of the past. That is what we offer to America. And I pledge to you tonight that the first priority foreign policy objective of our next Administration will be to bring an honorable end to the war in Vietnam.

TABLE 11-1  Ideology of Voters and National Convention Delegates, by Party, 1988

| Ideology | Democratic Delegates | Democratic Voters | All Voters | Republican Voters | Republican Delegates |
|---|---|---|---|---|---|
| Liberal | 39% | 25% | 20% | 12% | 1% |
| Conservative | 5 | 22 | 30 | 43 | 60 |

SOURCE: *New York Times*, August 14, 1988, 32.

more ideologically oriented (see Table 11-1). To satisfy these primary voters and convention delegates, candidates must sometimes take strong stands that they might otherwise try to avoid. Moreover, as we will discuss in detail in Chapter 19, the structure of the present nominating process increases the likelihood that the party's choice will be a candidate with immoderate views, such as a McGovern or a Reagan.

## PARTY COALITIONS

The groups and interests that support a party are collectively referred to as the **party coalition.** In multiparty systems, each party is supported by a rather narrow range of interests. European parties tend to divide along class lines, with the center and right parties drawing most of their votes from the middle and

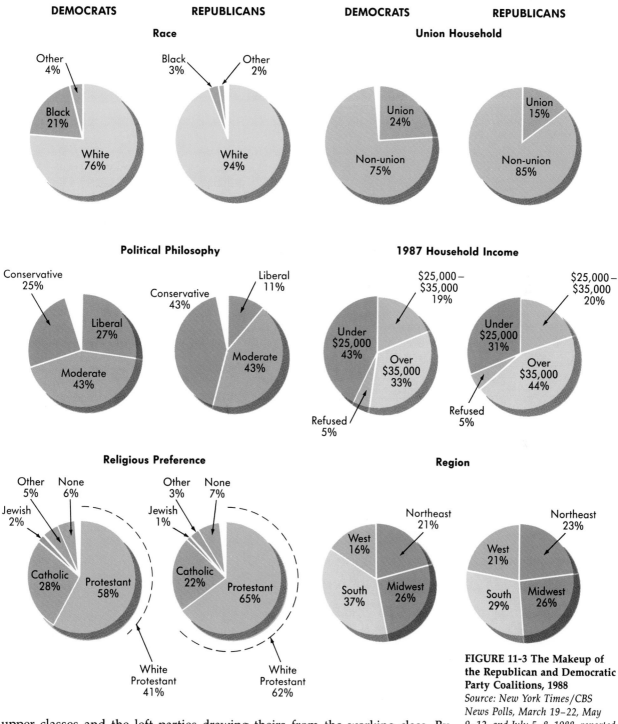

**FIGURE 11-3 The Makeup of the Republican and Democratic Party Coalitions, 1988**

*Source: New York Times/CBS News Polls, March 19–22, May 9–12, and July 5–8, 1988, reported in New York Times, July 17, 1988, 16. Data are based on responses of self-identified Democrats (n = 1,177) and self-identified Republicans (n = 994).*

upper classes and the left parties drawing theirs from the working class. By comparison, America's two-party system requires each party to accommodate a wide range of interests in order to gain the voting plurality necessary to win elections. The art of campaigning is to persuade people who think differently to vote alike. The Republican and Democratic coalitions are therefore very broad.

Each includes voters of every racial, ethnic, religious, regional, and economic grouping (see Figure 11-3). Only one sizable group aligns itself overwhelmingly with one party: 90 percent of black Americans have voted Democratic in recent presidential elections.[28]

Although the Republican and Democratic coalitions overlap, they are hardly identical. Each party likes to appear to be all things to all Americans, but in fact each builds its coalition through a process of both unification and division. If a party did not stand for something—if it never took sides—it would lose all support.

The 1988 presidential campaign demonstrated that the parties differ significantly even if their differences are not so broad and fundamental as those of parties in some other democracies. Michael Dukakis and George Bush stood apart on several key issues, including affirmative action, military assistance to the Nicaraguan guerrillas, the proper role of the CIA, a requirement that businesses give workers sixty days' notice before plant closings or layoffs, tax rates on capital gains, tax breaks for energy producers, military spending levels, and farm subsidies.

Since the 1930s, the major policy differences between the Republicans and the Democrats have involved the national government's role in solving social and economic problems. Each party has supported government action to promote economic security and social equality, but the Democrats have consistently favored a greater degree of governmental involvement. Major social-welfare and civil rights programs have been enacted during Democratic administrations, particularly those of Franklin Roosevelt and Lyndon Johnson. To some extent, the national Democratic party's coalition reflects this tradition:

[28]For thorough analyses of where the Republican and Democratic parties have found their votes in recent presidential campaigns, see Robert Axelrod, "Where the Votes Come From: An Analysis of Electoral Coalitions," *American Political Science Review* 66 (March 1972): 11–20; "Communications," *American Political Science Review* 68 (June 1974): 717–720; "Communications," *American Political Science Review* 76 (June 1982): 393–396.

Major-party candidates Michael Dukakis (*right*) and George Bush (*left*) debate on national television during the fall 1988 presidential campaign. No minor-party candidates were invited to participate in the debate. (Ira Wyman/Sygma)

it draws support disproportionately from society's "underdogs"—blacks, union members, the poor, city dwellers, Jews, and other "minorities."[29] Of course, many formerly underprivileged groups that are now part of the middle class have remained loyal to the Democratic party, which also includes a significant proportion of the nation's better-educated and higher-income voters.

Throughout the 1970s, the Republican coalition consisted mainly of white, middle-class Protestants. Richard Scammon and Ben Wattenberg described the Republicans as the party of the unpoor and the unblack—in short, the exact opposite of the Democratic party.[30] This characterization ignored the overlapping nature of the parties; if three-fifths of Catholics in 1970 were Democrats, then two-fifths—a hefty proportion—were Republicans. The same was true of working-class Americans. Nevertheless, the Republican coalition was, overall, remarkably homogeneous for an American major party.[31] However, the GOP has recently made inroads among such traditionally Democratic groups as Catholics, Hispanics, and blue-collar workers and is currently challenging the Democrats' majority position (see Chapter 10).

There is a self-limiting feature to the national party coalitions. The larger party can dominate the other only by building a broader coalition, but this broader base can ultimately be its undoing: the party cannot continue indefinitely to satisfy all the groups in its coalition.[32] As a party attracts more interest groups, the likelihood of conflict among them increases. The Democratic party, for example, could not possibly have met the demands of both black Americans and white southerners over the long term. Perhaps the surprising aspect of the Democrats' New Deal coalition was not its eventual decline but its longevity— its survival for almost fifty years. If the Republican party should gain majority status, it too can be expected to have problems in managing its coalition. Indeed, a source of internal division may already exist in the growing role of fundamentalist Christians within the GOP. In the presidential elections of 1980 through 1988, 75 percent of fundamentalists voted Republican, but the fundamentalists' strong views on school prayer, abortion, and other social issues are not shared by many traditional Republicans.

> **★ ANALYZE THE ISSUE**
>
> **Two Parties, Limited Choice**
> The public's only hope for sustained, predictable influence is concerted action. The Democratic and Republican parties provide the opportunity for such action, but at the cost of a substantial narrowing of the options. On what major issues do you think the parties are furthest apart? Closest together? Which issues are the most significant—those on which the parties' positions are most similar or those on which they most differ?

## Popular Influence and America's Two-Party System

"It is the competition of political organizations that provides the people with the opportunity to make a choice," E. E. Schattschneider once wrote. "Without this opportunity popular sovereignty amounts to nothing."[33] Thus the competitive nature of America's two major parties is a central issue in any evaluation of the nation's politics. For practical purposes, the Republican and Democratic parties

---

[29]See Richard L. Rubin, *Party Dynamics: The Democratic Coalition and the Politics of Change* (New York: Oxford University Press, 1976).
[30]Richard M. Scammon and Ben J. Wattenberg, *The Real Majority* (New York: Coward, McCann & Geohegan, 1970), chs. 4–5.
[31]Everett Carll Ladd, *Where Have All the Voters Gone?* (New York: Norton, 1978), xxii.
[32]See John R. Petrocik, *Party Coalitions: Realignments and the Decline of the New Deal System* (Chicago: University of Chicago Press, 1981).
[33]Schattschneider, *Semisovereign People*, 140.

**Party Systems**

For nearly 150 years, electoral competition in the United States has centered on the Republican and Democratic parties. By comparison, most democracies have a multiparty system, in which three or more parties receive substantial support from voters. The difference is significant. In a two-party system, the parties tend to have overlapping coalitions and programs, because each party must appeal to the middle-of-the-road voters who provide the margin of victory. In multiparty systems, particularly those with four or more strong parties, the parties tend to separate themselves, as each tries to secure the enduring loyalty of voters who have a particular viewpoint. Whether a country has a two-party or multiparty system depends on several factors, including its traditions, its social composition, and the nature of its electoral system. A few democracies have essentially a one-party system. Mexico's dominant party, the PRI (Institutional Revolutionary party), has held power since 1929, although it came close to losing a national election in 1988.

| Number of Competitive Parties | | | |
|---|---|---|---|
| One | Two | Three | Four or More |
| India | New Zealand | Canada | Belgium |
| Mexico | United States | Great Britain | Denmark |
|  |  | West Germany | France |
|  |  |  | Israel |
|  |  |  | Italy |
|  |  |  | Netherlands |
|  |  |  | Norway |
|  |  |  | Sweden |

provide our only political alternatives on broad policy issues. Do the parties in fact give the public a meaningful choice?

Critics who contend that public policy in America is controlled by a wealthy elite argue that the two parties do not offer a real alternative.[34] These critics emphasize the tendency of Republican and Democratic policies to converge and, when it comes to potentially divisive issues, to be less than clear-cut.[35] In truth, the U.S. two-party system does not produce the range of alternatives offered by Europe's multiparty systems. For nearly a century, for example, Europe has had major socialist parties, whereas the U.S. party system has never offered socialism as a serious alternative. Each U.S. major party has embraced private enterprise to a degree not found elsewhere. Of course, the American public has shared this attachment to private initiative, although from time to time polls have indicated public support for social-welfare alternatives. In the two decades following World War II, for example, the American public, by a bare majority and apparently without much intensity, indicated a preference for a comprehensive system of government-paid health care. President Truman did propose legislation for such a health-care system in the late 1940s, but the plan never came close to receiving the necessary congressional approval.

Noting such examples, leftist critics argue that America's major parties are tools of upper-class interests. Ironically, the Republican and Democratic parties have not been spared by critics on the right, either. After all, it was George Wallace, a conservative, who made the slogan "Not a dime's worth of difference between them" the basis for a third-party campaign. Wallace contended that the Republican and Democratic parties were both overly solicitous of the opinions of minorities and liberals. Indeed, until Ronald Reagan's election in 1980, most

[34]See G. William Domhoff, *Who Rules America Now?* (Englewood Cliffs, N.J.: Prentice-Hall, 1983), 117–129.
[35]Donald M. Wittman, "Parties as Utility Maximizers," *American Political Science Review 67* (June 1973): 498.

of the attacks on the parties from political circles (as opposed to academic circles) came from the right, not the left.

Nonetheless, the Republican and Democratic parties do offer somewhat different alternatives and, at times, a clear choice. When Roosevelt was elected president in 1932, Johnson in 1964, and Reagan in 1980, the parties were relatively far apart in their priorities and programs. Roosevelt's New Deal was an extreme alternative within the American political tradition and caused a decisive split along party lines. Similarly, voters had a real choice between Johnson's Great Society initiatives and the alternatives proposed by Goldwater. And Reagan's tax, spending, and defense priorities pitted Republicans against Democrats in bitter debate. In each case, the nature of the conflict was predictable, given the two parties' differing policy traditions and electoral coalitions.

America's parties tend to draw apart as public dissatisfaction and demands for new alternatives grow. In such periods of unrest as the 1930s, 1960s, and 1980s, the Democratic and Republican parties have clearly promoted different interests within society. When the parties later began to converge again, that trend was always in part a reflection of a change in the distribution of public attitudes.

The continuous adjustment of America's two parties to the mood of the electorate reflects their competition for power. Each party has a realistic chance of winning a national election, and thus has an incentive to respond to changes in public opinion. Viewed differently, a competitive opposition party is the public's best protection against an unresponsive government; the out-party provides the electorate with an alternative. Even in its weakened position after the Roosevelt years, the Republican party was strong enough to provide an alternative when the public's dissatisfaction with the Democrats rose, as in 1952, 1968, and 1980 at the presidential level and in 1946, 1952, and 1980 at the congressional level.

In sum, America's parties do offer the public a real choice, even if the alternatives are not so sharply defined as those in some other democratic nations. Without political parties the American public would be in a weak position to influence the broad direction of public policy through elections. However, the capacity of America's party system to propose coherent and consistent alternatives may be undergoing a long-term decline. The candidate-selection process in the United States has become more and more individualistic: within each party, candidates are increasingly free to define for themselves the policies on which they will campaign. The significance of this development to the public and to the parties is discussed in the next chapter.

> ★ ANALYZE THE ISSUE
>
> **The Similarity of the Two Major Parties**
> George Wallace attacked the Republican and Democratic parties by saying that "there's not a dime's worth of difference" between them. Do you agree with Wallace's contention? Would it make much difference today if the Republicans rather than the Democrats had majorities in both the House and the Senate?

## Summary

Political parties serve to link the public with its elected leaders. In the United States this linkage is provided by a two-party system; only the Republican and Democratic parties have any chance of winning control of government. Most other democracies have a multiparty system. The fact that the United States has only two major parties is explained by several factors: an electoral system— characterized by single-member districts—that makes it difficult for third parties to compete for power; each party's willingness to accept political leaders of differing views; and a political culture that stresses compromise and negotiation rather than ideological rigidity. America's two major parties are also maintained by laws and customs that support their domination of elections.

Because the United States has only two major parties, each of which seeks to gain majority support, they normally tend to avoid controversial or extreme political positions. The parties typically pursue moderate and somewhat overlapping policies. Their appeals are designed to win the support of a diverse electorate with moderate opinions. This form of party competition is reflected in the Republican and Democratic coalitions.

Although the two parties' coalitions are not identical, they do overlap significantly: each party includes large numbers of individuals who represent nearly every significant interest in the society. Nonetheless, the Democratic and Republican parties sometimes do offer sharply contrasting policy alternatives, particularly in times of political unrest. It is at such times that the public has its best opportunity to make a decisive difference through its vote.

## Major Concepts

| | |
|---|---|
| multiparty system | proportional representation |
| party coalition | single-member districts |
| party competition | two-party system |
| political party | |

## Suggested Readings

Binkley, Wilfred E. *American Political Parties: Their Natural History,* 2d ed. New York: Knopf, 1945. A dated but still valuable history of America's two-party system.

Duverger, Maurice. *Political Parties.* New York: Wiley, 1954. A classic analysis of types of party systems, their origins, and their effects.

Eldersveld, Samuel J. *Political Parties in American Society.* New York: Basic Books, 1982. An overview of the organization, role, and activities of America's two major parties.

Jewell, Malcolm, and David Olson. *American State Political Parties and Elections,* 2d ed. Homewood, Ill.: Dorsey Press, 1982. A broad overview of state parties with comparative information on the competitiveness of the two-party system at the state level.

Mazmanian, Daniel A. *Third Parties in Presidential Elections.* Washington, D.C.: Brookings Institution, 1984. An assessment of the influence of America's third-party movements, including George Wallace's 1968 campaign.

Page, Benjamin I. *Choices and Echoes in Presidential Elections.* Chicago: University of Chicago Press, 1978. A study of the campaign appeals of the major parties' presidential nominees from 1932 to 1976.

Rosenstone, Steven J., Roy L. Behr, and Edward H. Lazarus. *Third Parties in America.* Princeton, N.J.: Princeton University Press, 1984. An analysis of America's third parties and their impact on the two-party system.

Sorauf, Frank J. *Party Politics in America,* 5th ed. Boston: Little, Brown, 1984. A comprehensive text on America's political parties.

# Chapter 12

## PARTY ORGANIZATIONS: CONTESTING ELECTIONS

*By the standards of political parties of most Western democracies, the American party organizations are comparatively weak and insubstantial.*

—*Frank J. Sorauf*[1]

The 1968 Democratic convention was a last hurrah for party leaders. Led by Mayor Richard Daley, the boss of Chicago's powerful political machine, they delivered the presidential nomination to Lyndon Johnson's vice-president, Hubert H. Humphrey, who had not entered a single primary. His chief opponent for the nomination was Senator Eugene McCarthy, who had fought his way through a dozen state primaries. Party leaders such as Daley regarded McCarthy as a spoiler whose attacks on the Johnson administration's handling of the Vietnam war had driven a wedge in party unity, jeopardizing the Democratic party's chances in the fall election. Rejecting McCarthy's bid, they turned to Humphrey.

Four years later it was Mayor Daley's turn to be voted down at a Democratic convention. After the 1968 campaign, which ended in Humphrey's narrow defeat by Richard M. Nixon, reform elements within the Democratic party forced a change in the rules for selecting convention delegates. Party leaders in a state would no longer be permitted to hand-pick a slate of delegates. All states would have to choose their delegates openly, either through primary elections or through caucuses in which all party voters were invited to participate. Daley defied the new rules and arrived at the 1972 convention as head of an Illinois delegation of old-line party regulars. The convention was controlled by delegates loyal to George McGovern, and they voted to unseat the Daley

[1]Frank J. Sorauf, *Party Politics in America*, 5th ed. (Boston: Little, Brown, 1984), 61.

delegation. In a classic scene of confrontation between the old order and the new, Daley shook his fist in rage at the podium and stalked out of the convention, vowing that his Chicago machine would not participate in the fall campaign.

Daley's fall from national power symbolizes the fate of party leaders and organizations in the twentieth century. As the century began, the parties were in firm control of U.S. elections, but individual candidates gradually took command. By the 1960s, the presidential nominating convention was the last party stronghold in national politics. When party leaders after 1968 were denied control of convention delegates, the transition from **party-centered politics** to **candidate-centered politics** was virtually complete. The reality of today's national elections is that candidates have most of the initiative and influence. Candidates for the presidency and for Congress raise most of their own funds, form their own campaign organizations, and choose for themselves the issues that they will emphasize. Parties still play a part in election campaigns, but their role has become secondary.

The public's hostility toward political parties is the main reason for their decline. The individualistic and egalitarian elements of the nation's political culture create resentment among the public against any concentration of power, including the power of party bosses.[2] Americans have sought to control party organizations through restrictive laws (such as those requiring primary elections) that no other democracy has imposed on its parties. As a result, U.S. **party organizations** are among the weakest in the world and U.S. candidates are among the most independent. Americans prefer a more nearly direct form of democracy—one in which their relationships with candidates are not mediated by party organizations.

Each U.S. party is really three parties in one. There is, first, the party in the electorate, which consists, as we saw in Chapter 10, of the voters who identify with it. Second, there is the party in office, which consists, as was evident in Chapter 11, of those officials elected under its label. And third, there is the party as organization staffed and led by activists, which is the subject of this chapter. The following points are emphasized in the chapter:

★ *The ability of America's party organizations to control nominations, campaigns, and platforms has declined substantially.* Although the parties continue to play an important role, elections are now controlled largely by the candidates, each of whom is relatively free to go his or her own way. This situation is distinctly American. In other democracies, party organizations continue to dominate elections.

★ *U.S. party organizations are decentralized and fragmented. The national organization is a loose collection of state organizations, which in turn are loose associations of autonomous local organizations.* This feature of U.S. parties can be traced to federalism and the nation's diversity, which have made it difficult for the parties to act as instruments of national power.

★ *Candidates' relative freedom to run on platforms of their own devising diminishes the electorate's capacity to influence national policy in a predictable direction.* The candidate choice made by voters in any one constituency has no necessary relation to the choices of voters in other constituencies.

---

[2]Judson L. James, *American Political Parties* (New York: Pegasus, 1969), 60.

## Elections and the Decline of Party Control

The main business of America's major parties is the contesting of elections. Unlike some European parties, which contribute to public education by publishing newspapers and conducting issue forums, U.S. parties concentrate almost entirely on election campaigns. Ironically, U.S. parties do not completely control any aspect of these campaigns, not even the selection of candidates to run on their tickets. In 1978 Bill Bradley, former New York Knicks basketball star, entered the U.S. Senate race in New Jersey against a candidate supported by Democratic party leaders and the state's governor. Bradley defeated the party's choice in the primary and then went on to win the general election. This is not an isolated example. Candidates who are not recruited by the party often run and sometimes win. Even candidates who have the party's backing are more concerned with marketing themselves than with promoting their party.[3] As William Crotty has noted:

> It is a politics of every candidate for himself, each with an individual campaign organization loyal only to the candidate and disbanded after the election. It is an antiparty politics of fragmentation and transitory candidate organizations. It is a politics with no core, no sense of collective effort. And, it should be added, it is a politics that has captured the political world.[4]

In the nineteenth and early twentieth centuries, the situation was very different. The party organizations were in control of nominations, elections, and platforms. The story of how and why they lost their commanding position is basic to an understanding of the parties' present role and influence.

### CONTROL OF NOMINATIONS

**Nomination** refers to the selection of the individual who will run as the party's candidate in the general election. The legendary William Marcy ("Boss") Tweed of New York City's Tammany Hall machine once remarked, "I don't care who does the electing just so I can do the nominating."[5] Tweed was merely stating the obvious. His Democratic machine so thoroughly dominated New York City elections in the late nineteenth century that his hand-picked nominees were virtually guaranteed election. Even in constituencies where the parties are competitive, the nominating decision is a critical choice because it narrows a large field of potential candidates down to the final two, one Republican and one Democrat.

---

[3]See Robert Agranoff, "The New Style of Campaigning: The Decline of Party and the Rise of Candidate-Centered Technology," in Robert Agranoff, *The New Style in Election Campaigns*, 2d ed. (Boston: Holbrook Press, 1976), 3–48.

[4]William Crotty, "The Party Symbol and Its Changing Meaning," in William Crotty, ed., *The Party Symbol* (San Francisco: W. H. Freeman, 1980), 13.

[5]James W. Davis, *National Conventions in an Age of Party Reform* (Westport, Conn.: Greenwood Press, 1983), 4.

"Boss" Tweed, the head of Tammany Hall (New York City's Democratic party machine), is caricatured at left in this 1871 Thomas Nast cartoon. (Historical Pictures Services)

## Party-Controlled Nominations

Until the early twentieth century, nominations were the responsibility of party organizations. In smaller communities where voters had personal knowledge of potential candidates, the parties often had no practical alternative but to nominate popular individuals who wanted to run. In the cities, however, the party organizations were in a commanding position. Party label was the prime influence on urban voters, so it was essential for candidates to have party backing. To receive nomination, an individual had to be loyal to the party organization, a requirement that included a willingness to share with it the spoils of office—government jobs and contracts.

Political spoils enabled party organizations to acquire campaign workers and funds, but were also the foundation of party corruption. Unscrupulous party leaders were in a position to extort money from those seeking political favors. When Richard Croker, a Tammany leader, was asked his opinion of the unrestricted coinage of silver, the major political issue of the 1890s, he replied, "I'm in favor of all kinds of money—the more the better."[6]

Widespread corruption made the party organizations targets of Progressive reformers, who had, in addition to a desire for clean government, a partisan objective. The Progressive movement was led by native-born Protestant Republicans whose values were at odds with those of the big-city machines, which were Democratic organizations founded on the support of working-class Catholic immigrants. The machines operated not on the high principle of the public interest, but on the low principle of exchange.[7] They took contributions from business interests in return for favors from City Hall, and then used those

[6]William L. Riordon, *Plunkitt of Tammany Hall* (New York: Dutton, 1963), xvi.
[7]Dennis R. Judd, *The Politics of American Cities* (Boston: Little, Brown, 1984), ch. 3; for a discussion of the machines' policy orientations, see John Allswang, *Bosses, Machines, and Urban Voters* (Baltimore: Johns Hopkins University Press, 1986).

contributions to woo the ethnic voters whose support enabled them to control city government. In their day, the machines were the closest things that the United States had to full-service welfare agencies. Jim Pendergast's Kansas City machine, for example, handed out more than government jobs to the party faithful. When they were penniless in winter, the Pendergast machine delivered fuel to their homes. Hundreds of families had turkey and trimmings at the free dinners that "Big Jim" staged each Christmas.[8]

The Progressives fumed over the power of the machines and sought to destroy them through the principle of "party democracy"—the idea that party organizations should properly be run by ordinary voters and not by entrenched bosses. The idea appealed to Americans' sense of individualism and egalitarianism, and gained strong support in many state legislatures. Laws were passed requiring the parties to choose their organizational leaders by secret ballot, to print public notices of their meetings, and to make all major policy decisions in public session.

### Primary Elections

The most serious blow struck by the Progressives against the power of the party bosses was the **primary election** (or direct primary) as a method of choosing party nominees. In place of the older system of party-designated nominees, the primary system placed nominations in the hands of voters. In an 1897 speech, Robert M. La Follette, Sr., the Progressive movement's acknowledged leader, advised, "Go back to the first principles of democracy: go back to the people. Substitute for both the caucus and convention a primary election."[9]

[8]Lyle W. Dorsett, *The Pendergast Machine* (New York: Oxford University Press, 1968), 42.
[9]Robert M. La Follette, Sr., *La Follette's Autobiography* (Madison, Wis.: R. M. La Follette, 1913), 197–198; quoted in Sorauf, *Party Politics in America*, 210.

Senator Robert M. La Follette of Wisconsin pushed for Progressive reforms, including the use of primary elections to select the parties' candidates. (State Historical Society of Wisconsin)

# LIMITING PARTY ACTIVITIES DURING PRIMARIES

Primary elections are the major reason America's parties have so little leverage with candidates. A candidate no longer needs the support of the party organization to become the party's nominee because primaries enable candidates to win nominations by appealing directly to the voters. Some states have even taken steps to limit party activities during primary election campaigns in order to help ensure that nominations will not be controlled by organizational leaders. California and Oregon, for instance, prohibit party organizations from endorsing candidates in primary elections. Utah requires the parties to nominate two candidates for each office unless one candidate receives 70 percent of the vote at the state party convention. Other states, including New York and Colorado, allow parties to endorse candidates for nomination but require them also to list on the primary ballot any candidate who gets the support of a certain proportion of the delegates at the state convention (25 percent in New York). New York's parties are also prohibited by law from giving financial support to primary election candidates. The loss of party influence is reflected in the fact that in a number of recent New York races for governor and U.S. senator, the party-endorsed candidates have lost the primary elections.

The first primary election law was enacted in 1903 by Mississippi. Within a decade most states had adopted primaries as the means of choosing party nominees for some public offices. Today all states but Virginia have primary elections for contested nominations for U.S. Senate and House seats, and about thirty states use primaries to select their delegates to the presidential nominating conventions (see Chapter 19). Most states have "closed" primaries, in which participation is limited to voters registered or declared at the polls as members of the party whose primary is being held. Less than a fifth of the states use "open" primaries, a form that allows independents and voters of either party to vote in a party's primary, although voters are prohibited by law from participating in both parties' primaries simultaneously.*

Primaries have not completely eclipsed the party organizations. Successful candidacies are normally built on more than raw ambition.[10] Many politicians begin their careers as party volunteers; in this capacity they gain the attention of party leaders, who help them to win their first elective office. From there they move up the ladder. Nevertheless, primaries were the severest blow imaginable to party organizations. Because of primaries, candidates have the option of seeking office on their own, and, once elected (whether with or without the party's help), they can build an independent electoral base that effectively places them beyond the party's control.[11]

The absence of primaries in Europe is one of the main reasons the parties there have remained strong. They control nominations, and European candidates have no choice but to operate within the party organizations. The European philosophy of party democracy has been unlike that of the United

★ ANALYZE THE ISSUE

**Parties in the American Political Culture**
The modern political party originated in America and is a cornerstone of democratic government. Yet Americans have never fully accepted parties. What do you think accounts for this reluctance? What is your own opinion of parties? On what is your opinion based?

*Alaska and Washington have a third form of primary—the "blanket" primary. Primary voters in these states are provided a single primary ballot listing both the Republican and Democratic candidates by office. Each voter can cast only one vote per office, but can select a candidate of either party. Louisiana has a variation on this form in which all candidates are listed on the ballot but are not identified by party.
[10]James, *American Political Parties*, 68.
[11]Sarah McCally Morehouse, "The Effect of Pre-Primary Endorsements on State Party Strength," paper delivered at the 1980 meeting of the American Political Science Association, August 1980, 17.

States. Rather than imposing legal restrictions on party activities, European nations have allowed the parties to regulate their own affairs, counting on the threat of electoral defeat to keep them in line. By all accounts, European parties are no less honest than U.S. parties, and are considerably more effective.[12]

## CONTROL OF ELECTION CAMPAIGNS

Workers, money, and media have always been the key resources in campaigns, but their relative importance has changed over time, as has their control by parties and candidates.

### Party Workers

From their grass-roots inception in the Jacksonian era, U.S. parties have depended on a relatively small number of active members. The parties have never had the large dues-paying memberships that characterize some European socialist and labor parties. Even the party machines in their heyday did not attempt to enroll the party electorate as active members. The machine's lowest organizational echelon was the precinct-level unit. Each precinct had several hundred voters but only two party workers, a precinct captain and his assistant.

Patronage was the traditional source of party workers. To get or keep government employment, individuals had to work for the party during election campaigns. Instituted during Andrew Jackson's presidency, this "spoils system" was a perennial target of reformers, and when antiparty sentiment intensified around 1900, the Progressives saw an opportunity to deprive party leaders of their work force. About 10 percent of federal jobs had been placed under civil service in 1883, and the Progressives demanded that merit-based hiring be expanded. As government jobs in the early twentieth century shifted from the patronage to the merit category, the party organizations lost vigor. Today, because of the expanded size of government, thousands of patronage jobs still exist. These government employees help to staff the parties, but many of them are more loyal to the politician for whom they work than to a party organization.

The parties today get help from volunteers as well as from patronage workers. However, many volunteers are more interested in debating the issues than in distributing party leaflets, and because they are not patronage employees, they cannot be compelled to perform tedious campaign tasks or to work long hours.[13] Another problem with volunteers is that they often have more interest in a particular candidate than in the party.[14] In 1972 anti–Vietnam war activists took over numerous Democratic party organizations in order to secure national-convention delegates for George McGovern, but then abandoned those organizations after he failed to win the presidency.

### Money and Media

Campaigns for higher office have changed fundamentally in recent decades. The "old politics," which emphasized party rallies and door-to-door canvass-

---

[12]Samuel J. Eldersveld, *Political Parties in American Society* (New York: Basic Books, 1982), 96–97.
[13]See James Q. Wilson, *The Amateur Democrat* (Chicago: University of Chicago Press, 1962); Robert S. Hirschfield, Bert E. Swanson, and Blanche D. Blank, "A Profile of Political Activists in Manhattan," *Western Political Quarterly* 15 (1962): 489–506.
[14]Joseph Schlesinger, *Ambition and Politics* (Chicago: Rand McNally, 1966), 125–133.

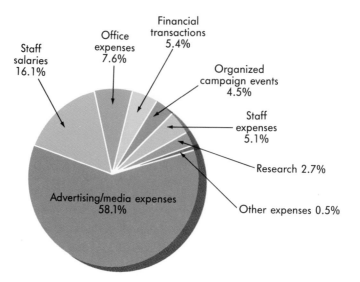

**FIGURE 12-1 Allocation of Campaign Expenditures in Races for the U.S. House of Representatives**
More congressional campaign funds are spent on the mass-communications media than on grass-roots organization. *Source: Edie N. Goldenberg and Michael W. Traugott,* Campaigning for Congress *(Washington, D.C.: Congressional Quarterly Press, 1984), 86.*

ing, was based on a large supply of workers. The "new politics" centers on the media and depends on money—lots of it. Most U.S. Senate candidates spend more than $1 million on their campaigns, and U.S. House candidates spend about $500,000 on average.

Candidates for major office spend a larger percentage of their budgets on televised political advertising and other media activities than they do on grass-roots organizing (see Figure 12-1). The key operatives in the modern campaign are television consultants, pollsters, and direct-mail fund-raising specialists, all of whom operate outside the formal party organizations. These advisers and their services have loosened the parties' hold on candidates.[15] Televised advertising in particular enables candidates to communicate directly and easily with the electorate, thereby reducing the need for grass-roots party workers.[16]

The news media reflect the increase in candidate-centered campaigns. Election news is devoted almost entirely to what the candidates say and do.[17] In earlier times, news coverage of campaigns during the nominating stage was filled with speculation as to what party kingmakers might do. Now, because the nominees are decided in primaries, party leaders are barely visible in election news. Press coverage simply mirrors the reality of today's campaigns: they are candidate-centered, so the news is, too.

Candidates also dominate election fund-raising. At the turn of the century, when party machines were at their peak, most campaign funds passed through the hands of party leaders. Today the parties provide only 10 percent of the money spent on congressional campaigns. Candidates now get most of their funds through direct solicitation of individual contributors and interest groups.

In European democracies, parties continue to dominate campaign resources. British parties, for example, hire and assign the campaign manager for each of their parliamentary candidates. These managers are party agents and are expected to see that the party's interests, as well as those of the candidates, are

[15]Alan R. Gitelson, M. Margaret Conway, and Frank B. Feigert, *American Political Parties* (Boston: Houghton Mifflin, 1984), 84.
[16]See David S. Broder, *The Party's Over* (New York: Harper & Row, 1972).
[17]See Peter Clarke and Susan Evans, *Covering Campaigns: Journalism in Congressional Elections* (Stanford, Calif.: Stanford University Press, 1983); Thomas E. Patterson, *The Mass Media Election* (New York: Praeger, 1980), chs. 3–5.

In organizing their campaigns, candidates for major office depend more heavily on professional consultants than on party leaders. One of these consultants is Richard Viguerie, who pioneered the use of computerized mailings to raise funds for Republican candidates. (Dennis Brack/Black Star)

adequately represented in parliamentary campaigns. Further, European nations allot free television time for campaign messages, which is granted directly to the parties rather than to candidates. Such differences reflect the fact that European elections are party-centered. European candidates do not have the freedom to organize and run on their own, and this constraint has kept them from taking control of campaign media and money.

## CONTROL OF PARTY PLATFORMS

Beginning in the 1830s and for more than a century thereafter, U.S. parties had control of the national platforms adopted at the presidential nominating conventions held every four years. Each state party sent a delegation to the national convention, and most of the delegates were high-ranking organizational and elected party officials. The first real business at each convention was the formulation of the policy proposals that made up the platform, and the delegates took the platform seriously as a statement of their common interests and commitments. (Ticket balancing—the practice of choosing a vice-presidential nominee from a different region and wing of the party than the presidential choice—served the same purpose.)

Modern platforms have a somewhat different status than earlier ones because national conventions themselves have changed. Until Franklin D. Roosevelt went to the 1932 Democratic convention to accept his party's nomination in person, prospective nominees by tradition did not attend the convention.* The

*To me, party platforms are contracts with the people.*
Harry S Truman

*William Jennings Bryan was not an exception. He was present at the 1896 Democratic convention, but was not regarded as a presidential contender until he gave his electrifying platform speech.

convention was the showcase of the party, not of the nominee. Today the convention is essentially controlled by the candidate who has accumulated the support of a majority of delegates in the state primaries and caucuses that precede the convention. The loyalty of these delegates, most of whom are *not* high-ranking party organizational and elected leaders, is mainly to the prospective nominee, not to the party.

Accordingly, the modern platform is tailored to the views of the potential nominee. For purposes of party unity, recent nominees-to-be have accepted platform compromises with their opponents and have even given their own followers leeway in drafting the platform. But recent nominees have insisted that major "planks" in the platform conform to their own views and that controversial minor planks be omitted. In addition, the vice-presidential nominee can no longer be regarded as the party's choice: the delegates now accept whomever the presidential nominee designates for the second spot on the ticket. In the 1988 Democratic race, for example, Michael Dukakis, who had accumulated a majority of the delegates before the Democratic convention, hand-picked Lloyd Bentsen as his running mate and directed that three platform planks proposed by his chief rival, Jesse Jackson, be rejected by the Democratic national convention. Bentsen was chosen and the Jackson planks were defeated, just as Dukakis instructed.

National platforms have never been officially binding on presidential candidates, much less on candidates for the House and Senate, who have traditionally embraced, ignored, or rejected platform planks as it suited their purposes to

Like many other politicians, State Senator Gonzalo Barrientos of Texas (at right) relies more on his own efforts than on his party organization to raise funds and to conduct election campaigns. (Bob Daemmrich/The Image Works)

In 1988 George Bush picked a relatively obscure senator, Dan Quayle of Indiana, to be his running mate. Delegates to the Republican party convention had no say in the selection, but they ratified it by nominating Quayle unanimously. (UPI/Bettmann Newsphotos)

do so. However, the transition from party-centered to nominee-centered conventions has reduced the applicability of the national platform to congressional campaigns. When the parties' organizational and elected leaders, including members of Congress, had control of the platform, they aimed to persuade the delegates to approve planks on which they could campaign. And by virtue of participation in the deliberations, they had a commitment to the platform. Today most candidates for Congress do not pay much attention to the national platform. They run on a platform of their own choosing.

In European democracies, a party's candidates are expected to campaign on the national platform and, if elected as a governing majority, to support its planks, which are formulated in conjunction with organizational leaders, particularly in the case of labor and socialist parties. In Great Britain's Labour party, for example, the national platform is prepared by an executive committee dominated by organizational leaders but also including elected party representatives.

## Party Organizations Today

U.S. parties have declined, but they are not about to die out. Political leaders and activists need an ongoing organization through which they can communicate and work together, and the parties meet that need. Moreover, certain activities, such as voter registration drives, benefit all of a party's candidates and are therefore more efficiently conducted through party organizations. Indeed, efficiency is an important reason that national and state party organizations are staging a comeback of sorts. They have recently developed the capacity to assist

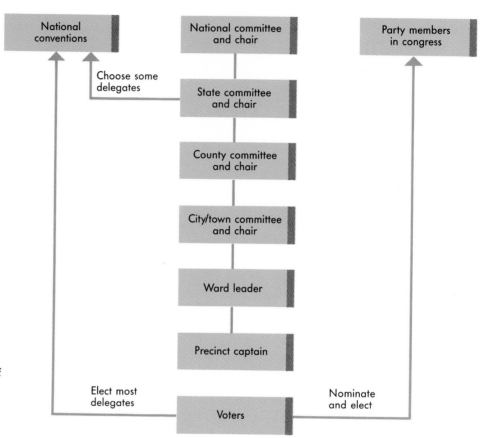

**FIGURE 12-2 Organization of the Political Party**
U.S. parties today are loosely structured as alliances of national, state, and local organizations.

candidates with polling, research, and media production, which are costly but essential ingredients of a successful modern campaign.

Structurally, U.S. parties are loose associations of national, state, and local organizations (see Figure 12-2). The national party organizations have almost no say in the decisions of state organizations, and the latter, in turn, cannot tell the local organizations what to do. By comparison, European parties tend to be hierarchical: national parties in Great Britain, for example, have the power to select parliamentary nominees, although they usually follow the recommendations of the local organizations. The major reason that U.S. parties are not hierarchical is the nation's federal system and tradition of local autonomy. Because each governing level in the United States is a competing center of power and ambition, the parties at the national, state, and local levels are able to reject the authority of other levels.

## LOCAL PARTY ORGANIZATIONS

U.S. parties are organized from the bottom up, not from the top down. There are about 500,000 elective offices in the United States, of which fewer than 500 are contested statewide and only two—the presidency and vice-presidency—are contested nationally. All the rest are local offices, so, not surprisingly, at least 95 percent of party activists work within local organizations.

It is difficult to generalize about local parties because they vary greatly in their structure and activities. But local parties tend to be strongest in urban areas and in the Northeast and Midwest, where parties traditionally have been more highly organized.[18] In any case, local parties tend to specialize in elections that coincide with local electoral boundaries. Campaigns for mayor, city council, state legislature, county offices, and the like activate local parties to a greater degree than do statewide and national contests. Local parties are not highly involved even in campaigns for the U.S. House of Representatives because most congressional districts overlap the boundaries of several local party organizations, and they are not accustomed to working together closely. Besides, congressional candidates run personal campaigns, taking help from the parties when they can get it but relying primarily on their own staffs.

### The Decline of the Big-City Machines

For most Americans, local party organizations are synonymous with the party machines that once flourished in the nation's cities. Well-staffed and tightly disciplined, the machines were welfare agencies for the poor, vehicles of upward mobility for newly arrived immigrant groups, and brokers of public jobs, contracts, and policies for those willing to meet the price. But above all, the machines could win elections, even if victory required stuffing ballot boxes with fraudulent votes.

The party machines deserve their notoriety, but they should not be viewed as representative of party politics in America. Their reign was relatively short: machines emerged during the latter half of the nineteenth century and within a few decades were in retreat in the face of economic and political changes. Moreover, the party machines were located primarily in the big cities of the Northeast and Midwest. Many southern and western cities did not have machinelike parties, and smaller communities rarely had highly organized parties.

Today only a few local parties, including the Democratic organizations in Albany, Philadelphia, and Chicago, deserve to be thought of as machines. Of these organizations the most famous is Chicago's, which is less formidable than it was under the first Mayor Daley (see box) but is still a force to be reckoned with. The Daley machine was built on more than 30,000 patronage jobs in Cook County and Chicago government. Each of Chicago's 3,500 precincts had a precinct captain, and nearly all of them held government jobs. Each captain's responsibility was to get to know the precinct's voters and gain their support. The precinct captains reported to fifty ward leaders, who also held patronage positions and were the link between City Hall and the voters, offering them services in exchange for support at the polls.[19]

### Nonmachine Local Organizations

In most urban areas the party organizations are important but bear no resemblance to the old-style machines. These organizations do not have enough

> ★ ANALYZE THE ISSUE
>
> **The Effect of Decentralization on the Political Parties**
> E. E. Schattschneider wrote, "Decentralization is by all odds the most important characteristic of the American party system." What do you think is the basis for this observation? How does decentralization affect the parties' ability to serve as instruments of national policy?

---

[18]Richard J. Tobin and Edward Keynes, "Institutional Differences in the Recruitment Process," *American Journal of Political Science* 19 (November 1975): 674.
[19]See Milton Rakove, *Don't Make No Waves, Don't Back No Losers* (Bloomington: Indiana University Press, 1975).

# THE LAST BIG-CITY BOSS: MAYOR DALEY OF CHICAGO

During his twenty-year reign (1956–1976) as boss of Chicago's Democratic machine, Richard J. Daley gained a national reputation as a political kingmaker. His support was instrumental in the success of John F. Kennedy's drive for the 1960 Democratic presidential nomination. He may even have "stolen" the general election for Kennedy. Daley delayed reporting some of Chicago's returns until the vote totals from downstate Illinois were nearly complete, buying himself time to calculate how many Chicago votes were needed to swing the state in Kennedy's favor. Kennedy narrowly won Illinois, the result, some observers have claimed, of ballot-box stuffing by the Daley machine. It is a fact that without Illinois's votes, Kennedy would have lost the election to Richard Nixon.

During Daley's tenure, Chicago was widely known as "the best-run city in America." As both the mayor and the head of Chicago's Democratic organization, Daley could count on the full support of the city council for his policy decisions. Daley's power also reached into the city's various regulatory commissions and agencies, so that private interests subject to their rulings had to have a healthy respect for Daley. Chicago's business community was highly responsive to Daley's leadership, in recognition of both his political power and his belief that a thriving business sector was the key to Chicago's prosperity. Daley also had close ties with labor, which enabled him to bring labor and business into a cooperative alliance.

Daley's importance in national and Illinois politics made him a powerful force in Washington and Spring-field. Chicago received billions of dollars in federal and state assistance during the Daley years. With these funds, Daley promoted business through construction loans, built a superhighway system for Chicago, and greatly expanded the city's social services.

Although Chicago was the envy of other cities, Daley was not without his critics, both in and out of the city he ruled. Outsiders attacked him as a symbol of an outdated form of corrupt politics. Insiders acknowledged that a concentration of power was what enabled Daley to get things done, but they disagreed with his priorities. Minority leaders in Chicago argued that he showed favoritism in developing white sections of the city rather than improving living conditions in the ghetto and was more interested in building highways and office buildings than in assisting the poor.

In 1972 Daley suffered humiliation when he and his hand-picked delegation were denied seats at the Democratic National Convention. Daley died in 1976 without having anointed an undisputed successor. The ensuing infighting among machine, reform, and minority factions greatly weakened the Daley organization. Today the Chicago Democratic organization is still one of the most formidable in the country, but it is a dim shadow of what it was during Daley's heyday. In 1989, Daley's son and namesake, Richard J. Daley, Jr., was elected Chicago's mayor and took over its Democratic organization. Whether the second Daley can repeat his father's mastery of party politics remains to be seen.

workers to staff even a majority of precincts regularly and become truly active only during campaigns, when they open campaign headquarters, conduct voter registration drives, send mailings or deliver leaflets to voters, and help get out the vote (see Table 12-1). In most cities the party organizations also play a role in the nomination of candidates for local office. Many nominees come from party ranks or are solicited by party leaders. Sometimes the organization's backing of a candidate will discourage others from waging a primary fight, and even if a nomination for local office is contested, the party organization is likely to prevail. Most local campaigns are not well funded, and the party's backing of a candidate often spells the difference.

In other localities the party's role is less substantial. In many suburbs, wards, and smaller communities, the parties exist organizationally but make no concerted effort to influence elections.[20] They hold meetings, but because they

[20]Robert L. Huckshorn, *Party Leadership in the States* (Amherst: University of Massachusetts Press, 1976), 234.

**TABLE 12-1  Characteristics and Activities of Local Democratic and Republican Parties**

|  | Local Democratic Parties | Local Republican Parties |
|---|---|---|
| Chairperson devotes at least six hours per week to party business during election periods | 77% | 78% |
| Chairperson devotes at least six hours per week to party business during nonelection periods | 24 | 26 |
| Organization has formal annual budget | 20 | 31 |
| Organization has paid, full-time staff | 3 | 4 |
| Organization has a telephone listing | 11 | 16 |
| Organization has a campaign headquarters during election periods | 55 | 60 |
| Organization contributes money to candidates | 62 | 70 |
| Organization prepares press releases during campaigns | 55 | 55 |
| Organization sends mailings to voters | 47 | 59 |
| Organization conducts voter registration drives | 56 | 45 |

SOURCE: Adapted from James L. Gibson, Cornelius P. Cotter, John F. Bibby, and Robert L. Huckshorn, "Whither the Local Parties?" *American Journal of Political Science* 29 (February 1985): 149–151.

have little money and few workers, they are not able to operate effectively as electoral organizations. The individual candidates must carry nearly the full burden. As one candidate in such a locality remarked, "I cannot count on the party to do what it should—like registration, hand out literature, arrange coffees and meetings, and turn out the vote. The party should also at least provide poll watchers, but often [does not]."[21]

Finally, in many places party organizations barely exist. Even the top positions, such as party chair and treasurer, are unfilled or occupied by inactive members. These organizations, such as they are, are found primarily in smaller towns and rural areas.

## STATE PARTY ORGANIZATIONS

At the state level, each party is headed by a central committee made up of members of local party organizations and local and state officeholders. These state central committees do not meet regularly, and they provide only general policy guidance for the state organizations. Day-to-day operations and policy are directed by a chairperson, who is a full-time, paid employee of the state party. The central committee appoints the chairperson, but it often accepts the individual recommended by the party's leading politician, usually the governor or a U.S. senator.[22]

[21]Quoted in Malcolm Jewell and David Olson, *American State Political Parties and Elections*, 2d ed. (Homewood, Ill.: Dorsey Press, 1982), 185.
[22]Ibid., 67–70.

In recent decades the state parties have expanded their budgets and staffs considerably, and so have been able to play a more active electoral role. On average, state parties now have an annual budget of about $500,000 and a staff of about ten people.[23] In contrast, thirty years ago about half of the state party organizations had no permanent staff at all. Heightened party competition is one reason that state party staffs have expanded. For example, Georgia's Democratic leaders in the early 1980s felt they had no choice but to enlarge their state organization because the Republicans had bolstered theirs and were making inroads on public offices that Democrats had held since the Reconstruction era, after the Civil War.[24] The increase in state party staffs is due largely to improvements in communication technology, such as computer-assisted direct mail, which have made it easier for political organizations of all kinds, parties included, to raise funds. Having acquired an ability to pay for permanent staffs, state parties have developed them in order to expand their activities, which range from polling to issues research to campaign management. (These activities are discussed in detail later in this chapter.)

State party organizations concentrate on statewide races, including those for U.S. senator, and races for the state legislature. They play only a small role in campaigns for national or local offices, and in most states they do not endorse candidates in statewide primary contests. Some states, such as New York and Connecticut, hold party conventions to endorse candidates for nomination, but these are not state-organization conventions but gatherings of local party organizations—in fact, the local organizations designate the delegates to these conventions.

## NATIONAL PARTY ORGANIZATIONS

The national party organizations are structured much like those at the state level: they have a national committee, a national party chairperson, and a support staff (see Figure 12-3). The national headquarters for the Republican and Democratic parties are located in Washington, D.C. Although in theory the national parties are run by their committees, neither the Democratic National Committee (DNC) nor the Republican National Committee (RNC) has great power. "A national committee," the columnist Thomas Stokes once said, "never nominated anybody, never elected anybody, never established party policy."[25] Although Stokes's claim is a slight exaggeration, it is true that the RNC (with 162 members) and the DNC (with more than 300 members) are too cumbersome to act as deliberative bodies. Besides, neither party can afford the expense of having its national committee meet for the long periods that would be required to forge party policy. Consequently, the national committees are convened only periodically, to ratify decisions made by a smaller core of party leaders.

[23]James L. Gibson, Cornelius P. Cotter, John F. Bibby, and Robert J. Huckshorn, "Assessing Party Organizational Strength," *American Journal of Political Science* 27 (May 1983): 200; John F. Bibby, Cornelius P. Cotter, James L. Gibson, and Robert J. Huckshorn, "Parties in State Politics," in Virginia Gray, Herbert Jacob, and Kenneth N. Vines, eds., *Politics in the American States* (Boston: Little, Brown, 1983), 77.
[24]Robin Toner, "Georgia Democrats Say Lance Move Helps Party," *New York Times*, July 8, 1985, A-13.
[25]Quoted in Hugh A. Bone, *American Politics and the Party System*, 3d ed. (New York: McGraw-Hill, 1965), 202.

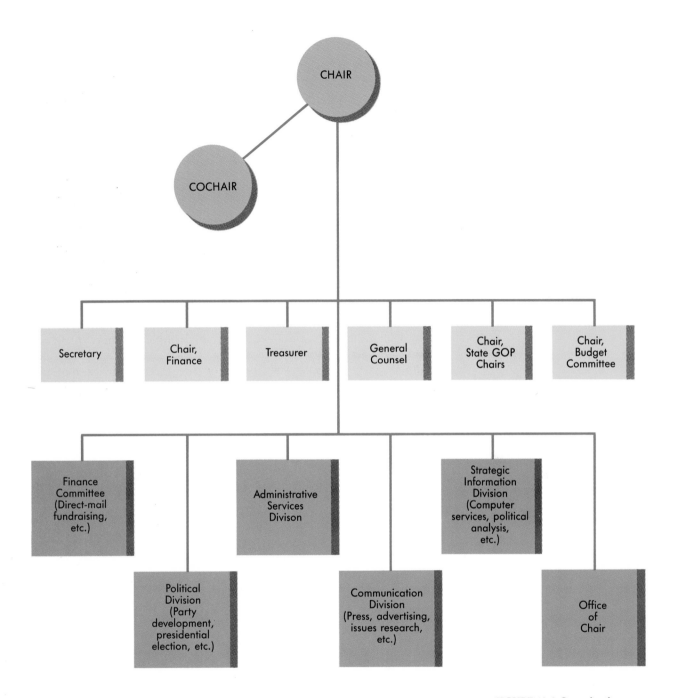

The RNC and the DNC include members chosen by each of the state parties and recently have striven for demographic representation as well. "Each national committee," Samuel Eldersveld wrote, "seeks to include blacks, women, persons from labor, business, and farm organizations, as well as representatives from different ethnic, socioeconomic, and age groups."[26] With all these efforts to achieve balance in other areas, the DNC and RNC are still not ideologically representative. Democrats on the DNC are more liberal as a whole

**FIGURE 12-3 Organization Chart of the Republican National Committee**
*Source: Graham Paterson, Republican National Committee (1989).*

[26]Eldersveld, *Political Parties in American Society*, 106.

Today, a major function of national party organizations is to provide campaign services for candidates. (Paul Conklin)

than rank-and-file Democrats, and Republicans on the RNC are more conservative than rank-and-file Republicans.[27]

The national party's day-to-day operations are directed by a national chairperson chosen by the national committee. When a party controls the White House, the president's choice for chairperson is accepted by the committee. The position of party chair was once highly coveted because its occupant was expected to run the party's presidential campaign and coordinate patronage appointments. These responsibilities have since been assigned elsewhere, so the position of chair has declined in importance.

The national party administers the quadrennial presidential nominating convention. This is a major responsibility, but it carries no political power. Influence at the national conventions rests with the delegates, who are chosen in the states they represent, although the national party organizations are legally empowered to tell state organizations how to choose and certify their national convention delegates.[28] When it comes to electoral activity, the national party organizations concentrate on campaigns for national office—the Senate, House, and presidential races. Both the Republican and Democratic national parties raise campaign funds and distribute them directly to their candidates for Congress.

## A NEW PARTY ROLE: SERVICING CANDIDATE-CENTERED CAMPAIGNS

Facing the fact that campaigns have become candidate-centered, the national and state parties have assumed a service role, helping candidates to conduct their personal campaigns. A key figure in this development was William Brock, who became the GOP's national committee chair in 1976. He believed that one

[27]William Crotty, "National Committees as Grass-Roots Vehicles of Representation," in Crotty, *Party Symbol*, 33–49.
[28]*Cousins* v. *Wigoda*, 419 U.S. 477 (1975); *Democratic Party of the United States* v. *La Follette*, 450 U.S. 107 (1975).

way to revive the Republican party, which was in disarray after the Watergate scandal and Nixon's resignation, was to strengthen the national organization. With its close ties to business and upper-middle-class interests, the Republican party has always had a fund-raising advantage over its rival party, and Brock sought to capitalize on this advantage through a nationwide direct-mail fund-raising campaign. By 1982 the Republican party's mailing list included over one million names and had been used to raise $130 million for the party's election efforts.[29]

Brock also decided that the GOP would take full advantage of new campaign technologies. The national Republican organization developed campaign management "colleges" for candidates and their staffs, compiled massive amounts of electoral data, sent field representatives to assist state and local party leaders, and established a media production division. The media division prepares advertising packages for candidates and assists them in buying commercial time on television and radio. In 1980 the Republican party used its in-house media capacity to produce a national advertising campaign, the first time that a party had done so. Based on the theme "Vote Republican—for a Change," the $9.5 million campaign attacked the Democrats for their handling of national government.[30]

In 1982 the Democratic party followed Brock's lead, mounting a national advertising campaign against Ronald Reagan's economic policies, but its later start and less affluent followers have kept the Democrats behind the GOP in spending (see Figure 12-4).[31] Modern campaigns, as David Adamany notes, are based on a "cash economy," and Democrats are relatively cash-poor.[32]

Fund-raising problems are not the only reason for the Democratic party's inability to match the Republicans' organizing efforts. The Democrats are a more deeply divided party, and the national organization has been preoccupied

[29]Larry Sabato, "New Campaign Techniques and the American Party System," in Vernon Bogdanor, ed., *Parties and Democracy in Britain and America* (New York: Praeger, 1984), 202–206.
[30]Ibid.
[31]See Peter Byrne Edsall, *The New Politics of Inequality* (New York: Norton, 1984).
[32]David Adamany, "Political Parties in the 1980s," in Michael J. Malbin, ed., *Money and Politics in the United States* (Chatham, N.J.: Chatham House, 1984), 114.

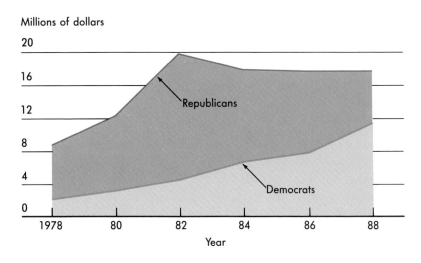

Millions of dollars

FIGURE 12-4 Democratic and Republican Party Spending, 1978–1988
The Republican party significantly outspends the Democratic party. The figures include spending on behalf of congressional candidates by national, state, and local party committees. *Source: Federal Elections Commission.*

with the issue of fair representation of the party's various factions, including organized labor, women, racial minorities, and southerners.[33] Also, the Democrats have long been the nation's majority party, and its leaders for a time felt that its candidates did not need expensive, sophisticated campaign techniques in order to be elected.[34]

Because of their expanded activities, the national parties now play a more important role in election campaigns, but their influence over candidates has not increased appreciably.[35] The relationship of parties to candidates is one of service, not of power.[36] Rather than lose an office to the opposition, a party will even contribute to the campaign of a party maverick. In 1986 the national Democratic party made the U.S. Senate race in Florida a top priority, even though its candidate, Bob Graham, had some policy views that were closer to those of Senate Republicans than of his fellow Democrats.

**Party Organizations**
The Republican and Democratic parties are weak organizationally. They do not have full control over the nomination of candidates and are not the centers of campaign organization. For the most part, candidates in the United States set up their own campaigns, raise their own funds, and determine their own platforms. This pattern is unusual. In most other democracies, party organizations choose the nominees, devise platforms on which candidates must run, and coordinate campaign activities. The United States is atypical for many reasons, among them a cultural bias against political parties and a federal system and demographic diversity that make party unity difficult to achieve. The United States even places legal restrictions on the scope of political parties' influence. The most significant restriction is the legally mandated primary election, which denies parties control over nominations and thus weakens their hold on candidates. No democracy in Western Europe has primary elections, and the parties there are organizationally strong.

## Party Organizations and the Public's Influence

Strong political parties give the public its greatest potential for influence. When a party is cohesive and disciplined enough to adopt a national platform on which all its candidates are willing to run, the electorate has its best opportunity to decide the policies by which the nation will be governed. Voters in all constituencies have a common choice and thus can act together in the election.

Because European parties are strong, national organizations, they can offer this type of choice to their electorates. U.S. parties have not provided it, and today's campaigns do not come anywhere near doing so. Each candidate is almost completely free to establish a personal platform. Because candidates of the same party in different constituencies stand for different things, the electorate nationally has no real chance to elect a lawmaking majority pledged to a common set of policies. Of course, U.S. elections produce governing majorities, and it is safe to assume that most elected officials of a particular party share certain ideas. There are common bonds among elected representatives of the same party even when they run and win on their own.[37] But this is a far cry from a system in which voters everywhere have the same choice.

As could be predicted by the shift from party-centered to candidate-centered campaigns, party voting by members of Congress has declined in the past century.[38] When party organizations were at their peak in the late nineteenth century, votes in Congress were often divided along party lines, with 90 percent of Democrats on one side of an issue and 90 percent of Republicans on the other

---

[33]See Dennis G. Sullivan, Jeffrey L. Pressman, Benjamin I. Page, and John J. Lyons, *The Politics of Representation: The Democratic Convention, 1972* (New York: St. Martin's Press, 1974).
[34]William J. Crotty and Gary C. Jacobson, *American Parties in Decline* (Boston: Little, Brown, 1980), 207.
[35]Charles H. Longley, "National Party Renewal," in Gerald M. Pomper, ed., *Party Renewal in America* (New York: Praeger, 1980), 69–86.
[36]Gibson et al., "Assessing Party Organizational Strength," 206.
[37]William J. Keefe, *Congress and the American People* (Englewood Cliffs, N.J.: Prentice-Hall, 1980), 101.
[38]See, for example, David Brady et al., "The Decline of Party in the House of Representatives, 1887–1968," *Legislative Studies Quarterly* 4 (August 1979): 384.

side. In recent decades, however, party divisions in Congress have averaged in the 60 to 70 percent range on key votes.

## THE ADVANTAGES AND DISADVANTAGES OF CANDIDATE-CENTERED CAMPAIGNS

Candidate-centered campaigns have some advantages. First, they contribute flexibility and new blood to electoral politics. When political conditions and issues change, self-directed candidates quickly adjust, bringing new problems and possible solutions to the forefront. By comparison, strong party organizations sometimes have difficulty adapting to new realities. For example, the British Labour party in recent years has been controlled by old-line activists who have been unwilling to recognize that weaknesses in the British economy call for changes in the party's employment and welfare policies.

Second, candidate-centered campaigns encourage national officeholders to be responsive to local interests. Where strong national parties exist, overarching national interests take precedence over local concerns. In France, the Basque and Brittany regions are severely underdeveloped, but their calls for a greater share of the country's resources have gone largely unheeded by major-party representatives in the National Assembly. Members of the U.S. Congress, in contrast, are keenly sensitive to subnational interests. In building personal followings among their state and district constituents, members of Congress respond to local needs. Nearly every significant domestic program enacted by Congress is adjusted to accommodate the interests of states and districts that would otherwise be hurt by the policy.

In other respects, however, candidate-centered campaigns are decidedly inferior to party-centered ones. Officeholders' accountability to the public is diminished by candidate-centered politics. If national policy goes awry, an individual member of Congress can always blame the problem on "others" in Congress or on the president.[39] Responsibility is less easily evaded when parties are stronger, because governing success or failure is then a party matter and members of the majority party must share in the credit or blame.

Candidate-centered campaigns are also characterized by the prominent influence of special interests. In a party-based system, power can rest on sheer numbers, so heavy emphasis is placed on appeals to the mass public. In a candidate-based system, by contrast, superior campaign funding is prized. In U.S. elections, money increasingly has come from special interests; in the last decade alone, group contributions have increased threefold in congressional campaigns. When the narrow demands of special interests predominate, candidates are less able to respond to broader national needs. (Chapter 14 discusses the relationship between candidates and interest groups more fully.)

Finally, candidate-centered campaigns can easily degenerate into meaningless showmanship. The 1986 congressional elections are a case in point. Many candidates chose to duck controversial issues and concentrated instead on character assassination. The result has been widely characterized as one of the most negative campaigns in history, as candidates filled the television airwaves with paid commercials condemning their opponents for every imaginable personal misdeed and misjudgment. One U.S. Senate candidate publicly

[39]David E. Price, *Bringing Back the Parties* (Washington, D.C.: Congressional Quarterly Press, 1984), 116.

accused his opponent of lesbianism. The 1986 campaign was also marked by what Nelson Polsby has called a "policy craze," which is an issue of the moment that is guaranteed to appeal to voters.[40] The policy craze in 1986 was illegal drugs, which was an ideal issue in that no candidate can lose votes for condemning drug dealers. When the news media began to focus on the spread of "crack," a new and inexpensive form of cocaine, congressional candidates quickly jumped on the bandwagon. So did President Ronald Reagan, who was actively campaigning for Republican Senate candidates. Reagan proposed and Congress passed legislation allocating millions of dollars to combat drug trafficking and drug abuse. Incumbent members of Congress held hastily scheduled news conferences to announce that they had voted for the new legislation, and many of them stressed the drug issue in their campaign advertising. After the election, however, the issue died out almost as quickly as it had flared up. When he submitted his budget to Congress the following January, Reagan had deleted all funding for the new drug programs. Only a few members of Congress strenuously objected.

Of course, expediency has always been a characteristic of election politics, whatever the time and whatever the nation. But it peaks when candidates work on their own for election. Unconstrained by a strong party's policy tradition and commitments, candidates are tempted to do whatever it takes to get elected.

★ ANALYZE THE ISSUE

**Presidents and Their Parties' Agendas**
Recent presidents have all but ignored their parties' agendas in favor of their own. Ronald Reagan was the exception. Why do you think Reagan sought to strengthen the Republican party for the long run? To the degree that you think Reagan had in mind the perpetuation of his own policy agenda, what do his efforts suggest about the value of strong, enduring parties?

## THE PRESIDENT AS PARTY SURROGATE

As campaigns in the United States have become increasingly candidate-centered, competition over policy issues has focused on the president. On broad national issues, his initiatives have come to serve as a basis of division, with candidates aligning themselves either with or against the president's policies. This tendency for the president to act as a surrogate for the parties as the center of policy debate has lent a degree of commonality to electoral competition in various parts of the nation. It can also give continuity to policy conflict, as it did in the early 1980s, when Reagan's policies resulted in relatively stable coalitions in Congress and created a policy debate that bridged the elections of 1980, 1982, and 1984.

In at least three respects, however, presidential politics is inferior to party politics. First, whatever the president's policy preferences and personal idiosyncrasies, they overshadow the ideas of all other individuals and define national debate. In contrast, a party agenda is formulated by a broader spectrum of leadership and thus provides a more fully representative set of views. Second, presidential politics lacks permanence: when a president leaves office after four or eight years, his policy agenda goes with him. In party politics, policy commitments outlast the term of any single administration. Finally, modern presidents have had difficulty maintaining their power throughout their terms of office: all presidents since Franklin D. Roosevelt have suffered prolonged periods of incapacity or loss of the public's confidence. When the president is unable to lead, the country has no other obvious source of guidance. In party politics, party tradition and philosophy are continuing sources of direction.

[40]Nelson Polsby, *Consequences of Party Reform* (New York: Oxford University Press, 1983), 147.

## THE PARADOX OF MODERN U.S. ELECTIONS

Wistful longings for a return to the party politics of yesteryear have a touch of both unreality and amnesia. The parties are never going to regain their former level of influence, and they were far from perfect in the first place. After all, it was abusive practices by party leaders that led to the introduction of primary elections—America's drastic cure for the mischiefs of party.

Yet, and this is the central point, the electorate's opportunity to have a broad and consistent influence on national policy has been weakened by the decline of parties. Election outcomes now depend more heavily than in the past on incumbency, personality, and campaign spending. These factors are not necessarily trivial, but they are inferior in importance to the sustained issues of party politics. Popular rule is not a question of a Congress filled with incumbents or ingratiating personalities but of a Congress filled with members committed to policy directions that the people through their votes have had a reasonable chance to accept or reject. The common belief that it is better to vote "for the person, not the party" conforms with Americans' trust in individualism but makes little sense as a guideline for collective voting. When candidates run personal campaigns, and are judged on them, the effect is to shift the point of decision from the electoral process to the legislative process, where 100 senators and 435 representatives finally bring their separate agendas together. This is the great paradox of modern U.S. elections: they appear to strengthen the public's hold on the policy agenda by making the candidate–voter relationship in any given constituency a more direct one; yet they actually weaken that hold by making it more difficult for voters in different constituencies to act together.

Of course, as we noted in Chapter 11, the two parties differ in their policy tendencies and constituency interests, so party labels still provide the electorate with a guide to candidates' policy leanings. Voters in different constituencies are thus given some opportunity for collective action, and their choice of a Democratic or Republican majority in Congress does affect the direction of national policy. Yet the history of democratic societies indicates that the potential for popular influence cannot be fully realized without effective organization.[41] Grass-roots parties—"the people's constitution," in the historian James MacGregor Burns's phrase—were established in the early nineteenth century to enable the mass public to assert its collective voice more forcefully.[42]

Americans either never learned this history lesson very well or have forgotten it. The public today has no real appreciation of parties and would welcome their further decline. A majority of Americans, for example, say that presidential nominees should be chosen by national primaries rather than in party conventions. Most candidates also have no desire to see a return of strong parties. Although they approve of the parties' new service role, candidates would not welcome any change that placed them in a position subordinate to the parties.

Parties survived the shift to candidate-centered campaigns and will persist, but their heyday has passed. A continuation of candidate-centered politics is the outlook for the future.

> ★ ANALYZE THE ISSUE
>
> **The Decline of Parties**
> Grass-roots political parties were created in order to "make" majorities. Are parties the only institution that can build majorities effectively and on a continuing basis? Many analysts of American politics have concluded that parties are declining in power and importance. Does this necessarily mean that the power of the majority has also been declining?

[41]Benjamin Ginsberg, *The Consequences of Consent* (New York: Random House, 1982), 145.
[42]James MacGregor Burns, *The Vineyard of Liberty* (New York: Knopf, 1982), 351.

# Summary

America's political parties are relatively weak organizations. They lack control over nominations, elections, and platforms. Candidates can bypass the party organization and win nomination through primary elections. Individual candidates also control most of the organization and money necessary to win elections and run largely on personal platforms.

Primary elections are the major reason for the organizational weakness of America's parties. Once the parties lost their hold on the nominating process, they became subordinate to candidates. More generally, the political parties have been undermined by election reforms, some of which were intended to weaken the party and others of which have unintentionally done so. Recently the state and national party organizations have expanded their capacity to provide candidates with modern campaign services and are again playing a prominent role in election campaigns. But this role is less influential than it once was, because party organizations at all levels have few ways of controlling the candidates who run under their banner. They assist candidates with campaign technology, workers, and funds, but cannot compel candidates' loyalty to organizational goals.

America's parties are decentralized, fragmented organizations. The relationship among local, state, and national party organizations is marked by paths of common interest rather than lines of authority. The national party organization does not control the policies and activities of the state organizations, and they in turn do not control the local organizations. The fragmentation of parties prevents them from acting as cohesive national organizations. Traditionally the local organizations have controlled most of the party's work force because most elections are contested at the local level. Local parties, however, vary markedly in their vitality; today only a few can be described as active, powerful machines, while most are understaffed and underfunded.

America's party organizations are flexible enough to allow diverse interests to coexist within them; they can also accommodate new ideas and leadership, since they are neither rigid nor closed. However, because America's parties cannot control their candidates or coordinate their policies at all levels, they are unable to present the voters with a coherent, detailed platform for governing. The national electorate as a whole is thus denied a clear choice among policy alternatives and has difficulty influencing national policy in a predictable and enduring way through elections.

# Major Concepts

candidate-centered politics  
nomination  
party-centered politics  

party organizations  
primary election (direct primary)  

# Suggested Readings

Allswang, John. *Bosses, Machines, and Urban Voters.* Baltimore: Johns Hopkins University Press, 1986. A penetrating study of the party machines that once flourished in America's cities.

Broder, David. *The Party's Over.* New York: Harper & Row, 1972. One of America's leading journalists discusses the declining influence of parties on election campaigns.

Crotty, William, ed. *The Party Symbol.* San Francisco: W. H. Freeman, 1980. A series of articles by leading scholars on the activities and influence of contemporary American parties.

Davis, James W. *National Conventions in an Age of Party Reform.* Westport, Conn: Greenwood Press, 1983. An assessment of how the role of national conventions has changed as a result of the changes in the parties and nominating system.

Eldersveld, Samuel J. *Political Parties: A Behavioral Analysis.* Chicago: Rand McNally, 1964. A behavioral study of the activities of the Democratic and Republican organizations in Detroit.

Epstein, Leon D. *Political Parties in Western Democracies.* New Brunswick, N.J.: Transaction Books, 1980. A comparative analysis of political parties, with special emphasis on those of the United States and Great Britain.

Frantzich, Stephen E. *Political Parties in the Technological Age.* New York: Longman, 1989. An insightful analysis of how parties are adapting to the information age.

Huckshorn, Robert L. *Party Leadership in the States.* Amherst: University of Massachusetts Press, 1976. A study of parties in the states based on a survey of party leaders.

Kayden, Xander, and Eddie Mahe, Jr. *The Party Goes On.* New York: Basic Books, 1985. An assessment of how the two major parties have adapted to the political changes of recent decades.

Pomper, Gerald M., ed. *Party Renewal in America.* New York: Praeger, 1980. Essays by scholars on recent changes in American political parties.

Sullivan, Dennis G., Jeffrey L. Pressman, Benjamin I. Page, and John L. Lyons. *The Politics of Representation: The Democratic Convention, 1972.* New York: St. Martin's Press, 1974. An empirical study of the representative nature of delegates to the 1972 Democratic convention.

# Chapter 13

## THE INTEREST-GROUP SYSTEM: ORGANIZING FOR INFLUENCE

*The flaw in the pluralist heaven is that the heavenly chorus sings with a strong upper-class bias.*

—*E. E. Schattschneider*[1]

Until Candy Lightner came along in May 1980, they had not thought of themselves as a group, even though they had something tragically important in common—the death of children or other family members in traffic accidents caused by drunk drivers. Lightner taught them to view themselves as a political lobby and gave them a name—Mothers Against Drunk Driving (MADD).

Perhaps no other small group in recent times has pressed its view so forcefully as MADD. Its intense grass-roots campaign resulted in a 1984 law that withholds federal highway funds from states with a legal drinking age under twenty-one. Through appearances on television news shows, letters to key members of Congress, and personal appeals to President Ronald Reagan, MADD won a campaign that at first appeared unlikely to succeed because of opposition by powerful restaurant and liquor lobbies. Since then, MADD has pressured state legislatures and local law-enforcement officials to toughen penalties for people convicted of driving while intoxicated.

MADD is one of thousands of organizations known as interest groups. An **interest group** is a set of individuals who are organized to promote a shared political interest. Also called a "faction" or "pressure group" or "special interest," an interest group is characterized by its formalized organization and by its pursuit of policy goals that stem from its members' shared interest. Thus college students as a whole do not constitute an interest group, because they are

[1]E. E. Schattschneider, *The Semisovereign People: A Realist's View of Democracy in America* (New York: Holt, Rinehart and Winston, 1960), 35.

Candy Lightner, founder of Mothers Against Drunk Driving (MADD). (AP/Wide World Photos)

not an organized collectivity. Similarly, a bridge club is not an interest group, because it does not seek to influence the political process. However, the organizations listed below—corporations, industry associations, nonprofit social-service agencies, lobbying organizations—*are* interest groups because, despite their differences, they all meet the definition's two criteria: each is an organized entity and each seeks to further its members' interests through political action.

| | |
|---|---|
| AFL-CIO | The National Grange |
| U.S. Chamber of Commerce | AT&T |
| Sierra Club | Planned Parenthood |
| Association of Wheat Growers | American Petroleum Institute |
| American Association of University Professors | Common Cause |
| Mobil Oil | Liberty Foundation |
| National Organization for Women | Americans for Democratic Action |
| American Civil Liberties Union | General Motors |
| American Bar Association | American Realtors Association |

Interest groups promote public policies, encourage the political participation of their members, support candidates for public office, and work to influence policymakers. Interest groups are thus similar to political parties in certain respects, but the two types of organizations differ in important ways. Major political parties address a broad range of issues so as to appeal to diverse blocs of voters. By comparison, interest groups focus on specific issues of immediate concern to their members; farm groups, for example, concentrate on agricultural policy.

The fact that interest groups exist to promote the interests of their members has given them a dubious reputation. However, blanket criticisms of interest groups are misplaced. Such groups are a basic means for people to achieve the ideal of self-government. Although citizens have common concerns, they also have disparate ones, and it is appropriate for them to look to government to protect their special interests. The elderly, for instance, have certain needs, such as financial security, that can be met only through government policies for the aged. The same can be said of farmers, consumers, corporations, minorities—indeed, of nearly every interest in society. Without groups to articulate and pursue the goals of various interests in society, government would be less aware of those interests and less able to promote them. Thus the issue is not whether government should be responsive to groups but whether particular groups have undue political influence.

A leading theory of American politics—**pluralism**—holds that society's interests are substantially represented through the activities of groups. An extreme statement of this view was Arthur F. Bentley's claim in 1908 that society is "nothing other than the complex of groups that compose it."[2] Although modern pluralists make far less sweeping claims, they do contend, on balance, that the group process is open to a great range of interests, nearly all of which benefit from organized activity in one significant way or another.

This chapter examines the degree to which various interests in American society are represented by organized groups. These groups will be considered to constitute a group *system*, much as political parties make up a party system. The major question about the group system is its representativeness. Which interests are highly organized through groups? Which are not? The chapter argues that the pluralist viewpoint exaggerates the representativeness of the group system. Economically powerful interests dominate the group system. The main points made in the chapter are the following:

★ *Although nearly all interests in American society are organized to some degree, those associated with economic activity, particularly business enterprises, are by far the most thoroughly organized.* Their advantage rests partly on the fact that their economic activities provide them with resources (especially money) that can be used for political purposes. Also, economic organizations are relatively easy to maintain because they provide individuals with private goods (such as wages and jobs) that are tangible incentives for membership.

★ *Groups that do not have economic activity as their primary function often have organizational problems.* They pursue public or collective goods (such as a safer environment) that are available even to individuals who are not group members, so individuals may choose not to pay the costs of membership.

[2]Quoted in Norman J. Ornstein and Shirley Elder, *Interest Groups, Lobbying, and Policymaking* (Washington, D.C.: Congressional Quarterly Press, 1978), 11.

★ *The interest-group system overrepresents business interests and higher income groups,* although their advantage has diminished in recent decades.

## Types of Interest Groups

In the 1830s the Frenchman Alexis de Tocqueville wrote that the "principle of association" was nowhere more evident than in America.[3] Tocqueville's observation has been echoed many times since then, for an obvious reason: organized groups have always flourished in the United States. The country's tradition of free association has made it easy for Americans to join together for political purposes, and their diverse interests have given them reason to seek influence through specialized groups. Perhaps no other nation has so many separate economic, ethnic, religious, social, and geographic interests as the United States. Moreover, the nation's fragmented political system provides numerous points of access for interest groups; because of federalism and separation of powers, numerous political institutions at all levels of government are available for groups to lobby. Not surprisingly, manufacturing, labor, agriculture, and other leading interests have not only national organizations but also separate state and local lobbies.

The extraordinary number of groups in the United States does not indicate, however, that the nation's various interests are equally well organized. Organizations develop when people with shared interests have the opportunity and the incentive to join together.[4] Some individuals have the skills, money, contacts, or time to participate effectively in group politics, but others do not. Moreover, some groups are inherently more attractive to potential members than others and thus find it easier to build large or devoted followings. Finally, organizations differ in their access to financial resources and thus differ also in their capacity for political action.

These differences are of critical importance. Group politics is the politics of organization. Interests that are highly organized stand a good chance of having their views heard by policymakers. Poorly organized interests stand a good chance of being ignored. Thus a first consideration in regard to group politics in America is the issue of how thoroughly various interests are organized.

### ECONOMIC GROUPS

No interests are more fully or effectively organized than those that have economic activity as their primary purpose. Corporations, labor unions, farm groups, and professional associations are organized primarily for economic reasons (see Table 13-1). They exist to make profits, provide jobs, improve pay, or protect an occupation. They do not exist for political purposes, but they do lobby government. Their political activity is secondary to their economic activity. For example, although corporations routinely seek favorable policies from government, they function chiefly to produce economic goods and

> ★ ANALYZE THE ISSUE
>
> **The Differences between Groups and Parties**
> Political parties and interest groups are the organizations through which people have traditionally obtained representation. How do groups differ from parties? How are groups like parties? Can either substitute for the other?

---

[3] Alexis de Tocqueville, *Democracy in America* (Garden City, N.Y.: Doubleday/Anchor, 1969), bk. II, ch.4.
[4] See Peter Clarke and James Q. Wilson, "Incentive Systems: A Theory of Organizations," *Administrative Science Quarterly* (1961): 129–166; William P. Browne, "Benefits and Membership: A Reappraisal of Interest Group Activity," *Western Political Quarterly* 29 (June 1976): 258–273.

**TABLE 13-1  Number of Members of Some Large Economic Groups**

| Group | Number of Members |
|---|---|
| AFL-CIO | 14,400,000 |
| Council of Better Business Bureaus | 125,000* |
| National Association of Manufacturers | 13,250* |
| United Farm Workers | 100,000 |
| United Mine Workers of America | 240,000 |
| American Medical Association | 258,000 |
| American Bar Association | 325,807 |
| Chamber of Commerce | 200,000 |
| American Farm Bureau Federation | 3,300,000 |

*Firms.

SOURCE: *Encyclopedia of Associations, 1988,* 22d ed. (Detroit: Gale Research, 1987).

services. For the sake of discussion, such organizations will be called **economic groups,** although it is important to recognize that their political goals can include policies that transcend narrow economic interests. Thus the AFL-CIO concentrates on labor objectives, but it also takes positions on broader issues of foreign and domestic policy.

### Business Groups

Writing in 1929, E. Pendleton Herring noted, "Of the many organized groups maintaining offices in [Washington], there are no interests more fully, more comprehensively, and more efficiently represented than those of American industry."[5] Although corporations do not dominate the group system to the same degree as they did in the past, Herring's general conclusion still holds: more than half of all groups formally registered to lobby Congress are business organizations. Nearly all large corporations and many smaller ones are politically active. They concentrate their activities on policies that touch directly on business interests, such as tax, tariff, and regulatory decisions.

Business organizations are also represented through associations. Some of these "organizations of organizations" seek to advance the general interests of business and industry and to articulate a business perspective on broad policy issues.[6] One of the oldest associations is the National Association of Manufacturers (NAM), which was formed in 1894. The NAM includes 13,000 manufacturers and has worked to restrain labor unions, to reduce federal taxes on corporations, and to block unfavorable regulation of business by government. Another large business association is the U.S. Chamber of Commerce, which represents more than 200,000 medium-sized and small businesses.[7] The

[5]E. Pendleton Herring, *Group Representation before Congress* (Washington, D.C.: Brookings Institution, 1929), 78.
[6]Kay Lehman Schlozman and John T. Tierney, *Organized Interests and American Democracy* (New York: Harper & Row, 1986), 41; see also Graham Wooton, *Interest Groups, Policy, and Politics in America* (Englewood Cliffs, N.J.: Prentice-Hall, 1985), 103.
[7]Schlozman and Tierney, *Organized Interests,* 24, 41.

Chamber has a Washington headquarters located near the White House with a support staff of more than four hundred employees. Because the Chamber of Commerce and the NAM represent firms of various types, they generally lobby for policies beneficial to the business sector as a whole.

Business is also organized through trade associations confined to a single industry. These associations vary enormously in their lobbying budgets; for example, the American Petroleum Institute and the National Association of Home Builders have annual budgets of $10 million each, whereas the Bow Tie Manufacturers Association and the Post Card Manufacturing Association each spend only $10,000 annually. Trade associations carry on the bulk of corporate lobbying. Because each trade association represents a single industry, it can promote the interests of member corporations even when these interests conflict with those of business generally. Thus, while the Chamber of Commerce promotes a free-trade policy, some trade associations seek protective tariffs because their member firms need barriers against foreign competition.

## Labor Groups

Since the 1930s, organized labor has been politically active on a large scale. Its goal has been to promote policies that benefit workers in general and union members in particular. In 1988, for example, organized labor worked hard and successfully for passage of legislation requiring companies to give workers sixty days' notice before they closed a plant or laid off employees.

Although some independent unions, such as the United Mine Workers, lobby actively, the dominant labor group is the AFL-CIO, which maintains its national headquarters in Washington, D.C. The AFL-CIO has more than one hundred affiliated unions, including the International Brotherhood of Electrical Workers, the Sheet Metal Workers, the Communication Workers of America, and, as of 1987, the giant International Brotherhood of Teamsters.

The AFL-CIO has the largest membership of any organization devoted to promoting the interests of labor. (Jim West/Impact Visuals)

The AFL-CIO has about 15 million members, which represents a considerable decline in recent years. At one time about a third of the U.S. work force was unionized, but only about one-sixth of all workers currently belong to unions. Skilled and unskilled laborers have been the core of organized labor, and their numbers are decreasing. Professionals, technicians, and service workers are increasing in number and, because of their educational backgrounds or employment situations, are more difficult to organize into unions.

However, unions have made important inroads in recent decades in their efforts to organize public employees. Teachers, postal workers, police, firefighters, and social workers are among the public-employee groups that have become increasingly unionized. The effectiveness of these unions is limited by federal and state laws forbidding public employees to strike. In 1981 the Professional Air Traffic Controllers Organization (PATCO) called a strike over pay and working conditions; President Reagan responded by firing 11,500 federally employed controllers.

### Agricultural Groups

Farm organizations are another large economic lobby. The American Farm Bureau Federation is the largest of the farm groups, with more than 2.5 million members. The National Farmers Union, the National Grange, and the National Farmers Organization are smaller farm lobbies. Agricultural groups do not always agree on policy issues. For instance, the Farm Bureau has sided with agribusiness and owners of large farms, while the Farmers Union has promoted the interests of smaller, "family" farms.

This 1873 lithograph illustrates the benefits of membership in the National Grange, an agricultural interest group. (Library of Congress)

There are also numerous specialty farm associations, including the Association of Wheat Growers, the American Soybean Association, and Associated Milk Producers. Each association acts as a separate lobby to try to obtain policies beneficial to its members' narrow agricultural interests. For example, the Tobacco Growers Association in 1984 successfully lobbied for increased government price supports for tobacco.

### Professional Groups

Most professions have lobbying associations. Perhaps the most powerful of these groups is the American Medical Association (AMA), which includes 250,000 of the nation's 550,000 physicians among its members. The AMA has opposed government involvement in medical practices and is widely held responsible for blocking comprehensive government-paid medical care in the United States. Other professional groups are the American Bar Association and the American Association of University Professors, each of which maintains a lobbying office in Washington.

## NONECONOMIC GROUPS

Although economic interests are the best-organized and most conspicuous groups, they have no monopoly on group activity. There are a great number and variety of other organized interests, which we shall refer to collectively as **noneconomic groups** (see Table 13-2). The members of groups in this category are drawn together not by the promise of direct economic gain but by **purposive incentives**—opportunities to promote a cause in which they believe.[8] Whether a group's goal is to protect the environment, reduce the threat of nuclear war, return prayer to the public schools, feed the poor at home or abroad, outlaw or retain abortion, or whatever, there are citizens who are willing to participate simply because they believe the policy goal is a worthy one.[9] Purposive incentives are powerful enough that nearly every conceivable interest within

[8]See Clarke and Wilson, "Incentive Systems," 135.
[9]Jeffrey M. Berry, *The Interest Group Society* (Boston: Little, Brown, 1984), 77.

**TABLE 13-2  Number of Members of Some Large Noneconomic Groups**

| Group | Number of Members |
|---|---|
| National Organization for Women | 260,000 |
| American Civil Liberties Union | 250,000 |
| National Association for the Advancement of Colored People | 400,000 |
| John Birch Society | 50,000 |
| Amnesty International of the United States | 225,000 |
| National Urban League | 50,000 |
| Ralph Nader's Public Citizen | 100,000 |
| Common Cause | 225,000 |

SOURCE: *Encyclopedia of Associations, 1988,* 22d ed. (Detroit: Gale Research, 1987).

American society has a group that claims to represent it. Most noneconomic groups are of three general types: public-interest groups, single-issue groups, and ideological groups.

### Public-Interest Groups

Public-interest groups are those that attempt to act in the broad interests of society as a whole. Despite their label, public-interest groups are not led by people elected by the public at large, and the issues they target are ones of their own choosing, not the public's. Nevertheless, there is a basis for distinguishing such groups from economic groups: the latter seek direct material benefits for their members, while the former seek benefits that are less tangible and more broadly shared. For example, the National Association of Manufacturers, an economic group, seeks policies favorable to large corporations, while the League of Women Voters, a public-interest group, seeks policies—such as simplified voter registration—that can benefit the public in general.

The League of Women Voters has existed for decades, but more than half of the currently active public-interest groups have been formed since 1960. Among the more visible of these newer organizations are Common Cause and Ralph Nader's Public Citizen. Each of these groups gets some of its resources from small contributors. Common Cause has about 225,000 members, whose annual dues help to support a large national staff of lobbyists, attorneys, and public relations experts. Founded in 1970 by John Gardner (formerly Lyndon Johnson's secretary of health, education, and welfare), Common Cause concentrates on political reform in such areas as campaign finance. Nader first came to national attention in 1965, when his book *Unsafe at Any Speed* exposed the poor safety record of General Motors' Corvair automobile. His Public Citizen group works primarily on consumers' issues, including pollution control, auto safety, and pure food and drugs.

THE LEAGUE
OF WOMEN VOTERS

Public Citizen, a public-interest group founded by Ralph Nader (at right), promotes consumer interests by working for such measures as laws requiring juice-drink producers to reveal on labels the amount of natural fruit juice in their products. (UPI/Bettmann Newsphotos)

## Single-Issue Groups

A single-issue group is organized to influence policy in just one area. Notable current examples are the various right-to-life and pro-choice groups that have formed around the issue of abortion. The number of single-issue groups has risen sharply in the past two decades, and they now lobby on almost every conceivable issue, from nuclear arms to day-care centers to drug abuse.

Environmental groups are sometimes classified as public-interest groups, but they may also be considered single-issue organizations in that most of them seek to influence public policy in a specific area, such as pollution reduction, wilderness preservation, or wildlife protection. The Sierra Club is one of the oldest of such groups; it was formed in the 1890s to promote the preservation of scenic areas. Also prominent are the National Audubon Society, the Wilderness Society, the Environmental Defense Fund, and the Izaak Walton League. Between 1960 and 1970, membership in environmental groups tripled in response to increased public concern about the quality of the environment.[10]

## Ideological Groups

Some groups are concerned with a broad range of policies from a general philosophical or moral perspective. Americans for Democratic Action (ADA), for example, supports liberal positions on social, economic, and foreign policy issues. Like many other groups, ADA rates members of Congress according to how closely their votes on various issues match its own positions. The Moral Majority, formed in 1979 by the Reverend Jerry Falwell and supported by fundamentalist Christians, is another example of an ideological group; it was formed to restore "Christian values" to American life and policy. Ideological groups on both the left and the right have proliferated since the 1960s.[11]

Groups such as the National Organization for Women (NOW) and the National Association for the Advancement of Colored People (NAACP) can also be generally classified as ideological groups. Their aim is to promote the broad interests of a particular demographic segment of society. The NAACP was formed in 1909 to promote the political interests of racial minorities, primarily through initiating lawsuits on their behalf.

## A SPECIAL CATEGORY OF INTEREST GROUP: GOVERNMENTS

While the vast majority of organized interests in the United States represent private concerns, a growing number of interest groups represent governments, both foreign and subnational.

The U.S. federal government makes policies that directly affect the economic development, political stability, and security of nations throughout the world. Arms sales, foreign aid, immigration, and import restrictions and other trade

[10]Carol S. Greenwald, *Group Power* (New York: Praeger, 1977), 181; Robert Cameron Mitchell, "National Environmental Lobbies and the Apparent Logic of Collective Action," in Clifford S. Russell, ed., *Collective Decision Making* (Baltimore: John Hopkins University Press for Resources for the Future, 1979), 93–98.
[11]See Alan Crawford, *Thunder on the Right* (New York: Pantheon, 1980).

consumers could join together in a single group, but they also realize the impossibility of forming such an organization. Getting millions of people to work together is infinitely more difficult than getting a few firms to collaborate.

## THE LURE OF INCENTIVES

Many economic groups offer prospective members a powerful incentive to join: **private goods** (or individual goods), which are the benefits that a group can grant directly to the individual member. For example, workers in the state of Michigan cannot hold automobile assembly jobs unless they belong to the United Auto Workers (UAW). Union membership is the qualification that enables an individual to obtain an auto worker's job, which is a private good.

Not all economic groups are in such a monopoly position. Agricultural organizations, for example, provide crop insurance, marketing arrangements, farming information, and other private goods to members, but these are benefits that farmers can obtain elsewhere. As a result, most farmers are not dues-paying members of a farm group. In general, however, the incentives provided by economic groups are stronger than those offered by other types of groups. Economic interests are highly organized in part because they serve the individual economic needs of potential members. A secure job or a higher income is, for most individuals, a powerful incentive to join a group.

Most noneconomic groups, in contrast, offer **collective goods** (or public goods) as an incentive for membership. These goods are benefits in which everyone can share. An environmental group that seeks tougher air-pollution laws, for example, is seeking a collective good; if government should enact such legislation, the resulting benefit—cleaner air—is provided to all citizens, whether or not they belong to the group. This characteristic of collective goods reduces the incentive of individuals to contribute to a group's efforts because they can get a "free ride," receiving the benefits but paying none of the costs. This situation, accordingly, is called the **free-rider problem.**

The free-rider problem arises because it is not rational, in the economic sense, for people to join a group that pursues a collective good.[16] If such a group succeeds in its goals, individuals will get the benefit even if they have not contributed to the cause. Participation in such groups is not rational in another sense as well: the contribution of any individual is so small that it does not affect the group's success in any significant way. Common Cause is no more or less effective if it gains or loses a single contributor. Why, then, should an individual bother to join such a group?

The free-rider problem becomes less troublesome when an issue is so compelling or a leader so charismatic that many potential members are roused to join a group. Membership in Common Cause rose to 350,000 in 1974, when the group conducted a nationwide direct-mail membership drive during the televised coverage of the Senate Watergate hearings. Common Cause subsequently lost more than 100,000 members, however, as public concern over honesty in government abated.

Another way in which noneconomic groups can overcome the free-rider problem is to create individual benefits, akin to those offered by economic

[16]Ibid., 64.

The Sierra Club is a single-issue group that attracts members by offering them such individual benefits as weekend outings. (John Eastcott/Yva Momatiuk/The Image Works)

groups, to make membership more attractive. The Sierra Club, for example, provides wilderness treks and other social benefits (known as "solidarity incentives") to its members. Many groups provide an organizational newsletter or magazine to their members. Such individual incentives are apparently more important to an organization's capacity to retain existing members than to its ability to attract new ones. The Environmental Defense Fund (EDF) is the only large environmental group that offers no newsletter or other services to individual members. Perhaps as a result, EDF also has the highest membership turnover among major environmental groups.

## ACCESS TO RESOURCES

Finally, economic groups have the advantage of ready access to the resources that facilitate organization. Political activity does not come cheap. If a group is to make its views known, it normally must possess a headquarters, an expert staff, and a communication capacity. Economic groups can siphon the requisite money and expertise from their economic activities. For example, a portion of the dues that unions, farm groups, and professional associations receive from their members can be used for lobbying purposes. Corporations have the greatest natural advantage: they can apply corporate funds to the support of their political activities. In the late 1970s, when gasoline prices were at an all-time high, the nation's oil companies spent some of their additional income on a nationwide advertising campaign aimed at dampening public anger, which the oil companies feared would provoke Congress to force them to rebate their windfall profits. The multimillion-dollar television and newspaper campaign blamed the high gasoline prices on Middle East oil-producing countries and told of the billions that U.S. firms were investing in oil exploration in order to free America from its dependence on Arab oil.

Noneconomic groups have a harder time gathering the resources that are necessary for effective political activity. Changes in communication technology have eased the free-rider problem somewhat and have contributed to the sharp increase in the number of noneconomic groups in recent decades. The power of television to dramatize issues and personalities has given a boost to some noneconomic groups. Without television's coverage, such issues as civil rights and the environment would have attracted less interest, and such figures as Jerry Falwell and Ralph Nader would have had smaller followings.

Even more important than television are computers. In the past, a fledgling organization almost had to locate potential members one by one and persuade them personally to join. Today, however, group organizers can buy mailing lists and flood the mails with computer-typed "personal" letters asking recipients to pay a small annual membership fee. For some citizens, a donation of $25 to $50 represents no great sacrifice and offers the personal satisfaction of involvement in a worthy cause.

From the organization's perspective, a direct mailing does not have to produce an extraordinary response to be successful. The immediate goal is to raise enough money to maintain the organization and its lobbying efforts; the goal can be met if only a small percentage of the people who receive fund-raising letters respond to them. Yet a weak response, which is the typical case, limits an organization's activities and its claim to represent a vital interest. In fact, some noneconomic groups could not survive if they depended on financial support from the general public; these organizations get most of their funds from charitable foundations or wealthy donors.[17]

On the whole, however, the organizational advantage rests with economic groups. In resources as in other respects, they have the edge on noneconomic groups.

## *The Group System: Indispensable but Flawed*

As we noted in the introduction to this chapter, pluralist theory holds that organized groups provide for the representation of society's many and diverse interests. On one level, this claim is beyond dispute. Without groups to carry the message, most of society's interests would have great difficulty in gaining government's attention and support. Yet the issue of representation is also a question of whether all interests in society have a fair chance to succeed, and here the pluralist argument is less compelling.

### THE CONTRIBUTION OF GROUPS TO SELF-GOVERNMENT

Group activity is an essential part of self-government. A major obstacle to popular sovereignty is the sheer difficulty that public officials encounter in trying to discover what the people want from government. As we saw in Chapter 8, public opinion cannot be accurately observed directly. To discover it, lawmakers consult public opinion polls, talk with experts, meet with constituents, follow the news, and assess the meaning of recent elections. Organized groups are an additional means of determining popular sentiment. Through their political activities, they provide policymakers with a heightened sense of

[17]Jack L. Walker, "The Origins and Maintenance of Interest Groups in America," *American Political Science Review* 77 (June 1983): 398–399.

the policy concerns of various interests in society. Groups communicate with an uncommon clarity and vigor.[18] On any given issue, the policy positions that are likely to be expressed most clearly and directly are those held by organized interests.

Organized groups also give officials an indication of the intensity with which popular opinions are held. Officials may ignore an issue that evokes almost no intensity, while an issue that provokes strong feelings, whether from a large or small portion of the public, is likely to require action.[19] Here again, organized groups provide policymakers with relevant cues. When organized interests feel strongly about an issue, they contrive to attract policymakers' attention.

Government does not exist simply to serve majority interests. Smaller interests too have a legitimate claim on public policy. The fact that most people are not retirees or labor union members or farmers or college students or Hispanics does not mean that the special needs and concerns of such "minorities" are undeserving of attention. And what better instrument exists for promoting the interests of such "minorities" than organizations formed around them? Groups are not antithetical to the democratic process: they are basic to it.

## THE ECONOMIC BIAS OF THE GROUP SYSTEM

The flaw in the pluralist argument resides in its claim that the group system is representative. Pluralists contend that society's interests compete on a reasonably equal footing through organized groups, that numerous winners emerge from the competition, and that society's general interest is ultimately served by government's responsiveness to a multitude of particular interests. Pluralists recognize that better-organized interests have more influence, but argue that the

---

[18]V. O. Key, Jr., *Public Opinion and American Democracy* (New York: Knopf, 1961), 428.
[19]Ibid.

---

# COMMUNICATION BY ORGANIZED AND UNORGANIZED INTERESTS

Democracy assumes that public officials will pay heed to the policy views of the people, but it is often difficult for officials to discover what the people want. Organized interest groups communicate their policy goals much more clearly than do unorganized interests.

| ORGANIZED INTERESTS | UNORGANIZED INTERESTS |
|---|---|
| Often communicate to officials specific policy actions they desire. | Rarely communicate specific policy actions they favor; at best, provide only an indication of their preferred policy ends. |
| Often communicate firm and consistent opinions on policies of concern. | Rarely communicate firm and consistent opinions; their opinions are often changeable and vague. |
| Often communicate the intensity of their opinions on policy matters through letter-writing campaigns, high levels of lobbying activity, and other means. | Rarely communicate the intensity of their opinions on policy issues; officials must infer it by indirect means. |

**Interest Group Systems**
A century and a half ago,
Alexis de Tocqueville noted
that the United States was
unrivaled in the range and
number of its groups. The
point remains valid today
and is a reflection of the
diversity of American society.
The United States has more
economic, social, religious,
ethnic, and other interests
than the countries of Europe.
The greater diversity of the
United States is evident in
particular areas of group
organization. For example,
whereas U.S. farmers are
represented through several
large general organizations
(among them the Farm
Bureau, the National Grange,
the Farmers Union, and the
National Farm Organization),
British farmers are
represented through only one
such organization (the
National Farmers Union).
Moreover, the group systems
of the United States and
Western Europe differ in their
socioeconomic bias. Because
of strong labor unions and
other working-class
organizations, lower-status
Europeans are only
marginally underrepresented
through groups. By
comparison, the group system
in the United States has a
decided tilt toward persons of
higher income and education.

SOURCES: Russell J. Dalton,
*Citizen Politics in Western
Democracies* (Chatham, N.J.:
Chatham House, 1988), ch. 3;
Thomas Rochon, "Political
Change in Ordered Societies,"
*Comparative Politics* 15 (1983):
351–353.

group process is relatively open and fluid and that few interests are at a serious disadvantage. Each of these claims contains an element of truth, but each is far from the complete truth.

Chiefly, as we have seen, organization is a political resource that is distributed unequally across society. Economic interests, particularly corporations, are the most highly organized, and some analysts argue that group politics works almost entirely to the advantage of business.[20] This generalization was perhaps valid before the 1930s but is less so today. In fact, many of the public-interest groups formed in the 1960s and early 1970s were deliberately created to check and balance the influence of existing groups, particularly corporate lobbies.[21]

Big government has also brought the group political system into closer balance. "Interest group activity," Benjamin Ginsberg writes, "is often more a consequence than an antecedent of the state's programs." In other words, groups form not only to influence policy but also to respond to it. When new programs were created in the 1960s for the benefit of less advantaged interests in society, these interests tended to mobilize to protect their newly acquired benefits. An example is the National Welfare Rights Organization, which was formed during the 1960s *after* new welfare programs were established.[22]

Many of the newer interest groups have had a significant impact in such areas as civil rights, the environment, social-welfare programs for the elderly and the poor, public morality, national security, and business regulation. Moreover, as Chapter 14 indicates, policy is less often decided today by the actions of one or a few groups. The group system is thus not closed and rigid; it is open to new interests and new patterns of influence.

Nevertheless, it would be inaccurate to conclude that the group system is now fully competitive or fully representative of society's interests. Interests differ significantly in their level of organization and degree of influence through group activity. Well over half of all lobbying groups in Washington are still business-related. The interest-group system has a decided tilt toward America's economically oriented groups, particularly its corporations.

The group system is also slanted toward upper-middle-class interests.[23] Studies indicate that individuals of higher socioeconomic status are disproportionately represented among group members and even more so among group leaders (see Table 13-4). These tendencies are predictable. Educated and affluent Americans have the skills and money that give organizational form to special-interest politics. Less advantaged Americans find it harder to contribute to organized activity even when they sense a need or desire to do so. They lack the money, information, contacts, and communication skills to participate. The nation's traditionally disadvantaged, including the poor, minorities, women, and the young, are greatly underrepresented in the group-politics system. When the Reagan administration in 1981 proposed large reductions in federal spending on programs for the poor and disadvantaged, a weak lobby emerged

[20]See G. William Domhoff, *Who Rules America Now?* (Englewood Cliffs, N.J.: Prentice-Hall, 1983).
[21]See Andrew McFarland, *Public Interest Lobbies* (Washington, D.C.: American Enterprise Institute, 1976); Berry, *Interest Group Society.*
[22]Benjamin Ginsberg, *The Consequences of Consent* (New York: Random House, 1982), 214; see also Frances Fox Piven and Richard A. Cloward, *Poor People's Movements* (New York: Random House, 1979), ch. 5.
[23]Sidney Verba and Norman H. Nie, *Participation in America: Political Democracy and Social Equality* (New York: Harper & Row, 1972), 181.

TABLE 13-4 **Extent of Participation of Americans in Organizations, by Socioeconomic Status**

| | SOCIOECONOMIC STATUS | | |
| --- | --- | --- | --- |
| | *Lowest Third* | *Middle Third* | *Highest Third* |
| Nonmember | 56% | 34% | 20% |
| Passive member | 23 | 22 | 21 |
| Active member of only one organization | 16 | 28 | 24 |
| Active member of more than one organization | 6 | 16 | 35 |
| | 101% | 100% | 100% |

*Note:* Socioeconomic status is a combined measure based on educational level of respondent and occupation and income of head of household. Membership is based on activity in *any* organization, not just political organizations. The active–passive distinction is based on respondents' own claims to take an active part in the organization or to be merely a passive member.
SOURCE: Sidney Verba and Norman H. Nie, *Participation in America: Political Democracy and Social Equality* (New York: Harper & Row, 1972), 204.

to fight these cuts. In contrast, a 1985 Reagan proposal to reduce federal loans to college students, most of whom are middle-class, triggered substantial organized opposition.

A lack of organization does not ensure an interest's failure, just as the existence of organization does not guarantee success. However, organized interests are obviously in a better position to make their views known. They have at hand the means to get the attention of policymakers. In contrast, underorganized interests must first collect themselves before they can communicate their opinions. Often they are not even able to establish themselves organizationally. Of course, the underorganized are sometimes represented by proxy.[24] For example, the Southern Poverty Law Center, which works solely on behalf of minorities and the poor who run afoul of the justice system, gets most of its funding from upper-middle-class whites. Interest groups of this sort are uncommon, however, and groups organized and funded directly by low-income Americans are even rarer.

The business and class bias of the group system is especially significant because the most highly organized interests are, in a sense, those least in need of political clout. Corporations and affluent citizens are already favored in the distribution of society's material resources. Left alone, market forces operate to increase the concentration of wealth and power; the rich do indeed get richer. The group system does not alter that basic fact.

## A MADISONIAN DILEMMA

James Madison recognized the dilemma inherent in group activity. Although he worried that government would fall under the control of a dominant interest, whether of the majority or of the minority, he realized that a free society is

★ ANALYZE THE ISSUE

**The Decline of Voting and the Rise of Groups**
Between the 1960s and the 1980s, voter turnout in the United States steadily declined as group activity increased. Is it possible to look upon these trends as the institutionalization of middle-class politics? (Consider not only which citizens tend to participate in groups but also which ones have tended to drop out of the voting electorate—see Chapter 9.)

[24]See Charles McCarry, *Citizen Nader* (New York: Signet, 1972).

*The diversity in the faculties of men . . . is . . . an insuperable obstacle to a uniformity of interests. The protection of these faculties is the first object of government.*
                *Federalist* No. 10

obliged to permit the advocacy of self-interest. Unless people can promote the separate opinions that stem from differences in their talents, needs, values, and possessions, they do not have liberty.

Madison added, however, that "the regulation of these various and interfering interests forms the principal task of modern legislation." Government must attempt to check and balance the demands of groups to ensure that the special interest not rule the general interest. Madison was arguing, in effect, that government, although obliged to foster the conditions that promote self-advocacy, must also operate to keep groups in their proper place. Government is the only institution in society that can greatly alter or offset private power. Among the topics of the next chapter is whether the U.S. government adequately constrains group demands.

## Summary

A political interest group is a set of individuals organized to promote a shared political concern. Most interest groups owe their existence to factors other than politics. They form for economic reasons, such as the pursuit of profit, and maintain themselves by making profits (in the case of corporations) or by providing their members with private goods, such as jobs and wages. Their lobbying for political advantage is an outgrowth of their economic activity. Such interest groups include corporations, trade associations, labor unions, farm organizations, and professional associations. Collectively, economic groups are by far the largest set of organized interests, accounting for about three-fourths of registered Washington lobbies.

Other groups do not have the same organizational advantages. They depend on voluntary contributions from potential members who may lack interest and

resources, or who recognize that they will get the collective good from a group's activity even if they do not participate (the free-rider problem).

Noneconomic groups include public-interest, single-issue, and ideological groups. Their numbers have increased dramatically since the 1960s despite their organizational problems.

In general, America's group system is relatively open and encompasses nearly all interests in society. However, interests are not equally well organized. Economic interests, particularly corporations, are more fully organized than other interests, and relatively affluent Americans are more fully organized than poorer Americans. As a result, the group system tends to favor interests that are already economically and socially advantaged.

## Major Concepts

collective (or public) goods
economic groups
free-rider problem
interest group

noneconomic groups
pluralism
private (or individual) goods
purposive incentives

## Suggested Readings

Berry, Jeffrey M. *Lobbying for the People.* Princeton, N.J.: Princeton University Press, 1977. An insightful analysis of public-interest lobbying groups.

Dahl, Robert. *Who Governs?* New Haven, Conn.: Yale University Press, 1961. A study of political influence whose major conclusion is that the policy process is open to participation and influence by many interests.

McFarland, Andrew S. *Common Cause: Lobbying in the Public Interest.* Chatham, N.J.: Chatham House, 1984. A case study of a public interest group, Common Cause.

Moe, Terry N. *The Organization of Interests.* Chicago: University of Chicago Press, 1980. An analysis of economic interest groups and their incentive structures.

Olson, Mancur. *The Logic of Collective Action.* Cambridge, Mass.: Harvard University Press, 1965. An insightful analysis of why some interests are more fully and easily organized than others.

Schattschneider, E. E. *The Semisovereign People: A Realist's View of Democracy in America.* New York: Holt, Rinehart and Winston, 1960. An analysis of bias in the interest-group system and a critique of pluralist democracy.

Schlozman, Kay Lehman, and John T. Tierney. *Organized Interests and American Democracy.* New York: Harper & Row, 1986. A recent survey of interest groups and their activities.

# Chapter 14

## GROUP ORGANIZATION: LOBBYING FOR SPECIAL BENEFITS

*The emerging public philosophy, interest group liberalism, has sought to solve the problems of public authority in a large modern state by defining them away . . . and by parceling out to private parties the power to make public policy.*

*Theodore Lowi*[1]

They first met over breakfast in 1978 at Washington's Sheraton-Carlton Hotel and thereafter were known as the "Carlton Group." Each member was a lobbyist for a major U.S. corporation, and collectively they were determined to reestablish business power.

The late 1960s and early 1970s had been unusually difficult times for U.S. corporations. Over their objections, Congress had passed tough new laws that required firms to spend billions to safeguard workers' health and safety and to reduce industrial pollution. U.S. industry was operating at less than 75 percent of capacity as a result of softened consumer demand stemming from high rates of inflation and unemployment. To make matters worse, Japanese and European firms were cutting into the United States' share of world markets. Not since the 1930s had American business been at such a low ebb.

The Carlton Group had a strategy for halting the decline. The lobbyists would push for continued deregulation of U.S. business, which had begun in 1977 with the airline industry. Their major objective, however, was a change in the tax laws. Although corporate tax rates had declined steadily since the 1950s, the Carlton Group sought the virtual elimination of business taxes. Under its plan, corporations would receive an accelerated depreciation allowance on new equipment and other tax breaks that would allow many of them to avoid taxes almost entirely.

The Carlton Group spent three years refining its plan and convincing legislators of its merits. Seminars were held, publications distributed, and

[1]Theodore Lowi, *The End of Liberalism*, 2d ed. (New York: Norton, 1979), 43–44.

private meetings arranged with key officials. In 1981 the Carlton Group achieved its goal. At the urging of the new Reagan administration, Congress enacted the accelerated depreciation allowance for business. General Electric was one of hundreds of major corporations that benefited from the change. Although GE made a profit of $6.5 billion in 1981–1983, it paid no federal taxes at all during the period; in fact, the company received $283 million in federal tax rebates.

Supporters of the 1981 tax change claimed that it enabled U.S. corporations to replace outmoded plants and equipment with new ones that would help America compete more effectively with Japan and West Germany. Critics maintained that business had instead used much of its additional capital to take over existing companies and to build plants in such countries as Mexico and Taiwan, where labor costs are lower than in the United States.

This sequence of events illustrates both the attractiveness of interest-group lobbying and the reasons for concern about it. By and large, interest groups have a better understanding of their problems and needs than public officials do. It is therefore important that public policy decisions be informed by the views of the interests likely to be affected by them. Lobbying enables groups to bring their views to policymakers' attention. Yet the logic of democratic politics implies that policies of benefit to special interests should also be broadly beneficial and should promote definable public goals. Lobbying, then, should not merely serve the narrow interests of particular groups.

This chapter examines the lobbying process by which interest groups seek to promote their advantage and then evaluates the impact of this process on national policy. The chapter demonstrates that the group process is indispensable and produces narrowly beneficial policies, but that groups have acquired too much policy influence and have significantly reduced government's capacity to respond effectively to society's broad interests. The main points made in the chapter are the following:

★ *Lobbying and electioneering are the traditional means by which groups communicate with and influence political leaders. Recent developments, including "grass-roots lobbying" and PACs, have given added visibility to groups' activities.*

★ *Groups can exert influence in a wide variety of ways and through many points of access to the legislative, executive, and judicial branches.*

★ *Most public policies are decided through iron triangles and issue networks, which facilitate the influence of interest groups.*

★ *When public policy is decided solely by group demands, the group process does not serve the collective interest, regardless of the number of separate interests that benefit from the process.*

## Inside Lobbying: Seeking Influence through Official Contacts

Modern government provides a supportive environment in which interest groups can seek to achieve their policy goals. First, modern government is involved in so many interest areas—business regulation, income maintenance, urban renewal, cancer research, and energy development, to name only a

The action orientation of goverment enhances the influence of interest groups. When a severe drought struck the United States in 1988, the federal government quickly stepped in with aid to farmers. (George Mars Cassidy/The Picture Club)

few—that hardly any interest in society could fail to benefit significantly from having influence over federal policies or programs. Moreover, most of what government does is decided without much publicity and with the participation of a relatively small group of officials. These conditions, as E. E. Schattschneider noted, are conducive to group influence.[2]

Second, modern government is oriented toward action. Officials are inclined to look for policy solutions to problems rather than to let problems linger. For example, when a severe drought caused a decline in farm production and income in many parts of the country in 1988, Washington did not leave farmers to sink or swim, but quickly mobilized to help them out through government programs. As a result of this action orientation, groups can expect officials to be predisposed to act on their claims.

A group's ability to take advantage of its opportunities for influence depends on any number of factors, including its size, its financial strength, and the nature of its policy demands.[3] Although groups cannot control all these factors, they can choose their persuasive strategies. According to Norman Ornstein and Shirley Edler, the two main strategies may be thought of as "inside lobbying" and "outside lobbying."[4] Each strategy involves communication between public officials and group lobbyists, but the strategies differ in what is communicated, who does the communicating, and who receives the communication (see Table 14-1). Let's begin by discussing **inside lobbying,** which is based on group efforts to develop and maintain close ("inside") contacts with policymakers. (Outside lobbying will be described in the next section.)

## ACQUIRING ACCESS TO OFFICIALS

Inside lobbying is designed to give a group direct access to officials in order to influence their decisions. Access is a critical first step. Unless a group can get the

[2]E. E. Schattschneider, *The Semisovereign People: A Realist's View of Democracy in America* (New York: Holt, Rinehart and Winston, 1960), 20–46.
[3]Jeffrey Berry, *Lobbying for the People* (Princeton, N.J.: Princeton University Press, 1977), 62
[4]Norman Ornstein and Shirley Elder, *Interest Groups, Lobbying, and Policymaking* (Washington, D.C.: Congressional Quarterly Press, 1978), 82–86.

**TABLE 14-1 Tactics Used in Inside and Outside Lobbying Strategies**

| *Inside Lobbying* | *Outside Lobbying* |
|---|---|
| Developing contacts with legislators and executives | Encouraging group members to write or phone their representatives in Congress |
| Providing information and policy proposals to key officials | Seeking favorable coverage by news media |
| Forming coalitions with other groups | Encouraging members to support particular candidates in elections |
| | Targeting group resources on key election races |
| | Making PAC contributions to candidates |

attention of officials, it has no chance of persuading them to support its position.

In the early nineteenth century, agents for interest groups would wait in the lobbies of legislative buildings to talk with officials. These agents came to be known as lobbyists, and that label is still applied to group representatives. Groups themselves are sometimes referred to as lobbies. The process in which groups and their representatives engage is called **lobbying.** The term refers broadly to efforts by special interests to influence public policy through contacts with public officials.

Lobbying once depended significantly on tangible inducements, sometimes including bribes. This approach is not unknown today, but modern lobbying is generally more subtle and sophisticated. It focuses on supplying officials with information and indications of group strength which will persuade them to

Access to public officials and the capacity to provide them with useful information are crucial to effective "inside" lobbying. (Dennis Brack/Black Star)

adopt the group's perspective. As one lobbyist explained: "To a large extent, the three B's—booze, bribes, and broads—have disappeared. . . . Today, a good lobbyist must have the ability to draw up factual information—a lot of it—in a short period of time for people on [Capitol] Hill who want it. . . . Nowadays, taking someone to a football game or a goose hunt just doesn't quite make it."[5] Few policymakers today are going to support a group's claim simply because it asks them to. For a group to gain its objectives, it must win out against competing interests and alternative objectives.

A group's chances of success are enhanced if it has effective lobbyists working on its behalf. Some of the best lobbyists are longtime Washington lawyers from prestigious firms who have built effective working relationships with top officials.[6] Former presidential assistants are also in demand as lobbyists, particularly if the president they served is still in the White House. Lyn Nofziger was charged in 1986 with illegal influence-peddling because, after leaving his position as a top aide to President Ronald Reagan, he had not waited one year, as the law required, before attempting to influence policy on behalf of group clients. Former members of Congress do not have to wait before they can lobby legally, and they, too, are in great demand as lobbyists. They have the unique right to go directly onto the floor of the House or Senate to speak with current members. Former members usually represent groups with which they had close ties while they were in office. Representative Fred B. Rooney (D-Pa., 1963–1979), known as an advocate for the railroads while he was in Congress, later became a consultant for the Association of American Railroads. Representatives Richard Ichord (D-Mo., 1961–1981) and Bob Wilson (R-Calif., 1953–1981) stepped from senior posts on the House Armed Services Committee to jobs with a lobbying firm that represented seven of the nation's major defense contractors.[7]

Money is the essential ingredient of inside lobbying efforts. The American Petroleum Institute, for example, with its abundant financial resources, can afford a downtown Washington office staffed by lobbyists, petroleum experts, and public relations specialists who help the oil companies to maintain access to and influence with legislative and executive leaders.[8] Other groups survive with much less, but it is hard to run a first-rate lobbying campaign on less than $100,000 a year. That figure is roughly what Guam paid a firm in 1988 to lobby for legislation that would change Guam's status from that of U.S. territory to U.S. commonwealth in order to give it more control of the policies governing it.[9] Given the costs of maintaining a Washington lobby, the domination by corporations and trade associations is understandable. They have the money to retain high-priced lobbyists, while many other interests do not. The best that some groups can manage is to buy a small share of a lobbyist's time.

[5]Quoted in Kay Lehman Schlozman and John T. Tierney, *Organized Interests and American Democracy* (New York: Harper & Row, 1986), 24.
[6]See Joseph Goulden, *The Superlawyers* (New York: Dell, 1973).
[7]Bill Keller, "Former House Members Ichord, Wilson Sign Up with Top Defense Contractors," *Congressional Quarterly,* June 13, 1984, 1052.
[8]Ornstein and Elder, *Interest Groups, Lobbying, and Policymaking,* 70.
[9]Steven Waldman, "The 'Designer Lobbyists,'" *Newsweek,* April 4, 1988, 22.

## PERSUASION THROUGH CONTACT AND INFORMATION

The medium of exchange for most inside lobbying activity is information. Lobbyists focus on supplying officials with information that will persuade them to adopt the interest group's perspective. The lobbyist's job is to build a persuasive case for the group's viewpoint, and this goal can rarely be achieved without convincing information. An argument that is not solidly based on facts is not likely to get very far, so the foundation of effective lobbying is necessarily the presentation of a strong supporting argument for the group's objective. This argument could conceivably be targeted at legislative, executive, or judicial officials.

### Lobbying Congress

Members of Congress are frequent targets of inside lobbying efforts. Lobbyists are required by the Federal Regulation of Lobbying Act of 1946 to register with Congress before they can lawfully engage in persuasive activities. The 1946 act is filled with loopholes, however, and the number of lobbyists who actually lobby Congress is substantially greater than the roughly 5,300 (representing 9,200 separate groups) who are formally registered to do so.

The benefits of a close relationship with members of Congress are substantial. Through its supporters in Congress, a group can obtain the legislative help it needs to achieve its policy goals. By the same token, members of Congress can gain from working closely with lobbyists. The volume of legislation facing Congress is enormous, and members rely on lobbyists they trust to identify bills that deserve their attention and support. Some members of Congress even involve lobbyists directly in their legislative work. One congressional aide explained:

> My boss demands a speech and a statement for the *Congressional Record* for every bill we introduce or co-sponsor—and we have a lot of bills. I just can't do it all myself. The better lobbyists, when they have a proposal they are pushing, bring it to me along with a couple of speeches, a *Record* insert, and a fact sheet.[10]

As would be expected, lobbyists work primarily with members of Congress who share their views.[11] Union lobbyists work most closely with pro-labor legislators, just as business lobbyists work mainly with pro-business legislators. In recent years, in order to improve communication with their congressional allies, some groups have organized informal caucuses.[12] These caucuses meet periodically to discuss pending issues and coordinate legislative strategy. There are about eighty such caucuses in the House and Senate, including, for example,

**Regulation of Lobbying**
Lobbying presents the risk that special interests will get undue favors through shady influence peddling. As a result, lobbying reform is often discussed, although the idea of regulating lobbying raises First Amendment issues of free speech and petition. To what extent should lobbying be regulated? What forms might regulation take?

[10]Quoted in Schlozman and Tierney, *Organized Interests and American Democracy*, 85.
[11]For the classic study of this process, see Raymond A. Bauer, Ithiel de Sola Pool, and Lewis Anthony Dexter, *American Business and Public Policy* (New York: Atherton, 1963); see also Lester Milbrath, *The Washington Lobbyists* (Chicago: Rand McNally, 1963), 212.
[12]Susan Webb Hammond, Arthur G. Stevens, Jr., and Daniel P. Mulhollan, "Congressional Caucuses: Legislators as Lobbyists," in Allan J. Cigler and Burdett A. Loomis, eds., *Interest Group Politics* (Washington, D.C.: Congressional Quarterly Press, 1983), 275–297.

the Oil Caucus, which consists of pro-industry members of Congress from such oil-producing states as Texas, California, Louisiana, and Oklahoma.

Lobbyists' effectiveness with members of Congress depends in part on their reputation for fair play. An effective lobbyist knows when and how to compromise. No group can expect to get everything it seeks and risks complete failure by insisting that all its demands be met. The goal, as one lobbyist put it, is "solution searching": finding a position that is beneficial to the group without conceding more than is necessary.[13] Lobbyists are also expected to play it straight with members of Congress. Said one congressman: "If any [lobbyist] gives me false or misleading information, that's it—I'll never see him again."[14]

Of course, lobbying is more than a process of information sharing and solution searching. Through lobbyists, members of Congress have been known to receive favorable stock options, free trips on corporate jets, jobs for friends, low-interest loans, and nearly every other imaginable benefit. The mistake is to assume that such giveaways are the ordinary means by which lobbyists win support. Such practices can violate the law and subject both lobbyist and legislator to adverse publicity and loss of position. It is also a mistake to think of lobbying as arm-twisting. A group that regularly throws its weight around creates resentment and loses access to members of Congress. The safe lobbying strategy is the aboveboard strategy: provide information, rely on longtime friends among members of Congress, and push steadily but not too aggressively for legislative goals.

## Lobbying Executive Agencies

> ★ ANALYZE THE ISSUE
>
> **The Mutual Dependency of Lobbyists and the Bureaucracy**
> As government has expanded, lobbying has increasingly been directed at the bureaucracy. Groups and bureaucrats have come to depend on each other for information and support. Is this development inherently more troubling than the traditional pattern of lobbying, which focuses on legislators? Does frequent contact between unelected bureaucrats and interest-group lobbyists have public benefits as well as costs?

As the scope of the federal government has expanded, lobbying of the executive branch has increased in importance. Bureaucrats make key administrative decisions and develop policy initiatives that the legislative branch later makes into law. By working closely with government agencies, groups can influence policy decisions at the implementation and initiation stages. In return, groups assist government agencies by providing them with information and lending support to their funding and programs.[15]

Nowhere is the link between groups and the bureaucracy more evident than in the regulatory agencies that oversee the nation's business sectors. For example, the Interstate Commerce Commission (ICC), which regulates the nation's railroads and truckers, uses information provided by these interests to decide many of the policies governing their activities. The ICC was created in 1887 to protect the public from price fixing and other corrupt practices then prevalent among the railroads. Yet at times—as when it has permitted trucking companies to set high shipping rates—the ICC has acted more as an agent of industry than as a watchdog for the public. The ICC is often cited as an example of agency "capture." The capture theory posits that regulatory agencies pass through a series of phases that constitute a "life cycle." Early in an agency's existence, it regulates an industry on the public's behalf, but as the agency matures, its vigor declines until at best it protects the status quo and at worst it falls captive to the very industry it is supposed to regulate.[16]

---

[13]Jeffrey M. Berry, *The Interest Group Society* (Boston: Little, Brown, 1984), 121–122.
[14]Quoted in Ornstein and Elder, *Interest Groups, Lobbying, and Policymaking*, 77.
[15]See Elizabeth Drew, "Charlie," in Cigler and Loomis, *Interest Group Politics*, 217–250.
[16]See Marver Bernstein, *Regulating Business by Independent Commission* (Princeton, N.J.: Princeton University Press, 1955).

The trucking industry is regulated by the Interstate Commerce Commission, which is widely viewed as a "captive" agency. (Johnson/ Gamma-Liaison)

Research on executive agencies has shown that the capture theory describes only some agencies and then only some of the time.[17] "Bureaucratic agencies," John Chubb writes, "need not be pawns of the interest organizations that confront them." In analyzing energy policy, Chubb found that agencies selectively cooperate with or oppose interest groups, depending on which strategy better suits agency purposes.[18] The first concern of any agency is its own well-being, and agency officials are aware that they can lose political support if they show too much favoritism to a special interest. In 1988 it became known that some Pentagon officials had lost sight of this cardinal rule when they gave inside information on weapons-contract bidding to defense corporations, thus allowing these firms to rig their bids and reap millions in illicit profits. Congress responded to the ensuing scandal by demanding new restrictions on defense contracts, thereby reducing the Pentagon's discretionary authority in securing new weaponry.

## Lobbying the Courts

Recent broad rulings by the courts in such areas as education and civil rights have made interest groups recognize that the judiciary, too, can help them reach their goals. Interest groups have several judicial lobbying options, including efforts to influence the selection of federal judges. "Right-to-life" groups pressured the Reagan administration to make opposition to abortion a prerequisite for nomination to the federal bench. Although the administration announced no such policy, it did require that nominees be political conservatives—most of whom had antiabortion views.

*Amicus curiae* ("friend of the court") briefs are another method of judicial lobbying. An *amicus* brief is a written document in which a group states its

[17]Paul J. Quirk, *Industry Influence in Federal Regulatory Agencies* (Princeton, N.J.: Princeton University Press, 1981); James Q. Wilson, ed., *The Politics of Regulation* (New York: Basic Books, 1980).
[18]John E. Chubb, *Interest Groups and the Bureaucracy: The Politics of Energy* (Stanford, Calif.: Stanford University Press, 1983), 200–201.

position on a particular case and thus makes the court aware of a view in addition to those of the plaintiff and defendant. For example, in the landmark affirmative action case *Regents of the University of California* v. *Bakke* (1978), fifty-eight *amicus* briefs representing the positions of more than one hundred organizations were filed with the Supreme Court at its invitation.

Finally, and most significant, groups can influence public policy through the courts by filing lawsuits. For some organizations, such as the National Association for the Advancement of Colored People (NAACP) and the American Civil Liberties Union (ACLU), legal action is the primary means of lobbying government. The ACLU devotes itself to defending the constitutional rights of individuals, whatever their beliefs. When the predominantly Jewish town of Skokie, Illinois, sought to bar the American Nazi party from marching through its streets in 1977, as we saw in Chapter 5, the ACLU defended the Nazis' First Amendment right to do so.

As interest groups increasingly resort to legal action, they often find themselves pitted against one another in court. Such environmental litigation groups as the Sierra Club Legal Defense Fund, the Environmental Defense Fund, and the Natural Resources Defense Council have frequently sued large oil, timber, and mining corporations.

Although court action is expensive, it can be less costly and more rewarding than legislative lobbying. The NAACP, for example, has emphasized legal action since its founding in 1909 because it recognizes that minorities often lack influence with elected officials. As we saw in Chapter 7, the NAACP financed the 1954 *Brown* case, in which the Supreme Court declared that racial segregation of public schools is unconstitutional. Had the NAACP tried to achieve the same result by lobbying state legislators in the South, it almost certainly would have failed.

## WEBS OF INFLUENCE: GROUPS IN THE POLICY PROCESS

Lobbying efforts provide an incomplete picture of how groups obtain influence. To get a fuller picture, it is necessary to consider also two policy processes, iron triangles and issue networks, in which many groups are enmeshed.

### Iron Triangles

An **iron triangle** consists of a small and informal but relatively stable set of bureaucrats, legislators, and lobbyists who are preoccupied with the development of policies beneficial to a particular interest.[19] The three "corners" of one such triangle are the Department of Veterans Affairs (bureaucrats), the veterans' affairs committees of Congress (legislators), and veterans' groups such as the American Legion and the Veterans of Foreign Wars (lobbyists), which together determine most of the policies affecting veterans. Of course, others, including the president and the majority in Congress, are needed to enact new programs to benefit veterans. However, they tend to defer to the policy preferences voiced by the veterans' triangle, because the triangle's members best understand the programs, problems, and policy needs of veterans.

---

[19]See J. Leiper Freeman, *The Political Process* (New York: Random House, 1965); Keith E. Hamm, "Patterns of Influence among Committees, Agencies, and Interest Groups," *Legislative Studies Quarterly* 8 (August 1983): 378–426.

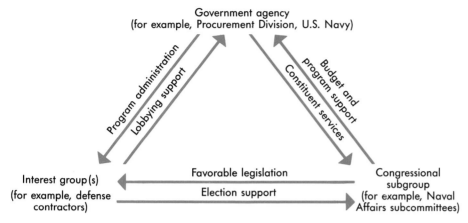

An iron triangle works to the advantage of each of its participants—an interest group, a congressional subgroup, and a government agency.

When a group is part of an iron triangle, it has an inside track to those legislators and bureaucrats who are in the best position to promote its cause. And because it has something of value to offer each of them in return, the relationship tends to be ironclad. The group provides lobbying support for the bureaucrats when their agency's funding and programs are at issue, and it has campaign contributions to give its congressional allies. The American Dairy Association, for example, contributes more than $1 million each election year to members of Congress (nearly all of them from farm states) who serve on the House and Senate Agriculture committees. Figure 14-1 summarizes the benefits that flow to each member of an iron triangle.

## Issue Networks

An iron triangle represents the pattern of influence only in certain policy areas, such as aspects of agriculture and public works. A more common pattern is that of the issue network. An **issue network** is an informal relationship among officials and lobbyists who are linked by common expertise and concern with a given policy area, such as energy, communication, the environment, or trade. Issue networks differ from iron triangles in that their memberships are less stable and less clearly defined, are based more on shared policy expertise than on a common goal, and cut across several agencies, committees, and groups.[20] An issue network on a question of energy policy, for example, would probably include bureaucrats, members of Congress, and lobbyists in the energy, environmental, and commerce areas.[21]

Issue networks are a consequence of the complexity of America's society and of its government, which has produced highly technical policy issues. To have influence on such issues, it is almost essential that a participant be "well informed about the ins and outs of a particular policy debate."[22]

Interest groups are at home within issue networks. In fact, because groups

[20]Hugh Heclo, "Issue Networks and the Executive Establishment," in Anthony King, ed., *The New American Political System* (Washington, D.C.: American Enterprise Institute, 1978), 87–124; Thomas L. Gais, Mark A. Peterson, and Jack L. Webb, "Interest Groups, Iron Triangles, and Representative Institutions in American National Government," *British Journal of Political Science* 14 (1984): 161–185.
[21]See Walter A. Rosenbaum, *Energy, Politics, and Public Policy* (Washington, D.C.: Congressional Quarterly Press, 1981).
[22]Heclo, "Issue Networks," 103.

★ ANALYZE THE ISSUE

**The Relative Influence of Iron Triangles and Issue Networks**
Some observers claim that issue networks are signs that government has become overly subject to stalemate and specialization. The argument has some validity, but is it too one-sided? Consider agricultural policy. When iron triangles were at their peak, agricultural policy was decided chiefly by agricultural groups and officials. Today, in the era of issue networks, consumer- and environment-oriented groups and officials also play major parts in setting agricultural policy. Are issue networks therefore an improvement on iron triangles?

focus narrowly and constantly on the particular policy area of concern to them, their level of expert knowledge often exceeds that of officials. Economic groups have a particular edge because of their direct involvement in policy areas affecting them. The staffs of oil companies, for example, include experts in nearly every conceivable aspect of energy, from exploration to depletion. When energy policy is the issue, the oil companies have no trouble joining in the debate.

## Outside Lobbying: Seeking Influence through Public Pressure

Although interest groups may rely on their Washington lobbying alone, this approach is not likely to be successful unless it is backed up by evidence of a connection to the public. Elected officials particularly, but also bureaucrats, are always more receptive to a lobbying group if it can demonstrate convincingly that its concerns reflect those of a vital constituency. Accordingly, groups make use of constituency connections when it seems advantageous to do so. They engage in **outside lobbying,** which involves bringing public ("outside") pressure to bear on policymakers.[23] The "outside" approach typically takes the form of either *constituency advocacy* or *electoral action.*

[23]Ornstein and Elder, *Interest Groups, Lobbying, and Policymaking,* 88–93; Berry, *Interest Group Society,* 151.

A representative of the National Organization for Women applies "outside" lobbying pressure on Congress. (John Troha/Black Star)

## CONSTITUENCY ADVOCACY: GRASS-ROOTS LOBBYING

Some groups depend heavily on **grass-roots lobbying**—that is, pressure designed to convince government officials that a group's policy position has broad public support.[24] To mobilize constituents, groups can mount advertising and public relations campaigns through the media. They can also encourage their members to write or call their elected representatives. A more dramatic grass-roots lobbying tactic consists of public protest or demonstration—as when in 1978 a group of 2,000 farmers attracted national attention to agricultural problems by driving their tractors around the White House and the

[24]Kay Lehman Schlozman and John T. Tierney, "More of the Same: Washington Pressure Group Activity in a Decade of Change," *Journal of Politics* 45 (May 1983): 363–364.

# INTEREST-GROUP LOBBYING AND NEW TECHNOLOGIES

Interest groups are discovering that new technologies can help their lobbying efforts. Television satellites, computers, and high-speed printers are changing the way interest groups operate.

In the area of telecommunications, the U.S. Chamber of Commerce broke new ground with Biznet, its closed-circuit satellite TV network. The network links together the Chamber's member organizations throughout the country. "Think of the increase in influence on the public policy-making process when we have real-time access to our members and they have real-time access to Washington," noted Richard Lesher, the Chamber's president. With the network, the Chamber can alert its members rapidly to events on Capitol Hill. Grass-roots campaigns can be developed in a matter of days rather than weeks. The Chamber's network also enables companies to set up two-way televised meetings with members of Congress to discuss bills. Biznet has inspired at least one imitator, the AFL-CIO's Solidarity Satellite Network. The network is used for closed-circuit meetings at which labor leaders in various cities confer on labor policy.

Computers have greatly simplified the job of compiling mailing lists and targeting people for direct-mail campaigns. Sophisticated computer systems allow organizations to identify their members by congressional district and even by precinct, as well as by occupation, age, party registration, and any other variable that is of interest to them. The Chamber of Commerce uses its computers and detailed information on member firms—such as number of employees, revenues, and plant locations—to refine its mail campaigns to include only those firms directly affected by pending legislation.

Changes in printing technology, such as high-speed laser printers, make it possible to increase the number of

letters sent while making each one look personalized. In one direct-mail campaign, a high-speed printer produced personalized form letters with slightly varying messages, each printed with the individual constituent's name and address, for the constituents to sign and send on to their representatives in Congress. Proxy mailings are sometimes sent without the constituent's direct knowledge. The National Education Association (NEA) got the permission of 100,000 teachers to sign their names to NEA-generated letters on a variety of issues. The NEA signs and sends out the letters and telegrams as they are needed. This method has its drawbacks, however. When Senator William Cohen of Maine responded to proxy letters generated by an organization, he discovered that some of the constituents who had supposedly just written to him were dead.

These expensive innovations cannot guarantee an increase in the political clout of an interest group. As one printer candidly admitted, "The best technology in the world cannot make a dead issue look like it's alive, or a badly written letter look like it's well written."

SOURCES: Jeffrey M. Berry, *The Interest Group Society* (Boston: Little, Brown, 1984), 154–155; Burdett A. Loomis, "A New Era: Groups and the Grass Roots," in Allan J. Cigler and Burdett A. Loomis, eds., *Interest Group Politics* (Washington, D.C.: Congressional Quarterly Press, 1983), 169–190; *New York Times*, October 12, 1983, B-9; Bill Keller, "Computers and Laser Printers Have Recast the Injunction: 'Write Your Congressman,'" *Congressional Quarterly Weekly Report*, September 11, 1982, 2245–2247; William J. Lanouette, "Chamber Ponderous Decision Making Leaves It Sitting on the Sidelines," *National Journal*, July 24, 1982, 1298–1301; Mark Green and Andrew Buchsbaum, "How the Chamber's Computers Con the Congress," *Washington Monthly*, May 1980, 48–50.

Capitol building in Washington. Grass-roots efforts increasingly have involved coalitions of interest groups. For example, Common Cause, the National Education Association, Ground Zero, the Council for a Livable World, and other groups joined together in the early 1980s to promote the idea of a nuclear weapons freeze.

As with other forms of influence, the impact of grass-roots lobbying is difficult to assess.[25] Some members of Congress downplay the influence it has on them, but nearly every congressional office monitors letters and phone calls from constituents as a way of tracking public opinion. In early 1988 Senator William Cohen (R-Maine) received 9,000 letters on the issue of military assistance for the Contra rebels in Nicaragua. Most of the letters were prompted by Neighbor to Neighbor, a grass-roots group that opposed U.S. aid to the Contras.[26] Cohen voted against the appropriation. In a few instances grass-roots lobbying has spurred Congress as a whole to action. In 1983, after receiving a million bank-supplied postcards from savers, Congress repealed a law requiring automatic withholding on savings-account interest in order to reduce tax evasion.

Grass-roots lobbying has occasionally been known to backfire. In 1983 insurance companies initiated a grass-roots campaign of 500,000 form letters to selected members of Congress. The letters demanded a stop to pending legislation that would require insurance companies to alter their property and casualty coverage. Angered by the tone and volume of the letters, some members of Congress threatened to close tax loopholes that benefited insurance companies.[27] The campaign stopped abruptly.

Grass-roots lobbying works better for groups whose members are well-educated and thus more likely to write or phone their representatives. In the early 1980s the Sierra Club and other environmental groups, which have an educated membership, employed a successful letter-writing campaign that helped alter the Reagan administration's policies regarding the commercial use of federal lands.

## TRYING TO DELIVER THE GROUP VOTE

"Reward your friends and punish your enemies" is a political adage that describes roughly how interest groups view election campaigns. As part of an "outside" strategy, organized groups work to elect their supporters and defeat their opponents. Although they are less influential than they are commonly assumed to be, they can have some real impact on an election. The mere possibility of electoral opposition from a powerful group can keep an officeholder from openly obstructing its interests.

Groups with a large membership try to exert influence by urging their members to vote for or against particular candidates. Many candidates are not willing to test whether a group's vote will hurt their chances of victory. Opposition from the National Rifle Association (NRA) is a major reason the

[25]Richard E. Cohen, "Controlling the Lobbyists," *National Journal*, December 31, 1983, 2591; Burdett A. Loomis, "A New Era: Groups and the Grass Roots," in Cigler and Loomis, *Interest Group Politics*, 184.
[26]Nancy Cooper, "Nowhere to Run, Nowhere to Hide," *Newsweek*, February 1, 1988, 31.
[27]Steven Pressman, "Critics Attack Industry Drive against Unisex Insurance Bills," *Congressional Quarterly*, July 9, 1983, 1401–1403.

The Washington headquarters of the National Rifle Association, which is one of America's wealthiest and best-organized interest groups. The NRA is consistently able to mobilize its membership to work against the passage of gun-control legislation. (Paul Conklin)

United States does not have strict federal handgun laws, although polls show that most Americans favor such laws. The NRA has staunch supporters in every congressional district and is determined to work for the defeat of candidates who favor gun control. The NRA even has a "test" that it offers candidates. Allen O'Donnell, a Nebraska college professor, received an A-minus on his NRA test, while his primary election opponent got an A and received the NRA's support. O'Donnell lost the primary.[28]

## THE RISE OF PACs: CONTRIBUTING MONEY

Another way in which interest groups try to gain influence is by contributing money to candidates' campaigns. As one lobbyist said, "Talking to politicians is fine, but with a little money they hear you better."[29] By this standard, groups are coming through loud and clear: they contribute millions of dollars to political campaigns.

Because the potential for abuse is high, the role of interest groups in campaign finance has long been a matter of controversy. In the late nineteenth century corporations poured millions into legislative election campaigns in order to block attempts at business regulation. In 1907 Congress passed legislation that prohibited corporate contributions to candidates for federal office. However, under-the-table corporate payments became common, and there was no law

[28]Allen O'Donnell, personal communication.
[29]Quoted in Mark Green, "Political PAC-Man," *New Republic*, December 13, 1982, 20.

prohibiting a wealthy businessman from giving a large personal donation to a candidate. The Watergate affair helped to change these practices. President Richard Nixon's reelection campaign was heavily underwritten by wealthy donors and corporate money that had illegally been channeled ("laundered") through Mexican banks. In response, Congress strengthened laws requiring candidates to account for the sources of their funds and placed a ceiling on the contributions they could receive from a single source.

However, these reforms opened the door to a larger overall funding role for interest groups through provisions that relaxed legal restrictions on **political action committees (PACs).** Through its PAC, a group can raise money for election campaigns by soliciting *voluntary* contributions from members or employees. A group cannot give organizational funds (such as corporate profits or union dues) to candidates, but it can give funds that it raises by soliciting voluntary contributions.

PACs are admired by those who believe that a campaign finance system based on pooled contributions by individuals is superior to one in which candidates rely heavily on a few wealthy donors.[30] However, critics claim that PACs give interest groups altogether too much influence over public officials.[31] Whichever view is accepted, there is no doubt that the emergence of PACs as a leading source of campaign funds is one of the most significant developments of recent elections.[32]

### PAC Spending as a Factor in Election Campaigns

Before the reforms of the early 1970s, PACs were a modest component of campaign financing. As late as 1974 there were only about 600 PACs, and their contribution to congressional candidates was $11.6 million—about 15 percent of all funds received by those candidates. The number of PACs increased sharply in the late 1970s, however (see Figure 14-2), and so did their contributions. By 1988 more than 4,000 PACs gave more than $125 million to congressional campaigns—roughly 30 percent of total contributions.

As PAC money can be raised earlier and more quickly than money from individual contributors, PACs have become a critical factor in getting congressional campaigns off the ground. Their role is less significant in presidential campaigns, which are larger in scale and publicly funded in part, and therefore depend on a wider range of funding sources than do congressional campaigns. (Chapters 16 and 19 examine congressional and presidential campaigns in greater depth.)

A PAC is legally limited in the amount it can contribute to the campaign of a candidate for federal office. The ceiling is $10,000 per candidate—$5,000 in the primary campaign and $5,000 in the general election campaign. However, there is no legal limit on how many candidates a PAC can support.

[30]See Michael J. Malbin, "Of Mountains and Molehills," in Michael J. Malbin, *Parties, Interest Groups, and Campaign Finance Laws* (Washington, D.C.: American Enterprise Institute, 1981), 157–177.
[31]See Fred Wertheimer, "Common Cause Declares War on Political Action Committees," *Common Cause*, March/April 1983; Elizabeth Drew, *Politics and Money: The New Road to Corruption* (New York: Macmillan, 1983).
[32]See Drew, *Politics and Money*; Larry Sabato, *PAC Power: Inside the World of Political Action Committees* (New York: Norton, 1984); Ronald J. Hrebenar and Clive S. Thomas. eds., *Interest Group Politics in the American West* (Salt Lake City: University of Utah Press, 1987).

Number of PACs

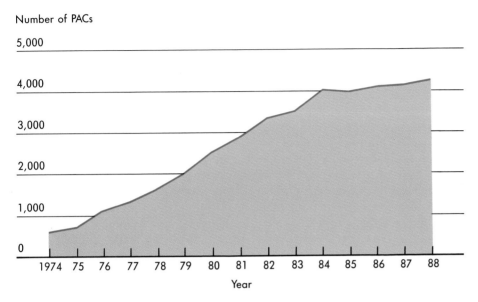

**FIGURE 14-2 Growth in the Number of PACs, 1974–1988** The number of PACs began to increase sharply after campaign finance reforms were enacted in the early 1970s. *Source: Federal Elections Commission.*

PACs have conducted increasing numbers of "independent" campaigns on behalf of certain candidates. In such cases, provided that the PAC's campaign is not coordinated with the candidate's own effort, the PAC is not bound by the $10,000 spending limit. The National Conservative Political Action Committee (NCPAC) has led the way in independent campaigns by developing its own television advertising and grass-roots efforts to elect conservatives and defeat liberals. NCPAC has spent several million dollars in each congressional election year since 1980, and it ran a $12 million independent campaign in 1984 to reelect President Reagan. In 1980 NCPAC claimed credit for the defeat of a half-dozen liberal senators, including George McGovern of South Dakota and Frank Church of Idaho. Again in 1982 NCPAC targeted several liberal members of Congress for defeat, but this time its extreme views and negative tactics actually appeared to help those officeholders in their reelection bids. Democratic Senator Paul Sarbanes of Maryland linked his opponent, former representative Larry Hogan, to NCPAC, and Hogan spent much of his losing campaign disavowing the connection.

### PAC Support for Incumbents

Members of Congress who seek reelection have an extraordinary success rate—over 70 percent for senators and over 90 percent for representatives. In 1988 the reelection rate for House incumbents was 99 percent.[33] PACs are well aware of the fact that incumbents are likely to win and thus to remain in a position to make policy. For this reason, about three-fourths of all PAC contributions are given to incumbents seeking reelection. Among the congressional incumbents who sought reelection in 1988 were John Dingell (D-Mich.), chairman of the House Energy and Commerce Committee, and Claude Pepper (D-Fla.), chairman of the House Rules Committee; the two received $507,000 and $402,000, respectively, from PACs—even though each was running unopposed.[34]

[33]"Of Debuts and Dead Heats," *Newsweek*, November 21, 1988, 16.
[34]George Hackett and Eleanor Clift, "For Members Only," *Newsweek*, November 14, 1988, 22–23.

*That these PACs feel compelled to contribute to lawmakers who have no opponent shows that what is being sought is access and influence.*

    Joan Claybrook, President
    of Public Citizen

The tendency of PACs to back incumbents has blurred long-standing partisan divisions in campaign funding. Business interests traditionally have been pro-Republican, but corporate PACs have been reluctant to anger Democratic incumbents. The result is that Democratic candidates for Congress, particularly in the House, have received nearly as much support from business-related PACs as have Republicans.[35] An exception was the House elections of 1978, when, correctly sensing a Republican surge, many corporate and trade PACs abandoned their strategy of supporting incumbents and increased their contributions to Republican challengers.[36]

Other PACs, especially those organized to promote a particular public policy or ideology, are less pragmatic than corporate PACs. The Christian Moral Government Fund, for example, backs only candidates who take conservative stands on such issues as school prayer, abortion, and pornography. A few PACs even demand that candidates commit themselves in writing to the group's policies. In 1982 PeacePAC required recipients of its contributions to sign a pledge to support a nuclear freeze and to oppose funding of the B-1 bomber and the MX missile.[37]

### Assessing PACs: The Corporate Advantage

More than 40 percent of all PACs are associated with corporations (see Table 14-2). Examples include the Ford Motor Company Civic Action Fund, the Sun Oil Company Political Action Committee (Sunpac), and the Coca-Cola PAC. The next largest group of PACs consists of those linked to noneconomic groups (that is, public-interest, single-issue, and ideological groups), such as the liberal People for the American Way and the conservative NCPAC. Ranking third are PACs tied to trade and professional associations, such as AMPAC (American Medical Association) and R-PAC (National Association of Realtors). Labor unions were once the major source of group contributions, but they now rank fourth. In terms of monetary contributions to candidates, economic PACs hold a 7-to-1 advantage over noneconomic PACs.

[35]Michael Barone and Grant Ujifusa, *The Almanac of American Politics, 1986* (Washington, D.C.: National Journal, 1985), 2147–2152.
[36]Maxwell Glen, "At the Wire, Corporate PACs Come Through for GOP," *National Journal*, February 3, 1979, 174–177.
[37]Larry Sabato, "Parties, PACs, and Independent Groups," in Thomas E. Mann and Norman Ornstein, eds., *The American Elections of 1982* (Washington, D.C.: American Enterprise Institute, 1983), 92.

**TABLE 14-2  Number and Percentage of Political Action Committees (PACs) in Six Categories**

| Category | Number | Percentage |
|---|---|---|
| Corporate | 1,734 | 42% |
| Noneconomic | 1,063 | 26 |
| Trade/membership association | 707 | 17 |
| Labor | 386 | 10 |
| Agriculture | 56 | 1 |
| Other | 146 | 4 |
| All categories | 4,092 | 100% |

SOURCE: Federal Election Commission figures, July 14, 1986.

## SINGLE-ISSUE POLITICS AND THE DECLINE OF POLITICAL PARTIES

As the growth of PACs illustrates, group activity has expanded rapidly in recent decades. Group politics now intrudes on the policymaking and electoral processes to such an extent that some analysts describe the situation as the triumph of **single-issue politics:** separate groups organized around nearly every conceivable policy issue, with each group pressing its demands and influence to the utmost.

Why have groups become so much more visible and powerful than ever before? As we discussed earlier, modern communication technology has made it easier for groups to organize for influence, and modern government offers numerous benefits that groups have a stake in maintaining. Of equal significance, however, is the fact that political parties have declined in importance. Whereas candidates in U.S. elections once turned to the parties for help, they now increasingly turn to groups. The candidate-centered campaigns of today run on money and media appeals, not on volunteer labor and party loyalty. Groups have an abundance of the resource—money—that is the foundation of the modern campaign for public office. Until recent decades, interest groups in Washington confined their efforts largely to inside lobbying. The outside lobbying of today—grass-roots pressure and PAC contributions—is a relatively new development and coincides with the decline of parties.

Group politics differs from party politics. As we noted in Chapter 12, parties seek to forge a majority, and this effort draws them naturally toward an emphasis on broad issues and interests. Parties do not ignore narrow interests, but they must subordinate any particular interest to a wider interest so that they can offer platforms that will appeal to the public in general. Thus democratic countries that have stronger political parties tend to have weaker interest groups. Power in these societies flows through the parties; to get a share of power, a group is forced to tone down its demands. U.S. parties have never been strong enough to control groups fully, but they have less control over them now than at nearly any time in the past. Parties are even losing the competition for citizens' loyalties; today most adult Americans believe they are better represented by interest groups than by parties (see Table 14-3).

**TABLE 14-3  Responses to the Question "Do Political Parties or Interest Groups Better Represent Your Political Interests?" by Age Group**

| Age Group | Interest Groups Better Represent My Interests | Political Parties Better Represent My Interests |
|---|---|---|
| All ages | 45% | 34% |
| 18–24 | 56 | 21 |
| 25–34 | 56 | 27 |
| 35–44 | 44 | 41 |
| 45–65 | 41 | 40 |
| Over 65 | 27 | 42 |

SOURCE: Survey conducted by Advisory Commission on Intergovernmental Relations, as reported in *National Journal*, March 10, 1984, 492.

Underlying the decline of parties and the upsurge of groups are the individualism and diversity that characterize American society. Groups represent the differences among citizens, not their similarities. Groups might be termed the organizational form of individualism: they are a means by which people in a pluralistic society find it possible to advance their particular political concerns.

## Groups and the Collective Interest

In *Federalist* No. 10 James Madison considered the conditions under which the pursuit of self-interest could also serve the collective interest of society. We noted at the end of Chapter 13 that although Madison lamented the tendency of a given group to further its own interests at the expense of other interests in society, he did not believe that groups could ever be persuaded as a matter of routine to subordinate their cause to the good of the whole society. And the thought that the power of government might be used to repress group interests was abhorrent to Madison.

Madison concluded that the only feasible solution to the problem of self-interested factions was a governing system that prevented groups from judging the worth of their own cause. Liberty required that any groups be allowed to act as "advocate," but good sense required that it not be allowed also to act as "judge." As we saw in Chapter 3, Madison's constitutional solution was a separation of powers which would make it nearly impossible for a single group to gain full control of government and thus be in a position to judge the merits of its own cause. Each group would have to work with others, and they would decide the merits of a given group's particular claim in the course of deciding issues of policy.

Madison's concerns are as relevant today as they were two centuries ago. Groups are a means by which society's various interests obtain representation. Yet the role of groups must also be assessed by their contribution to society's collective interest. Do the policies that result from group politics serve the common good? Pluralism and interest-group liberalism offer opposing opinions on this question.

### A FAVORABLE VIEW OF GROUP INFLUENCE: PLURALISM

As we noted in Chapter 13, pluralism holds that society is roughly the sum of the separate interests that constitute it. Pluralists even question whether such terms as "the common good" and "the collective interest" are very useful. If people disagree on the goals of society, as they always do, how can it be said that people have a "common" or "collective" concern? As an alternative, pluralists would substitute the sum of people's separate interests as a rough approximation of society's collective interest.

The relevant question then becomes not whether a single interest gets its way in a particular instance, but whether many and varied (that is, plural) interests win out at one time or another. The logic of this proposition is that, because society has so many interests, the common good is ultimately served by a process that enables a great many interests to gain favorable policies. Thus if manufacturing interests prevail on one issue, environmentalists on another, farmers on a third, minorities on a fourth, and so on until a wide range of particular interests are served, the collective interest of society has been promoted.[38]

As pluralist theory maintains, it is a mistake to assume that the only meritorious policies are those, such as national defense and public education, that broadly affect nearly everyone in society. In fact, few policies apply to the public generally; most bestow a particular benefit on a specific interest. Examples include government loans to students, price supports for farmers, national parks for vacationers, protective tariffs for steelmakers, and school lunch programs for the children of poor families. Representation in a complex society requires attention to special needs, and the policies that address these needs can also advance broader objectives. For example, when government intervened in the mid-1980s to protect thousands of farms threatened by bankruptcy, the action also brought greater stability to the general economy and protected the production of food grains and other commodities on which the country as a whole depends.

## AN UNFAVORABLE VIEW OF GROUP INFLUENCE: INTEREST-GROUP LIBERALISM

Although pluralist theory offers some compelling arguments, it also has questionable aspects. In a direct attack on pluralism, Theodore Lowi argues that there is no concept of society's collective interest in a system that allows special interests to determine for themselves which policy benefits they receive, regardless of how many interests are served.[39] The fact that a great number and variety of interests receive a slice of the pie is beside the point if each group decides for itself what its slice is going to be. When each group makes its own choice, the basis of decision in each case is not majority (collective) rule but minority (special-interest) rule.

In making his argument, Lowi accepts Madison's point that no interest should be allowed to be both advocate and judge. But whereas Madison's major concern was about a single interest that might capture full political control, Lowi's observation is based on the ability of various groups to come close to monopolizing power in their special areas. The policies that result favor the interests not of a majority but of a series of minorities. The iron triangle is the clearest example, with a particular group working in tandem with legislators and bureaucrats who have a stake in promoting the group's interest. Of course, the policy proposals that emerge from an iron triangle must still gain the acceptance of other officials, and this necessity serves as a restraint. But the sheer volume of modern legislation prevents most such policies from being studied closely and thus from acquiring the support of a true deliberative majority.

It is seldom safe to assume that what a popular majority favors is what a special-interest group wants. Consider the case of the federal law that required auto dealers to list the known defects of used cars on window stickers. The law was repealed after an extensive lobbying campaign financed by contributions of more than $1 million by the National Association of Automobile Dealers to the reelection campaigns of nearly 200 members of the U.S. House of Representa-

[38]See Robert Dahl, *Who Governs?* (New Haven, Conn.: Yale University Press, 1961); Robert Dahl, *Dilemmas of Pluralist Democracy* (New Haven, Conn.: Yale University Press, 1982); William Kelso, *American Democratic Theory: Pluralism and Its Critics* (Westport, Conn.: Greenwood Press, 1978).
[39]Lowi, *End of Liberalism.*

★ ANALYZE THE ISSUE

**Special and General Interests**

Is the sum of special interests nearly the same as the general interest? An answer to this question requires a judgment about the degree to which people's interests are more separate than general. An answer also requires a judgment about the degree to which government's response to special interests limits its ability to respond to general needs.

tives.[40] Although an overwhelming majority of the general public would surely have favored retention of the law, the car dealers' view prevailed. As Mancur Olson said of such situations, "Small groups . . . can often defeat the large groups . . . which are normally supposed to prevail in a democracy."[41]

Lowi uses the term **interest-group liberalism** to describe the tendency of officials to support the policy demands of the interest group or groups that have a special stake in a policy. Interest-group liberalism constitutes a partial abdication by government of its authority over policy. In practical terms, it is the group, not the government, that is deciding policy. The adverse effects include a weakening of majoritarian institutions and an inefficient use of society's resources: groups get what they want, whether or not their priorities are those of society as a whole. Lowi also points out that interest-group liberalism dulls the public spirit: a concern for justice (doing the "right thing") gives way to a concern for jurisdiction (deciding which groups have the "right" to prevail in a particular policy area).[42]

## HOW MADISON'S SOLUTION IS NOW PART OF THE PROBLEM

Ironically, Madison's constitutional solution to the problem of factions has become part of the problem. The American system of checks and balances, with a separation of powers at its core, was designed primarily to block control by a *majority* faction. Madison did not believe that a minority posed a significant threat, because "if a faction consists of less than a majority, relief is supplied by the republican principle, which enables the majority to defeat its [that is, the

[40]Berry, *Interest Group Society*, 172.
[41]Mancur Olson, Jr., *The Logic of Collective Action: Public Goods and the Theory of Groups*, rev. ed. (Cambridge, Mass.: Harvard University Press, 1971), 127–128.
[42]Lowi, *End of Liberalism*, 295–298; see also Ornstein and Elder, *Interest Groups, Lobbying, and Policymaking*.

Sometimes the interests of a group clearly diverge from majority opinion, as when the National Association of Auto Dealers lobbied successfully against legislation that would have required auto dealers to inform customers about any defects in used cars. (Sam Pierson/ Photo Researchers)

minority faction's] sinister views by regular vote." Yet by the same token a majority faction, by definition, has enough votes to get its way and thus to be in a position to sacrifice "both the public good and the rights of other citizens" to its selfish ends.[43]

Madison's solution to this problem has more or less worked as planned. Throughout U.S. history majorities have been frustrated in their efforts to gain full power by America's elaborate system of divided government. This same system, however, has made it relatively easy for minority factions—or, as they are called today, special-interest groups—to get their way. Madison did not anticipate that divided government would lead to the delegation of authority in particular policy areas to small sets of officials. Nevertheless, this development occurred, and it provides an almost perfect context for group influence. A group with a special interest in a particular policy area does not have to win majority backing; it has only to persuade the small set of officials in charge. And because these officials are likely also to benefit from actions beneficial to the group, they are inclined to serve its purposes. Only by great effort—more effort than any official can muster for each and every policy decision—can society's broad interest be imposed on decisions made in these small policy realms. Chapters 18 and 23 will discuss this problem further.

[43]*Federalist* No. 10.

## Summary

Organized interests seek influence largely by lobbying public officials and contributing to election campaigns. Lobbying serves primarily to provide policymakers with information and to alert them to group members' views. Using an "inside strategy," lobbyists develop direct contacts with legislators, government bureaucrats, and members of the judiciary in order to persuade them to accept their group's perspective on policy. Through iron triangles and issue networks particularly, groups develop the access to and influence with policymakers which result in policies favorable to them.

Groups also use an "outside strategy," seeking to mobilize public support for their goals. This strategy relies in part on grass-roots lobbying—encouraging group members and the public to communicate their policy views to officials. "Outside" lobbying also includes efforts to elect officeholders who will support group aims. Groups endorse candidates and urge their members to vote for them and, most important, contribute money to candidates' election campaigns. Through political action committees (PACs), organized groups now provide nearly a third of all contributions received by congressional candidates.

Public policy has increasingly been decided through the activities of organized groups. As society has become more complex and its sectors more interdependent, public policy has become more technical and increasingly targeted at particular problems. This situation works to the advantage of organized interests because they concentrate their attention on specific policy areas and have the expertise necessary to participate in the making of complex policy decisions. Interest groups have also gained strength because of the decline of political parties. Elected officials have turned to groups for campaign assistance, and this development has enhanced the influence of groups on policy.

The policies that emerge from the group system bring benefits to many of society's interests, and in some instances these benefits also serve the general interest. But when groups can essentially dictate policies, the common good is not served. A major challenge of democratic politics is to keep special interests in their proper place. They must be allowed to advocate their point of view, but they cannot also be permitted to judge the merits of their claims. Increasingly, interest groups have become both advocate and judge, and this is a development that cannot serve the common good.

## Major Concepts

| | |
|---|---|
| grass-roots lobbying | lobbying |
| inside lobbying | outside lobbying |
| interest-group liberalism | political action committees (PACs) |
| iron triangle | single-issue politics |
| issue network | |

## Suggested Readings

Berry, Jeffrey M. *The Interest Group Society.* Boston: Little, Brown, 1984. A general review of the formation, activity, and pervasiveness of interest groups in American society.

Chubb, John E. *Interest Groups and the Bureaucracy: The Politics of Energy.* Stanford, Calif.: Stanford University Press, 1983. An assessment of interest groups' influence which refutes the common idea that the bureaucracy is captive to groups.

Cigler, Allan J., and Burdett A. Loomis, eds. *Interest Group Politics.* Washington, D.C.: Congressional Quarterly Press, 1983. A useful set of readings on the activities and influence of America's interest groups.

Eismeier, Theodore J., and Philip H. Pollock III. *Business, Money, and the Rise of Corporate PACs in American Elections.* Westport, Conn.: Quorum Books, 1988. An analysis of the role and influence of corporate PACs in U.S. campaigns.

Lowi, Theodore J. *The End of Liberalism,* 2d ed. New York: Norton, 1979. A thorough critique of interest groups' influence on American politics.

McFarland, Andrew A. *Public Interest Lobbies: Decision-making on Energy.* Washington, D.C.: American Enterprise Institute, 1976. A study of public-interest groups' lobbying on energy policy.

Malbin, Michael J., ed. *Parties, Interest Groups, and Campaign Finance Laws.* Washington, D.C.: American Enterprise Institute, 1980. A collection of readings on the role of interest groups and political parties in campaign finance.

Milbrath, Lester W. *The Washington Lobbyists.* Chicago: Rand McNally, 1963. A study of Washington lobbyists, based on interviews with them.

Ornstein, Norman, and Shirley Elder. *Interest Groups, Lobbying, and Policymaking.* Washington, D.C.: Congressional Quarterly Press, 1978. A review of interest-group activities which discusses the strategies of groups' attempts to exert influence.

Sabato, Larry. *PAC Power: Inside the World of Political Action Committees.* New York: Norton, 1984. An assessment of the factors that have led to an increase in the numbers and influence of PACs.

# Chapter 15

## THE NEWS MEDIA: LINKING THE PEOPLE AND THEIR LEADERS

*The press in America . . . determines what people will think and talk about—an authority that in other nations is reserved for tyrants, priests, parties and mandarins.*

—*Theodore H. White*[1]

In November 1979, Islamic fundamentalists stormed the U.S. embassy in Iran, seized fifty-two of its occupants, and held them hostage for more than a year. Each day of the hostage crisis, every newspaper and television news program in the United States gave the story prominent play. One television news program, ABC's *Nightline,* was born of the crisis; the newscast's initial purpose was to provide Americans with a daily update on the situation, and its anchorman, Ted Koppel, began each night's report by noting the number of days that had elapsed since the hostages had been taken. By the time Koppel presented "America Held Hostage: Day 365," his news program was firmly established, and the American people were thoroughly disillusioned by their government's handling of the crisis. They blamed President Jimmy Carter, and he lost his bid for a second presidential term. (The hostages were finally released after 444 days, minutes after Ronald Reagan was inaugurated as president.)

Not all significant developments receive such intense media coverage. After World War II, black Americans in the rural South began to head for the urban North in search of better jobs. Each day, hundreds of blacks left such states as Mississippi, Georgia, and North Carolina for cities such as Detroit, New York, and Chicago. As they moved in, large numbers of whites moved out, in response both to the lure of the suburbs and to racial fears. By the end of the 1950s the political, economic, and social composition of urban America had

[1]Theodore H. White, *The Making of the President, 1972* (New York: Bantam Books, 1973), 327.

The mass movement of American blacks from the rural South to the cities of the North during the 1940s and 1950s is portrayed in this painting, one of a series collectively entitled *The Migration of the Negro* by the black artist Jacob Lawrence. Although the black migration had a decisive impact on American politics, it was not front-page news. (The Phillips Collection, Washington)

been fundamentally changed. Few developments in this century have had so large or lasting an impact on the nation as the postwar black migration. Yet this major population shift was seldom even mentioned in the news, let alone emblazoned in the headlines.

Although the news has been compared to a mirror held up to society,[2] it is actually a highly selective reflection of reality. The news is mainly an account of overt, obtruding events, particularly those that can be immediately seen as significant and dramatic.[3] Thus the situation in Iran became headline news at the instant the U.S. embassy was seized, and it remained newsworthy until the hostages were released. The black migration to the North was not considered news, because it was a slow and steady process, dramatic only in its long-term implications. The columnist George Will once suggested that the postwar migration of black Americans could have become news only if a ribbon had been stretched across the Mason-Dixon line as the one-millionth black person crossed it on the way north.[4] Reporters would then have had an event to cover.

News organizations and journalists, of either the print media (newspapers and magazines) or the broadcast media (radio and television), are referred to collectively as the *press* or the *news media.* The press has become an increasingly visible and powerful institution in American politics. Its heightened influence is attributable both to developments within the media themselves, particularly the emergence of television in the 1960s as a politically important medium, and to developments within politics, notably the trend toward individualistic leadership. As political leaders have begun to operate independently of political parties (see Chapter 12), they have turned to the media to help them build public support.

[2]See Sig Mickelson, *The Electronic Mirror* (New York: Dodd, Mead, 1972).
[3]Walter Lippmann, *Public Opinion* (New York: Free Press, 1965), 215, 221, 226.
[4]Comment at the annual meeting of the American Association of Political Consultants, Washington, D.C., 1977.

Like political parties and interest groups, the press has thus become a key link between the public and its leaders. This chapter will argue, however, that the news media are a very different kind of intermediary than either parties or groups and that problems arise when the press is expected to perform the same functions as a party or an interest group. The chapter begins with a review of the news media's historical development and current tendencies in reporting. Examination of these topics helps to explain the nature of the press and to distinguish its foundations from those of other linking mechanisms, such as political parties. The final section indicates what roles the news media can and cannot be expected to perform adequately in the American political system. The main ideas presented in this chapter are the following:

★ *The American press was initially tied to the nation's political party system (the partisan press) but gradually developed an independent position (the objective press).* In the process, the news shifted from a political orientation, which emphasized political values and ideas, to a journalistic orientation, which stresses newsworthy information and evaluations.

★ *Although the United States has thousands of separate news organizations, they present a common version of the news which reflects journalists' shared view of what the news is.* Freedom of the press in the United States does not result in a robust marketplace of ideas.

★ *In fulfilling its responsibility to provide public information, the news media effectively perform three significant roles—those of signaler (the press brings relevant events and problems into public view), common carrier (the press serves as a channel through which political leaders can address the public), and watchdog (the press scrutinizes official behavior for evidence of deceitful, careless, or corrupt acts).* These roles are within the news media's capacity because they fit with the values, incentives, and accountability of the press.

★ *The press cannot do the job of political institutions, even though it sometimes tries to do so.* The nature of journalism is incompatible with the characteristics required for the role of public representative (spokesperson for and advocate of the public).

## *The Development of the News Media: From Partisanship to Objective Journalism*

Democracy requires a free flow of information. Communication enables a free people to keep in touch with one another, with their leaders, and with important events. Recognizing the vital role of the press in the building of a democratic society, Thomas Jefferson wrote in 1787, "Were it left to me to decide whether we should have a government without newspapers, or newspapers without a government, I should not hesitate a moment to prefer the latter."[5]

America's early leaders were quick to see the advantages of promoting the establishment of newspapers. At Alexander Hamilton's urging, the *Gazette of the United States* was founded by John Fenno to promote the policies of George Washington's administration. Hamilton was secretary of the treasury and supported Fenno's paper by granting it the Treasury Department's printing contracts. Jefferson, who was secretary of state and Hamilton's adversary, complained that the newspaper's content was "pure Toryism." Jefferson

---

[5]Thomas Jefferson to Colonel Edward Carrington, January 16, 1787.

persuaded Philip Freneau to start the *National Gazette* as the opposition Republican party's publication and supported it by granting Freneau authority to print State Department documents.[6] Leaders of the U.S. Senate and House later came to have their own newspapers of record, to which they granted printing contracts and from which they received editorial support.[7]

Early newspapers were printed on hand presses, a process that limited production and kept the cost of each copy beyond the reach of ordinary citizens—most of whom could not read anyway. Leading papers such as the *Gazette of the United States* had fewer than 1,500 subscribers and could not have survived without party support. Not surprisingly, the "news" they printed was a form of party propaganda.[8] In this era of the **partisan press,** publishers openly took sides on partisan issues. Their employees were expected to follow the party line. President James K. Polk once persuaded a leading publisher to fire an editor who was critical of Polk's policies.[9]

## THE DECLINE OF THE PARTISAN PRESS

Technological changes helped bring about the gradual decline of America's partisan press. After the invention of the telegraph in 1837, when editors could receive timely information on developments in Washington and the state capital, they had less reason to fill their pages with partisan harangues.[10] Another major innovation was the high-speed rotary press (invented in 1845), which enabled publishers to print their newspapers rapidly and cheaply. The *New York Sun* was the first paper to pass on this benefit to subscribers by reducing the price of a daily copy from six cents to a penny. The *Sun*'s circulation rose to 5,000 in four months and to 10,000 in less than a year.[11] Increased circulation and revenues gave newspapers independence from government and parties, a change that some political leaders welcomed. "The freedom and independence of the press," a congressional committee concluded in 1873, "is best maintained by the people, and their subscriptions are a more legitimate means of support than the patronage of the federal government."[12]

By the late nineteenth century, several American newspapers were printing 100,000 or more copies a day, and their large circulation enabled them to charge high prices to advertisers. This development increased the profitability of newspapers but put pressure on editors and publishers to voice the political opinions of major advertisers, just as they had earlier reflected the views of party leaders. "One set of masters," V. O. Key, Jr., wrote, "had been replaced by another."[13]

---

[6]Culver Smith, *The Press, Politics, and Patronage* (Athens: University of Georgia Press, 1977), 2, 15, 39–55.
[7]Robert O. Blanchard, *Congress and the News Media* (New York: Hastings House, 1974), 8.
[8]Frank Luther Mott, *American Journalism, a History: 1690–1960* (New York: Macmillan, 1962), 114–115.
[9]Smith, *Press, Politics, and Patronage*, 163–168.
[10]Doris A. Graber, *Mass Media and American Politics* (Washington, D.C.: Congressional Quarterly Press, 1980), 36.
[11]Mott, *American Journalism*, 122–123, 220–227.
[12]Quoted in Smith, *Press, Politics, and Patronage*, 241.
[13]V. O. Key, Jr., *Public Opinion and American Democracy* (New York: Knopf, 1961), 388.

## AMERICA'S NEWSPAPERS: LOCALISM AND CONCENTRATION

America's great size influenced the development of its first newspapers. In England during the late eighteenth century, a few newspapers had already developed national circulations. However, national newspapers were not feasible in a nation the size of the United States at a time when it took more than a week to travel from New York to South Carolina. Thus separately owned dailies were established in all cities and in many small towns. Today systems of high-speed transportation and communication make national newspapers possible in the United States, as evidenced by the *Wall Street Journal* and *USA Today*. However, Americans retain a preference for local newspapers. There are about 1,700 local-circulation dailies in the United States, and they account for more than 95 percent of newspaper readership—a reflection of the public's interest in news of the community as well as of the nation.

Despite its local-circulation base, however, the ownership of newspapers has become increasingly concentrated. In 1935 only one in six newspapers was part of a publishing chain; now about two of every three dailies are owned by a chain. Of the nation's 155 publishing groups, a few—such as Knight-Ridder and Newhouse—own more than fifteen dailies. The largest chain is Gannett News, which in 1983 had eighty-six dailies in thirty-two states, Guam, and the Virgin Islands. Chain-owned newspapers account for nearly 75 percent of daily newspaper circulation in the United States. Local editors in these groups depend for some of their news on the chain's Washington news bureau and are occasionally instructed by the national chain on editorial policy. Endorsements of presidential candidates by a chain's local newspapers, for example, are sometimes decided by the chain's ownership.

The newspaper industry has also become concentrated in a second way. For most of the nation's history, larger communities had competing newspapers. New Yorkers in 1920 could choose from more than a dozen dailies. Now they have only four—the *Times*, the *Daily News*, the *Post*, and *Newsday*. Even at that, New Yorkers have more options than readers elsewhere. In the past decade, major newspapers in Chicago, Philadelphia, and Washington have folded. Newspaper competition still exists in most larger cities, and a third of the nation's population continues to have a choice among local newspapers; but the high costs of newspaper publishing have gradually narrowed Americans' newspaper options.

SOURCES: Edwin Emery and Michael Emery, *The Press in America* (Englewood Cliffs, N.J.: Prentice-Hall, 1984), 680; Donald Paneth, *The Encyclopedia of American Journalism* (New York: Facts on File, 1983), 328; Daniel B. Wackman, Donald M. Gillmor, Cecilie Gaziano, and Everette E. Dennis, "Chain Newspaper Autonomy as Reflected in Presidential Campaign Endorsements," *Journalism Quarterly* 52 (Fall 1975): 411–420.

The years around 1900 marked the height of newspapers' power and the depths of their sense of public responsibility.[14] A new style of reporting—"yellow journalism"—had emerged as a way of boosting circulation: the "yellow" press—so called because some of these newspapers were printed on cheap yellow paper—emphasized coverage of disasters, scandals, violence, sex, and sports.[15] One newspaper historian has described yellow journalism as "a shrieking, gaudy, sensation-loving, devil-may-care kind of journalism which lured the reader by any possible means."[16] A circulation battle between William Randolph Hearst's *New York Journal* and Joseph Pulitzer's *New York World* is widely blamed for the outbreak of the Spanish-American War through sensational (and largely inaccurate) reports on the cruelty of Spanish rule in Cuba. A young Frederic Remington (who later became a noted painter and sculptor),

[14]Commission on Freedom of the Press, *A Free and Responsible Press* (Chicago: University of Chicago Press, 1974), 62–63.
[15]Mott, *American Journalism*, 220–227, 241, 243.
[16]Edwin Emery, *The Press and America: An Interpretive History of the Mass Media* (Englewood Cliffs, N.J.: Prentice-Hall, 1977), 350.

Yellow journalism was characterized by its sensationalism. William Randolph Hearst's *New York Journal* whipped up public support for a war in Cuba with Spain through inflammatory reporting on the sinking of the battleship *Maine* in Havana Harbor in 1898. (Historical Pictures Services)

working as a news artist for Hearst, planned to return home because Cuba appeared calm and safe; but Hearst cabled back, "Please remain. You furnish the pictures and I'll furnish the war."[17]

## THE RISE OF OBJECTIVE JOURNALISM

The excesses of yellow journalism led some publishers to consider how the news could be reported more responsibly. Their goal was to establish the newspaper as an unbiased medium of timely public communication. One step they took was to separate the newspaper's advertising department from its news department, thus reducing the influence of advertisers on news content. A second development was a new model of reporting called **objective journalism,** which was based on the reporting of "facts" rather than opinions and was "fair" in that it presented all sides of partisan debate.[18]

A chief advocate of this new form of journalism was Adolph Ochs of the *New York Times*. Ochs bought the *Times* in 1896, when its circulation was 9,000; four years later, its subscriptions had grown to 82,000. Ochs told his reporters that he "wanted as little partisanship as possible . . . as few judgments as possible."[19] The *Times*'s approach to reporting appealed to educated readers particularly, and by the early twentieth century it had acquired a reputation as the country's premier newspaper.

Objective reporting was also promoted through newly formed journalism schools. Among the first of these professional schools were those at Columbia University and the University of Missouri. The Columbia School of Journalism opened in 1912 with a $2 million grant from Pulitzer.

---

[17]Mott, *American Journalism*, 529.

[18]See Theodore Peterson, "The Social Responsibility Theory of the Press," in Fred Siebert, Theodore Peterson, and Wilbur Schramm, eds., *Four Theories of the Press* (Urbana: University of Illinois Press, 1956).

[19]Quoted in David Halberstam, *The Powers That Be* (New York: Knopf, 1979), 208–209.

# THE *MANCHESTER UNION LEADER:* A THROWBACK TO THE DAYS OF THE PARTISAN PRESS

A few American newspapers continue to cover politics in much the manner of the nineteenth-century press. The *Manchester* (N.H.) *Union Leader* is noted for its partisan reporting of New Hampshire's pivotal presidential primary. In one notorious incident, the *Union Leader* helped to bring down the campaign of Senator Edmund Muskie of Maine, the early favorite for the 1972 Democratic presidential nomination. In a front-page editorial titled "Sen. Muskie Insults Franco-Americans," the paper made reference to a letter (later discovered to be a forgery) that claimed Muskie had laughed upon hearing an ethnic slur referring to French-Canadian Americans, who are a sig-

nificant portion of New Hampshire's population, as "Canucks." The next day the paper alleged that Muskie's wife had a foul mouth and drank heavily. Muskie went to the front steps of the newspaper's building and made a speech defending his wife, appearing to weep as he spoke. The national press widely interpreted Muskie's reaction as a sign that he did not have the emotional stability required of a president.

SOURCE: David H. Everson, *Public Opinion and Interest Groups in American Politics* (New York: Franklin Watts, 1982), 101–102.

Today most newspaper publishers emphasize objective reporting. Although publishers invariably slant the news slightly in favor of their own political position, they report both Republican and Democratic views and stress factual descriptions of news events. Many publishers even try to achieve some balance in their opinion columns. In the early 1970s, for example, the *New York Times* hired the conservative columnist William Safire as a counterweight to such liberal columnists as Tom Wicker and Anthony Lewis. Newspapers' partisan bias has traditionally been most evident in their endorsements of candidates during election campaigns, but even this form of advocacy has diminished. One-fourth of America's daily newspapers no longer endorse candidates, while most of the others do so without regard for the candidates' party affiliations.[20]

## THE DEVELOPMENT OF THE BROADCAST MEDIA

### Radio and Television: The Truly National Media

Until the early twentieth century, the print media were the only form of mass communication. Within a few decades, however, there were hundreds of radio stations throughout the nation, many of which were linked in national networks, such as the Red and Blue networks of the National Broadcasting Corporation (NBC). Franklin D. Roosevelt used radio for his famous "fireside chats" with the American people. Business-minded newspaper editors had been critical of his New Deal programs, and Roosevelt found that radio was a way of getting his messages directly to the people, without having to filter them through editors and reporters. Broadcasting was also revolutionary in a second

---

[20]Roger Gafke and David Leathold, "A Caveat on E & P Poll on Newspaper Endorsements," *Journalism Quarterly* 56 (Summer 1979): 384; Joseph E. Pillegge, Jr., "Two-Party Endorsements in a One-Party State," *Journalism Quarterly* 58 (Autumn 1981): 449–453.

During the 1920s radio became a common source of news for ordinary citizens. (UPI/Bettmann Newsphotos)

way: it was the first truly *national* mass medium. Newspapers had local circulation bases, whereas radio could reach millions of Americans across the country simultaneously.

Television followed radio, and by the late 1950s almost every American home had a television set. The political potential of television was evident as early as 1952, when 17 million homes tuned in to the national Republican and Democratic party conventions.[21] However, television newscasts of the 1950s were brief, lasting no more than fifteen minutes, and relied on news gathered by other organizations, particularly the Associated Press and other wire services. In 1963 CBS expanded its evening newscast to thirty minutes in an effort to overtake NBC's lead in audience ratings.[22] The popularity of President John F. Kennedy's televised press conferences helped to persuade CBS executives that the American people were eager for more television news. NBC and ABC followed suit by expanding their evening newscasts to thirty minutes, and the audience ratings of all three networks rose. Since then, the television networks have greatly increased their news-division staffs, and television has become the principal news medium of national politics.

### Government Licensing of Broadcasters

At first the government did not carefully regulate broadcasting. The result was chaos. A common problem was that nearby stations often used the same or adjacent radio frequencies, interfering with each other's transmissions. Finally, in 1934, Congress passed the Communications Act, which requires that broadcasters be licensed and meet certain performance standards. The Federal Communications Commission (FCC) was established to administer the act and

[21]Leo Bogart, *The Age of Television* (New York: Frederick Unger, 1956), 213.
[22]Theodore H. White, *America in Search of Itself: The Making of the President, 1956–1980* (New York: Harper & Row, 1982), 172–173.

In the 1950s television began to replace radio as Americans' primary source of broadcast news. (The Bettmann Archive)

to develop regulations pertaining to such matters as signal strength, advertising rates and access, and political coverage.

The principle of scarcity justifies the licensing and regulation of broadcast media. Because the number of available broadcasting frequencies is limited, those few individuals who are granted a broadcasting license are expected to serve the public interest in addition to their own. In principle, licensing is a means of controlling broadcasting. If a station fails to comply with federal broadcast regulations, the FCC can withdraw its license.

The government's licensing power, however, has not significantly undermined broadcasters' independence. During the early 1970s, for example, the Nixon administration allegedly pressured the FCC to refuse to renew the licenses of broadcast stations owned by the *Washington Post*, which was leading the investigation of the Watergate scandal. The FCC took no action. The FCC seldom even threatens to revoke a license, for fear of being accused of restricting freedom of the press. A broadcast station can apply for renewal of its license by postcard and is virtually guaranteed FCC approval, which covers seven years for radio and five for television.

## Government Regulation of Political Content

Because broadcast frequencies are a scarce resource, licensees are required by law to be politically evenhanded. Section 315 of the Communications Act imposes on broadcasters an "equal time" restriction, which means that they cannot sell or give air time to a political candidate without granting equal opportunities to other candidates running for the same office. (Election debates are an exception; broadcasters can sponsor them and limit participation to nominees of the Republican and Democratic parties only.) During campaigns broadcasters are also required to make air time available for purchase by candidates at the lowest rate charged to commercial advertisers.

John F. Kennedy was the first president to recognize fully the power of television as a means of public communication. He held more televised press conferences than any other president, before or since. (UPI/Bettmann Newsphotos)

Until 1987 broadcasters were also bound by the "fairness doctrine," an FCC regulation that compelled broadcasters to provide "reasonable" opportunities for the airing of opposing opinions on major public issues. The fairness doctrine did not prohibit broadcasters from taking sides on public issues; it required only that they also air opposing views. Moreover, a broadcaster could decide who would be allowed to voice their views, and when.

In effect, broadcasters have been required by law to adhere to roughly the same norms of news reporting that most newspapers practice voluntarily, giving air time to varying partisan views and concentrating on the objective "facts" of politics. In 1987 broadcasters finally persuaded the FCC to rescind the fairness doctrine, on the grounds that it infringed on press freedom. The FCC's decision was opposed by many members of Congress, who have threatened to reinstate the fairness doctrine through an amendment to the Communications Act.

### ★ ANALYZE THE ISSUE

**Broadcasting without the Fairness Doctrine**
In 1987 the FCC rescinded the fairness doctrine, which had required broadcasters to air opposing opinions on major issues. The FCC concluded that broadcasters should be free to cover issues as they wish, even if this means that some opinions do not get aired. Do you agree with the FCC's position? Consider whether the scarcity of broadcast frequencies compels different interpretations of freedom of the press for broadcasters and for print journalists.

## Freedom and Conformity in the U.S. News Media

Some democracies impose significant legal restraints on the press. The news media in Britain are barred from reporting on anything that the government has labeled an "official secret," and the nation's tough libel laws inhibit the press from publishing any allegation about an individual unless it can provide supporting evidence. In France the public television channel is under the directorship of the government and seldom criticizes the party in power. When Valéry Giscard d'Estaing was France's president (1974–1981), he reportedly had a telephone "hot line" from his office to the network's editorial room which he could use to influence news coverage.

In the United States, as we saw in Chapter 5, the First Amendment gives the press substantial protection. The courts have consistently upheld the right of U.S. newspapers to report on politics as they choose. The government cannot block publication of a news story unless it can demonstrate in court that the

**The Media**

The United States ranks first in the world in several media categories, including the number of radio receivers (2.10) and television sets (0.62) per capita. The United States ranks lower than nearly twenty other countries in daily newspaper circulation (0.28 per capita). Japan has the highest rate of newspaper circulation (0.57 per capita), and all the remaining countries in the top ten are European.

All democracies have vigorous news systems, but their characteristics vary somewhat. Whereas most Western European countries have strong public broadcasting networks, the United States depends almost entirely on private broadcast organizations, such as ABC, CBS, NBC, and CNN. Party-based newspapers are strong in many countries, including Norway, which subsidizes them from public funds. By comparison, the partisan press in the United States is nearly dead.

Many governments censor their news media, exercising daily control over news content and closing down news organizations that criticize official policy. News media in democratic societies, including the United States, have much greater freedom.

As for public attitudes about the media, a 1988 study indicated that 69 percent of Americans have confidence in their media whereas less than 50 percent of German, British, French, and Spanish citizens have confidence in their media. In addition, a plurality of Americans, Spaniards, and Britons said that their media have too much power, while pluralities in France and Germany held that the media have "just about the right amount" of power.

SOURCES: *The New Book of World Rankings* (New York: Facts on File, 1984), 395, 398, 408; Laurence Parisot, "Attitudes about the Media: A Five-Country Comparison," *Public Opinion*, January/February 1988, 19.

information would jeopardize national security. U.S. libel laws also strongly favor the press. A public figure who is attacked in a news story cannot collect libel damages unless he or she can demonstrate convincingly that the news organization was false in its accusations, careless in its search for the truth, and malicious in its intent.

Moreover, the U.S. government provides the news media with indirect economic support. Newspapers and magazines have a special postal rate that helps them to keep their circulation costs low, and broadcasters pay only a few dollars annually in license fees. Such policies have contributed to the development of a truly enormous news industry in the United States: 1,700 daily newspapers, 7,500 weeklies, 9,000 radio stations, five national television news networks, 1,000 local television stations, and 6,000 cable television systems.[23] The audience reach of leading news organizations is truly substantial (see Table 15-1).

In view of the great number and the freedom of news organizations in the United States, it might be expected that there would be great variation in the national news that Americans receive. And certainly the argument for a free press hinges on the expectation that a robust "marketplace of ideas" will result. Press freedom is intended to produce full and open debate, in which all significant opinions on leading issues are widely disseminated and thoroughly voiced so that the public can weigh the competing arguments and choose among them on their merits. To encourage the airing of diverse points of view, U.S. laws prohibit any owner from monopolizing print and broadcast media within a community or from holding more than a few broadcast licenses nationwide.

[23]Ernest C. Hynds, *American Newspapers in the 1980s* (New York: Hastings House, 1980); Annual Report, Federal Communications Commission, fiscal year 1985.

tend toward sensationalism. For example, when New York City's government faced bankruptcy in the mid-1970s and President Gerald Ford rejected a request for a federal bailout, the *New York Daily News* gave its whole front page to the headline: "Ford to City: Drop Dead." The *New York Times*, in contrast, gave the story a standard-size front-page headline. Such differences in approach, however, do not disguise the fact that most news organizations tell their audiences the same stories each day.

## DOMINATION OF NEWS PRODUCTION

Another reason for the lack of diversity in national news reporting is that a small number of news organizations generate most of it. The Associated Press (AP) and United Press International (UPI) are the major producers of news stories. They have reporters stationed throughout the country and the world to gather news stories, which are relayed by satellite to subscribing newspapers and broadcast stations. More than 99 percent of the nation's dailies are serviced by AP or UPI, and some also subscribe to other wire services, such as Reuters and the New York Times.[24]

Smaller dailies lack the resources to gather news outside their own localities and thus depend almost completely on wire-service reports for their national and international coverage.[25] They may give these reports a local or partisan slant, but most of what they say is reprinted word for word from the wire-service dispatches. Even major news organizations, such as the *New York Times*, depend heavily on AP and UPI for reports about developments in the more remote areas of the country and the world. The *Times* has fewer than fifty full-time political correspondents, compared with AP's 300 full-time reporters.[26]

Television news production is similarly dominated by just a few organizations. The five major networks—ABC, CBS, NBC, PBS, and CNN—generate most of the news coverage of national and international politics. For news of the nation and the world, local stations depend on videotransmissions fed to them by the networks. The quintessential case of concentrated news production is radio, with its "canned," network-provided news; almost no local radio station in the country produces its own national news reports.

## NEWS VALUES AND IMPERATIVES

Competitive pressures also lead the producers of news to report the same stories. No major news organization wants to miss an important story that others are reporting. The pressures *not* to be different are overwhelming. "Even at the best newspapers," Timothy Crouse notes, "the editor always gauges his own reporters' stories against the expectations that the stories [of other news organizations] have aroused."[27] Television news, too, displays a follow-the-leader tendency.[28]

[24]Graber, *Mass Media and American Politics*, 36.
[25]Maxwell E. McCombs and Donald L. Shaw, "Structuring the 'Unseen Environment,'" *Journal of Communication*, Spring 1976, 18–22.
[26]Lawrence W. Lichty, "The News Media: Video versus Print," *Wilson Quarterly* 6 (1982): 53.
[27]Timothy Crouse, *The Boys on the Bus* (New York: Ballantine, 1973), 20.
[28]Edward J. Epstein, *News from Nowhere: Television and the News* (New York: Random House, 1973), 37.

The networks, wire services, and a few elite dailies, including the *New York Times, Washington Post, Wall Street Journal, Los Angeles Times,* and *Chicago Tribune,* establish a national standard of story selection. Whenever one of them uncovers an important story, the others jump on the bandwagon. The chief trendsetter among news-gathering organizations is the *New York Times,* which has been described as "the bulletin board" for other major newspapers, newsmagazines, and television networks.[29] Herbert Gans notes, "The *Times* is treated as the professional setter of standards. When editors and producers are uncertain about a selection decision, they will check whether, where, and how the *Times* has covered the story; and story selectors see to it that many of the *Times'* front-page stories find their way into television programs and magazines."[30]

The imperatives of the fast pace of daily journalism also tend to make the news homogeneous.[31] Journalists have the task each day of filling a newspaper or broadcast with stories. Their job is to produce an edition every twenty-four hours. Thus editors assign reporters to such beats as the White House and Congress, which can be relied on for a steady supply of news. On these beats the reporters of various news organizations see and hear the same things, exchange views on what is important, and, not surprisingly, produce similar news stories.

Finally, a common set of professional values guides journalists in their search for news.[32] Reporters are on the lookout for aspects of situations that lend themselves to interesting news stories—novel, colorful, and compelling developments.[33] Long practice at storytelling leads journalists to find significance in the same things. Experienced journalists claim that they "know news when they see it," which is to say that they have a common understanding of what the news is.[34] After the White House press corps has listened to a presidential speech, for example, nearly all of the journalists in attendance are in agreement on what was most newsworthy about the speech, often only a single statement within it.

> ★ ANALYZE THE ISSUE
>
> **Distortion of the News**
> The news industry thrives on dramatic stories. Which types of issues, events, institutions, and interests are likely to be downplayed because of the media's need for exciting news? Which types tend to be overplayed? What are the likely political consequences of these news distortions?

## The News Media as Link: Roles the Press Can and Cannot Perform

When the objective model of reporting came to dominate American news coverage, the relationship between the press and the public was fundamentally altered. The nineteenth-century partisan press gave its readers blatant cues as to how to evaluate political issues and leaders. In the presidential election campaign of 1896, the *San Francisco Call* devoted 1,075 column-inches of photographs to the Republican ticket of McKinley-Hobart and only 11 inches to

[29]White, *Making of the President, 1972,* 346–348.
[30]Quoted in Kathleen Hall Jamieson and Karlyn Kohrs Campbell, *The Interplay of Influence* (Belmont, Calif.: Wadsworth, 1983), 9–10.
[31]See David Manning White, "The Gatekeeper," *Journalism Quarterly* 27 (Fall 1950): 383–388; Joseph S. Fowler and Stuart W. Showalter, "Evening Network News Selection," *Journalism Quarterly* 51 (Winter 1974): 712–715; John Chancellor and Walter R. Mears, *The News Business* (New York: Harper & Row, 1983).
[32]David L. Paletz and Robert M. Entman, *Media Power Politics* (New York: Free Press, 1981), 16.
[33]James David Barber, "Characters in the Campaign: The Literary Problem," in James David Barber, ed., *Race for the Presidency* (Englewood Cliffs, N.J.: Prentice-Hall, 1978), 114–115.
[34]Bernard Rushko, *Newsmaking* (Chicago: University of Chicago Press, 1975), 105.

the Democrats, Bryan and Sewell.[35] Many European newspapers still function in this way, guiding their readers by applying partisan or ideological values to current events. The *Daily Telegraph,* for example, is an unofficial but fiercely loyal voice of Britain's Conservative party.

In contrast, the U.S. news media act primarily as transmitters of information. Objective journalism places the American reporter in the role of nonpartisan observer, and the media are thus very different from the political parties and interest groups, the other major links between the public and its leaders. The force that drives the media is the search for interesting and revealing stories; parties and interest groups exist to articulate particular political opinions and values.

This distinction provides a basis for determining what roles the media can and cannot be expected to perform. The press is capable of fulfilling only those public responsibilities that are compatible with journalistic values: the signaler role, the common-carrier role, and the watchdog role. The media are less successful in their attempts to perform the politically oriented role of public representative.

### THE SIGNALER ROLE

As journalists see it, one of their responsibilities is to play the **signaler role,** alerting the public to important developments as soon as possible after they happen: a state visit to Washington by a foreign leader, a bill that has just been passed by Congress, a change in the nation's unemployment level, a demand by dairy farmers for higher milk prices, a terrorist bombing in a foreign capital.

[35]Lippmann, *Public Opinion,* 214.

# THE WASHINGTON JOURNALIST

Service in the nation's capital is the crowning ambition of most journalists, just as it is of politicians. For reporters, Washington provides more arenas of power and scenes of action than the rest of the nation combined: more than half of all reported national news emanates from the nation's capital, most of it from the White House and Congress. Altogether, about 10,000 people in Washington work in the news business. The key figures are the leading correspondents of the television networks and major newspapers, the heads of the Washington news bureaus, and a few top editors, such as Benjamin Bradlee of the *Washington Post.*

In the early nineteenth century, most Washington journalists, like their counterparts elsewhere, learned their trade on the job, starting as copy boys and working up to positions as reporters. Today almost all Washington reporters (93 percent) have a college degree, nearly half (48 percent) have gone to graduate school, and 6 percent have law degrees or doctorates. Traditionally, reporters were generalists, able to report on almost any subject. But as journalism has become increasingly professionalized, the reporter has increasingly become a specialist—someone who can claim expert knowledge in a particular area, such as national economic policy. Forty percent of Washington reporters now define themselves as specialists. These reporters demand the autonomy that professionals in other occupations have; they expect editors to accept their news judgments.

SOURCES: Allen Barton, "Consensus and Conflict among American Leaders," *Public Opinion Quarterly* 38 (Winter 1974–1975): 507–530; Stephen Hess, "A Washington Perspective," 5, paper presented at the Donald S. McNaughton Symposium, sponsored by Syracuse University, New York City, April 1985.

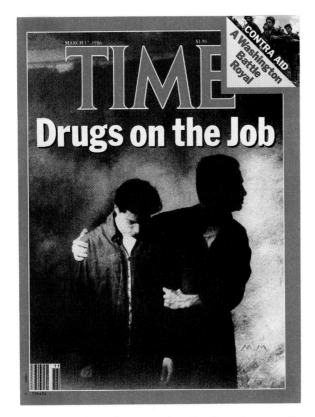

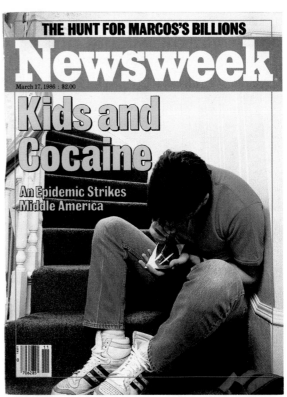

The signaler role is one that the American media perform extremely well. U.S. news organizations compete to be the first to discover and communicate news developments, and they have the resources to do the job effectively; in Washington, D.C., alone there are nearly 10,000 journalists—reporters, editors, photographers, news researchers, and others (see box). The press is poised to converge on any fast-breaking major news event anywhere in the nation and nearly anywhere in the world. For instance, within a few hours of the near-meltdown at the Three Mile Island nuclear power plant in Pennsylvania in 1979, every major national news agency had reporters on the scene.

*In their signaler role, the news media serve the public interest by identifying major problems, such as drug abuse. (Left, courtesy of* Time *Inc.; right, courtesy of* Newsweek *magazine)*

### Agenda Setting

Studies indicate that the press, in its capacity as signaler, has the power to focus the public's attention. The term "agenda setting" has been used to describe the media's ability to influence what is on people's minds. By covering the same events, problems, issues, and leaders—simply by giving them space or time in the news—the media place them on the public agenda. The press, as Bernard Cohen notes, "may not be successful much of the time in telling people what to think but it is stunningly successful in telling them what to think about."[36]

*You [that is, journalists] deal in the raw material of opinion, and, if my convictions have any validity, opinion ultimately governs the world.*

Woodrow Wilson

This influence is most obvious in such situations as the Three Mile Island accident, an event that quickly aroused widespread public concern. But the press's agenda-setting capacity is also evident in less dramatic circumstances. In March 1986, for example, both *Time* and *Newsweek* ran cover stories on drug abuse and then ran two more cover stories on drugs within six months.

[36]See Bernard C. Cohen, *The Press and Foreign Policy* (Princeton, N.J.: Princeton University Press, 1963), 13.

Newspapers around the country picked up the drug theme, as did radio and television stations. *U.S. News & World Report* devoted its July 28 cover story to drug abuse, calling it "the nation's no. 1 menace." On September 2 CBS ran a news documentary on drugs titled *48 Hours on Crack Street*. This mounting coverage of drugs had a clear impact on the public agenda. Gallup polls taken early in 1986 indicated that drug abuse was of small concern to most citizens, but by September 1986 a Gallup poll indicated that drug abuse had become the national problem of greatest concern to Americans. The only explanation for the change was the media's attention to the issue: statistics showed that the actual level of drug abuse in 1986 was no higher than it had been during the previous five years.[37]

### Forecasting

In another extension of the signaler role, the press attempts to alert the public to what lies ahead. The press often performs poorly in this area. Its forecasts are often off the mark or ignore alternative scenarios. The 1968 Tet offensive during the Vietnam war is a classic example. Vietnamese communists used the Tet holiday lull to catch American forces off guard and launch attacks on major South Vietnamese cities. In Saigon, they penetrated the U.S. embassy's inner perimeter before being driven back. The embassy attack was widely interpreted by the media as a symbol of the futility of America's presence in Vietnam and led many prominent journalists to conclude that the war was unwinnable.[38] However, the real story of Tet, Peter Braestrup has concluded, was that the Vietnamese communists suffered such heavy troop losses that they were unable to mount another major offensive for four years. Braestrup concludes that if the press had emphasized enemy casualties during Tet, the United States might have been encouraged to pursue the Vietnam conflict to victory.[39]

Whether in this particular case the press was right or wrong is of secondary significance. The main point is that the press has no crystal ball. Journalists work too rapidly and with too few facts to do well what even experts (such as military intelligence analysts) have difficulty doing. Journalists may be denied access to information, especially on issues of national security, without which reasonable predictions cannot be made. It is not surprising, then, that the media's forecasts are often inaccurate. For example, at some point during each of the five presidential elections from 1968 to 1988, the consensus in the press as to who would become the Republican or Democratic nominee turned out to be wrong.[40] After the Iowa caucuses, which began the formal campaign in 1988, the press seemed to be convinced that George Bush, who had finished third behind Robert Dole and Pat Robertson, was in deep trouble. "Bush is dead," said NBC's Ken Bode. A week later Bush easily won New Hampshire's primary, and he breezed to his party's nomination.

---

[37]The example is from Adam Paul Weisman, "48 Hours on Crock Street: I Was a Drug-Hype Junkie," *New Republic*, October 6, 1986, 15.
[38]See George Bailey, "Television War: Trends in Network Coverage of Vietnam, 1965–70," *Journal of Broadcasting* 20 (1976): 147–158; James Reston, "The End of the Tunnel," *New York Times*, April 30, 1975, 41.
[39]See Peter Braestrup, *The Big Story*, 2 vols. (Boulder, Colo.: Westview Press, 1977).
[40]See Gary Orren, "The Nomination Process: Vicissitudes of Candidate Selection," in Michael Nelson, ed., *The Elections of 1984* (Washington, D.C.: Congressional Quarterly Press, 1985), 27–82.

In their common-carrier role, the news media provide the president and other political leaders with a means of communicating with the public. (SIPA Pool/Black Star)

## THE COMMON-CARRIER ROLE

Journalists base many of their news stories on the words of political leaders. The press thus plays what is labeled a **common-carrier role,** serving as an open channel through which political leaders and the public can communicate. "It is my job," a reporter explained, "to report the position of the politician whether I believe it or not."[41]

The value of the media's common-carrier role to the public is obvious. Citizens cannot very well support or oppose what their leaders are planning and doing if they do not know what those plans and actions are. The importance of the press's function as a common carrier is also obvious from the viewpoint of political leaders. If leaders are to gain the public's attention, they must have news exposure. Not surprisingly, leaders go out of their way to build relationships with reporters: they brief them on important plans, grant them access to confidential matters, and provide them working space in Congress, the White House, and other government offices.[42]

The press reciprocates the interest of political leaders in developing a close relationship.[43] Journalists are always on the lookout for fresh stories, and political leaders are their prime source. Franklin D. Roosevelt, an early master of the art of media manipulation, held twice-weekly press conferences in the Oval Office to release information about his upcoming programs. Reporters called

[41]Quoted in Richard Davis, "News Media Coverage of National Political Institutions," Ph.D. dissertation, Syracuse University, 1986.
[42]William Rivers, *The Other Government: Power and the Washington Media* (New York: Universe Books, 1982), ch. 1; Michael Baruch Grossman and Martha Joynt Kumar, *Portraying the President* (Baltimore: Johns Hopkins University Press, 1981), 83.
[43]See Leon V. Sigel, *Reporters and Officials* (Lexington, Mass.: D. C. Heath, 1973); Hugh Heclo, "Introduction: The Presidential Illusion," in Hugh Heclo and Lester M. Salamon, *The Illusion of Presidential Government* (Boulder, Colo.: Westview Press, 1981), 8; Ben H. Bagdikian, "Congress and the Media: Partners in Propaganda," *Columbia Journalism Review* 12 (January/February 1974): 3–10.

these sessions "the best show in town" and eagerly sought to participate, even though Roosevelt's ground rules were strict. When he gave reporters confidential information, he expected it not to appear in the next day's headlines.[44]

Media critics complain that the press neglects its responsibilities as a common carrier by failing to allocate its coverage fairly.[45] The press virtually ignores all political parties except the Democrats and Republicans and devotes disproportionate amounts of coverage to established interest groups, such as the AFL-CIO; and it devotes substantially more attention to the president than to all the members of Congress combined. As the one political figure known to nearly all Americans, the president is presumed to be newsworthy whether he is at work in the White House or at play on vacation. Helen Douglas, the UPI's White House correspondent, has described her job as the "body watch"—keeping track of where the president is and what he is doing.[46] Congress fares poorly by comparison. Congress is an institution that is not personified by a single individual, and the press is less interested in reporting on institutions than on people. Reflecting on the press's tendency to downplay the newsworthiness of Congress, Thomas P. "Tip" O'Neill said, "If I could accomplish one thing as Speaker of the House of Representatives, it would be to teach the American public that the Congress is a coequal branch of the federal government."[47]

<table>
<tr><td>

**★ ANALYZE THE ISSUE**

**Journalistic Advocacy**
During the race for the Republican nomination in 1988, George Bush refused to admit that he had played any role in the Iran-Contra affair. In a controversial on-the-air shouting match with Bush, CBS news anchor Dan Rather tried to force Bush to acknowledge an involvement. Who was Rather representing in this instance—Bush's Republican rivals, the Democratic party, the American people, CBS, himself? What does this incident suggest to you about the proper limits of journalistic advocacy?

</td></tr>
</table>

## THE WATCHDOG ROLE

Traditionally the American press has accepted responsibility for protecting the public from deceitful, careless, incompetent, and corrupt officials.[48] In this **watchdog role** the press stands ready to expose any official who violates accepted legal, ethical, and performance standards.

The most notable exercise of the watchdog role in recent decades took place during the Watergate scandal. Bob Woodward and Carl Bernstein of the *Washington Post* spent months uncovering evidence that high-ranking officials in the Nixon White House were lying about their role in the burglary of the Democratic National Committee's headquarters and in the subsequent cover-up. Virtually all of the nation's media picked up on the *Post*'s revelations. In the end, even the most diehard Republicans found it all but impossible to deny that President Nixon had acted unlawfully. Nixon was forced to resign, as was his attorney general, John Mitchell. The Watergate episode is a dramatic reminder that a vigilant press is one of society's best safeguards against abuses of political power.

## THE PUBLIC REPRESENTATIVE ROLE

The mass media are an increasingly important and powerful institution in American society. They have become more influential as some other institu-

---

[44]B. H. Winfield, "Franklin D. Roosevelt's Efforts to Influence the News during His First-Term Press Conferences," *Presidential Studies Quarterly* 9 (Spring 1981): 189–199. See also George Juergens, *News from the White House* (Chicago: University of Chicago Press, 1981), 65.
[45]See Herbert I. Schiller, *Mass Communications and American Empire* (Boston: Beacon Press, 1971); Epstein, *News from Nowhere.*
[46]Grossman and Kumar, *Portraying the President,* 420.
[47]Thomas P. O'Neill, Jr., "Congress: The First 200 Years," *National Forum* 64 (Fall 1984): 20–21.
[48]See Rivers, *The Other Government;* Douglass Cater, *The Fourth Branch of Government* (Boston: Houghton Mifflin, 1955).

CBS News anchor Dan Rather is a "public figure," not a "public representative." Like other journalists, he has an allegiance to his news organization and to the norms of news reporting, not to an ideal of public advocacy. (UPI/Bettmann Newsphotos)

tions, most notably the political parties, have lost strength. Traditionally the **public representative role**—that of spokesperson for and advocate of the public—belonged to political leaders, political institutions, and political organizations. Today, however, many reporters seem to believe that *they* represent the public. "[Our] chief duty," the newscaster Roger Mudd claims, "is to put before the nation its unfinished business."[49]

Although the press has to some degree always acted as a stand-in for the people, the tendency for journalists to play the role of public advocate has increased significantly since the 1960s.[50] Vietnam and Watergate convinced many journalists that their judgments were superior to those of political leaders. "The press," declared Ben Bradlee, executive editor of the *Washington Post*, "won on Watergate."[51] The *New York Times*'s James Reston said much the same thing about Vietnam: "Maybe historians will agree that the reporters and the cameras were decisive in the end. They brought the issue of the war to the people, before the Congress and the courts, and forced the withdrawal of American power from Vietnam."[52]

Are reporters really in a position to know what is best for the American people? There are at least two basic reasons for concluding that the media are not well suited to the role of public representative: they do not promote a consistent point of view, and they are not adequately accountable to the public.

### "News from Nowhere"

First, representation requires a point of view. Politics is essentially the mobilization of bias—that is, it involves the representation of particular values and

[49]Quoted in Max Kampelman, "The Power of the Press," *Policy Review* 6 (1978): 19.
[50]Ibid.; Leonard Downie, Jr., *The New Muckrakers* (New York: New American Library, 1976); James Boylan, "Newspeople," *Wilson Quarterly* 6 (1982).
[51]Quoted in Kampelman, "Power of the Press," 18.
[52]Reston, "End of the Tunnel," 41.

**FIGURE 15-1 Network News Coverage of Policy Issues and of the "Horse Race" during the 1988 Presidential Campaign**
The media emphasize the "horse race" rather than the issues in reporting on election campaigns. During the 1988 presidential campaign, the news media never came close to giving the same amount of coverage to the policy issues as they did to the "horse race" aspects—which candidates were pulling ahead and which were falling behind. *Source: Figures based on author's content analysis of 1988 election news coverage.*

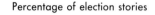
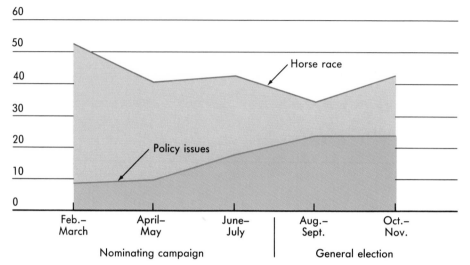

interests. Political parties and interest groups, as we saw in Chapters 11–14, exist to represent particular interests in society. But what political interests do the media represent? CBS News executive Richard Salant once said that his reporters covered stories "from nobody's point of view."[53] What he was saying in effect was that journalists do not consistently represent the political concerns of any group in particular. They respond to news opportunities, not to political interests.

Presidential elections provide an example. News coverage of presidential campaigns does not focus on the policy and leadership choices facing the American people but instead emphasizes the "horse race" between the candidates—who is winning and who is losing (see Figure 15-1). Moreover, the candidates' blunders and gaffes tend to make more news headlines than their stands on domestic and foreign policy.[54] In the 1984 campaign, for example, a major controversy was the refusal of the Democratic vice-presidential candidate, Geraldine Ferraro, to make public her family's income-tax returns. In 1987 Gary Hart, the preelection favorite for the 1988 Democratic nomination, was driven out of the race when the press ran stories on his extramarital affairs. Such stories meet the press's standards for newsworthiness because they are novel, controversial, and dramatic—but they hardly contribute to the fulfillment of the role of public representative.

The press is better geared to the role of critic. Studies indicate that journalists tend to be more liberal and Democratic in their preferences than are other elite groups, such as corporate executives and lawyers,[55] but there is no clear evidence that the news itself reflects journalists' personal biases. For example, the Democratic president Jimmy Carter took more of a bashing from the press than did the Republican president Ronald Reagan. The media do not consistently build up liberal and Democratic positions and tear down conservative and

*Without criticism and reliable and intelligent reporting, the government cannot govern.*
Walter Lippmann

[53]Quoted in Epstein, *News from Nowhere*, ix.
[54]See Thomas E. Patterson, *Mass Media Election* (New York: Praeger, 1980), chs. 3–5.
[55]S. Robert Lichter and Stanley Rothman, "Media and Business Elites," *Public Opinion*, October/November 1981, 42.

Republican ones, or vice versa. Journalists tend to criticize *all* sides—liberals as well as conservatives, Democrats as well as Republicans.[56]

Such criticism has value: a public that is aware of the policy failures and personal shortcomings of its political leaders is better equipped to hold them accountable for their actions. Yet political criticism is not the same as public representation, which involves advocacy of certain interests and values.

### Lack of Accountability

Second, the news media do not have the level of public accountability required of a public representative. Political institutions are made responsible to the public by formal mechanisms of accountability, particularly by regular elections. If representatives fail to serve as effective advocates, their constituents can vote them out of office. The vote thus provides officeholders with an incentive to discover what the people want and gives the public an opportunity to indicate whether it agrees with what officials are doing in its name. The public has no comparable hold over the press. Irate citizens can stop reading or viewing when they disagree with what journalists are advocating, but no daily newspaper or television station has ever gone out of business as a result.

The First Amendment virtually negates the press's claim to represent the public. Freedom of the press places the media beyond the control of popular majorities, and the people's representatives cannot properly be a self-appointed group, whether journalists or anyone else.

## *Organizing the Public in the Media Age*

The mass media increasingly mold Americans' ideas about politics. The United States is in a "media age," in which communication is instantaneous, the news is omnipresent, and journalists can become national celebrities. The press seems at times to be all-knowing and all-powerful, an illusion that leads its critics and defenders alike to expect the press to give coherence to the nation's politics. This expectation is unrealistic. The problem is that the news media are not truly a political institution and have no stake in organizing public opinion and policy choices. The press is a private institution that is in the public news business. And the business of news is as different from the practice of politics as being a stockholder is from running a corporation. Walter Lippmann once noted:

> The press is no substitute for [political] institutions. It is like the beam of a searchlight that moves restlessly about, bringing one episode and then another out of darkness into vision. Men cannot do the work of the world by this light alone. They cannot govern society by episodes, incidents, and interruptions.[57]

Lippmann's point was not that news organizations are somehow inferior to political organizations but that each has a different role and responsibility in society. Democracy cannot operate effectively without a free press that is acting

> ★ ANALYZE THE ISSUE
>
> **The News Media's Rights and Responsibilities**
> The news media have a favored position in law. They are the only private institution that enjoys special constitutional protection. Does the First Amendment's guarantee of freedom of the press place a special obligation on the media to behave responsibly? The media have become an increasingly powerful force in American politics. Is there a corresponding need for new checks and balances on the power of the media?

---

[56]See C. Richard Hofstetter, *Bias in the News* (Columbus: Ohio State University Press, 1976); Michael J. Robinson and Margaret A. Sheehan, *Over the Wire and on TV* (New York: Russell Sage Foundation, 1983); Michael J. Robinson and Austin Ranney, eds., *The Mass Media in Campaign '84* (Washington, D.C.: American Enterprise Institute, 1985).

[57]Lippmann, *Public Opinion*, 221.

effectively in its signaler, common-carrier, and watchdog roles. To keep in touch with one another and with government, citizens must have access to timely and uncensored news about public affairs. In other words, the media must do their job well if democratic government is to succeed. However, the media cannot also be asked to do the job of political institutions. For reasons already noted, the task is beyond the media's capacity.

As previous chapters have emphasized, the problem of citizen influence is the problem of organizing the public so that people can act together effectively. The news media merely appear to solve this problem. The fact that millions of people each day receive the same news about their government does not mold them into an organized community. The news creates a pseudocommunity: citizens feel they are part of a functioning whole until they try to act upon their news awareness. The futility of media-centered democracy was dramatized in the movie *Network* when its central character, a television anchorman, became enraged at the nation's political leadership and urged his viewers to go to their windows and yell, "I'm mad as hell and I'm not going to take it anymore!" Citizens heeded his instructions, but the main effect was to raise the network's ratings. It was not clear what officials in Washington were expected to do about several million people leaning out their windows and shouting a vague slogan at the top of their lungs. The film vividly illustrated the fact that the news can raise public consciousness as a prelude to organization, but the news itself cannot organize the public in any meaningful way. When public opinion is already formed, the media can serve as a channel for the expression of that opinion. But when public opinion is lacking, the media cannot establish it.

## Summary

In the nation's first century, the press was allied closely with the political parties and helped the parties to mobilize public opinion. Gradually the press freed itself from this relationship and developed a form of reporting, known as objective journalism, that emphasizes the fair and accurate reporting of newsworthy developments. The foundation of modern American news rests on the presentation and evaluation of significant events, not on the advocacy of partisan ideas. The nation's news organizations do not differ greatly in their reporting; broadcast stations and newspapers throughout the country emphasize many of the same events, issues, and personalities, following the lead of the major broadcast networks, a few elite newspapers, and the wire services.

The press performs four basic roles in a free society. In their signaler role, journalists communicate information to the public about events and problems that they consider important, relevant, and therefore newsworthy. The press also serves as a common carrier, in that it provides political leaders with a channel for addressing the public. Third, the press acts as a public protector or watchdog by exposing deceitful, careless, or corrupt officials. The American media can and, to a significant degree, do perform these roles adequately.

The press is less well suited, however, to the other role it plays, that of public representative. This role requires a consistent political viewpoint and public accountability, neither of which the press possesses. The media cannot be a substitute for effective political institutions. The press's strength lies ultimately in its capacity to inform the public, not in its claims to represent the people.

## *Major Concepts*

common-carrier role          public representative role
objective journalism         signaler role
partisan press               watchdog role

## *Suggested Readings*

Barber, James David. *The Pulse of Politics.* New York: Norton, 1980. A study of presidential elections from 1900 to 1976, focusing on the news media's role.

Entman, Robert M. *Democracy without Citizens.* New York: Oxford University Press, 1989. Analysis of the limits of media-based politics.

Epstein, Edward J. *News from Nowhere: Television and the News.* New York: Random House, 1973. A behind-the-scenes look at the organizational influences affecting the production of network television news.

Graber, Doris A. *Mass Media and American Politics.* Washington, D.C.: Congressional Quarterly Press, 1980. An overview of the media's role and impact on politics.

Grossman, Michael Baruch, and Martha Joynt Kumar. *Portraying the President.* Baltimore: Johns Hopkins University Press, 1981. A study of relations between the White House and the press.

Hofstetter, C. Richard. *Bias in the News.* Columbus: Ohio State University Press, 1976. A study of television news content that examines whether TV networks are ideologically biased in their news coverage.

Paletz, David L., and Robert M. Entman. *Media Power Politics.* New York: Free Press, 1981. A penetrating study of the links among the press, political elites, and the public in modern America.

Patterson, Thomas E., and Robert D. McClure. *The Unseeing Eye.* New York: Putnam, 1976. An analysis of television coverage of a presidential election campaign.

Robinson, Michael J., and Margaret A. Sheehan. *Over the Wire and on TV.* New York: Russell Sage Foundation, 1983. Analysis of television and wire-service news coverage of the 1980 presidential election.

# Has the Rise of Interest Groups Offset the Decline of Political Parties?

**ROBERT H. SALISBURY**

*The growth in the number and variety of interest groups in Washington has run parallel with a decline in their net impact on policy.*

Does the explosion of private-interest presence in the nation's capital signal a comparable increase in the influence of these groups? Do they now dominate the policymaking process to the exclusion of other considerations? Have they replaced political parties as the main mechanisms driving the political system? I think the answer to each of these questions is no; indeed, I think that the growth in the number and variety of interest groups in Washington has run parallel with a decline in their net impact on policy.

Part of this decline in influence has resulted from the great expansion in the number and effectiveness of various types of citizens' groups. Citizens' groups draw heavily upon well-educated middle-class Americans for support, and as this segment of society has grown, so have the organizing possibilities for such groups. These groups often disrupt the older established linkages between government officials and private groups. The links among congressional committees, executive agencies, and interest groups have been destabilized and often undermined by the vocal participation of groups that point out adverse third-party or externality effects of policy—harm to the environment from pesticide runoff, for example, or the high costs consumers must pay for zealous enforcement of workplace safety rules. The increasing number of groups has often meant that particular policy issues get bogged down in intergroup conflict, and the organized interests that used to dominate policy outcomes now find themselves confronted by vigorous opposition that sometimes results in policy stalemate.

As interest groups have grown, the structures of government with which they must deal have changed. In Congress, power has been broadly decentralized. Committee chairs have had to share their authority with subcommittee chairs, and every member has come to possess significant staff resources. Moreover, most incumbents have managed to insulate themselves against electoral defeat. From the perspective of the interest groups, there are now many more members who must be persuaded before any policy can be enacted. From the members' perspective, most of them are less dependent for reelection on the support of particular interest groups. Meanwhile, in the executive branch there has been a steady shift of power toward the Executive Office of the President and, indeed, the White House Office itself. These are much more difficult for lobbyists to penetrate than the operating units of cabinet departments or the independent agencies and commissions.

Finally, federal policy itself has immensely greater import for nearly every person or institution than it did a few decades ago. This fact helps to explain why, despite decreased clout, the number of interest groups in Washington has continued to grow. All sorts of groups—universities, business corporations, local governments, churches—need to know the potential impact of policy, not just in order to influence policy decisions but to adapt their own actions more effectively. Accordingly, they must send people to Washington to monitor the policymaking process. A great deal of what today's interest groups seek from their representatives is information, not influence. Shaping the future has become more and more difficult for them to do; if they can obtain the information needed to predict it and then adjust to it, their investment in Washington representation will be amply repaid.

*Robert H. Salisbury is Chair and Souers Professor of American Government at Washington University. Articles on the role of interest groups in American politics, the focus of his recent work, have appeared in the* American Political Science Review, *the* National Journal of Political Science, *the* American Journal of Political Science, *and other journals.*

**FRANK J. SORAUF**

*The rise of groups and the decline of parties have meant a new mix in the influence of these intermediaries between citizens and their government.*

When two changes, both of enormous political importance, occur more or less simultaneously, one can't avoid looking for connections. The decline of American political parties and the proliferation of interest groups both became evident in the 1960s and 1970s, so we naturally ask: Has one replaced the other? Has one trend offset the other? Has one *caused* the other?

Rather than being cause and effect, the rise of groups and the decline of parties seem to reflect the same changes in American society. Parties flourished when we were a less educated, less politically sophisticated society. Parties gave a simple and easily grasped structure to the complexities of American politics. Truth or wisdom was in one party or the other; for the individual partisan, the party defined the good guys and the bad guys. Today, however, many Americans would rather pick and choose among candidates and issues than accept the whole "package" of party candidates and issues. They find in groups a more specific and focused kind of choice, for groups seem better able to reflect the politics of a complex and heterogeneous society.

Americans, then, are exchanging one kind of politics, one kind of representation, for another. The change has enormous consequences. It means a more specialized, precise, and targeted representation of the political goals of individual Americans; it is, indeed, now much easier for the individual with a single interest to find representation for it. It also means a system in which relatively small but intense and committed groups can outweigh much larger groups; the successes of the National Rifle Association in forestalling gun control testify to that. And it means a kind of representation in which the interests of middle-class Americans are better represented, if only because they have the time and resources that permit them to join and work for groups. That is why we have seen the rise of a middle-class agenda—issues of the environment, lifestyle, equality, and morality, for instance —along with the rise of group politics.

However, the increase in group activity has not really "offset" the decline of political parties. Rather, the changes in the fortunes of the two have altered the nature of representation in American politics. Because both serve as mobilizers of individual Americans, the rise of groups and the decline of parties have meant a new mix in the influence of these intermediaries between citizens and their government.

Inevitably, the new mix affects the operation of the American democracy. The greater specialization and effectiveness of interest groups necessarily results in a fragmentation of the American electorate, a fragmentation that many observers think leads to deadlock in American legislatures. Whatever may be the shortcomings of the two major parties in trying to encompass a majority of Americans in a single coalition, they were in their heyday unsurpassed vehicles for mobilizing majorities. Their decline shifts the burdens of majority building from political intermediaries to increasingly burdened institutions of government.

*Frank J. Sorauf is a member of the Department of Political Science at the University of Minnesota. He is the author of* Money in American Elections.

# Part Five

## ELECTED REPRESENTATIVES

American democracy, it is sometimes said, is government by the people. So it is, but in a figurative sense. Direct democracy is a practical impossibility in a nation of the size and complexity of the United States. Americans are governed through representatives. There is no alternative.

As we indicated in Chapters 4 and 8, a debate has long raged over the proper relationship between a people and its representatives. One view holds that the representative must follow the expressed opinion of the constituency. Another view, first elaborated two centuries ago by the English theorist Edmund Burke, holds that the representative is obligated to exercise personal judgment in making policy decisions. The debate is essentially an issue of which interests will be the objects of public policy. The notion that representatives should take instructions from their constituents is based on the assumption that if they do not, they will promote the interests of themselves and their class over the true interests of the people. In contrast, Burke's idea that representatives should follow their consciences is based on the assumption that if they listen too closely to their electors, they will serve local or narrow interests rather than the national or general interest.

The governing system of the United States, partly by design and partly by accident, embodies elements of both these concepts of representation. The presidency is a truly national office that inclines its incumbent to take a national view of issues, while Congress is both a national institution and a body that is subject to powerful constituency influence. U.S. senators and representatives are elected from states and from districts within states, so that they are subject to strong local pressures. Chapters 17 and 18 show how the organization and policymaking of Congress reflect both national and local influences. In contrast, Chapters 20 and 21 reveal how the president's role, leadership, and power are affected by the office's national political base. Collectively, these four chapters indicate how local and national factors come together in relations between the executive and legislative branches.

Popular influence on both Congress and the president begins with the electoral process. It is through their ability to elect their representatives that citizens first acquire a hold over them. As we discussed in Chapter 10, elections are a blunt instrument of self-government: they enable the public to choose officeholders, not policies. Thus, to understand the contribution of elections to the American system of government, it is necessary to look not only at voters but also at candidates. Who runs and who wins? What effect do elections have on the relationship between representatives and the people they serve? Chapter 16 focuses on congressional elections, with particular attention to the considerable advantages of incumbency. Chapter 19 examines presidential selection, emphasizing the lengthy, intricate, and highly political process that, every four years, gives Americans their president.                    ★   ★   ★

# Chapter 16

## CONGRESSIONAL OFFICE: GETTING ELECTED, STAYING ELECTED

*. . . Nearly everything pertaining to [congressional] candidates and campaigns is profoundly influenced by whether the candidate is an incumbent, challenging an incumbent, or pursuing an open seat.*

*Gary C. Jacobson[1]*

Hundreds of pork-barrel projects were embedded in the $600 billion annual appropriations bill that Congress passed in late 1987. Through the intervention of Senator Ted Stevens, Alaska fishermen got $2.6 million in federal funds to "develop fishery products." The University of Massachusetts at Amherst received $60,000 for its Belgian Endive Research Center, thanks to the efforts of Congressman Silvio Conte, the ranking minority member on the House Appropriations Committee. Senator James McClure produced a $6.4 million federal grant for development of a ski resort in his state of Idaho.

Congress has a long tradition of pork-barrel legislation—laws designed primarily to help members of Congress get reelected by authorizing federal projects that benefit their constituents. The pork barrel has many critics outside Congress and a few inside, but it persists year after year. "I have spent my career trying to get Congressmen to spend the public's money as if it was their own, and I have failed," said Senator William Proxmire of Wisconsin, who retired in 1989 after thirty years in Congress.[2]

It would be a mistake to conclude that members of Congress are obsessed by pork-barrel legislation. But it would be only a slight exaggeration to say that most members of Congress are preoccupied with any and all factors, including pork-barrel projects, that will help them to stay in office. Getting reelected is the

---

[1]Gary C. Jacobson, *The Politics of Congressional Elections* (Boston: Little, Brown, 1983), 26.
[2]Quoted in "Is the Pork Barrel a Must?" *Newsweek*, January 18, 1988, 24.

first priority of members of Congress because that is what makes the attainment of their other political goals possible. In Lawrence Dodd's phrase, members of Congress strive for **electoral mastery**—a strong base of popular support that will free them from constant worry over reelection.[3] Without such a base, incumbents have little choice but to do those things that will win them votes. In 1984, for example, Jesse Helms promised North Carolina's voters that if he were reelected he would remain as head of the Senate Agriculture Committee, even though he would have preferred the chairmanship of the more prestigious Foreign Relations Committee. Helms was locked in a close (but ultimately successful) election fight with the state's former governor, James Hunt, and he believed that he needed to hold on to his Agriculture chairmanship in order to win the support of the many farmers—especially tobacco growers—in his state.[4]

Fortunately for members of Congress, a seat in the House or Senate is itself a springboard to reelection. While on the job and at public expense, members of Congress have frequent opportunities to publicize themselves, to claim credit for Congress's achievements, and to perform services for their constituents. Incumbency also has its liabilities, particularly for U.S. senators, whose greater visibility and more desirable office make them more attractive targets for potential opponents. On balance, however, incumbency is a substantial advantage.

A central argument of this chapter is that voters in many congressional races are not presented with a real choice: the advantages of incumbency and party competition so strongly favor one candidate that the outcome is hardly in doubt. Another central argument is that congressional elections produce senators and representatives who are highly responsive to their own constituencies but less responsive to the needs of Congress as a national policymaking body. The main points presented in this chapter are the following:

★ *Congressional office provides incumbents with substantial resources (free publicity, staff, and legislative influence) that help them to win reelection.* Members of Congress can promote themselves by claiming credit for Congress's achievements, performing services for constituents, and garnering publicity.

★ *The nature and outcome of congressional races depend on many influences, but particularly on whether the incumbent is running, whether the state or district is electorally competitive, and whether a strong challenger enters the race.* House campaigns tend to be less competitive than Senate campaigns.

★ *In most congressional races, circumstances (especially party competition and incumbency) so strongly favor one candidate that voters have no real alternative but to confirm that candidate as their choice.*

★ *Members of congress achieve reelection by paying close attention to constituency interests.* Although they serve in a national institution, they are also representative of state and local interests, and for many of them, these interests take precedence over national concerns.

[3]Lawrence C. Dodd, "A Theory of Congressional Cycles," in Gerald Wright, Leroy Rieselbach, and Lawrence C. Dodd, *Congress and Policy Change* (New York: Agathon, 1986).
[4]David R. Mayhew, *Congress: The Electoral Connection* (New Haven, Conn.: Yale University Press, 1974), 16.

## *Congress as a Career: The Impact of Party Competition and Incumbency*

In the nation's first century, service in the Congress was not a career for most of its members. Before 1900 at least a third and sometimes as many as half of the seats in Congress changed hands at each election. Most members left voluntarily. Because travel was slow and arduous, serving in the nation's capital required them to spend months away from their families. Many were glad to leave Washington, which, because it was built on a swamp, was chillingly damp in the winter and mosquito-ridden in the summer. And because the national government was not the center of power and politics that it is today, many politicians preferred to serve in state capitals.

The modern Congress is very different.[5] Congress is a career for most of its members. They are professional politicians, and a seat in the U.S. Senate or House is as far as most of them can expect to go in politics. The pay (about $90,000 a year) is reasonably good, and the prestige of their office is substantial, particularly if they serve in the Senate. A lengthy career in Congress is what most of its members aspire to attain.

Today the biggest obstacle to having a lengthy career in Congress is winning a seat in the first place. Incumbents, particularly members of the House, have a good chance of being returned to office again and again (see Table 16-1).[6] In recent House elections, about 90 percent of incumbents, on average, have decided to seek reelection, and fewer than 10 percent of them have lost. An all-time record was established in 1986 when only 2 percent of House incumbents seeking reelection were defeated; that record was tied in 1988. Senate seats are less secure. Since 1970 the success rate of incumbent senators has ranged from a low of 55 percent (1980) to a high of 93 percent (1982). Nevertheless, Senate incumbents who seek another term have, statistically speaking, a better than 2-to-1 chance of victory.

> ★ ANALYZE THE ISSUE
>
> **"Safe Seats"**
> As a result of the advantages of office and weakened partisanship, congressional incumbents can now be more confident than ever before about their chances for reelection. To what extent is this situation a danger to democracy? What might be done to change it? Does it offer any advantages?

[5]See John R. Hibbing, "Voluntary Retirements from the House in the Twentieth Century," *Journal of Politics* 44 (November 1982): 1020–1034.

[6]Robert S. Erikson, "Is There Such a Thing as a Safe Seat?" *Polity* 8 (Summer 1976): 627–628; James L. Payne, "The Personal Electoral Advantage of House Incumbents, 1936–1976," *American Politics Quarterly* 8 (October 1980): 465–482; see also Stephen E. Frantzich, "Opting Out: Retirement from the House of Representatives," *American Politics Quarterly* 6 (July 1978): 251–273.

# CONSTITUTIONAL QUALIFICATIONS FOR SERVING IN CONGRESS

*Representatives:* "No person shall be a Representative who shall not have attained to the age of twenty-five years, and been seven years a citizen of the United States, and who shall not, when elected, be an inhabitant of that State in which he shall be chosen" (Article I, section 2).

*Senators:* "No person shall be a Senator who shall not have attained to the age of thirty years, and been nine years a citizen of the United States, and who shall not, when elected, be an inhabitant of the State for which he shall be chosen" (Article I, section 3).

Congressional incumbents, particularly members of the House of Representatives, are usually reelected. Claude Pepper of Florida had been returned to the House every two years from 1962 to 1988. He had previously served in the U.S. Senate. Pepper died in May of 1989 at the age of eighty-eight. (Gamma Liaison)

**TABLE 16-1   House and Senate Incumbents Reelected and Not Seeking Reelection, 1954–1988**

| | HOUSE INCUMBENTS | | SENATE INCUMBENTS | |
|---|---|---|---|---|
| | Percent Not Seeking Reelection | Percent Reelected of Those Seeking Reelection | Percent Not Seeking Reelection | Percent Reelected of Those Seeking Reelection |
| 1954 | 6% | 93% | 18% | 75% |
| 1956 | 5 | 95 | 18 | 86 |
| 1958 | 8 | 90 | 18 | 64 |
| 1960 | 6 | 93 | 15 | 97 |
| 1962 | 6 | 92 | 12 | 83 |
| 1964 | 8 | 87 | 6 | 85 |
| 1966 | 5 | 88 | 9 | 88 |
| 1968 | 5 | 97 | 18 | 71 |
| 1970 | 7 | 95 | 12 | 77 |
| 1972 | 9 | 94 | 18 | 74 |
| 1974 | 10 | 88 | 21 | 85 |
| 1976 | 11 | 96 | 24 | 64 |
| 1978 | 11 | 94 | 30 | 60 |
| 1980 | 8 | 91 | 15 | 55 |
| 1982 | 9 | 90 | 9 | 93 |
| 1984 | 6 | 96 | 12 | 90 |
| 1986 | 10 | 98 | 18 | 75 |
| 1988 | 6 | 98 | 21 | 85 |

SOURCE: *Congressional Quarterly Weekly Report*, various dates.

The high reelection rates of congressional incumbents can be explained primarily by two factors: the existence of "safe" seats and the resources bestowed by congressional office.

## WEAK PARTY COMPETITION AND "SAFE" CONGRESSIONAL SEATS

Some states and districts are so heavily Republican or Democratic that the candidate of the majority party nearly always wins. Perhaps a fifth of all Senate seats and a larger proportion of House seats are safely in the hands of one party or the other. Democratic nominees in Louisiana, for example, have won every U.S. Senate election since the Reconstruction era of the 1870s. Republicans thought they could break the Democrats' hold on Louisiana when the popular Russell Long, first elected to the Senate in 1948, retired in 1986. President Ronald Reagan made two personal appearances on behalf of the Republican candidate, W. Henson Moore, in the election's closing days, but Moore still lost to the Democrat John B. Breaux. Republicans concede that Breaux, who was forty-two years old when he was elected, may well hold the Louisiana seat until his death or retirement.

In one-sided states and districts, primary elections are the main threat to incumbents. However, voters rarely abandon a member of Congress in a primary election unless the incumbent is embroiled in scandal or is widely perceived to have lost touch with local interests. Although one-fourth of congressional incumbents face primary challenges in an average election year, few of them lose.[7]

House elections have become less competitive in recent decades.[8] Although nearly half of all House races in the 1950s were decided by a victory margin of less than 60 percent, only a fourth of House races have been that close in more recent elections (see Table 16-2). One reason is that House incumbents have increasingly been protected by **gerrymandering**—the deliberate redrawing of an election district's boundaries to give a particular party or candidate an advantage. Every ten years, after each population census, states must rearrange their House electoral districts in order to make them as nearly equal in population as possible. This procedure is called **redistricting,** and it is a potentially explosive issue; if either party believes it is being grossly mistreated, it will fight a redistricting proposal with every political weapon available, including court action. As a consequence, Republicans and Democrats in state legislatures tend to draw district boundaries so as to protect House incumbents of both parties. They achieve this goal by creating heavily Republican districts around Republican incumbents and heavily Democratic districts around Democratic incumbents.

[7]Harvey L. Schantz, "Contested and Uncontested Primaries for the U.S. House," *Legislative Studies Quarterly* 5 (November 1980): 548; Arthur D. McNitt and Jim Seroka, "Intraparty Challenges of Incumbent Governors and Senators: 1956–1976," *American Politics Quarterly* 9 (July 1981): 321–340.

[8]David R. Mayhew, "Congressional Elections: The Case of the Vanishing Marginals," *Polity* 6 (1974): 295–317; see also Joseph Cooper and William West, "The Congressional Career in the 1970s," in Lawrence C. Dodd and Bruce I. Oppenheimer, eds., *Congress Reconsidered*, 2d ed. (Washington, D.C.: Congressional Quarterly Press, 1981), 99; Melissa P. Collie, "Incumbency, Electoral Safety, and Turnover in the House of Representatives, 1952–1976," *American Political Science Review* 75 (March 1981): 119–131.

When Massachusetts was redistricted in 1812, Governor Elbridge Gerry had the lines of one district redrawn in order to ensure that a candidate of his party would be elected. The cartoonist Elkanah Tinsdale, noting that the strangely shaped district resembled a salamander, called it a "Gerry-mander." (The Bettmann Archive)

**TABLE 16-2   Percentage of House and Senate Incumbents Who Won Reelection by 60 Percent or More of the Vote, 1956–1988**

| | House Incumbents | Senate Incumbents |
|---|---|---|
| 1956 | 59% | |
| 1958 | 63 | 43% |
| 1960 | 59 | |
| 1962 | 64 | |
| 1964 | 59 | 44 |
| 1966 | 68 | |
| 1968 | 72 | |
| 1970 | 77 | 45 |
| 1972 | 78 | |
| 1974 | 66 | |
| 1976 | 72 | 41 |
| 1978 | 78 | |
| 1980 | 73 | |
| 1982 | 69 | 39 |
| 1984 | 77 | |
| 1986 | 86 | |
| 1988 | 87 | 45 |

SOURCES: Date for 1956–1982 from Norman Ornstein et al., *Vital Statistics on Congress, 1984–1985* (Washington, D.C.: American Enterprise Institute, 1984), 53–54; for 1984, *Congressional Quarterly Almanac*, vol. 40 (Washington, D.C.: Congressional Quarterly, 1984), 7B–31B; for 1986, *Congressional Quarterly Weekly Report* 44 (November 8, 1986): 2864–2870; for 1988, Federal Election Commission.

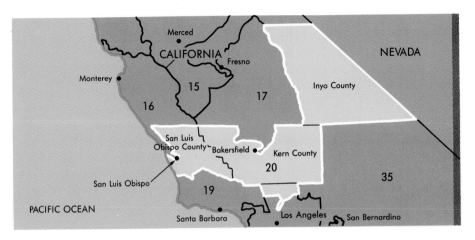

**FIGURE 16-1 Gerrymandering California's 20th Congressional District**
California Democrats adjusted congressional district lines after the 1980 census to include more of the conservative farmers and military workers of the Central Valley region in one district, the 20th. The result is a district that zigzags across the width of the state and is lopsidedly Republican. With the Democrats conceding this district, its Republican representative, William Thomas, was in office throughout the 1980s, winning reelection in 1988 with 72 percent of the vote. *Source: U.S. Bureau of the Census.*

Even when Republican and Democratic party leaders choose not to divide the spoils in advance, incumbents of both parties usually benefit from gerrymandering. After the 1980 census, Republican leaders in California made the mistake of rejecting a bipartisan redistricting plan. Although the Democrats had a majority in the state legislature, Republicans believed that Hispanic Democratic legislators could be persuaded to support a redistricting plan favorable to the GOP. It was a major miscalculation. Democrats in the state legislature held firm and eventually produced a redistricting plan favorable to their own party. Their strategy placed Republican incumbents in such lopsidedly Republican districts that few Democratic votes were "wasted" in these contests. (For an example of such a district, see Figure 16-1.) Democratic incumbents were also given safe districts, but ones that included no more Democratic voters than were needed to ensure the incumbents' reelection. Finally, the districts in which an incumbent was not seeking reelection were stacked with Democratic voters so that Democratic challengers had an advantage. The strategy worked as planned. In the 1982 congressional elections in California, Democrats received about 50 percent of the statewide congressional vote but gained 62 percent of the House seats.

Of course, gerrymandering is not a tool that can be applied to U.S. Senate races. The electoral district for such races is defined not by population but by geography: it consists of the entire state, and each state elects two senators. For this reason and others, the competitiveness of Senate races has remained relatively steady in recent decades.[9] In the majority of Senate contests, the winner receives less than 60 percent of the vote (see Table 16-2).

## USING INCUMBENCY TO STAY IN CONGRESS

Members of Congress say that they are in Washington primarily to serve the interests of their state or district.[10] As natural as this claim may appear, it is noteworthy that members of the British House of Commons or the French National Assembly would not be likely to make it: they consider their chief responsibility to be service to the nation, not to their localities. The unitary governments and strong parties of Britain and France give their politics a

[9]Cooper and West, "Congressional Career in the 1970s," 99.
[10]See Richard Fenno, *Home Style: House Members in Their Districts* (Boston: Little, Brown, 1978).

national orientation. The federal system and weak parties of the United States force members of Congress to take responsibility for their own reelection campaigns and to serve local interests as well as national ones.

## Claiming Credit for Congress's Achievements

One way in which members of Congress can please their constituents is by being instrumental in the enactment of legislation favorable to local interests. Many senators and representatives sit on congressional committees that formulate policies of special importance to their constituencies. Almost all members of the House and Senate Agricultural committees, for example, are from the farm states. In his 1984 reelection campaign, Jesse Helms emphasized the increase in tobacco price supports which he had steered through Congress for the benefit of many of his North Carolina constituents.

Members of Congress also seek **pork-barrel legislation.** As we indicated at the beginning of the chapter, this term refers to laws whose tangible benefits are targeted solely at a legislator's **constituency**—the body of citizens eligible to vote for him or her. ("Pork" was the term for political graft or corruption in the late nineteenth century; when legislators adopted the practice of placing numerous items of pork into a single bill, people began to say, "Now the pork is all in one barrel.") It is always good politics for a member of Congress to make sure that the home state or district gets as many federal dollars as possible. Constituents may disagree on issues of national policy, but no one objects when federal pork-barrel projects pour into their area. David Martin is one congressman who has built his reputation almost entirely on pork-barrel politics. He concentrates on securing federal funds for Fort Drum, a major military installation located in his rural district in upstate New York.

## Performing Services for Constituents

Each member of Congress is provided with a personal staff at taxpayers' expense.* House members receive office allowances of about $500,000 a year, which enable each of them to hire about twenty full-time staff members. Senators have budgets two or three times larger, depending on the populations of their states, and their personal staffs average about forty employees.[11]

Congressional staffs doubled in size during the 1960s, when members of Congress decided they needed more help to keep pace with their growing legislative load (see Table 16-3). However, most members of Congress use their personal staffs primarily to perform services in order to build support among constituents, a practice that is known as **service strategy.** Congressional staffers spend the bulk of their time not on legislative matters but on constituency relations, including responding to the thousands of letters that each member of Congress receives annually from individual constituents.[12] When citizens

---

*There are two types of congressional staffs: the personal staff, whose members work for the individual member, and the committee staff, whose members are assigned to particular congressional committees rather than to individual members. The discussion in this chapter refers only to personal staffs.

[11]Norman Ornstein et al., *Vital Statistics on Congress, 1984–1985* (Washington, D.C.: American Enterprise Institute, 1984), 1221.

[12]See John S. Saloma III, *Congress and the New Politics* (Boston: Little, Brown, 1969), 185; Harrison W. Fox and Susan Webb Hammond, "The Growth of Congressional Staffs," in Harvey C. Mansfield, ed., *Congress against President*, vol. 32, no. 1, of *Proceedings of the Academy of Political Science* (1975), 119.

**TABLE 16-3  Approximate Number of Personal Staff Members Employed by Members of Congress, 1960–1990, by Chamber**

| Year | Senate | House |
|------|--------|-------|
| 1960 | 1,275  | 2,875 |
| 1970 | 2,250  | 4,950 |
| 1980 | 3,925  | 7,200 |
| 1990 | 4,400  | 7,475 |

SOURCE: Staff, Senate Finance Section and Office of Clerk of the House.

encounter delays or other obstacles in applying for social security, government loans, and other federal benefits, their representative or senator can often assist by persuading the bureaucracy to act quickly or favorably.[13] In rare cases, members of Congress have personally intervened at the highest administrative levels. Congressman Wayne Hays of Ohio once earned the gratitude of a constituent by storming into the office of Secretary of State Dean Rusk to demand, successfully, that the State Department expedite the constituent's passport application.[14]

Some critics suggest that service-minded members of Congress are nothing more than "errand boys" for their constituents. This criticism overlooks the fact that the members themselves do not have to neglect legislative duties in order to serve constituents' personal needs. Most of this work can be delegated to staff

[13]Fenno, *Home Style,* 101.
[14]Morris P. Fiorina, *Congress: The Keystone of the Washington Establishment* (New Haven, Conn.: Yale University Press, 1977), 45–49.

Congressional staffers sort letters from constituents, many of whom are requesting information or assistance. Each member of Congress gets thousands of such requests every year, and prompt attention to them is presumed to result in votes and contributions at reelection time. (Art Stein/Photo Researchers)

members and has increasingly been shifted out of Washington offices to district offices. At one time these local offices were open only when the representative was in town; now they are open every day and serve as local congressional headquarters for constituents who need help.[15]

House members, especially, find that service to constituents is a natural extension of their political careers. Local politics is the traditional path to House election, and most House members maintain strong local ties and have a natural interest in constituents' personal needs. The bottom line, however, is that constituency service produces votes on election day. Congressional observers disagree on exactly how many votes can be won through these small favors,[16] but there is no doubt that constituency service helps—particularly in House races, in which the incumbent's attentiveness to local people and problems is often a major campaign issue.

### Garnering Publicity

Finally, members of Congress boost their chances of reelection by keeping their names before the voters. They do so in part by making personal appearances at local events and gatherings. At public expense, each House member is allowed twenty-six visits to his or her district each year and each senator can take about forty trips home. In addition, each member of Congress is permitted several free mailings annually to constituent households; not surprisingly, the use of this privilege (known as the frank) peaks during election years.[17] Congressional staffs also churn out newsletters and press releases designed to publicize the member for whom they work.[18] Some congressional offices are quite shameless in their use of the frank to get free publicity. Certain House members, for

---

[15]Ibid., 58.
[16]For the opposing views, see ibid., ch. 7, and John R. Johannes, *To Serve the People* (Lincoln: University of Nebraska Press, 1984), ch.8.
[17]Congressional Quarterly, *How Congress Works* (Washington, D.C.: Congressional Quarterly Press, 1983), 142–143.
[18]See Diana Evans Yiannakis, "House Members' Communication Styles," *Journal of Politics* 44 (November 1982): 1049–1073.

Representative Tom McMillen (D-Md.) at a ribbon-cutting ceremony. Such public occasions enable members of Congress to keep themselves highly visible to their constituents. (UPI/Bettmann Newsphotos)

example, routinely send congratulatory letters to all graduating high school seniors in their districts, an effort that is designed to impress these newly eligible voters and their parents.

The news media also publicize members of Congress. All U.S. senators and most House members receive reasonably close attention from local news media. Except for House members from large cities such as New York, Chicago, and Los Angeles, which have numerous congressional districts within their boundaries, members of Congress are locally prominent and are thus considered newsworthy.[19] Although the national media tend to be critical of Congress as an institution, most individual members of Congress get favorable coverage from the press and fare particularly well with local reporters.[20]

Name recognition alone can be an electoral advantage, particularly in House races. When voters' party loyalties declined after the early 1960s, other factors, such as voters' familiarity with individual candidates, became increasingly important (see Chapter 10).[21] In the typical House election campaign, about two-thirds of the voters cannot recall the challenger's name, let alone his or her political record or policy positions. Fewer people have difficulty recalling the incumbent's name, and once they enter the polling booth, 95 percent of voters recognize the incumbent by name.[22] When partisanship is weak, name recognition apparently has a large influence on voting decisions. In the 1950s, fewer than 10 percent of partisan voters defected to the House candidate of the opposing party. Now about 20 percent do so, and most of them are attracted to incumbents—presumably because they attach more significance to their sense of familiarity with the incumbent than to his or her party affiliation.[23]

## THE BURDENS OF INCUMBENCY

The blessings of incumbency can be decidedly mixed. The potential problems are several: personal misconduct, troublesome issues, and strong challengers.[24]

### Improper Conduct

Corruption is less common in Washington than most Americans assume, but it does occur. As a result of the FBI's ABSCAM sting operation in 1979, Senator Harrison Williams (D-N.J.) and several House members were convicted of accepting bribes in return for legislative promises.

The roots of improper behavior among members of Congress can often be traced to the social and financial demands placed on them. They interact with

[19]See Charles M. Tidmarch and Brad S. Karp, "The Missing Beat: Press Coverage of Congressional Elections in Eight Metropolitan Areas," *Congress and the Presidency* 10 (Spring 1983): 47–61.

[20]Peter Clarke and Susan Evans, *Covering Campaigns* (Stanford, Calif.: Stanford University Press, 1981), 2–6.

[21]John A. Ferejohn, "On the Decline of Competition in Congressional Elections," *American Political Science Review* 71 (March 1977): 166–175.

[22]Kent L. Tedin and Richard W. Murray, "Public Awareness of Congressional Representatives: Recall v. Recognition," *American Politics Quarterly* 7 (October 1979): 509–517.

[23]Albert D. Cover and David R. Mayhew, "Congressional Dynamics and the Decline of Competitive Congressional Elections," in Dodd and Oppenheimer, *Congress Reconsidered*, 74–75; Robert S. Erikson, "The Advantage of Incumbency in Congressional Elections," *Polity* 3 (1971): 395–405.

[24]See Thomas E. Mann, *Unsafe at Any Margin: Interpreting Congressional Elections* (Washington, D.C.: American Enterprise Institute, 1978).

The Democratic leadership in the House, June 1989: Majority Whip William H. Gray III (Pa.), Majority Leader Richard A. Gephardt (Mo.), and Speaker Thomas S. Foley (Wash.). (*George Tamas/NYT Pictures*)

lobbyists, attorneys, consultants, correspondents, and other persons who have much higher incomes than theirs, and they are expected to keep pace. They naturally feel pressure to find ways to supplement their congressional salary. For some, this extra income is provided by personal wealth they had acquired before election to Congress. Others find legitimate ways to supplement their salaries, such as accepting fees for giving public lectures.

However, there is a thin line between legal and illegal activity. Members of Congress cannot accept bribes, for example, but they can accept gratuities. In 1986 several congressmen were flown by corporate jet to the headquarters of the United Coal Company in Bristol, Virginia. They dined with company executives, were given a tour of the mines, and were handed $2,000 each upon departure. William Weld, an assistant attorney general who was newly arrived in Washington, learned of the incident and proposed that the congressmen be indicted for violating an antigratuities statute. Weld was surprised to learn from his staff that the congressmen had done nothing illegal: the law allowed them to accept up to $2,000 plus their travel expenses for participating in such a meeting.[25]

Ethics in Washington is obviously a complex moral and legal issue, and it is perhaps not surprising that some members of Congress engage in illegal or questionable activities. Even the top leaders are not immune, as evidenced by former Speaker of the House Jim Wright. In addition to being accused in 1988 of conflict of interest between his private business dealings and some of his legislative efforts, Wright was criticized for receiving $55,000 in "royalties" from a book written in his name by an aide and published by a friend. Almost

[25]"Congress Faces an Ethics Gap," *Newsweek,* July 4, 1988, 16.

all the copies sold were bought by interest groups, such as the Teamsters union, which bought 2,000 copies.[26]

In view of the legal and moral tightrope that members of Congress walk, the irony, perhaps, is that their constituents and colleagues often exact a stiff price when they are caught breaking the law. Nobody, it seems, wants to be associated with a certifiably rotten apple.

## Troublesome Issues

Powerful issues can also undermine incumbents. In the two centuries of Congress's existence, hundreds of members have lost their positions as a result of political upheaval. During the depression of the 1890s, for example, the issue of free silver divided the electorate sharply along class and regional lines, causing unprecedented turnover in Congress. Going into the 1894 congressional elections, Democrats held forty-four House seats in the Northeast; they emerged with only seven seats in the region.[27] Although turnover has been nowhere near that level in any recent election, disruptive issues are a potential threat to incumbents. Richard Nixon was not the only Republican who paid a high price for the Watergate scandal: in the 1974 election that came three months after his resignation, forty-nine House seats held by Republicans were lost to Democrats.

Of all policy issues, the economy has the largest bearing on congressional races. A strong economy strengthens the position of all incumbents, whereas a weak economy makes congressional incumbents of the president's party vulnerable.[28] In 1980 Jimmy Carter was in the White House and inflation was at record levels; that fall Carter's fellow Democrats lost a net total of thirteen Senate seats and thirty-three House seats. Economic conditions also have an indirect effect on election outcomes: potentially strong opponents are more likely to run against incumbents when a weak economy favors such a move.[29]

The influence of national issues on congressional races helps to explain the phenomenon called "presidential coattails."[30] The term commonly refers to the greater electoral success of congressional candidates who belong to the same party as the winning presidential candidate: they are said to ride into office on the president's coattails. Although the pattern is often said to occur because a presidential candidate's popularity rubs off on his party's congressional candidates, this factor actually has only a little to do with it. A larger factor is policy issues. The same issues (notably the condition of the economy) that contribute to the success of the party's presidential candidate can also benefit its congressional candidates.

In 1980, with the economy in a downturn and Democrat Jimmy Carter in the White House, Democrats in Congress were more vulnerable than incumbents normally are. Among the Democratic losers in that year's elections was George McGovern of South Dakota, who had been his party's presidential nominee in 1972. (AP/Wide World Photos)

[26]Ibid.

[27]Paul W. Glad, *McKinley, Bryan, and the People* (Philadelphia: Lippincott, 1964), 92.

[28]Morris P. Fiorina, *Retrospective Voting in American National Elections* (New Haven, Conn.: Yale University Press, 1981), 81.

[29]Gary C. Jacobson and Samuel Kernell, *Strategy and Choice in Congressional Elections* (New Haven, Conn.: Yale University Press, 1981), 2–3.

[30]See James E. Campbell, "Explaining Presidential Losses in Midterm Congressional Elections," *Journal of Politics* 47 (November 1985): 1140; James E. Campbell, "Predicting Seat Gains from Presidential Coattails," *American Journal of Political Science* 30 (February 1986): 165.

In most congressional races, the incumbent has the edge in fundraising. Pete Wilson (R-Calif.) was the top spender among U.S. Senate candidates in 1988. He spent $13 million on his campaign—twice as much as his Democratic opponent—and was reelected, 53 percent to 44 percent. (UPI/Bettmann Newsphotos)

## INCUMBENCY AND MONEY

A study by *Congressional Quarterly* found that only 10 percent of incumbents said they had had trouble raising enough money to conduct an effective campaign, compared with 70 percent of challengers.[38] In fact, many challengers are able to raise only enough money for a token campaign. In 1988 about half of House challengers had less than $100,000 with which to try to unseat an incumbent. "Spending is particularly important for non-incumbents," Barbara Hinckley notes. "It significantly increases recognition and affects the vote."[39] Challengers who spend heavily have at least a chance of victory; those who spend little are almost certain to lose. In contrast, incumbents normally spend heavily only when they face a serious challenger.[40]

Incumbents find it easier than challengers to raise money. First, they are more likely to have compiled lists of individuals from whom they can solicit campaign contributions.[41] Second, PACs overwhelmingly favor incumbents (see Figure 16-3). "We have a friendly incumbent policy," said one PAC director, expressing a common view. "We always stick with the incumbent when we agree with them both."[42]

Although Senate races tend to attract well-funded challengers, incumbent senators are usually better funded than their opponents. They derive their financial advantage from a variety of funding sources, including individual contributors, PACs, and political party sources. In recent years Senate incumbents have filled large campaign "war chests" well in advance of their Senate reelection campaigns, partly in order to discourage potentially strong challeng-

[38]*Congressional Quarterly Guide to Congress*, 3d ed. (Washington, D.C.: Congressional Quarterly Press, 1982), 666.
[39]Hinckley, *Congressional Elections*, 29.
[40]Edie N. Goldenberg and Michael W. Traugott, *Campaigning for Congress* (Washington, D.C.: Congressional Quarterly Press, 1984), 81.
[41]See David A. Leuthold, *Electioneering in a Democracy* (New York: Wiley, 1968).
[42]Quoted in Larry Sabato, *PAC Power* (New York: Norton, 1984), 72.

**FIGURE 16-3 Proportion of PAC Contributions Going to Incumbents and to Challengers in Congressional Races, 1972–1988**
In allocating campaign contributions, PACs favor incumbent members of Congress over their challengers by a wide margin. *Source: Estimated from Federal Election Commission data.*

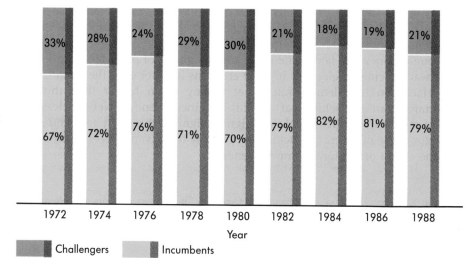

ers from running against them. Senator Daniel Patrick Moynihan raised more than $3 million before his 1988 New York race and eventually faced a weak challenger who had difficulty raising enough money to run a credible race.

## PARTY COMPETITIVENESS AND MONEY

The electoral competitiveness of a state or district affects the flow of campaign funds. If a House or Senate race promises to be reasonably close, it is likely to attract a strong challenger, considerable attention, and a lot of money. In allocating their funds, PACs and the political parties target campaigns in which the incumbent has a chance of being defeated. One PAC director stated, "[We] challenge uncooperative incumbents only when research shows they are vulnerable."[43]

A race without an incumbent—called an **open-seat election**—nearly always brings out a strong candidate from each party and involves heavy spending, especially when party competition in the state or district is strong. In 1988, for example, there were twenty-seven open-seat races for the House; on the average, each pair of major-party candidates spent $910,000 for the House races. These averages were about twice the amounts spent on other House races in the same year.

## Congressional Elections and the Relationship between Representatives and Voters

What does the nature of congressional elections imply for the relationship between members of Congress and the nation's voters? The principal effect of congressional elections is to orient individual members of Congress toward the state or district they represent. Congressional campaigns are not so much national events as "local events with national consequences."[44] They are local events in the sense that candidates act as individuals who aim to please local voters in 50 states and 435 districts, not as members of a national party addressing a national electorate on a common platform. These candidate-centered campaigns serve to decentralize the voters' choice: each congressional campaign, in effect, is a separate event (although the outcome in some cases is influenced by national events, such as the condition of the economy). Candidate-centered campaigns also serve to convince the winners that their victories were personal triumphs that demonstrated the strength of their policy views and personalities.[45]

This parochialism is carried into office. Reelection is the member's personal responsibility and is most reliably pursued by devotion to constituency needs and interests. Members of Congress always keep the home state or district in mind, a tendency that has become increasingly evident in recent decades as elections have become less party-oriented and more candidate-oriented.[46]

---

**The Influence of PACs**
Many people believe that PACs exercise too much influence over politics and government. However, attempts by some members of Congress to curb the power of PACs have not attracted majority support. Is it likely that such congressional support will ever materialize? Why, or why not? Does the fact that members of Congress set the ground rules for congressional campaigns, including levels of PAC support, represent a threat to democracy?

*Any government is free to the people under it where the laws rule and the people are a party to the laws.*

William Penn

---

[43]Quoted in ibid., 79.
[44]Randall B. Ripley, *Congress: Process and Policy*, 3d ed. (New York: Norton, 1983), 76.
[45]John Kingdon, *Candidates for Office: Beliefs and Strategies* (New York: Random House, 1968), 29.
[46]James Reston, "This Is Democracy?" *New York Times*, November 6, 1986.

In today's candidate-centered congressional campaigns, the key operatives are professional consultants rather than party leaders. Roger Ailes is in great demand as a consultant to Republican candidates. (Phil Huber/Black Star)

★ ANALYZE THE ISSUE

**The Public's Influence on Representatives**
Members of Congress now win election largely through their own efforts rather than through political parties. In this situation, does the influence that constituents have on their particular representative in Congress have any necessary relation to the larger question of whether the public as a whole has influence over Congress as a whole? In answering, bear in mind that each member of Congress is but one of 435 House members or 100 senators.

The point can be overstated. Representation is a complex process, and local and national interests complement each other more often than they conflict with each other. Moreover, changes in campaign technology and congressional staffing have enabled members of Congress to pursue local interests aggressively while also paying attention to national issues. Members of Congress have no good reason to ignore the vote-getting potential of pork-barreling and the service strategy; the legwork these efforts require can usually be delegated to staff and interested groups, while the member gets the credit for their accomplishments. The goodwill that a member accumulates through such activities can give him or her greater confidence about reelection and thus more freedom to address national problems of personal interest. To be sure, some members of Congress choose to play it safe once they attain office, contenting themselves with service to constituents and the advocacy of uncontroversial policy positions, while avoiding speaking out on difficult national issues.[47] Their purpose is simply to stay in Congress, basking in the prestige and forgoing a record of real accomplishment. But for most members, the ideal situation is to have enough electoral mastery to pursue national policy objectives without fear of defeat in the next election. For all members, however, the starting point is attention to constituency interests: this is the common denominator in an institution where each member must see to his or her own reelection.

From the public's perspective, the local orientation of Congress's members has mixed implications. On the one hand, local interests achieve greater representation than they would if members of Congress were preoccupied with national issues. The Johnson administration's Model Cities program of the 1960s, for example, was originally formulated as a way to revitalize the nation's depressed urban centers, such as New York, Detroit, and Chicago. However, members from states and districts with no large cities refused to vote for the program until it was modified to include smaller and thriving cities within their constituencies, such as Cody, Bangor, and San Jose. On the other hand, this localism raises troubling issues of self-government, not the least of which is the efficient use of society's resources. The Model Cities program became less cost-effective when eligibility was extended to cities that were not in dire need of federal assistance.

Localism also has the effect of reducing collective accountability in Congress. Members who say they are in Washington primarily to take care of the needs of their constituents are in a position to deny responsibility for Congress's governing failures. In the absence of strong and cohesive national parties, U.S. senators and representatives are not obligated to adhere to a national agenda but instead can act as free agents. In fact, incumbents often campaign against Congress itself, criticizing its policy failures while denying any personal responsibility for them.[48] Members of Congress can have it both ways, aligning themselves with the institution's successes and disavowing any part in its shortcomings. The voters are left to wonder where they should assign the real responsibility for Congress's collective performance.

Accountability is further diminished by the capacity of incumbents to insulate

[47]Morris P. Fiorina, "Electoral Margins, Constituency Influence, and Policy Moderation: A Critical Reassessment," *American Politics Quarterly* 1 (1973): 479–498.
[48]Fenno, *Home Style*, 167.

★ HOW THE UNITED
STATES COMPARES

**National Office, Local Orientation**

Whereas legislators in most other democracies are preoccupied with national affairs, members of the U.S. Congress divide their attention between national and local concerns. Membership in Congress provides U.S. senators and representatives with the large personal budget and staff they need to retain the support of constituents in the home state or district—support that they must have if they are to be reelected. Incumbency also makes it relatively easy for members of Congress to raise money for their reelection campaigns—typically half a million dollars or more for representatives and several million dollars for senators. Many members focus so intently on constituent services and public relations that, in effect, their reelection campaigns last as long as their term of office.

In contrast, members of the British Parliament's House of Commons concentrate on national matters because their chances of reelection depend more on their party's nationwide popularity than on their services to local constituents. Each member has just one secretary instead of a large staff. Most members of Parliament spend only a few thousand dollars on reelection campaigns that last just a few weeks.

themselves by obtaining pork-barrel projects and services for constituents. The electorate is then likely to judge an incumbent more on his or her ability to deliver such benefits than on his or her policy positions.[49] Sometimes the resources of office also enable incumbents to scare off strong challengers, thus reducing the voters' alternatives even further.

Without a doubt, the mere fact that incumbents maintain close contact with their constituents in order to secure reelection helps keep them responsive to the public. However, this form of popular influence is much weaker than that associated with the replacement of incumbents by new legislators who are more in step with current opinions. For example, because of the advantages of incumbency, the House of Representatives remained securely in Democratic control when voters turned to Republican presidents in 1980, 1984, and 1988. Before the modern era of congressional careerism and secure incumbency, the outcomes of House races were more responsive to changes in popular opinion. In 1894, for example, when economic hard times and the issue of free silver were working to the Republicans' advantage, they turned a 218–127 Democratic majority in the House of Representatives into a 244–105 majority of their own.[50]

In sum, a crucial fact about elections to Congress is that the people who are already in Congress have an interest in remaining there and, at least in the case of House members, have the resources to stay there. The consequences of this situation will be examined further in the next two chapters.

[49]Cover and Mayhew, "Decline of Competitive Congressional Elections," 79.
[50]R. Hal Williams, *Years of Decision* (New York: Wiley, 1978), 162.

## Summary

Members of Congress, once elected, are likely to be reelected. Many states and districts are heavily Republican or Democratic, and candidates of the majority party in these situations almost always win. Incumbency itself provides important advantages. Members of Congress have large staffs and can pursue a "service strategy" of responding to the needs of individual constituents. They also can secure pork-barrel projects for their state or district and thus demonstrate their concern for constituents. House members gain a greater advantage from these activities than do senators, whose larger constituencies make it harder for them to build close personal relations with voters. Incumbency does have some disadvantages. Members of Congress must take positions on controversial issues, may blunder into a political scandal or indiscretion, or may face strong challengers, any of which can reduce their reelection chances. By and large, however, the advantages of incumbency far outweigh the disadvantages, particularly for House members.

Incumbents' advantages extend into their reelection campaigns. Their influential positions in Congress make it easier for them to raise campaign funds. Only in competitive races can challengers count on being able to raise enough money to conduct effective campaigns. Senate races tend to be more competitive than House races, in part because Senate challengers are more likely to have a strong political base and other resources.

The congressional election process encourages members of Congress to be highly responsive to the interests of their respective states and districts. They campaign independently, so their campaigns are local events and thus are subject to local demands and expectations. Although this localism encourages members of Congress to remain attentive to constituency interests when they address national issues, it also results in cost inefficiencies and a lack of collective responsibility for what takes place in Congress. Moreover, because of the advantages of incumbency, Congress is somewhat insulated from changes in the political environment.

## Major Concepts

constituency              pork-barrel legislation
electoral mastery         redistricting
gerrymandering            service strategy
open-seat election

## Suggested Readings

Clem, Alan L. *The Making of Congressmen.* North Scituate, Mass.: Duxbury Press, 1976. An analysis of seven congressional campaigns in different states during 1974.

Fenno, Richard F., Jr. *Home Style: House Members in Their Districts.* Boston: Little, Brown, 1978. A penetrating analysis of the varying relationships between House members and their constituents.

Fiorina, Morris P. *Congress: Keystone of the Washington Establishment.* New Haven, Conn.: Yale University Press, 1977. An analysis of how incumbent congressmen use their office to win reelection.

Fowler, Linda L., and Robert D. McClure. *Political Ambition: Who Decides to Run for Congress.* New Haven, Conn.: Yale University Press, 1989. A study of why potentially strong challengers often choose *not* to run against a House incumbent, thereby reducing the voters' alternatives.

Gertzog, Irwin N. *Congressional Women: Their Recruitment, Treatment, and Behavior.* New York: Praeger, 1984. A study of women in Congress as candidates and representatives.

Hinckley, Barbara. *Congressional Elections.* Washington, D.C.: Congressional Quarterly Press, 1981. An evaluation of why particular congressional candidates win election.

Jacobson, Gary C. *Money in Congressional Elections.* New Haven, Conn.: Yale University Press, 1980. An analysis of the sources and impact of money in congressional campaigns.

Maisel, Louis Sandy. *From Obscurity to Oblivion: Running in the Congressional Primary.* Knoxville: University of Tennessee Press, 1982. A look at the frustrating experiences of candidates who run and lose in congressional primaries.

Mann, Thomas E. *Unsafe at Any Margin: Interpreting Congressional Elections.* Washington, D.C.: American Enterprise Institute, 1978. An assessment of the dynamics of congressional election outcomes.

Mayhew, David R. *Congress: The Electoral Connection.* New Haven, Conn.: Yale University Press, 1974. Analysis of how legislative activity is influenced by and affects the reelection of members of Congress.

# Chapter 17

## THE ORGANIZATION OF CONGRESS: DIVIDING THE WORK AND THE POWER

*A decentralized system [of power serves] the immediate needs of members of a professionalized Congress.*

*Lawrence Dodd and Richard Schott[1]*

In 1981, soon after taking office, Republican President Ronald Reagan pressed Congress for drastic cuts in domestic spending. His budget proposals included stricter eligibility requirements for social security recipients, cuts in public-service jobs and child nutrition programs, the disqualification of a million food-stamp recipients, the reduction of the maximum term of unemployment benefits from thirty-nine weeks to twenty-six, and cuts in federal loan programs for college students. Reagan argued that only deep budget cuts would restore the nation's faltering economy, and the U.S. Senate had a Republican majority that was prepared to follow his leadership. The House of Representatives was a different matter. It had a 243–192 Democratic majority, and the Speaker of the House was Thomas P. "Tip" O'Neill, a feisty liberal Democrat.

O'Neill had served in Congress during the period when Democratic presidents and congressional majorities had initiated many of the programs that Reagan proposed to chop, and O'Neill had supported all of them. He believed firmly that government was obligated to help society's underdogs and was determined to fight Reagan's proposals with all the authority of the Speaker's office. Appealing to the Democratic majority that had placed him in the House's top position, O'Neill called for the defeat of Reagan's plan. O'Neill himself describes the outcome:

---

[1]Lawrence C. Dodd and Richard L. Schott, *Congress and the Administrative State* (New York: John Wiley and Sons, 1979), 326.

I screeched and I hollered and I fought his [Reagan's] program every way I could, but there are times that you just can't buck a trend. I got clobbered so badly that I felt like the guy in the old joke who gets hit by a steamroller. Somebody runs to tell his wife about the accident.

"I'm taking a bath right now," she says. "Could you just slip him under the door?"

That's what happened to me during the President's first year, except that they didn't bother to slip me under the door. They just left me lying out on the street.[2]

Speaker O'Neill's clobbering, as Congress enacted into law one Reagan proposal after another, illustrates the key fact that congressional power is diffused. In most democratic countries, power in the national legislature is centralized: there is a dominant chamber and the top leaders are powerful, the committees weak, and the parties unified.[3] The U.S. Congress is unusual in being such a fragmented institution: it has two equal chambers, elected leaders with limited powers, a vast network of relatively independent and powerful committees and subcommittees, and members who are free to follow or ignore other members of their party.[4]

Although power is widely dispersed in Congress, national policies must still be decided by Congress. If our national legislature were completely splintered —with its 435 House members and 100 senators each going a separate way—the only result would be chaos. Congress must be able to legislate resolutions of national issues, an imperative that requires a degree of centralization. Thus it should be no surprise that Congress has periodically tightened its organization to enhance its capacity to govern.[5] As recently as the 1970s, Congress enacted major reforms: the budgetary process was altered to give Congress greater control over national spending priorities; the power of committee chairs was reduced in order to increase the influence of the membership as a whole; the Senate filibuster was weakened to make it more difficult for a handful of senators to obstruct legislation; and the top party leadership, particularly the House Speaker, was given more control over the policy agenda.

Yet the natural long-term trend in Congress has been toward fragmentation. Junior and mid-career members—who constitute the large majority of all legislators—have resisted reforms that would greatly centralize power. In fact, the most significant of the 1970s reforms may have been a decentralizing measure: the number and authority of congressional subcommittees were expanded. There are now about 250 subcommittees in Congress, each with its separate leader and policy jurisdiction. Furthermore, whenever Congress has enacted centralizing reforms, fragmenting pressures have soon made themselves felt. Most members of Congress do not acquire power as rapidly as they

[2]Thomas P. (Tip) O'Neill with William Novak, *Man of the House: The Life and Political Memoirs of Speaker Tip O'Neill* (New York: Random House, 1987).

[3]See John E. Schwarz and L. Earl Shaw, *The United States Congress in Comparative Perspective* (Hindsdale, Ill.: Dryden Press, 1976).

[4]Ibid.

[5]See Lawrence C. Dodd, "A Theory of Congressional Cycles: Solving the Puzzles of Change," in Gerald Wright, Leroy Rieselbach, and Lawrence C. Dodd, *Congress and Policy Change* (New York: Agathon, 1986).

wish and thus seek ways to hasten their ascendancy, a goal that can be achieved most easily through organizational changes that give more power to less senior members.[6]

This chapter's main purpose is to describe how Congress is organized to do its work, a subject that must be understood if Congress's contribution to the American system of self-government is to be properly understood. Congress must translate public needs and demands into legislation. The way in which Congress is organized has a major influence on this process. In the next chapter we will discuss how the fragmented organization of Congress serves the personal power and reelection needs of its members but weakens the institution's collective power and makes it better suited to handle narrow policy issues than broad ones. This chapter establishes a basis for that discussion by describing the decentralized structure of Congress. The following points are emphasized in the chapter:

★ *Congress is organized in part along political party lines; its collective leadership is provided by party leaders of the House of Representatives and the Senate.* However, these party leaders do not have great formal powers. Their authority rests mainly on the fact that they have been entrusted with leadership responsibility by other senators or representatives of their party.

★ *The work of Congress is done mainly through its committees and subcommittees, each of which has its leader (a chair) and its policy jurisdiction.* The committee system of Congress allows a broad sharing of power and leadership, which serves the power and reelection needs of Congress's members but fragments the institution.

★ *Because Congress is organizationally fragmented, it is better designed to block or delay legislation than to enact legislation and is better suited to handle narrow policy issues than broad ones.*

## Congressional Leadership

The writers of the Constitution feared any concentration of power, including an overly powerful legislative branch, so they divided Congress into two separate and equal houses. One result is that Congress has many leaders, no one of whom speaks authoritatively for the whole institution. Although the Speaker of the House is that chamber's chief spokesman, he would not presume to act as the voice of the Senate, just as the Senate majority leader would never claim to be spokesman for the House. Furthermore, these chamber leaders do not even monopolize leadership in their separate houses. In both the House and the Senate, there are minority-party leaders *plus* another and independent set of leaders: the chairs of Congress's powerful committees and subcommittees.

### PARTY LEADERSHIP IN CONGRESS

The House and Senate are organized along party lines. When members of Congress are sworn in at the start of a new two-year session, they automatically join either the Democratic or Republican caucus in their chamber. These

[6]Ibid.

**TABLE 17-1 Number of Democrats and Republicans in House of Representatives and Senate, 1971–1990**

|  | 1971–72 | 1973–74 | 1975–76 | 1977–78 | 1979–80 | 1981–82 | 1983–84 | 1985–86 | 1987–88 | 1989–90 |
|---|---|---|---|---|---|---|---|---|---|---|
| **House** | | | | | | | | | | |
| Democrats | 255* | 243* | 290* | 293 | 276 | 243* | 269* | 253* | 258* | 262* |
| Republicans | 180 | 192 | 145 | 142 | 159 | 192 | 166 | 182 | 177 | 173 |
| **Senate** | | | | | | | | | | |
| Democrats | 54* | 57* | 61* | 61 | 59 | 47 | 45 | 47 | 54* | 55* |
| Republicans | 44 | 43 | 39 | 39 | 41 | 53 | 55 | 53 | 46 | 45 |

*Chamber not controlled by the president's party.

caucuses select **party leaders** to represent the party's interests in the full chamber and to give some central direction to the body's deliberations.

## The House Leadership

The main party leaders in the House are the Speaker, majority leader, majority whip, minority leader, and minority whip. The Constitution provides only for the post of Speaker, who is to be chosen by a vote of the entire House. In practice, this means that the Speaker is selected by the majority party's members, since they have enough votes to choose one of their own. (Table 17-1 shows the party composition of Congress during the past two decades.)

The Speaker is often said to be the second most powerful official in Washington. The Speaker has the right to speak first on legislation during House debate and has the power to recognize members—that is, give them permission to speak from the floor. Since the House places a time limit on floor debate, not everyone has a chance to speak on a bill, and the Speaker can sometimes influence legislation simply by exercising his power to decide who will speak

The U.S. Capitol in Washington, D.C., with the Senate wing in the foreground. The House of Representatives meets in the wing at the left of the central rotunda (under the dome). The offices of the House and Senate party leaders—Speaker, vice-president, majority and minority leaders and whips—are located in the Capitol; other members of Congress have offices in buildings nearby. (Ellis Herwig/Stock, Boston)

and when.[7] The Speaker also chooses the chairperson and majority-party members of the powerful House Rules Committee, which controls the scheduling of bills for debate.[8] Legislation the Speaker wants passed is likely to reach the floor under conditions favorable to its enactment; for example, he may ask the Rules Committee to delay sending a bill to the floor until he has lined up enough votes for its passage. The Speaker has other ways of directing the work of the House. He assigns bills to committees, can place time limits on the reporting of bills out of committees, and assigns members to conference committees. (The importance of these powers over committee action will become apparent later in the chapter.)

The Speaker is active in developing his party's position on issues and in persuading his fellow party members in the House to follow his lead.[9] The Speaker chairs the House Steering and Policy Committee, which has ongoing responsibility for developing and promoting the majority party's legislative program. Although the Speaker cannot compel party members to support this program, they look to him for leadership. He can draw upon shared partisan views and has a few rewards at his disposal for cooperative party members; he can, for instance, help them obtain pork-barrel projects and committee assignments.

The Speaker is assisted by the House majority leader, who is elected by the majority party's members. The majority leader acts as the party's floor leader, organizing the debate on bills. He also works in other ways to advance his party's goals in the House; for example, he may urge individual party members to support or defeat a legislative measure. Typically, the majority leader is a highly experienced and skilled legislator.[10] Jim Wright served in the House for twenty-two years before he was chosen majority leader in 1977 (he became Speaker in 1987 upon O'Neill's retirement).

There is also a majority-party whip, who has the important job of soliciting votes from party members and of informing them when critical votes are scheduled. Whips have been known to track down members who are out of town and persuade them to rush back to Washington for an important vote. As voting is getting under way on the House floor, whips will sometimes position themselves where they can easily be seen by party members and let them know how the leadership wants them to vote by giving a thumbs-up or thumbs-down signal.

The minority party, currently the Republicans, has its own leaders in the House. The House minority leader heads his party's caucus and policy committee and plays the leading role in developing his party's legislative positions. If the president is also of the minority party, the minority leader will work closely with him on legislative issues. The minority leader is assisted by a

---

[7]Barbara Sinclair, *Majority Leadership in the U.S. House* (Baltimore: Johns Hopkins University Press, 1983), 34–41.

[8]See Bruce Oppenheimer, "The Rules Committee: New Arm of Leadership in a Decentralized House," in Lawrence C. Dodd and Bruce I. Oppenheimer, eds., *Congress Reconsidered* (New York: Praeger, 1977), 96–116; Spark M. Matsuna and Ping Chen, *Rulemakers of the House* (Urbana: University of Illinois Press, 1976).

[9]Barbara Hinckley, *Stability and Change in Congress*, 2d ed. (New York: Harper & Row, 1978), 113–114; Sidney Waldman, "Majority Leadership in the House of Representatives," *Political Science Quarterly*, Fall 1980, 377.

[10]Roger H. Davidson and Walter J. Oleszek, *Congress and Its Members* (Washington, D.C.: Congressional Quarterly Press, 1981), 171.

minority whip, who is responsible for lining up party members' support on legislation and informing them when votes are scheduled.

## The Senate Leadership

In the Senate, the most important party leadership position is that of the majority leader, who heads the majority-party caucus. His role is much like that of the Speaker of the House, in that he formulates the majority's legislative policies and strategies and seeks to develop influential relationships with his colleagues. Like the Speaker, the Senate majority leader chairs the party's policy committee and acts as the party's voice in his chamber.[11] He works closely with the president in developing legislative programs if they are of the same party. When Howard Baker was the Senate majority leader, he said that part of his job was to act as President Reagan's "point man" in the Senate.[12] For example, when the Reagan administration in 1981 sought congressional approval for the sale of sophisticated radar planes (AWACS) to Saudi Arabia, Baker advised the White House not to press for a vote in order to give undecided senators enough time to study the effect of the sale on the security of Israel. Reagan agreed to hold off, and the sale was eventually approved.[13]

Unlike the Speaker of the House, the Senate majority leader is not the presiding officer of his chamber. The Constitution assigns this responsibility to the vice-president of the United States. However, since the vice-president is allowed to vote in the Senate only to break a tie, he seldom presides over Senate debates. The Senate has a president *pro tempore,* who, in the absence of the vice-president, has the right to preside over the Senate. President *pro tempore* is

[11]Robert L. Peabody, *Leadership in the Congress: Stability, Succession, and Change* (Boston: Little, Brown, 1976), 35.
[12]CBS News, February 27, 1987.
[13]Davidson and Oleszek, *Congress and Its Members,* 185.

Robert Dole (R-Kans.), minority leader of the U.S. Senate. (Paul Conklin)

largely an honorary position that by tradition is usually held by the majority party's senior member. The presiding official has limited power, since each senator has the right to speak at any length on bills under consideration.

The Senate's tradition of unlimited debate stems mainly from its relatively small size (only 100 members, compared to the House's 435 members). Moreover, senators like to view themselves as the equals of all others in their chamber and are thus reluctant to take orders from their leadership.[14] For such reasons, the Senate majority leader's position is weaker than that of the Speaker of the House. Robert Byrd, former Senate majority leader, jokingly called himself a "slave," saying that he served his fellow Democrats' needs without commanding their votes.[15]

The Senate majority leader's actual power depends significantly on his persuasive skills.[16] Lacking strong formal powers, he must convince party members that their interests coincide with his. Lyndon B. Johnson, who served as Senate majority leader from 1955 to 1960, had an exceptionally intense face-to-face style of persuasion which came to be known as "The Treatment":

> The Treatment could last ten minutes or four hours. It came, enveloping its target, at the LBJ Ranch swimming pool, in one of LBJ's offices, in the Senate cloakroom, on the floor of the Senate itself—wherever Johnson might find a fellow Senator within his reach. Its tone could be supplication, accusation, cajolery, exuberance, scorn, tears, complaint, the hint of threat. It was all of these together. It ran the gamut of human emotions. Its velocity was breathtaking, and it was all in one direction. Interjections from the target were rare. Johnson anticipated them before they could be spoken. He moved in close, his face a scant millimeter from his target, his eyes widening and narrowing, his eyebrows rising and falling. From his pockets poured clippings, memos, statistics. Mimicry, humor, and the genius of analogy made The Treatment an almost hypnotic experience and rendered the target stunned and helpless.[17]

No majority leader since Johnson has tried the same approach, partly because junior senators have become more independent of their party leadership.[18]

Like the House, the Senate has a majority whip; however, this position is less important in the Senate because that body's members are less subject to persuasive tactics. Nevertheless, the Senate majority whip sees to it that members know when important votes are scheduled and ensures that the party's strongest advocates on a legislative measure are present for the debate. "The leadership must have the right members at the right place at the right time," said Senator Byrd.[19]

Finally, the Senate has a minority leader and minority whip, whose roles are comparable to those performed by their counterparts in the House. As befits "a chamber of equals," the majority leadership in the Senate usually consults the

---

[14]See Randall B. Ripley, *Power in the Senate* (New York: St. Martin's Press, 1969), 104–106.
[15]Frank H. Mackamar, *Understanding Congressional Leadership: The State of the Art* (Pekin, Ill.: Dickson Center, 1981), 9.
[16]Randall B. Ripley, *Party Leaders in the House of Representatives* (Washington, D.C.: Brookings Institution, 1967), 12–14.
[17]Rowland Evans and Robert Novak, *Lyndon B. Johnson: The Exercise of Power* (New York: New American Library, 1966), 104, cited in Peabody, *Leadership in the Congress*, 341–342.
[18]Davidson and Oleszek, *Congress and Its Members*, 178.
[19]Quoted in ibid., 185.

**TABLE 17-2  Majority and Minority Party Leaders in House and Senate, 1989–1990**

| *Majority* | *Minority* |
|---|---|
| *House (Democrats)* | *House (Republicans)* |
| Speaker: Thomas S. Foley (Wash.) | |
| Majority leader: Richard A. Gephardt (Mo.) | Minority leader: Robert Michel (Ill.) |
| Whip: William H. Gray 3d (Pa.) | Whip: Newt Gingrich (Ga.) |
| *Senate (Democrats)* | *Senate (Republicans)* |
| President *pro tempore*: Robert C. Byrd (W.Va.) | |
| Majority leader: George Mitchell (Maine) | Minority leader: Robert Dole (Kans.) |
| Whip: Alan Cranston (Calif.) | Whip: Alan Simpson (Wyo.) |

minority leadership on the scheduling of legislation. (The Senate and House majority and minority leaders for the 101st Congress (1989–1990) are listed in Table 17-2.)

## COMMITTEE CHAIRPERSONS

Party leaders are not the only top leaders in Congress. Most of the work of Congress takes place in the meetings of its thirty-eight standing (permanent) committees and their numerous subcommittees, each of which is headed by a chairperson. These chairpersons are largely free from control by the party leadership.[20]

### The Seniority Principle

Committee chairs are always members of the majority party, and they almost always have the most **seniority**—the most consecutive years of service on a particular committee. The seniority principle for selecting committee chairs began in the Senate in the mid–nineteenth century but was not formally applied in the House until the early twentieth century.[21] Before that time, the Speaker picked all committee chairs, who were then expected to back his policies. Abuses of authority by Speaker Joseph Cannon led the House to end this practice in 1911.

The seniority principle remained virtually absolute until the House Democratic majority decided in the early 1970s that committee chairs would henceforth be chosen by secret ballot. Even so, the House majority has deviated from the seniority principle in only a few exceptional cases. Three House chairs were stripped of their leadership positions in 1975 for abuses of power. In 1985 Mel Price of Illinois was voted out of the chairmanship of one of the House's most important committees, Armed Services; although Price was liked by his Democratic colleagues on Armed Services, he was eighty years old and unable to represent the committee effectively on television.

Dan Rostenkowski (D-Ill.), chairman of the House Ways and Means Committee. (Dennis Brack/Black Star)

[20]See Barbara Hinckley, *The Seniority System in Congress* (Bloomington: Indiana University Press, 1971), 112.

[21]See Nelson W. Polsby, Miriam Gallagher, and Barry S. Rundquist, "The Growth of the Seniority System in the U.S. House of Representatives," *American Political Science Review* 63 (September 1969): 787–807.

A committee chair schedules committee meetings, determines the order in which committee bills are considered, presides over committee discussions, directs the committee's majority staff, and can choose to lead the debate when a committee bill reaches the floor. For many members, a committee chairmanship is the highest congressional position they can hope to attain. Because length of tenure on a committee is normally the deciding factor in the selection of its chair, members of Congress often stay on the same committees indefinitely.

### The Advantages and Disadvantages of the Seniority System

The reason for the persistence of the seniority system lies in the substantial advantages it affords: the seniority principle reduces the number of bitter power struggles that would occur if chairmanships were decided by open competition, provides experienced committee leadership, and enables members to look forward to the reward of a chairmanship after years of committee service.[22]

Yet the seniority system is not without problems. For one thing, seniority can elevate an individual who is unsuited for leadership, often simply because of advanced age. Carl Hayden of Arizona was first elected to Congress in 1912, the year the state was admitted to the Union. Hayden served fifteen years in the House and another forty-two years in the Senate. By the time he retired as chairman of the Senate Appropriations Committee in 1969, at the age of ninety-two, Hayden could barely hear or see and often dozed off during committee meetings.

The seniority system has also been criticized as favoring members from districts and states where party competition is minimal. Legislators from such areas are easily reelected to one term after another, thereby accumulating the seniority that can elevate them to the top of committees. Before the early 1970s, many of these safe seats were in the South; nearly half of the standing committees were chaired by southern Democrats, who were substantially more conservative than the Democratic membership as a whole. Virginia's Howard Smith chaired the House Rules Committee in the 1950s and 1960s; when civil rights legislation reached his committee, Smith would leave Washington for his Virginia farm. Because the Rules Committee could not meet unless he called it into session, Smith's absence was sometimes enough to persuade the full committee to table a bill. Speaker of the House Sam Rayburn complained that he often had to "beg" Smith to release a bill from the committee so that it could be voted on by the full membership of the House. Smith's tactics were a contributing factor in the House's 1975 decision to allow the Speaker to appoint the Rules Committee's chair and majority-party members. Moreover, a chair now has less discretionary power; for example, a majority of the committee members can vote to convene meetings in the chair's absence. Because these reforms greatly reduced the worst abuses, the seniority system has not been criticized much in recent years.

### SUBCOMMITTEE CHAIRPERSONS

Congressional organization and leadership extend into subcommittees, which are smaller units within each committee formed to conduct specific aspects of the committee's business. The House has nearly 150 subcommittees and the

---

[22]Hinckley, *Seniority System in Congress,* 111.

Senate about 100, each with a chair who decides its order of business, presides over its meetings, and directs its staff.

Before the reforms of the 1970s, subcommittees were controlled largely by committee chairs. Some committee chairs appointed themselves to head each of their subcommittees. A few committees, such as House Ways and Means (taxation), did not even have subcommittees: all power was vested in the full committee and thus was concentrated in its chair.

In 1973, in a move intended partly to limit the power of Ways and Means chairman Wilbur Mills of Arkansas, whose alcoholism had made him erratic, House Democrats adopted the so-called Subcommittee Bill of Rights, which requires each House committee of more than twenty members to maintain at least four subcommittees. The House also determined that no representative can chair more than one committee and one subcommittee at a time, and it placed selection of subcommittee chairs in the hands of majority-party members of each committee.[23] These measures give House subcommittees a substantial degree of independence from their committee and its chair.

In 1977 the Senate altered its subcommittee structure, limiting to three the number of committee and subcommittee chairmanships that a senator can hold at the same time. In both the House and the Senate, seniority on the full committee is a primary criterion, but not always the decisive one, in the selection of a subcommittee's chair.[24]

Reform leaders contended that these subcommittee changes would make Congress "more democratic."[25] Indeed, an effect of the subcommittee reforms has been to create a broader congressional leadership corps. At present about half of the majority party's House members chair a committee or subcommittee. In the smaller Senate, all members of the majority party, even those newly elected, normally head at least one committee or subcommittee. However, members of Congress had more than democracy on their minds in enacting the reforms of the 1970s. By creating more leadership positions, they were serving their personal reelection and power needs.[26] Less senior members would no longer have to wait many years before rising to a position of institutional authority.

## CONGRESSIONAL LEADERSHIP TODAY: WIDER DISTRIBUTION OF POWER

The reforms of the 1970s have given Congress the look of a feudal system, with more than 200 senators and representatives presiding as committee or subcommittee chairs over separate "kingdoms," or policy spheres. These leaders take a proprietary attitude toward the legislation that falls within the jurisdiction of

[23]See Steven H. Haeberle, "The Institutionalization of the Subcommittee in the United States House of Representatives," *Journal of Politics* 40 (November 1978): 1054–1065.

[24]Thomas R. Wolanin, "Committee Seniority and the Choice of House Sub-committee Chairmen, 80th–91st Congresses," *Journal of Politics* 36 (1974): 687–702.

[25]David Rohde, "Committee Reform in the House of Representatives and Subcommittee Bill of Rights," *Annals of the American Academy of Political and Social Sciences* 411 (1974): 39–47; Leroy N. Rieselbach, "Assessing Congressional Change, or What Hath Reform Wrought or Wreaked?" in Dennis Hale, ed., *The United States Congress* (Boston: Boston College Press, 1982), 179–181.

[26]David E. Price, "Congressional Committees in the Policy Process," in Lawrence C. Dodd and Bruce I. Oppenheimer, eds., *Congress Reconsidered*, 2d ed. (Washington, D.C.: Congressional Quarterly Press, 1981), 162.

their committees or subcommittees, and they naturally seek to influence its content and to get it placed high on the congressional agenda. Of course, bills of major national importance receive more attention from the whole chamber than do other legislative measures, but the wide distribution of power within Congress reduces its capacity to focus its work.

The enduring tendency for seniority to serve as the basis for allocating the chairmanships of committees and subcommittees places these leaders largely outside the power of the House or Senate's elected leaders.[27] The Speaker of the House and the Senate majority leader have little choice but to defer to senior committee and subcommittee members on policy issues within their jurisdictions.[28] Seniority in committee also reduces the power of party leaders in another way: the principle ensures that the persons who chair the committees will normally not be replaced. Party leaders have tended to leave the committees alone and only later to work for the passage, defeat, or amendment of the legislation they propose.[29]

The increased importance of subcommittees has multiplied the problems of the elected congressional leadership. The Speaker of the House and the Senate majority leader have limited formal powers in any case, and the rise of the subcommittees has tested the limits of informal authority. James Sundquist concludes:

> The headlong trend toward democracy, and dispersal of power, in the Senate and the House has changed the task of leadership. . . . The problem . . . is to organize the new individualism—or new fragmentation—into some kind of working whole. And the leaders must do that without seeming to grasp for power, because the resistance of the rank and file of the new-style congressman to any hint of bossism would be instant. . . . Junior members will accept leadership only on their terms.[30]

## Congressional Committees and Subcommittees

When Congress first met in 1789, it had no committees. However, committees formed within a few years in the House, and the first Senate committees were established in 1816. At present there are twenty-two standing committees in the House and sixteen in the Senate (see Table 17-3). A **standing committee** is a permanent committee with responsibility for a particular area of public policy. Both the House and the Senate, for example, have a committee that specializes in handling foreign policy issues. Other important committees are those that deal with agriculture, commerce, the national budget, the interior (natural resources and public lands), defense, government spending, labor, the judiciary, and taxation. House committees, which average about thirty-five members each, are larger than the Senate committees, with about eighteen members.

In addition to its standing committees, Congress has a number of temporary

★ ANALYZE THE ISSUE

**Institutional Power vs. Individual Power**
The history of congressional organization, at least in the twentieth century, is the history of conflict between institutional power and individual power. Can this conflict ever be resolved? Is it possible for Congress as a whole and its individual members to be strong at the same time? Which position—a strong Congress or individually powerful members—appears to win out generally? Why? What are the consequences for the American governing system?

[27]Hinckley, *Seniority System in Congress*, 111.
[28]Lawrence C. Dodd and Bruce I. Oppenheimer, "The House in Transition: Change and Consolidation," in Dodd and Oppenheimer, *Congress Reconsidered*, 2d ed., 46–55.
[29]Randall B. Ripley, *Congress*, 3d ed. (New York: Norton, 1983), 242–243.
[30]James L. Sundquist, *The Decline and Resurgence of Congress* (Washington, D.C.: Brookings Institution, 1981), 395.

**TABLE 17-3  The Standing Committees of Congress**

| House of Representatives | Senate |
| --- | --- |
| Agriculture | Agriculture, Nutrition, and Forestry |
| Appropriations | Appropriations |
| Armed Services | Armed Services |
| Banking, Finance, and Urban Affairs | Banking, Housing, and Urban Affairs |
| Budget | Budget |
| District of Columbia | Commerce, Science, and Transportation |
| Education and Labor | Energy and Natural Resources |
| Energy and Commerce | Environment and Public Works |
| Foreign Affairs | Finance |
| Government Operations | Foreign Relations |
| House Administration | Governmental Affairs |
| Interior and Insular Affairs | Judiciary |
| Judiciary | Labor and Human Resources |
| Merchant Marine and Fisheries | Rules and Administration |
| Post Office and Civil Service | Small Business |
| Public Works and Transportation | Veterans' Affairs |
| Rules | |
| Science, Space, and Technology | |
| Small Business | |
| Standards of Official Conduct | |
| Veterans' Affairs | |
| Ways and Means | |

committees called **select committees,** which are created to perform specific tasks and are disbanded after they have done so. They generally do not have legislative authority but can conduct hearings and investigations. At present the

The Senate Select Committee on Indian Affairs reviews legislation that affects Native Americans living on reservations, including the Taos Pueblo in New Mexico. (Paul Conklin)

Members of Congress from tobacco-growing states dominate the congressional subcommittees that have jurisdiction over the federal government's tobacco policy. The same tendency is reflected in the makeup of other committees. (J. P. Laffont/Sygma).

experience, party loyalty, ideology, region, length of congressional service, and work habits weigh heavily in the determination of appointments to these prestigious committees. In both the House and the Senate, however, the choice rests with the special party committees established for the purpose of deciding standing-committee assignments.[38]

### Obtaining a Subcommittee Assignment

Subcommittee assignments are handled differently. The members of each party on a committee decide who among them will serve on each of its subcommittees. The members' preferences, seniority, and backgrounds and the interests of their constituencies are key influences on subcommittee assignments. Of the thirteen members of the Tobacco and Peanuts Subcommittee of the House Agriculture Committee, for example, all but three are from the South—the region where most of the nation's tobacco and peanut crops are grown.

## Institutional Support for the Work of Congress

The range and complexity of the policy issues that Congress must confront have greatly increased in this century. To manage their work load, Congress's standing committees and their subcommittees have a large number of staff members, and four congressional agencies have been formed to advise Congress.

[38]Irwin N. Gertzog, "The Routinization of Committee Assignments in the U.S. House of Representatives," *American Journal of Political Science* 20 (1976): 693–712.

## COMMITTEE STAFFS

More than 3,000 people are employed by the House and Senate committees and subcommittees (see Figure 17-1). Unlike the members' personal staffs—which, as we saw in Chapter 16, concentrate on constituency relations—the committee staffs perform an almost entirely legislative function. They help to draft legislation, prepare reports, and participate in altering bills within committee. Committee staffs are also responsible for organizing legislative hearings— inviting witnesses, preparing questions, informing committee members of proposed legislation, and sometimes participating in hearings when members are absent.[39]

Although its institutional staff enhances Congress's legislative capacity, it also contributes to the fragmentation of congressional power. By specializing in their committees' or subcommittees' policy areas, staff members increase Congress's emphasis on a narrow range of issues. They are often more familiar with the technical details of legislation than are the members themselves.[40]

A committee's or subcommittee's employees are hired and fired by its chair or its ranking minority member. As a result, they usually adapt to his or her way of doing things.[41] Nevertheless, staff members' knowledge of a committee's or subcommittee's work enables them to influence its decisions. Some staff members, on their own initiative, even prepare drafts of legislation; by thus acting as "unelected representatives," they blur Congress's lines of authority even further.[42] Upon leaving the Senate in 1986, Barry Goldwater of Arizona complained that some staff members "don't have anything to do, so they sit

[39]Michael J. Malbin, "Delegation, Deliberation, and the New Role of Congressional Staff," in Thomas E. Mann and Norman Ornstein, eds., *The New Congress* (Washington, D.C.: American Enterprise Institute, 1981), 156–160; see also Harrison W. Fox and Susan Webb Hammond, *Congressional Staffs* (New York: Free Press, 1977).

[40]Robert H. Salisbury and Kenneth A. Shepsle, "Congressional Staff Turnover and the Ties-That-Bind," *American Political Science Review* 75 (June 1981): 381–396.

[41]Thomas P. Murphy, *The Politics of Congressional Committees* (Woodbury, N.Y.: Barron's, 1978), 38.

[42]Michael J. Malbin, *Unelected Representatives* (New York: Basic Books, 1980), 28.

Number of staff members

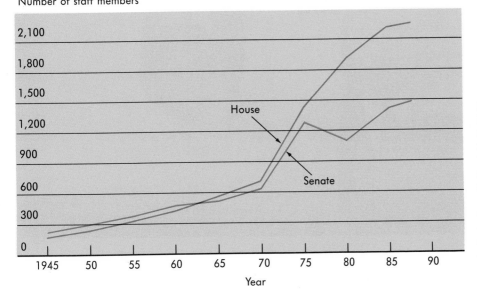

**FIGURE 17-1 Number of Staff Members Employed by Congressional Committees, 1947–1988**
The number of committee staff members has increased sharply since the mid-1960s. *Sources: 1947–1980, Roger H. Davidson and Walter J. Oleszek,* Congress and Its Members *(Washington, D.C.: Congressional Quarterly Press, 1981), 238; 1985, 1990, Staff, Clerk of House Office and Senate Finance Section.*

down and write amendments and bills. My god, the number of bills on the calendar every year is unbelievable."[43]

However, congressional staffers work within an institution where loyalty and deference to elected representatives are the norm. Staff members have room to initiate and advocate policy, but they can find themselves out of a job if they try to force their ideas on the elected members of Congress.[44]

## CONGRESSIONAL AGENCIES

Congress has four agencies to provide it with information and technical advice. The 6,800 employees of these agencies help to lessen Congress's dependence on the executive branch for information relevant to legislative decisions.

The General Accounting Office (GAO), with about 5,400 employees, is the largest congressional agency. Formed in 1921, it has the primary responsibility of overseeing executive agencies' spending of money that has been appropriated by Congress.[45] Recently the GAO was much in the news for bringing abuses by defense contractors to Congress's attention. (In one notorious instance, the GAO reported that the government was paying more than $1,000 apiece for wrenches available in hardware stores for less than $10.) In the past decade Congress has broadened the GAO's responsibilities to include program evaluations, such as a major study on the need to reform government-paid health programs.

[43]Quoted in *Time*, November 10, 1986, 25.
[44]Samuel C. Patterson, "The Professional Staffs of Congressional Committees," *Administrative Science Quarterly* 15 (1970): 22–37.
[45]See Frederick C. Mosher, *The GAO* (Boulder, Colo.: Westview Press, 1979).

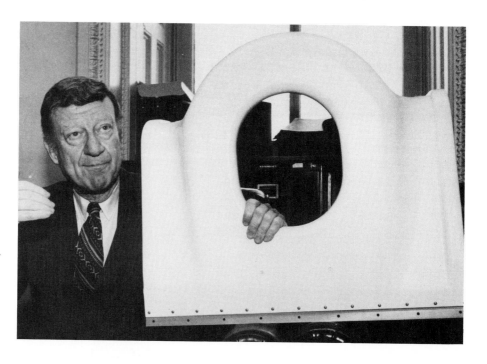

Findings by the General Accounting Office in the mid-1980s triggered a congressional investigation of wasteful defense spending. Here Senator William Roth (R-Del.) displays a plastic toilet-seat cover for a P-3 airplane, for which the Lockheed Corporation had tried to charge the U.S. Navy $640 apiece; Lockheed later agreed to drop the price to $100. (AP/Wide World Photos)

Created in 1914, the Congressional Research Service (CRS) is the oldest congressional agency and is part of the Library of Congress. (The CRS was originally the LRS—Legislative Reference Service.) The CRS is a nonpartisan reference agency. If a member of Congress wants historical or statistical information for a speech or bill, the CRS will provide it. It also prepares reports on pending legislative issues, although it makes no recommendations as to what action Congress should take. Finally, the CRS provides members with status reports and summaries of all bills currently under consideration in Congress. The 1,000-member staff of the CRS sometimes complains that it is too much Congress's errand boy (responding, for example, to a member's request for information with which to reply to a constituent's letter) and not enough of a research institute.

The Congressional Budget Office (CBO) is the newest agency, created by the Congressional Budget and Impoundment Control Act of 1974. The main role of the CBO's 200 employees is to provide Congress with projections of the nation's economic situation and of government expenditures and revenues.[46] The Office of Management and Budget (OMB) furnishes similar projections to the president, who incorporates them into the annual budget he submits to Congress. The CBO's figures enable Congress to scrutinize the president's budget proposals more thoroughly. During the Reagan years, the CBO consistently disagreed with the OMB on economic, tax, and spending trends, and nearly always turned out to be the more accurate of the two agencies.[*]

The Office of Technology Assessment (OTA), established in 1972, assesses technology policies and evaluates policy proposals in such areas as oil exploration and communications. Most of the work of the OTA's 200 employees could be done by other agencies, and some members of Congress have proposed that it be abolished.

In some ways, congressional agencies have strengthened Congress's ability to act as a collective body. Before the CBO was formed, for example, Congress lacked the authoritative information that is needed to challenge the president's budget proposals. Congress is still at a disadvantage, but the CBO's budget estimates give the House and Senate Budget committees (also formed in 1974) a basis for an institutional response. These committees propose spending ceilings that, once approved by the full House and Senate, establish the broad limits of the federal budget.

In other ways, however, congressional agencies contribute to the fragmentation of Congress. These organizations are not controlled by the top leadership but are designed mainly to serve individual members, committees, and subcommittees.

---

[*]During Reagan's first administration the CBO and OMB estimates on unemployment, inflation, and interest rates often differed greatly. These estimates are very important in the budgetary process. If interest rates are higher than anticipated, for example, the government will pay more than expected for the money it borrows to balance the budget. Since the anticipated budget deficit affects the amount of government spending that Congress is willing to authorize, it is important for interest-rate projections to be as accurate as possible. In the early 1980s, the CBO's estimates were consistently more accurate than the OMB's. Critics alleged that the OMB's estimates were based on the Reagan administration's hopes rather than on realistic assessments.

[46]See Joel Havemann, *Congress and the Budget* (Bloomington: Indiana University Press, 1978), ch.6.

## How a Bill Becomes Law

The power to legislate, to decide the laws by which the United States will be governed, is an extraordinary opportunity that falls to only a tiny fraction of Americans. Amid all their jockeying for reelection, committee assignments, and leadership positions, members of the House and Senate realize, in their reflective moments, that lawmaking is their highest responsibility.

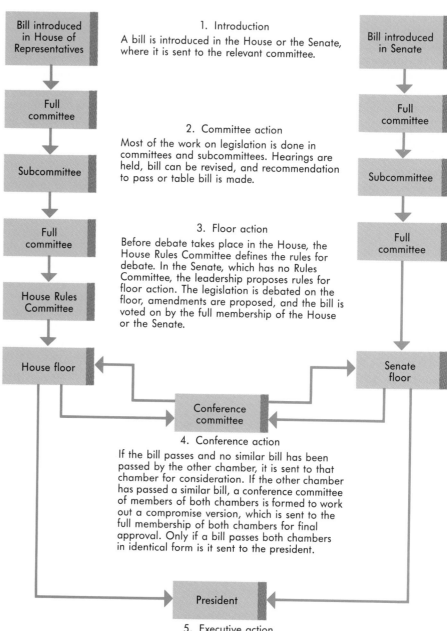

**FIGURE 17-2 How a Bill Becomes a Law**
Although the legislative process can be short-circuited in many ways, this diagram describes the most typical way in which a bill becomes law.

1. Introduction
A bill is introduced in the House or the Senate, where it is sent to the relevant committee.

2. Committee action
Most of the work on legislation is done in committees and subcommittees. Hearings are held, bill can be revised, and recommendation to pass or table bill is made.

3. Floor action
Before debate takes place in the House, the House Rules Committee defines the rules for debate. In the Senate, which has no Rules Committee, the leadership proposes rules for floor action. The legislation is debated on the floor, amendments are proposed, and the bill is voted on by the full membership of the House or the Senate.

4. Conference action
If the bill passes and no similar bill has been passed by the other chamber, it is sent to that chamber for consideration. If the other chamber has passed a similar bill, a conference committee of members of both chambers is formed to work out a compromise version, which is sent to the full membership of both chambers for final approval. Only if a bill passes both chambers in identical form is it sent to the president.

5. Executive action
If the president signs the bill, it becomes law. A presidential veto can be overridden by a two-thirds majority in each chamber.

The basic steps in enacting a law are summarized in Figure 17-2. The first step in the legislative process is the creation of a bill. A **bill** is a proposed legislative act. Many bills are prepared by executive agencies, interest groups, or other outside parties, but members of Congress also draft bills and only they can formally submit a bill for consideration by their chamber. If a bill is passed by both the House and Senate and signed by the president, it becomes a **law** and thereby takes effect.

## FROM COMMITTEE HEARINGS TO FLOOR DEBATE

Once a bill is introduced in the House or Senate, it is given a number and a title. The bill is then sent to the appropriate committee, which assigns it to one of its subcommittees. Most bills that reach a subcommittee are tabled on the grounds that they are not worthwhile. If a bill seems to have merit, the subcommittee will schedule hearings on it. This is a critical stage in a bill's development. The subcommittee invites testimony on the proposed legislation by lobbyists, administrators, and experts, who inform members about the policy in question, provide an indication of the support the bill has, and may disclose weaknesses in the proposal. After the hearings, if the subcommittee still feels that the legislation is warranted, members recommend the bill to the full committee, which can hold additional hearings. The full committee may decide to kill the bill by taking no action on it, but usually accepts the subcommittee's recommendation for passage. In the House, both the full committee and a subcommittee can "mark up," or revise, a bill; in the Senate, markup is usually reserved for the full committee.

Once a bill is reported out of committee, it needs to be scheduled for floor debate by the full chamber. In the House, the Rules Committee determines when the bill will be voted on, how long the debate on the bill will last, and whether the bill will receive a "closed rule" (no amendments will be permitted), an "open rule" (members can propose amendments relevant to any of the bill's sections), or something in between (for example, only certain sections of the bill will be subject to amendment). The Rules Committee has this scheduling power because the House is too large to operate effectively without strict rules for the handling of legislation by the full chamber.

By comparison, the smaller Senate relies on the majority leader to schedule bills. All bills are subject to unlimited debate unless a three-fifths majority of the full Senate votes for **cloture,** which limits debate to 100 hours. Cloture is a way of thwarting a Senate **filibuster,** a procedural tactic whereby a minority of senators prevent a bill from coming to a vote by holding the floor and talking until other senators give in and the bill is withdrawn from consideration. Filibustering is an honored tradition in the Senate, and in the past the chamber rarely voted to invoke cloture. Although the filibuster remains an important weapon of the Senate minority, successful cloture votes are now more common; in a recent eight-year period, cloture was voted on eighty-seven times and was invoked on thirty-one of those occasions.[47]

The Senate also differs from the House in that its members can propose *any* amendment to *any* bill. Unlike House amendments, those in the Senate do not have to be germane to a bill's content. For example, a senator may propose an antiabortion amendment to a bill dealing with defense expenditures. Such amendments are called *riders* and are frequently introduced.

[47]Ripley, *Congress,* 148–149.

Strom Thurmond of South Carolina leaves the Senate cloakroom after setting the record for the longest filibuster by a single senator. Thurmond spoke against the Civil Rights Act of 1957 for an uninterrupted twenty-four hours and nineteen minutes. (AP/Wide World Photos)

★ HOW THE UNITED
STATES COMPARES

**Legislative Authority**
Every bill must pass the U.S. House and Senate in identical form before it can become law. This equal division of legislative authority is not found in most democracies. Although many of them have a bicameral legislature like the U.S. Congress, nearly all power is vested in just one of the two chambers. In the British Parliament, for example, the House of Commons is far more powerful than the House of Lords; the latter can delay legislation but cannot kill it. In such a situation legislative power is more concentrated and easier to exercise. Thus in Great Britain the party that controls the House of Commons decides national policy. In the United States a party must control both the House of Representatives and the Senate if it is to exercise such power.

| Country | Form of Legislature |
| --- | --- |
| Canada | One house dominant |
| France | One house dominant |
| Great Britain | One house dominant |
| Israel | One house only |
| Italy | Two equal houses |
| Japan | One house dominant |
| Mexico | Two equal houses |
| United States | Two equal houses |
| West Germany | One house dominant (except on regional issues) |

## FROM FLOOR DEBATE TO ENACTMENT INTO LAW

To become law, a bill must be passed in identical form by both the House and the Senate. About 10 percent of all proposals that are approved by both chambers—the proportion is larger for major bills—differ in some respects in their House and Senate versions and are referred to a **conference committee** to resolve their differences. Each conference committee is formed temporarily to handle a particular bill; its members are usually appointed from the House and Senate standing committees that worked on the bill originally. The conference committee's job is to bargain over the differences in the House and Senate versions and to develop a compromise version. It then goes to the House and Senate floors, where it can be passed, defeated, or returned to conference, but not amended. Nongermane amendments, however, can be voted on separately, so that each chamber has an opportunity to reject part of a conference committee's proposed version of a bill while accepting another part.

After identical versions of a bill have passed both houses, the bill goes to the president for signature or veto. If the president signs the bill, it immediately becomes law. If the president exercises the *veto*, the bill is sent back to its originating chamber with the president's reasons for the veto. Congress can *override* a veto by vote of a two-thirds majority of each chamber; the bill then becomes law. If the president fails to sign a bill within ten days and Congress has remained in session, the bill automatically becomes law anyway. If the president fails to sign a bill within ten days and Congress has adjourned for the term, the bill does not become law. This last situation is called a *pocket veto* and forces Congress in its next session to start from the beginning: the bill must again pass both chambers and is again subject to presidential veto.

A program or project enacted into law may require an appropriation of funds. For instance, if Congress authorizes the United States Navy to build a new aircraft carrier, the carrier cannot be built unless Congress also appropriates the necessary funds. *This funding legislation must go through the same steps as the earlier authorizing legislation:* passage of identical appropriations bills in both houses, subject to presidential veto. Should the appropriations bill be defeated, as such bills occasionally are, the authorizing law is effectively negated.

## CONSEQUENCES OF THE LEGISLATIVE PROCESS

The congressional lawmaking process contains a built-in bias favoring the status quo and forestalling major policy changes. Legislation must pass so many hurdles before it becomes law that Congress finds it easier to block legislation or to force modifications in it than to enact it. If a bill can be stopped at any one of several points—committee or floor, House or Senate, authorization step or appropriations step—it usually *is* stopped, unless its backers reach a compromise with its opponents. The two-year time cycle in which Congress operates— from one congressional election to the next—gives the opponents of policy change an additional advantage: they can delay a legislative proposal until it dies at the session's end.

The conservative bias of the congressional process is particularly important in regard to legislation involving broad and controversial national objectives.

★ ANALYZE THE ISSUE

**The Slowness of Congress**
Congress has been called the "slow" branch of the national government. How do its fragmentation and the complexity of the process by which it enacts a bill into law help account for Congress's reputation? What are the advantages and disadvantages of this slow institutional pace?

The MX missile program survived repeated congressional challenges in 1985 at both the authorization and appropriation stages. An unfavorable vote at either stage could have meant the end of the MX program. (Gamma Liaison)

Major bills inevitably face obstacles erected by legislators who are trying to protect partisan, local, or special interests. By the same token, narrow legislation—a proposal that fits within the jurisdiction of a single committee and serves special interests of concern to the committee's members—is more likely to pass unimpeded through Congress.

If Congress, then, is not particularly well designed to take a national perspective on the formulation of broad national policy, its organization is compatible with the power and reelection needs of individual members. By investing substantial authority in committees and subcommittees, and then enabling representatives and senators to gain seats on those committees where they can be of greatest help to their constituents, Congress offers its members a golden opportunity to impress voters with their records on issues of local concern. The next chapter examines further how national and local concerns come together in Congress.

## Summary

Congress is a highly fragmented institution. It has no single leader; the House and Senate have separate leaders, neither of whom can presume to speak for the other chamber. The principal party leaders of Congress are the Speaker of the House and the Senate majority leader. Of the two, the Speaker has the greater powers, but even his formal authority is limited. The party leaders derive their influence mainly from having been entrusted by other members of their party with the tasks of formulating policy positions and coordinating party strategy. However, individual party members can choose to follow or ignore their leader's requests.

The committee system is a network of about 40 committees and 250 subcommittees, each with its separate chairperson. Each chair has influence on the policy decisions of the committee or subcommittee through the scheduling of bills and control of staff. Although the seniority principle is not absolute, the chair of a committee or subcommittee is usually the member from the majority party who has the longest continuous service. Party loyalty is not normally a criterion in the selection of chairs. As a result, committee and subcommittee leaders may or may not have the same national policy objectives as the leaders their party colleagues have elected.

It is in the committees that most of the work of Congress is conducted. Each standing committee of the House and Senate has jurisdiction over congressional

policy in a particular area (such as agriculture or foreign relations), as does each of its subcommittees. In most cases, the full House and Senate accept committee recommendations about passage of bills, although amendments to bills are quite common. In effect, small numbers of representatives make many of the decisions that the entire institution later confirms. Legislation in Congress is less the product of top-down leadership in the full House or Senate than of bottom-up leadership in the committees and subcommittees. Congress is a legislative system in which influence is widely dispersed, an arrangement that suits the power and reelection needs of its individual members. It is also a legislative system that works to the advantage of those who oppose policy change: if they can stop legislation at any level in either chamber, they can defeat it or force its supporters to accept substantial modifications.

In recent decades, the individualistic nature of Congress has been intensified by staffing changes. Larger committee and subcommittee staffs now make it easier for members of Congress to pursue their separate power and reelection goals. Congressional agencies strengthen the ability of Congress to act as a collective body by lessening the institution's dependence on the executive branch for information relevant to legislative issues, but they also make it easier for members of Congress to function independently.

## Major Concepts

| | |
|---|---|
| bill | law |
| cloture | party leaders |
| conference committee | select committee |
| filibuster | seniority |
| jurisdictions | standing committee |

## Suggested Readings

Cooper, Joseph, and G. Calvin Mackenzie, eds. *The House at Work.* Austin: University of Texas Press, 1981. A series of essays on the House of Representatives.

Davidson, Roger H., and Walter J. Oleszek. *Congress against Itself.* Bloomington: Indiana University Press, 1977. An assessment of the congressional reform movement of the early 1970s.

Dodd, Lawrence C., and Bruce I. Oppenheimer, eds. *Congress Reconsidered,* 3d ed. Washington, D.C.: Congressional Quarterly Press, 1985. Essays and analyses of Congress by leading legislative scholars.

Fenno, Richard F., Jr. *Congressmen in Committees.* Boston: Little, Brown, 1973. A detailed study of standing committees in Congress and their members' norms and behaviors.

Fox, Harrison W., and Susan Webb Hammond. *Congressional Staffs.* New York: Free Press, 1977. A study of congressional staff members, focusing on their personal backgrounds and legislative influence.

Jones, Charles O. *The United States Congress.* Homewood, Ill.: Dorsey Press, 1982. A thorough overview of the organization and activities of Congress.

Malbin, Michael J. *Unelected Representatives: Congressional Staff and the Future of Representation.* New York: Basic Books, 1980. A careful assessment of the impact of congressional staffs on the legislative process.

Matthews, Donald R. *U.S. Senators and Their World.* Chapel Hill: University of North Carolina Press, 1960. One of the first "behavioral" studies of Congress.

Oleszek, Walter J. *Congressional Procedures and the Policy Process.* Washington, D.C.: Congressional Quarterly Press, 1978. A detailed description of how Congress does its work.

Smith, Steven S., and Christopher J. Deering. *Committees in Congress.* Washington, D.C.: Congressional Quarterly Press, 1984. A comprehensive look at the House and Senate committee systems.

# Chapter 18

## CONGRESSIONAL POLICYMAKING: BALANCING NATIONAL GOALS AND LOCAL INTERESTS

*There are really two Congresses, not just one. Often these two Congresses are widely separated; the tightly knit, complex world of Capitol Hill is a long way from the world of [the member's district or state]—not only in miles, but in perspective and outlook as well.*
*Roger Davidson and Walter Oleszek[1]*

In 1987 Congress began work on legislation that would address the growing U.S. trade imbalance; the trade deficit had hit a yearly high of $171 billion. At one time the United States had the greatest trade surplus in the world, which fueled unprecedented prosperity at home and influence abroad, but by the early 1980s the United States had become a debtor country, with a huge trade deficit. Congress was determined to reverse the trend. The proposed legislation was based on the principle of free trade and provided for economic penalties for countries that exported goods to the United States but erected barriers to the importation of American goods. In its original form the bill was relatively straightforward and just 200 pages long. By the time it reached the floors of the House and Senate in 1988, however, the bill had been loaded down with so many amendments that it ran to more than 1,000 pages.

The trade bill had ballooned because, in a classic case of doing special favors for local interests, many members of Congress had succeeded in creating exceptions to the free-trade principle that underlay the legislation. At the same time that the bill threatened reprisals against countries that practiced trade protectionism, it provided protections of its own for U.S. interests. Senator Max Baucus of the lamb-producing state of Montana proposed a provision that called for federal payments to sheep producers who were damaged by imports.

[1]Roger H. Davidson and Walter J. Oleszek, *Congress and Its Members*, 2d ed. (Washington, D.C.: Congressional Quarterly Press, 1985), 7.

Representative Don Bonker of the lumber-rich state of Washington developed a measure that would protect certain U.S. wood products, including plywood paneling, from foreign imports. Representative Beryl Anthony, whose state of Arkansas has a Timex assembly plant, inserted a provision that would protect foreign watch companies with production facilities in the United States.[2]

The story of the trade bill illustrates the dual nature of Congress: it is both a lawmaking institution for the country and a representative assembly for states and districts. Members of Congress must bargain and compromise in the process of producing legislation because they have both an individual duty to serve the interests of their separate constituencies and a collective duty to protect the interests of the country as a whole.

This chapter examines how the conflicting demands on members of Congress come together in the policymaking process. Because Congress is a large and complex organization whose members vary widely in their concerns and positions, the observations made in this chapter are necessarily broad. There are exceptions to every generalization that is made about Congress except one: members of Congress have no choice but to balance national and local concerns. With this idea at its center, this chapter describes Congress's policymaking role in the context of the institution's three major functions: lawmaking, representation, and oversight. The main points made in the chapter are the following:

★ *Congress is limited by the lack of direction and organization usually necessary for the development of comprehensive national policies.* Congress looks to the president to initiate most broad policy programs but has a substantial influence on the timing and content of those programs.

★ *Congress is well organized to handle policies of relatively narrow scope.* Such policies are usually worked out by small sets of legislators, bureaucrats, and interest groups.

★ *Individual members of Congress are extraordinarily responsive to local interests and concerns,* although they also respond to national interests. These responses often take place within the context of party tendencies.

★ *Congress oversees the bureaucracy's administration of its laws,* but this oversight function is of less concern to members of Congress than is lawmaking or representation.

★ *Congress is admired by those who favor negotiation, deliberation, and the rewarding of many interests, particularly those with a local constituency base. Critics of Congress say that it hinders majority rule, fosters policy delay, and caters to special interests.*

## The Lawmaking Function of Congress

The Framers of the Constitution expected Congress to be the leading branch of the national government. It was to the legislature—the embodiment of representative government—that the people were expected to look for policy leadership. Moreover, Congress was granted the **lawmaking function**—the authority to make the laws necessary to carry out the powers granted to the national government. The capacity to make the laws is, beyond doubt, the greatest power of a civil government. During most of the nineteenth century,

---

[2]"The Making of a Mishmash," *Time*, March 28, 1988, 49.

Congress, not the president, was clearly the dominant national institution.[3] Aside from a few strong leaders such as Jackson and Lincoln, presidents did not play a major legislative role. In fact, Congress frequently made it clear that presidential advice was not wanted. Then, as national and international forces combined to place greater leadership and policy demands on the federal government, the president became a vital part of the national legislative process.

Today Congress and the president substantially share the lawmaking function. However, their roles differ greatly. The president's major contribution is made on the small number of broad legislative measures that arise each year, although Congress also plays a large part in the disposition of such bills. In addition, Congress has the lead—and in most cases nearly the full say—on the narrower legislation that constitutes the great majority of the roughly 10,000 bills introduced during a two-year congressional session.

## CONGRESS IN RESPONSE: BROAD POLICY ISSUES

Some of the policy issues addressed by the national government transcend local or group boundaries. A sluggish economy, for example, affects Americans of all regions and of most occupational groups. Such issues normally call for a broad and well-coordinated policy response. Congress is not well suited to the development of such policies. Its strengths are deliberation and compromise, not comprehensive planning.

### Fragmentation as a Policymaking Limitation

*Congress remains organized to deal with narrow problems but not with broad ones.*

James Sundquist

Fragmentation makes it difficult for Congress to take the lead in developing policies that address broad national problems. "Congress remains organized," James Sundquist notes, "to deal with narrow problems but not with broad ones."[4] Congress is not one house but two, and each chamber has its separate

[3]See Ernest Griffith and Francis Valeo, *Congress: Its Contemporary Role,* 5th ed. (New York: New York University Press, 1975), ch.1.
[4]James L. Sundquist, "Congress and the President: Enemies or Partners?" in Lawrence C. Dodd and Bruce I. Oppenheimer, eds., *Congress Reconsidered* (New York: Praeger, 1977), 240.

Sam Nunn, chairman of the Senate Armed Services Committee. Nunn's knowledge of and opinions on defense-related issues are respected by other senators of both parties. (Gamma Liaison)

leadership. Moreover, neither the Speaker of the House nor the Senate majority leader has the authority to bind the chamber's majority to a legislative program. Not surprisingly, the party leaders in Congress seldom initiate major legislative programs. Their offices are not even staffed with the broad range of policy experts who could enable them to undertake such a policy role consistently.

The committee system of Congress is likewise not designed to handle broad national issues. Such issues transcend committee jurisdictions, and neither the House nor the Senate has any institutionalized way for its committees to work together to originate major bills. The House has experimented with ad hoc committees formed for this purpose, with mixed results. In 1977 House Speaker Thomas P. ("Tip") O'Neill appointed a temporary committee to develop a broad welfare bill. The committee negotiated a bill, which passed the House but was never acted on by the Senate.[5] More successful was the ad hoc energy committee, also appointed by O'Neill in 1977, which produced a broad bill that passed Congress.[6] However, the bill had begun as President Jimmy Carter's energy program. It had been split among five standing committees upon reaching the House, and the temporary committee's job was mainly to put the five pieces together once the standing committees had done their work.[7]

The reelection needs of members of Congress are a further obstacle to its initiation of national solutions to national problems. It is difficult for senators or representatives to look beyond the special needs of their own districts or states.

[5]James L. Sundquist, "Congress, the President, and the Crisis of Competence in Government," in Lawrence C. Dodd and Bruce I. Oppenheimer, eds., Congress Reconsidered, 2d ed. (Washington, D.C.: Congressional Quarterly Press, 1981), 362–364.

[6]See Bruce I. Oppenheimer, "Congress and the New Obstructionism: Developing an Energy Program," in ibid., 275–295.

[7]For a broader perspective on committee and policy initiatives, see Gerald Wright, Leroy Rieselbach, and Lawrence C. Dodd, Congress and Policy Change (New York: Agathon, 1986).

Oil shortages during the mid-1970s led to debate in Congress between members from oil-producing states and those from other states. Such differences of opinion, which arise from the country's great diversity, make it difficult for Congress to take the lead on broad issues of national policy. (Owen Franken/Stock, Boston)

The energy crisis of the 1970s, for example, required decisions on the pricing of oil and natural gas, on taking the windfall profits that oil producers had made from higher oil prices, and on funding research on synthetic fuels. The view of the nation's energy policy needs held by members of Congress from oil-producing states such as Texas and Louisiana differed sharply from that of members from other states, whose ideas also varied in accordance with their states' energy resources and requirements.[8]

To be sure, Congress sometimes does take the lead on large issues.[9] Except during Roosevelt's New Deal, Congress has been a chief source of major labor legislation, including the Taft-Hartley Act of 1947 (which legalized state right-to-work laws), the Landrum-Griffin Act of 1959 (which holds union officials to sound administrative and democratic practices), and plant-closing legislation in 1988 (which requires companies to notify workers sixty days before a plant closing or mass layoff). Congress also developed the Water Pollution Control Act of 1964, the Clean Air Act of 1963, and other environmental legislation.[10] Federal aid to education, atomic energy, and urban development are other areas in which Congress has played an initiating role.[11] But Congress does not ordinarily develop broad policy programs and carry them through to passage. "Congress," Arthur Maass notes, "is limited by the lack of resources and organization typically needed for these tasks."[12]

### Presidential Leadership, Congressional Response

In general, Congress depends on the president to initiate broad policy proposals, and for good reason: the president is strong in ways that Congress cannot match.

First, whereas Congress's authority is fragmented, the president is a singular authority.[13] The president seeks the advice of others within the executive branch, but ultimately the decision is his to make. His decision may not be easy: some national problems are difficult to understand fully, let alone to manage effectively.[14] Runaway inflation admittedly bewildered President Carter, who proposed program after program—five in all—in a frantic effort to control it. Nevertheless, the president does not have to have a majority consensus within the executive branch in order to act. As sole chief executive, he can choose a course of action on his own and direct his assistants to prepare a legislative proposal for implementing it. Accordingly, the presidency is capable of a degree of policy planning and coordination that is far beyond the normal capacity of Congress. "It is the difference," one congressman said, "between an organization headed by one powerful man and a many-headed organization."[15]

[8]Oppenheimer, "Congress and the New Obstructionism," 282–285.

[9]Ronald C. Moe and Steven C. Teel, "Congress as Policy-Maker," *Political Science Quarterly* 85 (1970): 467–468.

[10]See Charles O. Jones, *Clean Air: The Policies and Politics of Pollution Control* (Pittsburgh: University of Pittsburgh Press, 1975).

[11]See Gary Orfield, *Congressional Power: Congress and Social Change* (New York: Harcourt Brace Jovanovich, 1975).

[12]Arthur Maass, *Congress and the Common Good* (New York: Basic Books, 1983), 14.

[13]See Paul C. Light, *The President's Agenda* (Baltimore: Johns Hopkins University Press, 1982).

[14]Hugh Heclo, "Introduction: The Presidential Illusion," in Hugh Heclo and Lester M. Salamon, *The Illusion of Presidential Government* (Boulder, Colo.: Westview Press, 1981), 1–2.

[15]Quoted in Randall B. Ripley, *Congress*, 3d ed. (New York: Norton, 1983), 326.

---

★ ANALYZE THE ISSUE

**Institutional Reform of Congress**

In the opinion of some observers, Congress can no longer make satisfactory policy decisions. Today's problems are supposedly too big and too technical to be handled by an institution that has no strong central authority. Is this argument persuasive? Have the Congressional Budget Office and other modernizing efforts helped Congress respond more promptly and effectively to urgent issues? Can you think of other changes that would help?

Flanked by congressional leaders of both parties, President George Bush announces a budget compromise that all have agreed to support. The president often takes the lead in proposing legislative solutions to the nation's major problems. (John Ficara/Woodfin Camp & Associates)

Another advantage that the president enjoys is his national political base which focuses public attention on his actions and lends a national perspective to his choices. The president must take regional and state concerns into account, but they do not affect his decisions as much as they influence those of members of Congress. In a way, the president's situation is the reverse of that of a member of Congress: the president cannot ignore state and local interests, but he must concentrate on national ones if he hopes to retain power.

Presidential leadership means that Congress will pay attention to the White House, not that it will accept whatever the president proposes. But Congress welcomes presidential initiatives as a starting point for its own deliberations. Frequently Congress will delay action on a problem until the president submits his plan. In the early 1980s, for example, several tax-simplification plans, including the Kemp-Roth and Bradley-Gephardt bills, were initiated in Congress, but Congress did not commit itself to a full airing of the issue until President Reagan introduced his tax plan in 1985. The result was the Tax Reform Act of 1986, a comprehensive overhaul of the personal and corporate tax codes.

Organizational changes have improved Congress's ability to evaluate and modify presidential proposals. For example, as we mentioned in Chapter 17, the Congressional Budget Office (CBO) was created as part of the Budget and Impoundment Control Act of 1974, which also established the House and Senate budget committees. These committees propose spending ceilings that, when approved by the full Congress in a concurrent resolution (see Table 18-1), determine the size of the federal budget, both overall and within major categories, such as defense and interior.[16]

★ ANALYZE THE ISSUE

**The Line-Item Veto**
Several modern presidents, including Reagan and Bush, have wanted Congress to give them the line-item veto on budgetary legislation. As things stand, the president can either veto a whole bill or let it become law in its entirety. A line-item veto would enable the president to veto particular budget items while affirming others. What is your view on the line-item veto? Would it greatly undermine Congress and thereby upset the balance of power between the executive and the legislative branches?

[16]See Allen Schick, *Congress and Money* (Washington, D.C.: Urban Institute, 1980); Lance T. LeLoup, *The Fiscal Congress* (Westport, Conn.: Greenwood Press, 1980).

**TABLE 18-1   Annual Congressional Budget Schedule**

| Target Date | Action |
| --- | --- |
| November 10 | President submits figures on current budget. |
| 15th day after Congress convenes | President gives Congress his budget proposal. |
| March 15–April 1 | Budget committees receive reports from Congressional Budget Office and other committees. |
| April 15 | Budget Committee submits first concurrent resolution on budget to full chamber. |
| May 15 | Congress adopts first concurrent resolution. |
| September 15 | Congress adopts second concurrent resolution. |
| September 25 | Congress concludes budget action in accord with second concurrent resolution. |
| October 1 | Start of fiscal year. |

However, Congress's budgetary role is necessarily a reactive one. Congress cannot play the initiating role because it lacks the unified leadership that would enable it to set priorities among hundreds of agencies and programs. In 1986 President Reagan submitted to Congress a budget that he knew was unacceptable to its Democratic leaders and challenged them to write a budget of their own. After six months they threw in the towel, acknowledging that differences of opinion within Democratic ranks made the task impossible. They settled on the same program allocations that the previous year's budget had contained.

Of course, the same factors that make it difficult for Congress to initiate broad policy also make it difficult for the president to persuade Congress to accept his initiatives. There is no permanent congressional majority waiting eagerly to line up behind the president's programs. As we will discuss in Chapter 21, Congress has rejected outright roughly half of all major presidential proposals in recent decades and has modified others substantially. Congressional majorities must constantly be created because each member has his or her own reelection base and does not have to take orders from any congressional leader. Much talk and bargaining precede the passage of comprehensive legislation, which also normally requires the stimulus of an urgent, major problem.[17] When a president tries to act ahead of events and public opinion, Congress is likely to drag its feet. Gerald Ford attempted to awaken congressional concern over the looming problems of inflation and energy during the mid-1970s but could not get Congress to move. Said Ford, "There are just roadblocks up there [on Capitol Hill] that are apparently unbreakable until we get a real crisis. . . . That is the way [the system works], right or wrong."[18]

Determined opposition from a sizable minority will often defeat a presidential initiative because so many tactics for blocking legislation are available in Congress.[19] A bill must pass through two legislatures that differ from each other in size, constituency, and term of office and even, at times, in majority party.[20]

[17]Light, *President's Agenda*, 90–91.
[18]Interview in *Newsweek*, December 9, 1974, 33–34.
[19]Lewis A. Froman, Jr., *The Congressional Process* (Boston: Little, Brown, 1967), 18.
[20]Benjamin Page, "Cooling the Legislative Tea," in Walter Dean Burnham and Martha Wagner Weinberg, *American Politics and Public Policy* (Cambridge, Mass.: MIT Press, 1978), 171–187.

Inaction or rejection by either chamber is sufficient to kill a bill. Senator Robert Dole (R-Kans.) compared Congress to a wet noodle: "If it doesn't want to move, it's not going to move."[21]

## CONGRESS IN THE LEAD: NARROW POLICY ISSUES

Only a small proportion of the bills addressed by Congress deal with broad national issues of widespread interest.* The rest cover smaller problems of less general interest. The leading role in the disposition of these bills falls not on the president but on Congress and, in most cases, on a relatively small number of its members.

The standing committees of Congress decide most legislative issues.[22] Interest groups and bureaucratic agencies with a stake in a particular policy issue tend to concentrate their persuasive efforts on the committee that is responsible for formulating legislation in that policy area. Hearings on proposed legislation are held by a committee or subcommittee, not by the full membership of Congress. The testimony introduced at the hearings is published, but transcripts of congressional hearings run to over a million pages annually, far more than any

[21]Quoted in Martin Tolchin, "How Senators View the Senate," *New York Times*, November 25, 1984, 40.
*Congress has two kinds of bills, public and private. *Private bills* are relatively unimportant; they grant privileges or payments to individuals. (For example, a private bill might allow someone who does not meet immigration requirements to immigrate to the United States anyway.) *Public bills* deal with programs and broad categories of people and are what is normally meant by "legislation." The discussion in this chapter focuses on public bills.
[22]See George Goodwin, *The Little Legislatures* (Amherst: University of Massachusetts Press, 1970); Joseph K. Unekis and Leroy N. Rieselbach, *Congressional Committee Politics* (New York: Praeger, 1984); Richard F. Fenno, Jr., *Congressmen in Committees* (Boston: Little, Brown, 1973).

Congress is particularly adept at handling issues that are narrow in scope and that coincide with the jurisdiction of a particular committee. Price supports for agricultural products are an example. (Dennis Stock/Magnum Photos)

The effects of acid rain on forests and lakes are mainly a concern of people who live in northeastern states and, accordingly, to members of Congress from those states. (Peter Miller/Photo Researchers)

the nation as a whole or those of his or her own constituency.[27] These interests always overlap to some degree but rarely coincide exactly. Policies that are of maximum benefit to the full society are not always equally advantageous to particular localities, and can even be of harm to some constituencies. To the writers of the Constitution, the higher duty was to the nation. James Madison said in *Federalist* No. 10 that members of Congress should be those persons "least likely to sacrifice" the national interest to "local prejudice." But the choice is not a simple one, even for a legislator who is inclined to focus on national concerns. To be fully effective, a member of Congress must be reelected time and again, a necessity that compels him or her to pay attention to local concerns. Most members of Congress, it appears, tend toward a local orientation, albeit one that is modified by both overarching and partisan concerns, as the following discussion explains.

## REPRESENTATION OF STATES AND DISTRICTS

Members of Congress represent particular states or districts and are wary of antagonizing local interests.[28] They are particularly reluctant to oppose local

[27]See David J. Vogler and Sidney R. Waldman, *Congress and Democracy* (Washington, D.C.: Congressional Quarterly Press, 1985); David C. Kozak, *Contexts of Congressional Decision Behavior* (Lanham, Md.: University Press of America, 1984).

[28]See Thomas A. Flinn and Harold L. Wolman, "Constituency and Roll Call Voting," *Midwest Journal of Political Science*, May 1966, 193–199; Richard F. Fenno, Jr., *Home Style: House Members in Their Districts* (Boston: Little, Brown, 1978), ch. 1; John W. Kingdon, *Congressmen's Voting Decisions* (New York: Harper & Row, 1981), 19; Randall B. Ripley, *Party Leaders in the House of Representatives* (Washington, D.C.: Brookings Institution, 1967), 140–141.

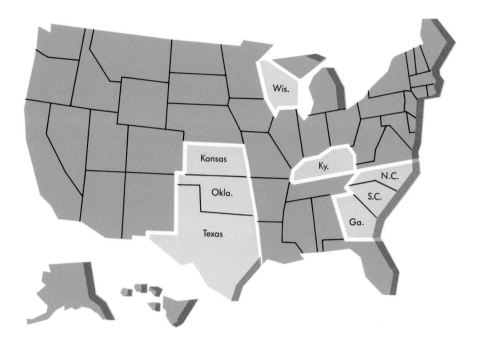

**FIGURE 18-1 States Represented by Membership on the House Tobacco and Peanut Subcommittee, 1989–1990** Members of Congress try to get assigned to committees and subcommittees whose jurisdictions allow them to help their constituents. Nearly all the members of the Tobacco and Peanut Subcommittee of the House Agriculture Committee are from the states (singled out on map) in which most of the nation's peanuts and tobacco are grown. *Source: Staff, House Agriculture Committee.*

sentiment on issues of intense concern, even when larger national objectives are at stake.[29] For example, the Civil Rights Act of 1964, which forbids racial discrimination in public accommodations such as hotels and restaurants, was supported by only twelve House members from the South.

The committee system of Congress promotes representation of local rather than national interests.[30] Many senators and representatives sit on committees and subcommittees with policy jurisdictions that coincide with state or district interests (see Figure 18-1). For example, farm-state legislators dominate the membership of the House and Senate Agriculture committees, while westerners dominate the Interior committees (which deal with federal lands and natural resources, most of which are concentrated in the West).

Constituency interests are also advanced by **logrolling,** the common practice of trading one's vote with another member so that each gets what he or she most wants. The term dates to the early nineteenth century, when a settler would ask neighbors for help in rolling logs off farmland, with the understanding that the settler would reciprocate when the neighbors were cutting trees. In Congress, logrolling often occurs in committees where constituency interests vary from member to member. Senator Sam Ervin of North Carolina expressed the general attitude of many committee members when he said to Senator Milton Young of North Dakota, his colleague on the Agriculture Committee, "Milt, I would just like you to tell me how to vote about wheat and sugar beets and things like that, if you just help me out on tobacco and things like that."[31]

[29]Thomas E. Cavanaugh, "The Calculus of Representation," *Western Political Quarterly,* March 1982, 120–129.
[30]Roger H. Davison, "Representation and Congressional Committees," *Annals of the American Academy of Political and Social Science,* January 1974, 48–62.
[31]Quoted in Charles O. Jones, "Representation in Congress: The Case of the House Agriculture Committee," *American Political Science Review* 55 (1961): 358–367.

Nevertheless, representation of constituency interests has its limits. A representative's constituents have little interest in most issues that come before Congress and even less information about them.[32] Whether the government should appropriate a few million dollars in foreign aid for the Central African Republic or should alter patent requirements for copying machines is not the sort of issue that local people are likely to know or care about. Moreover, members of Congress often have no choice but to go against the wishes of a significant portion of their constituency. Congress sometimes delays action on controversial issues, forcing the president to take the heat from the opposing sides. Congress cannot always duck such issues, however, and when its members are forced to vote, they know that by agreeing with one portion of their constituency they will antagonize another.

*The happiness of society is the end [that is, the purpose] of government.*

John Adams

## REPRESENTATION OF "THE COMMON GOOD"

"The two biggest lies," Senator Thomas Eagleton once remarked, are "one, to say a senator never takes into account the political ramifications of a vote and secondly, almost an equal lie, is to say the only thing a senator considers is politics."[33] Arthur Maass agrees that Congress's concern for the common good is vastly underestimated by most observers. He notes, for example, that committees routinely weigh the impact of special-interest legislation on other interests and on the nation as a whole. Moreover, one-third of all bills are amended on the floor of the House or Senate, often for the purpose of adapting a committee's work to national interests.[34] Yet members of Congress admit that when they deliberate on highly visible issues, they only occasionally feel free to place national interests ahead of local concerns.[35]

★ ANALYZE THE ISSUE

**Party Unity and Fragmentation in Congress**
The best predictor of the way individual members of Congress will respond to legislation is their party affiliation, Republican or Democratic. In view of this fact, do you think it makes sense for voters in congressional elections to "vote for the person, not the party"? Why, or why not? Then consider this question: Can anything but party unity overcome the fragmentation that besets Congress?

## REPRESENTATION THROUGH POLITICAL PARTIES

To this point, local and national constituencies have been discussed as if each, though differing from the other, were consistent in itself. This is obviously not the case, even in relatively homogeneous local constituencies. The interests of small and large farmers in an agricultural state, for example, can differ considerably. Rarely can a member of Congress choose an action that will be acceptable to everyone in his or her constituency. Thus the whole constituency is not a very useful reference point for representation. The legislator must take sides. In other words, the member of Congress must decide which interests he or she will represent within the constituency and the nation. By and large, the basis of this representation is partisanship.

[32]See Aage R. Clausen, *How Congressmen Decide* (New York: St. Martin's Press, 1973).
[33]Quoted in Davidson and Oleszek, *Congress and Its Members*, 398.
[34]Maass, *Congress and the Common Good*.
[35]See Davidson and Oleszek, *Congress and Its Members*, ch.4.

Percentage of roll-call votes

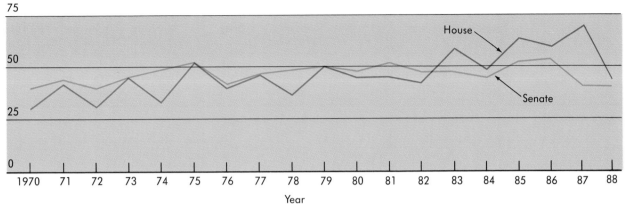

FIGURE 18-2 Percentage of
Roll-Call Votes in House and
Senate in Which a Majority of
Democrats Voted against a
Majority of Republicans,
1970–1988
As a result of partisan traditions,
Democrats and Republicans in
Congress are often on opposite
sides of issues. *Source:*
Congressional Quarterly Weekly,
*November 19, 1988, 3334–3335.*

Although members of Congress, unlike their counterparts in many European legislatures, are not bound to a legislative program of their party, they share partisan traditions and viewpoints, which affect their policy choices (see Figure 18-2). Roll-call votes in Congress often align a majority of Democrats against a majority of Republicans.[36] The typical member of Congress votes with his or her party's majority about 70 percent of the time.[37] Divisions along party lines are common in committee voting as well.[38]

Party influence is also evident in the president's relationship with Congress. He serves as a legislative leader not so much for the whole Congress as for members of his party.[39] More than half of the time, opposition and support for presidential initiatives divide along party lines. A president can expect problems with Congress when it is controlled by the opposing party or when divisions within his own party prevent him from fully mobilizing its support (see Chapter 21).

The influence of partisanship is also evident in the liberal or conservative pattern of the individual member's voting record (see Table 18-2). For example, on major economic legislative issues during the 1987-1988 congressional sessions, 83 percent of Senate Democrats and 82 percent of House Democrats had an overall liberal voting record, compared to only 9 percent of Senate Republicans and 3 percent of House Republicans.[40] The differences between

[36]Richard E. Cohen, "Rating Congress—A Guide to Separating the Liberals from the Conservatives," *National Journal*, May 8, 1982, 800–810.

[37]See Keith T. Poole and R. Steven Daniels, "Ideology, Party, and Voting in the U.S. Congress 1959–1983," *American Political Science Review*, 79 (June 1985): 373–399; *Congressional Quarterly Weekly Report*, January 15, 1983, 107; David E. Price, *Bringing Back the Parties* (Washington, D.C.: Congressional Quarterly Press, 1984), 54.

[38]Glenn R. Parker and Suzanne L. Parker, "Factions in Committee: The U.S. House of Representatives," *American Political Science Review*, March 1979, 52–63.

[39]See Steven A. Shull, *Domestic Policy Formation: Presidential-Congressional Partnership?* (Westport, Conn.: Greenwood Press, 1983); Matthews and Stimson, *Yeas and Nays.*

[40]Helmut Norpoth, "Exploring Party Cohesion in Congress," *American Political Science Review*, December 1976, 1171; John W. Kingdon, *Congressmen's Voting Decisions*, 19.

TABLE 18-2   Liberal/Conservative Voting Pattern of Senate and House Democrats and Republicans, 1987-1988

| VOTING PATTERN | ECONOMIC LEGISLATION | | | | NONECONOMIC LEGISLATION | | | |
|---|---|---|---|---|---|---|---|---|
| | *Senate Democrats* | *Senate Republicans* | *House Democrats* | *House Republicans* | *Senate Democrats* | *Senate Republicans* | *House Democrats* | *House Republicans* |
| Liberal | 83% | 9% | 82% | 3% | 74% | 22% | 80% | 9% |
| Conservative | 17 | 91 | 18 | 97 | 26 | 78 | 20 | 91 |
| | 100% | 100% | 100% | 100% | 100% | 100% | 100% | 100% |

SOURCE: Adapted from "Ideological Portrait of Congress," *National Journal*, January 28, 1989, 206.

---

### ★ HOW THE UNITED STATES COMPARES

**Party Unity in the Legislature**

All democratic legislatures are organized by party, but they differ greatly in the degree of control exercised by parties. At one extreme are those countries in which a single legislative chamber dominates, one party has a majority in that chamber, and the members of the majority party display a high level of unity. In such countries, which currently include Great Britain and West Germany, the majority party in the legislature essentially dictates national policy. At the other extreme are multiparty systems in which no party has a legislative majority and national policy is worked out in bargaining among a coalition of parties. If the parties find themselves unable to agree on national policy, however, the government may collapse. Belgium's coalition government was disbanded in 1987 for this reason.

With its fixed terms for legislators, the U.S. system precludes a collapse of government, but party control of Congress is always somewhat uncertain. For one thing, the Republicans may control one chamber while the Democrats control the other, as was the case in 1981–1986. For another, Congress is not characterized by a high level of party unity. It is common for one-fourth or more of Democratic or Republican members to vote against their party's position on important legislative issues. The effect of this lack of a reliable party majority is to weaken Congress's ability to provide national leadership.

---

Republicans and Democrats were less pronounced on noneconomic issues but were still very substantial.

## The Oversight Function of Congress

Although Congress enacts the laws governing the nation and appropriates the money to implement them, the administration of these laws is entrusted to the executive branch. Congress has the responsibility to see that the executive carries out the laws faithfully and spends the money properly, a supervisory activity that is referred to as the **oversight function** of Congress.

### THE PROCESS OF LEGISLATIVE OVERSIGHT

Oversight is carried out largely through the committee system of Congress and is facilitated by the parallel structure of the committees and the executive bureaucracy: the Foreign Affairs committees of Congress oversee the work of the State Department, the Agriculture committees look after the Department of Agriculture, and so on. The Legislative Reorganization Act of 1970 spells out each committee's responsibility for overseeing its parallel agency:

A witness testifies at a congressional hearing that investigated why the government was charged several hundred dollars apiece for coffee makers that the manufacturer would have sold for a much lower price in retail stores. Such investigations are part of the congressional oversight process. (Shepard Sherbell/Picture Group)

Each standing committee shall review and study, on a continuing basis, the application, administration, and execution of those laws, or parts of laws, the subject matter of which is within the jurisdiction of that committee.

However, oversight is easier to mandate than to carry out. If congressional committees were to try to monitor all the bureaucracy's activities, they would have no time or energy to do anything else. Most members of Congress are more interested in working out new laws and looking after constituents than in laboriously keeping track of the bureaucracy. As a result, oversight normally is not pursued aggressively unless members of Congress are annoyed with an agency, have discovered that a legislative authorization is being grossly abused, or are reviewing a program for possible major changes.[41]

If a committee believes that an agency has mishandled a program, it can investigate the matter.[42] When it suspects serious abuses, the committee is likely to hold hearings. Except in cases involving "executive privilege" (the right to withhold confidential information affecting national security), executive-branch officials are compelled to testify at these hearings. If they refuse, they can be cited for contempt of Congress, which is a criminal offense. In 1982, in response to allegations that the Environmental Protection Agency (EPA) was permitting some corporations to circumvent laws regulating the disposal of toxic wastes, Congress scheduled hearings on the question. When the EPA's top administrators refused to provide requested information, Congress issued subpoenas. When it was rebuffed again, Congress forced the resignation of the EPA

★ **ANALYZE THE ISSUE**

**Congressional Oversight of Executive Lawmaking**
Oversight has traditionally ranked behind lawmaking and representation in Congress's priorities, but most legislation now originates in the executive branch, which has the expertise and working knowledge of government programs that are the foundation of modern public policy. Is Congress's chief role, like it or not, coming to be that of overseer of the executive's legislative ideas and administrative actions?

[41]See Morris S. Ogul, *Congress Oversees the Bureaucracy* (Pittsburgh: University of Pittsburgh Press, 1976); Morris S. Ogul, "Congressional Oversight Structures and Incentives," in Dodd and Oppenheimer, *Congress Reconsidered*, 2d ed., 317–331.
[42]See James Hamilton, *The Power to Probe: A Study of Congressional Investigations* (New York: Vintage Books, 1976).

(Susan Van Etten/The Picture Cube)

Among these casualties of presidential politics were George Romney, Lyndon Johnson, Edmund Muskie, Hubert Humphrey, Henry "Scoop" Jackson, Gerald Ford, Jimmy Carter, Edward Kennedy, and Gary Hart.

The major justification for America's elaborate presidential election system is **legitimacy**—the idea that the voters must choose the party nominees as well as the final winner if the outcome is truly to reflect the people's choice.[3] Because of popular participation in the nominating process, presidential campaigns are necessarily long and involve large fields of contending candidates. This chapter traces the origins of the current system of electing presidents, describes how the system works in practice, and assesses its impact on the nature of presidential leadership. A basic question about this process, one addressed in the chapter's conclusion, is whether it is designed to produce exceptional presidents, as opposed to presidents who have successfully endured an exhausting campaign. The major ideas discussed are these:

★ *The United States has had four presidential selection systems in its history, and each succeeding one has been designed to be more legitimate—that is, more responsive to the people.*

★ *In the nominating phase of the campaign the candidates' basic strategy is to make a strong showing in the early state caucuses and primaries and to let the "momentum" of this early success carry over to later stages. Whether candidates are likely to get off to a fast start can depend on their records of accomplishment, policy positions, ideological positioning, group support, campaign organization, and media coverage.*

★ *The outcome of the general election is decided mainly by the cohesiveness of the party coalitions, national conditions (particularly the state of the economy), and the candidates' campaign efforts.*

[3]James W. Ceaser, *Presidential Selection: Theory and Development* (Princeton, N.J.: Princeton University Press, 1979), 19.

Jesse Jackson campaigns in Iowa in 1988. Iowa's party caucuses kick off the presidential nomination race. (UPI/Bettmann Newsphotos)

★ *The present selection system is not designed specifically to produce capable presidents (that is, presidents who have the talent, experience, and character to provide strong national leadership), but the system does give the victorious candidate a reservoir of popular support and an opportunity to act as national policy leader.*

## The Development of the Presidential Selection Process

The process by which the United States selects its chief executive has evolved through four cumulative stages, or systems, all of which were expected to yield skillful presidents (see Table 19-1). However, only the first system had this as its overriding goal. Each succeeding system resulted from popular reforms that were aimed chiefly at making the selection process more legitimate by granting the American people a larger voice in choosing the president.[4]

### THE FIRST SYSTEM: THE ELECTORAL COLLEGE

The delegates to the Constitutional Convention of 1787 were steadfastly opposed to popular election of the president. Although James Wilson of Pennsylvania twice proposed the idea, it was rejected each time by a large majority. The delegates believed that ordinary citizens, most of whom could neither read nor write, were too poorly informed to choose wisely. More important, the Framers feared that popular election could enable a tyrant to capture the presidency by appealing to the people's fears and prejudices. The Framers also ruled out the selection of the president by Congress because that procedure would undermine the principle of separation of executive and legislative powers.

[4]Thomas R. Marshall, *Presidential Nominations in a Reform Age* (New York: Praeger, 1981); James W. Ceaser, *Reforming the Reforms: A Critical Analysis of the Presidential Selection Process* (Cambridge, Mass.: Ballinger, 1982), 81; Ceaser, *Presidential Selection.*

TABLE 19-1    The Four Systems of Presidential Selection

| Selection System | Period | Features |
|---|---|---|
| 1. Original | 1788–1828 | Party nominees are chosen in congressional caucuses. Electoral College members act somewhat independently in their presidential voting. |
| 2. Party convention | 1832–1900 | Party nominees are chosen in national party conventions by delegates selected by state and local party organizations. Electoral College members cast their ballots for the popular-vote winner in their respective states. |
| 3. Party convention, primary | 1904–1968 | As in system 2, except that a *minority* of national convention delegates are chosen through primary elections (the majority still being chosen by party organizations). |
| 4. Party primary, open caucus | 1972– present | As in system 2, except that a *majority* of national convention delegates are chosen through primary elections. |

Having thus rejected the two methods—popular election and legislative selection—that the states used to choose their governors, the Framers devised a new system, which came to be called the Electoral College. Under the Constitution, the president is chosen by a vote of electors who are appointed by the states. Each state is entitled to as many electors as it has members of Congress, and each state determines its own method for selecting its electors. The Framers envisioned that the states would choose only thoughtful and informed electors, who in turn would choose talented and experienced presidents. "It will not be too strong to say," Alexander Hamilton wrote in *Federalist* No. 68, "that there will be a constant probability of seeing the [presidency] filled by characters pre-eminent for ability and virtue."

In the first two presidential elections, the electors unanimously selected George Washington, the only presidential candidate in history to receive the votes of all electors. Nevertheless, the Framers anticipated that in some elections no candidate would gain the electoral majority required by the Constitution, in which case the House of Representatives (with each state having one vote) would select the president from among the top five votegetters (later changed to the top three by the Twelfth Amendment). The House soon did decide an election, choosing Thomas Jefferson in 1800.

Jefferson's election by the House resulted from a development that the Framers had not anticipated. In its original form, the Constitution provided that each elector would cast two ballots. The candidate who placed first, provided that he received the votes of a majority of electors, would become president, and the second-place finisher would become vice-president. The Framers had not anticipated the emergence of political parties and the formation of party tickets. In 1800 Jefferson teamed with vice-presidential candidate Aaron Burr on the Republican party's ticket, and each elector who voted for Jefferson also voted for Burr, thus creating a tie. With no winner, the election was left to the House of Representatives. At this point, Burr decided that he wanted the presidency, not the vice-presidency, and encouraged the support of Federalists in Congress.

*It will not be too strong to say that there will be a constant probability of seeing the [presidency] filled by characters pre-eminent for ability and virtue.*

Alexander Hamilton,
*Federalist* No. 68

Thirty-five ballots were cast, with neither candidate receiving the necessary majority. Finally Hamilton persuaded enough of his fellow Federalists to back Jefferson to give him the election. Hamilton and Jefferson were political foes, but Hamilton had an even stronger dislike for Burr, whom he called "the most unfit man in the United States for the office of President"[5] (and who in 1804 killed Hamilton in a pistol duel). After Jefferson took office, the Twelfth Amendment was enacted to prevent similar deadlocks in the future; the amendment provides that each elector shall cast one ballot for a presidential candidate and one ballot for a vice-presidential candidate.

The emergence of political parties in the 1790s also created a need for a presidential nominating system. Unless a party's electors were united behind a single nominee, its chances of gaining an electoral majority were diminished. The power to name nominees was assumed by party members in Congress, who caucused before each election to choose among the alternatives. Their decision was not binding on the electors, who could vote as they pleased, but the need for party unity and the prestige of the Congress led most electors to follow the recommendation of their party's congressional caucus, earning it the title of "King Caucus."[6] All presidents from John Adams through James Monroe were caucus nominees.

In 1824, however, Republican congressional leaders made known their intention to bypass the war hero Andrew Jackson and Secretary of State John Quincy Adams, who had emerged as the leaders of the party's rival factions, and nominate instead Secretary of the Treasury William Crawford of Georgia, who they believed would be easy to control once he was in the White House. Angered by this development, congressional supporters of Jackson and Adams boycotted the caucus. The stage was now set for a four-candidate race among Crawford, Jackson (who was nominated by the legislature of his home state, Tennessee), Adams (the pick of several New England legislatures), and Speaker of the House Henry Clay (nominated by the Kentucky legislature). A number of states had established popular voting for president, and the four candidates took their campaigns to the people. Jackson polled 152,933 popular votes to Adams' 115,696, while Crawford and Clay each received fewer than 50,000 votes. Jackson also placed first in the electoral voting (which was separate from the popular voting) but had less than a majority; so the final decision passed to the House of Representatives, which chose John Quincy Adams on the first ballot.[7]

## THE SECOND SYSTEM: THE PARTY CONVENTION

Jackson was outraged by Adams' election, believing that an elite conspiracy had denied him the presidency. Claiming that the people's will had been thwarted, Jackson prepared for the 1828 campaign, which he won. Jackson then set about altering the presidential election system so that it would give the people a stronger voice.

Jackson first tried to abolish selection by electors in favor of direct election by

---

[5]Quoted in Lucius Wilmerding, *The Electoral College* (New Brunswick, N.J.: Rutgers University Press, 1953), 32.
[6]See Noble E. Cunningham, Jr., "Presidential Leadership, Political Parties, and the Congressional Caucus, 1800–1824," in Patricia Bonami, James MacGregor Burns, and Austin Ranney, eds., *The American Constitutional System under Strong and Weak Parties* (New York: Praeger, 1981), 1–20.
[7]Neal R. Pierce and Lawrence Longley, *The People's President* (New Haven, Conn.: Yale University Press, 1981), 49–52.

the people. Unable to get Congress to support a constitutional amendment mandating these changes, Jackson pursued the next-best alternative: he persuaded the states to tie their electoral vote to the popular vote. Before that time, popular voting provided an opportunity for the people in a state to express their preference, which the electors could weigh along with any other factors they considered relevant when they cast their ballots. Their votes were the deciding ones. Under Jackson's reform, which is still in effect today, each party in a state has a separate slate of electors who gain the right to cast a state's electoral votes if their party's candidate places first in the state's popular voting. Thus the popular vote directly affects the electoral vote, and one candidate is likely to win both forms of the presidential vote. Since Jackson's time, only Rutherford B. Hayes (in 1876) has won the presidency after having lost the popular vote.

Jackson was also determined to kill King Caucus. He had changed the name of his party from Republican to Democratic and in 1832 he convened a national party convention to choose the Democratic presidential nominee. To Jackson, the grass-roots political party was in close touch with the people, whereas Congress was a distant tool of the establishment. Congress was dominated by men of wealth and social distinction and, in the House, by the representatives of a few large states. All presidents except Jackson had come from Virginia or Massachusetts, and the destruction of the caucus system was Jackson's way of breaking the hold that the "aristocracy" of those two states had on the presidency. Since Jackson's time, presidential nominees have been formally chosen at national party conventions.

## THE THIRD SYSTEM: THE EMERGENCE OF STATE PRIMARIES

Jackson's presidential selection system remained intact until the early twentieth century, when the Progressives initiated primary elections as a way of wrestling control over presidential nominations from party bosses. In 1904 Florida became the first state to choose its national convention delegates through a presidential primary. Some other states followed suit, but most either stayed with the older system of party selection or adopted nonbinding primaries. As a result, party leaders continued to control a majority of the convention delegates who selected the presidential nominees.

Through 1968, a strong showing in the primaries enabled a candidate to demonstrate popular support but did not guarantee nomination. The party leadership had to be persuaded that the candidate was deserving of nomination. In 1952 Senator Estes Kefauver won twelve of the thirteen state primaries he entered, but still lost the Democratic nomination to Adlai Stevenson, governor of Illinois, whom the party leaders preferred because his views on social welfare and labor policy were more consistent with the party's tradition. In contrast, state primaries were pivotal in John F. Kennedy's drive for the Democratic nomination in 1960. "He had to prove to [party leaders] he could win," said Kennedy's assistant Theodore Sorensen.[8] No Catholic had ever won the presidency, and it took Kennedy's primary victories in the largely Protestant states of Wisconsin and West Virginia to convince party leaders that his religion would not prevent a Democratic victory in November.

---

[8]Quoted in Theodore H. White, *The Making of the President, 1960* (New York: Atheneum, 1961), 61.

John F. Kennedy was the first president whose nomination clearly derived from victories in the primaries. As a Catholic and a junior senator, Kennedy had no chance of winning the Democratic presidential nomination in 1960 unless his primary campaign was successful. Kennedy is shown campaigning in West Virginia, a heavily Protestant state whose primary he won. (AP/Wide World Photos)

## THE FOURTH SYSTEM: PRIMARIES AND OPEN CAUCUSES

Recognizing the drama inherent in Kennedy's run for the presidency, the news media covered the 1960 Democratic primaries heavily, contributing to a growing sense in some circles that primaries were "the *democratic* way to make nominations."[9] This perception was heightened when Barry Goldwater won the 1964 Republican nomination in an open contest. In 1968, however, the Democratic nomination went to Vice-President Hubert Humphrey, who had not entered a single primary. The 1968 Democratic nominating campaign was bitterly fought. President Lyndon Johnson had mired the nation in a war in Vietnam that increasingly seemed unwinnable, and he was challenged for nomination by Senators Eugene McCarthy and Robert Kennedy, who did well enough in the Democratic primaries to help force Johnson to withdraw from the race. Kennedy's assassination in early June left McCarthy to carry the challenge, but he was viewed by party leaders as a spoiler who had split the party and jeopardized the likelihood of a Democratic victory in November. The delegate selection rules favored the leaders. They controlled the delegates in most nonprimary states, and they even had control of a share of the delegates in some primary states. For example, McCarthy won nearly 80 percent of the popular vote in Pennsylvania's primary but, because of the state's rules, received the support of less than 20 percent of its national convention delegates.

When the party leadership's choice, Humphrey, narrowly lost the 1968 general election to Richard Nixon, reform-minded Democrats forced changes in the nominating process. The new rules gave rank-and-file party voters more

[9]Richard Rubin, *Press, Party, and President* (New York: Norton, 1981), ch. 7.

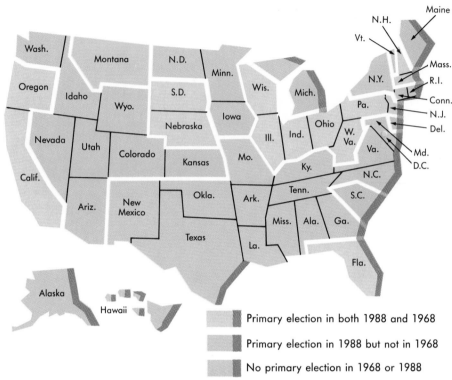

**FIGURE 19-1 Use of Primary Elections to Select Presidential Candidates, by State, 1968 and 1988**
The number of presidential primaries has increased greatly in recent decades.

Primary election in both 1988 and 1968

Primary election in 1988 but not in 1968

No primary election in 1968 or 1988

control by requiring that states choose their delegates through either primary elections or **open party caucuses** (meetings open to all rank-and-file party voters who want to attend). Although the Democrats initiated the change, the Republicans were also affected by it. Most states that adopted a presidential primary in order to comply with the Democrats' new rules required Republicans, too, to select their convention delegates through a primary.

Today the voters, through state primaries and open caucuses (see Figure 19-1), largely determine who will be chosen as the Democratic and Republican presidential nominees. Some rule changes since the early 1970s have altered the system slightly,* but nominating campaigns today are nearly national plebiscites. Presidential hopefuls must win the people's support, a process that guarantees long and grueling campaigns that sometimes have surprising outcomes.

## The Campaign for Nomination

Many leading politicians yearn to be president but most of them choose not to make a run for the nation's highest office.[10] A presidential campaign is lengthy

---

*In 1982, for example, the Democratic party's Hunt Commission changed that party's nominating system somewhat to increase the likelihood that its presidential nominee wound be an established political leader. The Hunt Commission's major change was to set aside 15 percent (since changed to 20 percent) of delegate positions for local, state, and national party officials. These "superdelegates" would hold the balance of power if the nominating race was close. Presumably they would use their influence to choose a nominee who by background and policy positions would represent the party tradition.

[10]John H. Aldrich, *Before the Convention* (Chicago: University of Chicago Press, 1980), ch. 2; Thomas E. Cronin, *State of the Presidency* (Boston: Little, Brown, 1980), 28.

The Democratic presidential field in 1988 included seven active candidates, who are shown here moments before a televised debate in Houston. (John Makely/Sygma)

and demanding, and there can be only one winner.[11] Nevertheless, recent nominating campaigns, except those in which an incumbent president is seeking reelection, have attracted a half-dozen or more contenders. They begin planning their campaigns almost as soon as the last presidential election is over and hit the campaign trail six to twelve months in advance of the first primaries and caucuses. The 1988 Republican campaign started earlier than usual when the Michigan Republican party decided to conduct a nonbinding ballot at its 1986 state convention. Vice-President George Bush, who was the leading Republican presidential contender in national polls, believed that he could not risk the embarrassment of a defeat in the Michigan balloting and spent $800,000 lining up votes.

Most presidential contenders are not well known to the nation's voters before the campaign, and many of them have no significant record of national accomplishment. They enter the race out of personal ambition and with hopes that a strong showing in the earliest state contests will propel them into the national spotlight. In the race for the 1988 Democratic nomination, Gary Hart and Jesse Jackson were the only active contenders who had national reputations when their campaigns began. Michael Dukakis, Bruce Babbitt, Richard Gephardt, Albert Gore, and Paul Simon were complete unknowns to most Americans.

## GAINING THE MEDIA'S ATTENTION

For candidates to acquire public support, they must first get the public's attention. The news media are therefore an influential force in the nominating process and have been called "the Great Mentioner": a candidate who is regularly mentioned in the news has a chance of nomination, whereas one who is ignored by the press is effectively out of the race from the beginning.[12]

---

[11]See Robert E. DiClerico and Eric M. Uslaner, *Few Are Chosen* (New York: McGraw-Hill, 1984).
[12]Ronald Berkman and Laura W. Kitch, *Politics in the Media Age* (New York: McGraw-Hill, 1986), ch. 5.

★ ANALYZE THE ISSUE

**The New Elite in the Nomination Process**
The process of choosing presidential nominees has greatly changed in the past few decades. Among other things, the old elite of party leaders—governors, mayors, members of Congress, and party chairmen—has given way to a new elite of journalists and the candidates' hired consultants—pollsters, media specialists, and the like. What are the implications of this shift? In regard to this change alone, is the new system an improvement over the old?

★ ANALYZE THE ISSUE

**The Importance of New Hampshire's Primary**
George Bush and Michael Dukakis won the New Hampshire primaries of their respective parties in 1988 and went on to become the presidential nominees. This pattern has become common. In the past four presidential elections, only the Democrat Walter Mondale in 1984 has become the nominee without winning the New Hampshire primary. What accounts for New Hampshire's importance? Is it really as important as it appears to be? Should New Hampshire, or any other state, be allowed to have a disproportionate impact on the presidential campaign? How might the nominating system be changed to reduce this impact?

National opinion polls guide the news media in deciding whom to cover closely. Bush was the leading candidate among Republicans in opinion polls before the 1988 primaries and received heavier news coverage than his opponents. The media also take their cues from the candidates' ability to raise funds, build an effective organization, gain the support of important groups, and articulate critical issues. George McGovern had only limited support among Democrats in national polls before the 1972 race but received more attention from the media than other low-ranking contenders because of his strong grass-roots support among anti-Vietnam activists.

## MOMENTUM

A key to success in the nominating campaign is what candidates and journalists call **momentum**—a strong showing in the early contests which leads to a buildup of public support in subsequent ones. If a candidate starts off poorly, reporters will lose interest in covering him, contributors will deny him funding, political leaders will not endorse him, and voters will not give further thought to supporting him.

For these reasons, presidential contenders now give extraordinary attention to the early contests, particularly the first ones, in Iowa and New Hampshire.[13] They may make dozens of trips to Iowa and New Hampshire in the year or two before these contests are held. The media also give these two contests close scrutiny (see Figure 19-2). Even though New Hampshire's primary selects less than 1 percent of the national convention delegates, it receives more news coverage than any other presidential primary.[14]

A victory in Iowa or New Hampshire is a media bonanza for the winner. After narrowly winning New Hampshire's 1976 Democratic primary, for example, Jimmy Carter was on the front covers of *Time* and *Newsweek* and received 2,600 lines of coverage, compared to 300 lines for all five of his Democratic challengers combined. Within a week of his New Hampshire triumph, Carter's name recognition nationwide jumped from 20 percent to 80 percent, and his support among Democratic voters tripled.[15] In the same week, all of Carter's opponents either stood still or dropped in the polls.

Candidates in primary elections are assisted by the Federal Election Campaign Act of 1974 (as amended in 1979). This act provides for federal "matching funds" to be given to any candidate who raises at least $5,000 in contributions of up to $250 in each of twenty states. In general, this federal support mainly helps lesser-known contenders—the sort who in the past had trouble raising enough money to compete effectively. Now any candidate who raises funds in the legally prescribed way is given an equal amount by the U.S. Treasury. Candidates are restricted in their spending during the nominating campaign if they accept matching funds. In 1988 the spending limit was roughly $22 million, which is about what Bush and Dukakis each spent on their nominating campaigns.

---

[13]See Hugh Winebrenner, *The Iowa Precinct Caucuses* (Ames: Iowa State University Press, 1987); Gary R. Orren and Nelson W. Polsby, eds., *Media and Momentum: The New Hampshire Primary and Nomination Politics* (Chatham, N.J.: Chatham House, 1987).
[14]Michael J. Robinson and Margaret A. Sheehan, *Over the Wire and on TV* (New York: Russell Sage Foundation, 1983), 174.
[15]Thomas E. Patterson, *The Mass Media Election* (New York: Praeger, 1980), ch. 5.

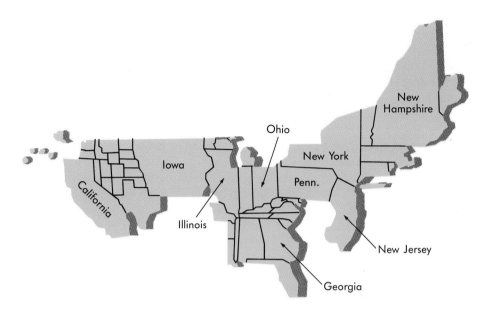

**FIGURE 19-2 States Sized in Proportion to News Coverage Given Their Presidential Nominating Contests, 1984**
The Iowa caucuses and the New Hampshire primary dominate news coverage of state nominating contests. *Source: William C. Adams, "As New Hampshire Goes . . .," in Gary R. Orren and Nelson W. Polsby, eds.,* Media and Momentum: The New Hampshire Primary and Nomination Politics *(Chatham, N.J.: Chatham House, 1987), ch. 3.*

## THE POLITICS OF NOMINATION RACES

Voter turnout for presidential primaries has increased since primaries became decisive in the outcomes of the nomination races. Yet the primary electorate includes only about a third of potential voters and is hardly representative of the American public. Primary voters are more ideological in their beliefs than nonvoters, a fact that can work to the benefit of candidates of the left or right. It is unlikely that either George McGovern, a liberal, or Ronald Reagan, a conservative, would have won nomination had party leaders remained in control of the process; party leaders tend to prefer moderates, on the assumption that such nominees appeal to a wider range of the full electorate and thus have a better chance of winning the election.

Voting in primaries is somewhat unpredictable because voters must choose among candidates within the same party. Partisanship gives stability to the vote in the general election; each nominee can expect the support of voters faithful to the party. This component is missing in primaries, so vote swings can be substantial. After Dukakis won the New Hampshire primary in 1988, his nationwide support among Democratic voters in polls jumped from 16 percent to 34 percent. Most New Hampshire winners in recent elections have, like Dukakis, gained significant public support immediately after this primary.[16]

A candidate's early triumph can often be parlayed into continued success, particularly when there is no strong, well-known opponent. When the voters are poorly informed about the contenders, the attention that comes to a candidate because of an early win can move millions of voters in his direction. Their gaze is focused on one contender, so, not surprisingly, those without an existing strong preference may be inclined to support him.[17] In 1976 Carter apparently gained half or more of his votes in subsequent early primaries from the momentum achieved by his victory in New Hampshire's primary.[18]

---

[16]William C. Adams, "As New Hampshire Goes . . . ," in Orren and Polsby, *Media and Momentum,* ch. 3.
[17]See Larry Bartels, *Presidential Primaries and the Dynamics of Public Choice* (Princeton, N.J.: Princeton University Press, 1988), ch. 8.
[18]Patterson, *Mass Media Election,* ch. 11.

**The Relative Importance of Primary and General Elections**
Voter turnout is roughly 20 percentage points lower in presidential primaries than in the general election. This pattern suggests that the public regards the general election as the more important of the two—but is it? Consider the fact that the nominating races eliminate all the presidential alternatives except two, one of whom is certain to win.

Although the dynamics of momentum help to explain why the early leader often wins nomination, it does not account for initial success or enduring appeal. Why does one candidate start strongly or maintain strength while another does not? There is no single answer, but a candidate must have strength of one kind or another to prevail. Issues can be important: the main reason McGovern won the Democratic nomination in 1972 was that his anti-Vietnam stance attracted a stable and committed voting bloc. Ideology can also matter: the division between Ford and Reagan in 1976 reflected a long-standing split between moderate and conservative Republicans. Critical events can further influence nominations: the international crisis resulting when Iranian militants took control of the U.S. embassy in Tehran in late 1979 gave President Carter's popularity a temporary boost that enabled him to turn back Senator Edward Kennedy's challenge for the 1980 Democratic nomination. Group support is sometimes a factor: Mondale's 1984 campaign became strong in late 1983 when powerful labor, teachers', and women's groups backed his candidacy. Public familiarity is another factor: Bush's successful drive to the 1988 Republican nomination owed mainly to support built up during his vice-presidency.

In short, political influences of varying kinds have a strong impact on nominating races. Presidential nominations are not decided strictly by momentum and superior strategy. Since 1968 the preprimary poll leader in contested nominations has won about half the time. Nevertheless, Carter's 1976 campaign and Dukakis's 1988 campaign are reminders that a well-organized candidate with no national reputation or previous strong base of support can sometimes maneuver successfully through the maze of state caucuses and primaries.

## THE NATIONAL PARTY CONVENTIONS

National party conventions were once tumultuous affairs where lengthy, heated bargaining took place before a presidential nominee was chosen. An extreme case was the Democratic convention of 1924, which, after 103 ballots, ended up nominating an unknown "dark horse," John W. Davis. Today's conventions are relatively tame; not since 1952 has a nomination gone past the first ballot.* Nevertheless, the party convention is a major event. It brings together the delegates elected in state caucuses and primaries, who then vote to approve a party platform and to nominate the party's presidential and vice-presidential candidates.

### Party Unity and Disunity

Some recent conventions have been the scenes of major disputes. The strategies and issues of nominating campaigns can so alienate the losers that they cannot accept defeat gracefully. In 1968, when the Vietnam war was at issue, the Democratic contender Eugene McCarthy at first refused to support the party's nominee, Hubert Humphrey, even though they were both from Minnesota and

---

*Through 1932, the Democrats required their nominee to have a two-thirds majority of convention delegates to win nomination. Now only a simple majority is required. This is the main reason that recent nominations have been decided on the first ballot. In addition, the shift toward primaries and caucuses has reduced strategic voting at the convention; at one time it was common for party leaders to withhold their state's delegate votes until concessions were granted. Finally, the winnowing process in today's campaigns quickly reduces the field, in most cases, to two leading contenders, and one of them is likely to have the support of 50 percent or more of the delegates by the time the convention begins.

Presidential nominees are formally chosen at national party conventions. (Matthew McVay/Picture Group)

had been personal friends. Also, when the nominee is extremely liberal or conservative, deep ideological cleavages can keep the opposing sides apart. In 1964, after the GOP had nominated the conservative Barry Goldwater, his chief opponent, the moderate Nelson Rockefeller, stood up at the convention to pledge his support for Goldwater. Goldwater's delegates, who had come to regard Rockefeller as their archenemy, booed him so long and loudly that he was unable to make himself heard; after several vain attempts he stalked off the podium, leaving the national television audience with the image of the GOP as a party divided against itself.

However, national conventions are ordinarily an occasion for cementing party unity. Carter delegates in 1980 accepted several platform planks proposed by Edward Kennedy's backers, including a commitment to a $12 billion public jobs program, in order to heal antagonisms that had developed during the Carter–Kennedy primary battles. Conventions also provide nominees with an opportunity to build bridges to party voters. As many as 150 million Americans watch part of the proceedings on national television, and for many of them it is a time of decision. About a fourth of voters solidify their presidential choice during the convention, and most of them decide to back the nominee of their preferred party.[19]

## The Vice-presidential Nomination

The party conventions choose the vice-presidential nominees as well as those for president. Nomination to run for the vice-presidency was once scorned by leading politicians, including Daniel Webster and Henry Clay. Said Webster, "I do not propose to be buried until I'm really dead."[20] No politician today shares this view of the vice-presidency. Although it is a relatively powerless office, it

[19]William Flanigan and Nancy Zingale, *Political Behavior of the American Electorate*, 4th ed. (Boston: Allyn & Bacon, 1979), 172–173.
[20]Quoted in Steven J. Wayne, *Road to the White House*, 2d ed. (New York: St. Martin's Press, 1984), 131.

In 1984 Geraldine Ferraro was chosen as the Democratic party's vice-presidential candidate, the first woman ever to be selected for the national ticket by a major party. Ferraro's nomination as Walter Mondale's running mate initially helped to unite the party, but her effectiveness during the fall campaign was impaired by questions about her family's finances. (Art Stein/ Photo Researchers)

has become the inside track to the presidency: five of the nine presidents between 1948 and 1988 were former vice-presidents (Truman, Johnson, Nixon, Ford, and Bush).

By tradition, the choice of the vice-presidential nominee rests with the presidential nominee. His decision can reflect any number of considerations, including the experience, reputation, political beliefs, ethnic background, and home region of a possible running mate. Mondale in 1984 chose Geraldine Ferraro, the first female vice-presidential nominee of a major party, because his private polls indicated that a woman would be a stronger addition to the ticket than any of the available men.

At times the vice-presidential nominee has been selected hastily because the presidential nominee was preoccupied until the last moment with securing his own nomination. This situation can be risky. In 1972 George McGovern picked Senator Thomas Eagleton as his running mate, a decision reached at the convention when McGovern talked with Eagleton by phone and was assured that there were no skeletons in Eagleton's closet. Within a few days of the convention, however, it became known that Eagleton had a history of depression and years earlier had received electroshock therapy. Eagleton was dumped from the ticket and replaced by Sargent Shriver, a brother-in-law of the Kennedys. Polls revealed that the Eagleton affair created a no-win situation for McGovern: he stood to lose public support whether he kept Eagleton or dropped him. The Eagleton incident was almost repeated in 1988, when Bush's running mate, Senator Dan Quayle of Indiana, was discovered to have pulled strings to avoid the draft during the Vietnam war. Bush rejected pleas that Quayle be dropped from the ticket, but kept him in the background during the fall campaign.

It has been questioned whether the vice-presidential nomination should rest in the hands of a single individual, the presidential nominee. The vice-president stands a good chance of becoming president someday, so it has been argued that the vice-presidential nomination should be decided in open competition at the party convention. The chief argument for keeping the existing system is that the presidential nominee, if elected, needs a vice-president in whom he has complete confidence.

## The Campaign for Election

The winner in the November general election is almost certain to be either the Republican or the Democratic nominee. A minor-party or independent candidate, such as George Wallace in 1968 or John Anderson in 1980, can draw votes away from the major-party nominees but stands almost no chance of defeating them.

A major-party nominee has the critical advantage of support from the party faithful. Earlier in the twentieth century, this support was so unwavering that the victory of the stronger party's candidate was almost a certainty. Warren G. Harding accepted the 1920 Republican nomination at his Ohio home and stayed there throughout most of the campaign. Like another Ohio nominee, William McKinley in 1896, Harding spoke on his front steps to visiting groups but made little effort to run a national campaign. Harding won a landslide victory simply because most of the voters of his time were Republicans.

Party loyalty has declined sharply in recent decades, but more than two-thirds of the nation's voters still identify themselves as Democrats or Republicans, and most of them support their party's presidential candidate (see Table

Questions that emerge about a vice-presidential candidate can cast doubt on a presidential candidate's judgment. George Bush was criticized in 1988 after it was revealed that Dan Quayle, his choice of a running mate, had used family influence to avoid the draft by joining the National Guard during the Vietnam war. (Dennis Brack/Black Star)

TABLE 19-2   Percentage of Voters Identifying with a Party Who Voted for That Party's Candidate, 1960–1988

| Year | Candidates | Democratic Identifiers | Republican Identifiers |
|------|-----------|------------------------|------------------------|
| 1960 | Kennedy (D)–Nixon (R) | 80% | 93% |
| 1964 | Johnson (D)–Goldwater (R) | 89 | 76 |
| 1968 | Nixon (R)–Humphrey (D) | 73 | 88 |
| 1972 | Nixon (R)–McGovern (D) | 58 | 94 |
| 1976 | Carter (D)–Ford (R) | 80 | 86 |
| 1980 | Reagan (R)–Carter (D) | 67 | 86 |
| 1984 | Reagan (R)–Mondale (D) | 75 | 93 |
| 1988 | Bush (R)–Dukakis (D) | 82 | 91 |

SOURCES: 1960–1976, SRC/CPS Election Studies; 1980–1988, *New York Times*, November 10, 1988, B6.

19-2).[21] Even McGovern, who had the lowest level of party support among recent nominees, was backed in 1972 by 58 percent of his party's voters.[22]

## BUILDING A WINNING COALITION: THE IMPACT OF PARTY, ISSUES, AND IMAGE

Nevertheless, partisan loyalty alone will not carry today's presidential nominee to victory. A winning coalition is built on party, issues, and image.

### Party

Democratic party identifiers have outnumbered Republicans since the realigning election of 1932, and the Democratic candidate has been able to win the election when the party has held together. However, the Democratic party is currently made up of a somewhat unstable coalition of groups with differing values and political attitudes. Southerners and Catholics are among the traditional Democrats who have strayed from their party in significant numbers in recent presidential elections. In fact, southerners can no longer be described as Democrats in presidential politics. The Democratic presidential nominee has carried the formerly "Solid South," including the border states, in only one presidential election since 1964.

Democratic nominees have normally emphasized basic economic issues, such as unemployment and social security, in hopes of keeping the party's coalition together. Dukakis followed this strategy in 1988, arguing that newer service-sector jobs offered neither a livable wage nor employment security. This claim helped to prevent large-scale defections, but 17 percent of registered Democrats nevertheless voted for Bush. Traditional economic appeals have simply become less effective for Democratic nominees because of improvements in Americans' economic security and standard of living since the 1930s.

Republican nominees find it easier to keep their party's loyalists in line. The

[21]See Norman H. Nie, Sidney Verba, and John Petrocik, *The Changing American Voter* (Cambridge, Mass.: Harvard University Press, 1979), 48–59.
[22]Herbert Asher, *Presidential Elections and American Politics*, rev. ed. (Homewood, Ill.: Dorsey Press, 1980), 92.

GOP is now relatively homogeneous; its members share many attitudes on economic, social, and foreign policy issues. Appeals to traditional social values, patriotism, restrained government spending, lower taxes, and a strong defense against communism will usually maintain the Republican vote. In 1964 Barry Goldwater lost some Republican support because of his extreme policy stands —yet more than 75 percent of the nation's Republicans still voted for him.[23] A Republican candidate, however, cannot win with Republican votes alone and must make substantial inroads among independent and Democratic voters.

## Issues

Presidential nominees identify key issues on which to build their campaigns. For incumbents and challengers alike, some of these issues will be questions of past performance, such as the condition of the economy. Whether candidates benefit by raising such issues depends largely on national conditions. In 1980 Reagan asked whether voters wanted "four more years" of Carter, a telling slogan in view of the nation's reeling economy. Reagan employed the same slogan in 1984, with the idea that voters would respond favorably to the improvements in the nation's economy which had occurred during his first term.

Prospective issues also enter into every nominee's campaign, although they vary in importance. In 1988, for example, Bush struck a responsive chord when he claimed that a Dukakis administration would be soft on crime. As evidence, Bush's advertising campaign repeatedly referred to the case of Willie Horton, a convicted murderer who, while out of prison on a furlough program during Dukakis's incumbency as governor of Massachusetts, had brutally assaulted a Maryland couple.

Presidential nominees have more than raw ambition in mind when they seek the nation's highest office, and their issue positions indicate where they intend to lead the nation. Although cynics often claim that presidential campaign promises are mere vote-getting ploys, the evidence indicates that in fact newly elected presidents do fulfill most of their promises (see Figure 19-3). When they fail to deliver on a commitment, it is usually because of circumstances beyond their control, such as Congress's refusal to cooperate.[24]

## Image

One of the great myths of modern campaigns is that candidates must look good on television if they are to win.[25] Among television-age presidents, only John F. Kennedy and Ronald Reagan were physically handsome men who were entirely at ease on television. Image is far more than a matter of personal appearance and style. The essence of a presidential image resides in the candidate's ability to project an impression of strong and forthright leadership. In large part, this impression depends on external factors rather than on a candidate's personal characteristics. During his first two years in office, an economic recession caused Reagan to lose public approval faster than any president since polling began in

> ★ ANALYZE THE ISSUE
>
> **Why Did Dukakis Lose?**
> In midsummer of 1988 Michael Dukakis had a clear lead in the polls over George Bush. When Dukakis lost that lead, and ultimately lost the election, many analysts said that it was his own fault—that, among other mistakes, he had campaigned poorly and had let Bush define the issues. Is this explanation convincing? As an alternative, consider the state of the economy and the world. The United States in 1988 was in its fifth year of an economic upswing, the longest in fifty years. And in 1988 tensions between the United States and the Soviet Union were at their lowest in decades. Is it realistic to think that the out-party's nominee, Dukakis, should have won in 1988?

[23]Gerald Pomper, *Voter's Choice* (New York: Dodd, Mead, 1975), 37.
[24]Gerald Pomper with Susan Lederman, *Elections in America* (New York: Longman, 1980), ch. 8.
[25]See Thomas E. Patterson, "The Mistaken Image," *Television Quarterly*, Spring 1987, 29–34.

Percentage of campaign pledges

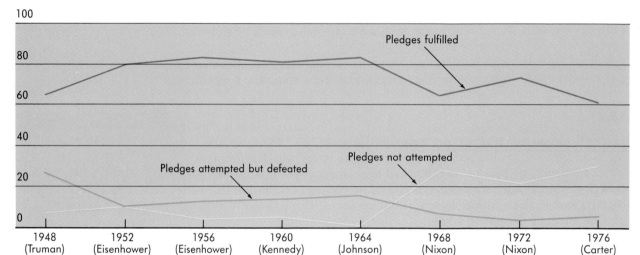

FIGURE 19-3 Percentage of Platform Pledges Fulfilled, Defeated, and Not Attempted, 1948–1976
Contrary to widespread belief, winning presidential candidates keep most of their campaign promises. *Source: Gerald M. Pomper with Susan S. Lederman,* Elections in America *(New York: Longman, 1980), 162–163.*

the 1930s. When the economy rebounded in 1983, so did the public's sense that Reagan was an able leader.

Candidates do have some control over the way the public perceives their leadership. To maintain a positive image, candidates must avoid mistakes in judgment and the appearance of character weakness. The Eagleton incident in 1972, for example, severely undermined public confidence in McGovern's judgment. The lesson that candidates have drawn from such episodes is that they must avoid mistakes at all costs, which in practice means that they have to consider carefully everything they say and do.

## DEVISING A WINNING STRATEGY

In their choice of party, issue, and image appeals, candidates act strategically. In deciding whether to pursue a course of action, they try to estimate its likely impact on the voters.

Strategic choices take place within the context of certain realities, one of which is the constitutional provision that each state shall have electoral votes equal in number to its representation in Congress. Each state thus gets two electoral votes for its Senate representation and a varying number of electoral votes depending on its House representation. North Dakota, which has only one House member, is one of several states with three electoral votes; California, which has forty-five House members, has the most electoral votes—forty-seven (see Figure 19-4). Altogether, there are 538 electoral votes (including three for the District of Columbia, even though it has no voting representatives in Congress). To win the presidency, a candidate must receive at least 270 votes, an electoral majority.

Because the popular-vote winner in a state receives all of that state's electoral votes, candidates are particularly concerned with winning the more populous states, such as California (47 electoral votes), New York (36), Texas (29), Pennsylvania (25), Illinois (24), and Florida (17). Victory in the twelve largest

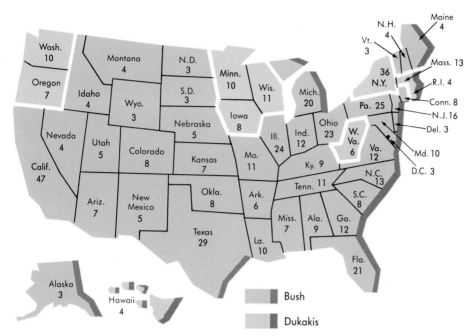

**FIGURE 19-4 Electoral Votes in the Fifty States, and States Carried by the Presidential Candidates in the 1988 Election** The larger a state's population is, the more electoral votes it has—and the more important it is to presidential candidates. Each state's electoral votes are shown here, along with the states carried by candidates George Bush and Michael Dukakis in the 1988 election. To win the presidency, a candidate must receive 270 of the national total of 538 electoral votes. Bush won forty states for 426 electoral votes, while Dukakis took ten states and the District of Columbia, which had a total of 112 electoral votes.

states alone would provide an electoral majority, and presidential candidates therefore spend most of their time campaigning in the larger states.[26]

Incumbent presidents can avoid strenuous campaigning by making news at the White House. This option, sometimes known as the "Rose Garden strategy," capitalizes on the prestige and power of the presidential office. In his 1980 reelection campaign, President Carter made a dramatic announcement of a breakthrough in the Iranian hostage crisis at a 7:00 A.M. White House news conference on the morning of Wisconsin's primary, in which he faced a strong challenge from Edward Kennedy. The hostage breakthrough did not materialize, but news of Carter's announcement contributed to his victory in Wisconsin. President Nixon pursued the Rose Garden strategy almost exclusively in 1972, making only seven appearances outside Washington during the entire general election campaign. A week before election day, Nixon announced from the White House that the Vietnam peace talks in Paris were nearing a breakthrough; the tactic strengthened his position with voters.

On paper, the incumbent president would seem to have so many advantages that he should never lose.[27] Indeed, a second term was almost guaranteed until recently. Among twentieth-century presidents, only William Howard Taft and Herbert Hoover failed to win reelection until Lyndon Johnson saw the wisdom of not seeking nomination in 1968 and Jimmy Carter lost his bid for a second term in 1980. A president's chances for reelection are somewhat worse today than they were in the past because the public has come to have higher expectations of the president and tends to blame him for national problems, a point that will be discussed in Chapter 21.

[26]Raymond Tatalovich, "Electoral Votes and Presidential Campaign Trails, 1932–1976," *American Politics Quarterly*, October 1979, 489–498.
[27]James W. Davis, *The American Presidency* (New York: Harper & Row, 1987), 84.

## MONEY AND MEDIA

In the 1988 general election Dukakis and Bush each spent about $46 million on his campaign. In view of the scope of these national campaigns, expenditures of this magnitude are not surprising. A presidential campaign requires a large staff, mass mailings, opinion polls, a chartered jet to carry the nominee around the country, media production, television time, and so on. In an age when some U.S. Senate campaigns within a single state cost $10 million or more, presidential campaigns might even be considered underfunded by comparison.

### Federal Funding of Campaigns

Until 1976, presidential candidates had no choice but to raise campaign funds on their own. The need for large infusions of cash led them to rely on "fat cats"—wealthy private donors such as W. Clement Stone, a Chicago insurance firm owner, who donated $2 million to Nixon's 1972 campaign, and Stewart Mott, a General Motors heir, who contributed nearly $750,000 to McGovern's 1972 campaign. In 1974, in response to revelations about campaign finance irregularities, Congress passed legislation providing for federal funding of major presidential candidates.

The Republican and Democratic nominees are each entitled to the same level of federal funding. The only string attached to this funding is that a candidate who accepts it can spend no additional funds on his campaign (though his party can spend additional money on his behalf). In the 1976 campaign, the first to which the new rules applied, Jimmy Carter and Gerald Ford each received $21 million. The amount has been increased in each subsequent presidential election by the level of inflation during the preceding four years, reaching $46 million per major-party candidate in 1988. Presidential candidates can choose not to accept public funding, in which case the amount they spend is limited only by their ability to raise money privately. However, all major-party nominees since 1976 have accepted public funding.

The current arrangement works to the disadvantage of independent and minor-party candidates. The law requires them to get at least 5 percent of the popular vote in order to qualify for public funds and then permits them to receive only an amount equal to the ratio of their vote total to the average vote total of the two major-party nominees. John Anderson, an independent candidate, received $4.2 million after he won 7 percent of the 1980 presidential vote. Reagan and Carter had seven times as many votes, on average, and each received $29 million. Moreover, Reagan and Carter were given their money in late summer, after the major-party conventions, whereas Anderson did not become eligible for his public funds until after the November election and had to conduct his fall campaign on borrowed money.

### Television Campaigns

Presidential candidates allot a large proportion of their campaign funds to televised political advertising.[28] Since 1976, political television commercials have accounted for about half of the candidates' expenditures in the general

---

[28]George C. Edwards and Stephen J. Wayne, *Presidential Leadership* (New York: St. Martin's Press, 1985), 64.

★ HOW THE UNITED STATES COMPARES

**Television Campaign Advertising**
Unlike the United States, most other democracies have a parliamentary system of government based on strong parties. If a single party wins a legislative majority, it chooses the prime minister from among its legislators. If not, all the parties represented in the legislature bargain to fill the post of chief executive. In either case, the prime minister is chosen by the parties, not elected directly by the voters. The contrast between party-centered methods of selecting the chief executive and the candidate-centered nature of U.S. presidential elections is evident even in the use of television. In most democracies, televised campaigning on behalf of candidates takes place through the parties, which receive free air time to make their appeals to the voters. U.S. presidential candidates do not receive unrestricted free time, but instead must buy advertising time with their campaign funds. Some other democracies prohibit politicians from buying television time to promote their own candidacies.

| Country | Paid TV Ads Allowed? | Unrestricted Free TV Time Provided? |
| --- | --- | --- |
| Canada | Yes | Yes |
| France | No | Yes |
| Great Britain | No | Yes |
| Italy | No | Yes |
| Japan | Yes | Yes |
| Mexico | Yes | Yes |
| United States | Yes | No |
| West Germany | No | Yes |

election. Bush and Dukakis each spent more than $20 million on television advertising in 1988.

Television also provides the focal point of the fall campaign: presidential debates. The first of these televised encounters took place in 1960 between Kennedy and Nixon, and an estimated 80 percent of all eligible voters saw at least one of their four debates.[29] Televised debates resumed in 1976 and have apparently become a permanent fixture of presidential campaigns. Studies indicate that presidential debates influence the votes of only a small percentage of the electorate. However, presidential elections are sometimes decided by a few percentage points, and the lesser-known candidate usually benefits more than his opponent from televised debates. In 1960, for example, Kennedy gained support among undecided Democrats when his debate performance convinced them that, despite his youth, he had the skills and knowledge required of a president.[30] Debate performance can also hurt a candidate's chances. In 1976 President Ford became so rattled during a televised debate that he said that Eastern Europe was "not under the domination of the Soviet Union," a claim that hurt his image as a master of foreign affairs.

## THE IMPACT OF THE CAMPAIGN ON THE FINAL VOTE

In the 1940s and 1950s, when voters' party loyalties were stronger than they are today, presidential campaigns changed few people's minds. About 80 percent of the voters made their choice early in the campaign and stayed with it. Even the

[29]Sidney Kraus, ed., *The Great Debates* (Bloomington: Indiana University Press, 1962), 190.
[30]Ibid., 315–317.

The Kennedy–Nixon debates of 1960 were the first televised debates between presidential candidates. The poised, handsome Kennedy was much more attractive to viewers than Nixon, who looked ill at ease and evasive on television. Some observers believe that this difference gave Kennedy his narow margin of victory. (UPI/Bettman Newsphotos)

late deciders were not entirely open to persuasion; the large majority ended up supporting the candidate of their party.[31]

Because of the recent decline in partisanship, voters are now more easily influenced by a campaign's issues, events, and candidates. Most votes are not won or lost in the campaign (as in the case of a diehard Democrat who always has and always will vote for the Democratic nominee), but large percentages of the vote have been up for grabs in recent campaigns. In 1976, for example, more than 40 percent of all voters at one time or another during the campaign considered voting for the candidate—Jimmy Carter or Gerald Ford—who was *not* their final choice.[32] In 1988 Dukakis at one time led Bush by 15 points, but a few weeks later had fallen 10 points behind.

Not all recent campaigns have shown such high volatility, and many partisans are not entirely serious when they claim to be thinking about defecting to the other party's candidate. In 1976, for example, most Republicans who toyed with the idea of voting for Carter decided in the end to back Ford, just as most wavering Democrats finally voted for Carter.

The impact of the campaign on voters is also limited by incumbency and national conditions, particularly the state of the economy (see Chapter 10). In 1984 no campaign strategy or amount of effort could have carried Mondale to victory against the personally popular incumbent, Reagan, at a time when the national economy was on an upward swing. Similarly, Richard Nixon was unbeatable in 1972, as was Lyndon Johnson in 1964.

Nevertheless, campaign effort and maneuvering have become more significant in recent decades. More votes are available to be won today: partisanship is

[31]See Bernard Berelson, Paul Lazarsfeld, and William McPhee, *Voting* (Chicago: University of Chicago Press, 1954), 18.
[32]See Steven Chaffee and Sun Yuel Chou, "Time of Decision and Media Use during the Ford–Carter Campaign," *Public Opinion Quarterly* #44 (Spring 1980), 55; Bruce Campbell, *The American Electorate* (New York: Holt, Rinehart and Winston, 1979), 262.

less of a guide to presidential choice, and the issues and personalities of the moment have increased in importance. Today, if an election is close for other reasons, victory is likely to go to the candidate who campaigns more effectively.[33]

## Are Great Leaders Elected President?

The presidency of the United States has always been a restricted office. All presidents have been white males, and the great majority have been well-to-do Anglo-Saxon Protestants who were married and over fifty years of age.[34] Except for four army generals, no man has won the presidency who has not first held high public office. Nearly a third of the nation's presidents had previously been vice-presidents, and most of the rest were former U.S. senators, state governors, or top federal executives (see Table 19-3).

Although past presidents have had privileged backgrounds, not all have been men of great talent, experience, and character. In an 1891 essay titled "Why Great Men Are Not Elected President," James Bryce argued that the presidential selection process itself was a major reason why the United States did not regularly elect talented men to its highest office.[35] Bryce claimed that the party bosses were more interested in maintaining personal power than in picking nominees of exceptional ability. Today's nominating system is also not designed to produce great nominees. Its foundation is legitimacy: above all, the people must have the decisive voice in the choice of nominees.

The nominating decisions are the critical ones, because they narrow a very large number of presidential possibilities down to two, and one of them, the Republican or the Democratic nominee, is virtually certain to become the next

*After a long struggle, to which he gave a lot and for which he paid a price, George Bush has realized his life's dream of becoming President. Now he has to govern.*

Elizabeth Drew (*The New Yorker*, December 12, 1988)

---

[33]See Joe McGinniss, *The Selling of the President, 1968* (New York: Trident Press, 1968).
[34]Benjamin I. Page and Mark P. Petracca, *The American Presidency* (New York: McGraw-Hill, 1983), 90.
[35]Bryce, *American Commonwealth*, 2:70–77.

# FORMAL AND INFORMAL REQUIREMENTS FOR BECOMING PRESIDENT

*Formal Requirements.* Article II of the U.S. Constitution requires a president to be:

   at least thirty-five years old

   a natural-born U.S. citizen

   a resident in the United States for at least fourteen years

*Informal Requirements.* In the nation's history, presidents have been:

   male, without exception

   white, without exception

   Protestant, with the exception of John F. Kennedy

   married, with the exceptions of James Buchanan and Grover Cleveland (who married in the White House)

   career public servants—four were army generals, thirteen were vice-presidents (seven succeeded upon a president's death, one upon a president's resignation), eight were federal administrators, and the remainder were U.S. senators, U.S. representatives (only one), or state governors.

**TABLE 19-3   The Path to the White House for Twentieth-Century Presidents**

| President | Years in Office | Highest Previous Office | Second-Highest Office |
|---|---|---|---|
| William McKinley | 1897–1901 | Governor | U.S. representative |
| Theodore Roosevelt | 1901–1908 | Vice-president[a] | Governor |
| William Howard Taft | 1909–1912 | Secretary of war | Federal judge |
| Woodrow Wilson | 1913–1920 | Governor | None |
| Warren G. Harding | 1921–1924 | U.S. senator | Lieutenant governor |
| Calvin Coolidge | 1925–1928 | Vice-president[a] | Governor |
| Herbert Hoover | 1929–1932 | Secretary of commerce | War relief administrator |
| Franklin D. Roosevelt | 1933–1945 | Governor | Assistant secretary of navy |
| Harry S. Truman | 1945–1952 | Vice-president[a] | U.S. senator |
| Dwight D. Eisenhower | 1953–1960 | None (Army general) | None |
| John F. Kennedy | 1961–1963 | U.S. senator | U.S. representative |
| Lyndon Johnson | 1963–1968 | Vice-president[a] | U.S. senator |
| Richard Nixon | 1969–1974 | Vice-president | U.S. senator |
| Gerald Ford | 1974–1976 | Vice-president[a] | U.S. representative |
| Jimmy Carter | 1977–1980 | Governor | State senator |
| Ronald Reagan | 1981–1988 | Governor | None |
| George Bush | 1989– | Vice-president | Director, Central Intelligence Agency |

[a]Became president on death or resignation of incumbent.

president. As we noted earlier, chance and circumstance, even outright luck, now play a large part in deciding the outcome of nominating races. With slight changes in circumstance, there might not have been a McGovern or Carter or Reagan or Mondale or Dukakis or Bush nomination. A different candidate might have prevailed in each case. Stated another way, there is not much about the present system that guarantees that the candidate best suited to the presidency will emerge as the victor.

The nature of the modern presidential campaign makes it difficult even for political leaders who hold high office to make a serious bid for nomination. A successful campaign requires careful planning and necessitates frequent campaign appearances in Iowa, New Hampshire, and other primary states in the year preceding the nominating conventions. In 1980 Howard Baker's duties as Senate minority leader prevented him from campaigning effectively, and he was easily defeated. In recent campaigns, the strongest candidates for nomination have often been individuals who were out of public office; this was the case, for instance, with Carter (1976), Reagan (1980), and Mondale (1984). A year before the 1988 campaign, Mario Cuomo withdrew as a possible Democratic contender, saying that he could not fulfill his duties as governor of New York and also find the time to run a nomination campaign. No other nation has a system of selecting its chief executive which in effect penalizes those who currently hold a responsible office.

The assumptions that underlie the present system are altogether different from the premises that guided the Framers. They envisioned a system in which a candidate's popularity was secondary to his ability and background. In *Federalist* No. 68, Alexander Hamilton expressed the Framers' optimism about the effectiveness of the Electoral College:

> The process of election affords a moral certainty that the office of President will never fall to the lot of any man who is not in an eminent degree endowed with the requisite qualifications. Talents for low intrigue, and the little arts of popularity, may alone suffice to elevate a man to the first honors in a single State; but it will require other talents, and a different kind of merit, to establish him in the esteem and confidence of the whole Union, or of so considerable a portion of it as would be necessary to make him a successful candidate for the distinguished office of President of the United States.

In fact, the nation's first system of presidential selection did produce several of the nation's finest chief executives, including Washington, Jefferson, and Jackson.

The present system was established formally by 1972, although it dates in spirit to the hotly contested nominating races of the 1960s. Too few presidents have been elected under the existing system to permit a final judgment, but it can be said that its early products have not been overly qualified. Carter was a one-term state governor who was largely unfamiliar with the workings of the federal government, and historians have already ranked him below average in terms of performance in office (see Table 19-4). Reagan was a more experienced politician than Carter and had more success in the presidency, but he was less

★ ANALYZE THE ISSUE

**Characteristics of Candidates and of Presidents**
What personal and political characteristics of candidates does the current system of electing presidents seem to reward? Are the same characteristics desirable in a president? Why, or why not? If you think they are not, what changes in the process of selecting presidents would you suggest to improve the situation?

**TABLE 19-4  Performance Rankings of U.S. Presidents, by System of Selection**

| Selection System[a] | Great/ Near-Great | Above Average | Below Average | Bad/ Failure |
|---|---|---|---|---|
| 1. Original (1788–1828) | Washington Jefferson Jackson[c] | J. Adams Madison Monroe J. Q. Adams | | |
| 2. Party convention (1832–1900) | Lincoln T. Roosevelt[b,c] | Polk Cleveland McKinley[c] | Van Buren Taylor Hayes Arthur[b] Harrison | Tyler[b] Pierce Fillmore[b] Buchanan A. Johnson[b] Grant |
| 3. Party convention, primary (1904–1968) | Wilson F. Roosevelt Truman[b] | Eisenhower Kennedy[c] L. Johnson[b,c] | Taft Hoover | Harding Coolidge[b] Nixon[c] |
| 4. Party primary, open caucus (1972–present) | | Reagan | Ford[b] Carter | |

[a]See Table 19-1.
[b]Became president upon death or resignation of incumbent.
[c]Was president when electoral process was in transition to next system.

SOURCE: Based on author's interpretation of rankings compiled by various historians.

# Chapter 20

---

## THE OFFICE OF THE PRESIDENT: LEADING THE NATION

---

*[The president's] is the only voice in national affairs. Let him once win the admiration and confidence of the people, and no other single voice will easily overpower him.*

*Woodrow Wilson[1]*

In 1972 Richard Nixon demonstrated why the presidency has been described as "both the most dynamic and most dangerous of our political institutions."[2] At the same time that Nixon was reopening relations with China, suspended since the Communist takeover in 1949, he was ordering the saturation bombing of large areas of Cambodia. The two policies began in secrecy, but they led in opposing directions and had vastly different consequences. The opening to China was a brilliant diplomatic move that heightened tensions between China and the Soviet Union, drew China toward the West, and contributed to developments that led the Soviet Union, more than a decade later under Mikhail Gorbachev, also to reach out to the West. The bombing of Cambodia, in contrast, violated international law, rained death and destruction on the people of that tiny nation, and, when it became publicly known, undermined relations between the United States and its allies and created tension between the executive and legislative branches of the national government.

The characterization of the presidency as "both the most dynamic and most dangerous" of U.S. political institutions refers to the leeway inherent in the office's constitutional authority. The writers of the Constitution sought to establish an energetic presidency but also wanted to constrain the powers of the office. The Framers knew what they wanted from a president—national leadership, statesmanship in foreign affairs, command in time of war or insurgency, enforcement of the laws—but could devise only general phrases to describe the president's constitutional authority. Compared with Article I,

---

[1]Woodrow Wilson, *Constitutional Government in the United States* (New York: Columbia University Press, 1908), 67.
[2]Robert Hirschfield, ed., *The Power of the Presidency*, 3d ed. (New York: Aldine, 1982), 3.

President Richard Nixon and his wife, Pat, visit the Great Wall of China in 1972. Nixon resumed U.S. diplomatic relations with China, even as he was secretly intensifying U.S. involvement in the war in Southeast Asia—a demonstration of why the presidency is characterized as the most dynamic and yet most dangerous of U.S. institutions. (AP/Wide World)

which enumerates Congress's specific powers, Article II of the Constitution contains relatively vague statements on the president's powers. This constitutional ambiguity, James W. Davis says, gives presidents "wide latitude in defining their executive duties."[3]

Political power holds such allure that it is perhaps not surprising that, over time, presidents have expanded the authority of their office. Each of the president's constitutional powers has been broadened in practice beyond the Framers' intention. For example, the Constitution grants the president command of the nation's military, but only Congress can declare war. In *Federalist* No. 69 Alexander Hamilton wrote that a surprise attack on the United States was the only justification for war by presidential action. President Thomas Jefferson disputed even this exception, claiming that he could respond to invasion only with defensive action unless Congress declared war. Since Jefferson, however, the nation's presidents have sent troops into military action abroad more than 200 times. Of the eleven wars included in that figure, only five were declared by Congress.[4]

The Constitution also empowers the president to act as diplomatic leader. He is granted the authority to receive ambassadors, and thus has the power to decide which nations will have the formal diplomatic recognition of the United States. The president is further empowered to appoint U.S. ambassadors and to negotiate treaties with other countries, subject to approval by the Senate. The Framers anticipated that Congress would have responsibility for developing foreign policy, while the president would oversee its implementation.[5] Howev-

[3]James W. Davis, *The American Presidency* (New York: Harper & Row, 1987), 13.
[4]See Barry M. Blechman and Stephen S. Kaplan, *Force without War* (Washington, D.C.: Brookings Institution, 1978).
[5]Edward S. Corwin, *The President: Office and Powers, 1787–1957*, (New York: New York University Press, 1959), 180–181.

er, the president has become the principal architect of U.S. foreign policy and has even acquired the power to make treaty-like arrangements with other nations, in the form of executive agreements. In 1937 the Supreme Court ruled that such agreements, signed and approved only by the president, have the same legal status as treaties, which require approval by a two-thirds vote of the Senate.[6] Since World War II, presidents have negotiated more than 9,000 executive agreements, as compared with roughly 500 treaties ratified by the Senate.[7]

The Constitution also vests "executive power" in the president, granting him the power to execute the laws and to appoint major administrators, such as heads of the various departments of the executive branch. In *Federalist* No. 76 Hamilton indicated that the president's real authority as chief executive was to be found in this appointive capacity. Presidents have indeed exercised substantial power through their appointments, but they have found their administrative authority—the power to execute the laws—to be of even greater value, because it enables them to determine how laws will be interpreted and applied.

Finally, the Constitution provides the president with legislative authority, including use of the veto and the opportunity to recommend proposals to Congress. The Framers expected this authority to be used in a limited and largely negative way. George Washington acted as the Framers anticipated: he proposed only three legislative measures and vetoed only two acts of Congress. Modern presidents have a different, more activist view of their legislative role. They routinely submit legislative proposals to Congress and often veto legislation they find disagreeable. The champion of the veto is Franklin D. Roosevelt, who during his twelve years in office rejected 635 acts of Congress.

This chapter explains why the presidency has become a stronger office than the Founders envisioned. It argues that the president's prominence stems primarily from his unique relationship with the American people. The president is the only truly nationally elected leader in the U.S. political system, and the public looks first to him for national leadership. The responsibility thus accorded presidents has enabled them, as the executive demands on government have increased during the past century, to assume broad powers that have helped to transform the office. Ironically, as the president's responsibilities have grown, so have his difficulties in controlling his office. The modern president necessarily depends on a great many assistants to help him carry out his duties, but, as the chapter's concluding section explains, the staff's large size frustrates the president's attempts to control everything that is done in his name. The main ideas of the chapter are these:

★ *Public expectations, national crises, and changing national and world conditions have required the presidency to become a strong office. Underlying this development is the public support that the president acquires from the circumstance that he is the only nationally elected official.*

★ *The modern presidency could not operate without a large staff of assistants, experts, and high-level managers, but the sheer size of this staff makes it impossible for the president to exercise complete control over it.*

---

[6]*U.S.* v. *Belmont*, 57 U.S. 758 (1937).
[7]Raymond Tatalovich and Byron W. Daynes, *Presidential Power in the United States* (Monterey, Calif.: Brooks/Cole, 1984), 263.

# THE PRESIDENT'S CONSTITUTIONAL AUTHORITY

*Commander in chief.* Article II, section 2: "The President shall be commander in chief of the Army and Navy of the United States, and of the militia of the several states."

*Chief executive.* Article II, section 2: "He may require the opinion, in writing, of the principal officer in each of the executive departments, upon any subject relating to the duties of their respective offices, and he shall have power to grant reprieves and pardons for offences against the United States, except in cases of impeachment."

Article II, section 2: "He shall have power, by and with the advice and consent of the Senate, to make treaties, provided two thirds of the senators present concur; and he shall nominate, and by and with the advice and consent of the Senate, shall appoint ambassadors, other public ministers and consuls, judges of the Supreme Court, and all other officers of the United States, whose appointments are not herein otherwise provided for, and which shall be established by law."

Article II, section 2: "The President shall have power to fill up all vacancies that may happen during the recess of the Senate, by granting commissions which shall expire at the end of their next session."

Article II, section 3: "He shall take care that the laws be faithfully executed, and shall commission all the officers of the United States."

*Chief diplomat.* Article II, section 2: "He shall have power, and with the advice and consent of the Senate, to make treaties, provided two thirds of the senators present concur."

Article II, section 3: "He shall receive ambassadors and other public ministers."

*Legislative promoter.* Article II, section 3: "He shall from time to time give to the Congress information of the state of the Union, and recommend to their consideration such measures as he shall judge necessary and expedient; he may, on extraordinary occasions, convene both houses, or either of them, and in case of disagreement between them, with respect to the time of adjournment, he may adjourn them to such time as he shall think proper."

## Foundations of the Modern Presidency

The writers of the Constitution chose to vest executive authority in a single individual in order to create an energetic presidency. The Framers debated the possibility of a three-person executive (one president each from the northern, middle, and southern states) but rejected the idea on the grounds that a joint office would be rendered useless by constant dissension and intrigue. They also believed that only a single executive could provide decisive action in case of a military attack on the United States. "Unity," Alexander Hamilton wrote in *Federalist* No. 70, "is conducive to energy." The Framers worried that a single executive might become too powerful but believed that adequate protection against such a threat was provided by the separation of powers and the president's selection by electors. Although the president would represent the people, he would not be chosen directly by them. This arrangement would protect him against excessive public demands and at the same time deny him the reserve of power that direct public election could confer.

The Framers failed to anticipate that the president someday would in effect be chosen through popular election (see Chapter 19). The Framers also underestimated the significance of the fact that the presidency is a national office. Senators and representatives are chosen by voters within a single state or district, a limitation that diminishes the claim of any one of them to national leadership. Moreover, since the House and the Senate are separate bodies, no member of Congress can speak for the whole institution. The president, in contrast, is a nationally elected official and the sole chief executive. More than anything else, these features of the office—national election and singular authority—have enabled presidents to claim the position of national leader.

## AN EMERGING TRADITION OF STRONG PRESIDENTS

The first president to assert this view forcefully was Andrew Jackson, who in many ways was the first "people's president." He was swept into office in 1828 on a tide of public support that broke the hold of the upper classes on the presidency. Jackson used his popular backing to challenge Congress's claim to national policy leadership, contending that he was "the people's tribune."

Jackson's view of the presidency, however, was not shared by most of his successors during the nineteenth century, because national conditions did not routinely call for strong presidential leadership. The prevailing conception of the presidency was the **Whig theory.** In this view, the presidency was a limited or constrained office whose occupant was confined to the exercise of expressly granted constitutional authority. The president had no implicit powers for dealing with national problems, but was primarily an administrator, charged with carrying out the expressed will of Congress. "My duty," said President James Buchanan, a Whig adherent, "is to execute the laws . . . and not my individual opinions."[8]

Theodore Roosevelt rejected the Whig tradition when he took office in 1901. He embraced the **stewardship theory,** which called for a strong, assertive presidential role. As "steward of the people," Roosevelt said, he was obliged "to do anything that the needs of the Nation demanded unless such action was *forbidden* by the Constitution or by the laws."[9] Thus, in Roosevelt's view, presidential authority was not limited by any restrictions inherent in expressed grants of power; it stopped only at points specifically prohibited by law. Moreover, the stewardship view holds that the presidency includes the role of legislative initiator, a leader who formulates policy proposals and prods Congress to act on them. Accordingly, Roosevelt, among other initiatives, attacked the business trusts, promoted conservation, and persuaded Congress to enact standards for the safety of foods, drugs, and transportation.[10]

Roosevelt's image of a strong presidency was shared by Woodrow Wilson, but his other immediate successors reverted to the Whig notion of the limited presidency.[11] William Howard Taft wrote, "The true view of the executive function is, as I conceive it, that the president can exercise no power which cannot be fairly and reasonably traced to some specific grant of power or justly implied."[12] Herbert Hoover's restrained conception of the presidency prevented

*The president can exercise no power which cannot be fairly and reasonably traced to some specific grant of power or justly implied.*

William Howard Taft

[8]Quoted in Wilfred E. Binkley, *President and Congress*, 3d ed. (New York: Vintage, 1962), 142.
[9]Theodore Roosevelt, *An Autobiography* (New York: Scribner's, 1931), 383.
[10]George C. Edwards and Stephen J. Wayne, *Presidential Leadership* (New York: St. Martin's Press, 1985), 6–7.
[11]See Richard M. Pious, *The American Presidency* (New York: Basic Books, 1979), 83.
[12]William Howard Taft, *Our Chief Magistrate and His Powers* (New York: Columbia University Press, 1916), 138, cited in Pious, *American Presidency*, 7.

Perceiving himself as the people's steward, President Teddy Roosevelt took on the business trusts that were using their domination of markets to gouge consumers. (Culver Pictures)

him from taking decisive action even during the economic devastation that followed the Wall Street crash of 1929. Hoover argued that he had no authority to establish public relief programs for jobless and penniless Americans.

Hoover's successor, Franklin D. Roosevelt, shared the stewardship theory of his distant cousin Theodore Roosevelt, and FDR's New Deal signaled the end of the limited presidency. Today the presidency is an inherently strong office.[13] The modern presidency becomes a more substantial office in the hands of a persuasive leader such as Lyndon Johnson or Ronald Reagan, but even a less forceful person such as Gerald Ford or Jimmy Carter is now expected to act assertively. This expectation not only is the legacy of former strong presidents but also stems from the need for presidential leadership in periods of national crisis and from changes that have occurred in the federal government's national and international policy responsibilities.

## THE NEED FOR PRESIDENTIAL LEADERSHIP IN NATIONAL CRISES

National crises have enabled presidents to assume powers beyond those provided in the Constitution. Emergencies usually demand speed of action and singleness of purpose. Congress—a large, divided, and often unwieldy institution—is poorly suited to such a response. In contrast, the president, as sole head of the executive branch, can act quickly and decisively. Abraham Lincoln's response to the outbreak of the Civil War is a notable example. Acting on his own authority, Lincoln called up the militia, blockaded southern ports,

[13]Robert Hirschfield, "The Power of the Contemporary President," in Aaron Wildavsky, ed., *The Presidency* (Boston: Little, Brown, 1969), 137.

Japanese Americans assemble for evacuation from San Francisco to inland detention camps in April 1942. President Franklin Roosevelt ordered this drastic program in the crisis atmosphere that followed the Japanese attack on Pearl Harbor. His order was upheld by the Supreme Court as a lawful exercise of the president's authority as commander-in-chief. (Library of Congress)

increased the size of the Army and Navy, ordered conscription, suspended the writ of *habeas corpus,* and placed part of the nation under martial law. When Congress convened in 1861, after Lincoln's war orders had already taken effect, it acknowledged the validity of his actions by passing a law stating that his directives had the same authority "as if they had been issued and done under the previous express authority and direction of the Congress of the United States."[14]

Similarly, Congress formally endorsed Franklin Roosevelt's directive, issued in the wake of the Japanese attack on Pearl Harbor in 1941, that ordered the evacuation of 135,000 Japanese Americans living on the West Coast. Fearing subversive activities among these Japanese Americans, Roosevelt instructed federal authorities to seize their property and relocate them in detention camps farther inland until the war's end. Japanese Americans challenged the legality of Roosevelt's order, but the Supreme Court upheld their forced evacuation from coastal areas (although it voided their involuntary detention).[15]

In such instances the other branches of government have had little choice but to accept presidential claims to extraordinary powers. Constitutionality has given way to perceived necessity in times of crisis. Lincoln's critics called him a dictator, but a congressional majority affirmed that his extraconstitutional actions had been necessary to save the Union. On the one occasion when the Supreme Court did clearly reject a president's claim to emergency powers, the issue was not national survival. In 1952 the Court invalidated President Harry S Truman's order for the takeover of the nation's steel mills by federal troops.

[14]Tatalovitch and Daynes, *Presidential Power,* 322–323.
[15]*Korematsu* v. *U.S.,* 323 U.S. 214 (1944); *Ex parte* Endo, 323 U.S. 283 (1944).

Steelworkers had gone on strike, jeopardizing steel production that Truman believed was essential to the Korean war effort. Truman contended that the "sum of his powers" as commander in chief and chief executive and "his unique responsibility for the conduct of foreign affairs" justified his order. The Supreme Court disagreed with Truman's position, noting that the circumstances did not constitute a grave national emergency, that the United States was technically at peace (Congress had not declared war on North Korea), and that Truman had a lawful alternative—the Taft-Hartley Act—that he could have invoked to suspend the strike.[16]

National crises have had a lasting impact on the conduct of the executive office. Modern presidents are expected to be powerful in part because some of their predecessors assumed extraordinary powers in critical times. Lincoln, Roosevelt, and other strong presidents left a legacy for later presidents. Every strong president has seen his power as flowing from a special relationship with the American people. As Truman noted in his memoirs, "I believe that the power of the President should be used in the interest of the people and in order to do that the President must use whatever power the Constitution does not expressly deny him."[17]

*The President must use whatever power the Constitution does not expressly deny him.*

Harry S Truman

## THE NEED FOR PRESIDENTIAL LEADERSHIP OF AN ACTIVIST GOVERNMENT

During most of the nineteenth century the United States did not need a strong president. The federal government's policymaking role was small, as was its bureaucracy. Moreover, the nation's major issues were of a sectional nature (especially the North–South split over slavery) and thus suited to action by Congress, which represented state and local interests. The U.S. government's role in world affairs was also small. Today the situation has greatly changed. The federal government has such broad national and international responsibilities that strong leadership from presidents is essential.

### Foreign Policy Leadership

The president has always been the foreign policy leader of the United States, but during the nation's first century that role was a rather undemanding one. The United States avoided getting entangled in the turbulent politics of Europe, and though it was involved in foreign trade, its major preoccupation was its internal development. By the end of the nineteenth century, however, the nation was seeking to expand the world market for its goods, and the size and growing industrial power of the United States was attracting more attention from other nations. President Theodore Roosevelt advocated an American economic empire, looking south toward Latin America and west toward Hawaii, the Philippines, and China (the "Open Door" policy) for new markets. However, the United States' tradition of isolationism remained a powerful influence on national policy. The United States fought in World War I but immediately thereafter demobilized its armed forces. Over President Woodrow Wilson's

---

[16]*Youngstown Sheet and Tube Co.* v. *Sawyer,* 343 U.S. 579 (1952).
[17]Harry S Truman, *1946–1952: Years of Trial and Hope* (New York: Signet, 1956), 535.

objections, Congress then voted against the entry of the United States into the League of Nations.

World War II fundamentally changed the nation's international role and the president's role in foreign policy. In 1945 the United States emerged as a global superpower, a giant in world trade, and the recognized leader of the noncommunist world. The United States today has formal diplomatic relations with three times as many nations as it did in the 1930s; a military presence in nearly every part of the globe; and an unprecedented interest in trade balances, energy supplies, and other international issues affecting the nation's economy (see Chapter 26).[18]

The effects of these developments on America's political institutions have been largely one-sided. Because of the president's constitutional authority as chief diplomat and military commander and the special demands of foreign policy leadership, he, not Congress, has taken the lead in addressing the United States' increased responsibilities in the world. Congress is a blunt instrument, capable of enacting policies but unable to monitor their implementation. Congress can decide, for example, that the interests of the United States require a global military capacity but cannot effectively determine, on an ongoing basis, where military force should be deployed and applied. If congressional approval were required each time a naval task force had to be repositioned in response to some emerging threat, U.S. security interests would be continually compromised by the inevitable slowness of the response. By comparison, the president has the capacity to act quickly and decisively; so, not surprisingly, he makes most of the nation's defense policy decisions. (The special demands of foreign policy and how they work to the president's advantage are discussed more fully in Chapter 21.)

### Domestic Policy Leadership

The change in the president's domestic leadership has also been substantial. Throughout most of the nineteenth century Congress jealously guarded its constitutional powers, making it clear that domestic policy was its business. James Bryce wrote in the 1880s that Congress paid no more attention to the president's views on legislation than it did to the editorial positions of prominent newspaper publishers.[19]

By the early twentieth century, however, the national government was taking on regulatory and policy responsibilities imposed by the nation's transition from an agrarian to an industrial society, and stronger presidential leadership was becoming necessary. In 1921 Congress conceded that it lacked the centralized authority to coordinate the growing national budget and enacted the Budget and Accounting Act, which provided for an executive budget. Federal departments and agencies would no longer submit their annual budget requests directly to Congress. The president would oversee the initiation of the budget, compiling the various agencies' requests into an overall budget, which he would submit to Congress for its approval. As James W. Davis notes, this centralization strengthened the president's hand in dealing both with Congress and with the agencies of the executive branch.[20]

[18]Davis, *American Presidency*, 25–26.
[19]James Bryce, *The American Commonwealth* (New York: Commonwealth Edition, 1908), 230.
[20]Davis, *American Presidency*, 20.

The federal government has become an active force in the nation's economy. Today virtually every economic activity is subject to federal regulation. (Richard Wood/The Picture Cube)

During the Great Depression of the 1930s, Franklin D. Roosevelt's New Deal responded to the public's demand for economic relief and involved a level of policy planning and coordination that was beyond the capacity of Congress. In addition to initiating public works projects and social-welfare programs aimed at providing immediate relief, the New Deal made the government a partner in nearly every aspect of the nation's economy. If economic regulation was to work, unified and continuous policy leadership was needed, and only the president could provide it. Later Congress institutionalized the president's economic role with the Full Employment Act of 1946, which assigns to the president an ongoing responsibility for economic growth. This act entrusts the president with the authority "to use all practicable means . . . to promote maximum employment, production, and purchasing power."

Roosevelt's power, like that of the strong presidents before him, rested on the support of the American people.[21] In the early 1930s the nation was in such desperate condition that Americans would have supported almost anything Roosevelt did. "If he burned down the Capitol," said the humorist Will Rogers, "we would cheer and say 'Well, we at least got a fire started.' "[22]

Presidential authority has continued to grow since Roosevelt's time. The main reason for this expansion is that the public has placed greater demands on the national government in such areas as education, health, welfare, safety, and protection of the environment.[23]

[21]Ibid., 25.

[22]Quoted in Arthur M. Schlesinger, Jr., *The Coming of the New Deal* (Boston: Houghton Mifflin, 1958), 13.

[23]Hugh Heclo, "Introduction: The Presidential Illusion," in Hugh Heclo and Lester M. Salamon, eds., *The Illusion of Presidential Government* (Boulder, Colo.: Westview Press, 1981), 6.

★ ANALYZE THE ISSUE

**The Increase in Presidential Power**
It has been said that constitutionality bends to necessity. How does this axiom help to explain the increased power and responsibility that the president has acquired during the twentieth century? Is the axiom strictly accurate, given that the provisions for presidential authority in Article II of the Constitution are relatively vague in any case?

The president's preeminence as domestic policy leader does not mean that Congress no longer plays a significant role.[24] As we saw in Chapter 18, some major policy initiatives of recent decades—including labor–management relations, public housing, atomic energy, and environmental protection—have emanated from Congress, which has also modified or rejected many presidential proposals during this period.[25] Moreover, Congress tends to seek the president's leadership only on particular types of legislative measures—principally those that address truly national issues from a national perspective.[26] (The president's domestic policy role is discussed further in Chapter 21.)

## Staffing the Presidency

The duties of the modern presidency far exceed the capacity of one person. Thus the president must rely on an increasingly large staff to carry out the responsibilities of his office, a situation that Thomas Cronin calls the "swelling" of the presidency.[27]

The president gains important advantages from his authority to appoint more than 2,000 assistants, experts, and administrators. First, his appointees are a source of policy information. Modern policymaking depends on detailed information, and control of information is a source of considerable power.

[24]James Sundquist, The *Decline and Resurgence of Congress* (Washington, D.C.: Brookings Institution, 1981), 150.
[25]Richard M. Pious, "Sources of Domestic Policy Initiatives," in Harvey C. Mansfield, ed., *Congress against the President* (New York: Praeger, 1975), 108–109.
[26]John Kingdon, *Congressmen's Voting Decisions* (New York: Harper & Row, 1973), 170–171.
[27]Thomas E. Cronin, *The State of the Presidency*, 2d ed. (Boston: Little, Brown, 1980), 243.

The White House contains, on the first floor, the president's Oval Office, other offices, and ceremonial rooms. The First Family's living quarters are on the second floor. (Jake McGuire)

Second, the president's appointees extend his reach into the huge federal bureaucracy, helping him exert some influence on the day-to-day workings of government. Quite simply, the president puts "his people" in top positions of the executive branch. Not surprisingly, presidents have tended to appoint individuals who share their partisan views. However, the degree to which presidents have stressed partisanship has varied considerably. Among recent presidents, Reagan was the most adamant about partisan loyalty as a criterion for appointment; he perceived career bureaucrats as hostile to many of his ideas and believed that he needed Republicans as conservative as himself in top positions. Of Reagan's first-term appointees, 82 percent were Republicans, 15 percent were unaffiliated, and 3 percent were Democrats. By comparison, of Carter's appointees, 58 percent were fellow Democrats, 35 percent were unaffiliated, and 7 percent were Republicans.[28]

## PRESIDENTIAL APPOINTEES AND THE PROBLEM OF CONTROL

Although the president's appointees are a valuable asset, they also pose a problem: because they are so numerous, they represent a challenge to his control of the presidential office. Most appointees are not under the president's direct supervision and have considerable freedom to act on their own initiative —not necessarily in accord with the president's wishes. Truman had a wall chart in the Oval Office listing more than 100 officials who reported directly to him, and often told visitors, "I cannot even see all of these men, let alone actually study what they are doing."[29] Since Truman's time the number of bureaucratic agencies has more than doubled, compounding the problem of presidential control over subordinates.

To assist him in administering the executive branch of the federal government, the president appoints the members of the organizations that make up the Executive Office of the President and the heads of the various cabinet departments. These and other presidential appointees differ in their backgrounds, proximity to the Oval Office, duties, and policy views. All these factors affect the president's ability to control their activities, as can be seen from a closer examination of who his appointees are and what they do.

*No one who has not had the responsibility can really understand what it is like to be President, not even his closest aides or members of his immediate family. There is no end to the chain of responsibility that binds him, and he is never allowed to forget that he is President.*

Harry S Truman

### The Executive Office of the President

In 1939 Congress created the Executive Office of the President (EOP) on the recommendation of a committee formed in 1936 by Franklin D. Roosevelt and headed by the management expert Louis Brownlow.[30] The Brownlow committee had concluded that the effective functioning of the executive branch required a level of coordination that only a well-staffed presidency could provide.[31]

Since 1939 the EOP has become the command center of the executive

---

[28]Davis, *American Presidency*, 296.
[29]Quoted in James MacGregor Burns, "Our Super-Government—Can We Control It?" *New York Times*, April 24, 1949, 32.
[30]Edwards and Wayne, *Presidential Leadership*, 187.
[31]Adapted from Richard P. Nathan, *The Administrative Presidency* (New York: Wiley, 1983), 36. Based on *Report of the President's Committee on Administrative Management* (Washington, D.C., January 1973).

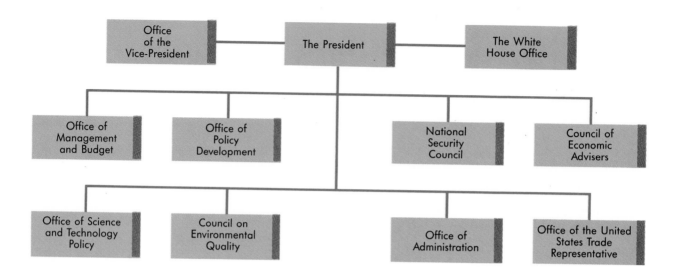

| Office of the Vice-President | The President | The White House Office |
| --- | --- | --- |

| Office of Management and Budget | Office of Policy Development | National Security Council | Council of Economic Advisers |
| --- | --- | --- | --- |

| Office of Science and Technology Policy | Council on Environmental Quality | Office of Administration | Office of the United States Trade Representative |
| --- | --- | --- | --- |

**FIGURE 20-1 Executive Office of the President**
The Executive Office of the President acts as the president's personal bureaucracy, helping him to manage the rest of the executive branch. *Source:* U.S. Government Manual, 1987/1988 *(Washington, D.C.: U.S. Government Printing Office, 1988),* 86.

branch[32] and is itself a small bureaucracy. It currently consists of ten organizations (see Figure 20-1). The leading ones are the White House Office (WHO), which consists of the president's closest personal advisers; the Office of Management and Budget (OMB), which consists of experts who formulate and then administer the federal budget; the National Security Council (NSC), which assists the president on foreign and military affairs; and the Council of Economic Advisers (CEA), which advises the president on the national economy.[33]

*Presidential Assistants*     Of the EOP's ten organizations, the White House Office serves the president most directly and personally. The WHO consists of the president's personal assistants, including his close personal advisers, press agents, legislative and group liaison aides, and special assistants for domestic and international policy. They work in the White House, and the president can hire and fire them at will. Total loyalty to the president is expected of these staff members.

A president's personal assistants do much of his legwork for him and serve as his main source of advice. Because of their closeness and loyalty to the president, they are among the most powerful individuals in Washington. They are not expert advisers in the sense of having studied or worked for years in a specialized policy field, but they often possess political savvy. When George Bush took office, he appointed John Sununu as his top White House assistant. Sununu had been governor of New Hampshire for six years. Before becoming Bush's chief of staff, he had headed Bush's victorious New Hampshire primary campaign, which was widely seen as the turning point in Bush's drive toward the 1988 Republican nomination.

Although no modern president could function effectively without his close assistants, they can also cause problems. In trying to conserve the president's time, they may withhold views or information that he could use. At times advisers have also presumed to undertake important initiatives without first

[32]Davis, *American Presidency,* 240.
[33]Hugh Heclo, "The Changing Presidential Office," in Arnold J. Meltsner, ed., *Politics and the Oval Office* (San Francisco: Institute for Contemporary Studies, 1981), 163.

## THE VICE-PRESIDENT AS POLICY ADVISER

Though the vice-president works in the White House, he is not necessarily a member of the president's inner circle of advisers. The Constitution assigns the vice-president no policy authority. Accordingly, whether the vice-president plays a large or small role is the president's choice. Jimmy Carter gave Walter Mondale more responsibility than any previous vice-president had received, and Mondale served as one of his confidants. George Bush was given fewer duties than Mondale, but he played a substantial role in the Reagan administration as a liaison with Congress and as chairman of the crisis-management team within the National Security Council. When he became president, Bush gave Dan Quayle many of the duties he had performed during his vice-presidency.

Other vice-presidents have played much smaller roles. Many of them were selected for their ability to attract votes rather than because of their close association with the president. Lyndon Johnson was Senate majority leader before becoming John Kennedy's vice-president and was selected because Kennedy believed that he would not win the presidency unless he carried Texas, Johnson's home state. As vice-president, Johnson was given few tasks and responsibilities, playing second fiddle to Kennedy's personal advisers, such as Ted Sorensen and McGeorge Bundy. When Kennedy was assassinated in 1963, Johnson suddenly was president, and Kennedy's advisers may have wished that they had been more attentive to Johnson while he was vice-president.

obtaining the president's approval, leading others to question whether he is actually in charge of his office. Finally, advisers have sometimes been so intent on maintaining their close relationship with the president that they have done him a disservice by not challenging his views. Recognizing this possibility, President John F. Kennedy, during the Cuban missile crisis of 1962, sometimes asked his advisers to meet without him. His purpose was to allow the discussion of possibilities that might not be raised if he were present. Kennedy had not used this approach in planning the disastrous Bay of Pigs operation of 1961, and he was determined to have the benefit of opposing opinions during the new crisis.[34]

[34]Stephen Hess, *Organizing the Presidency* (Washington, D.C.: Brookings Institution, 1976), 162–163.

The president's personal advisers can provide valuable guidance, but they can also be a source of embarrassment. Ronald Reagan is shown early in his first term with his "Big Four" aides, James Baker, William Clark, Edwin Meese III, and Michael Deaver (*left to right*). By the time Reagan left office, Deaver had been convicted of perjury and Meese was under a cloud for various kinds of questionable behavior. (Paul Conklin)

If presidential appointees are to influence career bureaucrats, they must gain their confidence. However, career bureaucrats are likely to be more committed to their agencies' goals than to the president's.[39] The civil service system protects careerists, so they cannot easily be removed from their positions even if they work against the president's objectives. To gain their cooperation, presidential appointees must achieve a working compromise between the president's goals and those of the bureaucratic organizations. Such delicate maneuvering requires managerial skills that many inexperienced appointees lack. Chapters 22 and 23 examine more closely the relationship between presidential appointees and career bureaucrats.

## ORGANIZING THE EXTENDED PRESIDENCY

Effective use of appointees by the president requires two-way communication. The president cannot possibly meet regularly with all his appointees or personally oversee their activities. Yet if he is to be in control, he must receive essential advice from his subordinates and have means of communicating his views to them.

### Patterns of Organization

Presidents have relied on a variety of techniques to regulate the flow of information to and from the Oval Office. One arrangement, used by Eisenhower, Nixon, Reagan, and Bush, resembles the way the military and most corporations are organized. It places the president at the top of an organizational pyramid and his closest personal advisers, each of whom is assigned specific responsibilities, at the second level (see Figure 20-2). All information and

[39]Joel D. Aberbach and Bert A. Rockman, "Clashing Beliefs within the Executive Branch," *American Political Science Review* 70 (June 1976): 461.

---

★ HOW THE UNITED STATES COMPARES

**Heads of State and Heads of Government**

Most democracies divide the executive office between a head of state, who is the ceremonial leader, and a head of government, who is the policy leader. In Great Britain these positions are filled by the queen and the prime minister, respectively. In democracies without a hereditary monarchy, the position of head of state is usually held by an individual chosen by the legislature. West Germany's head of state, for example, is a president, who is elected by the Federal Assembly; the head of government is a chancellor, who is chosen by the majority party in the lower house (Bundestag) of the Federal Assembly. The United States is one of a few countries in which the roles of head of state and head of government are combined in a single office, the presidency. The major disadvantage of this arrangement is that the president must devote considerable time to ceremonial functions, such as dinners for visiting heads of state. The major advantages are that the president alone is the center of national attention and that his power as head of government is enhanced by his prestige as the personification of the American state.

| Country | Head of State | Head of Government |
|---|---|---|
| Canada | Governor general (representative of the British monarch) | Prime minister |
| France | President | Premier |
| Great Britain | Queen | Prime minister |
| Italy | President | Prime minister |
| Japan | Emperor | Prime minister |
| Mexico | President | President |
| Sweden | King | Prime minister |
| United States | President | President |
| West Germany | President | Chancellor |

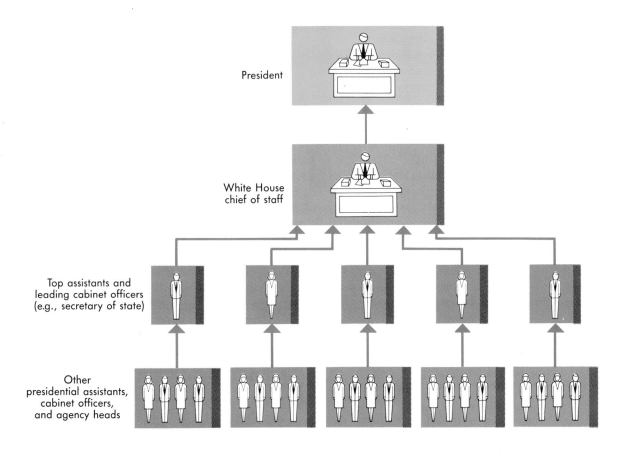

President

White House chief of staff

Top assistants and leading cabinet officers (e.g., secretary of state)

Other presidential assistants, cabinet officers, and agency heads

recommendations from lower levels must be submitted to these top aides, who decide whether these reports should be forwarded to the president. This hierarchical arrangement, with its multiple levels of supervision, permits more effective control of subordinates. Hierarchical organization also has the advantage of freeing the president from the need to deal with the many small issues that reach the White House.

A major disadvantage of the pyramid form is the danger that presidential advisers will make decisions that should be passed along for the president to make. Another disadvantage is that the pyramid form can result in misdirected or blocked information.[40] The president may be denied access to opinions that his close advisers decide are wrong or unimportant. The risk is that he will not be able to take important views and facts into account as he makes his policy decisions, so that the chances that they will prove ineffective are increased.[41]

A second approach to staff organization was developed by Franklin D. Roosevelt and adapted by Presidents Kennedy, Johnson, Ford, and Carter. Each placed himself at the center of the organization, accessible to a fairly large number of advisers (see Figure 20-3). This "hub-of-the-wheel" (or circular) form allows more information to reach the president and provides him with a greater range of options and opinions. Roosevelt and Kennedy were particularly adept at operating within this organizational framework; each surrounded himself with talented advisers and knew how to make them work together as a team even while they generated competing ideas.

**FIGURE 20-2 Managing the Presidency: The Pyramid (Hierarchical) Form of Organization**
In the pyramid form that some presidents have used to organize their staffs, information and recommendations that lower-level advisers wish to communicate to the president must be transmitted through —and thus "filtered" by— first top-level aides and then the White House chief of staff.

[40]Richard T. Johnson, *Managing the White House* (New York: Harper & Row, 1974), 238.
[41]See Irving Janis, *Victims of Groupthink* (Boston: Houghton Mifflin, 1972).

The Reagan case is the latest in the saga of the ups and downs of the presidential office. Lyndon Johnson's and Richard Nixon's dogged pursuit of the Vietnam war led to talk of "the imperial presidency," an office so powerful that constitutional checks and balances were no longer an effective constraint on it.[2] Within a few years, because of the undermining effects of Watergate and of changing international conditions on the Ford and Carter presidencies, the watchword was "the imperiled presidency," an office too weak to meet the nation's demands for executive leadership.[3] Reagan's policy successes before 1986 renewed talk heard in the Roosevelt and Kennedy years of "a heroic presidency," an office that is the inspirational center of American politics.[4]

No other political institution has been subject to such varying characterizations as the modern presidency. One reason is that the formal powers of the office are somewhat limited, and thus presidential power changes with national conditions, political circumstances, and the office's occupant. The American presidency is always a *central* office in that the president is constantly a focus of national attention. Yet the presidency is not an inherently powerful office in the sense that presidents always get what they want. Presidential power is conditional. It depends on the president's personal capacity but even more on the circumstances—on whether the situation demands strong leadership and whether the political support for that leadership exists. When conditions are favorable, the president will appear to be almost invincible. When conditions are adverse, the president will seem vulnerable. This chapter examines the correlates of presidential success and failure in policymaking, focusing on the following main points:

★ *Presidential influence on national policy is highly variable.* Whether a president succeeds or fails in getting his policies enacted depends heavily on the force of circumstances, the stage of his presidency, his partisan support in Congress, and the foreign or domestic nature of the policy issue.

★ *The president's election by national vote and his position as sole chief executive ensures that others will listen to his ideas; but, to lead effectively, he must have the help of other officials and, to get their help, must respond to their interests as they respond to his.*

★ *The president often finds it difficult to maintain the high level of public support that gives force to his leadership.* The American people have unreasonably high expectations of the president and tend to blame him for national problems.

## *Presidential Leadership*

At times presidents can make critical decisions on their own authority.[5] In 1963 John F. Kennedy met secretly with his advisers to plan a response to the Soviet

---

[2]Arthur M. Schlesinger, Jr., *The Imperial Presidency* (Boston: Houghton Mifflin, 1973).
[3]See Thomas Franck, ed., *The Tethered Presidency* (New York: New York University Press, 1981); Richard M. Pious, *The American Presidency* (New York: Basic Books, 1979); Harold M. Barger, *The Impossible Presidency* (Glenview, Ill.: Scott, Foresman, 1984); George Reedy, *The Twilight of the Presidency* (New York: New American Library, 1970).
[4]See Grant McConnell, *The Modern Presidency* (New York: St. Martin's Press, 1967); Clinton Rossiter, *The American Presidency* (New York: Harcourt, Brace & World, 1960).
[5]George C. Edwards III and Stephen J. Wayne, *Presidential Leadership: Politics and Policy Making* (New York: St. Martin's Press, 1985), 291.

Percentage of bills on which Congress
supported president's position

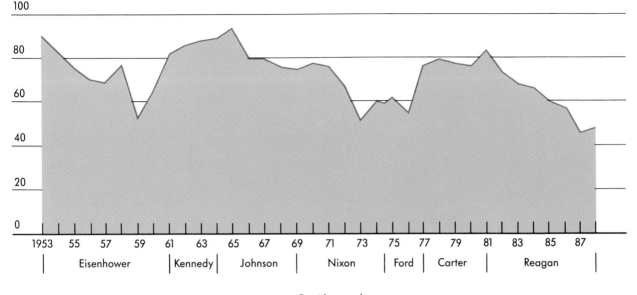

President and year

FIGURE 21-1 Percentage of
Bills Passed by Congress on
Which the President
Announced His Position,
1953–1988
In most years the president is
supported by Congress on a
majority of policy issues on
which he takes a stand. *Source:*
Congressional Quarterly Weekly,
*November 19, 1988, 3327.*

Union's deployment of nuclear missiles in Cuba. Kennedy decided to impose an air and sea blockade and ordered U.S. Navy ships into position around Cuba. Congressional leaders were told of the plan only minutes before Kennedy announced it on television to the American people. On his own, Kennedy had committed the country to a course of action that might very well have led to a war between the superpowers.

Such dramatic initiatives as Kennedy's moves during the Cuban missile crisis suggest that presidents regularly have the power of command, but in fact such unilateral policymaking is uncommon. The president operates within a system of separate institutions that share power. Thus significant presidential action normally depends on the approval of Congress, the cooperation of the bureaucracy, and sometimes the acceptance of the judiciary. Since other officials have their own priorities, the president does not always get his way. His responsibility to initiate and coordinate policy places him at the center of attention, but other institutions have the authority that can make his leadership effective. Congress in particular—more than the courts or the bureaucracy—holds the key to presidential success. Without congressional authorization and funding, most presidential proposals are nothing but ideas, empty of substance. Theodore Roosevelt expressed a wish that he could "be the president and Congress, too," if only for a day, so that he would have the power to enact as well as propose policies.

Given that the president must elicit support from others if he is to succeed, what is the record of presidential success? One way to judge is to measure the extent to which Congress backs legislation on which the president has taken a stand. By this indicator, presidents are reasonably successful (see Figure 21-1). Congress has agreed with the president in more than 50 percent of its votes in recent decades, with just one exception. The low year was 1987, when only 45 percent of the proposals backed by Reagan won congressional approval. The

President Lyndon Johnson addresses a joint session of Congress in 1965. Johnson had an extraordinary record of success with Congress, which adopted the great majority of his legislative proposals. (Rene Burri/Magnum)

previous low had occurred in 1973, during the Watergate crisis, when Congress agreed with Nixon only on slightly more than half of legislative issues. The high point of presidential–congressional agreement was 1965, when Lyndon Johnson's positions coincided with Congress's votes in 93 percent of cases.[6]

A tougher test of presidential success is the proportion of White House initiatives that are enacted by Congress. It is one thing for a president to take a stand on a bill that is already before Congress, but quite another thing for the president to develop a legislative proposal and then see Congress enact it into law. No president has come close to getting enactment of all the programs that he placed before Congress. The average success rate is just below 50 percent, but there has been wide variation.[7] Johnson saw 69 percent of his 1965 initiatives enacted, whereas Nixon attained only 20 percent in 1973. Moreover, presidents have had markedly less success on their more ambitious proposals than on lesser ones.[8]

Whether a president's initiatives are likely to succeed or fail depends on several factors, including the force of circumstance, the stage of the president's term, the president's partisan support in Congress, and the foreign or domestic nature of the policy proposal. Let us examine each of these factors.

### THE FORCE OF CIRCUMSTANCE

During his first months in office and in the midst of the Great Depression, Franklin D. Roosevelt accomplished the most sweeping changes in domestic

[6]*Congressional Quarterly Almanac, 1983* (Washington, D.C.: Congressional Quarterly Press, 1984), 19C.
[7]George C. Edwards III, *Presidential Influence in Congress* (San Francisco: W. H. Freeman, 1980), 14.
[8]Robert J. Spitzer, "The Presidency and Public Policy," *Political Science Quarterly*, Fall 1979, 441–457.

policy in the nation's history. Congress moved quickly to pass nearly every New Deal initiative he proposed. In 1964 and 1965 Lyndon Johnson pushed landmark civil rights and social-welfare legislation through Congress on the strength of the civil rights movement, the legacy of the assassinated President Kennedy, and large Democratic majorities in the House and Senate. When Reagan assumed the presidency in 1981, high unemployment and inflation had greatly weakened the national economy and created a mood for significant change, which enabled Reagan to persuade Congress to enact some of the most drastic taxing and spending laws in history.

From presidencies such as these has come the popular impression that presidents singlehandedly decide national policy. However, each of these periods of presidential dominance was marked by a special set of circumstances: a decisive election victory that gave added force to the president's leadership, a compelling national problem that convinced Congress and the public that bold presidential action was needed, and a president who was mindful of what was expected and who vigorously advocated policies consistent with those expectations.

When conditions are favorable, the power of the presidency appears awesome. The problem for most presidents is that conditions are not normally conducive to strong leadership. Erwin Hargrove suggests that presidential influence depends largely on circumstance.[9] Some presidents serve in periods when important problems are surfacing in American society but have not yet become critical. Such a situation, Hargrove contends, produces a "president of preparation," who opens the way for major policy changes but is no longer in office by the time the change is made. Kennedy was one such president; he recognized that federal intervention would be necessary to bring social justice to black Americans, but because conditions were unfavorable, he could not get Congress to act. The legislation was passed after his death, when Lyndon Johnson was president. Johnson is an example of what Hargrove calls a "president of achievement." Such a president is likely to have an activist view of his office, but a more crucial factor is that he serves at a time when other leaders and the public are generally agreed on a compelling issue, such as the need for civil rights legislation. This climate of opinion enables the president, if he seizes the moment, to achieve great success. Finally, there is the "president of consolidation," who by personal inclination and circumstance solidifies past achievements. One such president was Dwight D. Eisenhower, who proposed few innovative policies of his own but did consolidate the policy changes accomplished two decades earlier under Franklin Roosevelt, a president of achievement.

Of course, presidents have some control over their fate. Through effective leadership they can sometimes rally the public and Congress behind goals that they believe are important. In general, however, presidential achievement is heavily dependent on circumstance. Had Franklin Roosevelt been elected in 1960 rather than 1932, his place in American history would be very different and probably much less conspicuous. Roosevelt's genius lay in the devising of extraordinary policies, not in the creation of conditions that led to their acceptance.

★ **ANALYZE THE ISSUE**

**Presidential Greatness**
A perennial question is whether the president shapes events or is shaped by them. In his inaugural address, President Bush said that Americans should not expect too much from him because the mountainous budget deficits precluded most policy initiatives. Do the times dictate that Bush will be less than a great president? What does history suggest to you about the general question of presidential greatness?

[9]Erwin Hargrove, *The Power of the Modern Presidency* (New York: Knopf, 1974).

## THE STAGE OF THE PRESIDENT'S TERM

If conditions conducive to great accomplishments occur infrequently, it is nonetheless the case that nearly every president has favorable moments. Such moments tend to come during the first months in office. A newly elected president enjoys a "honeymoon" period during which Congress, the press, and the public expect him to propose programs and are predisposed to support them.[10] Not surprisingly, presidents have put forth more new programs in their first year in office than in any subsequent year.[11]

Later in their terms, presidents tend to do less well in presenting initiatives and getting them enacted. They may run out of good ideas or, more likely, deplete their political resources—the momentum of their election is gone and sources of opposition have emerged. Furthermore, if the president blunders or conditions turn sour—and it is hard for a president to serve for any length of time without a serious setback of one kind or another—he will lose some of his credibility and public support. Even highly successful presidents tend to have weak records in their final years. Franklin Roosevelt began his presidency with a remarkable period of achievement—the celebrated "Hundred Days"—but during his last six years in office, few of his major domestic proposals were enacted.

## THE PRESIDENT'S PARTISAN SUPPORT IN CONGRESS

The fact that they represent separate state or district constituencies can place individual members of Congress at odds with one another as well as with the president, whose constituency is a national one. Representatives of urban and rural areas, wealthier and poorer communities, and different regions of the country have conflicting views on some policy issues. To succeed, the president must convince enough members of Congress that their disparate interests can be reconciled with his singular purpose.

No source of division is more important to presidential success than partisanship. The fact that the president belongs or does not belong to the same party as the House and the Senate majorities and the absolute sizes of those majorities are crucial factors. Between 1952 and 1988, each Republican president—Eisenhower, Nixon, Ford, and Reagan—had to contend with a Democratic majority in one or both houses of Congress. Congress passed a smaller percentage of the initiatives proposed by each of these presidents than by any Democratic president of the period—Kennedy, Johnson, or Carter.[12]

Democratic presidents have not always had an easy time with Congress, either. The chief obstacle has been southern Democrats, who tend to be more conservative than congressional Democrats from other regions and thus more likely to break party ranks and vote with their Republican colleagues. Even Jimmy Carter, who was from the South himself, had appreciably less support from his fellow southern Democrats. In 1978, for example, his legislative positions were supported by an average of only 50 percent of southern

[10]See Charles McCall, "Political Parties and Popular Government," in George J. Graham, Jr., and Scarlett G. Graham, *Founding Principles of American Government* (Chatham, N.J.: Chatham House, 1984), 299; Stephen J. Wayne, *The Road to the White House*, 2d ed. (New York: St. Martin's Press, 1984), 264.
[11]Paul C. Light, *The President's Agenda* (Baltimore: Johns Hopkins University Press, 1982), 41–45.
[12]*Congressional Quarterly Almanac, 1983*, 20C.

congressional Democrats, compared with nearly 70 percent of congressional Democrats from other regions.[13] On such issues as social welfare and individual rights, southern Democrats have frequently combined with Republicans (in the "conservative coalition") to block many of the legislative initiatives of Democratic presidents. Over the past two decades, a majority of Republicans and a majority of southern Democrats have voted together on about a fifth of all congressional votes. When they have done so, they have prevailed most of the time.[14]

Nevertheless, Democratic majorities in Congress have given Democratic presidents an advantage. Of post–World War II presidents, Lyndon Johnson had the highest success rate with Congress. When his advisers cautioned him about proposing what was to become the Voting Rights Act of 1965, Johnson told them he would push legislation as fast and hard as he could before his "window of opportunity" with Congress closed. Party loyalty and the urgency of poverty and civil rights issues carried the day for Johnson.

## THE FOREIGN OR DOMESTIC NATURE
## OF THE POLICY PROPOSAL

In the 1960s Aaron Wildavsky wrote that, while the nation has only one president, it has two presidencies: one domestic and one foreign.[15] Wildavsky was referring to Congress's differential responses to domestic and foreign presidential initiatives. He found that since World War II, only 40 percent of

[13]*Congressional Quarterly Almanac, 1978* (Washington, D.C.: Congressional Quarterly Press, 1979), 24C–25C.
[14]See Mark C. Shelley, *The Permanent Majority: The Conservative Coalition in the United States Congress* (University: University of Alabama Press, 1983).
[15]Aaron Wildavsky, "The Two Presidencies," *Trans-action*, December 1966, 7.

---

### ⋆ HOW THE UNITED STATES COMPARES

**Systems of Executive Policy Leadership**

The United States instituted a presidential system in 1789 as part of its constitutional checks and balances. This form of executive leadership was copied in Latin America but not in Europe. European democracies adopted parliamentary systems, in which executive leadership is provided by a prime minister, who is a member of the legislature. In recent years some European prime ministers have campaigned and governed as if they were a singular authority rather than the head of a collective institution. France in the 1960s created a separate chief executive office, but retained its parliamentary form of legislature.

The policy leadership of a president can differ substantially from that of a prime minister. As a singular head of an independent branch of government, a president does not have to share executive authority but nevertheless depends on the willingness of the legislative branch to support his leadership. By comparison, a prime minister shares executive leadership with a cabinet, but once agreement within the cabinet is reached, he or she is almost assured of the legislative support necessary to carry out policy initiatives.

| Presidential System | Presidential/Parliamentary System | Parliamentary System |
|---|---|---|
| Mexico | France | Australia |
| United States | Finland | Belgium |
| Venezuela | | Canada |
| | | Great Britain |
| | | Israel |
| | | Italy |
| | | Japan |
| | | Netherlands |
| | | West Germany |
| | | Sweden |

presidential proposals in the domestic policy area had been enacted by Congress, compared with 70 percent of foreign policy initiatives. It must be noted that Wildavsky was analyzing a period when there was general agreement on U.S. foreign policy objectives. After World War II, Republican and Democratic leaders alike were agreed on the desirability of containing Soviet communism and establishing U.S. diplomatic, military, and economic influence around the world (see Chapter 28). Accordingly, presidents had strong backing for their foreign policy leadership. By the late 1960s, however, the Vietnam war had disrupted the policy consensus and made it more difficult for presidents to lead.

The two-presidencies thesis is now regarded as an oversimplified conception of presidential influence. Many of the same factors, such as the composition of Congress, that affect a president's success on foreign policy also affect his success on domestic policy.[16] Nevertheless, presidents do have a general advantage in the foreign policy area. Some members of Congress believe that partisanship ends "at the ocean's edge" and will side with any foreign policy position the president takes unless they find it substantially objectionable.[17] The Senate's historical response to treaty proposals illustrates this point.[18] The Senate has voted to reject only 1 percent of the treaties proposed by presidents; it has ratified another 15 percent after modifying them; and some treaties have been withdrawn because of Senate opposition. The Senate supports the president on the great majority of treaties in part as a signal to other nations that they can negotiate with the United States through its president. The defeat of a treaty is a rebuke not only to the president but also to the other country or countries that are parties to the treaty.

The Supreme Court has recognized the special requirements of foreign policy, conceding to the president the power to take action not expressly forbidden by law. As a result, presidents are able to make some major policy decisions—including those on trade agreements, deployments of military forces, and the granting of diplomatic recognition—on their own authority. For example, Richard Nixon's 1972 agreement with China's premier, Chou En-lai, to renew diplomatic relations between their countries was worked out in secret and presented to Congress after the fact.

The president also owes his advantage in foreign and defense policy to his commanding position with the defense, diplomatic, and intelligence agencies. These are sometimes labeled "presidential agencies." As chief executive, the president is in charge of all federal agencies, but in practice his influence is strongest in those agencies that connect with his constitutional authority as chief diplomat and commander in chief, such as the Departments of State and Defense and the CIA. They have a tradition of deference to presidential authority which is not found in agencies that deal primarily with domestic policy. The Department of Agriculture, for example, responds to presidential

[16]Lance T. LeLoup and Steven A. Shull, "Congress versus the Executive: The Two Presidencies 'Reconsidered,'" *Social Science Quarterly*, March 1979, 707 (for 1965–1975); Harvey G. Zeidenstein, "The Two Presidencies Thesis Is Alive and Well and Has Been Living in the U.S. Senate Since 1973," *Presidential Studies Quarterly* 2 (1981): 511–525; see also Michael Mumper, "The President and Domestic Policy-making," *Congress and the Presidency*, Spring 1985, 75–80.
[17]Aage Clausen, *How Congressmen Decide* (New York: St. Martin's Press, 1973), ch. 8; see also Lee Sigelman, "A Reassessment of the Two Presidencies Thesis," *Journal of Politics* 41 (1979): 120.
[18]See Raymond Tatalovich and Byron W. Daynes, *Presidential Power in the United States* (Monterey, Calif.: Brooks/Cole, 1984), 262.

Richard Nixon's administration is a recent example of the fact that Congress and the Supreme Court tend to give presidents more cooperation on foreign policy proposals than on domestic matters. Here Nixon dines with Chinese leaders during his visit to China in 1972, which was part of his successful initiative to resume diplomatic relations between the United States and China. (Dirck Halstead)

direction but is also responsive (perhaps even more responsive) to farm-state senators and representatives. As Chapter 23 describes, bureaucratic support is important to a president's success with Congress, and that support is more likely to be forthcoming when the agency in question is part of the defense, diplomatic, or intelligence bureaucracy.

## Staying Strong: How Presidents Help and Hurt Themselves

Although presidents are not nearly so powerful as the news media make them appear, their capacity to influence the agenda of national debate is unrivaled, reflecting their unique claim to represent the whole country. Whenever presidents direct their attention to a particular issue or program, the attention of others usually follows. But will those others pay attention for long? And will they follow the president's lead? As we have noted, a president's support varies with conditions, some of which are clearly beyond his control. Yet presidents are not entirely at the mercy of history. As sole chief executive, a president is an active participant in his fate and can increase his chances of success by having an appropriate outlook on the presidency, by working to create effective relationships with Congress, and by developing a strong rapport with the American people.

### DISPLAYING PRESIDENTIAL CHARACTER

Because the presidential office is vested in a single individual, a president's personal traits can have a profound effect on his performance. In his landmark book *The Presidential Character*, James David Barber suggests that a president's orientation toward power ("active" or "passive," in Barber's terms) and politics ("positive" or "negative") affects his capacity to lead.[19]

[19]James David Barber, *The Presidential Character: Predicting Performance in the White House,* 3d ed. (Englewood Cliffs, N.J.: Prentice-Hall, 1985).

In Barber's view, "active" presidents are more effective than "passive" presidents. Active presidents have a drive to lead and succeed. They devote great energy to the presidency, apply its power fully, and have clear objectives in mind. Passive presidents feel less need to take command. They do not work so hard, are more willing to accept the direction of others, and do not make full use of the office's resources. Barber also regards "positive" presidents as more effective than "negative" presidents. Positive presidents thrive on the give-and-take, the limelight, and the thrill of victory that politics can offer. In contrast, negative presidents are driven by an inner compulsion or sense of duty rather than by enjoyment of politics.*

Barber's distinctions take on added meaning when one reflects on the American system's pluralism and the resulting fragmentation of authority. Although presidents like to claim that they have a policy mandate because they are elected by national vote, the fact is that no clear mandate is possible in American politics. For one thing, members of Congress are elected independently of the president, so that the claim of a congressional majority to a leadership mandate is as valid as the president's. For another, the fragmentation and pluralism of the U.S. political system result in weak parties, so that there is no agreed-upon platform, or policy mandate, among those elected to office. Power is always an open question in the American system of government. It must be won and rewon. If presidents are to succeed fully in the open-ended struggle for power in Washington, they must be aggressive in their pursuit of goals and must relish political maneuvering—that is, they must be active-positive, in Barber's terms.

And in fact, active-positive presidents have tended to be more successful than any others. Franklin D. Roosevelt was the archetypical active-positive president. He relished politics and was tireless in his pursuit of his policy agenda. When he had setbacks, as when the Supreme Court struck down one of his early New Deal programs, Roosevelt simply regrouped and came back with another policy proposal to deal with the same problem. Harry Truman and John Kennedy are other presidents whom Barber has classified as active-positives. Each was dogged in his pursuit of policy goals, tireless in his attempts to master the presidential office, and energized by the politicking required to get others to accept his leadership.

Barber regards active-negative presidents as potentially the most dangerous. Although they are active in their drive to succeed, their negative traits of compulsiveness and distaste for the routines of politics can result in confrontation, stalemate, or deviousness. Barber places Woodrow Wilson and Richard Nixon in this category. In Wilson's case, unyielding self-righteousness led to a fight with the Senate over joining the League of Nations which destroyed his physical and emotional health and ended in bitter defeat. Wilson refused to compromise on the issue, preferring to stand by what he regarded as strictly an issue of principle. In a system of divided powers, Wilson's rigidity was a recipe for failure. As for Nixon, his personal insecurity and unwillingness to accept the legitimacy of opposing views led him to develop an "enemies list" and

*Barber's typology is not without problems. No president fits any of Barber's categories precisely, and situational factors as well as character traits affect a president's behavior. Barber predicted in 1980 that Reagan would be a passive-positive president, but Reagan's performance in some ways placed him in the active-positive category. Nevertheless, Barber's classification of personality types is helpful in efforts to understand differences in presidential performance.

Examples of James David Barber's presidential characterizations: Jimmy Carter, active-positive; Richard Nixon, active-negative; Ronald Reagan, passive-positive; Dwight Eisenhower, passive-negative. (top two, UPI/Bettmann Newsphotos; bottom l., White House Photo/Black Star; bottom r., D.D.E./National Archives)

poisoned the atmosphere in the White House, fostering wrongdoing by subordinates and culminating in the Watergate scandal.

Passive presidents, whether of the positive or negative type, are less likely to get into political trouble but are also less likely to achieve. Calvin Coolidge (passive-negative) decided not to seek a second term. He was relieved to be free of the office, which he had taken upon President Warren Harding's death out of a sense of duty rather than a love of politics or a desire to achieve policy goals.

## SEEKING COOPERATION FROM CONGRESS

Presidents cannot assume that support for their policies will automatically materialize. They have to build a following by taking into consideration the interests of other policymakers, who have their own jobs to do and their own interests to satisfy. As obvious as this point seems, presidents sometimes lose sight of it. As the center of national attention, a president can easily start to think that his ideas ought to prevail because they are somehow innately superior.

This line of reasoning invariably gets the president into trouble. Jimmy Carter had not held national office before he was elected, so he had no clear understanding of how Washington operates. In his memoirs, House Speaker Thomas P. "Tip" O'Neill, a fellow Democrat, said of Carter:

> Jimmy Carter was the smartest public officer I've ever known. The range and extent of his knowledge was astounding; he could speak with authority about energy, the nuclear issue, space travel, the Middle East, Latin America, human rights, American history, and just about any other topic that came up. Time after time, and without using notes, he would tick off the arguments on both sides of a question. His mind was exceptionally well developed, and it was open, too. He was always willing to listen and to learn. *With one exception.* When it came to the politics of Washington, D.C., *he never really understood how the system worked.*[20]

Soon after taking office, Carter had vetoed nineteen public works projects that he believed were a waste of taxpayers' money, ignoring the importance that members of Congress attach to obtaining federally funded projects for their home states and districts. Carter's action set the tone for a conflict-ridden relationship with Congress.

### The Veto

One instrument by which presidents can try to force their views on Congress is the veto (see Table 21-1). Congress can seldom muster enough votes to override a presidential veto, so the threat of a veto can force Congress to accept a presidential demand. When the Tax Reform Act of 1986 was being debated in Congress, Reagan said flatly that he would veto any bill that had the effect of raising taxes; this ultimatum forced Congress to limit itself to considering revenue-neutral provisions. Congress will often accept some compromise with the president in return for his support of a legislative proposal.[21] However, Richard Neustadt argues that the veto is actually a sign of presidential weakness, not strength, because it usually comes into play when Congress has refused to go along with the president's ideas.[22] The frequency with which Gerald Ford resorted to the veto kept the Democratic-controlled Congress from getting its way, but it was a strong indication that Ford was failing to get Congress to accept his leadership.

[20]Thomas P. (Tip) O'Neill, with William Novak, *Man of the House: The Life and Political Memoirs of Speaker Tip O'Neill* (New York: Random House, 1987), 297; emphasis added.
[21]Robert J. Spitzer, *The Presidential Veto: Touchstone of the America Presidency* (Albany: State University of New York Press, 1988).
[22]Richard E. Neustadt, *Presidential Power: The Politics of Leadership from FDR to Carter* (New York: Wiley, 1980), 67.

TABLE 21-1  **Number and Override of Presidential Vetoes, 1933–1988**

| President | Years in Office | Number of Vetoes | Number of Vetoes Overriden by Congress |
|---|---|---|---|
| Franklin Roosevelt | 1933–1945 | 635 | 9 |
| Harry Truman | 1945–1952 | 250 | 12 |
| Dwight Eisenhower | 1953–1960 | 181 | 2 |
| John Kennedy | 1961–1963 | 21 | 0 |
| Lyndon Johnson | 1963–1968 | 30 | 0 |
| Richard Nixon | 1969–1974 | 43 | 7 |
| Gerald Ford | 1974–1976 | 66 | 12 |
| Jimmy Carter | 1977–1980 | 31 | 2 |
| Ronald Reagan | 1981–1988 | 78 | 9 |

SOURCE: *Congressional Quarterly Weekly Report,* January 7, 1989, 7.

## The War Powers Act

The Vietnam war is the clearest illustration of the dangers to the nation and to the presidency when a president tries to force his policies on others. The war taught Congress a bitter lesson about presidential usurpation of its constitutional authority to declare war. Presidents Johnson and Nixon repeatedly told Congress that victory was near, providing military estimates of enemy casualties as evidence. Congressional support changed abruptly in 1971 with the publication of *The Pentagon Papers.* These secret government documents revealed that Johnson and Nixon had systematically distorted facts to put the Vietnam situation in a more favorable light. To prevent future presidential wars, Congress in 1973 passed the War Powers Act. Nixon vetoed the measure, but his veto was overridden by two-thirds majorities in the House and Senate. The War Powers Act stipulates that:

- Within 48 hours of committing combat troops, the president must inform Congress in writing of his reasons for doing so.
- Unless Congress acts to extend the period, hostilities involving American troops must end in sixty days, although the troops can remain for an additional thirty days if the president declares that extra time is needed for their safe withdrawal.
- Within the extra thirty days, Congress can demand the immediate withdrawal of the troops by passing a concurrent resolution, which is not subject to presidential veto.
- In every possible instance, the president must consult with Congress before dispatching troops into hostile situations or into areas where such situations are likely to arise.

The War Powers Act is perhaps Congress's most significant effort to curb presidential authority in the nation's history. Not surprisingly, every president from Nixon to Reagan has claimed that the act infringes on his constitutional power as commander in chief, and each has refused to comply fully with its provisions. For example, Congress was not formally consulted before Reagan's invasion of Grenada in 1983, Carter's military mission to rescue hostages in Iran in 1979, or Ford's action to free the crew of the *Mayaguez* in 1975. In each case the president obeyed the requirement to report the military commitment to

★ ANALYZE THE ISSUE

**Foreign Policy: The President vs. Congress**
In his first State of the Union address, President Bush said that Congress should stop trying to "micro-manage" foreign policy. Presidents Reagan, Carter, and Ford had the same complaint, holding that the president should have broad discretion in carrying out foreign policy. Should Congress take an active role in setting precise limits on foreign policy, or should the president have this responsibility? What are the advantages and disadvantages of each arrangement?

During its investigation into the Iran-Contra scandal, Congress made clear its displeasure with any exercise of presidential authority that was designed to circumvent the law. (Christopher Morris/Black Star)

Congress within forty-eight hours, but at the same time refused to acknowledge limits on his authority.

Nevertheless, the lessons of Vietnam have been a significant curb on presidential warmaking. Congress has shown no willingness to give the president anything approaching a free hand in the use of military force. This posture was plainly evident when, in response to news of covert arms dealings in the Iran-Contra affair, Congress began a full-scale investigation that threw the Reagan administration into disarray. Thus the effect of executive efforts to circumvent congressional authority in the warmaking area is heightened congressional opposition. Even if the president gains in the short run, he undermines his capacity to lead in the long run by failing to keep in mind that Congress is a coequal branch of the American governing system.

### Congress as a Presidential Constituency

*A President needs political understanding to run the government, [although] he may be elected without it.*
Harry S Truman

Without question, the powers of the presidential office are insufficient by themselves to keep the president in a position of power. He must have the help of other officials, particularly members of Congress, and in order to get their help, he must respond to their interests as they respond to his. Congress is a constituency that the president must serve if he expects its backing.[23]

A classic illustration of what presidents can do to help themselves with Congress is the Marshall Plan, a program to aid European countries devastated by World War II. The plan was enacted by Congress in 1948 at the request of Harry S Truman. Truman had become president upon the death of Franklin Roosevelt and was widely regarded in Washington as just a caretaker president who would be replaced by a Republican. (The Republicans had made substantial gains in the 1946 congressional elections.) Truman knew he could not simply demand that Congress make a commitment to the postwar rebuilding of

[23]On the leadership role of the president, see Harold Laski, *The American Presidency* (New York: Harper, 1940), and Nicholas D. Berry, "The Foundation of Presidential Leadership: Teaching," *Presidential Studies Quarterly* 11 (Winter 1981): 99–105.

## IMPEACHMENT AND REMOVAL OF THE PRESIDENT

Congress's ultimate control over the president is its power to impeach and remove him from office. The procedure is spelled out in Article I of the Constitution. The House of Representatives decides whether the president should be placed on trial by the Senate for what the Constitution calls "high crimes and misdemeanors." If the House impeaches the president, the Senate becomes a tribunal presided over by the chief justice of the Supreme Court and can remove the president from office by a two-thirds vote.

Congress has undertaken action to impeach and remove two presidents. In 1868 Andrew Johnson came within one Senate vote of being removed from office for his opposition to Congress's harsh Reconstruction policies in the wake of the Civil War. In 1974 Richard Nixon's involvement in the Watergate cover-up led to a recommendation of impeachment by the House Judiciary Committee. Before the full House could vote on his impeachment, however, Nixon resigned the presidency.

Europe, in view of the cost of such a program (roughly $100 billion in today's dollars) and of its novelty (historically, the United States had stayed free of permanent European entanglements). Truman succeeded in getting congressional approval by subordinating his position to that of others.

First, rather than announce the program himself, Truman gave the task to General George C. Marshall, who had been chief of staff of the armed forces during World War II and was one of America's most widely admired leaders. Second, Truman made a special effort to gain the support of Arthur Vandenberg, a leading Republican senator and chairman of the Senate Foreign Relations Committee. Truman accepted Vandenberg's request that "politics" not embroil the plan, followed Vandenberg's advice on changes in financial and administrative aspects of the plan, and allowed Vandenberg to choose a Republican, Paul Hoffman, to head the U.S. agency responsible for administering the plan. Through Vandenberg's backing, Truman gained the Republican congressional support that made the Marshall Plan possible.

From cases such as the Marshall Plan, Richard Neustadt, a political scientist, concluded that presidential power, at base, is "the power to persuade."[24] More recently the presidential scholar Fred Greenstein offered the same general conclusion: "Whatever else his qualities, the president needs to be a working politician who can work with or otherwise win over the Washington community."[25]

### NURTURING PUBLIC SUPPORT

Public support can have a powerful effect on the president's ability to achieve his policy goals. Much of his power rests on his claim to national leadership, and the legitimacy of that claim is roughly proportional to public support of his performance. As long as the public is behind him, the president's leadership cannot easily be dismissed by other Washington officials. If his public support sinks, they are less inclined to accept his leadership.[26]

[24]Neustadt, *Presidential Power*, 33.
[25]Fred I. Greenstein, ed., *Leadership in the Modern Presidency* (Cambridge, Mass.: Harvard University Press, 1988), ch. 10.
[26]Harvey G. Zeidenstein, "Presidents' Popularity and Their Wins and Losses on Major Issues: Does One Have a Greater Influence over the Other?" *Presidential Studies Quarterly*, Spring 1985, 287–300.

# Does the President Have Too Much Power in Relation to Congress?

**LOUIS FISHER**

*The central goal of the War Powers Act—to bring about government by 'collective judgment' of the president and Congress—remains an essential objective.*

Deciding how to restrain presidential power, especially in foreign affairs, remains one of the thorniest issues of the twentieth century. Even though numerous statutes designed to curb and regulate executive power have been enacted, recent decades have featured a succession of presidential initiatives in Korea and Southeast Asia, the Watergate and Iran-Contra scandals, and several other events that have been costly to the nation and to the prestige of the presidency.

In times of crisis, presidential power naturally expands to meet the emergency. So it was with Abraham Lincoln during the Civil War and with Woodrow Wilson during World War I. However, after each of those conflicts Congress resumed its status as a coequal branch of government. In contrast, the powers transferred to Franklin D. Roosevelt during the Great Depression and World War II did not revert to Congress. What Congress had earlier accepted as a temporary disequilibrium now became a permanent feature of executive–legislative relations.

Particularly disturbing to Congress was the continuation of presidential war powers after World War II ended in 1945. Harry Truman retained various emergency authorities on the grounds that a "state of war" or a "state of emergency" still existed. Not until 1952 did Truman sign a statement terminating the state of war with Japan, and by that time he had already involved U.S. troops in Korea without congressional authority. In 1951 he also announced his intention to send ground forces to Europe, again without seeking congressional approval.

For three months in 1951, the Senate engaged in a "Great Debate" over the president's authority to engage the nation in war. The senators concluded that the policies of the federal government require the approval of Congress and the people after full and free discussion. Secret executive agreements and initiatives, they argued, threaten the liberties of the people. Both chambers of Congress were also stimulated to rethink their own role in foreign affairs.

Dwight Eisenhower tried to forge a common front with Congress. He pointed out that a military commitment by the United States has much greater impact on allies and enemies alike if it represents the collective judgment of the president and Congress.

Under John Kennedy and Lyndon Johnson, however, the relationship between the two branches became progressively more strained and combative. After Richard Nixon had taken several steps to widen the war in Southeast Asia, Congress passed the War Powers Act of 1973 over Nixon's veto.

More than fifteen years of experience with the War Powers Act have proved that its success depends on the willingness of executive officials and members of Congress to cooperate. Some have complained that the act has "failed" because the required presidential reports to Congress are inadequate, because presidents have not consulted sufficiently with Congress, and because the "legislative veto" conferred by the act is unconstitutional. However, the central goal of the act—to bring about government by "collective judgment" on the part of Congress and the president—remains an essential objective. Moreover, the act seems to have succeeded in confining presidential initiatives to short-term military actions, as in Grenada and Libya.

The main lesson of the post–World War II period is that the president needs to secure the understanding and support of Congress and the American people before engaging U.S. forces in hostilities. Such cooperation is in the interest not only of the country and the world but also of the presidency itself.

*Louis Fisher is affiliated with the Congressional Research Service. He is the author of* **American Constitutional Law.**

**GEORGE C. EDWARDS III**

*It is precisely because national security policy is so fundamental that Congress needs to be involved in it.*

The controversy over the relative power of the president and Congress becomes most heated in the area of national security policymaking. Congressional assertiveness in national security policy during the 1980s, broad claims of executive power made by the Reagan administration, the dispute generated by the Iran-Contra affair—all these recent developments show that this venerable question is still relevant.

Those who believe that Congress should play a subsidiary role in national security policymaking often argue that the nature of national security policy is such that Congress cannot exercise wise judgment and thus should defer to the president. However, careful examination reveals the weakness of this argument.

In theory, the executive branch has several advantages over the legislature in determining national security policy. Congress is an institution organized for open deliberation and the articulation of diverse views. In contrast, the executive branch, with its hierarchical and specialized organization, has greater potential for secrecy, speed, expertise, and coherence in the development and implementation of public policy.

Those who propose that Congress play only a modest role in national security policy argue that because most members of Congress lack expertise in foreign policy, they should rely on the judgments of national security specialists in the executive branch. Yet most members of Congress are not specialists in other complex policy areas, either—health care, social security financing, economics, or agriculture—but no one argues that they should defer to the executive branch in these areas. Why should they do so when questions of national security are involved?

The response might be that national security policy is different because, at bottom, it involves matters of life and death and basic freedoms. Yet it is precisely because national security policy is so fundamental that Congress needs to be involved in it, in order to ensure that the people's interests are represented. Only congressional debate can bring out broad perspectives, diverse views, and full discussion of the possible consequences of alternatives and the likely trade-offs involved in policy alternatives. In addition, Congress sometimes has a moral obligation to nudge a reluctant administration in a particular direction, such as toward arms-control negotiations.

In an emergency that requires an immediate response, such as a nuclear attack, Congress in effect must yield to the president. It does not follow, however, that Congress should not be involved in situations that allow more time for deliberation. Members of Congress are no less able than officials in the executive branch to listen to experts on, say, the Strategic Defense Initiative (SDI). In addition, they are better positioned to represent the will of the people and to assess the true costs and benefits of such a program.

Those who assert that increased participation by Congress will produce inconsistency in policy often are really only complaining about Congress's failure to support the policy proposals they favor. When Congress refused to appropriate any or all of the funds the president requested for aid to the Contras, SDI research, or the MX missile, did the Reagan administration drop these initiatives in the interests of policy continuity? Of course not. Instead, it continued to fight for the funds, hoping thereby to create a discontinuity in policy.

Congress has been intimately involved in national security policy from the beginning of our history. It is not an illegitimate intruder into the president's proper domain, but rather a constitutionally sanctioned participant whose involvement is widely—and wisely—supported by the American people.

*George C. Edwards III is a member of the Department of Political Science at Texas A&M University. He is the author of* The Public Presidency *and* At the Margins: Presidential Leadership of Congress, *and co-editor (with Wallace E. Walker) of* National Security and the U.S. Constitution.

# Part Six

## APPOINTED OFFICIALS

Early in the twentieth century the Supreme Court of the United States was restricted by laws that effectively determined the issues it would address. The great majority of cases reached the Court as mandatory appeals. The Court had no choice but to hear and rule upon these cases, even if they had legal significance only to the parties directly involved. During this period, the policymaking discretion of bureaucratic agencies was also under substantial limits. These agencies administered laws passed by Congress and assessed situations arising under the laws, but were effectively blocked from issuing regulations that would give new definition to public policy.

Times have changed. Today bureaucratic agencies routinely develop and implement broad regulations. In fact, the number and volume of regulations issued by bureaucratic agencies far exceed the legislative output of Congress. In addition, some of these regulations are as far-reaching as the statutes from which they derive. Affirmative action programs, for example, began when federal agencies required recipients of federal funds to take steps to ensure that members of minority groups would share in the opportunities provided by this funding.

The Supreme Court is also a more substantial policymaker today than it was in the past. The Court is more or less free to decide which cases it will hear—and thus which legal issues it will address. Busing to achieve racial integration in the public schools is but one significant public policy that was established through action by the Supreme Court.

Chapters 22 and 23 examine the federal bureaucracy, which is undoubtedly the least appreciated and the most widely misunderstood of the nation's institutions. Chapters 24 and 25 consider the judiciary, which is also misunderstood but is more widely respected than the bureaucracy. The discussion of both the bureaucracy and the judiciary concentrates on the nature of these institutions, their historical development, their roles in modern politics, the recruitment of their officials, their impact on public policy, and their accountability to the public they serve.

The accountability of judges and bureaucrats is a particularly critical issue. These officials are not elected to their positions, yet they affect Americans' daily lives in direct and substantial ways. No observer of American politics would argue that the judiciary and the bureaucracy are more powerful than Congress or the president, but at the same time no observer would say that their power is a secondary concern. Bureaucrats and judges are important government officials, and whether these appointees properly serve the people they represent is a very compelling question in American society today.     ★   ★   ★

# Chapter 22

## BUREAUCRACY AND BUREAUCRATS: ADMINISTERING THE GOVERNMENT

*[No] industrial society could manage the daily operations of its public affairs without bureaucratic organizations in which officials play a major policymaking role.*

*Norman Thomas[1]*

When Neil Armstrong set foot on the moon in 1969, most Americans were watching the historic event on television. Armstrong instantly became a national hero, just as Americans had earlier made heroes of Alan Shepard, the first U.S. astronaut to fly into space, and John Glenn, the first American to orbit the earth. Through the power of the press, the space program would continue to make celebrities, if not heroes, of the men and women who risked their lives to fly into space. Then on January 28, 1986, the television cameras made America a witness to tragedy. Seventy-one seconds after liftoff, the space shuttle *Challenger* exploded, killing all seven crew members, including a schoolteacher, Christa McAuliffe.

The *Challenger* disaster led the press, for the first time, to peer deep inside the bureaucracy of the National Aeronautics and Space Administration (NASA). The picture that emerged was one of careless administration, flawed safety procedures, competition over jurisdiction, and denial of responsibility. The presidential commission that was appointed to investigate the tragedy reached the same conclusions. But the news media's portrayal of NASA was incomplete. However courageous America's astronauts might have been, they were not the main force behind the space program. It was the NASA bureaucracy—the aeronautical engineers, the rocket scientists, the top managers, and thousands of other people—that had developed the delivery and control systems that

[1]Norman Thomas, *Rule 9: Politics, Administration, and Civil Rights* (New York: Random House, 1966), 6.

The space shuttle *Challenger* explodes—a human tragedy and an example of bureaucratic blundering. (AP/Wide World)

made space missions possible. Yet not until the *Challenger* explosion was NASA's organization brought squarely into public view, and then in a wholly critical way.

The U.S. space program illustrates two points about the federal government's bureaucracy. The lesser point is that it rarely gets publicity unless it makes a mistake. The news media infrequently cover the bureaucracy's successes but often report its failures. The bureaucracy also takes a regular beating from politicians. The president and members of Congress have the highly visible role of enacting policy, and they are quick to claim credit when things go well but are often just as quick to shift the blame to the bureaucracy when things go badly. For the most part, their charges are unfair. The federal bureaucracy is far from perfect, but it does not deserve many of the criticisms directed at it.

The more important point that can be drawn from the example of the space program is that the U.S. government could not accomplish its goals without the bureaucracy's contributions. The writers of the Constitution made no mention of a bureaucracy. Modern government, however, would be unthinkable without one. It is America's organizational capacity that makes it possible for us to have such ambitious programs as space exploration, social security, and interstate highways.

This chapter describes the nature of the federal bureaucracy and the personnel who staff it. The discussion aims to clarify the bureaucracy's responsibilities, organizational structure, and personnel management practices. But the chapter also shows that the bureaucracy is very much involved in the play of politics. A recognition of the bureaucracy's political nature is essential to an understanding not only of the bureaucracy's development, which is a focus of this chapter, but also of the bureaucracy's influence, which is the subject of the next chapter. The main points in this first of two chapters on the bureaucracy are the following:

★ *Bureaucracy is an inevitable consequence of complexity and scale.* Modern government could not function without a large bureaucracy. Through hierarchy, specialization, and rules, bureaucracy provides an efficient means for managing thousands of workers and activities.

★ *Government agencies have developed in response to changing national conditions and political demands.* The result is a bureaucracy with hundreds of agencies that are involved inevitably and deeply in the play of politics.

★ *The federal bureaucracy's primary responsibilities are initiation and development of policy, delivery of services, evaluation of programs, regulation, and adjudication.* Bureaucrats necessarily exercise discretion in carrying out these responsibilities. The bureaucracy does not simply administer policy, it also *makes* policy.

★ *The bureaucracy is expected simultaneously to respond to the direction of partisan officials and to administer programs fairly and competently.* These conflicting demands are addressed through a combination of personnel management systems: the patronage, merit, and executive leadership systems.

## The Federal Bureaucracy: Form, Personnel, and Activities

Bureaucracy is essentially a method of organizing people and work. As a form of organization, bureaucracy is the most efficient means of getting people to work together on tasks of great magnitude and complexity.

**Bureaucracy** is a system of organization and control that is based on three principles: hierarchical authority, job specialization, and formalized rules. **Hierarchical authority** refers to a chain of command, whereby the officials and units at the top of a bureaucracy have control over those in the middle, who in turn control those at the bottom. In **job specialization,** the responsibilities of each job position are explicitly defined, and there is a precise division of labor within the organization. **Formalized rules** are the standardized procedures and established regulations by which a bureaucracy conducts its operations.

These features are the reason that bureaucracy, as a form of organization, is unrivaled in the efficiency and control it provides. Hierarchy speeds action by reducing conflict over the power to make decisions: the higher an individual's position in the organization, the more decisionmaking power he or she has. Hierarchy is also the basis by which superiors control subordinates and maintain a commitment to organizational goals. Specialization yields efficiency because each individual is required to concentrate on a particular job: specialization enables workers to develop advanced skills and expert knowledge. Formalized rules enable workers to act quickly and precisely because decisions are made on the basis of predetermined guidelines. Formalized rules also enhance control: workers make decisions according to established organizational standards rather than their personal inclinations.[2]

The characteristics of bureaucratic organizations were first described by the noted German sociologist Max Weber (1864–1920), who concluded that bureaucratic efficiency is achieved at a high price. Bureaucracy transforms people from social beings to rational actors: they perform not as whole persons but as parts of an organizational entity. Their behavior is dictated by position, specialty, and rule. A bureaucracy grinds on, heedless of the personal feelings of its members. In the process, they lose a sense of the place of their narrow role and specialty within the larger context and become bound to rules without

[2]H. H. Gerth and C. Wright Mills, eds., *From Max Weber: Essays in Sociology* (New York: Oxford University Press, 1946).

policy problems. NASA, for example, could conceivably be located in the Department of Defense, but this placement would suggest that the space program is intended almost solely for military purposes rather than also for civilian purposes, such as space exploration and satellite communication. And if NASA tried to balance its defense and civilian missions within the Department of Defense, the balancing act would not last long. Agencies located within a cabinet department inevitably place that department's goals ahead of those of other units of the bureaucracy.

## Regulatory Agencies

**Regulatory agencies** have been created when Congress has recognized the importance of close and continuous regulation of an economic activity. Because such regulation requires more time and expertise than Congress can provide, the responsibility is delegated to a regulatory agency. The oldest regulatory agency is the Interstate Commerce Commission (ICC), which was created in 1887 to control price fixing and other unfair practices of the nation's railroads. The ICC today regulates all surface transportation affecting interstate commerce. Other regulatory agencies include the Securities and Exchange Commission (SEC), which oversees the stock and bond markets, and the Federal Reserve Board, which regulates federal banks and the nation's money supply.

Unlike these and other older agencies, which are charged with overseeing a certain industry, the regulatory agencies created since the 1960s are concerned with the business sector in general. Among them are the Occupational Safety and Health Administration (OSHA), which promotes job safety, and the Environmental Protection Agency (EPA), which regulates industrial pollution.

Beyond their executive functions, regulatory agencies have certain legislative and judicial functions. They issue regulations, implement them, and then judge whether individuals or organizations have followed them. Some regulatory agencies, particularly the older ones, are "independent" by virtue of their relative freedom from ongoing political control. They are headed by a commission of several members appointed by the president and confirmed by Congress but are not subject to removal by the president. Commissioners serve a fixed term, a legal stipulation intended to free their agencies from political interference. The newer regulatory agencies lack such autonomy. They are headed by a single administrator, who can be removed from office by the president and is therefore more responsive to the president's goals. (Regulatory agencies are discussed more fully in Chapter 26.)

## Government Corporations

**Government corporations** are similar to private corporations in that they charge clients for their services and are governed by a board of directors. However, government corporations receive federal funding to help defray operating expenses, and their directors are appointed by the president with Senate approval. The largest government corporation is the U.S. Postal Service, with roughly 800,000 employees. Other government corporations include the Federal Deposit Insurance Corporation (FDIC), which insures savings accounts against bank failures, and the National Railroad Passenger Corporation (Amtrak), which provides passenger rail service.

# U.S. REGULATORY AGENCIES, INDEPENDENT AGENCIES, GOVERNMENT CORPORATIONS, AND PRESIDENTIAL COMMISSIONS

ACTION

Administrative Conference of the U.S.

African Development Foundation

American Battle Monuments Commission

Appalachian Regional Commission

Board for International Broadcasting

Central Intelligence Agency

Commission on the Bicentennial of the United States Constitution

Commission on Civil Rights

Commission of Fine Arts

Commodity Futures Trading Commission

Consumer Product Safety Commission

Environmental Protection Agency

Equal Employment Opportunity Commission

Export-Import Bank of the U.S

Farm Credit Administration

Federal Communications Commission

Federal Deposit Insurance Corporation

Federal Election Commission

Federal Emergency Management Agency

Federal Home Loan Bank Board

Federal Labor Relations Authority

Federal Maritime Commission

Federal Mediation and Conciliation Service

Federal Reserve System, Board of Governors of the

Federal Trade Commission

General Services Administration

Inter-American Foundation

Interstate Commerce Commission

Merit Systems Protection Board

National Aeronautics and Space Administration

National Archives and Records Administration

National Capital Planning Commission

National Credit Union Administration

National Foundation on the Arts and the Humanities

National Labor Relations Board

National Mediation Board

National Railroad Passenger Corporation (Amtrak)

National Science Foundation

National Transportation Safety Board

Nuclear Regulatory Commission

Occupational Safety and Health Review Commission

Office of Personnel Management

Panama Canal Commission

Peace Corps

Pennsylvania Avenue Development Corporation

Pension Benefit Guaranty Corporation

Postal Rate Commission

Railroad Retirement Board

Securities and Exchange Commission

Selective Service System

Small Business Administration

Tennessee Valley Authority

U.S. Arms Control and Disarmament Agency

U.S. Information Agency

U.S. International Development Cooperation Agency

U.S. International Trade Commission

U.S. Postal Service

SOURCE: *The U.S. Government Manual, 1987–88* (Washington, D.C.: U.S. Government Printing Office, 1988), 21.

## Presidential Commissions

Some **presidential commissions** are permanently established and provide ongoing recommendations to the president in particular areas of responsibility. Two such commissions are the Commission on Civil Rights and the Commission on Fine Arts. Other presidential commissions are temporary and disband after making recommendations on specific issues. Temporary commissions during the 1980s included the President's Commission on Central America (charged with recommending a broad Central American policy) and the President's Private Sector Survey on Cost Control, commonly known as the Grace Commission (asked to suggest ways of reducing waste in the administration of federal programs).

## FEDERAL EMPLOYMENT

The 3 million civilian employees of the federal government include professionals who bring their expertise to the problems of governing a large and complex society, service workers who perform such tasks as the typing of correspondence and the delivery of mail, and middle and top managers who supervise the work of the various federal agencies.

More than 90 percent of federal employees are hired by merit criteria, which include educational attainment and performance on competitive tests (such as the civil service and foreign service examinations). Merit hiring protects government workers from being fired for partisan reasons. The Supreme Court has ruled that "non-policymaking" public employees cannot be dismissed "on the sole ground of political belief."[7] Their job security is further enhanced by a limited right to a hearing in dismissal actions.[8]

Although federal employees were once underpaid in comparison with their counterparts in the private sector, they now receive reasonably competitive salaries, except at the top levels. The large majority of federal employees have a GS (Graded Service) job ranking. The rankings, ranging from GS-1 to GS-18, are determined by job position and the employee's qualifications, such as level of education. Generally, a bachelor's degree is required for a GS-5 appointment, a master's degree for GS-9, and a doctorate for GS-11. A GS-5 starting salary is approximately $16,000, a GS-9 salary about $25,000, and a GS-11 about $30,000. An employee's salary increases with length of service. Public employees receive substantial fringe benefits, including full health insurance, liberal retirement plans, and generous vacation time and sick leave.

Public service has its drawbacks. Unlike civil servants in, say, Great Britain or West Germany, U.S. bureaucrats are not held in high esteem. Americans tend to look upon government employees as somehow less talented and industrious than people who hold comparable positions in the private sector. The evidence does not justify this perception, but it persists nonetheless and diminishes the satisfaction that federal bureaucrats derive from a career in public service.

Moreover, career bureaucrats are denied some opportunities that are available to workers in the private sector. The Hatch Act of 1939, as amended, prohibits federal employees from holding key positions (such as campaign manager or publicity director) in election campaigns.

In addition, federal employees have few rights of collective action.[9] They can join labor unions, but their unions by law have limited authority: the government maintains full control of job assignments, compensation, and promotion. Moreover, the Taft-Hartley Act of 1947 prohibits strikes by federal employees and permits the firing of workers who do go on strike.[10] In 1981 the 13,000-member Professional Air Traffic Controllers Organization (PATCO) decided to ignore the ban and went on strike over pay and working conditions, particularly the strain of monitoring air traffic for long hours without relief. President Reagan immediately invoked the Taft-Hartley Act, officially ordering the 11,500 striking controllers back to work. When they refused, Reagan fired all of them

---

[7]*Elrod* v. *Burns*, 727 U.S. 347 (1976).
[8]*Board of Regents* v. *Roth*, 408 U.S. 564 (1972).
[9]Sar A. Levitan and Alexandra B. Noden, *Working for the Sovereign* (Baltimore: Johns Hopkins University Press, 1983), 28–29, 39.
[10]See Wilson R. Hart, *Collective Bargaining in the Federal Civil Service* (New York: Harper & Row, 1961), ch. 3.

As the members of the Professional Air Traffic Controllers Organization discovered in 1981, federal employees do not have the same labor rights as do union members in the private sector. President Reagan summarily fired all 11,500 striking PATCO members. (Charles Steiner/Sygma)

and replaced them with supervisors, military and retired controllers, and nonstriking PATCO members. By 1982, as a rush training program began to provide additional controllers, the union was effectively broken. PATCO eventually filed for bankruptcy, and the striking controllers permanently lost their jobs.[11]

## THE FEDERAL BUREAUCRACY'S POLICY RESPONSIBILITIES

We have noted that although the federal bureaucracy is a key policymaking institution, the Constitution does not mention it. Its policymaking authority derives from grants of power to the constitutional branches: Congress, which has legislative power; the president, who has executive power; and the courts, which have judicial power.

[11]Levitan and Noden, *Working for the Sovereign*, 101–103.

---

### ★ HOW THE UNITED STATES COMPARES

**Bureaucratic Performance**
In a 1986 Harris poll, only one in four respondents expressed confidence in the performance of the U.S. federal bureaucracy. A comparison with other national bureaucracies, however, suggests that the U.S. federal bureaucracy is relatively effective. In fact, Charles Goodsell, a public administration expert, concludes that America's bureaucracy is among the best in the world. "Some national bureaucracies," he writes, "may be roughly the same [as the U.S. bureaucracy] in quality of overall performance, but they are few in number." In some countries, the bureaucracy is thoroughly inefficient and corrupt. Tasks are completed slowly and sometimes not at all unless a bribe has been paid. In other countries, the bureaucracy is overly rigid, centralized, and remote. The rules are more important than the policy goals these rules are designed to achieve. Neither of these extreme tendencies is characteristic of the U.S. federal bureaucracy.

Comparisons of national postal services, for example, confirm that the U.S. postal bureaucracy is among the world's best. The U.S. mail usually arrives on time, at the right destination, and with the right postage. In many countries, the mail is chronically late, often misrouted, frequently lost, and sometimes posted at the wrong rate.

SOURCE: Charles T. Goodsell, *The Case for Bureaucracy*, 2d ed. (Chatham, N.J.: Chatham House, 1985), 55–60.

could undoubtedly produce "evidence" that the cuts would have disastrous consequences for the environment.

### Regulation

The bureaucracy's policy role is perhaps clearest in its regulatory activities.[16] Lacking the necessary expertise and time, Congress has delegated regulatory responsibilities to specialized agencies. The Federal Communications Commission (FCC), for instance, is authorized by Congress to control broadcasting practices and licensing. Among the FCC's regulations was the "fairness doctrine," which (as we saw in Chapter 15) required broadcasters to present opposing views on controversial and important issues of public policy. In 1987 the FCC removed the restriction, despite objections by many members of Congress. The FCC's decision would have been overridden by Congress in late 1987, but President Reagan's threat of a veto caused the legislation to be set aside.

Regulation is not confined to specialized agencies. All executive agencies issue binding regulations of one kind or another. The Department of Health and Human Services (HHS), for example, requires health institutions that receive federal assistance to comply with its affirmative action guidelines for the hiring and promotion of women and minorities.

### Adjudication

Through reviews and hearings, bureaucrats exercise their responsibility to adjudicate, deciding whether individuals or groups have complied with federal law or have been wrongfully denied federal services and benefits. For example, the EPA can fine a company that is not complying with antipollution standards and can refer serious cases to the Justice Department for further action. Agencies possess considerable discretion in their adjudicatory function. Consider the differences in the performance of the EPA under presidents Jimmy Carter and Ronald Reagan. The number of cases of industrial pollution referred by the EPA to the Justice Department for prosecution declined from 252 in 1980, Carter's last year, to 78 in 1981, Reagan's first year.[17]

## The Development of the Federal Bureaucracy: Politics and Administration

The federal bureaucracy has been two centuries in the making, although most of its development has occurred since the 1930s. A more significant fact is that the organization and staffing of the bureaucracy have been administrative *and* political issues throughout the country's history. Agencies are responsible for carrying out programs that serve the society, and yet each agency was created and is maintained in response to partisan interests. Each agency thus confronts two simultaneous but incompatible demands: that it administer programs fairly and competently and that it respond to partisan claims.

[16]See Gary C. Bryner, *Bureaucratic Discretion: Law and Policy in Federal Regulatory Agencies* (Elmsford, N.Y.: Pergamon, 1987).
[17]Kenneth J. Meier, *Regulation* (New York: St. Martin's Press, 1985), 164.

TABLE 22-2 Justifications for Major Systems for Managing the Bureaucracy

| System | Justification |
|---|---|
| Patronage | Makes the bureaucracy more responsive to election outcomes by allowing the president to appoint the top officials of executive agencies. |
| Merit | Provides for *competent* administration in that employees are hired on the basis of ability and allowed to remain on the job and thereby become proficient at their work, and provides for *neutral* administration in the sense that civil servants are not partisan appointees and thus are expected to do their work in an evenhanded way. |
| Executive leadership | Provides for presidential leadership of the bureaucracy in order to make it more responsive and to give it greater coordination and direction (left alone, the bureaucracy tends toward fragmentation). |

Historically, this conflict has worked itself out in ways that have made the organization of the modern bureaucracy a blend of the political and the administrative. This dual line of development is clearly reflected in the mix of management systems that characterizes the bureaucracy today—the *patronage, merit,* and *executive leadership* systems (see Table 22-2).

## SMALL GOVERNMENT AND THE PATRONAGE SYSTEM

The federal bureaucracy was originally small. Under the U.S. Constitution, the states retained responsibility for nearly all domestic policy areas. The federal government's role was confined mainly to defense and foreign affairs, currency and interstate commerce, and the postal system. Accordingly, the First Congress established departments of State, Treasury, and War. Shortly thereafter, a few other agencies were created, including the Department of the Navy and the offices of postmaster general and attorney general. By 1800 the federal government had only 3,000 civilian employees, more than a third of whom were involved in delivering the mail (see Figure 22-2).[18] By 1828 federal employment had risen to a mere 11,000.

In this early period, a large bureaucracy was not required because many of the major federal programs were discrete rather than continuous. Most of the early federal assistance to the states, for example, took the form of land grants. Once the land was deeded to the states, the federal government's role ended. One of the few ongoing activities of the federal government was the delivery of mail, which accounts for the fact that a large proportion of U.S. employees in this period were in the postal service. Until the Civil War, in fact, presidents personally made many of the decisions that today are handled by bureaucrats. President Martin Van Buren, for example, once had to choose the contractor who would build a fire engine that had been authorized by Congress.[19]

The nation's first six presidents, from George Washington through John Quincy Adams, believed that only distinguished men should be entrusted with the administration of the national government. Nearly all top presidential appointees were men of considerable talent, education, and political experience,

[18]Paul Van Riper, *History of the United States Civil Service* (Evanston, Ill.: Row, Peterson, 1958), 19.
[19]Benjamin Ginsberg, *The Consequences of Consent* (New York: Random House, 1982), 208.

Number of civilian federal employees

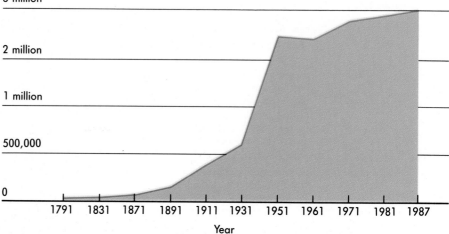

**FIGURE 22-2 Number of Persons Employed by the Federal Government, 1791–1987** The federal bureaucracy grew slowly until the 1930s, when an explosive growth began in the number of programs that required ongoing administration by the federal government. *Source:* Historical Statistics of the United States *and* Statistical Abstract of the United States 1986, 322; 1987 *figure from* Workforce Analysis and Statistics Division, U.S. Office of Personnel Management.

*The duties of all public office are so plain and simple that men of intelligence can readily qualify themselves for their performance.*

Andrew Jackson

and many of them were members of socially prominent families. They often remained in their jobs year after year.

The nation's seventh president, Andrew Jackson, did not share his predecessors' faith in the abilities of the wellborn.[20] In Jackson's view, government would be more responsive to the people if it were administered by common men of good sense. "The duties of all public office," Jackson claimed, "are so plain and simple that men of intelligence can readily qualify themselves for their performance."[21] Jackson also believed that top administrators should remain in office for short periods, so that there would be a steady influx of fresh ideas. Jackson's version of the **patronage system** was popular with the public, but critics labeled it a **spoils system**—a device for placing political cronies in high office as a reward for partisan service. In truth, Jackson's desire to reward partisan supporters was tempered by his concern for democratic government. Later presidents, however, were more interested in distributing the spoils of victory. Although Jackson left most lower officials in office, his successors extended patronage to these lesser positions.[22] Party bosses thus had plenty of federal jobs to give to their friends and loyalists, many of whom were incompetent or corrupt.[23] On balance, the patronage system may actually have decreased the bureaucracy's responsiveness to the public.

## GROWTH IN GOVERNMENT AND THE MERIT SYSTEM

The patronage system was compatible with the small federal government of the early nineteenth century. Because the government's activities were relatively few and of limited scope, they could be managed by employees who had little or no administrative training or experience. As the century advanced, however, the

[20]Fredrick C. Mosher, *Democracy and the Public Service,* 2d ed. (New York: Oxford University Press, 1982), 64–66.
[21]Quoted in Van Riper, *History of the U.S. Civil Service,* 36.
[22]Jay M. Shafritz, *Personnel Management in Government* (New York: Marcel Dekker, 1981), 9–13.
[23]Herbert Kaufman, "Emerging Conflicts in the Doctrine of Public Administration," *American Political Science Review* 50 (December 1956): 1060.

nature of the bureaucracy changed rapidly, as did the bureaucracy's personnel needs.

An impetus for change was the Industrial Revolution, which was creating a truly national economy and prompting economic groups to pressure Congress to protect and promote their interests. Farmers were initially one of the most demanding groups, looking to the federal government for market and price assistance; in response, Congress created the Department of Agriculture in 1862. Business and labor interests also pressed their claims, and in 1903 Congress established the Department of Commerce and Labor to "promote the mutual interest" of the nation's firms and workers. (The separate interests of business and labor proved stronger than their shared concerns, so in 1913 Labor became a separate department.)[24]

While various economic sectors were advancing their interests, other Americans were demanding protection from economic exploitation. Popular discontent with unfair practices by the railroad monopolies led Congress in 1887 to establish the Interstate Commerce Commission (ICC). The Food and Drug Administration (FDA) was created in 1907 to protect consumers against unsafe products. The Federal Trade Commission (FTC) was formed in 1914 to prevent businesses from limiting competition. Whereas previous agencies had been formed primarily to carry out specific programs enacted by Congress, the ICC, FDA, and FTC were assigned ongoing legislative and judicial functions in addition to administrative ones. That is, they were instructed to develop regulations governing business activity and to investigate alleged violations of federal laws and regulations.

Because of the increased need for continuous administration of government, an ever-larger bureaucracy was required. By 1931 federal employment had reached 600,000, a sixfold increase over the level of the 1880s.[25] With President Franklin Roosevelt's New Deal, the federal work force increased enormously, to 1.2 million by 1940. Roosevelt's programs were generated in response to public demands for relief from the economic hardship and uncertainty of the Great Depression. Administration of these programs necessitated the formation of economic and social-welfare agencies such as the Securities and Exchange Commission (SEC) and the Social Security Board. The effect was to give the federal government an ongoing responsibility for Americans' economic well-being.

A large and active government requires skilled and experienced personnel. This fact was evident long before the 1930s. During the Civil War (1861–1865), President Lincoln complained that the then-dominant patronage system was inadequate to the country's emerging administrative needs. Yet the spoils system survived the Civil War and would have lasted much longer had not President James Garfield been assassinated in 1881 by a disgruntled party worker who had been promised a federal job but had not received it. Garfield's death strengthened the reform movement that was pushing for a **merit system,** or **civil service system,** of government employment. In 1883 Congress passed the Pendleton Act, which established a merit system whereby certain federal employees were hired through competitive examinations or by virtue of having

[24]James Q. Wilson, "The Rise of the Bureaucratic State," *Public Interest* 41 (Fall 1975): 77–103.
[25]Nachmias and Rosenbloom, *Bureaucratic Government: U.S.A.,* 39; U.S. Bureau of the Census, *Historical Statistics of the United States: Colonial Times to 1970,* pt. 2 (Washington, D.C.: U.S. Government Printing Office, 1975), 1102.

special qualifications, such as an advanced degree in a particular field. The Pendleton Act was the first national legislation in the field of public personnel administration and was therefore historic. However, the transition to a career civil service was gradual. Only about 10 percent of federal positions in 1885 were filled on the basis of merit; more than 70 percent were merit-based in 1919; and since 1947 the proportion of merit employees has not dipped below 80 percent.[26]

The Pendleton Act created a Civil Service Commission to establish job classifications, administer competitive examinations, and oversee merit employees. The commission was abolished in 1978 and replaced by two independent agencies. The Office of Personnel Management now supervises the hiring and classification of federal employees, and the Merit Service Protection Board handles appeals of personnel actions, such as demotions and dismissals, involving civil service employees.

The merit system is designed to separate the administration of government from partisan politics. The administrative objective is **neutral competence.**[27] A merit-based bureaucracy is "competent" in the sense that employees are hired on the basis of ability and are allowed to remain on the job indefinitely and thereby to become proficient in their work, and it is "neutral" in the sense that employees are not partisan appointees and thus are expected to do their work on behalf of the general public, not just the segment of the public that is loyal to the incumbent administration.

Although the merit system has wide acceptance, it does not guarantee impartial administration. In the process of administering the laws, bureaucrats necessarily make policy choices. Programs are not self-executing; they must be developed and applied by bureaucrats—a fact that both enables and requires them to play a policy role. The issue of the merit system is not, as some of its early advocates claimed, how to eliminate politics from administration but whether bureaucratic politics will be played by partisan appointees or by career civil servants. There is another broad sense in which a merit-based bureaucracy is political: career civil servants stay in their jobs regardless of which party wins elections, and they develop close ties with the interests that benefit from the programs they run. These factors tend to make civil servants powerful advocates of their agencies. Each agency naturally gives higher priority to its concerns than to those of other agencies and to those of Congress or the president. The results include a more fragmented government and a loss of political accountability because bureaucrats are not subject to election.[28] (The next chapter discusses these consequences of bureaucratic government in detail.)

## BIG GOVERNMENT AND THE EXECUTIVE LEADERSHIP SYSTEM

As problems with the merit system surfaced after the early years of this century, reformers looked to a strengthened presidency—an **executive leadership system**—as a means of making the bureaucracy more responsive and better

---

[26]David H. Rosenbloom, *Federal Service and the Constitution* (Ithaca, N.Y.: Cornell University Press, 1971), 83.
[27]Kaufman, "Emerging Conflicts," 1060.
[28]Ibid., 1063.

Today the vast majority of government employees obtain their jobs by passing a competitive civil service examination. (Paul Conklin)

integrated.[29] The president was to provide the general leadership that would overcome agency fragmentation and give the bureaucracy a common direction. As we saw in Chapter 20, Congress in 1939 provided the president with some of the tools needed for fuller control of the bureaucracy. The Office of Management and Budget (OMB) was created to allow the president to examine and adjust the annual budget proposal of each executive agency. The president was also empowered to reorganize the bureaucracy, subject to congressional approval, in order to reduce duplication of activities and strengthen the chain of command from the president to the agencies. Finally, the president was authorized to develop the Executive Office of the President, which oversees the agencies' activities on the president's behalf and assists him in the development of policy programs.

The Senior Executive Service (SES) is a more recently created presidential management tool. Established by Congress in 1978 at the urging of President Jimmy Carter, the SES represents a compromise between two traditions: a president-led bureaucracy and an expert one.[30] The SES consists of roughly 8,000 top-level career civil servants who receive higher salaries than their peers but who can be assigned, dismissed, or transferred by order of the president. Unlike regular presidential appointees, however, SES bureaucrats cannot be fired; if the president relieves them of their jobs, they have "fallback" rights to their former rank in the regular civil service. The SES gives the president greater access to and control over individuals who are already expert in the bureaucracy's work. However, the SES is not a panacea: after years of work in the bureaucracy, many top-level bureaucrats have difficulty transferring their loyalty from an agency to the president.

Like the merit and patronage systems, the executive leadership system has brought problems as well as improvements to the administration of government. The chief drawback of placing additional power in the hands of the

[29]Ibid., 1062.
[30]See Mark W. Huddleston, "The Carter Civil Service Reforms," *Political Science Quarterly*, Winter 1981–82, 607–622.

president has been the possibility that he may abuse it. Richard Nixon did so by using the OMB to impound (that is, fail to spend) more than $40 billion in program funds appropriated by Congress. Nixon claimed that his purpose was to prevent the funds from being spent wastefully or in ways inconsistent with other spending. In reality, however, Nixon disliked the programs in question and withheld the funds in order to prevent their implementation. The impoundment ended only after the courts ruled that Nixon's action was an unlawful infringement on Congress's constitutional authority over spending. To prevent a recurrence of the problem, Congress in 1974 passed legislation that gives the president the authority to withhold funds for only 45 days unless Congress passes legislation to rescind the appropriation.

Other presidents have at times put their administrative management tools to dubious use, but Nixon's impoundment policy most clearly illustrates the weakness of the executive leadership concept. If carried too far, it can threaten the balance of executive power and legislative power on which the U.S. constitutional system is based, and it can make partisanship, not fairness, the criterion by which provision of services is determined.

Despite its potential for abuse, the executive leadership system is a necessary component of any effective strategy for managing the modern federal bureaucracy. Its size and range make the bureaucracy a management nightmare. Since the 1950s, the number of federal employees has been 2.5 million or more, and that figure actually understates the scope of national programs. In recent decades the federal government has developed many programs that are administered through state and local governments (see Chapter 27). In addition, the federal government has hired increasing numbers of private consultants and firms to do tasks that would once have been assigned to federal employees.[31] Finally, nearly a third of the bureaucracy's roughly 400 separate and semi-autonomous agencies have been established since the 1950s.[32]

Government agencies have proliferated largely in response to political demands that have arisen from the economic, technological, and social complexity of American society. Examples include the Department of Health and Human Services (which began as the Department of Health, Education, and Welfare in 1953), the Civil Rights Commission (1957), the National Aeronautics and Space Administration (1958), the Department of Housing and Urban Development (1965), the Department of Transportation (1966), the Environmental Protection Agency (1970), the Department of Energy (1977), and the Department of Education (1979).

In the 1980s an economic downturn contributed to a slowing of the bureaucracy's growth, but efforts to streamline the bureaucracy were affected by political demands. Although President Reagan had stated his determination to cut the size of the bureaucracy, he quietly shelved his plan as he learned the timeless lesson that agencies represent powerful constituencies. Reagan further acknowledged political realities when he proposed in 1987 that the Veterans Administration (VA), an independent agency, be elevated to cabinet status. The VA became the Department of Veterans Affairs by act of Congress in late 1988.

★ ANALYZE THE ISSUE

**The Bureaucracy's Responsiveness**

Opinion polls indicate that Americans are concerned about the bureaucracy's responsiveness. How do the patronage, merit, and executive leadership systems address the issue of responsiveness? Which system would you strengthen the most if you had the choice? Which interests would benefit if your change was enacted? Is this what you intended?

[31]See James T. Bennett, "How Big Is the Federal Government?" *Economic Review*, December 1981, 43–49.

[32]Herbert Kaufman, *Are Governmental Organizations Immortal?* (Washington, D.C.: Brookings Institution, 1976), 48–49.

Its annual budget of $30 billion includes funds for a medical care system, pensions, and loan benefits for veterans of military service, who, through national organizations such as the American Legion and Veterans of Foreign Wars, are a vocal and powerful, lobby.

## THE MODERN BUREAUCRACY: A MIX OF MANAGEMENT SYSTEMS

The executive leadership system of public administration has not replaced the merit system, just as the merit system did not eliminate the patronage system. The federal bureaucracy today retains aspects of all three systems, a situation that reflects the tensions inherent in governmental administration. The bureaucracy is expected to carry out programs fairly and impartially, but it is also expected to respond to political forces. The first of these requirements is addressed primarily through the merit system and the second through the executive leadership and patronage systems.

This blending of partisan and nonpartisan elements hardly settles the issues that surround the bureaucracy's influence. The bureaucracy is essentially America's permanent government. Its ongoing programs outlast any president or Congress, and its power, which derives from its size and specialization, is not easily brought under control. The next chapter examines the bureaucracy's power and the problems it poses for democratic government.

## *Summary*

Bureaucracy is a method of organizing people and work which is based on the principles of hierarchical authority, job specialization, and formalized rules. As a form of organization, bureaucracy is the most efficient means of getting people to work together on tasks of great magnitude and complexity.

The United States could not be governed without a large federal bureaucracy. The day-to-day work of the federal government, from mail delivery to provision of social security to international diplomacy, is done by the bureaucracy. The federal bureaucracy's 3 million employees work in roughly 400 major agencies, including cabinet departments, independent agencies, regulatory agencies, government corporations, and presidential commissions.

Yet the bureaucracy is more than simply an administrative giant. Bureaucrats exercise considerable discretion in their policy decisions. In the process of implementing policy—which includes initiation and development of policy, evaluation of programs, delivery of services, regulation, and adjudication—bureaucrats make important policy and political choices.

Each agency of the federal government was created in response to political demands on national officials. During the country's earliest decades, the bureaucracy was small, a reflection of the federal government's relatively few responsibilities outside the areas of national security and commerce. As the economy became increasingly industrialized and its sectors increasingly interconnected in the late nineteenth century, the bureaucracy expanded in response to the demands of economic interests and the requirement for regulation of certain business activities. During the Great Depression, social-welfare programs and further business regulatory activities were added to the bureaucracy's responsibilities. After World War II, the heightened role of the United States in world affairs and public demands for additional social services fueled the bureaucracy's growth. Government agencies continued to multiply in the 1970s in response to broad consumer and environmental issues as well as to technological change. The bureaucracy's growth slowed in the 1980s because of federal budget deficits and the philosophy of the Reagan administration.

Because of its origins in political demands, the bureaucracy is necessarily political. An inherent conflict results from two simultaneous but incompatible demands on the bureaucracy: that it respond to the demands of partisan officials but also that it administer programs fairly and competently. These tensions are evident in the three concurrent personnel management systems under which the bureaucracy operates: patronage, merit, and executive leadership.

## Major Concepts

bureaucracy
cabinet (executive) departments
executive leadership system
formalized rules
government corporations
hierarchical authority
independent agencies
job specialization

merit (civil service) system
neutral competence
patronage system
policy implementation
presidential commissions
regulatory agencies
spoils system

## Suggested Readings

Bryner, Gary C. *Bureaucratic Discretion: Law and Policy in Federal Regulatory Agencies.* Elmsford, N.Y.: Pergamon Press, 1987. An exploration of bureaucratic decision making, with an emphasis on regulatory policy.

Gerth, H. H., and C. Wright Mills, eds. *From Max Weber: Essays in Sociology.* New York: Oxford University Press, 1946. Weber's writings on bureaucracy are the classic analysis of this form of organization.

Goodsell, Charles T. *The Case for Bureaucracy.* Chatham, N.J.: Chatham House, 1983. A defense of the bureaucracy against many of the common complaints (e.g., red tape, wastefulness) about it.

Kaufman, Herbert. *Red Tape: Its Origins, Uses, and Abuses.* Washington, D.C.: Brookings Institution, 1977. An analysis of why bureaucratic rules and regulations are seemingly excessive, and why red tape frustrates some interests and benefits others.

Pressman, Jeffrey, and Aaron Wildavsky. *Implementation,* 3d ed. Berkeley: University of California Press, 1984. A case study of a federal job-creation program which assesses the problems of policy implementation.

Rosenbloom, David H. *Public Administration and Law.* New York: Marcel Dekker, 1983. A valuable review by a leading scholar of administrative law.

Rourke, Francis E. *Bureaucracy, Politics, and Public Policy,* 2d ed. Boston: Little, Brown, 1976. A textbook assessment of the bureaucracy and its influence on public policy.

Van Riper, Paul P. *History of the United States Civil Service.* Westport, Conn.: Greenwood Press, 1976. A history of the civil service by a scholar of public administration.

# Chapter 23

## BUREAUCRATIC POLICYMAKING: COMPETING FOR POWER

*The lifeblood of administration is power.*
*Norton E. Long[1]*

Congress enacted the Occupational Safety and Health Act of 1970 "to assure as far as possible every working man and woman in the nation safe and healthy work conditions." The legislation shifted the primary responsibility for occupational safety and health to the federal government from the states, which had addressed the issue largely through compensation payments to workers injured on the job or to the survivors of workers killed on the job. The federal program, in contrast, would focus on the prevention of job-related injuries, illnesses, and deaths. Firms would be subject to stringent health and safety standards and would have to submit to on-site visits by federal inspectors.[2]

The Occupational Safety and Health Administration (OSHA) was created to administer the program. OSHA was granted broad regulatory power and was authorized to hire specialists, such as safety engineers and industrial hygienists, who could be expected to look out for workers' interests. In its first year OSHA issued more than 4,000 health and safety standards. Most of the standards were based on accepted practices, such as the requirement that fire extinguishers be placed in work areas, but some standards were excessively elaborate or laughably out of date. For example, there were 140 standards for industrial

---

[1]Norton E. Long, "Power and Administration," *Public Administration Review* 10 (Autumn 1949): 257.
[2]Kenneth J. Meier, *Regulation* (New York: St. Martin's Press, 1985). The lead paragraphs in this chapter are based on Meier's ch. 8.

An OSHA Inspector checks the accuracy of instruments that measure the quality of the air inside a work site. (Richard Wood/The Picture Cube)

ladders, covering everything from construction materials to the distance between rungs. There was also a regulation that prohibited employers from placing ice in employees' drinking water, a legacy from the days when ice was cut from polluted lakes.

Some of this regulatory overkill was attributable to the growing pains that afflict any new organization. But OSHA's approach also reflected the values of its professional staff. The agency's safety engineers and industrial hygienists believed in the importance of reducing occupational hazards and were intent on vigorously pursuing that goal. A survey indicated that 80 percent of OSHA inspectors believed that business firms would try to evade safety and health requirements unless they were held to high standards of accountability.[3]

Congress was generally supportive of OSHA during its first years but held several hearings at which its overzealousness was criticized. President Jimmy Carter also backed OSHA but demanded that it give more consideration to whether the benefits of specific regulations justified the costs they imposed on businesses. When Ronald Reagan became president, OSHA came under sharp attack. Business had opposed OSHA's formation and welcomed Reagan's cutbacks in its personnel and regulations. Organized labor lashed out at Reagan, claiming that any curtailment of OSHA's activities was a blow to workers' safety and health. Congress held hearings at which witnesses criticized the Reagan administration's handling of OSHA. Meanwhile, the agency's health and safety specialists fought to maintain the effectiveness of their programs.

The battle over OSHA illustrates the nature of bureaucratic politics. The bureaucracy is caught between competing demands and conflicting power

[3]Steven Kelman, "Occupational Safety and Health Administration," in James Q. Wilson, ed., *The Politics of Regulation* (New York: Basic Books, 1980), 255.

centers. The American political system, with its plural interests and fragmented governing authority, requires bureaucrats to play politics. If administrators are to carry out the programs assigned to them, they must have the power to make decisions and put them into effect. Because different interests and officials will have widely varying opinions on the merits of an agency's programs, the agency must fight for power or it will be submerged by those who are working toward other goals and *are* willing to compete for power.

This chapter examines bureaucratic policymaking from the standpoint of the ways in which agencies acquire the power they need in order to maintain themselves and their programs. The chapter shows that career bureaucrats necessarily and naturally take an "agency point of view," seeking to promote their agency's objectives. Moreover, they have substantial resources—expertise, group support, and presidential and congressional backing—that help them to promote their agency's goals. The three constitutional branches of government impose a degree of accountability on the bureaucracy; but the U.S. system of government, with its fragmented authority, frees bureaucrats from tight control. The main points discussed in this chapter are the following:

★ *Because of America's diversity and fragmented system of government, bureaucrats must compete for the power required to administer programs effectively.*

★ *Bureaucrats are committed to the goals of their particular agencies.* Their expert knowledge, support from clientele groups, and backing by Congress and the president help them to promote agency goals.

★ *Agencies are subject to control by the president, Congress, and the judiciary, but these controls place only general limits on the bureaucracy's power.* A major reason agencies are able to achieve power in their own right is that Congress and the president often resist each other's attempts to control the bureaucracy.

★ *The bureaucracy's power is not easily reconciled with the principle of self-government.* Bureaucrats are not directly accountable to the people through elections.


## The Bureaucracy's Power Imperative

Agencies of the federal bureaucracy must fight for the power that they need if they are to conduct their programs effectively.[4] This fact cannot be understood without consideration of broader tendencies in the American political system, particularly diversity and the separation of powers.

Elections in the United States, unlike those in many other democracies, do not provide a clear mandate for either the winning party's platform or the president's leadership.[5] Because even candidates of the same party do not have a shared agenda and because the president and Congress are elected separately, the task of establishing programs and priorities is dealt with largely after elections and through a process of continuous bargaining and power wielding. The president will insist that his ideas should take precedence, but so will Congress. Moreover, conflicting interests will make claims on both the president and Congress. In short, the American political system produces not a

---

[4]Long, "Power and Administration." Long's argument provides the basis for the lead paragraphs of this section.
[5]Ibid., 259.

government of clear and accepted objectives, but a government in which objectives are always open to dispute.

## THE AGENCY POINT OF VIEW

If agencies are to operate successfully in this system, they must seek support where they can find it—if not from the president, then from Congress; if not from one interest, then from another; if not today, then tomorrow. In other words, agencies must play politics. They must devote themselves to building enough support to permit the effective administration of their programs. If they do not, their goals will suffer because other agencies that *are* willing to play politics will grab the available funding, attention, and support. Bureaucrats must look out for their agency's interests, a perspective that is called the **agency point of view.**[6]

This perspective comes naturally to most high-ranking civil servants. Their careers within the bureaucracy have taught them to do the job they are assigned, which in all cases is to do their part in making the organization effective. Many bureaucrats are also personally committed to their agency's objectives as a result of having spent years at work on its programs. More than 80 percent of all top careerists reach their high-level positions by rising through the ranks of the same agency.[7] As one top bureaucrat said in testifying before the House Appropriations Committee, "Mr. Chairman, you would not think it proper for me to be in charge of this work and not be enthusiastic about it . . . , would you? I have been in it for thirty years, and I believe in it."[8]

Professionalism also cements agency loyalties.[9] As public policymaking has become more complex, high-level positions in the bureaucracy have increasingly been filled by scientists, engineers, lawyers, educators, physicians, and other professionals. Most of them take jobs in an agency that has programs consistent with their professional values. Consider the case of John Nestor, a physician who tested drugs for the Food and Drug Administration (FDA). Dr. Nestor saw it as his medical and administrative duty to protect the public from unsafe drugs and became angry when a drug that had not been fully tested was approved for sale by the FDA's director, who was a presidential appointee and a supporter of the pharmaceutical industry. "I believe," said Nestor in testimony before a Senate committee, "that hundreds of people . . . suffer daily, and many die because [presidential appointees within the FDA have] failed utterly in . . . enforcing those sections of the law dealing with the safety and mishandling of drugs."[10]

Studies confirm that bureaucrats believe in the importance of their agency's

[6]See Robert Harasch, *The Institutional Imperative* (New York: Charterhouse Books, 1973); William A. Niskanen, Jr., *Bureaucracy and Representation* (Chicago: Aldine-Atherton, 1971), 38; Morton H. Halperin, *Bureaucratic Politics and Foreign Policy* (Washington, D.C.: Brookings Institution, 1974), 39–40; Anthony Downs, *Inside Bureaucracy* (Boston: Little, Brown, 1967), 212–218; Herbert Kaufman, *The Administrative Behavior of Federal Bureaucrats* (Washington, D.C.: Brookings Institution, 1981), 4.
[7]Hugh Heclo, *A Government of Strangers* (Washington, D.C.: Brookings Institution, 1977), 117–118.
[8]Quoted in Aaron Wildavsky, *The Politics of the Budgetary Process* (Boston: Little, Brown, 1964), 19.
[9]Frederick C. Mosher, *Democracy and the Public Service*, 2d ed. (New York: Oxford University Press, 1982), ch.2.
[10]Quoted in Kenneth Lassim, *Private Lives of Public Servants* (Bloomington: Indiana University Press, 1978), 96–97.

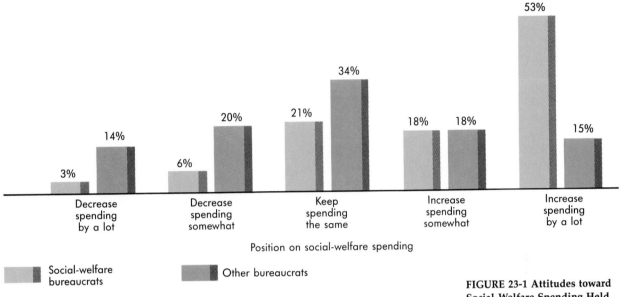

Social-welfare bureaucrats

Other bureaucrats

FIGURE 23-1 Attitudes toward Social-Welfare Spending Held by Bureaucrats in Social-Welfare Agencies and in Other Agencies
Bureaucrats who work in social-welfare agencies are much more likely than other bureaucrats to believe that spending on social-welfare programs should be increased. These survey results illustrate the "agency point of view." *Source: Adapted from Joel D. Aberbach and Bert A. Rockman, "Clashing Beliefs within the Executive Branch: The Nixon Administration Bureaucracy,"* American Political Science Review 70 (June 1976): 461.

work.[11] One study found that social-welfare administrators are three times as likely as other civil servants to believe that social-welfare programs should have a high budget priority (see Figure 23-1). Another survey found that 80 percent of administrators believe that their agency's budget deserved to be increased substantially.[12]

## SOURCES OF BUREAUCRATIC POWER

In promoting their agency's interests, bureaucrats rely on their specialized knowledge, the support of interests that benefit from the programs they run, and the backing of the president and Congress.

### The Power of Expertise

Many of the policy problems that the federal government confronts do not lend themselves to simple solutions. Whether the issue is space travel, hunger in America, or relations with the Soviet Union, expert knowledge is essential to the development of effective public policy. Much of this expertise is held by bureaucrats. Bureaucrats specialize in narrow policy areas, and many have had scientific, technical, or other specialized training that helps them to understand complex issues.[13]

*An expert is one who knows more and more about less and less.*

Nicholas Murray Butler

[11]See Kenneth J. Meier and Lloyd Nigro, "Representative Bureaucracy and Policy Preferences," *Public Administrative Review* 36 (July/August 1976): 446; Joel D. Aberbach and Bert A. Rockman, "Clashing Beliefs within the Executive Branch," *American Political Science Review* 70 (June 1976): 461.
[12]Advisory Commission on Intergovernmental Relations, *The Intergovernmental Grant System as Seen by Local, State, and Federal Officials,* A-54 (Washington, D.C.: U.S. Government Printing Office, 1977), 184.
[13]Joel D. Aberbach, Robert Putnam, and Bert A. Rockman, *Bureaucrats and Politicians in Western Democracies* (Cambridge, Mass.: Harvard University Press, 1981), 52.

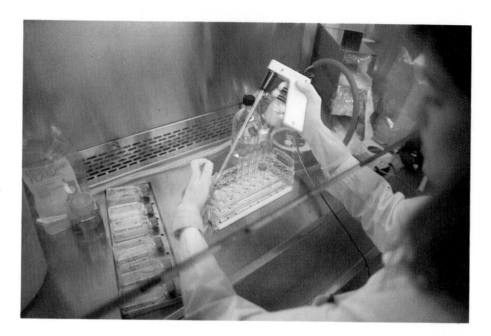

Research on AIDS conducted at the National Institutes of Health provided the expert knowledge that helped the agency to convince elected officials that AIDS-related policy measures were needed. (Shepard Sherbell/Picture Group)

By comparison, elected officials are generalists. To some degree members of Congress do specialize through their committee work, but they rarely have the time or inclination to acquire a commanding knowledge of a particular issue. The president's understanding of policy issues is even more general. Not surprisingly, bureaucrats are a major source of policy ideas. They are more likely than either the president or members of Congress to be aware of particular problems and to have policy solutions in mind. According to Richard Rose, the president's influence on policy is felt primarily through his decisions about which bureaucratic initiatives to embrace and which ones to ignore.[14] Congress is in somewhat the same situation; as we mentioned in Chapter 22, many of the bills proposed by members of Congress are conceived by careerists in the bureaucracy.

Not all agencies acquire a great amount of leverage from their staffs' expert knowledge. Those that do have an edge have highly specialized, professional staffs. For example, the expert judgments of the health scientists and physicians in the National Institutes of Health (NIH) are rarely challenged by elected officials. They may question the political assessments of these health professionals but are unlikely to question their scientific evaluations, which are sometimes decisive. For example, as much as some elected officials may have wanted to avoid the issues surrounding the AIDS epidemic during the 1980s, they were eventually forced into action by the warnings of health scientists about the dire consequences of a do-nothing policy.

The power of expertise is conditioned by the extent to which an agency's employees share the same goals. In many agencies, such as the NIH, careerists with different professional backgrounds have similar values. In other agencies professional infighting breaks down this cohesiveness and gives outsiders an opportunity to support the faction whose aims agree with their own. An example is the Federal Trade Commission (FTC), which is divided between its

[14]Richard Rose, *Managing Presidential Objectives* (New York: Free Press, 1976), 149.

lawyers, who tend to emphasize issues that can be quickly and successfully litigated, and its economists, who tend to stress larger and more complicated issues that have broad implications for national commerce.[15]

Nevertheless, *all* agencies acquire some power through their careerists' expertise. No matter how simple a policy issue may appear at first, it invariably involves more than meets the eye. For example, a recognition that millions of Americans are poor is a foundation for poverty programs but does not begin to address such basic questions as the form that such programs might take, their probable cost and effectiveness, and their connection to other social-welfare programs. Answers to these questions are fundamental to the formulation of sensible antipoverty programs, and the officials most likely to have the answers are social-welfare administrators. During the 1960s, in fact, welfare experts within the federal bureaucracy conceived a range of new antipoverty programs, encouraged President Lyndon Johnson to support them, and then helped him lobby Congress to enact them.[16]

## The Power of Clientele Groups

Most agencies have **clientele groups,** which are special interests that benefit directly from an agency's programs. Typically, whenever an agency or program is created, a clientele lobby springs up to protect it.[17] For example, the welfare programs that were part of Johnson's Great Society in the 1960s were quickly taken under the wing of such interest groups as the National Welfare Rights Organization and the American Association of Retired Persons. Clientele groups place pressure on Congress and the president to retain the programs on which they depend.[18] A result is that agency programs, once started, are difficult to terminate. "Government activities," as Herbert Kaufman says, "tend to go on indefinitely."[19]

In general, agencies lead and are led by the clientele groups that depend on the programs they administer.[20] Many agencies were created for the purpose of promoting particular interests in society and, because of their permanence, outlook, and resources, are the major channel of representation for these interests. For example, the Department of Agriculture's career bureaucrats are dependable allies of farm interests year after year. The same cannot be said of the president, Congress as a whole, or either political party; these other channels, while not antagonistic to the agricultural sector, must balance its demands against those of other interests. Department of Agriculture careerists have no such conflict: promoting agriculture is their only concern.

## The Power of Friends in High Places

Although members of Congress and the president sometimes appear to be at war with the bureaucracy, they need it as much as it needs them. An agency's

[15]Meier, *Regulation,* 16.

[16]Samuel Beer, "Political Overload and Federalism," *Polity* 10 (Fall 1977): 11.

[17]Matthew Holden, Jr., "'Imperialism' in Bureaucracy," *American Political Science Review* 60 (December 1966): 944.

[18]See Peter Woll, *American Bureaucracy,* 2d ed. (New York: Norton, 1977), ch.1.

[19]Herbert Kaufman, *Are Government Organizations Immortal?* (Washington, D.C.: Brookings Institution, 1976), 76.

[20]Long, "Power and Administration," 269.

The huge corporate "agribusinesses" that make up a large part of the nation's farm sector form a clientele group and are a powerful ally of the bureaucrats who administer agricultural programs. (Peter Menzel/Stock, Boston)

resources—its programs, expertise, and group support—can assist elected officials in their efforts to achieve their goals. When George Bush came to the White House, he was determined to maintain the existing level of defense spending and needed the support of Defense Department careerists to fend off the efforts of congressional Democrats to cut the defense budget. Of course, government defense agencies were more than eager to help Bush meet this goal.

Bureaucrats seek favorable relations with members of Congress, too. From the perspective of the bureaucracy, congressional support is vital because agencies' funding and programs are provided through legislation. Agencies that offer benefits to major constituency interests are particularly likely to have close ties to Congress. In some policy areas, more or less permanent alliances—"iron triangles"—form among agencies, clientele groups, and congressional subcommittees.[21] In other policy areas, temporary "issue networks" form among bureaucrats, lobbyists, and members of Congress.[22] As we saw in Chapters 14 and 18, these alliances enable agencies and interest groups to work toward programs they want and provide members of Congress with electoral support.[23] Not surprisingly, most members of Congress believe that government agencies should maintain close relationships with their clientele groups (see box).

A common misperception is that, because the president is the chief executive, he alone has a claim on the bureaucracy's loyalty. In fact, each of the elected institutions has reason to claim proprietorship: the president because of his

[21]See Harold Seidman, *Politics, Position, and Power: The Dynamics of Federal Organization*, 2d ed. (New York: Oxford University Press, 1975), 150.

[22]Hugh Heclo, "Issue Networks and the Executive Establishment," in Anthony King, ed., *The New American Political System* (Washington, D.C.: American Enterprise Institute, 1978), 102.

[23]Joel D. Aberbach and Bert A. Rockman, "Bureaucrats and Client Groups: A View from Capitol Hill," *American Journal of Political Science* 22 (November 1978): 821.

## CONGRESSIONAL VIEWS OF THE PROPER RELATIONSHIP OF BUREAUCRATS AND THEIR CLIENTELE GROUPS

Sixty-one members of Congress were asked: "Do you think it is desirable for a government agency to have close relations with its clientele or do you think this is unnecessary and undesirable?" Here are their responses:

| | |
|---|---|
| Close relations desirable | 34% |
| Close relations, with reservations | 39 |
| Depends on situation | 3 |
| Distant relations, with reservations | 10 |
| Distant relations desirable | 13 |
| | 99% |

SOURCE: Joel D. Aberbach and Bert A. Rockman, "Bureaucrats and Clientele Groups: A View From Capitol Hill," *American Journal of Political Science* 22 (November 1978): 821.

position as chief executive and Congress because it authorizes and funds the bureaucracy's programs. Neither elected branch is inclined to concede domination over agencies to the other branch.[24] Faced with a threat from either Congress or the president, agencies often find that the other becomes an ally. One Nixon appointee was bluntly informed of Congress's ability to protect the bureaucracy from intrusions by the executive. The appointee asked a congressional committee whether it had any problem with a planned reduction in his agency's authority. The committee chairman replied, "No, you have the problem, because if you touch that bureau I'll cut your job out of the budget."[25]

The president and Congress are often at odds over the bureaucracy partly as a matter of institutional rivalry. The American system of separate institutions sharing power results in a natural tendency for each institution to guard its turf. In addition, the president and members of Congress differ in their constituencies and thus in the interests to which they are most responsive. For example, although the agricultural sector is just one of many concerns of the president, it is a preoccupation of senators and representatives from farm states; they will fight a president's efforts to cut back agricultural programs. Finally, because the president and Congress are elected separately, the White House and one or both houses of Congress may be in the hands of opposing parties. Of late, this source of executive–legislative conflict has been more often the rule than the exception. Since 1968 there have been only four years in which the same party controlled the presidency and both houses of Congress.

When congressional and presidential ambitions collide, agencies often win out by having either Congress or the White House on their side. Consider the case of the Environmental Protection Agency (EPA) in the early 1980s. The EPA's career staff is dominated by employees who prize environmental protection: pollution-control engineers, health specialists, environmental scientists, and public-interest lawyers.[26] Their values conflicted with those of Reagan's EPA appointees, who were determined to relax the agency's enforcement of antipollution laws in order to benefit business. Through information

[24]Dean Alger, "The Presidency, the Bureaucracy, and the People," paper presented at the annual meeting of the American Political Science Association, New Orleans, 1985.
[25]Quoted in Heclo, *Government of Strangers*, 225.
[26]Meier, *Regulation*, 146.

Anne Burford Gorsuch was forced to resign as head of the Environmental Protection Agency in 1983 after some career employees of the agency leaked information to Congress and the press about her failure to enforce antipollution laws. (AP/Wide World)

leaked by EPA careerists, the news media disclosed that the EPA's partisan appointees had privately arranged lenient settlements for firms that had committed serious violations of toxic-waste disposal regulations. The ensuing congressional investigation resulted in the resignation, dismissal, or conviction in court of more than a dozen top EPA officials. Under pressure from Congress and the public, Reagan appointed a new EPA head, William Ruckelshaus, who put the EPA back on the track of vigorous enforcement of environmental protection standards, as its careerists wanted.

★ ANALYZE THE ISSUE

**The Career Bureaucracy's Authority**
It is sometimes said that bureaucrats should not have policy authority because they are not elected by the people. Is this perspective useful? Does it make any sense to pretend that all authority should rest with elected institutions when government depends also on the continuity, expertise, and impartiality that only a career bureaucracy can provide?

## Bureaucratic Accountability

Bureaucratic politics raises the specter of a huge, permanent, and uncontrollable organization run by entrenched unelected officials. Adapting the requirements of bureaucracy to those of democracy has been a persistent challenge for public administration.[27] The issue is **accountability:** the capacity of the public to hold officials responsible for their actions. In the case of the bureaucracy, accountability works primarily through other institutions: the presidency, Congress, and the courts (see box).

### ACCOUNTABILITY THROUGH THE PRESIDENCY

All presidents have found the bureaucracy an obstacle to some of their goals. As chief executive, the president may believe that the bureaucracy should be subject to his command, but it is never entirely under his control. "We can outlast any president" is a common view among bureaucrats. Each agency has its clientele and its congressional supporters, as well as statutory authority for its existence and activities. No president can unilaterally eliminate an agency or its funding and programs. Nor can the president be indifferent to the opinions

[27]See Bernard Rosen, *Holding Government Bureaucrats Accountable* (New York: Praeger, 1982).

# HOLDING THE BUREAUCRACY ACCOUNTABLE

The president can:

Appoint and fire agency heads and some other top bureaucrats.

Reorganize the bureaucracy (subject to congressional approval).

Adjust annual budget proposals of agencies.

Resist legislative initiatives originating within the bureaucracy.

Issue executive orders for the bureaucracy to follow.

Propose new policies or changes in existing ones which will, if enacted by Congress, affect the bureaucracy's activities.

Congress can:

Reduce agencies' annual budgets.

Pass new or revised legislation that affects the bureaucracy's activities.

Abolish existing programs.

Investigate the bureaucracy's activities and force bureaucrats to testify about their activities.

Influence the appointments of agency heads and some other top bureaucrats.

Write legislation (e.g., sunset laws) in ways that limit the bureaucracy's discretion.

The courts can:

Judge whether bureaucrats have acted within the law and force them to change their policies to accord with the law.

Force the bureaucracy to respect individuals' rights in hearings and other proceedings.

---

of career civil servants, because he needs their support and expertise to develop and implement his own policy objectives.

To encourage the bureaucracy to follow his lead, the president has important management tools that have developed out of the "executive leadership" concept discussed in Chapter 22. These tools include reorganization, presidential appointees, and the executive budget.

## Reorganization

The bureaucracy's extreme fragmentation—its hundreds of separate agencies—makes presidential coordination of its activities difficult. Agencies pursue independent, even contradictory paths, resulting in an undetermined amount of waste and duplication of effort. For example, some twenty-five units have responsibility for various aspects of national trade policy.[28] More than 100 units have pieces of education policy.

All recent presidents have tried to reorganize the bureaucracy to streamline it and make it more accountable.[29] The most ambitious reorganization plan was Nixon's proposal to combine fifty domestic agencies into four large departments, which would have given him tighter control over domestic policy by placing it under the direction of a few cabinet secretaries. Existing agencies fought Nixon's plan because it threatened their independence. Their clientele

---

[28]John Helmer, "The Presidential Office," in Hugh Heclo and Lester M. Salamon, eds., *The Illusion of Presidential Government* (Boulder, Colo.: Westview Press, 1981), 55.
[29]See Woll, *American Bureaucracy*, 207–229; Peter Szanton, *Federal Reorganization* (Chatham, N.J.: Chatham House, 1981).

groups joined the opposition because they feared the loss of programs. Members of Congress rejected Nixon's plan because of the objections of various interests and also because they recognized that centralization would reduce their influence with the bureaucracy.

Presidents have frequently been able to make less sweeping changes in the bureaucracy's organization, such as reducing the autonomy or number of employees of particular agencies.[30] However, minor changes tend merely to upgrade or downgrade programs or to shift activities from one agency to another. A reshuffling of agency responsibilities is usually no cure: the same problems of presidential control typically reemerge in a new place.[31]

Presidents have been more successful in creating new organizations than in eliminating old ones. Lyndon Johnson decided in 1965 that the nation's cities needed massive federal support because of their deteriorating physical condition and declining tax base. The situation helped to persuade Congress to accept Johnson's proposal for a cabinet-level Department of Housing and Urban Development to carry out his urban policies. Bureaucratic growth has been even more pronounced at the agency level. About a third of all federal agencies in existence today have been established since 1960.[32] Ironically, by forming new agencies to meet new problems, presidents have contributed to the bureaucracy's fragmentation and thus to the problem of controlling and coordinating its activities.

## Presidential Appointments

Although there is almost no direct confrontation with a bureaucrat that a president cannot win, he does not have time to deal personally with every troublesome careerist. Nor does he have time to make sure that the bureaucracy has complied with his every order. The president relies on his political appointees in the agencies to see that his policies are followed. Although presidential appointees hold the highest positions in each agency, many of them are inexperienced in the bureaucracy's ways and uninformed about the agencies they lead. Such appointees are unlikely to command the respect of career bureaucrats, have no real power to fire them because of civil service regulations, and depend on them for information.[33]

Presidents have increasingly come to recognize that appointments based strictly on patronage are not likely to help them govern. Patronage appointees typically have proven their loyalty to the president through service in his election campaign, but they rarely have the expertise to evaluate the claims of career bureaucrats. As a result, presidents have increasingly sought appointees who combine political loyalty with professional knowledge.[34] A tough-minded appointee who knows the work of an agency and shares the president's philosophy can be a powerful surrogate. Reagan had many such appointees. In 1981, for example, he appointed the economist James Miller III to head the

---

[30]Harvey C. Mansfield, "Federal Executive Reorganization: Thirty Years of Experience," *Public Administration Review*, July–August 1969, 339.
[31]James G. March and John P. Olson, "Organizing Political Life: What Administrative Reorganization Tells Us about Government," *American Political Science Review* 77 (June 1983): 281–296.
[32]Kaufman, *Are Government Organizations Immortal?* 48–49.
[33]Thomas Cronin, *The State of the Presidency* (Boston: Little, Brown, 1975), 168.
[34]Kathleen A. Kemp, "The Regulators: Partisanship and Public Policy," *Policy Studies Journal* 11 (March 1983): 386–397.

Federal Trade Commission (FTC). Miller was strong-willed and shared Reagan's belief that consumer protection policy had gone too far and was adversely affecting business interests. In Miller's first year as head of the FTC, the commission dropped one-fourth of its pending cases against business firms.[35]

Regulatory agencies, such as the FTC, are the clearest illustration of the power of presidential appointments. Because these agencies have broad discretion over regulatory policy, a change in their leadership can have substantial effects. Newly appointed members of regulatory commissions are usually eager to implement the president's regulatory philosophy.[36]

However, there are limits to what a president can accomplish through his appointments.[37] High-level presidential appointees number in the hundreds, and their turnover rate is high: the average appointee remains in the administration for less than two years before moving on to other employment.[38] No president can keep track of all his appointees, much less instruct them in detail on his intended policies. In addition, some presidential appointees will have a vested interest in the agencies they head. In choosing political appointees, the president is lobbied by groups that depend on agency programs. Rather than antagonize these groups, the president will accept their recommendations in some cases.

## The Executive Budget

Faced with the difficulty of controlling the bureaucracy, presidents have come to rely heavily on their personal bureaucracy, the Executive Office of the President (EOP). As we noted in Chapter 20, many decisions once made in agencies are now made by presidential appointees in the EOP.

In terms of presidential management, the key unit within the EOP is the Office of Management and Budget (OMB). Funding, programs, and regulations are the mainstays of every agency, and the OMB has substantial influence on each of them (see box). No agency can issue a major regulation without the OMB's verification that the regulation's benefits outweigh its costs, and no agency can propose legislation to Congress without the OMB's approval. However, the OMB's greatest influence over agencies derives from its budgetary role. At the start of the annual budget cycle the OMB assigns each agency a budget limit in accord with the president's directives. Before the agency's tentative allocation requests are sent back to the OMB, they must be approved by the agency head, who of course is a presidential appointee. The OMB then conducts a final review of all agencies' requests before sending the full budget to Congress in the president's name.

Agencies have certain advantages in budgetary matters which can offset the OMB's influence. Fewer than five OMB analysts monitor the budgets of the typical agency, and they generally know less about its activities than does the agency's larger staff of budgetary experts. Within the overall limits that the OMB places on an agency's budget, the agency has considerable leeway in

[35]Meier, *Regulation*, 110–111.
[36]See David Welborn, *Governance of Federal Regulatory Agencies* (Knoxville: University of Tennessee Press, 1977).
[37]See Richard P. Nathan, *The Plot That Failed: Nixon and the Administrative Presidency* (New York: Wiley, 1975).
[38]See Heclo, *Government of Strangers.*

# THE FUNCTIONS OF THE OFFICE OF MANAGEMENT AND BUDGET: HELPING THE PRESIDENT MANAGE THE BUREAUCRACY

The Office of Management and Budget is charged:

To assist the President in his program to develop and maintain effective government by reviewing the organizational structure and management procedures of the executive branch to ensure that they produce the intended results.

To assist in developing efficient coordinating mechanisms to implement Government activities and to expand interagency cooperation.

To assist the President in the preparation of the budget and the formulation of the fiscal program of the Government.

To supervise and control the administration of the budget.

To assist the President by clearing and coordinating departmental advice on proposed legislation and by making recommendations as to Presidential action on legislative enactments, in accordance with past practice.

To assist in the development of regulatory reform proposals and in programs for paperwork reduction, especially reporting burdens of the public.

To assist in the consideration and clearance and, where necessary, in the preparation of proposed Executive orders and proclamations.

To plan and develop information systems to provide the President with program performance data.

To plan, conduct, and promote evaluation efforts to assist the President in the assessment of program objectives, performance, and efficiency.

To keep the President informed of the progress of activities by Government agencies with respect to work proposed, initiated, and completed, together with the relative timing of work between the several agencies of the Government, all to the end that the work programs of the several agencies of the executive branch of the Government may be coordinated and that the moneys appropriated by the Congress may be expended in the most economical manner with the least possible overlapping and duplication of effort.

SOURCE: Reprinted from *The U.S. Government Manual, 1987/88* (Washington, D.C.: U.S. Government Printing Office, 1988), 91–92.

---

allocating funds among its various programs. If the person appointed to head the agency is knowledgeable enough, he or she can slant the budget toward the president's goals, but the sheer scope of these agency budgets—involving scores of programs and billions of dollars in some instances—restricts this indirect source of presidential control. Moreover, the work of the president's appointees can be undone by Congress: if the OMB denies an agency's request for a new program or a larger budget, sympathetic members of Congress can grant it anyway.

In most cases, an agency's overall budget does not change much from year to year.[39] This fact indicates that a significant portion of the bureaucracy's activities persist regardless of who sits in the White House or Congress.[40] At the program level within an agency, however, major year-to-year changes sometimes occur. A significant increase or decrease in the amount allocated to a program from one year to the next nearly always indicates a shift in the president's priorities.[41] The

★ ANALYZE THE ISSUE

**Overcoming Bureaucratic Resistance**
A president's policy goals often conflict with those of the careerists in a bureaucratic agency. Can you think of realistic ways in which a president might try to elicit cooperation from bureaucrats who do not share his policy goals?

[39]See Wildavsky, *Politics of the Budgetary Process.*
[40]Benjamin Ginsberg, *The Consequence of Consent* (New York: Random House, 1982), 207.
[41]Harvey J. Tucker, "Incremental Budgeting: Myth or Model?" *Western Political Quarterly* 35 (September 1982): 327–338.

president also has some authority, after the budget is approved by Congress, to reallocate funds within agencies and to place conditions on their use.

## ACCOUNTABILITY THROUGH CONGRESS

Congress has powerful means of influencing the bureaucracy. All agencies depend on Congress for their existence, authority, programs, and funding. The most extreme action that Congress can take is to eliminate an agency's budget or programs. Congress can also pass legislation that reduces an agency's discretion or voids administrative action. However, Congress has no choice but to allow bureaucrats considerable latitude. Congress lacks the institutional capacity to work out complex policies down to the last detail.[42] The bureaucracy would grind to a halt if it had to get congressional approval for all of its policy decisions. Having neither the time nor the capacity to review every regulation of every agency, Congress has no option but to give the bureaucracy a general heading and then let it proceed along that course.

### Correcting Bureaucratic Error: Legislative Oversight

Congress has statutory responsibility to oversee the bureaucracy's work, reviewing it to ensure compliance with legislative intentions.[43] As we noted in Chapter 18, however, most members of Congress place less emphasis on oversight than on other major duties. Keeping an eye on bureaucrats does not ordinarily help members of Congress to win reelection[44] and is less rewarding than working on new legislation. Oversight can also interfere with the benefits, such as favorable action on constituents' requests, that members of Congress derive from cooperating with the bureaucracy.[45] For the most part, congressional oversight occurs after the fact. Only when an agency has clearly gotten out of line is Congress likely to take decisive corrective action, holding hearings to ask tough questions and to warn of legislative punishment. Often the mere threat of a congressional investigation is enough to persuade an agency to mend its ways.

Congress has sometimes legislated its own authority to void bureaucratic decisions—a device called the *legislative veto*. When Congress authorized the Alaska oil pipeline, for example, it retained the authority to veto bureaucratic decisions about the pipeline's route. In 1983, however, the Supreme Court voided the use of a legislative veto as interference with the president's constitutional authority to execute the laws, but limited its ruling to the law in question. During the same year, the Court affirmed two lower-court rulings that the legislative veto was unconstitutional. Whether the Supreme Court in some situations will rule differently remains to be tested by future cases, but Congress has apparently concluded that the legislative veto is a dead issue; no recent legislation has contained it.

Because oversight is so difficult and unrewarding, Congress has shifted much

---

[42]Samuel H. Beer, "Modernization of American Federalism," *Publius* 3 (Fall 1973): 75.

[43]See Morris Ogul, *Congress Oversees the Bureaucracy* (Pittsburgh: University of Pittsburgh Press, 1976); Randall Ripley and Grace Franklin, *Congress, the Bureaucracy, and Public Policy* (Homewood, Ill.: Dorsey Press, 1976), 225.

[44]Morris Fiorina, *Congress: Keystone of the Washington Establishment* (New Haven, Conn.: Yale University Press, 1977), 91.

[45]Ripley and Franklin, *Congress, the Bureaucracy, and Public Policy*, 173–178.

In authorizing construction of the Alaska pipeline, Congress retained authority to veto the bureaucracy's decisions about the pipeline's route. The Supreme Court has since ruled that such legislative vetoes are unconstitutional in some forms and situations. (Michael G. Edrington/The Image Works)

of its oversight responsibility to the Government Accounting Office (GAO). The GAO's primary function once was to keep track of the funds spent within the bureaucracy; now it also monitors the implementation of policies. The Congressional Budget Office (CBO) also does oversight studies. When the GAO or CBO uncovers a major problem with an agency's handling of a program, it notifies Congress, which can then take remedial action.

### Restricting the Bureaucracy in Advance

Oversight takes place *after* the bureaucracy has acted. Of course, an awareness by bureaucrats that misbehavior can trigger a congressional response helps to keep them in line. Nevertheless, oversight cannot change mistakes or abuses that have already occurred. Recognizing this limit on oversight, Congress has devised ways to constrain the bureaucracy *before* it acts. The simplest method is to draft laws that contain very specific instructions as to how programs are to be administered. Such provisions limit bureaucrats' options when they implement policy.

Another restrictive device is the "sunset law," which, as we saw in Chapter 18, establishes a specific date when a law will expire unless it is reenacted by Congress. Advocates of sunset laws see them as a solution to the problem of the bureaucracy's reluctance to give up programs that have outlived their usefulness.[46] As members of Congress usually want their policies to last far into the future, however, only a few sunset laws have been enacted.

[46]See Theodore Lowi, *The End of Liberalism* (New York: Norton, 1979), 309–310.

## ACCOUNTABILITY THROUGH THE COURTS

The judiciary's influence on agencies is less direct than that of the elected branches, but the courts, too, can and do act to ensure the bureaucracy's compliance with Congress's requirements. Legally, the bureaucracy derives its authority from acts of Congress, and an injured party can bring suit against an agency on the grounds that it has failed to carry out the law properly. Judges can order an agency to change its interpretation of a law. Moreover, the courts have held that agencies must observe the legal standards of due process in making administrative decisions that affect a particular person or group.[47] Finally, the courts have ruled that the individual bureaucrat is required to respect citizens' constitutional rights.[48] A bureaucrat can be sued for monetary damages by a person whose rights have been violated.[49]

However, the Courts have tended to support the bureaucracy if its actions seem at all reasonable. "Courts typically provide agencies wide discretion," David Nachmias and David Rosenbloom conclude. "They greatly defer to the judgment and expertise of administrators."[50] The reason is simple enough: the administration of government would founder if the courts repeatedly reversed agency decisions. The judiciary promotes bureaucratic accountability primarily by encouraging bureaucrats to act responsibly in their dealings with the public and by protecting individuals and groups from the bureaucracy's worst abuses.

## ACCOUNTABILITY WITHIN THE BUREAUCRACY ITSELF

A recognition of the difficulty of achieving adequate accountability of the bureaucracy through the presidency, Congress, and the courts has led to the development of mechanisms of accountability within the bureaucracy itself. Two measures, whistle-blowing and demographic representativeness, are particularly noteworthy.

### Whistle-Blowing

The bureaucratic corruption that is rampant in some countries is relatively uncommon in the United States. However, in view of the fact that the federal bureaucracy has 3 million employees and thousands of programs, a certain amount of waste, fraud, and abuse is inevitable. **Whistle-blowing**, the act of reporting instances of corruption or mismanagement by one's fellow bureaucrats, is a potentially effective internal check. Whistle-blowing has not been highly successful, however, because superiors are seldom pleased to have their lapses made public. In 1988, when Felix Smith, a biologist in the Department of

[47]David H. Rosenbloom, *Public Administration and Law* (New York: Marcel Dekker, 1983); Rosen, *Holding Bureaucrats Accountable,* ch.6.
[48]*Goldberg* v. *Kelly,* 397 U.S. 254 (1970).
[49]*Wood* v. *Strickland,* 420 U.S. 308 (1975). In a few instances involving state and local governments, the Supreme Court has also indicated a willingness to make administrative policy itself. In *Wyatt* v. *Stickney,* the Court established conditions (for example, no more than six patients to a room) that a mental hospital had to meet in order to remain open.
[50]David Nachmias and David H. Rosenbloom, *Bureaucratic Government: U.S.A.* (New York: St. Martin's Press, 1980), 56.

★ *The Supreme Court of the United States is at the top of the federal court hierarchy and functions mainly as an appellate court.* As the Supreme Court has nearly complete freedom to decide which cases it will hear, it can concentrate on cases that involve significant legal issues.

★ *In addition to the Supreme Court, the federal judiciary includes district courts, which hold trials, and courts of appeal, which hear appeals.* These lower courts settle most federal legal cases and have substantial discretion in their actions—contrary to the popular belief that the Supreme Court is the only federal court of great consequence.

★ *Each state has a court system of its own, which for the most part is independent of supervision by the federal courts.* State courts, not federal courts, handle by far the larger proportion of legal cases that arise each year in the United States, and most of these state cases are not subject to appeal in federal courts.

★ *Political considerations are vitally important in the selection of federal judges and justices.* Because of concern about future judicial performance, presidents have tended to choose persons of their own party and philosophy for nomination to the federal bench.

## The Supreme Court of the United States

The writers of the Constitution were determined that the judiciary would be a separate and powerful branch of the federal government but were not certain what the extent of its case load would be. Each state already had its separate court system, and most legal disputes were expected to arise under state laws. A federal judiciary would be needed to resolve cases arising under federal law, but

The Supreme Court building is located across from the Capitol in Washington, D.C. The courtroom, the justices' offices, and the conference room are on the first floor. Administrative staff offices and the Court's records and reference materials occupy the other floors. (Dennis Brack/Black Star)

the writers of the Constitution had no way to predict precisely how many federal cases would occur. Accordingly, the Constitution established the Supreme Court of the United States and granted Congress the authority to establish lower federal courts of its choosing.

Congress also has the constitutional authority to determine the number of justices on the Supreme Court and since 1869 has held the number at nine justices. The chief justice of the United States presides over the Supreme Court and, like the eight associate justices, is appointed by the president with the approval of the U.S. Senate. The Constitution states that the justices "shall hold their offices during good behavior." However, the Constitution contains no precise definition of "good behavior," and no Supreme Court justice has ever been removed from office through impeachment and conviction by Congress. In practice, Supreme Court justices serve until they retire or die.

## THE SUPREME COURT'S JURISDICTION

The Constitution grants the Supreme Court both original and appellate jurisdiction. A court's **jurisdiction** is its authority to hear cases of a particular kind. Jurisdiction is determined partly by the stage of a legal dispute. **Original jurisdiction** is the authority to be the first court to hear a case (such courts are called trial courts). **Appellate jurisdiction** is the authority to review cases that have already been tried in lower courts and are appealed to it by the losing party; such courts are called appeals courts or appellate courts.

The Supreme Court's original jurisdiction embraces legal disputes involving foreign diplomats or two or more states. When such disputes arise, the Supreme Court can act as a trial court. However, the Court in its entire history has convened as a trial court only a few hundred times and has rarely done so in recent years.

The Court, then, does its most significant work through its appellate jurisdiction which extends to cases arising under the Constitution, federal law and regulations, and treaties. The Court also hears appeals involving admiralty or maritime issues and legal controversies that cross state or national boundaries, as when the parties are different states or citizens of different states or when one party is the U.S. government or a foreign government. Congress has constitutional authority over the Court's appellate jurisdiction. A first act of Congress in 1789, for example, gave the Supreme Court the authority to hear appeals of lower-court decisions upholding a state law that allegedly violates the Constitution. Various acts of Congress have empowered the Supreme Court to review almost any case originating in a lower federal court or in a state court when a federal question is involved.

The Constitution bars the Court from issuing decisions except on actual cases before it. This restriction prevents the Court from developing legal positions outside the context of the judicial process, a point that will be addressed more fully in the next chapter.

## THE SUPREME COURT'S PROCEDURES

The primary function of the judiciary is to interpret the law in such a way that rules made in the past (for example, the Constitution or legislation) can be applied reasonably in the present. This function gives the courts—all courts—a role in policymaking. Antitrust legislation, for example, is designed to prevent uncompetitive business practices, but like all such legislation, it is not self-enforcing. If government or another corporation should bring suit against a corporation for an alleged violation of antitrust laws, it is up to the courts to decide whether and how these laws apply to the case at hand.

As the nation's highest court, the Supreme Court is particularly important in determining the meaning and application of laws. Its rulings establish legal precedents that guide lower courts. A **precedent** is a judicial decision that serves as a rule for settling subsequent cases of a similar nature (see Chapter 25). Lower courts are expected to follow precedent—that is, to resolve cases of a like nature in ways consistent with Supreme Court rulings.

### Selecting Cases

The Supreme Court's ability to set legal precedent is strengthened by its authority to choose which cases it will hear. Before 1925 the Court did not have much control over its case load; most cases reached it by mandatory appeal—that is, the Court was required by law to hear them. This situation restricted the Court's capacity to choose cases on the basis of their legal significance. The Judiciary Act of 1925 freed the Court from the burden of mandatory appeals by limiting the types of cases that it was required to hear on appeal.*

Today the Supreme Court has broad discretion in choosing the cases it will hear. The large majority of cases reach the Court through a **writ of *certiorari*,** which the justices grant at their discretion. In applying for such a writ, the losing party in a lower-court case explains in writing why its case should be ruled upon by the Supreme Court. Four of the Court's nine justices must agree to accept a particular case before it is granted a writ. Each year roughly 4,000 parties apply for *certiorari*, but the Court accepts only about 150 cases for a full hearing and ruling. The Court issues another 100 to 200 *per curiam* (unsigned) decisions, which are made without a hearing and simply state the facts of the case and the Court's decision.

Case selection is a vital part of the Supreme Court's work. Through its review of applications for *certiorari*, the Court keeps abreast of legal controversies. Justice William Brennan noted that the *certiorari* process enables the Court to acquire a general idea of the compelling legal issues arising in lower courts and to address those that are most in need of immediate attention.[2]

The Court seldom accepts a routine case, even if the justices believe that a lower court has erred. The Supreme Court's job is not to correct every mistake of other courts but to resolve broad legal questions. As a result, the justices usually choose cases that involve substantial legal issues.[3] This criterion is vague but essentially means that a case must center on an issue of significance not merely to the parties involved but to the nation. As a result, most of the cases heard by the Court raise major constitutional issues, affect the lives of many Americans,

*The Supreme Court is now required by law to hear on appeal only cases that arise when a state or federal court declares a federal law unconstitutional or, in some circumstances, when a state court upholds a state law that is challenged on the grounds that it clashes with federal law.

[2]D. Marie Provine, *Case Selection in the United States Supreme Court* (Chicago: University of Chicago Press, 1980), 62–63.

[3]See Saul Brenner, "The New Certiorari Game," *Journal of Politics* 41 (1979): 649–655; Donald R. Songer, "Concern for Policy Outputs as a Cue for Supreme Court Decisions on Certiorari," *Journal of Politics* 41 (1979): 1185–1194; S. Sidney Ulmer, "Selecting Cases for Supreme Court Review: An Underdog Model," *American Political Science Review* 72 (1979): 902–910.

or address issues being decided inconsistently by the lower courts. The Court is also more likely to grant *certiorari* when the U.S. government is a party to the case and requests a hearing. Nearly half of all such cases are accepted by the Court, compared with less than 10 percent of cases requested by other parties.[4] When the Court does accept a case, chances are that most of the justices disagree with the lower court's ruling. In recent years about three-fourths of the Supreme Court's decisions have reversed the judgments of lower courts.[5]

Despite its control over its cases, the Supreme Court has a substantial work load. The time required to sift through 4,000 cases and then to consider fully about 150 of them each year is considerable. Law clerks assist the justices in these tasks. Each justice is entitled to four clerks, who are usually top-ranking recent graduates of the nation's most prestigious law schools. The clerks prepare memos that summarize each case referred to the Court and recommend whether or not the case should be granted *certiorari*. The chief justice and his staff then compile a list of cases that seem to involve sufficiently substantial issues. This list is circulated among the other justices, who can add cases to it. Cases not on this "Discuss List" are automatically dropped from further consideration.

Justices have complained of having insufficient time to study the legal issues of the cases before them, and several proposals have been put forward for reducing the Supreme Court's case load. Warren Burger, chief justice from 1969 to 1986, proposed the elimination of all mandatory appeals and restrictions on the types of cases eligible for *certiorari*. He also called for the creation of a special appeals court just below the level of the Supreme Court which would handle cases involving conflicting rulings in lower federal appellate courts. This court would be made up of judges chosen from these lower courts. All such proposals for reorganizing the judiciary require congressional approval and have political implications: curtailment of the Supreme Court's jurisdiction would place certain types of petitioners and problems outside the scope of its authority. So far, a majority in Congress has been reluctant to alter the Court's responsibilities.[6]

## Deciding Cases

Once the Supreme Court accepts a case, it sets a date on which the attorneys for the two sides will present their oral arguments. Strict time limits, usually thirty minutes per side, are placed on these arguments, because each side has already submitted written arguments to the justices.

This open hearing is much less important than the **judicial conference** that follows, which is attended only by the nine justices. Conferences normally take place on Wednesday afternoons and Fridays in the Court's private conference room, and the justices are not supposed to discuss the conference's proceedings with outsiders. This secrecy allows the justices to speak freely and tentatively about a case without having to worry that their thoughts will become public.

[4]Joseph Tanenhaus, Marvin Schick, Matthew Muraskin, and Daniel Rosen, "The Supreme Court's Certiorari Jurisdiction," in Glendon A. Schubert, ed., *Judicial Decision-Making* (New York: Free Press, 1963).
[5]Henry Glick, *Courts, Politics, and Justice* (New York: McGraw-Hill, 1983), 214.
[6]Henry J. Abraham, "The Judicial Function under the Constitution," *News for Teachers of Political Science* 41 (Spring 1984): 11, 15.

# THE ROLE OF THE CHIEF JUSTICE

The Supreme Court is presided over by the chief justice of the United States. Like the eight associate justices with whom he serves, the chief justice is appointed for life during good behavior on nomination of the president and approval by the U.S. Senate. The chief justice presides over sessions of the Court and acts as its principal spokesman outside the Court. By tradition, however, justices do not speak publicly about cases currently before the Court, so the chief justice's main responsibility is to manage the Court's work load, which includes chairing the conference hearing on each case. The chief justice is expected to provide leadership for his colleagues. His leadership is largely inspirational, as the chief justice's formal powers are nearly the same as those of the other justices on the Court. Consequently, the chief justice's intellectual capacities, knowledge of the law, political awareness, and persuasiveness are significant. Charles Evans Hughes is reputed to have been the most effective leader in the Court's history, although John Marshall is generally regarded as the greatest chief justice.

The chief justice presides over the conference and speaks first about a particular case. The other justices then speak in order of their seniority (length of service on the Court); this arrangement enhances the senior members' ability to influence the discussion. After the discussion, the justices vote in reverse order of seniority: the least senior justice votes first and the chief justice votes last.

## Issuing Decisions and Opinions

After the vote is taken, the Court prepares and issues its decision and one or more opinions. The **decision** indicates which party the Court sides with and by how large a margin. For example, in its landmark school desegregation ruling, *Brown* v. *Board of Education of Topeka* (1954), the Supreme Court ruled 9–0 in favor of Linda Brown, a schoolchild who claimed that she had been denied equal protection of the laws when she was refused admission to an all-white public school because she was black.[7] The decision meant that Topeka had to admit Linda Brown to a public school previously reserved for white children, and the unanimous vote made it clear that the Court was not likely to reverse its decision.

The Supreme Court's justices also issue **opinions,** which are explanations of the reasons behind their decisions. The reasons may be broad or narrow, but they are ultimately the most important part of a Supreme Court ruling because they inform others of the justices' interpretations of laws. When a majority of the justices agree on the legal basis of a decision, the result is a **majority opinion.** In the *Brown* case, for example, all the justices agreed that government-sponsored school segregation was unconstitutional because it violated the Fourteenth Amendment's guarantee that all Americans are entitled to equal protection of the laws. Enforced segregation of the public schools was therefore constitutionally impermissible. This opinion became the legal basis by which communities throughout the southern states were ordered by lower courts to end their policy of segregating students in their public schools by race.

[7]*Brown* v. *Board of Education of Topeka,* 347 U.S. 483 (1954).

When the chief justice votes with the majority, he decides which of the justices will write the majority opinion. Otherwise, the senior justice in the majority determines the author. Chief justices have often given themselves the influential task of writing the majority opinion in important cases. John Marshall did so often: *Marbury* v. *Madison* (1802) and *McCulloch* v. *Maryland* (1819) were among the opinions he wrote.

The justice who writes the Court's majority opinion has an important and difficult job, since the other justices who voted with the majority must agree with the written opinion. Because the vote on a case is not considered final until the decision is made public, plenty of compromising and old-fashioned horse-trading can take place during the writing stage. The majority opinion often goes through a series of drafts and is circulated among all nine justices. In *Brown* v. *Board of Education,* Justice Felix Frankfurter, the lone initial holdout, was persuaded to make the decision unanimous by the continued urgings of his colleagues and by their willingness to incorporate some of his concerns into the majority opinion.

In some cases there is no majority opinion because a majority of the justices agree on the decision but cannot agree on the legal basis for it. The result is a **plurality opinion,** which presents the view held by most of the justices who side with the winning party. In the *Bakke* case (discussed in Chapter 6), the Court ruled 5–4 that Alan Bakke, a white male, had been wrongly denied admission to medical school because of a quota system that reserved a certain number of admissions for minority students. However, the five justices who ruled in Bakke's favor were divided in their legal reasoning. Four of the justices concluded that Bakke's denial of admission was a violation of the 1964 Civil Rights Act; their view became the plurality opinion. Lewis Powell, the fifth justice who sided with Bakke, believed that Bakke's denial of admission violated a constitutional right. Powell set forth his reasoning in a **concurring opinion,** which is a separate opinion written by a justice who votes with the majority but disagrees with their reasoning.

A justice or justices on the losing side can write a **dissenting opinion** to explain their reasons for disagreeing with the majority position. Sometimes these dissents become a later Court's majority position. In a 1942 dissenting opinion, Justice Hugo Black wrote that defendants in state felony trials should have legal counsel, even if they could not afford to pay for it. Two decades later, in *Gideon* v. *Wainwright* (1963), the Court adopted this position.[8]

## *The American Judicial System*

During the Senate Judiciary Committee's confirmation hearings on Robert Bork, one of his supporters, Senator Gordon Humphrey (R-N.H.), became exasperated by the line of questioning being pursued by senators who opposed Bork. Noting that the Judiciary Committee had scrutinized Bork five years earlier when he was nominated for a lower-court appointment, Humphrey asked why certain objections to Bork had not been raised back then. Humphrey was particularly incensed by criticisms of legal positions that Bork had taken in lectures and articles written long before he had entered the federal judiciary. If

[8]*Gideon* v. *Wainwright,* 372 U.S. 335 (1963).

# TYPES OF SUPREME COURT OPINIONS

*Majority opinion:* a written opinion of the majority of the Court's justices stating the reasoning underlying their decision on a case.

*Plurality opinion:* a written opinion that in the absence of a majority opinion presents the reasoning of most of the justices who side with the winning party.

*Concurring opinion:* a written opinion of one or more justices who support the majority position but disagree with the majority's reasoning on a case. This opinion expresses the reasoning of the concurring justices.

*Dissenting opinion:* a written opinion of one or more justices who disagree with the majority's decision and opinion. This opinion provides the reasoning underlying the dissent.

Bork's earlier views were so questionable, Humphrey asked, why had they not been probed in the earlier hearings? Bork's opponents on the Senate Judiciary Committee ignored Humphrey's complaint, probably because they believed that the answer was obvious: a nominee to the Supreme Court needs much closer scrutiny than a lower-court nominee. After all, there are more than 100 federal courts but there is only one Supreme Court, and its position at the top of the country's judicial system gives Supreme Court appointments unparalleled importance.

It is a mistake, however, to conclude that the Supreme Court is the only court of consequence. Justice Jerome Frank once wrote of the "upper-court myth" that appellate courts and in particular the Supreme Court are the only truly significant judicial arena and that lower courts just dutifully follow the rulings handed down by the appellate level.[9] The reality is very different, as the following discussion will explain.

## FEDERAL DISTRICT COURTS

The lowest federal courts are the district courts (see Figure 24-1). There are more than ninety federal district courts altogether—at least one in every state and as many as four in some states. District-court judges, who number about 500 in all, are appointed by the president with the consent of the Senate.

Federal cases usually originate in district courts, which are trial courts, where the parties present their evidence and argue their sides and a decision is rendered in favor of one party or the other. District courts are the only courts in the federal system in which juries hear testimony in some cases, and most cases at this level are presented before a single judge. Some district-court cases involve issues of "private law" (relationships between individuals and between businesses), such as divorce and contract disputes. Other cases involve issues of "public law" (relationships of individuals to government and the rights and obligations of each), such as crimes, political rights, and the government's obligations under the Constitution and under statutes and administrative regulations.

[9]From a letter to the author by Frank Schwartz of Beaver College, 1986. This section reflects substantially Professor Schwartz's recommendations to the author, as does the later section that addresses the "federal-court myth."

The Supreme Court is not the only federal court that "matters" in the American judicial system. Most federal cases originate in district courts, and most appealed cases are settled in courts of appeals, never reaching the Supreme Court. (Eli Reed/Magnum)

In theory, federal district courts are bound by legal precedents established by the Supreme Court. This requirement was reiterated in a 1982 case, *Hutto* v. *Davis:* "Unless we wish anarchy to prevail within the federal judicial system, a precedent of this Court must be followed by the lower federal courts no matter how misguided the judges of those courts may think it to be."[10]

There is no question that lower federal courts rely on and follow Supreme Court decisions in their own rulings. However, the idea that lower courts are guided strictly by Supreme Court rulings is part of the "upper-court myth." District-court judges may misapply or misunderstand the Supreme Court's position and deviate from it for that reason. In addition, the facts of a case before a district court are seldom precisely the same as those of a similar case decided by the Supreme Court. In this situation, the lower-court judge must decide whether the facts of the current case are sufficiently different that a different legal principle must be invoked. In some cases, district-court judges have willfully disregarded Supreme Court precedent, finding a basis for decision that

[10]*Hutto* v. *Davis*, U.S. 370 (1982).

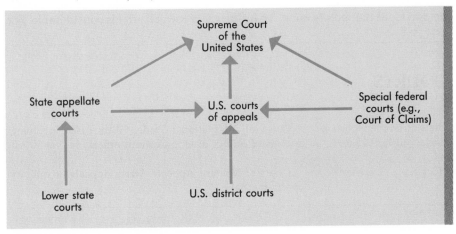

**FIGURE 24-1 The Federal Judicial System**
This simplified diagram shows the relationships among the various levels of federal courts and between state and federal courts. The losing party in a case can appeal a lower-court decision to the court at the next highest level, as the arrows indicate. A case can be appealed from state courts to federal courts only when a federal issue is involved.

allows them to reach a judgment they prefer. For example, after the Supreme Court declared in *Brown* v. *Board of Education* that racial segregation of public schools violated the Fourteenth Amendment's guarantee of equal protection under the law, several southern district-court judges concluded that the issue in question in subsequent school desegregation cases was not equal protection but the maintenance of public order, and that school desegregation could not be allowed because it would disrupt public order. Finally, it is not unusual for the Supreme Court to take a very general legal position, leaving it to the lower courts to decide their exact meaning in practice. Trial-court judges then have a creative role in judicial decision making which rivals that of appellate-court judges.

Most federal cases end with the district court's decision; the losing party does not appeal the decision to a higher court. This is another indication of the highly significant role of district-court judges.

## FEDERAL COURTS OF APPEALS

When cases are appealed from district courts, they go to a federal court of appeals. These appellate courts make up the second level of the federal court system. Courts of appeals do not use juries. No new evidence is submitted in an appealed case; appellate courts base their decisions on a review of lower-court records. Appellate judges act as supervisors in the legal system, reviewing trial-court decisions and correcting what they consider to be mistakes.

The United States has twelve general appeals courts, each of which serves an area consisting of between three and nine states, except the one that serves the District of Columbia only. There is also the U.S. Court of Appeals for the Federal Circuit, which specializes in appeals of decisions in cases involving patents and international trade. Between four and twenty-six judges sit on each court of appeals, but each case is usually heard by a panel of three judges. On rare occasions, all the judges of a court of appeals sit as a body (*en banc*) in order to resolve difficult controversies, typically ones that have resulted in conflicting decisions within the same circuit. The usual purpose of an *en banc* hearing is to ensure that the judges will decide similar cases in a consistent way.

Courts of appeals offer the only real hope of reversal for many appellants, since the Supreme Court hears so few cases. Fewer than 1 percent of the cases heard by federal appeals courts are later reviewed by the Supreme Court. "Because the Supreme Court only handles several hundred cases a year," Sheldon Goldman points out, "the influence of lower courts is considerable. For

## SPECIAL FEDERAL COURTS

In addition to the Supreme Court, the courts of appeals, and the district courts, the federal judiciary includes a few specialty courts:

Court of Claims: Hears cases in which the U.S. government is sued for damages.

Court of International Trade: Hears cases involving appeals of rulings of U.S. Customs offices.

Court of Military Appeals: Hears appeals of military courts-martial.

most intents and purposes, the courts of appeals function as regional Supreme Courts for the nation. As a result, we're talking about some major policy makers."[11]

## STATE COURTS

As a consequence of the United States' federal system of government, each state has a court system that exists apart from the federal courts. Like the federal courts, state court systems have trial courts at the bottom level and appellate courts at the top. Some states have two appellate levels, and others have only a single appellate court. States vary in the way they organize and label their courts, but tend to give some lower courts specialized titles and jurisdictions. Family courts, for example, settle such issues as divorce and child-custody disputes, and probate courts handle the disposition of the estates of deceased persons. Below such specialized trial courts are less formal trial courts, such as magistrate courts and justice of the peace courts. They handle a variety of minor cases, such as traffic infractions, and usually do not use a jury.

States vary also in their methods of selecting judges. In about a fourth of the states, judges are appointed by the governor, but in most states, judgeships are elective offices. Several states use the "Missouri Plan" (so called because Missouri was the first state to use it), under which a judicial selection commission provides a short list of acceptable candidates from which the governor selects one; after a year on the bench, the judge selected must be approved by the voters in order to serve a longer term. Some other states use nonpartisan or partisan elections to choose their judges. Federalism allows each state to decide for itself the structure of its courts and the method of judicial appointment. Thus, although all federal judges are appointed to office, states are not required to use this method.

Besides the upper-court myth, there exists a "federal-court myth," which holds that the federal judiciary is the most significant part of the judicial system and that state courts play a subordinate role. This view, too, is inaccurate. Upwards of 95 percent of the nation's legal cases are decided in state courts (or local courts, which are agents of the states). Most crimes (from shoplifting to murder) and most civil controversies (such as divorces and corporate disputes) are defined by state or local law. These cases are hardly insignificant, as the federal-court myth implies they are. Moreover, nearly all cases that originate in state courts also end there; the federal courts never come into the picture.

Cases that originate in state courts can be appealed to a federal court if a federal issue is involved and usually only after all avenues of appeal in the state courts have been exhausted. When a federal court does become involved in a state case, it often confines itself to the federal aspects of the matter, such as whether a suspect in a criminal case received the protections guaranteed by the U.S. Constitution. If the Supreme Court decides, for instance, that state authorities violated a person's constitutional right to a fair trail, the person is not necessarily acquitted; the Court's decision may require only that the state retry the accused.

When a state case is removed to a federal court and decided there, the federal court must apply state law as interpreted by the state's courts to any aspect of the

---

[11]Quoted in Howard Brownstein, "With or without Supreme Court Changes, Reagan Will Reshape the Federal Court," *National Journal*, December 8, 1984, 2238.

case to which state law, rather than federal law, applies. The federal court must also accept the facts determined by the state court unless such findings are clearly in error. In short, legal and factual determinations of state courts can bind the federal courts—a clear contradiction of the federal-court myth.

However, cases traditionally within the jurisdiction of the states can become federal cases through rulings of federal courts. In *Roe* v. *Wade* (1973), for example, the Supreme Court concluded that women had a right to abortion under the U.S. Constitution, thus taking away from the states an issue that they had previously decided.[12]

When court jurisdictions overlap, the governing principle is **comity**—the idea that the laws of a governing authority (such as a state) will be respected even though the dispute is being settled by a court of a different authority (such as another state or the national government). Adherence to this principle is essential if federalism is to work effectively and harmoniously. Consider a state civil suit involving residents of different states. In such situations, the plaintiff (the person who initiates a court suit) can choose to bring the suit either in his or her state court or in federal court; however, if the plaintiff brings the suit in state court, the defendant (the person against whom a suit is brought) can have the case removed to federal court if the suit involves a claim of $10,000 or more.* In such cases of multiple jurisdiction, confusion would result if no principle existed for deciding which laws apply—those of the plaintiff's state or the defendant's state. Accordingly, the principle of comity dictates that if such cases are removed to the federal judiciary, they are decided under the laws of the plaintiff's state and that the defendant's state must honor the decision.

## Federal Court Appointees

By the time President Ronald Reagan left office in January 1989, he had appointed almost half of all federal judges, filling vacancies that had resulted from resignations, retirements, and deaths (see Figure 24-2). Reagan selected

[12]*Roe* v. *Wade*, 410 U.S. 113 (1973).
*The idea that the federal judiciary should be able to hear such cases arose in 1787 because of fears that a state court would be biased toward the interests of its own citizens.

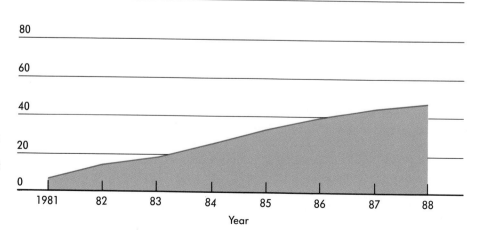

**FIGURE 24-2 Percentage of Federal Judges Who Were Appointed by President Reagan** Ronald Reagan's eight years as president enabled him to appoint nearly half of all federal judges and thus to go far in his efforts to remake the federal judiciary. *Source: Department of Justice data.*

his appointees with care; the new judges were expected to alter liberal principles that had been laid down by federal courts in the previous three decades. Among the areas in which Reagan hoped for significant change were abortion, school prayer, affirmative action, and the rights of the accused. Assistant Attorney General Stephen Markman, who coordinated Reagan's judicial appointments, said that the goal was to appoint judges who were "less likely to be engaged in broad social engineering policies" than their more liberal predecessors.[13]

Appointments of federal judges do represent a significant opportunity for a president to influence national policy because judges have considerable discretion. Although courts make their decisions on the basis of law, "the law" is not always clear-cut in its application to particular cases. In the course of deciding cases that arise under various laws, courts actively create policy. This subject is the focus of the next chapter; here it will suffice to note that no modern president has been willing to leave to chance the question of who will sit on the federal bench. Each president has sought appointees whose political beliefs reflected his own. The litmus test for Reagan appointees was their commitment to conservative principles.

As most judges retain their positions for many years, a president can influence judicial policy through his appointments long after he himself has left office. Reagan's appointees will be a force on the federal bench well into the twenty-first century. The careers of some Supreme Court justices provide even more dramatic testimony to the enduring effects of judicial appointments. Franklin D. Roosevelt appointed William O. Douglas to the Supreme Court in 1939, and for thirty years after Roosevelt's death in 1945 Douglas remained a strong liberal influence on the Court. John Marshall was appointed chief justice in 1801 by the second president, John Adams, and served until 1835, when the seventh president, Andrew Jackson, was in his second term.

William O. Douglas served as a Supreme Court justice for thirty-six years, from 1939 to 1975. (Laurence Willinger/ Fourth Estate Press/Black Star)

## SELECTING SUPREME COURT JUSTICES AND FEDERAL JUDGES

The formal mechanism for appointments to the Supreme Court and the lower federal courts is the same: the president nominates and the Senate confirms or rejects. Beyond that basic similarity, however, significant differences emerge.

### Supreme Court Nominees

Presidents have used a variety of approaches to the task of selecting a nominee to fill a vacancy on the Supreme Court. A president may choose to depend chiefly on his own counsel, ask the Justice Department for advice, or seek the views of interested parties who share his general philosophy.

Interest groups invariably become actively involved in the selection process after the president has announced his choice. When Reagan nominated Sandra Day O'Connor in 1981, her selection was endorsed by several groups that wanted a woman on the Supreme Court. Most nominees are confirmed by wide margins by the Senate, but interest groups occasionally play a significant role in the Senate's rejection of a nominee. In 1969 Clement F. Haynsworth, Jr., a Nixon nominee, was rejected 55–45 by the Senate after strong opposition by organized labor and minority groups (and amid allegations of conflict of interest in his financial dealings).

In 1967 Thurgood Marshall was the first and only black appointed to the Supreme Court. Marshall has been one of the Court's most liberal members. (Yoichi R. Okamoto/Photo Researchers)

[13]Quoted in Kathryn Kahler, "Will Numerous Reagan Appointees Mold a New Judiciary?" *Syracuse Herald-American,* January 24, 1988, E1, E4.

Sandra Day O'Connor is sworn in as the first and only female Supreme Court justice in 1981. O'Connor has tended to side with the Court's conservatives. (Sygma)

One group that always takes a stand on Supreme Court nominees is the American Bar Association (ABA). Its Committee on the Federal Judiciary investigates each nominee and assesses his or her qualifications for appointment to the Supreme Court. This evaluation is less meaningful than it might be, however, because the ABA committee has never judged a nominee to be not qualified—not even G. Harrold Carswell, an undistinguished and perhaps racially biased federal judge whom the Senate refused, 51–45, to confirm in 1970. Carswell's qualifications were so weak that one of his Senate supporters inadvertently contributed to his defeat by offering the now-infamous "mediocrity defense": "There are a lot of mediocre judges and people in Congress," Nebraska's Senator Roman Hruska said, "and they are entitled to a little representation [on the Supreme Court], aren't they?"[14]

Within the Senate, a key body is the Judiciary Committee, whose members have responsibility for conducting hearings on judicial nominees and recommending their confirmation or rejection by the full Senate. Nearly 20 percent of presidential nominees have been rejected by the Senate on grounds of judicial qualification, political views, personal ethics, or partisanship. Most of the rejections of nominees in the country's history occurred before 1900, and partisan politics was the main reason. Today a nominee with strong professional and ethical credentials is less likely to be blocked for partisan reasons alone. An exception was Robert Bork, whose rejection in 1987 was founded on strong opposition from Senate Democrats who disagreed with his judicial philosophy.

### Lower-Court Nominees

The president normally gives the deputy attorney general the task of screening potential nominees for lower-court judgeships.[15] Senatorial courtesy is also a

[14]Quoted in Lawrence Baum, *The Supreme Court* (Washington, D.C.: Congressional Quarterly Press, 1981), 37.
[15]For a study of lower-court appointments, see Harold W. Chase, *Federal Judges: The Appointing Process* (Minneapolis: University of Minnesota Press, 1972).

**Judicial Appointment**

U.S. courts are highly political by comparison with the courts of most other democracies. First, U.S. courts operate within a common-law tradition, which makes judge-made law (through precedent) a part of the legal code. Many democracies have a civil-law tradition, in which nearly all law is defined by legislative statutes. Second, because U.S. courts operate in a constitutional system of divided power, they are required to rule on conflicts between state and nation or between the executive and legislative branches, which thrusts the judiciary into the middle of political conflicts. U.S. courts have no choice but to act politically. It should not be surprising, then, that federal judges and justices are appointed through an overtly political process in which partisan views and activities are major considerations. Many federal judges, particularly at the district level, have no significant prior judicial experience and no claim to special legal talent or training.

The pattern is different in most European democracies. Judgeships there tend to be career positions. Individuals are appointed to the judiciary at an early age and then work their way up the judicial ladder largely on the basis of seniority. Partisan politics does not play a large role in appointment and promotion, partly because the courts themselves are less political than their U.S. counterparts. By tradition, European judges see their job as the strict interpretation of statutes, not the creative application of them.

consideration in these appointments: a senator from the state in which a vacancy has arisen is normally given a say in the nomination if the senator is of the same party as the president.[16]

Although the president does not become as personally involved in selecting lower-court nominees as in naming potential Supreme Court justices, lower-court appointments are collectively a significant factor in the impact of a president's administration. Reagan was able to fill more than 300 vacancies in district and appellate courts (compared with three Supreme Court openings), which, as we noted earlier, constituted about half of all judgeships at those levels. The Senate is more likely to confirm a president's lower-court nominees than his Supreme court nominees. Of Reagan's lower-court nominees, only one, Daniel Mannion, the son of the founder of the ultraconservative John Birch Society, was strongly opposed in the Senate. Mannion's critics maintained that he was unsuitable because he held extreme legal views and lacked the ability and experience expected of a federal appellate judge. Nevertheless, he was confirmed by a margin of one vote.

The ABA's Committee on the Federal Judiciary can play a key role in lower-court appointments. If the ABA committee unanimously approves a nominee, the Senate Judiciary Committee is not likely to examine the appointment exhaustively. However, when some members of the ABA's committee have reservations about a nominee, as was the case with Mannion, the Senate Judiciary Committee tends to investigate the president's choice more thoroughly.

## JUSTICES AND JUDGES AS POLITICAL OFFICIALS

In comparing the Supreme Court with the U.S. Senate, where he had served before his appointment to the Court, Justice Harold Burton said that it was the

---

[16]Stephen L. Wasby, *The Supreme Court in the Federal Judicial System*, 2d ed. (New York: Holt, Rinehart and Winston, 1984), 75.

★ ANALYZE THE ISSUE

**Ideology on the Supreme Court**

Supreme Court justices normally take ideological positions that are roughly in line with what the presidents who appointed them expected. Of recent justices who have *not* conformed to expectations—including Justices Warren, Blackmun, and Stevens—most have tended to be more liberal than expected, particularly on issues of civil liberties. Do you think this is just a coincidence, or does it suggest something basic about the Court's role in protecting the rights of the individual?

difference between a "monastery" and a "circus."[17] The quiet setting of the Court, the dignity of its proceedings, and the lack of fanfare with which it announces its decisions give the impression that the Court is about as far removed from the world of politics as a governmental institution can possibly be. Above all else, however, Supreme Court justices are political officials who exercise the authority of a separate and powerful branch of government. They are appointed through a political process, they bring their political views with them to the Court, and they have regular opportunities to promote their political beliefs through the cases they decide.

## The Role of Partisanship

Not surprisingly, partisanship is a critical test of potential jurists: presidents nearly always nominate someone from their own party in order to increase the chances of appointing a justice with political views similar to their own. Before nominating Oliver Wendell Holmes, Jr., to the Court, Theodore Roosevelt wrote to Henry Cabot Lodge for his opinion, saying, "I should hold myself as guilty of an irreparable wrong to the nation if I should put in his place any man who was not absolutely sane and sound on the great national policies for which we stand in public life."[18]

Presidents generally manage to appoint individuals who share their political philosophy. Although justices are free to go their own way on the Court, their legal philosophies can be inferred from their prior activities. Robert Scigliano found that about three of every four appointees have behaved on the Supreme Court approximately as presidents could have expected.[19] Of course, a president has no guarantee that a nominee will fulfill his hopes. Justices Earl Warren and William Brennan proved more liberal than President Dwight D. Eisenhower would have liked. When he was asked whether he had made any mistakes as president, Eisenhower replied, "Yes, two, and they are both sitting on the Supreme Court."[20]

Presidents also tend to nominate members of their own party to lower-court judgeships. All recent presidents except Gerald Ford have selected more than 90 percent of their district- and appeals-court nominees from among members of their own party.[21]

## Should "Merit" Play a Larger Role?

Over the years the partisanship evident in court appointments has occasionally come under attack. In the early nineteenth century, Progressive reformers persuaded some states to exclude their judgeships from party patronage positions. The Missouri Plan is a more recent reflection of the belief that partisan loyalty should not play a deciding role in the filling of judicial offices.

[17]Quoted in Mary Frances Berry, *Stability, Security, and Continuity: Mr. Justice Burton and Decision-Making in the Supreme Court* (Westport, Conn.: Greenwood Press, 1978), 27.
[18]Quoted in Walter Murphy and C. Herman Pritchett, eds., *Courts, Judges, and Politics,* 3d ed. (New York: Random House, 1979), 137.
[19]Robert Scigliano, *The Supreme Court and the Presidency* (New York: Free Press, 1971), 146.
[20]Quoted in Baum, *Supreme Court,* 37.
[21]C. Herman Pritchett, *The American Constitutional System* (New York: McGraw-Hill, 1967), 76; Herbert Jacob, *Justice in America: Courts, Lawyers, and the Judicial Process,* 4th ed. (Glenview, Ill.: Scott, Foresman, 1984), 122.

# THE SOCIAL CHARACTERISTICS OF FEDERAL JUSTICES AND JUDGES

Although the judiciary is a branch of the U.S. system of representative government, it is hardly demographically representative of the public it serves. White males are greatly overrepresented on the courts, just as they dominate Congress. In a study of appellate judges who served from 1933 to 1976, for example, John Schmidhauser found that fewer than 5 percent were women or members of minority groups. When Jimmy Carter became president in 1977, he was determined to appoint more women and blacks to the courts. Women totaled 20 percent of his appointees and blacks 16 percent—numerically, twice as many as had been appointed by all previous presidents.

Ronald Reagan was more concerned with nominees' ideology than with their race or sex. Nevertheless, women and blacks accounted for only 10 percent of his appointees. Reagan did seek younger people for the federal courts, knowing that such individuals are more likely to remain on the bench for many years, thus prolonging their influence on the law. Reagan's judicial appointees averaged about forty-five years of age, compared with the previous average of more than fifty years.

Justices of the Supreme Court have been overwhelmingly white, male, and Protestant. Until 1916, when Louis D. Brandeis was appointed to the Court, no Jewish justice had served. At least one Catholic, but at most times only one, has been on the Court almost continuously for nearly a century. Thurgood Marshall in 1967 became the first black justice, and Sandra Day O'Connor in 1981 became the first woman. Antonin Scalia in 1986 became the Court's first justice of Italian descent. No person of Hispanic or Asian descent has ever been a member of the Court.

The judicial scholar Henry J. Abraham has dismissed concerns about the Court's demographic makeup, saying that the Court was never meant to be a representative body. Another scholar, Sheldon Goldman, disagrees, saying that "the *best* bench may be composed of persons of all races and both sexes with diverse backgrounds and experiences." Goldman argues that the judiciary's sensitivity to society's diverse interests depends to a degree on the social backgrounds that the justices bring with them to the Court.

SOURCES: John Schmidhauser, *Judges and Justices: The Federal Appellate Judiciary* (Boston: Little, Brown, 1978), ch. 3; Henry J. Abraham, "The Judicial Function under the Constitution," *News for Teachers of Political Science* 41 (Spring 1984): 14; Sheldon Goldman, "Should There Be Affirmative Action for the Judiciary?" *Judicature* 62 (May 1979); 494.

No such thoroughgoing reform has taken place at the federal level, although Jimmy Carter used selection panels to compile lists of five candidates to fill appellate-court vacancies on the basis of merit. Carter selected from among these candidates, although he nearly always picked a Democrat. Carter's merit system was opposed by some senators, who believed that it reduced their influence on the selection process. Reagan returned to the earlier system after taking office in 1981.[22]

Increasing numbers of federal justices and judges have had prior judicial experience; the assumption is that such individuals are better qualified for appointment to the federal bench. Elective office (particularly a seat in the U.S. Senate) was once the typical route to the Supreme Court,[23] but now most justices have held an appellate-court judgeship or high administrative office in the Justice Department before their appointment (see Table 24-1). In addition, most recent appellate-court appointees have been district or state judges or have worked in the office of the attorney general.[24]

[22]Abraham, "Judicial Function under the Constitution," 12.
[23]Joseph B. Harris, *The Advice and Consent of the Senate* (Berkeley: University of California Press, 1953), 313.
[24]John Schmidhauser, *Judges and Justices: The Federal Appellate Judiciary* (Boston: Little, Brown, 1979), 84–85.

★ ANALYZE THE ISSUE

**Appointing Justices: Merit or Politics?**
The Supreme Court has had a few great jurists, such as Holmes and Cardozo, and many mediocre ones. Should merit be a larger consideration in appointments to the Court, or is it more important that justices be chosen on the basis of their policy views?

TABLE 24-1   Justices of the Supreme Court, 1989

| Justice | Year of Appointment | Nominating President | Position Before Appointment |
|---|---|---|---|
| William Brennan | 1956 | Eisenhower | Justice, Supreme Court of New Jersey |
| Byron White | 1962 | Kennedy | Deputy attorney general |
| Thurgood Marshall | 1967 | Johnson | Solicitor general |
| Harry Blackmun | 1970 | Nixon | Judge, U.S. Court of Appeals |
| William Rehnquist* | 1971 | Nixon | Assistant attorney general |
| John Paul Stevens | 1975 | Ford | Judge, U.S. Court of Appeals |
| Sandra Day O'Connor | 1981 | Reagan | Judge, Arizona Court of Appeals |
| Antonin Scalia | 1986 | Reagan | Judge, U.S. Court of Appeals |
| Anthony Kennedy | 1988 | Reagan | Judge, U.S. Court of Appeals |

*Appointed chief justice in 1986.

The official portrait of the 1988–1989 session of the Supreme Court of the United States: (*front row*) Thurgood Marshall, William Brennan, Jr., Chief Justice William Rehnquist, Byron White, Harry Blackmun; (*back row*) Antonin Scalia, John Paul Stevens, Sandra Day O'Connor, Anthony Kennedy. (Supreme Court Historical Society)

Not all observers agree that judicial experience is the best preparation for a federal jurist, particularly for a justice of the Supreme Court. Justice Felix Frankfurter claimed that "the correlation between prior judicial experience and fitness for the Supreme Court is zero," and felt that the greatest jurists, Oliver Wendell Holmes, Jr., and Benjamin Cardozo among them, were essentially "legal philosophers."[25] Frankfurter's observation has merit, in that many of the Court's most influential members—including John Marshall, Charles Evans Hughes, Louis Brandeis, Harlan Stone, Felix Frankfurter, Earl Warren, and

[25]Felix Frankfurter, "The Supreme Court in the Mirror of Justices," *University of Pennsylvania Law Review* 106 (1957): 781.

Hugo Black—had no significant judicial experience before being appointed to the Court.[26]

Because the issues facing the Supreme Court are both political and legal, their proper resolution may require a balancing of political and legal considerations. This prospect, says C. Herman Pritchett, a leading judicial scholar, is enhanced when the justices collectively have experience in both realms. Noting that the Warren Court (1953–1969) had a penchant for tackling issues that in some cases might have been better left to legislative bodies, while the Burger Court (1969–1986) often was preoccupied with narrow points of law, Pritchett observed, "Perhaps there were too many politicians on the Warren Court, but perhaps there [were] too many judges on the Burger Court."[27]

Judicial appointments are a critical issue because the judiciary is a political institution as well as a legal one—a point that will be developed in the next chapter.

[26]Schmidhauser, *Judges and Justices*, 95.
[27]C. Herman Pritchett, "High Court Selection," *New York Times*, January 12, 1976; reprinted in Murphy and Pritchett, *Courts, Judges, and Politics.*

> **★ ANALYZE THE ISSUE**
>
> **The Effect of Justices' Personal Characteristics**
> The United States is said to have "a government of laws, not of men." Yet the judges who interpret the laws are people. The justices of the Supreme Court have tended to be older white males of privileged and partisan backgrounds. How might these characteristics of Supreme Court justices have affected their rulings? Can you think of specific decisions that only judges with these characteristics would have been likely to make?

## Summary

At the lowest level of the federal judicial system are the district courts, where most federal cases begin. Above them are the federal courts of appeals, which review cases appealed from the lower courts. The U.S. Supreme Court is the nation's highest court. Each state has its own court system, consisting of trial courts at the bottom and one or two appellate levels at the top. Cases originating in state courts ordinarily cannot be appealed to the federal courts unless a federal issue is involved, and then the federal courts can choose to rule only on the federal aspects of the case.

The Supreme Court is unquestionably the most important court in the country. The legal principles it establishes are binding on lower courts, and its capacity to define the law is enhanced by the control it exercises over the cases it hears. The most important part of the Court's majority opinion in a case is the legal reasoning underlying the decision: this reasoning guides lower courts in their handling of similar cases. However, it is inaccurate to assume that lower courts are inconsequential (the upper-court myth). Lower courts have considerable discretion in their evaluation of the facts and applicable laws of the cases before them, and the great majority of their decisions are not reviewed by a higher court. It is also inaccurate to assume that federal courts are far more significant than state courts (the federal-court myth). The vast majority of legal cases that arise each year in the United States are decided in state courts.

Federal judges at all levels are appointed by the president and confirmed by the Senate. Once on the federal bench, they serve until they die, retire, or are removed by impeachment and conviction. Partisan politics plays a significant role in judicial appointments. Presidents are particularly alert to political philosophy in their selection of Supreme Court justices. The nation's top court makes broad policy decisions, and presidents have tried to ensure that appointees share their partisan goals.

## Major Concepts

appellate jurisdiction
comity
concurring opinion
decision
dissenting opinion
judicial conference
jurisdiction

majority opinion
opinions
original jurisdiction
plurality opinion
precedent
writ of *certiorari*

## Suggested Readings

Abraham, Henry J. *The Judicial Process*, 4th ed. New York: Oxford University Press, 1980. An explanation of how state and federal courts form the judicial system of the United States.

Ball, Howard. *Courts and Politics: The Federal Judicial System*, 2d ed. Englewood Cliffs, N.J.: Prentice-Hall, 1987. A text that describes the function, organization, and purpose of the federal judicial system.

Baum, Lawrence. *The Supreme Court*. Washington, D.C.: Congressional Quarterly Press, 1981. A survey of the personnel, procedures, and cases of the Supreme Court which assesses its policymaking function.

Carp, Robert A., and Ronald Stidham. *The Federal Courts*. Washington, D.C.: Congressional Quarterly Press, 1985. An analysis of the lower federal court system.

Chase, Harold W. *Federal Judges: The Appointing Process*. Minneapolis: University of Minnesota Press, 1972. An analysis of the process by which lower federal judges are appointed, and who receives these appointments.

Howard, J. Woodford, Jr. *Courts of Appeals in the Federal Judicial System*. Princeton, N.J.: Princeton University Press, 1981. A recent assessment of the role of federal courts of appeals.

Provine, D. Marie. *Case Selection in the United States Supreme Court*. Chicago: University of Chicago Press, 1980. An analysis of the process by which the Supreme Court chooses the cases it reviews.

Schmidhauser, John. *Judges and Justice: The Federal Appellate Judiciary*. Boston: Little, Brown, 1979. An examination of the backgrounds of Supreme Court justices and federal appeals-court judges.

Scigliano, Robert. *The Supreme Court and the Presidency*. New York: Free Press, 1971. A look at the relationship between the Supreme Court and the presidency, including the subject of presidential nominations of justices.

Woodward, Bob, and Scott Armstrong. *The Brethren*. New York: Simon & Schuster, 1979. An inside look at the Supreme Court from 1969 to 1976 by two Washington journalists.

# Chapter 25

## SUPREME COURT POLICYMAKING: DECIDING THE LAW

*Judges make choices, but they are not the "free" choices of congressmen.*
C. Herman Pritchett[1]

In its historic ruling in *Brown* v. *Board of Education* (1954), the Supreme Court declared that public school segregation was unconstitutional.[2] However, the Court did not require local officials to take positive steps to promote school integration; it merely forbade them to prevent black children from attending previously all-white schools. Because children of each race lived in segregated neighborhoods, most black children fifteen years after the *Brown* ruling were still not attending school with white children.

To remedy this situation, the Supreme Court held in *Swann* v. *Charlotte–Mecklenburg County Board of Education* (1971) that busing was an acceptable, though not required, means of bringing black and white children together in the public schools.[3] The Court reasoned that, where school segregation is a consequence of past public policies, busing is an appropriate remedy for the injustice. Shortly thereafter, lower courts in many parts of the nation, North and South, were ordering communities to use busing to correct the racial imbalance in their schools. Many whites in the affected communities reacted angrily and sometimes violently. Nevertheless, busing has remained public policy. Thousands of American schoolchildren are bused out of their neighborhoods in order to ensure racially mixed schools.

---

[1]C. Herman Pritchett, "The Development of Judicial Research," in Joel B. Grossman and Joseph Tanenhaus, eds., *Frontiers of Judicial Research* (New York: Wiley, 1969), 42.
[2]*Brown* v. *Board of Education of Topeka,* 347 U.S. 483 (1954).
[3]*Swann* v. *Charlotte–Mecklenburg County Board of Education,* 412 U.S. 92 (1971).

After the Supreme Court's *Swann* decision in 1971, which mandated busing to achieve public school integration, police had to be called out at South Boston High School to maintain order. Some legalists claim that this ruling exceeded the Court's authority. (Ira Wyman/Sygma)

Was the Supreme Court on solid legal ground when it sanctioned court-ordered busing? Some legalists believe that the Court's decision was justified. They argue that the judiciary should act when legislative majorities are afraid or unwilling to undertake policies that protect the basic rights of minorities. According to this view, the U.S. Constitution has strong moral language—for example, "equal protection of the laws"—that justifies decisions such as the busing ruling.[4] Without busing, many black children would be consigned to a life of permanent inequality.

Other legalists claim that the Court overstepped its authority in approving busing. From their perspective, the problem with court-ordered busing is that it primarily addresses segregation resulting not from law but from the racial, economic, and social differences that lead blacks and whites to live in separate neighborhoods. This situation is supposedly a political problem, not a legal one, and therefore is properly settled by elected officials, not judges.[5]

The Supreme Court's position on busing illustrates two key points about its decisions. First, the Court is an extremely important policymaking body; some of its rulings, including its busing decisions, are as consequential as nearly any law passed by Congress or any executive action taken by the president. Second, the Court has considerable discretion in its rulings. The *Swann* decision was not based on any literal reading of the law: the justices invoked *their* interpretation of the Fourteenth Amendment's equal-protection clause.

The Supreme Court's policymaking significance and discretion have been sources of controversy throughout the country's history, but the controversies have perhaps never been livelier than during recent decades. The Court has become more extensively involved in policymaking for many of the same

[4]See Michael J. Perry, *The Constitution, the Courts, and Human Rights: An Inquiry into the Legitimacy of Constitutional Policymaking by the Judiciary* (New Haven, Conn.: Yale University Press, 1982).
[5]Raoul Berger, *Government by Judiciary: The Transformation of the Fourteenth Amendment* (Cambridge, Mass.: Harvard University Press, 1977).

reasons that Congress and the president have been thrust into new policy areas and more deeply into old ones. Social and economic change have required government to play a larger role in society, and this development has generated a seemingly endless series of new legal controversies. The greater interconnectedness of society and policy has also meant that judicial action will have a more far-reaching impact than it had in early periods when American life was slower and more compartmentalized.

This chapter examines Supreme Court policymaking, describing how legal and political factors come together to influence the Court's decisions. The chapter also discusses the controversy surrounding the Court's policy role. The principle of self-government asserts that lawmaking majorities have the power to decide society's policies. Yet the principles of liberty and equality are checks on the power of lawmaking majorities and justify a significant policy role for the Court. A critical question is how far the Court's members, who are not elected, ought to go in substituting their policy judgments for those of officials who are elected by the people. The main points made in this chapter are the following:

★ *Although the justices of the Supreme Court have discretion in their decisions, their alternatives are constrained by existing law.* In deciding cases, justices are compelled to consider applicable constitutional law, statutory law, and precedent.

★ *Political factors have a major influence on the Supreme Court's decisions.* The Court is somewhat responsive to political officials and to the public, although the direction of the Court is set chiefly by the political beliefs of the justices themselves.

★ *The Supreme Court has become an increasingly powerful policymaking body in recent decades, although it still plays less of a policymaking role than Congress or the president.* Many of the Court's leading decisions have been controversial and have raised the question of whether the Court has usurped the powers of elected institutions. Advocates of judicial restraint claim that it has overstepped its authority, whereas judicial activists say that the Court's enlarged policy role is constitutionally appropriate.

## Legal Influences on Supreme Court Decisions

The justices of the Supreme Court are political officials: they head one of three coequal branches of the national government. Yet the justices are not political officers in the same sense as members of Congress or the president. The justices serve in a legal institution and make their decisions in a legal context. As a consequence, their discretionary power is less than that of elected officials. Existing laws constrain the Supreme Court by preventing it from making choices that cannot be justified in legal terms. The effect is that justices approach each decision as a matter of interpreting the law.[6] In deciding an issue, the justices rely not simply on personal preference but also on the legal principles that they see as applicable to the case they are considering. When asked by a friend to "do justice," Oliver Wendell Holmes, Jr., replied, "That is not my job. My job is to play the game according to the rules."[7] In playing according to the

> ★ ANALYZE THE ISSUE
>
> **The Political Becomes the Judicial**
> The Supreme Court has distinguished between political questions (within the authority of elected officials) and judicial questions (within the authority of the judiciary). However, the Court sometimes decides that a political question has become a judicial question, as in its rulings on abortion (1973), apportionment of state legislatures (1963), and school desegregation (1954). Is the political–judicial distinction therefore a phony one—merely a line drawn where the Supreme Court chooses to draw it at any given moment? Why, or why not?

[6]Lawrence Baum, *The Supreme Court* (Washington, D.C.: Congressional Quarterly Press, 1981), 117.
[7]Quoted in Charles P. Curtis, *Law and Large as Life* (New York: Simon & Schuster, 1959), 156–157.

rules, the justices engage in a creative legal process that requires them to identify the facts of the case, determine and sometimes formulate the relevant legal principles or rules, and then apply them to the case at hand.

## THE CONSTRAINTS OF THE FACTS

The Constitution prohibits the courts from ruling in the absence of a case brought before it. Thus the Supreme Court, unlike Congress or the president, is not free to make judgments at any time and on any issue it chooses. It can rule only on actual cases brought before it by persons who claim to be harmed by applications of existing law.

A basic distinction in any legal case is between "the facts" and "the laws." The **facts** of a case, as determined by trial courts, are the relevant circumstances of a legal dispute or offense. In the case of a person accused of murder, for example, key facts would include evidence about the murder and whether the rights of the accused were respected by police in the course of their investigation. The facts of a case are crucial because they determine which law or laws are applicable to the case.

The Supreme Court must respond to the facts of a dispute. Thus a case that centers on whether a defendant's right to a fair trial has been abridged cannot be used as an occasion to pronounce judgment on a corporate merger. This restriction is a very substantial one. Consider the period in the 1960s when the Supreme Court broadened most of the due-process protections in the Fourth through Eighth amendments to include states' criminal proceedings. The first of these rulings came in *Mapp* v. *Ohio* (1961), discussed in Chapter 5.[8] The case arose when the defendant claimed that police had violated her Fourth Amendment protection against unreasonable search and seizure. In deciding that the Fourteenth Amendment's due-process clause embraced this protection, the Court did not also rule that all other due-process guarantees were similarly protected. The facts of the *Mapp* case limited the Court's judgment to the search-and-seizure issue. Only through subsequent cases did the Supreme Court decide, one by one, that certain other rights were also protected by the Fourteenth Amendment's due-process clause.

## THE CONSTRAINTS OF THE LAW

In deciding cases, the Supreme Court is constrained by existing laws. As distinct from the facts of a case, the **laws** of a case are the constitutional provisions, legislative statutes, or judicial precedents that apply to the situation. To use an obvious comparison, the laws governing a case of alleged murder differ from the laws that apply to an antitrust suit. When addressing a case, the Supreme Court—or any other court, for that matter—must determine which laws are relevant.

### Interpretation of the Constitution

The Constitution is a sparsely worded document, and for that reason its language is open to interpretation. For example, the Constitution grants

---

[8]*Mapp* v. *Ohio*, 367 U.S. 643 (1961).

The Supreme Court is guided by the Constitution and yet is required to give meaning to it. In the 1930s, for example, the Court reversed its earlier position and held that Congress's commerce power (under Article I) applied to manufacturing practices, which thus became subject to federal regulation. (Joseph Nettis/Photo Researchers)

*We are under a Constitution, but the Constitution is what the judges say it is, and the judiciary is the safeguard of our liberty and of our property under the Constitution.*

Charles Evans Hughes

Congress the power to regulate interstate commerce, but the meaning of "commerce" is not spelled out, and the Court has defined it in various ways during the nation's history. Until the early twentieth century the Court held that factory practices were not "commerce" but "production" and were thus beyond Congress's legislative authority. Now, however, the Court holds that the commerce clause embraces nearly every business activity. The Court's varying interpretations of the commerce clause have reflected the nation's changing economic needs. A function of the judiciary is to apply rules made in the past in ways that are meaningful in the present. The U.S. industrial economy of today bears no resemblance to the agrarian economy of the late eighteenth century, and only an updated interpretation of the commerce clause could meet today's needs.

Nevertheless, the Court respects the purpose and intent of the Constitution: the justices strive for reasonable interpretations of its provisions. The question for the justices is not how the writers of the Constitution would settle today's disputes by yesterday's standards but what the Framers had in mind by a particular provision. For example, in deciding whether wiretapping and other electronic means of surveillance are covered by the Fourth Amendment's prohibition against unreasonable searches and seizures, the issue is what the amendment was designed to protect. Obviously, the Framers could not have meant to protect people against wiretapping per se; electronic surveillance was not invented until 150 years after the Fourth Amendment was ratified. But the Fourth Amendment was intended to protect individuals against snooping by government into their private lives; for this reason, the Court has held that government cannot indiscriminately tap people's telephones.

## Interpretation of Statutes

Most of the federal law that the Supreme Court rules upon is statutory law, enacted by Congress, and administrative regulations, developed by the bu-

★ ANALYZE THE ISSUE

**Busing as a Constitutional Issue**
Using your knowledge of the Constitution and the Supreme Court's role in the U.S. political system, defend the Court's reasoning in cases involving busing to achieve racial integration in the schools. Now, using that same knowledge, criticize the Court's reasoning in busing cases. Which constitutional argument seems more compelling to you?

reaucracy from statutory provisions. When a statute is challenged in a case, the Court will initially see whether its meaning can be determined by common sense (the "plain-meaning rule"). However, the Supreme Court seldom hears cases in which the law's meaning is unmistakable, because such cases are usually resolved in lower courts.

Congress occasionally structures its debate to ensure that courts will later be readily able to understand its intent. For example, the Civil Rights Act of 1964 was designed in part to prohibit racial discrimination in public accommodations, such as restaurants, hotels, and movie theaters. The act was based principally on the commerce clause, which the Court had already interpreted broadly. In the congressional debate, the legislation's supporters stressed the adverse effects of racial discrimination on the free flow of commerce. As its supporters in Congress had anticipated, the Civil Rights Act's ban on racial discrimination in public accommodations was later challenged in court. The Supreme Court upheld the law, noting that "the legislative history of the Act is replete with evidence of the burdens that discrimination by race or color places upon interstate commerce."[9]

The Court makes its mark on legislation by filling in the gaps left by Congress. Congress can seldom anticipate all the specific applications of a legislative act and therefore uses general language to state the act's purpose. Legislation is often a product of political compromise, which can also result in ambiguous provisions. Such vagueness can give rise to disputes over the implementation of laws, and an individual who is adversely affected by a law-enforcement or administrative official's judgment as to the meaning of a law can seek to have this assessment reversed in the courts.[10]

*What has once been settled by a precedent will not be unsettled overnight, for certainty and uniformity are gains not lightly to be sacrificed. Above all is this true when honest men have shaped their conduct on the faith of the pronouncement.*

Benjamin Cardozo

*The law must be stable, but it must not stand still.*

Roscoe Pound

### Interpretation of Precedent

We saw in Chapter 24 that the English common-law tradition that a court's decision on a case should be consistent with previous rulings is called **precedent.** The philosophy underlying the tradition of adherence to precedent is known as *stare decisis* (Latin for "to stand by things that have been settled")—the doctrine that principles of law, once established, should be accepted as authoritative in all subsequent similar cases.

Many cases brought before the Supreme Court do not have a clear precedent. When precedent is more or less obvious, lower courts usually apply it, and the Supreme Court is unlikely to review such cases. The cases that the Supreme Court selects for a full hearing and decision may interest it precisely because their facts differ significantly from those of previous cases. The justices may argue that they are following precedent, while actually they are modifying it substantially. In 1984, for instance, the Court said that the exclusionary rule (discussed in Chapter 5) did not apply to evidence obtained by an illegal search warrant if police obtained it "in good faith."[11] This ruling weakened and substantially modified precedent regarding the exclusion of evidence. At times

★ ANALYZE THE ISSUE

**Precedent as Assurance of Predictability**
Justice Oliver Wendell Holmes, Jr., claimed that law is founded on the precept of reasonable expectations: people make choices on the assumption that the law will not change overnight. In your judgment, is precedent as important as Holmes claimed it is? Why, or why not?

---

[9]*Heart of Atlanta Motel* v. *United States,* 371 U.S. 241 (1964).
[10]Samuel Krislov, *The Supreme Court in the Political Process* (New York: Macmillan, 1965), 76–77.
[11]*United States* v. *Leon,* 463 U.S. 1206 (1984).

## SOURCES OF LAW THAT CONSTRAIN THE SUPREME COURT'S DECISIONS

*U.S. Constitution:* The Supreme Court is bound by the provisions of the U.S. Constitution. The sparseness of its wording, however, requires the Constitution to be applied in the light of present circumstances. Thus the justices are accorded a substantial degree of discretion in their constitutional judgments.

*Statutory law:* The Supreme Court is constrained by statutes and by administrative regulations derived from the provisions of statutes. Most laws, however, are somewhat vague in their provisions and often have unanticipated applications. As a result, the justices have some freedom in deciding cases based on statutes.

*Precedent:* The Supreme Court is bound by precedent (or *stare decisis*), which is a legal principle developed in earlier court decisions. Because not all cases have a clear precedent, however, the justices have some discretion in their evaluation of the way earlier cases apply to a current case.

the Supreme Court disavows precedent entirely. In recent decades the Court has overturned an average of four precedents each year.[12]

Nevertheless, precedent is an important constraint on the Supreme Court. To persist in ignoring precedent would be to direct the law onto an unpredictable course, creating confusion and uncertainty among those who must make choices on the basis of their understanding of the law. Supreme Court justices are fully aware of their responsibility to help maintain legal consistency. "The life of the law has not been logic: it has been experience," Oliver Wendell Holmes, Jr., wrote. "In order to know what is [the law], we must know what it has been."[13]

## Political Influences on Supreme Court Decisions

Any Supreme Court opinion of reasonable length and importance contains references to previous rulings or to the language of the Constitution or statute law. It would be inaccurate to conclude, however, that the Court is merely following the path laid down by existing legal principles. The law, Martin Shapiro notes, "is never entirely clear," and the Court "always has some discretion."[14] The extent of the Court's discretion is most obvious in the frequency of disagreement among the justices over how cases should be settled. On most cases of major significance, the justices are divided in their opinions. Each side has legal arguments for its position, but existing law has not clearly led all justices to the same conclusion.

The principal reason for divisions among the justices is that Supreme Court opinions reflect not only legal influences but also political ones, which come from both outside and inside the Court.

[12]Congressional Research Service, *The Constitution of the United States of America: Analysis and Interpretation* (Washington, D.C.: U.S. Government Printing Office, 1979).
[13]Oliver Wendell Holmes, Jr., *The Common Law* (Boston: Little, Brown, 1881), 1.
[14]Martin Shapiro, *The Supreme Court and Administrative Agencies* (New York: Free Press, 1968), 71.

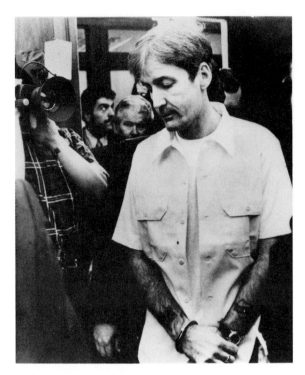

In 1976 the Supreme Court cited public opinion polls in a ruling that upheld the death penalty. The decision paved the way for the execution by firing squad of convicted murderer Gary Gilmore in Utah in 1977—the first execution in the United States in ten years. (AP/Wide World).

## "OUTSIDE" INFLUENCES ON COURT DECISIONS

The Court responds selectively to the expectations of the general public, interest groups, and elected officials, particularly the president and members of Congress. The precise impact of these outside pressures cannot be measured, but judicial experts agree that the Court is affected by them.

### The Force of Public Opinion

Supreme Court justices are responsive to public opinion, although much less so than are elected officials. In rare instances, public opinion becomes part of the formal basis for a decision. In its ruling in *Gregg* v. *Georgia* (1976), for example, the Court cited the results of public opinion polling in upholding the constitutionality of the death penalty.[15] In other cases the Court has tailored its rulings in an effort to gain public support or dampen public resistance. In the *Brown* case, for example, the justices, recognizing that school desegregation would be an explosive issue in the South, attempted to defuse the reaction by requiring only that desegregation take place "with all deliberate speed" rather than immediately or on a fixed timetable.

The Court's apparent strategy is to stay close enough to popular opinion to avoid seriously eroding public support for the judiciary.[16] To make some of its decisions effective, the Court depends almost entirely on voluntary compliance by the public. For example, the day still begins with a prayer in some public schools in the United States, but the practice was stopped in most schools in 1962, when the Supreme Court ruled that school prayers violated the First

[15]*Gregg* v. *Georgia,* 428 U.S. 153 (1976).
[16]Stephen L. Wasby, *The Supreme Court in the Federal Judicial System* (New York: Holt, Rinehart and Winston, 1978), 53.

Amendment provision that church and state must remain separate.[17] Most Americans have enough respect for the Supreme Court and the rule of law to abide by judicial decisions. This tendency, however, rests on the public's perception of the legitimacy of the Court's rulings, and this perception depends in part on the Court's sensitivity to public opinion.

The Court does not have to follow public opinion slavishly in order to keep its authoritative position. Only a few of its decisions affect a large portion of the public directly, and most Americans do not want to endure the legal difficulties that might attend violation of judicial policy. Moreover, the fact that public opinion on controversial issues is always divided means that the justices will not stand alone no matter which side of such an issue they favor. Recent polls, for example, indicate that Americans are about evenly split on the Court's position that women have the right to an abortion in the early months of pregnancy.

## Pressure from Interest Groups

The Supreme Court has become an attractive alternative for interests that would have difficulty achieving their policy goals through legislative action. Although legal action is expensive (the cost of carrying a case all the way to the Supreme Court can run as high as $500,000), it often costs less than lobbying Congress on a major issue. And obviously some interests, particularly those represented by persons who are in an unpopular or underprivileged minority, have a better chance of success in a legal suit than with an elected institution. Legislators usually avoid issues that may hurt them at the polls, whereas justices do not have to worry about reelection.

Some groups that have made extensive use of the judicial alternative are the American Civil Liberties Union, the Environmental Defense Fund, and the National Association for the Advancement of Colored People. Such groups are

[17]*Engel* v. *Vitale*, 370 U.S. 421 (1962).

Thurgood Marshall (*center*) was the special counsel for the NAACP lawyers who argued the *Brown* school desegregation case before the Supreme Court in 1954. Other members of the team were George E. C. Hayes (*left*) and James Nabret, Jr. (*right*). In 1967 Marshall was appointed to the Supreme Court. (UPI/Bettmann Newsphotos)

obviously more likely to succeed when they correctly perceive where the Supreme Court is heading. The NAACP, for example, noting that the Supreme Court was nibbling away at the "separate but equal" precedent of *Plessy* v. *Ferguson,* searched out cases that would test the precedent in the area of public school segregation. One of the cases undertaken by the NAACP was that of a Topeka, Kansas, schoolchild, Linda Brown. Brown's case, of course, became the vehicle by which the Court established a new precedent—namely, that state-sponsored racial segregation of public schools violates the equal-protection clause of the Fourteenth Amendment.

Through *amicus curiae* ("friend of the court") briefs the Supreme Court can obtain more precise expressions of a group's opinion. When invited by the Court to submit such a brief, an interest group gets an opportunity to explain its position on a pending case directly to the Court. In some cases (including *Brown*), the Supreme Court has requested such briefs from twenty or more interest groups in order to obtain a broad sense of how various interests line up on an issue.

## The Leverage of Public Officials

The influence of groups and the general public on the Court is usually registered indirectly, through the elected branches of government. In response to public and group pressure, elected officials try to persuade the Court to hand down rulings favored by their constituents. Both Congress and the president have powerful means of influencing the Court.

Congress is constitutionally empowered to establish the Court's size and appellate jurisdiction, and Congress can rewrite legislation that it feels the Court has misinterpreted. Although Congress has seldom confronted the Court directly, it has often demonstrated displeasure with Supreme Court rulings, in the hope that the justices would respond favorably. When the Court handed down its *Swann* decision endorsing busing, for example, members of Congress threatened to pass legislation that would prevent the Court from hearing appeals of busing cases. Although busing remains a Court policy, it has not been used to its full potential in part because it is unpopular with many members of Congress.

The president is responsible for implementing the decisions of the Court and also affects its work by pursuing or neglecting possible legal controversies, thereby influencing the justices' choice of cases to review. Under President Ronald Reagan, for instance, the Justice Department vigorously backed several suits challenging affirmative action programs and made no great attempt to push cases that would have expanded the rights of racial minorities and women. By these actions, the Reagan administration pressured the Court on issues of civil rights.

In general, the Court avoids intense conflicts with elected officials when it can do so without substantial damage to its authority or to legal principles. This approach is evident in the Court's restraint in its use of judicial review. In the course of its history, the Court has invalidated on constitutional grounds slightly more than 100 federal laws and 1,000 state laws and local ordinances (see Table 25-1), a rather small number in the context of two centuries of legislative output. The Court prefers to decide cases on statutory grounds whenever it can. This approach is less confrontational and gives elected officials

TABLE 25-1 Number of Federal Laws and of State and Local Laws Held to Be Unconstitutional Wholly or in Part, 1790–1983

| Period | Federal Laws | State and Local Laws |
|---|---|---|
| 1790–1839 | 1 | 19 |
| 1840–1889 | 17 | 121 |
| 1890–1919 | 19 | 194 |
| 1920–1939 | 28 | 232 |
| 1940–1959 | 6 | 126 |
| 1960–1969 | 16 | 140 |
| 1970–1979 | 19 | 193 |
| 1980–1983 | 8 | 63 |
| All periods | 114 | 1,088 |

SOURCE: Lawrence Baum, *The Supreme Court* (Washington, D.C.: Congressional Quarterly Press, 1985), 171, 173.

the option of changing the law if they disagree with the Court's interpretation of it.

Although it is willing to make such concessions, the Court views certain positions as basic to individual rights rather than as matters of majority opinion. In such instances the Court seldom lets the public or elected officials dictate its course of action. Despite continuing criticism of its 1962 decision on school prayer, for instance, the Court has not backed down from its position, refusing even to uphold a 1985 Alabama statute that provided for a minute of silent meditation each day in its public schools. The school-prayer issue illustrates the crucial distinction between the judiciary and the elected branches mentioned earlier, and helps to explain why the policies of the judiciary are more often at odds with public opinion: elected officials are chosen by popular majorities and remain in power through public support, whereas justices are not popularly elected and hold their appointments indefinitely.

The Supreme Court resists pressure from the public and from elected officials on some issues, such as school prayer, that it considers to be questions of individual rights rather than of majority opinion. (Bruce Flynn/Picture Group)

Supreme Court justice Harry Blackmun, who wrote the majority opinion in *Roe* v. *Wade* (1973). (Dennis Brack/Black Star)

## "INSIDE" INFLUENCES: THE JUSTICES' OWN POLITICAL BELIEFS

Most scholars contend that the justices' personal beliefs exercise the most significant influence on their legal opinions.[18] The justices are frequently divided in their opinions, and the nature of this division can often be predicted on the basis of the justices' differing political attitudes. The Court's "liberals" will be on one side of a given issue and its "conservatives" will be on the other. On fair-trial cases in the 1970s, for example, justices William Brennan and Thurgood Marshall, both Democrats when they were appointed to the Court, were "liberals," meaning that they were highly protective of the rights of persons accused of crimes. They were opposed most often on criminal rights cases by justices Warren Burger and William Rehnquist, both of whom were Republicans when they were appointed to the Court and were "conservative" in the sense that they usually sided with the police when police practices conflicted with the rights of the accused. In one four-year period Burger and Rehnquist agreed with each other on 80 percent of the Court's decisions and voted with Brennan and Marshall on less than 50 percent of the cases. Brennan and Marshall, for their part, agreed with each other on more than 90 percent of the cases.[19]

Although such patterns are revealing, the relationship between justices' political beliefs and their decisions is not a simple one. Liberalism and conservatism are not the same among justices as among elected officials. Because justices are constrained by legal principles, their political differences, though not small or inconsequential, are seldom total. For example, the conservative-leaning Burger Court modified substantially the criminal justice rulings of the more liberal Warren Court, but did not repudiate the Warren Court's most important legacy in this area—the principle that the Fourteenth Amendment provides substantial protections for the accused in state trial proceedings. Moreover, some justices may be liberal, moderate, *or* conservative, depending on the issue in question.[20] For example, Justice Byron White, who was appointed by the Democratic president John F. Kennedy, proved to be fairly conservative on civil liberties issues, particularly the rights of the accused, but moderate on questions of governmental regulation of the economy.

Most Supreme Court justices hold relatively stable political views during their tenure. Some justices, including Oliver Wendell Holmes, Jr., Earl Warren, and, more recently, Harry Blackmun, have taken a few years on the Court to establish their positions. When he first joined the Court, Blackmun had a voting record that was so close to Chief Justice Warren Burger's that he and Burger, who were from the same home state, were called "the Minnesota Twins." But Blackmun gradually moved toward the views of the Court's liberal members, particularly on issues of civil liberties. In general, however, most justices stick with their legal positions throughout their time on the nation's highest bench.

As a result, major shifts in the Court's position usually occur in conjunction with changes in its membership. In the late 1950s, for example, the Court

[18]For a general discussion of this research, see Henry R. Glick, *Courts, Politics, and Justice* (New York: McGraw-Hill, 1983), ch. 9.

[19]David Rhode and Harold Spaeth, *Supreme Court Decision Making* (San Francisco: W. H. Freeman, 1976), 138.

[20]See Glendon Schubert, *The Judicial Mind* (Evanston, Ill.: Northwestern University Press, 1965); Glendon Schubert, *The Judicial Mind Revisited* (New York: Oxford University Press, 1974).

moved away from its traditional position that Congress could impose curbs on political expression for reasons of national security. This development was largely an outgrowth of the appointment of new justices who believed that the First Amendment right of free expression deserved stronger judicial protection.

Shifts in the Court's direction are related to political trends. Although justices are more or less free to follow their own beliefs, they are political appointees who are nominated in part because their legal positions seem to be compatible with those of the president. Pointing out that a new justice has been appointed on average every two years in the Court's history, Robert Dahl infers that the policy views of the Court will never be substantially at odds for very long with those of elected officials.[21]

Nevertheless, the Court's membership has its unpredictable aspects. The turnover of justices depends on retirement and death, which occur irregularly. Whether a president will be able to appoint several, one, or no justices is never certain. The Republican president Richard Nixon made four Supreme Court appointments during his six years in office, whereas the Democratic president Jimmy Carter made none during his four-year term. Moreover, the influence of new appointees depends on the size of the Court's majority. Important issues have often been decided by 5–4 votes, and the addition of a single new justice has altered the majority. At other times, however, the existing majority has been more substantial, so two or more new members have been needed to shift the balance.

## Judicial Power and Democratic Government

The Supreme Court symbolizes John Adams' characterization of the U.S. political system as "a government of laws, and not of men." The characterization has value as myth—the vision of impartial justice is undeniably compelling—but the ideal has never fully described the reality. As John Schmidhauser has noted, "Laws are made, enforced, and interpreted by men."[22] The Supreme Court's decisions bear the indelible imprint of its justices' political beliefs.

The significance of the justices' power is enhanced by the fact that the Court is not a democratic institution. The justices are not elected and cannot easily be held accountable by the public for their decisions—a contradiction of the principle of majority rule. The justices' power is justified by the Court's authority to interpret the Constitution. Because the United States has a constitutional system that places checks on the will of the majority, there is obviously an important role in the system for a countermajoritarian institution such as the Court. Yet the Court's decisions invariably reflect the political philosophy of its justices. They constitute a tiny political elite that wields significant power.[23]

This power is most dramatically evident when the Court declares unconstitutional a law enacted by Congress. Such acts of judicial review place the

[21]Robert A. Dahl, "The Supreme Court and Majority Control," in S. Sidney Ulmer, ed., Courts, Law, and Judicial Processes (New York: Free Press, 1981), 214; see also Richard Funston, "The Supreme Court and Critical Elections," American Political Science Review 69 (September 1975): 795–811.
[22]John Schmidhauser, The Supreme Court (New York: Holt, Rinehart and Winston, 1964), 6.
[23]David M. O'Brien, Storm Center (New York: Norton, 1986), 14–15.

The courts are necessarily creative in formulating judicial policy in response to social and technological change. For example, despite objections from some the courts have held that adding color to black-and-white movies is not a violationg of copyright laws. Shown here are black-and-white and color-added versions of the same scene from the movie *Saint Joan*. (Colorization, Inc.)

judgment of nine unelected justices over the decision of 535 elected representatives. Moreover, the Court's judgment tends to be final. Although Court decisions can be reversed, the process, particularly in the case of constitutional rulings, is formidably difficult. In the nation's history only a few constitutional amendments (such as the Sixteenth, which permits a federal income tax) have reversed Supreme Court decisions.

## A CREATIVE POLICY ROLE

Of course, there are limits on the Court's power. As we have seen, the Court is constrained by procedures, legal principles, and the limits of what public officials and the American people will accept. Its range of discretion and effective action is narrower than that of either Congress or the president.

However, the judiciary is an important and creative policymaking branch of the government. Courts do more than apply the law: they establish law. The English tradition of common law, which was adopted by the United States and which defines most relationships between private parties, is judge-made policy. In addition, when a legislative body enacts a law, it necessarily does so without knowing all the circumstances in which the law may apply in the future. When unforeseen situations arise, judges must make creative decisions. For example, judges have recently had to decide whether copyright laws, enacted before the technological advances that made possible the "colorization" of black-and-white films, permit such coloring.[24]

The structure of the U.S. political system forces a creative role on the judiciary. When the U.S. Constitution established the judiciary as a coequal branch of government, it broke from the English tradition whereby courts had an active role in defining private relationships (*private law*) but were not allowed to define governmental relationships or the relationship of individuals to government (*public law*). Under the U.S. constitutional system, the judiciary in general and the Supreme Court in particular were granted a major role in the sphere of public-law policymaking. The Court has the responsibility of interpreting the Constitution, overseeing federalism and the separation of powers, and defining individual rights.

*The Court bows to the lessons of experience and the force of better reasoning, recognizing that the process of trial and error, so fruitful in the physical sciences, is appropriate also in the judicial function.*

Louis D. Brandeis

[24]Richard Posner, "What Am I? A Potted Plant?" *New Republic*, September 28, 1987, 24.

## THE DEBATE OVER THE PROPER ROLE OF THE SUPREME COURT

As we noted in this chapter's introduction, the Supreme Court's policy role has broadened substantially in recent decades in response to social change and new government programs. As a result, the Court's authority has been extended into areas that were once regarded as virtually the exclusive domain of elected officials.[25] The Supreme Court has declared, for example, that communities in some circumstances are compelled to bus students in order to integrate the public schools, that women have the right to an early abortion without state interference, and that welfare eligibility does not require a long period of residency in a state. Some of the Court's recent rulings have not merely forbidden lawmaking majorities to take certain actions but have prescribed actions they must take, such as providing better facilities and programs for inmates of prisons and mental hospitals.

The reactions of liberal and conservative groups to the Supreme Court's recent decisions have depended largely on the degree to which those rulings accord with their own views. However, the question of judicial power goes beyond partisan politics to the basic issue of **legitimacy**—the proper authority of the judiciary in a political system based on the principle of majority rule. In recent decades the Court at times has acted almost legislatively by ordering broad social policies, such as busing and prison reform. In doing so the Court has restricted the policymaking authority of the states, has narrowed legislative discretion, and has made judicial action an effective alternative to election victory for certain interests.[26]

The Court's actions have raised important questions. Has the Court exceeded its intended authority under the U.S. constitutional system? Has it robbed lawmaking majorities of decisions that are rightfully theirs to make? There are two general schools of thought on these issues: those of judicial restraint and

[25]Donald Horowitz, *The Courts and Social Policy* (Washington, D.C.: Brookings Institution, 1977), 5–9.
[26]See Stuart Sheingold, *The Politics of Rights* (New Haven, Conn.: Yale University Press, 1974).

★ ANALYZE THE ISSUE

**The Judiciary's Power**
Alexander Hamilton called the judiciary the weakest branch of government. How do the Supreme Court's responses in cases involving racial equality illustrate Hamilton's view? Does the Court's behavior also suggest that Hamilton, though correct in his comparison of the relative power of the judiciary as against that of the executive and legislative branches, may have underestimated the power inherent in judicial action?

A current controversy is whether the judiciary should get involved in decisions that were once regarded as reserved for legislatures. For example, should the courts be entitled to require the states to improve prison conditions, as by offering training programs like this computer course at Shawnee Prison in Illinois? (Rick Falco/ Black Star)

judicial activism. Although these terms are somewhat imprecise and often misused, they are helpful in efforts to clarify opposing philosophical positions on the Court's proper role.[27]

### The Doctrine of Judicial Restraint

The doctrine of **judicial restraint** holds that the judiciary should be highly deferential to the judgment of legislatures. The restraint doctrine rests on a presumption that elected lawmakers are acting constitutionally and should have broad discretionary authority to decide policy. Although the restraint doctrine does not insist that the judiciary should always defer to lawmaking majorities, it does hold that broad issues of the public good should be decided in nearly all cases by the majority through legislation enacted by elected officials. The job of judges is to work within the confines of these laws, seeking to discover their application to specific cases, rather than searching for new principles that essentially change these laws. In the words of a Reagan administration assistant, Stephen Markman, who was responsible for screening potential appointees to the federal bench: "We want judges who understand their role is not to act as munificent wise men imposing what they consider to be prudent public policy . . . and who respect the will of the popular branches of government."[28]

Advocates of judicial restraint support their position with two major arguments. First, they contend that when the Supreme Court assumes policy functions that traditionally belong to elected institutions, it undermines the fundamental premise of self-government: the right of the majority to choose society's policies.[29] Second, judicial self-restraint is admired because it protects the Court's authority. The power of the Court, it is argued, depends ultimately on public respect for its authority. The Court must be concerned with **compliance**—with whether its decisions will be respected and obeyed (see box). The Court's decisions can differ substantially in practice from what the justices had in mind.[30] The Court has no enforcement mechanism of its own and depends for its effectiveness on the support of the public, law-enforcement officials, and elected representatives. If the Court thwarts the majority's desires, public confidence in its legitimacy is endangered, and other officials may act to undermine the Court's decisions.[31]

Advocates of judicial restraint acknowledge that established law is never so precise as to provide exact answers to every question raised by every case or controversy, so the courts should be empowered to provide remedies in some instances. And in rare circumstances, decisive judicial action may be both appropriate and necessary, as in the historic *Brown* v. *Board of Education* decision (1954). Although the Constitution provides no explicit basis for school desegregation, government-supported racial discrimination violates the principle of

[27]The references cited in the following sections are taken substantially from Henry J. Abraham, "The Judicial Function under the Constitution," *News for Teachers of Political Science* 41 (Spring 1984): 12–14; see also Stephen C. Halpern and Charles M. Lamb, eds., *Supreme Court Activism and Restraint* (Lexington, Mass.: Lexington Books, 1982).
[28]Quoted in Kathryn Kahler, "Will Numerous Reagan Appointees Mold a New Judiciary?" *Syracuse Herald-American*, January 24, 1988, El.
[29]Abraham, "Judicial Function," 14.
[30]See Charles A. Johnson and Bradley C. Canon, *Judicial Policies* (Washington, D.C.: Congressional Quarterly Press, 1984).
[31]Alexander M. Bickel, *The Supreme Court and the Idea of Progress* (New Haven, Conn.: Yale University Press, 1978), 173–181.

# THE DIFFICULTIES OF COMPLIANCE: THE EXAMPLE OF *MAPP* v. *OHIO*

In making broad policy decisions, the Supreme Court encounters various limits, including its inability to ensure compliance. It must hope that lower officials will adhere faithfully to its rulings, as they do sometimes but not always. When the Court ruled in *Mapp* v. *Ohio* in 1961 that evidence obtained by police through illegal search and seizure is inadmissible in state trial proceedings, some police departments responded by developing careful search procedures for their officers to follow when they apprehended suspects or investigated alleged wrongdoings. Other police departments, however, looked for ways to evade the Court's ruling, usually by covering up instances in which police officers obtained evidence through illegal search and seizure. After researching the subject, Bradley Canon concluded that *Mapp* reduced the

national rate of illegal search and seizure only moderately and at the cost of encouraging other actions detrimental to the criminal justice system. Canon found documented evidence that some police officers perjured themselves when they were asked in court about search procedures, and some district attorneys encouraged defendants victimized by illegal search and seizure to plea-bargain rather than seek to have the illegally obtained evidence ruled inadmissible.

SOURCE: Bradley C. Canon, "Testing the Effectiveness of Civil Liberties Policies at the State and Federal Levels: The Case of the Exclusionary Rule," *American Politics Quarterly* 5 (January, 1977): 57–82.

equal justice under the law. Louis Lusky is among the advocates of judicial restraint who argue that the broad moral language of the Fourteenth Amendment, which says that no state shall deny any person the equal protection of its laws, was adequate justification for the Court to require state governments to end their policy of segregated public schools.[32]

Yet many other advocates of judicial restraint see no constitutional justification for the Court's busing and abortion decisions. In *Roe* v. *Wade* (1973), for example, the Court struck down state laws prohibiting abortion, and it has upheld its position in subsequent rulings. The Court has justified these rulings not only by citing common law and medical advances but also by claiming that the Fourteenth Amendment implicitly protects a "right of privacy." The Constitution enumerates many specific individual rights, but privacy is not among them. Although most advocates of judicial restraint agree that some right of privacy is implied by the Constitution's guarantee of personal liberty, they do not believe the right is as broad as the Court's majority in *Roe* v. *Wade* claimed it to be. In their view, abortion is an issue that should have been left in the hands of lawmaking majorities in the states.

To advocates of judicial restraint, *Roe* v. *Wade* is an example of judicial interference in the exercise of powers that belong rightfully to the majority through its elected representatives. The question of whether the majority's policies are enlightened or stupid is beside the point. The issue is simply the majority's right to decide for itself the policies, whatever their merits or defects, by which society will be governed. As Justice John Harlan argued in a 1964 opinion: "The Constitution is not a panacea for every blot upon the public welfare; nor should this Court, ordained as a legal body, be thought of as a general haven for reform movements."[33]

[32]Louis Lusky, *By What Right? A Commentary on the Supreme Court's Power to Revise the Constitution* (Charlottesville, Va.: Michie, 1975), 214–216.
[33]*Reynolds* v. *Sims*, 377 U.S. 533 (1964).

★ ANALYZE THE ISSUE

**Roe v. Wade as Judicial Activism**
*Roe* v. *Wade*, the 1973 decision that legalized abortion on the basis of a woman's right to privacy, is often cited as an example of judicial activism. Why? Would a Supreme Court decision that reversed *Roe* v. *Wade* also constitute judicial activism? (Consider the fact that the Supreme Court has never repudiated a right that has previously been established in law.)

Some advocates of judicial restraint believe that the Supreme Court had no consitutional basis for its *Roe v. Wade* decision legalizing abortion in 1973. (Erica Stone/Photo Researchers)

### The Doctrine of Judicial Activism

In contrast to the judicial-restraint position is the idea that the courts should take a generous view of judicial power and involve themselves extensively in interpreting and enlarging upon the law. Although advocates of this doctrine, which is known as **judicial activism,** acknowledge the principles of majority rule and legislative policymaking, they claim that the courts should not be overly deferential to the judgments of elected officials. While admitting the value of maintaining existing legal principles, advocates of judicial activism are inclined to believe that courts should not be too hesitant about developing new principles whenever they see a compelling need to do so, even if this action puts them into conflict with the executive and legislative branches.

The doctrine of judicial activism is associated primarily with legalists who believe that the Supreme Court is obligated to promote social justice by enlarging upon the rights of individuals. These liberal activists are in the centuries-old tradition of **equity,** which holds that courts should resort to general principles of fairness when existing law is insufficient. Liberal judicial activists argue, for example, that fairness for black children requires that in some circumstances some children should be bused to achieve school integration. This reasoning does not extend to all issues of social justice. For example, liberal judicial activists do not regard fundamental decisions about the distribution of wealth as falling within the realm of the judiciary. But in areas where social justice depends substantially on protection of the rights of the individual, the Court is said to have a responsibility to act positively and decisively.[34]

Not all judicial activists are of this liberal persuasion. When Robert Bork was being considered for a seat on the Supreme Court in 1987, his opponents called him a judicial activist, citing his expressed willingness to overturn established

[34]Abraham, ''Judicial Function,'' 13.

# JUDICIAL ACTIVISM AND THEORIES OF LAW

There are three major theories of law, two of which provide some justification for judicial activism.

The exception is *analytical jurisprudence,* which holds that the law should be applied not according to judges' subjective standards of good or bad, but according to logical applications of legislation. Chief Justice John Marshall expressed this principle when he said that judicial power is exercised "for the purpose of giving effect to the will of the Legislature."

A second theory, *natural law,* gives judges greater leeway. The natural-law theory reflects the belief that there are universal standards of right and wrong that can be discovered through reason. In this view, judicial power can be justified as upholding such standards.

The third theory of law, *sociological jurisprudence,* holds that human law consists of fallible rules made by society to resolve conflicts among competing values. This theory assumes that judges can take into account information about society provided by a broad range of sources, and need not base their decisions exclusively on narrow legal considerations.

---

legal principles, particularly those that had broadened civil liberties. Such a brand of judicial activism is obviously different from the legal philosophy that holds that the Court has a special obligation to enlarge upon individual rights. The Bork incident illustrates the difficulty of applying the terms "judicial activism" and "judicial restraint" in consistent ways. In fact, some observers argue that all justices are activists in the sense that their judgments are necessarily creative ones.

Activists who emphasize the Court's obligation to protect civil rights and liberties find justification for their position in the U.S. Constitution's strong moral language and several of its provisions.[35] They see the Constitution as a charter for liberties, not as a set of narrow rules. An activist interprets the Sixth Amendment's right to counsel, for example, not just as a negative right of a defendant to hire counsel but as a positive right to have a competent lawyer even if the defendant cannot afford one. When the Sixth Amendment was enacted in the late eighteenth century, criminal trials were short and straightfor-

[35]Ibid.

Liberal judicial activists maintain that the Supreme Court has an obligation to act aggressively and positively to safeguard individual rights, as in its 1963 ruling that the Sixth Amendment confers the right to free legal counsel on defendants who cannot afford to pay a lawyer. (Rene Burri/ Magnum)

# IS THE SUPREME COURT SUITED TO THE MAKING OF BROAD SOCIAL POLICY?

As the Supreme Court has extended its reach into areas that were once dominated by Congress and the president, some analysts have questioned whether the Court has the capacity (as distinct from the right) to devise workable policies in all these areas. The structure and procedures of the judiciary obviously differ greatly from those of elected institutions. The way in which the Supreme Court gathers information and formulates decisions bears little resemblance to the way in which Congress or the White House carries out its tasks. These differences, Donald Horowitz argues in *The Courts and Social Policy,* prevent the Supreme Court from being a fully effective policymaking body when it comes to such issues as school integration.

Horowitz notes that, unlike members of Congress or executive officials, who usually start their policy deliberations from a general perspective, justices of the Supreme Court start with a particular case, which often involves unusual or extreme circumstances. The Court's initial busing decision in the 1971 *Swann* case, for example, involved Mecklenburg County, North Carolina, which had a long history of government-sponsored racial segregation. Yet the *Swann* decision became binding on a great number of communities, many of which had nothing approaching the level of institutionalized racism in Mecklenburg County.

Horowitz also notes that the Court acts on the basis of less complete information than Congress, which often holds hearings, conducts research, and by other means considers a wide range of facts before deciding on policy. The basic function of courts is to resolve specific disputes, and admissible evidence is generally limited to material directly relevant to the case at hand. Research studies on social conditions, for example, cannot ordinarily be introduced in a court of law, because pieces of paper cannot be cross-examined on the witness stand. To be sure, the Supreme Court is more likely than lower courts to look for information beyond an immediate case. The justices can, for example, invite interested groups to submit *amicus curiae* ("friend of the court") briefs in the hope that the advice thus obtained will broaden their understanding of a case's implications. The Court has a heavy schedule, however, and time and procedural tradition usually permit only a cursory assessment of information beyond what is contained in the trial record of a lower court.

Nevertheless, limits on the Court's policymaking capacity need to be kept in perspective. If the criterion for deciding whether an institution should establish broad policies were the likelihood of complete success, no institution would qualify. Every problem associated with judicial policymaking is also a problem confronted by legislative and executive institutions. Congress and the president also must act on the basis of imperfect information. In view of their resources, organization, and incentives, the elected institutions are better at fact finding and are more representative than the Court, but they are not without flaws of their own. The difference is one of degree, not of kind.

SOURCE: Donald L. Horowitz, *The Courts and Social Policy* (Washington, D.C.: Brookings Institution, 1977).

ward, and it was at least possible for poor people to defend themselves competently. But criminal law and procedures today are so complex that a defendant without legal counsel would be at a serious disadvantage. Moreover, society today can afford to provide poor defendants with legal assistance. By such reasoning, the judicial-activist school would argue that the Supreme Court was acting properly when it ruled in *Gideon* v. *Wainwright* (1963) that state governments had to provide indigent defendants with counsel at public expense.[36] More generally, advocates of judicial activism contend that decisions such as busing are not usurpations of legislative power but are rather judicial protection of individual constitutional rights that elected officials have failed to protect.

Some proponents argue that judicial activism is more appropriate on procedural issues, such as protection of individuals' voting rights, than on substantive

[36]*Gideon* v. *Wainwright,* 372 U.S. 335 (1963). Example and argument are from Posner, "What Am I? A Potted Plant?" 25.

issues, such as busing and abortion.[37] Other advocates of judicial activism reject the distinction. For example, Arthur Selwyn Miller claims that abortion is clearly an issue of individual rights and is therefore within the policymaking domain of the judiciary. Miller supports the idea that the Constitution implies a broad right of privacy that the Court is obligated to protect. Like other strong supporters of activism, Miller views the Constitution as designed chiefly to protect people from unreasonable governmental interference in their lives—a goal that can be accomplished only by a Supreme Court that is willing to stand up to the lawmaking majority whenever the latter tries to restrict individual choice.[38]

## THE SUPREME COURT'S PROPER ROLE: A QUESTION OF COMPETING VALUES

The dispute between advocates of judicial activism and advocates of judicial restraint cannot be settled by factual analysis. The argument is a philosophical one that involves opposing values. Nevertheless, the debate is important because it addresses the normative question of what role the Supreme Court *ought* to play in American democracy. Should this unelected court of law involve itself deeply in policy by adopting a broad conception of individual rights, or should it give wide discretion to elective institutions? This question cannot be

[37]John Hart Ely, *Democracy and Distrust: A Theory of Judicial Review* (Cambridge, Mass.: Harvard University Press, 1980), 74.
[38]Arthur Selwyn Miller, *Toward Increased Judicial Activism: The Political Role of the Supreme Court* (Westport, Conn.: Greenwood Press, 1982), 111.

---

**★ ANALYZE THE ISSUE**

**Judicial Activism as Ideology**
Richard A. Epstein of the University of Chicago Law School has said that courts should strike down rent controls, zoning, the minimum wage, and social security on the grounds that these laws violate property and contract rights. Is Epstein's advocacy a form of judicial activism from the right? Why, or why not? (Consider that all the above-mentioned laws were enacted by representatives of the people.)

---

**★ HOW THE UNITED STATES COMPARES**

**Judicial Review**
The power of U.S. courts is nowhere more evident than in the exercise of judicial review—the voiding of a legislative or executive action on the grounds that it violates the Constitution. Judicial review had its origins in European experiences and thought, but it was first formally applied in the United States when, in *Marbury v. Madison* (1803), the Supreme Court declared an act of Congress unconstitutional. Judicial review was not immediately incorporated into legal doctrine elsewhere but has since become relatively common. Some democracies, including Great Britain, still do not allow broad-scale judicial review, but most democracies now provide for it.

In the so-called American system of judicial review, all judges can evaluate the applicability of constitutional law to particular cases and can declare ordinary law invalid when it conflicts with constitutional law. By comparison, the so-called Austrian system restricts judicial review to a special constitutional court. Judges in other courts cannot declare a law void on the grounds that it is unconstitutional: they must apply ordinary law as it is written. In the Austrian system, moreover, constitutional decisions are made mainly in response to requests for judicial review by political officials (such as the chief executive).

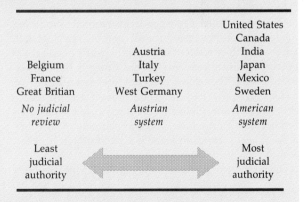

*Mexico is included under the American system even though its judiciary has elements of the Austrian system.

SOURCE: Mauro Cappelletti and William Cohen, *Comparative Constitutional Law* (Indianapolis: Bobbs-Merrill, 1979), ch.4.

answered simply on the basis of whether one personally agrees or disagrees with a particular Court decision. The answer necessarily depends on a value judgment about the role of the judiciary in a governing system based on the often-conflicting concepts of majority rule and individual rights.

The United States has a constitutional democracy that recognizes both the power of the majority to rule and the claim of the minority to protection of its rights. The Supreme Court was not established as the nation's moral conscience and does not have a monopoly on the issue of minority interests and rights. Yet the Bill of Rights was added to the Constitution to transform natural rights into civil liberties and thus to bring them under the judiciary's protection. In short, the constitutional question of how far the Supreme Court should be allowed to go in protecting the individual against the power of the majority is open to interpretation. The trade-off is significant on all issues: minority rights vs. majority rule, states' rights vs. federal power, legislative authority vs. judicial authority. The question of whether judicial restraint or judicial activism is more desirable is one that every student of American government should ponder.

## Summary

The Supreme Court has less discretionary authority than elected institutions. The Court's positions are constrained by the facts of a case and by what is stated in the Constitution, statutes and government regulations, and legal precedent. Yet existing legal guidelines are seldom so precise that the Court has no choice in its judgment. The state of the law narrows the Court's options in a particular case, but within these confines the justices have room for considerable discretion.

As a result, political influences have a strong impact on the Supreme Court. It responds to national conditions, public opinion, interest groups, and elected officials, particularly the president and members of Congress. But the chief political influence on the Court is the justices' own beliefs. They have personal preferences that are evident in the way they decide on issues before the Court. Most justices are relatively consistent in their positions during their Court tenure, and consequently major shifts in the Court's direction usually occur through appointment of new justices.

The Supreme Court is an important policymaking body because of gaps in the law that require interpretation and because of the Court's role in constitutional interpretation. Issues of federalism, separation of powers, majority power, and individual rights are often resolved through the Supreme Court. In recent decades the Court has issued broad rulings on individual rights, some of which have required governments to take positive action on behalf of minority interests. As the Court has crossed into areas traditionally left to lawmaking majorities, the legitimacy of its policies has been questioned. Advocates of judicial restraint claim that the justices' personal values are inadequate justification for exceeding the proper judicial role. They argue that the Constitution entrusts broad issues of the public good to elective institutions and that Court activism ultimately undermines public respect for the judiciary. Liberal judicial activists counter that the Court should promote social justice, a more open and fair political system, and individual rights. These goals, they maintain, are consistent with the purpose of the Constitution.

## Major Concepts

compliance  
equity  
facts (of a case)  
judicial activism  

judicial restraint  
laws (of a case)  
legitimacy  
precedent

## Suggested Readings

Berger, Raoul. *Government by Judiciary: The Transformation of the Fourteenth Amendment.* Cambridge, Mass.: Harvard University Press, 1977. A historical study of alleged misinterpretations of the Fourteenth Amendment by a controversial advocate of judicial restraint.

Bickel, Alexander M. *The Supreme Court and the Idea of Progress.* New Haven, Conn.: Yale University Press, 1978. A critical assessment of the policy rulings of the Warren Court from the perspective of an advocate of judicial restraint.

Ely, John Hart. *Democracy and Distrust: A Theory of Judicial Review.* Cambridge, Mass.: Harvard University Press, 1980. A theory of judicial review which advocates activism in some areas but not in others.

Glick, Henry R. *Courts, Politics, and Justice.* New York: McGraw-Hill, 1983. A general examination of the Supreme Court and the influences on its decisions.

Halpern, Stephen C., and Charles M. Lamb, eds. *Supreme Court Activism and Restraint.* Lexington, Mass.: Lexington Books, 1982. Readings on the issues of judicial activism and restraint.

Horowitz, Donald L. *The Courts and Social Policy.* Washington, D.C.: Brookings Institution, 1977. An analysis of the capacity of courts to make broad public policies.

O'Brien, David M. *Storm Center.* New York: Norton, 1986. An analysis of the Supreme Court in the context of the controversy surrounding the role of the judiciary in the U.S. political system.

Perry, Michael J. *Morality, Politics, and Law.* New York: Oxford University Press, 1988. An argument for judicial activism in the determination of individual rights.

Rhode, David, and Harold Spaeth. *Supreme Court Decision Making.* San Francisco: W. H. Freeman, 1976. An analysis of the Court's legal interpretations and decision making patterns.

# Is Too Much Public Policy Determined by Nonelected Officials in the Bureaucracy and the Judiciary?

**HUGH HECLO**

*As the power of direct democracy grows, the power of nonelected officials must keep pace if we are to keep our political system in balance.*

History taught our forebears three important reasons for designing a national political system with centers of semi-independent, nonelective power over the making of public policy. These reasons still apply today. First, we hope for conduct of the public's business—in the administration of both government programs and justice—that is impartial, or above partisan politics. Second, we desire stability and continuity to shield both public policy and minorities from capricious swings in majority public opinion. Third, expert knowledge—including expertise in impartial weighing of evidence—is needed to inform more partisan judgments about policy issues.

Obviously, impartiality is an elusive ideal; continuity can degenerate into stagnation; expertise can become exclusionary and self-serving in bureaucracies and courts. But the lapses that inevitably occur in practice do not mean that these goals should be abandoned or that these "nonpartisan" expectations should not be imposed on at least some participants in our multifaceted policymaking process.

Today the power of direct democracy—government by mass public opinion—is greater than anything ever imagined by the Founders when they designed our original constitutional structure. We live in a world of nonstop public opinion polling, popular elections to the Senate, an ever-lengthening cycle of presidential campaigns appealing directly to the people, and instantaneous media coverage of political affairs. All these developments would have astonished those early Americans, but their underlying idea of a balanced constitutional structure is far from outmoded. As the power of direct democracy grows, the power of nonelected officials must keep pace if we are to keep our political system in balance with the aid of those "old-fashioned" norms of impartiality, continuity, and expertise.

Today no American judge or bureaucrat, nor any combination of nonelected officials, can sustain a truly unpopular decision against the power of a determined majority. Both bureaucrats and judges depend largely on what is brought to them through legislation and cases; their power of initiating policy is meager. Both ultimately depend on popular consent to carry out their decisions; there is no enforcement power within the United States sufficient to carry out any arbitrary dictates of American bureaucrats or judges.

All of us can find reasons to complain about the decisions of nonelected officials, whether these apply to abortion and school prayer or environmental cleanup and taxes. However, if we try to be objective (or as impartial as a judge or a senior bureaucrat is supposed to try to be but probably never can be), we will see that our complaints are really about particular policy decisions that we dislike and not about some general usurpation of institutional power by nonelected officials.

How would we know if nonelected officials in the United States were determining too much public policy? There is one good test. If that were true, our political institutions would be experiencing a massive hemorrhage of legitimacy—not simply disputes about policy issues (a healthy thing in a cantankerous democracy), but an underlying alienation from elective *and* nonelective components of our constitutional structure. Despite all our complaints, that loss of legitimacy (a prominent feature of regimes from Eastern Europe to China) condition is not characteristic of late twentieth-century America. The important but limited power of nonelected officials is helping to keep representative democracy stable and healthy in the United States.

*Hugh Heclo is Clarence J. Robinson Professor of Public Affairs at George Mason University. He is the author of* A Government of Strangers: Executive Politics in Washington.

**MARTIN SHAPIRO**

*In a democracy, law ought to be made by the people through their elected representatives.*

It is a mistake to believe that because we settle disputes between two individuals by sending them to an impartial third party such as a judge, we should settle public policy disputes that way. Third parties settle individual disputes by applying existing law. Thus, in an auto accident case, the traffic code helps the judge decide which driver was at fault. Policy disputes, in contrast, are about the making of new law. In a democracy, law ought to be made by the people through their elected representatives. We don't want the "impartial" law that someone else thinks is good for us, but law that we devise for ourselves.

We guarantee impartiality in private disputes by finding a third party who knew nothing about the dispute or disputants before the case was brought to him or her. Who would want a dispute about nuclear power or abortion rights to be resolved by someone so out of touch that they had not thought about these important matters before the dispute reached them? Public issues ought to be resolved by people who know a lot about them, but if you know a lot, you will already have decided who is right and who is wrong. Thus, on public questions we need, not impartiality, but popular control; we need decisions to be made by

people who know a lot but are subject to election. That means legislators, not judges or bureaucrats.

Judges and bureaucrats themselves say that they resolve issues of public policy by balancing interests. For instance, the Supreme Court says that even the First Amendment right to free speech is not absolute. It is constitutional to arrest a speaker for inciting a riot, because the society's interest in preventing riots outweighs the individual's right to speak. If policy is arrived at by such balancing, it is illogical to try to achieve it in "impartial" judiciaries and bureaucracies rather than in legislatures that are set up specifically to represent various interests and to arrive at compromises, or balances, among those interests.

Bureaucratic and judicial impartiality is mostly a fake, anyway. When the Supreme Court decides that there either is or isn't a constitutional right to abortion, it is not being any more impartial about the issue than the rest of us are. Each of the justices is a human being with ideas about right and wrong. How else could the justices decide a question like abortion except by consulting their own values? Granted, in choosing between good and bad, they should choose the good; but what appears to each of them to be the good is going to depend a lot on their own ideas rather than on some impartial weighing of pros and cons.

Very few people who are in the business of making political decisions go through life keeping an open mind about everything. Instead, they arrive at fairly firm judgments about who and what would be best for the country. Once they do so, they are not impartial, but partial to what they think is right. That is as it should be, but it means that the law ought to reflect the public's sense of right and wrong as determined by elected representatives, not by the judiciary and the bureaucracy.

*Martin Shapiro is on the faculty of the School of Law at the University of California, Berkeley. He is the author of* Who Guards the Guardians: Judicial Control of Administration.

# Part Seven

## PUBLIC POLICY

The term *public policy* refers to action (or inaction) by government which is directed toward a particular goal or purpose. Busing to achieve racial integration in the public schools is an example of public policy—a goal-oriented governmental action.

In a sense, all the preceding sections of this book have led up to this one. Public policy is the major consequence of political activity. National policy is decided directly by public officials (discussed in Parts Five and Six), but these officials operate within a constitutionally established framework of governmental institutions (Part One) and individual rights (Part Two), and they make decisions in the context of public opinion (Part Three) and political organizations (Part Four). Accordingly, any realistic assessment of public policy requires that all these factors be taken into account; this fact is evident in this section's three chapters, on economic policy (Chapter 26), social-welfare policy (Chapter 27), and national security policy (Chapter 28).

These three chapters are designed mainly to provide insights into the specific policy areas that they discuss. However, some common patterns emerge. First, U.S. policy is never settled once and for all. As changes occur in society or in the balance of power between interests, public policy changes, sometimes substantially. During the 1980s, for example, U.S. policy toward the Soviet Union shifted from open hostility to cautious cooperation.

Second, U.S. policy tends to be piecemeal and reactive. The nation's fragmented governing structure, diverse interests, and cultural bias against intrusive government make it difficult for policymakers to deal with an issue except in small parts and until it has become a problem. As the unit makes clear, this tendency has advantages as well as disadvantages.

Third, U.S. policy is generated through a process of conflict and consensus. Americans differ in many of their interests, and accordingly they disagree over policy. Some of their differences—over abortion policy, for example—are so fundamental as to be irreconcilable. On most issues of policy, however, competing interests can find common ground if they are willing to search for it. The typical impulse in such situations is to seek compromise, a tendency that itself speaks volumes about the democratic governing process. Although politics is sometimes said to be mostly about conflict, it is actually mostly about problem solving. Public policy is the instrument by which people try to work out solutions to the complex problems of collective life.                                                    ★   ★   ★

# Chapter 26

## ECONOMIC POLICY: CONTRIBUTING TO PROSPERITY

*We the people of the United States, in order to . . . insure domestic tranquility . . .*
*—Preamble, U.S. Constitution*

On October 19, 1987, the Dow Jones industrial average plunged 508 points, the largest one-day drop in the history of the stock market. The panic on Wall Street awakened memories of another October crash nearly sixty years earlier, which had signaled the start of the Great Depression. Would history repeat itself? Was the United States on the verge of another economic collapse in which millions of Americans would find themselves without work and without hope?

There was one major difference between the late 1920s and the late 1980s. When the market plummeted in 1929, no substantial government programs were in place to stabilize and stimulate the U.S. economy. The response to the 1929 crash guaranteed that the economic disaster would worsen. Businesses cut back on production, depositors withdrew their savings, and consumers slowed their spending; all of these actions accelerated the downward spiral. In contrast, in 1987 government was there to assure depositors that their savings were insured, to encourage consumers to keep spending, to inform business that government would not allow interest rates to soar. "I don't anticipate a recession unless some of those doomsayers scare the people into one," said President Ronald Reagan, expressing his view that the economy would remain healthy as long as Americans did not panic. In fact, the stock market crash of 1987 did not trigger a plunge in the economy.

Nevertheless, the market crash of 1987 was a sign that the U.S. economy had severe problems. As Americans headed into the 1990s, huge budget, credit, and trade deficits threatened the high standard of living to which they had become accustomed. At the beginning of the 1980s, the United States had been the world's biggest creditor nation, holding a net positive international investment in excess of $100 billion. By the end of 1987, the United States was the world's largest debtor nation, owing $400 billion to foreign investors. In the same period, the U.S. balance of trade (that is, of imports against exports) declined steadily, and the trade deficit reached a record $170 billion in 1987. There was also the problem of the national debt. During the 1980s, the federal debt rose from less than $1 trillion to more than $2.5 trillion. In a widely noted article, Peter G. Peterson, former secretary of commerce in the Nixon administration, warned that America's economic imbalances could cripple its future: "The [worst] scenario, of course, is a huge plunge in the dollar, unaffordable imports, a long recession, garrison protectionism and a marked decline in American living standards."[1] Peterson contended that the leadership necessary to resolve the country's economic policies would have to come from Washington. On that point no politician, economist, or business leader disagreed.

This chapter examines the role of the government in the U.S. economy, focusing on its promotion and regulation of economic interests and its fiscal and monetary policies, which affect economic growth. Directly or indirectly, the federal government is a party to almost every economic transaction in which Americans engage. Although the private decisions of firms and individuals are the main force in the American economic system, these decisions are made in the context of government policy. Washington seeks to maintain high productivity, employment, and purchasing power; regulates business practices that would otherwise result in economic inefficiencies and inequities; and promotes economic interests. To an important extent, the condition of the U.S. economy depends on how well the government in Washington performs these roles. And certainly no issue is more politically significant than the state of the economy. Americans have high expectations about their financial well-being and, to a large degree, judge their national leaders by whether the economy is doing well or poorly. The main ideas presented in the chapter are the following:

★ *Through regulation, the U.S. government imposes restraints on business activity which are designed to promote economic efficiency and equity.* This regulation is often the cause of political conflict, which is both ideological and group-centered.

★ *Through promotion, the U.S. government helps private interests to achieve their economic goals.* Business in particular benefits from the government's promotional efforts, which take place largely in the context of group politics.

★ *Through fiscal and monetary policy, the U.S. government seeks to maintain a stable and prosperous general economy.* The overall condition of the U.S. economy is generally the leading issue in American electoral politics and has a major influence on each party's success.

## Regulating the Economy

An **economy** is a system of production and consumption of goods and services, which are allocated through exchange. When a shopper chooses groceries at a store and pays money in order to take them out the door, that transaction is one of the millions of economic exchanges that make up the economy. Underlying

[1]Peter G. Peterson, "The Morning After," *Atlantic Monthly*, October 1987, 46.

economic exchange is a vast system for the production and distribution of goods. In *The Wealth of Nations* (1776), Adam Smith presented the case for the **laissez-faire doctrine,** which holds that private individuals and firms should be left alone to make their own production and distribution decisions. Smith reasoned that when there is a demand for a good (that is, when people desire it), private entrepreneurs will respond by producing the good and distributing it to points where the demand exists. By the same token, when demand declines, producers will cut back on production and distribution.

In a capitalist economic system, the incentive that drives this process is profit. Smith argued that the desire for profit is the "invisible hand" that guides the system toward the greatest welfare for all. Left to itself, Smith said, a capitalist economy will produce "a universal opulence extending to the lowest reaches of society." Smith acknowledged that the doctrine of laissez-faire capitalism had a few limits. Certain areas of the economy, such as roadways and postal services, were natural monopolies and were better run by government than by private firms. In addition, by regulating banking, currency, and contracts, government could give stability to private transactions. Otherwise, Smith argued, the economy was best left in private hands.

Adam Smith. (National Portrait Gallery, London)

In contrast, Karl Marx proposed a worker-controlled economy. In *Das Kapital* (*Capital*, 1867) Marx argued that a free-market system is exploitive because producers, through their control of production and markets, can compel workers to labor at a wage below the value they add to production and can force consumers to pay higher prices for goods than are justified by the cost of production. The effect of capitalism, Marx argued, is to create two social classes—overprivileged owners (the bourgeoisie) and underprivileged workers (the proletariat). To end the exploitation of labor, Marx proposed a collective economy. When the workers owned the means of production, the economy would operate in the interest of all citizens equally.

*Political institutions are a superstructure resting on an economic foundation.*
Nikolai Lenin

Marx and Smith represent the extremes of economic theory. No country in the world has an economy that conforms fully to either the laissez-faire or the collectivist model because each has advantages and defects. All national economies today are of "mixed" form in that they contain elements of both private and public control. However, the world's economies vary greatly in their mix. The United States tends strongly toward the private side, whereas the Soviet Union tends strongly toward the collective side. In between, but closer to the American type of economy, are certain Western European countries whose governments, on behalf of their people, own and operate a number of key industries, including steel, airlines, banking, and oil.

Although the U.S. government owns only a few businesses (such as Amtrak and the Tennessee Valley Authority), it plays a substantial economic role through **regulation** of privately owned businesses. U.S. firms are not free to act as they please, but must operate within production and distribution bounds set by federal regulations. Regulatory policy is generally intended to promote either economic *efficiency* or *equity* (see Table 26-1).

Karl Marx. (German Information Center)

## EFFICIENCY THROUGH GOVERNMENT INTERVENTION[2]

Economic **efficiency** requires firms to fulfill as many of society's needs as possible while using as few of its resources as possible. Adam Smith and other classical economists believed that the free market was the optimal means of

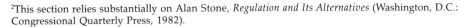

[2]This section relies substantially on Alan Stone, *Regulation and Its Alternatives* (Washington, D.C.: Congressional Quarterly Press, 1982).

**TABLE 26-1   The Main Objectives of Regulatory Policy: Efficiency and Equity**

| Objective | Definition | Representative Actions by Government |
|---|---|---|
| Efficiency | Fulfillment of as many of society's needs as possible at the cost of as few of its resources as possible. | Preventing restraint of trade; requiring producers to pay the costs of damage to the environment; reducing restrictions on business that cannot be justified on a cost-benefit basis. |
| Equity | A system of free and fair economic transactions in which each party gains equally. | Requiring firms to bargain in good faith with labor; protecting consumers in their purchases; protecting workers' safety and health. |

achieving efficiency. Competition among producers would compel them to use as few resources as possible in producing goods and to charge consumers the lowest possible prices. Inefficient entrepreneurs would be driven out of business by their more efficient competitors, and those who tried to overcharge would be unable to sell their goods and would thus be forced to lower the price to prevailing market levels.

### Preventing Restraint of Trade

The assumption that the market always determines price is flawed; the same incentive—the profit motive—that drives producers to respond to demand can drive them to corner the market on a good. If a producer gains a monopoly on a good or conspires with other producers to fix its price, consumers are forced to

The business trusts that controlled sectors of the American economy in the late nineteenth century seemed immune to government regulation. In this 1889 cartoon the trusts are depicted as being powerful enough to control the U.S. Senate. (The New York Historical Society)

pay an artificially high price. This form of inefficiency surfaced in the late nineteenth century, when large trusts came to dominate many areas of the U.S. economy, including the oil, steel, railroad, and sugar markets. The trusts were not true monopolies, but they controlled enough of their markets to be able to manipulate production and price levels. Railroad companies, for example, had no competition on short routes, and gouged their customers.[3] Farmers were especially hard hit because they depended on the railroads to get their crops and livestock to market.

In 1887, as the Progressive era dawned, Congress took a first step toward controlling the trusts through federal regulation. The Interstate Commerce Commission (ICC) was created and charged with regulating railroad practices and fares. Three years later, the Sherman Antitrust Act declared that any business combination or practice in restraint of trade was illegal. A hostile Supreme Court and the imprecision of the Sherman Act's provisions made the legislation less effective than anticipated, so the 1914 Clayton Act was passed to strengthen the government's regulatory powers by specifying the business practices that constituted restraint of trade.* The Federal Trade Commission (FTC) was established in 1914 to regulate trade practices.

Today the FTC is one of several federal agencies charged with regulating business competition. In a few cases, the government has prohibited mergers or required divestments in order to increase competition. The largest antitrust suit in the country's history was settled in 1984 when AT&T was forced to sell its regional Bell Telephone companies, which had enabled it to monopolize access to long-distance telephone service. AT&T must now compete for long-distance customers with MCI, Sprint, and other carriers.

In general, however, the government tolerates business concentration. Corporate takeovers and mergers are common, although most of them involve the joining of corporations that are not direct competitors. An example is the acquisition of Carrier, a manufacturer of air conditioners, and Otis, an elevator manufacturer, by United Technologies Corporation (UTC). UTC is a conglomerate—a business organization that consists of a number of noncompeting corporations. The government has concluded that conglomerates do not substantially threaten competitive trade practices. But the government has also permitted some recent mergers of competing firms, such as Chrysler's acquisition of AMC and Pennzoil's takeover of Getty Oil. Although such mergers reduce competition, the government tolerates concentrated ownership in such industries as oil and automobiles, where high capital costs make it difficult for smaller firms to compete successfully. The government's policy toward corporate giants that act in restraint of trade in these fields has been to penalize them financially. In 1986, for example, Exxon was ordered to rebate $2 billion to gasoline customers because of illegal price fixing. Government acceptance of corporate giants also reflects a realization that market competition no longer involves just domestic firms. For example, the "Big Three" U.S. automakers (General Motors, Ford, and Chrysler) face stiff competition from imports, particularly those from Japan and West Germany.

---

*The Interstate Commerce Act of 1887 also required strengthening, a task accomplished by the Mann-Elkins Act of 1911.

[3]James E. Anderson, *The Emergence of the Modern Regulatory State* (Washington, D.C.: Public Affairs Press, 1962), 408.

**Governmental Encouragement of Economic Efficiency**
Zenith and AT&T announced in 1989 that they would collaborate on the development of high-definition television. This venture is unusual because U.S. firms have a reputation for emphasizing short-term profits and corporate takeovers at the expense of long-term product development. By comparison, Japanese and European firms, supported by government subsidies and tax breaks, have been heavily involved in long-range product research. Should the U.S. government adopt similar approaches, or would such policies constitute unreasonable interference with free enterprise?

## Making Business Pay for Indirect Costs

Economic inefficiencies can result not only from restraint of trade but from the failure of businesses or consumers to pay the full costs of resources used in production. Classical economics assumed that market prices reflect all the costs of production, but this assumption is rarely warranted. Consider the case of persons who become disabled on the job. A large part of the cost of maintaining these now less productive persons is borne, not by their former employers, but by society through public welfare and health-care programs. Or consider companies that dump their industrial wastes in the nearest river. They are polluting a resource that belongs to society rather than to them. The price of these companies' products does not reflect the water pollution, so customers are not paying all the costs that society has incurred in the making of the products. Economists label such unpaid costs **externalities.**

Until the 1960s, the federal government made no great effort to force firms to pay such costs. The impetus to begin doing so came not only from lawmakers but also from the scientific community and public-interest groups. The Clean Air Act of 1963 and the Water Pollution Control Act of 1964 required industry to install antipollution devices to keep air and water pollutants within specified limits. In 1970 Congress created the Environmental Protection Agency (EPA) to monitor compliance with federal regulations governing air and water quality and the disposal of toxic wastes.

The government has shifted some of the cost of cleaning up toxic waste dumps and other kinds of pollution from the general public to the firms that discharge the pollutants. (Fred Ward/Black Star)

## EFFICIENCY THROUGH GOVERNMENT NONINTERVENTION

Although government intervention is intended to increase economic efficiency, the effect can be the opposite. If government places too many regulatory burdens on firms, they may waste resources in the effort to comply.

### Overregulation

In a speech to the National Federation of Industrial Business in 1975, President Gerald Ford claimed that business regulation was costing $150 billion annually, or $2,000 for every American family.[4] Ford's estimate was high, but the validity of his point was generally acknowledged.[5] The pace of business regulation had more than doubled in the early 1970s (see Figure 26-1). Firms had to hire additional employees simply to monitor and implement new federal regulations,[6] which in many instances also required them to buy and install expensive equipment. According to one estimate, compliance with regulations cut national productivity by one-half of 1 percent at a time when the U.S. economy was growing at an annual rate of only 2 percent.[7]

The first efforts at a rollback in regulations were directed at excessive ones, but sharper cutbacks were then sought as a way to stimulate business productivity. "There has been a swing of attitudes," Senator Robert Packwood (R-Ore.) said in 1980, "toward a necessity for relaxing regulation as a trade-off

[4]*U.S. News & World Report,* June 30, 1975, 25.
[5]William Cilley III and James Miller III, "The New Social Regulation," in Ellen F. Paul and Philip A. Russo, Jr., *Public Policy* (Chatham, N.J.: Chatham House, 1982), 214; David Vogel, "The 'New' Social Regulation in Historical and Comparative Perspective," in Thomas McGraw, ed., *Regulation in Perspective* (Cambridge, Mass.: Harvard University Press, 1981), 214.
[6]Murray Weidenbaum, "An Overview of Government Regulation," *Journal of Commercial Lending,* January 1981, 29.
[7]Timothy C. Clarke, "Fighting Inflation by Limiting Regulation," *National Journal,* August 28, 1978, 1283.

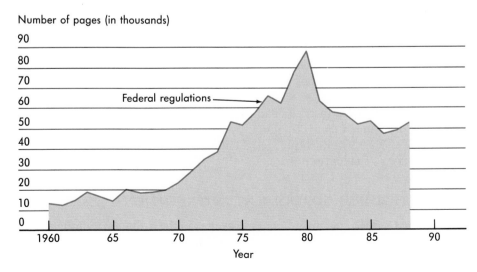

**FIGURE 26-1 Number of Pages of Federal Regulations, 1960–1988**
The number of federal regulations, as indicated by the number of pages they occupy in *The Federal Register,* more than doubled during the early 1970s, imposing new costs on U.S. businesses. *Source: Staff, Office of Federal Register.*

for economic growth."[8] This drive peaked in 1981, when President Reagan ordered a sixty-day moratorium on new regulations and the elimination of old ones that were particularly costly to business. Reagan also issued an executive order requiring any major new regulation to be justified on a cost-benefit basis.

### Deregulation

In the early 1930s the airline industry was struggling to get started. Airlines were competing for service between major cities because these routes were potentially the most profitable. However, the competition for these routes was so intense that airline companies were not profitable enough to accumulate the capital to build large fleets of up-to-date aircraft. In 1938 Congress established the Civil Aeronautics Board (CAB) to regulate airline routes and fares. Major routes were divided among existing carriers, and new flights on these routes were rarely authorized. The CAB also determined fares, setting them high in order to ensure the airlines' profitability. In exchange, airline carriers were required to provide service to smaller cities. The net result was the emergence of a few well-capitalized airline companies, including TWA, Pan Am, American, and United.

In the 1970s the idea of deregulating the airlines came under discussion in Congress. The airlines did not conform to any economist's model of a monopoly, so the argument in favor of regulating them for purposes of efficiency was always a weak one. Senator Edward Kennedy (D-Mass.) introduced an airline deregulation bill in 1977. The bill was opposed by established airlines, which correctly saw the legislation as a threat to their profits and exclusive routes. They argued that unrestricted competition would make the industry unprofitable. However, the idea of **deregulation**—the rescinding of the regulations then in force—had wide support in Congress. Conservatives favored any measure that would allow business to act more freely, and liberals were persuaded that deregulation would result in lower fares, which would benefit consumers. In 1978 Congress passed the Airline Deregulation Act and, soon thereafter, air travelers had more flights to choose from and paid lower fares.

Congress followed airline deregulation with partial deregulation of the trucking, banking, energy, and communications industries, among others. However, like all other approaches to efficiency, deregulation has not been an unqualified success.[9] The savings and loan industry is a prime example. When deregulation lifted restrictions on how savings and loan institutions could invest depositors' savings, many of them engaged in highly speculative ventures. By 1989 the industry was in crisis. Bad investments had resulted in an industry-wide loss of as much as $100 billion, by some estimates. In order to save the failing S&Ls, President Bush pledged a bailout plan that included the expenditure of billions of taxpayer dollars.

## EQUITY THROUGH GOVERNMENT INTERVENTION

As we noted earlier, the government intervenes in the economy to bring equity as well as efficiency to the marketplace. **Equity** occurs when an economic

[8]Quoted in *U.S. News & World Report*, June 2, 1980, 59.
[9]See Larry N. Gerston, Cynthia Fraleigh, and Robert Schwab, *The Deregulated Society* (Pacific Grove, Calif.: Brooks/Cole, 1988); Susan Tolchin and Martin Tolchin, *Dismantling America* (New York: Oxford University Press, 1985).

Government deregulation of the airlines has resulted in lower fares but has also increased congestion on the runways. (Kevin Horan/Picture Group)

transaction is fair to each party. A transaction can be considered fair if each party enters into it freely and is not unknowingly at a disadvantage (for example, if the seller knows a product is defective, equity requires that the buyer also know of the defect).

An early equity measure was the creation of the Food and Drug Administration (FDA) in 1907. Because consumers are often unable to tell whether foods and drugs are safe to use, the FDA works to keep adulterated foods and dangerous or ineffective drugs off the market. In the 1930s, financial reforms were among the equity measures enacted under the New Deal. The Securities and Exchange Act of 1934 and the Banking Act of 1934 were designed in part to protect investors and savers from dishonest or imprudent brokers and bankers. The New Deal also provided greater equity for organized labor, which previously had been in a weak position in its dealings with management. Under the terms of the 1935 National Labor Relations Act (also called the Wagner Act), employers could no longer refuse to negotiate pay and working conditions with employees' unions. The Fair Labor Standards Act of 1938 established minimum wages, maximum working hours, and constraints on the use of child labor.[10]

The 1960s and 1970s produced the greatest number of equity reforms. From 1965 to 1977, ten federal agencies were established to protect consumers, workers, and the public from harmful effects of business activity. Protection of consumers from defective or health-threatening products was a major thrust of this reform period. Among the products declared to be unsafe in the 1960s and 1970s were the insecticide DDT, cigarettes, the Chevrolet Corvair, phosphates, Firestone radial tires, and leaded gasoline.[11]

Business interests were strongly opposed to the expansion of equity regulation and gained an ally when Ronald Reagan was elected president. In the first weeks of his administration, Reagan issued an executive order that any new federal regulation had to be justified on a cost-benefit basis, a requirement that limited the number of new restrictions that could be placed on business. In

Health warnings on cigarette packages are an example of government regulation aimed at achieving equity by providing consumers with relevant product information. (George W. Gardner/Stock, Boston)

[10]Henry C. Dethluff, *Americans and Free Enterprise* (Englewood Cliffs, N.J.: Prentice-Hall, 1971), 257.

[11]Vogel, " 'New' Social Regulation," 162.

some cases, the Reagan administration used creative arithmetic in order to get a favorable cost-benefit calculation. In 1984, for example, the Office of Management and Budget blocked a proposed regulation to phase out the use of asbestos. In order to do so, the OMB had to show that the cost of an asbestos ban would exceed the benefit of lives saved by the ban. Although other agencies had placed the value of a human life as high as $2.5 million, the OMB assigned a value of only $208,000, reasoning that deaths from asbestos-caused cancer had to be "discounted" because they occurred years after exposure to asbestos. With the $208,000 figure, the cost to business of the proposed regulation exceeded the benefit to society of lives saved, so the OMB could kill the regulation.[12]

## THE POLITICS OF REGULATORY POLICY

Economic regulation has come in waves, as changes in national conditions have produced intermittent bursts of social consciousness.

### The Reforms of the Progressive and New Deal Eras

The first wave of regulation came during the Progressive era, when reformers sought to break the power of the trusts by placing constraints on unfair business practices. The second wave came in the New Deal era, when reformers sought to stimulate economic recovery by regulatory policies that they designed as much to save business as to reform it. For example, 1930s banking regulations were meant not only to protect depositors but also to save the banking system, which was threatened by bank closings arising from financial institutions' unsound investments and from mass withdrawals of funds by panicked depositors.

*We have always known that heedless self-interest was bad morals; we know now that it is bad economics.*
Franklin Delano Roosevelt

Although business fought Progressive and New Deal reforms, long-term opposition was lessened by the fact that most of the resulting regulation applied to a particular industry rather than to firms of all types. This pattern made it possible for an affected industry to gain influence with those officials who were responsible for regulating its activities. By cultivating close ties to ICC commissioners, for example, railroads eventually managed to gain the ICC's approval of uncompetitive shipping rates that gave them high and sustained profits. Although most industries have not coopted their regulators as fully as the shipping industry, it is generally true that business has not been greatly hampered by older forms of regulation and in fact has substantially benefited from it in some cases.

Most of the regulatory functions that were established during the Progressive and New Deal periods are organized in ways that facilitate group access and influence. Some regulatory functions are located within departments, such as the Department of Commerce, that are oriented toward the promotion of particular economic interests. Other functions are carried out by regulatory commissions, such as the ICC, whose sole responsibility is the regulation of a given activity or industry.* As we saw in Chapter 22, the commission members are appointed by the president with Senate approval but serve fixed terms and are not subject to removal by the president. In other words, regulatory

---

*The five most significant commissions are the Interstate Commerce Commission (ICC, established in 1887); the Federal Trade Commission (FTC, 1914); the Federal Communications Commission (FCC, 1934); the Securities and Exchange Commission (SEC, 1934); and the Civil Aeronautics Board (CAB, 1938).

[12]"Putting a Price Tag on Life," *Newsweek*, January 11, 1988, 40.

commissioners are relatively independent officials who have broad authority in their policy areas. A regulated interest that acquires influence with commissioners is positioned to obtain favorable policies.

### The Era of New Social Regulation

The third wave of regulatory reform, in the 1960s and 1970s, differed from the Progressive and New Deal waves in both its policies and its politics. The third wave has been called the era of "new social regulation" by some economists because of the social goals it addressed[13] in its three major policy areas: environmental protection, consumer protection, and worker safety.

Most of the regulatory agencies established during the third wave have much broader policy mandates than those created earlier. They have responsibility not for a single industry but for firms of all types, and their policy scope covers a wide range of activities. The Environmental Protection Agency (EPA), for example, is charged with regulating environmental pollution of almost any kind by almost any firm. Because newer agencies such as the EPA have a far-ranging clientele, no one firm or industry can easily maneuver itself into a position to influence agency policy to a great extent. There is also strong group competition in some of the newer regulatory spheres; for example, business lobbies must compete with environmental groups such as the Sierra Club for influence with the EPA.[14] The firms regulated by the older agencies, in contrast, face no powerful competition in their lobbying activities; broadcasters, for example, are largely unopposed in their efforts to influence the Federal Communications Commission, which was established during the New Deal era.

Unlike the older agencies that are run by a commission whose members serve for fixed terms, the newer agencies are headed by a single director, who is appointed by the president with Senate approval. Because this appointee can be removed from office at the president's discretion, the newer agencies are more responsive to partisan politics. Although much of their work occurs in the context of lobbying and other group activity, the broad direction of the newer regulatory agencies has been set in the context of party and ideological conflict. With its stronger commitment to business and economic individualism, the Republican party is less inclined toward regulatory activity than the Democratic party, which has a firmer attachment to labor and economic equity.

## How the Government Promotes Various Economic Interests

The U.S. government has always made important contributions to the nation's economy. The Constitution was written in part to provide for a national government strong enough to promote a sound economy. The Constitution stipulated that the government was to regulate commerce, create a strong currency, develop uniform commercial standards, and provide a stable credit system. The fledgling government also immediately demonstrated its concern for economic interests. Congress in 1789 gave a boost to the nation's shipping industry by placing a tariff on imported goods carried by foreign ships. Since

[13]Cilley and Miller, "New Social Regulation," 216.
[14]Vogel, " 'New' Social Regulation," 173.

Billion-dollar broadcasting corporations are built on the few dollars the government charges their affiliated stations for a license to use the public airwaves. (Guy Gillette/Photo Researchers)

that first favor, the U.S. government has provided thousands of direct benefits to economic interests.

In Chapters 14, 18, and 23 we described how congressional and bureaucratic politics results in the promotion of group interests. Here we will briefly examine a few illustrations of the scope of government's contribution to the interests of business, labor, and agriculture.

## PROMOTING BUSINESS

American business is not opposed to government regulation as such. It objects only to regulatory policies that are adverse to its interests. We have noted that, at various times and in differing ways, many federal regulatory agencies have served primarily the interests of the industries they are intended to regulate.

Government also promotes business through loans and loan guarantees. In 1979 the Chrysler Corporation was about to go under. The doctrine of laissez-faire economics would have dictated that any unprofitable and poorly managed company be allowed to fail. Instead, Washington guaranteed $1.5 billion in loans for Chrysler: the federal government would repay the lenders if Chrysler defaulted. Although this loan guarantee came under criticism, it was remarkable only in the amount of money involved. The federal government has guaranteed thousands of business loans and also makes direct loans to businesses. Many new high-technology firms have received loans from federal, state, or local government for construction and equipment costs.

The most significant contribution that government makes to business is the traditional services it provides, such as education, transportation, and defense. Colleges and universities, which are funded primarily by governments, furnish business with most of its professional and technical work force and with much of the basic research that goes into product development. The nation's interstate highway system, other road systems, waterways, and airports are other public-sector contributions without which business could not survive. There is an entire industry—defense contracting—that exists almost entirely on government money. The nation's military power, which is designed for national defense, also protects American business interests abroad. In short, America's business has no better promoter than government.

## PROMOTING LABOR

Laissez-faire thinking dominated government's approach to labor well into the twentieth century. The governing principle, developed by the courts in the early nineteenth century, was that workers had limited rights of collective action. Union activity was regarded as interference with the natural supply of labor and the free setting of wages. The extent of hostility toward labor can be seen in the use of federal troops to break up strikes. (Early labor–government relations are discussed in Chapter 7.)

The 1930s brought significant changes. The key legislation was the National Labor Relations Act of 1935, which guarantees workers the right to bargain collectively and prohibits business from discriminating against union employees and from unreasonably interfering with union activities. The Taft-Hartley Act of 1947 took away some of labor's gains, including compulsory union membership for workers whose workplace is unionized. Under the provisions of Taft-Hartley, each state can decide for itself whether all workers in work units that are unionized must become union members (union shop) or whether a worker can choose not to join the union (open shop). Despite these modifications, the National Labor Relations Act has remained a cornerstone of labor's power. The legislation not only requires that business bargain with organized labor but also established the National Labor Relations Board (NLRB), an independent regulatory commission that is empowered to enforce compliance

Organized labor has never enjoyed the same high level of government support as business has. As a consequence, strikes are an only moderately effective tactic. (Rob Nelson/Picture Group)

★ ANALYZE THE ISSUE

**Governmental Involvement in Economic Equity**

During a strike by its flight attendants, TWA airlines was able to stay in operation with the help of 1,200 unionized attendants who crossed the picket lines. After the strike, TWA kept all these employees and, on the basis of seniority, hired back about a third of the attendants who had stayed out on strike. The union took TWA to court, arguing that seniority alone should have determined which members of the union got their jobs back after the strike. In 1989, by a 6–3 vote, the Supreme Court upheld TWA's action. To what degree does the Court's decision undermine the effectiveness of strikes? Do you agree with the Court's decision? Why, or why not?

with labor law by both business and labor. Government has also aided labor by legislating minimum wages and maximum hours, unemployment benefits, safer and more healthful working conditions, and nondiscriminatory hiring practices.

Although government support for labor extends beyond these examples, it is not nearly so extensive as its assistance to business. America's individualistic culture has worked against efforts to organize labor and establish labor rights as strong as those in Western European democracies.

In the 1980s, backed by the Reagan administration, business launched a broad attack on organized labor which included efforts to undermine employee unions. In one such case, 5,000 striking TWA flight attendants were fired and replaced by new employees who were paid at roughly half the wage rate of the former employees. In labor–management disputes of the 1980s, the NLRB, which was dominated by pro-business Reagan appointees, generally upheld company actions. Some union leaders began to refer to the NLRB as the National Labor Repression Board. In one case labor had the NLRB on its side but lost out before the Supreme Court, which ruled in favor of a company that had filed for bankruptcy for the purpose of voiding its labor contracts.[15] After filing, the corporation resumed its operations with new workers hired at much lower wage and benefit levels.

## PROMOTING AGRICULTURE

Until well into the twentieth century, most Americans still lived on farms and in small rural communities. Agriculture was America's dominant business and was assisted by government's land policies. The Homestead Act of 1862, for example, opened government-owned lands to settlement, creating spectacular "land rushes" by offering 160 free acres of government land to each family that staked a claim, built a house, and farmed the land for five years.

[15]*National Labor Relations Board* v. *Bildisco and Bildisco*, 465 U.S. 513 (1984).

In America's first century or so, the government promoted agriculture by offering 160 acres of public land free to homesteaders like this family, photographed in Nebraska in 1877. (Solomon D. Butcher Collection, Nebraska State Historical Society)

Government promotion of agriculture has been complicated by two natural factors. First, farmers' income can fluctuate sharply from one year to the next, depending on market and growing conditions. Second, U.S. farmland is so fertile that it produces more of many crops than can be sold in the marketplace. U.S. agricultural policy has been designed to promote stable farm incomes and control agricultural production, an approach that is both complex and costly.

A brief look at government efforts to reduce farm surpluses in the 1980s provides some insight into the tangled web of agricultural tariffs, parity, price supports, and subsidies. Surpluses are a double problem: they keep market prices low because supply exceeds demand, and they require storage at an annual cost of hundreds of millions of dollars. Washington has developed numerous programs designed to reduce farm surpluses. In one such program during the 1980s, the government offered payments to dairy farmers who voluntarily destroyed their herds. Another program gave surplus commodities free to farmers who normally grew these commodities but who agreed to take land out of production. In addition, farmers received direct cash payments from government when market prices fell below a specified threshold; the condition for participating in this program, which gave stability to farmers' income, was the removal of some acreage from production. Farm programs cost the federal government a record $31.4 billion in 1986 (see Figure 26-2).

## *Maintaining a Stable Economy*

Until the 1930s, the federal government adhered to the prevailing free-market theory and made no attempt to maintain the stability of the economy as a whole. The economy was regarded as largely self-regulating. If sellers and buyers looked after their personal interests—with sellers seeking high profits and buyers seeking favorable prices—the result would be abundant goods, jobs, and income. The U.S. economy was indeed fairly prosperous, but periodically—in the late 1830s, early 1870s, and early 1890s—the nation experienced severe

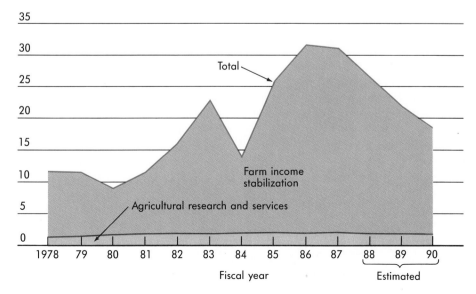

**FIGURE 26-2 Federal Expenditures for Agriculture, 1979–1990**
Federal assistance to farmers is substantial and is aimed chiefly at stabilizing their yearly income. *Source: Office of Management and Budget,* The United States Budget in Brief, Fiscal Year 1988 *(Washington, D.C.: U.S. Government Printing Office, 1988), 61.*

**Economic Policy and
Performance**

All Western democracies have market economies, as opposed to the state-run economies of communist nations. However, democratic countries vary significantly in the degree to which key industries are run by the government. In most democracies, the government owns and operates a number of leading industries, such as the airlines, steel, oil, or banking. But the U.S. government owns and operates very little in the way of industry. The United States also spends less on social welfare than do most other Western democracies, and consequently has a lower tax burden. The U.S. economy differs most obviously from those of other democracies in its sheer size. As measured by gross national product (total output of goods and services), the U.S. economy is far and away the world's largest. It is also a strong economy, although most experts rate it as less healthy than the economies of Japan and West Germany. A major reason is that the United States has an unfavorable balance of trade. Americans import more goods than they export. By comparison, Japan and West Germany are strong exporting nations.

*Sources:* OECD, 1988 (tax and trade data); *Statistical Abstract of the United States, 1988* (Washington, D.C.: U.S. Government Printing Office, 1987), 806 (GNP data); government ownership rankings are author's estimates.

| Country | Extent of Government Ownership of Industry | Total Tax Receipts (Percent of GNP, 1986) | Gross National Product (Billions of dollars, 1986) | Trade Balance: Exports Minus Imports (Billions of dollars, 1986) |
|---|---|---|---|---|
| Canada | Medium-low | 33.1 | $ 351 | $ +5.3 |
| France | High | 45.6 | 710 | −9.5 |
| Great Britain | Medium | 38.1 | 555 | −19.1 |
| Italy | High | 34.7 | 503 | −2.5 |
| Japan | Medium | 28.0 | 1,994 | +83.2 |
| Sweden | High | 50.5 | 128 | +4.6 |
| United States | Low | 29.2 | 3,911 | −152.6 |
| West Germany | Medium | 37.8 | 902 | +52.8 |

economic slumps that resulted in thousands of business failures and high unemployment. During the last of these nineteenth-century depressions, President Grover Cleveland, a Democrat, was urged to create a government jobs program to put the nation's unemployed back to work. He refused, saying that America was founded on self-reliance and that the government had no legitimate basis for interfering with the free market.

The greatest economic catastrophe in the nation's history—the Great Depression of the 1930s—finally brought an end to traditional economics. Franklin D. Roosevelt's emergency spending and job programs, designed to stimulate the economy and put Americans back to work, were in accord with the economic theories of John Maynard Keynes. In *The General Theory of Employment, Interest, and Money* (1936), Keynes noted that employers become overly cautious during a depression and will not expand production, even as wages drop. Challenging the traditional idea that government should draw back during depressions, Keynes claimed that severe economic downturns can be shortened only by increased government spending. By placing additional money in the hands of consumers and investors, government can stimulate production, employment, and spending and thus promote recovery.[16]

During the Great Depression of the 1930s, the federal government intervened on a massive scale to stabilize the economy. In one New Deal program, the Works Progress Administration, unemployed men were given jobs on public improvement projects, such as the building of roads and parks. (Bettmann Archive)

Roosevelt's efforts to stimulate the economy were controversial, but today government is expected to have ongoing policies for maintaining high economic production, employment, and growth and for controlling prices and interest rates. *Fiscal policy* and *monetary policy* are the economic approaches on which the government relies most heavily. Each approach is complex and has competing schools of thought. Accordingly, the following discussion attempts merely to outline some of the basic components of fiscal policy and monetary policy.

## FISCAL POLICY APPROACHES

The government's efforts to maintain a stable economy are made mainly through its taxing and spending decisions, which together are referred to as its **fiscal policy** (see Table 26-2).

[16]See Robert Lekachman, *The Age of Keynes* (New York: Random House, 1966).

**TABLE 26-2  Fiscal Policy: A Summary**

| | FISCAL POLICY ACTION | |
| *Problem* | *Demand Side* | *Supply Side* |
| --- | --- | --- |
| Low productivity and high unemployment | Increase spending<br>Cut personal income taxes | Cut business taxes<br>Encourage consumer saving and investment |
| Excess production and high inflation | Decrease spending<br>Increase personal income taxes | Uncertain |

### Demand-Side Economics

Keynes's economic ideas centered on fiscal policy and particularly on government's efforts to stimulate consumer spending. This **demand-side economics** emphasized the "demand" in the supply/demand equation. When the economy is sluggish, the government can increase its spending, thus placing more money in consumers' hands and stimulating demand. Increased demand in turn fosters rising production and employment. The New Deal, with its emphasis on public works jobs and social-welfare payments, was designed to spur the economy in this way. Government can also try to encourage demand through cuts in personal taxes.

High unemployment and low production are only two of the economic problems that government is called upon to solve. Another is inflation, which is an increase in the average level of prices of goods and services. Before the late 1960s, inflation was a minor irritant: prices rose by less than 4 percent annually. But inflation rose sharply during the last years of the Vietnam war and remained high throughout the 1970s, reaching a postwar record rate of 13 percent in 1979. As a result of inflation, the equivalent model of the $2,000 automobile of 1949 cost nearly $10,000 in 1979.

To fight inflation, government can apply remedies opposite to those used to fight unemployment and low productivity. Inflation normally occurs when jobs are plentiful and people have extra money to spend. Demand is high in such periods, and prices are pulled up in what is known as "demand-pull" inflation. By reducing its spending or by raising personal income taxes, government takes money from consumers, thus reducing demand and dampening prices. In response to rising inflation in the late 1960s, for instance, the federal government cut expenditures by $6 billion and imposed a 10 percent surcharge on personal income taxes.

### Supply-Side Economics

When President Ronald Reagan took office in 1981, the U.S. economy was in its worst slowdown in thirty-five years. Reagan turned to fiscal policy to bolster the economy, but his approach was somewhat unconventional. Previous presidents had emphasized consumption; by increasing or decreasing the amount of money in consumers' hands, government had stimulated or dampened consumer demand. In contrast, Reagan's policy was premised on stimulating the business sector. Thus his **supply-side economics** emphasized the "supply" in the supply/demand equation.[17]

"Reaganomics" included substantial tax cuts and credits for business, reflecting Reagan's belief that additional capital for business would result in economic expansion that would generate jobs and income. Provisions of the 1981 tax change were so generous to business that many corporations even received tax rebates. Tax loopholes enabled 128 corporations to cut their tax bills to less than zero in at least one of the years between 1981 and 1983. General Electric had profits of $6.5 billion in the 1981–1983 period, but instead of paying taxes, it received $283 million in tax rebates from the federal government.[18]

---

[17]See Bruce Bartlett, *Reaganomics: Supply-Side Economics* (Westport, Conn.: Arlington House, 1981).
[18]"Tax Reform Means End of the Line for Many Corporations' Free Ride," *Syracuse Post-Standard*, April 29, 1988, A-7.

Reagan's program also included the largest cut in personal income taxes in the nation's history. A 23 percent reduction was enacted for all income categories, so that higher-income Americans gained more in absolute terms; the tax saving for individuals in the $100,000 net-income category was nearly $5,000, compared with a $1,000 tax saving for individuals in the $20,000 net-income category. Higher-income Americans were expected to place more money in savings and investments, which would help business. The increased prosperity of wealthy Americans was expected to "trickle down" to those at the bottom as production increased and more jobs were created.

Although Reaganomics emphasized the supply side, the demand side was not neglected: government spending rose sharply as a result of the largest peacetime defense buildup in the nation's history. Whereas about $400 billion was spent on defense during Jimmy Carter's presidency, nearly $1 trillion was expended during Reagan's first term. Not since the New Deal had the government, through tax cuts and increased spending, stimulated the economy to such a great extent. During Reagan's first eighteen months in office, the economy weakened, but the downswing ended in 1982 and the economy grew progressively stronger. By 1987 the national unemployment rate was less than 6 percent (down from 11 percent in 1982) and the annual inflation rate was below 5 percent (down from the 1979 high of 13 percent). When Reagan left office in early 1989, the United States was in the sixth year of an uninterrupted economic upswing, the longest such period in the nation's history.

An ominous aspect of Reaganomics was the unprecedented size of the national debt, more than $2.5 trillion in 1988 (up from less than $1 trillion when Reagan took office). Reaganomics was based partly on the economist Arthur Laffer's prediction that a sizable federal tax cut would actually result in higher tax revenues. Laffer reasoned that lower tax rates would create such a vigorous economy that millions of unemployed people would find jobs and would thus be paying taxes rather than collecting unemployment and welfare payments. As it turned out, the additional tax revenues from new jobs did not, at least in the short run, make up for the tax revenues lost from the 23 percent cut in the tax

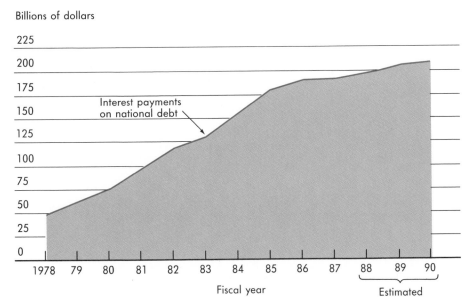

Billions of dollars

**FIGURE 26-3 Interest Payments on the National Debt, 1978–1990**
Interest on the national debt consumes a huge proportion of each year's federal budget.
SOURCE: *Office of Management and Budget,* The United States Budget in Brief, Fiscal Year 1988 *(Washington, D.C.: U.S. Government Printing Office, 1988), 107.*

rates, and the federal government went more deeply into debt. As a direct consequence, enormous sums are required each year to pay the interest on the national debt (see Figure 26-3). The interest payments were more than $200 billion in 1989, a sum larger than the entire federal budget as recently as 1969. Today only national defense and social security consume a larger share of the federal budget than does interest on the national debt.

## THE MAKING OF FISCAL POLICY

The annual federal budget is the foundation of fiscal policy. George Washington wrote his budget on a single sheet of paper, but the federal budget today is thousands of pages long and takes eighteen months to prepare and enact. The budget is a massive policy statement that allocates federal expenditures among thousands of government programs and provides for the revenues—taxes, social insurance receipts, and borrowed funds—to pay for these expenditures (see Figure 26-4). From one perspective, the budget is the national government's allocation of costs and benefits. Every federal program benefits some interest, whether it be farmers who get price supports, defense firms that obtain military contracts, or retirees who receive monthly social security checks. Not surprisingly, the process of enacting the annual federal budget is a highly political one. Agencies and groups have an obvious stake in promoting their interests.

From another standpoint, that of fiscal policy, the budget is a device for stimulating or dampening economic growth. Changes in overall levels of spending and taxing are means of keeping the economy's normal ups and downs from becoming extreme. However, there are practical limits to political leaders' ability to manipulate the budget. Cuts in the budget are particularly difficult to achieve, because many items, such as interest payments on the national debt, cannot be postponed and other items, such as social security benefits for retirees, federal employees' salary levels, and veterans' benefits, are politically untouchable.

Congress finds it easier to expand the budget than to contract it, but again there are limits. Higher expenditures eventually mean higher taxes. Political leaders have tended to expand the budget through increased borrowing rather than increased taxing. But this approach cannot be used indefinitely, because, in effect, it mortgages the future. The government currently is trying to deal with

**FIGURE 26-4 The Federal Budget Dollar**
*Source: Office of Management and Budget,* The United States Budget in Brief, Fiscal Year 1988, *(Washington, D.C.: U.S. Government Printing Office, 1988), i.*

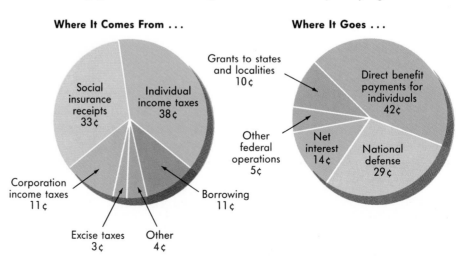

**Where It Comes From . . .**

Social insurance receipts 33¢
Individual income taxes 38¢
Corporation income taxes 11¢
Excise taxes 3¢
Other 4¢

**Where It Goes . . .**

Grants to states and localities 10¢
Direct benefit payments for individuals 42¢
Other federal operations 5¢
Net interest 14¢
National defense 29¢
Borrowing 11¢

the fiscal crisis created by the $1.5 trillion added to the federal debt between 1981 and 1988. Interest on the debt alone accounts for roughly 15 percent of all current federal spending and has discouraged the creation of new spending programs. In his inaugural address, George Bush said, in effect, that the government did not have the money to undertake any significant initiatives.

## The Fiscal Policy Structure

The president and Congress determine fiscal policy. The Constitution grants Congress the power to tax and spend, but the president normally initiates major policies in these areas and sits atop most of the fiscal policy structure.

The Employment Act of 1946 created the Council of Economic Advisers (CEA) and placed it within the Executive Office of the President (see Chapter 20). Appointed by the president with the approval of the Senate, the three members of the CEA advise the president on economic policy and assist him in preparing his annual Economic Report to Congress. This statement contains an assessment of the nation's economy and may include legislative proposals. The president also has the services of economic and revenue experts in the Treasury, Labor, and Commerce departments. The Office of Management and Budget (OMB), another presidential staff agency, is the chief instrument of fiscal policy; it prepares the annual budget that the president submits to Congress. The budget contains the president's recommendations on overall government spending and on the allocation of these expenditures among various programs. The combination of taxes and government borrowing necessary to finance this spending is also part of the president's annual budget message.

Congress's ability to affect fiscal policy was improved by the Employment Act of 1946, which established a joint House–Senate committee on the economy. Of much greater importance, however, was the Budget Control Act of 1974, which requires the president to provide Congress with detailed information on the spending and taxing proposals underlying his budget. The 1974 act also moved the starting date of the government's fiscal year from July 1 to October 1, giving Congress an additional three months to study the president's budget, which reaches the legislature in January. As we saw in Chapter 17, the act also established the Congressional Budget Office (CBO) to provide the House and Senate with budget analyses, which can be compared with those of the OMB. Finally, the act created the House and Senate Budget committees, which are responsible for proposing ceilings for various budget categories. Once the full House and Senate approve the proposals, Congress works within the constraints established by the budget resolutions, an approach that has increased Congress's ability to help shape the budget. Before 1974, areas of the budget were divided among congressional committees and subcommittees, and their separate actions were not coordinated so as to stay within specific budgetary limits.

## The Politics of Fiscal Policy

Politics plays a large part in the making of fiscal policy because Democrats and Republicans often disagree over the direction it should take.[19] The Democratic coalition has traditionally included the majority of lower-income and working-

[19]See Douglas Hibbs, "Political Parties and Macroeconomic Policy," *American Political Science Review* 77 (December 1977): 1467–1487.

TO APPLY FOR BENEFITS FROM WASHINGTON ST. COMPLETE FORM A & AND GO TO WINDOW 24

TO APPLY FOR BENEFITS FROM ANOTHER STATE COMPLETE FORM B & GO TO THE INFORMATION COUNTER

IF YOUR BENEFIT YE[A] HAS NOT END[I] & YOU WISH TO RE-OPEN YOUR CLAIM AFTER A PERIOD OF EMPLOYMENT COMPLETE FORM C AND GO TO WINDOW 22

Through spending and tax policies that are designed to stimulate economic growth, fiscal policy can reduce the nation's unemployment level. (Doug Wilson/Black Star)

class Americans. Accordingly, the party's leaders are sensitive to rising unemployment because blue-collar workers are usually the first and most deeply affected. Chronic unemployment is also characteristic of some largely Democratic groups, such as black Americans, whose rate of joblessness is roughly twice the overall rate. Democrats in Washington have usually responded to a sluggish economy with increased government spending, which offers direct help to the unemployed and stimulates demand.

Republican leaders are likely to be more concerned about inflation. It attacks the purchasing power of all Americans, including higher-income individuals who are usually untouched by rising unemployment rates. Inflation also raises the cost of doing business, because firms must pay higher interest rates for the money they borrow. With its electoral base in business and the middle class, the Republican party usually wants to hold government spending to a level where its inflationary effects are small. Thus, in response to the unusual combination of high inflation and high unemployment in the late 1970s and early 1980s, the Republicans Ford and Reagan placed more emphasis on fighting inflation, while the Democrat Carter concentrated initially on reducing unemployment. All these presidents would have preferred to hold down both unemployment and inflation if they could, but each attacked the problem that was of greatest concern to his party's constituents.

Tax policy also has partisan dimensions. Reagan's 1981 tax cut favored Republican constituencies—the business community and higher-income Americans. Although conservative Democrats in the House of Representatives supported the Reagan policy, liberal Democrats in 1981 wanted a tax cut that would be more beneficial to working-class and lower-middle-class Americans.[20]

[20]See Richard E. Cohen, "Rating Congress—A Guide to Separating the Liberals from the Conservatives," *National Journal*, May 8, 1982, 800–810.

In the House of Representatives, 99 percent of the Republicans but only 20 percent of the Democrats voted for the 1981 tax cut. Democrats generally have favored a progressive tax system, which progressively increases tax rates as incomes rise. Although Republicans have also supported this concept, they have preferred to keep the upper-income tax rate at a relatively low level, contending that this policy encourages the savings and investment that are necessary to foster economic growth. The American tax system does impose higher rates on higher income levels but also contains loopholes (such as tax deductions for interest paid on home mortgages) that benefit mostly higher-income taxpayers. The net effect is that Americans of modest and high incomes have traditionally paid taxes at about the same rate.

In comparison with high-income taxpayers in other democracies, wealthy Americans pay relatively little in taxes. The marginal tax rate on a taxpayer with a net income above $150,000 is only 28 percent, compared with 70 percent or more in some Western European countries. The powerful hold that the ideal of individualism has on Americans' thinking leads them to justify low taxes on the wealthy and makes taxation an explosive political issue. Few U.S. politicians are willing to say that taxes should be higher. Walter Mondale was widely criticized during his 1984 presidential campaign for proposing a tax increase to produce additional revenue that would be applied toward reducing the national debt. In contrast, a campaign promise like the one George Bush made in 1988, "No new taxes," is always a popular message.

### The Electoral Connection

We noted in Chapter 19 that the issues that affect Americans' pocketbooks have the most influence on their presidential voting decisions. As Seymour Martin Lipset writes, "Voters are disposed to credit or blame incumbent administrations for the state of the economy."[21]

Until recently, unemployment was the main concern of officials at election time. The attitude was that other economic problems might wound a politician, but high unemployment could be fatal. Studies of voting behavior supported this assumption; of all economic indicators, the joblessness rate has most consistently been related to swings in election outcomes.[22] In recent elections, however, taxes and inflation have also been major issues. The "taxpayers' revolt" of the late 1970s apparently contributed to the defeat of some incumbent officeholders.[23] In 1980, high inflation contributed to Jimmy Carter's failure to win reelection and to the loss of the Democrats' control of the U.S. Senate.

Officeholders get less credit when the economy is healthy than blame when it goes bad.[24] A stagnant economy can result in a drop of several percentage points

---

★ ANALYZE THE ISSUE

**Taxation to Redistribute Income**
It is often stated that a goal of taxes is to achieve a partial redistribution of income from wealthier people to poorer ones. According to U.S. Census Bureau figures from 1986, the richest one-fifth of Americans received 46.0 percent of household income, including government benefits, before taxes and still had 45.7 percent after taxes. Meanwhile, the poorest fifth had 3.8 percent of household income, including government benefits, before taxes and 4.7 percent after taxes. Does it surprise you that taxation does so little to redistribute income? Why do you think the effect is so slight?

*And having looked to Government for bread, on the very first scarcity they will turn and bite the hand that fed them.*
                    Edmund Burke

---

[21]Seymour Martin Lipset, "The Economy, Elections, and Public Opinions," *Tocqueville Review* 5 (Fall 1983): 431.

[22]D. Roderick Kiewiet, *Macro-Economics and Micro-Politics* (Chicago: University of Chicago Press, 1983), 154–158; Donald R. Kinder and D. Roderick Kiewiet, "Economic Discontent and Political Behavior," *American Journal of Political Science* 23 (1979): 495–527.

[23]Abraham Sharna, "Thomas Hobbes, Meet Howard Jarvis," *Public Opinion*, November/December 1978, 56–59.

[24]Howard S. Bloom and H. Douglas Price, "Voter Response to Short-Run Economic Conditions: The Asymmetric Effect of Prosperity and Recession," *American Political Science Review* 69 (1976): 1240–1254.

in the vote obtained by the party holding the presidency.[25] The problem for incumbents is the difficulty of getting the economy to respond to their efforts. If government could easily control it, the economy would always be strong. In reality, however, the economy has natural ups and downs that so far have defied mastery by economists and politicians.

## MONETARY POLICY

Fiscal policy is not the only instrument of economic management available to government; another is **monetary policy,** which is based on manipulation of the amount of money in circulation (see Table 26-3). Monetarists such as the economist Milton Friedman hold that control of the money supply is the key to sustaining a healthy economy. Too much money in circulation contributes to inflation because when too many dollars are chasing too few goods, prices are driven up. Too little money in circulation results in a slowing of the economy because consumers lack ready cash and easy credit. Monetarists believe in tightening or loosening the money supply as a way of slowing or invigorating the economy.

### The Federal Reserve System

Control over the money supply rests not with the president or Congress but with the Federal Reserve System (known as "the Fed"), which was created by the Federal Reserve Act of 1913. The Fed is directed by a board of governors whose seven members serve for fourteen years, except for the chair and vice-chair, who serve for four years. All members are appointed by the president with the approval of the Senate. The Fed regulates the activities of all national banks and those state banks that choose to become members of the Federal Reserve System—about 6,000 banks in all. The key policy decisions made by the Fed's board are carried out through twelve regional Federal Reserve banks, each of which has responsibility for the member banks in its region.

[25]Edward R. Tufte, *Political Control of the Economy* (Princeton, N.J.: Princeton University Press, 1978), ch. 5; Francisco Arcelus and Allen H. Meltzer, "The Effect of Aggregate Economic Variables on Congressional Elections," *American Political Science Review* 69 (1975): 1232–1239.

**TABLE 26-3  Monetary Policy: A Summary**

| *Problem* | *Monetary Policy Action by Federal Reserve* |
|---|---|
| Low productivity and high unemployment (require an increase in the money supply) | Buys securities<br>Lowers interest rate on loans to member banks<br>Lowers cash reserve that member banks must deposit in Federal Reserve System |
| Excess productivity and high inflation (require a decrease in the money supply) | Sells securities<br>Raises interest rate on loans to member banks<br>Raises cash reserve that member banks must deposit in Federal Reserve System |

The Fed controls the money supply primarily through three activities. First, it buys and sells securities on the open market. When it buys securities from the public, the Fed puts money into private hands to be spent or invested, thus stimulating the economy. When it sells securities to the public, the Fed takes money out of circulation, thereby slowing spending and investment. Second, the Fed affects the money supply by lowering or raising the interest charged when member banks borrow money from their regional Federal Reserve bank. When the Fed raises the interest rate for banks, they are discouraged from borrowing from the Federal Reserve, and so they have less money available to lend. Conversely, by lowering the interest rate, the Fed encourages its member banks to borrow, thus increasing their loan funds. When more credit is available, consumers and investors can obtain loans at lower rates and are thereby encouraged to borrow and spend. Third, the Fed can raise or lower the cash reserve that member banks are required to deposit with the regional Federal Reserve banks. This reserve is a proportion of each member bank's total deposits. By increasing the reserve rate, the Fed takes money from member banks and thus takes it out of circulation; when the Fed lowers the reserve rate, banks keep more of their money and can make more loans to consumers and investors. Essentially, the Fed decides how much money to add to or subtract from the economy, estimating the amount that will permit the most economic growth without leading to an unacceptable level of inflation.

Economists debate the relative effectiveness of monetary policy and fiscal policy, but monetary (money supply) policy has one obvious advantage: it can be implemented more quickly. The Fed can adjust interest and reserve rates on short notice. In contrast, changes in fiscal (taxing and spending) policy normally take time to implement because Congress is a slow-acting institution. Many economists believed, for example, that Lyndon Johnson's proposed tax increase, which Congress enacted in 1968 after months of delay, was the proper remedy for rising inflation but came too late to be fully effective.

## The Politics of Monetary Policy

The Fed's role in managing the national economy is controversial, because its officials are neither elected nor directly responsible to elected representatives. The Fed was established to give stability to the banking system. Only later, with the development of monetarism as a theory of economic management, did the Fed become an instrument for manipulating the national economy.

The Fed's policies are not always popular with elected officials. In 1979, for example, with inflation running at a 13 percent annual rate, the Fed sharply reduced the money supply. By 1981 inflation had come down, but the prime interest rate had soared to a record high of 20 percent.* Neither consumers nor investors could afford to take out many loans at such a rate; housing construction, business expansion, and consumer spending slowed dramatically, and unemployment rose. About the only satisfied group was the bankers; high inflation had been eroding the value of their outstanding bank loans. The Reagan administration and Congress pleaded with the Fed to increase the money supply. When Paul Volcker, then chairman of the Fed's board of governors, refused, the hostility of some interests toward him became so intense

> ★ ANALYZE THE ISSUE
>
> **Coordinating the Nation's Economic Policy**
> In 1989 the Fed hiked interest rates in response to rising consumer prices. The Bush administration criticized the Fed's anti-inflationary action, fearing that it would contribute to an economic slowdown and thereby reduce government revenues and worsen the budget deficit. What does this dispute suggest about the difficulty of achieving a coordinated national economic policy? Do you think that monetary policy, like fiscal policy, should be determined by elected officials? Why, or why not?

---

*The *prime rate* is the interest rate that commercial banks charge their major, most creditworthy corporate customers for short-term loans; it is used as an indicator of prevailing interest rates.

that he was placed under Secret Service protection.[26] In mid-1982 the Fed finally did increase the money supply. The nation's economy began to grow, while inflation remained low. In the judgment of some economists, the Fed's decision to loosen credit was a larger factor in the economic recovery that began in late 1982 than was the supply-side policy of the Reagan administration. If this is true, the obvious question is why the needs of the bankers were initially placed ahead of the needs of the nation.

Economic prosperity after 1982 eased official Washington's concern over the Fed, but the issue of its accountability to elected officials remains unsettled. Under the present arrangement, the Fed and elected officials can work at cross-purposes. Congress at some point may decide that an independent Fed can no longer be tolerated and enact a change that will bring monetary policy under the direct control of elected officials.

[26]*Newsweek*, February 24, 1986, 52.

## Summary

Although private enterprise is the main force in the American economic system, the federal government plays a significant role through the policies it selects to regulate, promote, and stimulate the economy.

Regulatory policy is designed to achieve efficiency and equity, which require government to intervene, for example, to maintain competitive trade practices (an efficiency goal) and to protect vulnerable parties in economic transactions (an equity goal). Many of the regulatory decisions of the federal government, particularly those of older agencies, are made largely in the context of group politics; business lobbies have an especially strong influence on the regulatory policies that affect them. In general, newer regulatory agencies have policy responsibilities that are broader in scope and apply to a larger number of firms than those of the older agencies. As a result, the policy decisions of newer agencies are more often made in the context of party politics; Republican administrations are less vigorous in their regulation of business than are Democratic administrations.

Business is the major beneficiary of the federal government's efforts to promote economic interests. Any number of programs, including those to provide loans and research grants, are designed to assist businesses, which are also protected from failure through such measures as tariffs and favorable tax laws. Labor, for its part, gets government assistance through laws concerning such matters as worker safety, the minimum wage, and collective bargaining; yet America's individualistic culture tends to put labor at a disadvantage, keeping it less powerful than business in dealing with the government. Agriculture is another economic sector that depends substantially on government's help, particularly in the form of income stabilization programs, such as those that provide subsidies and price supports.

Through its fiscal and monetary policies, the federal government attempts to maintain a strong and stable economy—one that is characterized by high productivity, high employment, and low inflation. Fiscal policy is based on government decisions in regard to spending and taxing, which are aimed at influencing either consumers (demand-side economics) or producers (supply-side economics). Fiscal policy is worked out through Congress and the president and is consequently responsive to political pressures. However, because of the difficulty of either raising taxes or cutting programs, there are limits to the government's ability to apply fiscal policy as an economic remedy. Monetary policy is based on the money supply and works through the Federal Reserve System, which is headed by a board whose members hold office for fixed terms. The Fed is a relatively independent body, a fact that has given rise to questions as to whether it should have such a large role in national economic policy.

## Major Concepts

demand-side economics
deregulatoin
economy
efficiency
equity
externalities

fiscal policy
laissez-faire doctrine
monetary policy
regulation
supply-side economics

## Suggested Readings

Friedman, Milton, and Walter Heller. *Monetary vs. Fiscal Policy.* New York: Norton, 1969. Opposing arguments by a leading monetarist and a leading Keynesian.

Gerston, Larry N., Cynthia Fraleigh, and Robert Schwab. *The Deregulated Society.* Pacific Grove, Calif.: Brooks/Cole, 1988. An assessment of deregulation and its effects.

Gilder, George. *Wealth and Poverty.* New York: Basic Books, 1984. A defense of the free-market system as economically and morally superior to the welfare state.

Harrington, Michael. *The Twilight of Capitalism.* New York: Simon & Schuster, 1976. A critique of the U.S. economy by one of the country's leading socialists.

Kiewiet, D. Roderick. *Macro-Economics and Micro-Politics.* Chicago: University of Chicago Press, 1983. An analysis of the relationship between general economic conditions and election outcomes.

Lekachman, Robert. *The Age of Keynes.* New York: Random House, 1966. A nontechnical assessment of the economic theories of John Maynard Keynes.

Lindbloom, Charles. *Politics and Markets.* An analysis of the challenges of a mixed economy.

Pechman, Joseph. *Federal Tax Policy,* 5th ed. Washington, D.C.: Brookings Institution, 1987. A description of federal tax policy by an expert.

Stone, Alan. *Regulation and Its Alternatives.* Washington, D.C.: Congressional Quarterly Press, 1982. A useful overview of regulatory policy and its purposes.

# Chapter 27

---

## SOCIAL-WELFARE POLICY: PROVIDING FOR PERSONAL SECURITY AND NEED

---

*We the people of the United States, in order to . . . promote the general welfare . . .*
*Preamble, U.S. Constitution*

John Jones is a fictitious retired businessman who has a company pension that pays him $1,500 a month. He also receives more than $1,000 a month in interest and dividends on his savings, bonds, and stocks. John's financial obligations are few. He is a widower, and the youngest of his three children graduated from college years ago.

Jane Smith is a fictitious recent divorcée with two children, aged eight and three. Jane had gotten married the summer after she graduated from high school. Jane had never worked outside the home before her husband left her; without special job skills and with a small child at home, the only work that she could take is a part-time job paying $4 an hour. Jane's net financial assets total less than $500.

John and Jane seem very different, but they do have one thing in common: each gets a monthly social-welfare check from government. Who, John or Mary, receives the larger government check? Who has fewer strings attached to continuing receipt of the check? Who incurs no stigma by taking government handouts? The answer to all of these questions is the same: John.

John is a social security recipient and gets about $750 each month from the government. He applied for social security upon retiring at age sixty-five, and the monthly checks have come regularly ever since. John does not have to worry that the checks will stop coming; he has a lifelong entitlement to them. If John moves to another state, or even to another country, his monthly check will follow. Jane, who lives in New Jersey, gets about $350 a month from the government through the Aid to Families with Dependent Children (AFDC) program. To get this money Jane had to provide proof of her divorce, low income, and lack of assets (she is allowed no more than $1,000 in assets), and she is required to report regularly on whether her economic status has changed. If her income should rise above the poverty level, she would lose her monthly AFDC support. If Jane should move, say, to Florida, she would have to reapply for AFDC and there would be a waiting period during which she would get no support. Moreover, by moving, she would take a cut in her monthly benefit, to about $225—$125 less than she gets in New Jersey. Finally, Jane carries the mark of a "welfare case" supported by the taxpaying public. John bears no such stigma. He "earned" his monthly check by paying social security taxes during his years of employment.

The U.S. welfare system reflects the country's individualistic culture, tinged with an element of egalitarian compassion. Most Americans are expected to provide for their own economic needs. Economic security is not a right of citizenship. In Western European nations a different welfare philosophy prevails. Of course, citizens of these countries are encouraged to work and benefit economically from doing so; but they are considered to be more or less entitled to a minimum standard of living, at government expense if necessary. For example, all citizens of these countries are eligible for government-funded health care. In contrast, Americans believe that it is somehow unfair for people to receive government support unless they have worked for it or are demonstrably unable to work. Moreover, Americans tend to feel that giving public support to able-bodied individuals discourages personal effort and produces welfare dependency. As a consequence, welfare programs based on need, such as AFDC, have less public support than programs based on personal tax contributions, such as social security.

*Few, save the poor, feel for the poor.*

Letitia Landon

Another powerful influence on U.S. welfare policy is the country's federal system of government. Welfare was traditionally a responsibility of state and local governments; only since the 1930s has the federal government played a major role. A few programs, such as social security, are run solely by the federal government, whereas most programs, such as AFDC, are joint federal–state programs. Because the continuing eligibility of AFDC recipients must be verified at regular intervals, the program is administered by state governments, which have the local offices and employees required for such a task. Each state provides some of the funding for the AFDC program and sets its own level of AFDC benefits. Because the states vary considerably in their ability and willingness to support the program, the amount that AFDC recipients receive depends on where they live. In contrast, as a national program, social security provides uniform benefits regardless of where a recipient resides.

America's traditional values and federal system of government have made welfare policy in the United States a web of complex, untidy, and sometimes logic-defying programs that many liberals and conservatives alike have described as a mess. This chapter accepts that judgment but concludes that the welfare system could hardly be otherwise, given the fact that social welfare is the arena in which nearly all the contending forces of American politics collide. The main points discussed in the chapter are the following:

One of the ironies of American domestic policy is that tax deductions on home mortgages for the middle and upper classes are government subsidies, just as are rent vouchers for the poor, but only the latter are stigmatized as "welfare handouts." (top, Sally Weigand/The Picture Cube; bottom, Charles Vergara/Photo Researchers)

★ *The federal government today is deeply involved in the provision of social welfare, which historically was the responsibility of states and localities.* The change resulted from economic and social trends and was facilitated by the federal government's superior capacity to tax and borrow. Officials at all levels—federal, state, and local—now work together to address welfare problems.

★ *Social-welfare programs are designed to reward and foster self-reliance or, when this is not possible, to provide benefits only to those individuals who are truly in need.* U.S. welfare policy is *not* based on the assumption that every citizen has a right to material security.

★ *Americans favor social insurance programs (such as social security) over public assistance programs (such as AFDC).* As a result, most social-welfare expenditures are not targeted toward the nation's neediest citizens.

★ *Social welfare policy embodies all the conflicts of American politics:* individualism vs. equality, Congress vs. president, national authority vs. local authority, public sector vs. private sector, Republicans vs. Democrats, poorer vs. richer. At best, social-welfare policy represents the politics of hope—an uneasy blend of opportunity and compassion.

## The Federal Government's Role in Social Welfare

Until the 1930s, state and local governments had almost complete responsibility for public welfare. Welfare policy was deemed to fall within the powers reserved to the states by the Tenth Amendment and to be adequately addressed by them because the provision of welfare services was constrained by the country's individualistic culture. Americans were expected to fend for themselves, and when they were unable to do so, they became the responsibility of relatives and friends. In large part, government services were reserved for society's "losers." The Great Depression was a turning point. A fourth of the nation's workers were jobless and even more were underemployed and inadequately paid. Private charity was no match for a problem of such magnitude, and state and local governments were nearly broke. Moreover, no part of the country escaped the economic devastation. Every city, village, and farm fell on hard times. There was no practical alternative to federal intervention.

### SOCIAL WELFARE AND AMERICANS AS A NATIONAL COMMUNITY

The Great Depression made it clear that Americans had become a national community with national welfare needs. During the nineteenth century it was possible, even desirable, to have a fully decentralized welfare system. Most

The federal government took on a major role in social-welfare policy during the Great Depression of the 1930s, when some Americans were so destitute that they had to live in shantytowns called "Hoovervilles," like this one in what is now New York City's Riverside Park. (Culver Pictures)

people lived on farms and in small towns, and families were large and tended to remain together in the same community when the children reached adulthood. Public-welfare needs accordingly were small. Americans raised much of their own food, and when they became old or sick, they could turn to family and friends for help.

By the time of the Great Depression, Americans were enmeshed in a complex and economically interdependent society. More than half of the population lived in cities (only 20 percent did so in 1860), and more than 10 million workers were employed by industry (only 1 million were so employed in 1860). Urban workers typically depended on landlords for their housing, on farmers and grocers for their food, and on corporations for their jobs. Farmers were more independent, but they, too, were increasingly part of a larger economic network. Their income depended on market prices and shipping and equipment costs.[1]

This economic interdependence enabled the United States to achieve unprecedented prosperity, but it also meant that no area of the economy could be protected if things turned sour. When the Depression hit in 1929, its effects could not be contained. A decline in spending was followed by a drop in production, a loss of jobs, unpaid rents and grocery bills, and a shrinking market for foodstuffs, which led to a further decline in spending and a continuation of the downward spiral. The universal impact of the Great Depression made it clear that Americans had become joined together in a national community.

Through its response, the government in Washington intensified the sense of national community. The New Deal was important not only for the immediate economic relief it provided but also for its impact on Americans' attitudes.[2] The public jobs projects and welfare programs of the New Deal encouraged Americans to look favorably upon Washington's help. For example, a 1936 Gallup poll indicated that 61 percent of Americans supported Roosevelt's old-age pension plan, while only 27 percent opposed it. "The Social Security Act," Andrew Dobelstein notes, "reflected [the new attitude] that the federal government had responsibility to *promote* the general welfare through specific public welfare programs funded with federal tax dollars."[3]

*Unfortunately many Americans live on the outskirts of hope—some because of their poverty, some because of their color, and all too many because of both. Our task is to help replace their despair with opportunity.*

Lyndon Johnson

The extent and permanence of the change in public attitudes became clear in the 1960s, when the second great wave of new federal welfare programs— President Lyndon Johnson's Great Society—was initiated. Public demands in the 1960s, as in the 1930s, were the driving force behind a larger federal role. Americans wanted more and better services from government, and when they recognized that federal officials were willing to venture into policy areas traditionally managed by the states, they pressured them to act.[4]

Johnson did not require much persuasion. As we mentioned in Chapter 10, he was an activist president who believed that the national government should be

[1]James E. Anderson, *The Emergence of the Modern Regulatory State* (Washington, D.C.: Public Affairs Press, 1962), 2–3.
[2]V. O. Key, Jr., *The Responsible Electorate* (Cambridge, Mass.: Belknap Press of Harvard University, 1966), 43.
[3]Andrew W. Dobelstein, *Politics, Economics, and Public Welfare* (Englewood Cliffs, N.J.: Prentice-Hall, 1980), 5.
[4]Lloyd A. Free and Hadley Cantril, *The Political Beliefs of Americans* (New York: Simon & Schuster, 1968), 21; see also Eva Mueller, "Public Attitudes toward Fiscal Programs," *Quarterly Journal of Economics* 77 (May 1963): 210–235.

deeply involved in social policy. The Great Society programs included federal initiatives in health care, education, public housing, nutrition, and other areas traditionally dominated by states and localities. In addition to providing direct benefits, these programs had the indirect goal of fostering racial equality. If states and localities wanted a share of federal program funds, they had to use the money in ways that were not racially discriminatory. Thus Johnson's vision of public welfare was broader than that of Roosevelt, whose programs had been aimed at economic recovery. In Johnson's view, Americans formed a national community and Washington had a responsibility to equalize the opportunities and social services available to them.[5] Johnson was not contending that Washington should run all social programs or that Americans belong only to the nation, not to their state or city. He was saying that times had changed and that it no longer made sense for the quality of Americans' public education, health care, or welfare services to depend largely on whether they resided in Mississippi or California or Iowa.

The idea that Americans are a national community has not gone unchallenged. In the 1930s, before bending to the imperative of national economic recovery, the Supreme Court used the Tenth Amendment to block some New Deal programs. Since then, opposition to federal authority has stemmed largely from political and philosophical considerations. Although national change has unquestionably required Washington to play a larger role, some people ask whether the federal government has gone too far in asserting its authority. Presidents Richard Nixon and Ronald Reagan spoke of their hope for a "new federalism" in which some decisions being made in Washington would be turned over to states and localities. In addition, state and local officials have frequently claimed that they understand their residents' requirements better than distant officials in Washington can.

Nevertheless, state and local governments have generally looked to the federal government for help. By and large, officials at all levels have learned to combine their efforts and resources to address common problems. Some of the federal programs, particularly those established in the 1970s, resulted from specific requests made by state and local officials, who, as we saw in Chapter 14, have become a strong lobbying group in Washington. The pragmatic outlook of state and local officials was clearly evident in 1982, when, as part of his "new federalism" philosophy, Reagan proposed a $50 billion takeover of federal welfare spending by the states. In return, the federal government would assume responsibility for about $20 billion in state Medicaid costs and provide a $30 billion first-year subsidy to the states to help them fund their new responsibilities. The federal subsidy would then gradually decline until, after ten years, the states would be on their own and would have to decide whether to keep or phase out the programs in question. Reagan's proposal was rebuffed by state and local officials, who did not want control of costly and popular programs. The prospect of gaining control over these policies was a weak incentive in comparison with a continuation of federal funding.

The American people are somewhat ambivalent about Washington's welfare role. Although more than 50 percent of Americans say in surveys that the federal government has become too large and powerful, more than 80 percent also say that they favor current or higher levels of federal spending on social

[5]See Michael Reagan, *The New Federalism* (New York: Oxford University Press, 1972).

★ ANALYZE THE ISSUE

**Big Government's Impact on the American Dream** According to a 1986 Roper poll, 80 percent of Americans believe that cuts in federal social-welfare programs would threaten the American dream. Yet 86 percent believe that this same dream is threatened by big government. Do these contradictory opinions represent public support for the status quo, or do they mean something else? Explain your interpretation.

programs.[6] Americans have a longing for smaller government and local control, but do not want to face the reality of fewer services.

## SOCIAL WELFARE AND WASHINGTON'S REVENUE-GENERATING POWER

The interdependence of the sectors of modern American society is one of two major factors that have compelled the federal government to assume a larger role in promoting the general welfare. The other is the federal government's superior capacity to tax and borrow. Although states and localities have a substantial tax base, they are in an inherently competitive situation. People and businesses faced with state or local increases can move to another state or locality where taxes are lower. The national government is less constrained by tax competition. Moreover, the federal government depends almost entirely on forms of taxation, such as personal and corporate income taxes, that automatically increase revenues as the economy expands. The net effect is that the federal government raises more tax revenues than do all fifty states and the thousands of local governments combined (see Figure 27-1). Finally, because it controls the American dollar, the federal government has a nearly unlimited line of credit. States and localities cannot so easily borrow to cover their budget deficits.

The New Deal was made possible by Washington's superior fiscal position. At a time when state and local governments were struggling to raise enough revenues to stay afloat, national officials funded welfare programs for the aged and disabled and mounted public jobs programs that at their peak employed a fifth of the country's entire work force. The federal government's fiscal strength was also crucial to the Great Society programs of the 1960s. When employment and income levels rose in the early 1960s, federal tax revenues increased sharply. To prevent the economic slowdown that would result if this revenue windfall were kept out of circulation, Johnson's chief economic adviser, Walter Heller, urged him to use it to help the states improve their services.[7]

Johnson accepted Heller's general advice but rejected his suggestion that funds be given outright to the states. Johnson preferred to supply states and localities with federal funds and to restrict the purposes for which they could be

[6]Warren E. Miller et al., *American National Election Studies Data Sourcebook* (Cambridge, Mass.: Harvard University Press, 1980), 171.
[7]Walter Heller, *New Dimensions of Political Economy* (Cambridge, Mass.: Harvard University Press, 1966), 72–73.

**FIGURE 27-1 Federal, State, and Local Shares of Government Revenue, 1987**
The federal government raises more revenues than all state and local governments combined.
*Source: Advisory Commission on Intergovernmental Relations,* Significant Features of Fiscal Federalism, *1988 ed., vol. 2 (Washington, D.C.: ACIR, 1989), 26.*

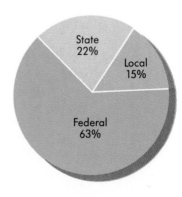

State 22%

Local 15%

Federal 63%

Federal school lunch programs are funded by Washington but administered by states and localities. (Susan Lapides/Design Conceptions)

used. The concept was not new. The funding for some of Roosevelt's New Deal programs, including survivors' benefits, had been channeled through the states. But Johnson carried the practice much further. Except for Medicare, the Great Society programs were based on grants to state governments or local governments. Thus a complex form of intergovernmental relations emerged in which Washington dealt directly with other governments at all levels—states, cities, counties, school districts, and others.[8] In addition to welfare services, these federal programs covered such policy areas as transportation, recreation, and law enforcement.

Viewed in a broad perspective, federal grants-in-aid have been the basis for nothing less than a quiet revolution in the relations among America's governments[9] and in the federal government's contribution to the general welfare. Federal restrictions on the policy decisions of state and local governments were relatively few before the 1950s, but they have proliferated in the form of conditions attached to the receipt of federal assistance. From a total of $5 billion in 1955, federal grants-in-aid passed the $100 billion level in 1985. In terms of constant dollars, federal aid has increased roughly sixfold since 1955 (see Figure 27-2). The federal government's recent debt problems, which were discussed in Chapter 26, have resulted in a modest cutback in assistance to states and localities, but federal funds still account for nearly $1 of every $5 spent by these governments.

Viewed from the opposite perspective, states and localities raise 80 percent of the money they spend. This figure should be a caution against the simplistic

[8]David B. Walker, *Toward a Functioning Federalism* (Cambridge, Mass.: Winthrop, 1981), 102.
[9]Ibid. See also Douglas D. Rose, "National and Local Forces in State Politics," *American Political Science Review* 67 (December 1973): 1162–1173; Morton Grodzins, "Centralization and Decentralization in the American Federal System," in Robert A. Goldwin, ed., *A Nation of States* (Chicago: Rand McNally, 1963), 1–4.

Billions of 1982 dollars

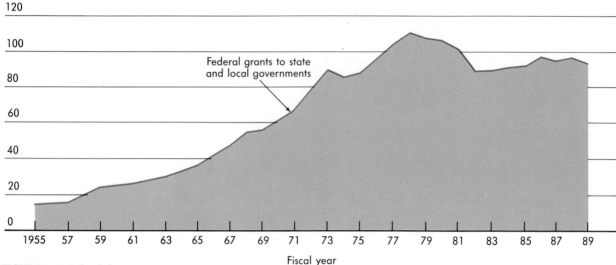

Fiscal year

**FIGURE 27-2 Federal Grants to State and Local Governments in Constant (1982) Dollars, 1955–1989**
Federal aid to states and localities has increased dramatically since the 1950s.
*Source: Advisory Commission on Intergovernmental Relations,* Significant Features of Fiscal Federalism, *1989 ed., vol. 1 (Washington, D.C.: ACIR, 1989), 15.*

conclusion that Washington dictates what states and localities do. The federal government's influence on domestic welfare policies has indeed increased dramatically, but state and local governments continue to make the largest contributions. For example, they determine most public education policies and provide about 90 percent of the funding for public schools (see Table 27-1).

## TYPES OF FEDERAL GRANTS: PURPOSES AND POLITICS

Federal grants-in-aid to states and localities have been of three major types, which are differentiated by the extent to which Washington defines the conditions of their use (see Table 27-2).

### Categorical Grants

Most federal aid programs have been in the form of **categorical grants,** so called because the funds can be used only for designated projects. State and local governments can refuse the money, but if they accept it, they must comply with federal restrictions on its use. Medicaid funds, for example, can be spent only on health care for the poor, and states that accept Medicaid funds are required to provide health-care coverage to all people on public welfare.

Categorical grants serve the power and reelection needs of members of Congress, who are national officeholders but are also representatives of state

**TABLE 27-1  Funds Provided by Federal, State, and Local Governments in Selected Policy Areas (Percent)**

| Policy Area | Federal Funds | State Funds | Local Funds |
|---|---|---|---|
| Education | 7% | 49% | 44% |
| Public welfare | 56 | 36 | 8 |
| Health and hospitals | 7 | 47 | 45 |

SOURCE: Advisory Commission on Intergovernmental Relations, *Significant Features of Fiscal Federalism* (Washington, D.C.: ACIR, 1987), 30, 34, 36.

**TABLE 27-2   Restrictions Associated with Types of Federal Grants-in-Aid to States and Localities**

| Type of Grant | Restrictions |
| --- | --- |
| Categorical grant | Funds can be used only for specific projects (such as the purchase of hospital equipment). |
| Block grant | Funds can be used only in a general policy area (such as health), with the choice of specific projects resting with state or local government. |
| Revenue-sharing grant | Funds can be used as the state or local government chooses. |

and local interests. Such grants are the best means of combining the two roles because they allow members of Congress to assist their constituents while imposing conditions designed to promote national goals. From another perspective, such grants allow members of Congress to act not only as national legislators but also, in effect, as state governors and local mayors: they have the power to decide some of the policy directions of states and localities.[10] Such grants also help members of Congress to build the constituent support necessary to stay in office. They can point to a local hospital wing or school lunch program as something for which they voted to contribute federal funds. Categorical grants are typically drafted so that as many communities as possible can qualify, because members of Congress are not likely to be interested in voting for a grant program that does not include their constituents.

Democrats, whether in Congress or in the White House, have been particularly inclined to favor categorical grants.[11] Important constituent groups within the Democratic party, such as the poor and minorities, often lose out in state and local politics because of the power of other interests or because of jurisdictional boundaries. The inner-city schools attended by poorer children, for example, are nearly always inferior to the suburban schools attended by more affluent children. Such disparities can be targeted for correction by means of categorical grants: the Elementary and Secondary Education Act of 1965, for example, provides disproportionate funding for schools in impoverished areas.

Welfare policy has generally been debated along partisan lines, a reflection of differences in the coalitions and philosophies of the Republican and Democratic parties. With its ties to labor, the poor, and minorities, the Democratic party has nearly always led on major federal welfare initiatives. As a dramatic example, the key House vote on the Social Security Act of 1935 found 85 percent of Democrats supporting it and 99 percent of Republicans against it.[12] Republicans gradually came to accept the idea that the federal government has a role in social welfare but have argued that the role should be kept as small as practicable. Thus, in the 1960s, Republican opposition to Johnson's Great Society was substantial. More than 70 percent of congressional Republicans voted against the 1964 Economic Opportunity Act and the 1965 Medicare and Medicaid programs. In the 1980s, against the opposition of congressional Democrats,

---

[10]Charles Schultze, "Federal Spending: Past, Present and Future," in Henry Owen and Charles Schultze, eds., *Setting National Priorities: The Next Ten Years* (Washington, D.C.: Brookings Institution, 1976), 323–369.

[11]See George Break, *Intergovernmental Fiscal Relations in the United States* (Washington, D.C.: Brookings Institution, 1967); Wallace Oates, *Fiscal Federalism* (New York: Harcourt Brace Jovanovich, 1972).

[12]Everett Carll Ladd, *American Political Parties* (New York: Norton, 1970), 205.

# FIVE ASPECTS OF FEDERAL GRANTS-IN-AID: THE LEGACY OF POST-1950s POLICIES

1. A massive increase in federal assistance.
2. A federalism increasingly dominated by the national government, which increasingly has bypassed the states to deal directly with local governments.
3. So great an expansion in the number of separate federal aid programs that most areas of government policy are now covered to a degree by one program or another.

4. An increase in the conditions that state and local governments meet in order to receive federal aid.
5. An extension of direct eligibility for federal assistance so that the large majority of the 80,000 state and local governments in the United States qualify.

social-welfare spending was the prime target of Reagan's efforts to cut the domestic budget.

## Block Grants

Although state and local officials welcome categorical grants, they naturally prefer federal money that comes with no strings attached. As a partial response to this sentiment, the Johnson administration developed the concept of **block grants.** The major feature of a block grant is that it allows state and local officials to choose how money will be spent within a specified general area. The first block grant program was established under the Partnership for Health Act of 1966. State and local officials were required to use the funds in the health area but could decide for themselves whether to spend the money on medical equipment, say, or on hospital construction. Congress has since authorized block grants in additional policy areas, including social services and community services.

## General Revenue Sharing

Richard Nixon began his presidency with a determination to shift a large share of control over domestic programs to the states.[13] The policy that was to make this objective possible was **general revenue sharing.** In Nixon's vision of the "new federalism," the federal government would simply give money to the states for them to use as they saw fit.[14] "After a third of a century of power flowing from the people and the states to Washington," said Nixon in announcing his plan, "it is time for a new federalism in which power, funds and responsibility flow from Washington to the states and to the people."[15] Nixon's plan was based on politics as much as on philosophy. Whereas the uses of categorical grants were decided in Congress, which had a Democratic majority,

[13]Samuel Beer, "In Search of a New Public Philosophy," in Anthony King, ed., *The New American Political System* (Washington, D.C.: American Enterprise Institute, 1978), 39.
[14]See Paul R. Dommel, *The Politics of Revenue Sharing* (Bloomington: Indiana University Press, 1976).
[15]Televised speech, August 8, 1969, reported in *New York Times*, August 9, 1969, 10.

the uses of revenue-sharing funds would be decided in state capitals, some of which were in Republican hands.

Nixon's revenue-sharing proposal met with some objections from Congress's Democratic majority, who were less than enthusiastic about granting funds without retaining some control over their use. Moreover, the idea that only states would receive the funds was unacceptable to congressional Democrats.[16] The Democratic party had control of most cities, and congressional Democrats preferred to see federal money in the hands of Democratic mayors and city councils rather than Republican governors and state legislatures. Congress in 1972 finally authorized $6 billion in revenue-sharing grants but stipulated that one-third of the money was for the use of state governments and two-thirds was for localities. The state governments were granted unrestricted use of their funds, whereas local governments could use theirs in any of nine general areas.

Revenue sharing did not become the dominant form of federal assistance, as Nixon had hoped. It accounted for about 15 percent of all federal grants in 1973 but then declined in proportion. In its desire to control the use of federal money, Congress funded most new and renewed programs thereafter through categorical grants. In 1985 revenue sharing was terminated, a casualty of the federal government's budget deficits.

## Individual-Benefit Programs

All spending to promote the general welfare is designed to help individuals, but much of it—such as federal funds for public school construction and hospital equipment—is not in the form of direct payments to individuals. However, many federal programs do provide benefits directly to individuals, such as social security payments to retired people. These individual-benefit programs are what most people have in mind when they speak of "social welfare." These programs require the payment of benefits to any individual who is entitled to payment by virtue of meeting the established criteria of eligibility. For this reason, each of these programs is termed an **entitlement program.**

The United States has a complex system of social-welfare programs addressing specific needs. No individual-benefit program is universal; each program applies only to those individuals who meet the eligibility criteria. For example, unemployment benefits are not available to all individuals who are out of work. A young person seeking a first job but unable to find one is not eligible for unemployment benefits. Eligible individuals are those who have been laid off from jobs covered by unemployment insurance, and they receive benefits only for a limited period. Such rules are common in the American welfare system and are designed to reward individualism and promote self-reliance or at least to ensure that laziness is not rewarded or encouraged—that is, to limit benefits to the "truly needy."

Individual-benefit programs are designed to alleviate the personal hardships associated with such conditions as joblessness, poverty, and old age. Some benefit programs, such as social security for retirees, provide cash payments to recipients. Other programs provide **in-kind benefits,** which are cash equivalents such as food stamps or rent vouchers. The purpose of in-kind benefits is to

[16]Suzanne Farkas, *Urban Lobbying* (New York: New York University Press, 1971), 41.

★ ANALYZE THE ISSUE

**Government Grants: No Strings Attached?**
What are the differences among categorical grants, block grants, and revenue sharing? Do you think Washington should attach conditions to the money it grants to states and localities? Why, or why not?

ensure that recipients use the support as Congress intended—on groceries or rent rather than on luxuries.

Individual-benefit programs fall into two general categories: social insurance and public assistance. The distinction is a critical one, because the two types of programs differ sharply in concept and degree of public support.

## SOCIAL INSURANCE PROGRAMS

Roughly 45 million Americans receive benefits from social insurance programs —including social security, Medicare, unemployment insurance, and workers' compensation. The two major programs, social security and Medicare, cost the federal government nearly $300 billion per year. Recipients attain eligibility for benefits by virtue of having paid special payroll taxes when they were employed. This is why such programs are labeled **social insurance:** recipients get an insurance benefit under a program that they have helped to fund. This self-financing feature of social insurance programs accounts for their strong public support.

### Social Security

The premier social insurance program is social security for retirees.[17] The program began with passage of the Social Security Act of 1935 and is funded through payroll taxes on employees and employers. Franklin D. Roosevelt emphasized that retiring workers would be getting an insurance benefit that they had earned through their payroll taxes, not a handout from the government. The result was a program that has gained respectability and permanence; that meets some of the financial needs of Americans upon retirement; and that gives promise of future financial security to those still working. Today social security has Americans' full support. A large majority oppose even small cuts in the program; in a 1984 survey conducted by the National Opinion Research Center, 91 percent of respondents said they favored current or higher levels of social security benefits for the elderly.

Social security is one of the few entirely federal welfare programs. Washington collects the payroll taxes that fund the program and sends monthly checks directly to recipients, who, on average, get roughly $600 a month. The 40 million social security recipients get a total of about $220 billion per year.

Although many people believe that an individual's social security benefits are financed by his or her past contributions, they are actually funded largely through payroll taxes on the current work force. The typical social security recipient gets far more money from the government than he or she has paid into the fund; thus it is necessary to use contributions from the current work force to finance the program. The average recipient takes only five years to recover his or her lifetime contributions plus interest and receives "free" benefits from that time forward (see Table 27-3). In the 1970s expenditures for social security began to exceed contributions as the number of retirees and the size of benefit payments increased. The program would have gone bankrupt in the late 1970s had the social security tax rate not been raised.

[17]See Martha Derthick, *Policy Making for Social Security* (Washington, D.C.: Brookings Institution, 1979).

**TABLE 27-3 Number of Months Required for Nonmarried Retiree with Average Earnings to Recover Social Security "Investment," 1982 and 2010**

| Investment | 1982 | 2010* |
|---|---|---|
| Lifetime taxes paid by employee only | 13 months | 23 months |
| Lifetime taxes paid by employee and employer | 26 months | 46 months |
| Lifetime taxes paid by employee and employer plus interest | 64 months | 149 months |

*Figures do not include changes made in the 1983 rescue bill, which increased the amount of time required to recover lifetime taxes.

SOURCE: *Federal Reserve Board of New York Quarterly Review,* Autumn 1982; adapted from Paul Light, *Artful Work: The Politics of Social Security Reform* (New York: Random House, 1985), 91.

In 1981 a bipartisan commission was appointed to study ways of keeping the social security system solvent. The commission recommended that all new federal employees and all employees of nonprofit organizations should be required to contribute to the program, that annual cost-of-living increases in benefits should be delayed by six months, that the payroll-tax increases scheduled throughout the 1980s should go into effect sooner, and that a percentage of the benefits going to retirees with annual incomes over $20,000 should be taxed. The commission's recommendations were enacted in 1983, but only time can tell whether they have solved the social security funding problem.[18] Because of medical and other advances, Americans live longer than they once did, and our longevity could create a social security crisis during the next century. Roughly 20 percent of the U.S. population—55 million people— will be over age sixty-five in the year 2030, and there may not be enough workers to fund the payout to retirees.

## Unemployment Insurance

The 1935 Social Security Act provides for unemployment benefits for workers who have lost their jobs involuntarily. Unemployment insurance is a joint federal–state program. The federal government collects the payroll taxes that fund unemployment benefits, but states have the option of deciding whether the taxes will be paid by employers only or by both employees and employers (most states use the first option). Individual states also set the tax rate, conditions of eligibility, and benefit level, subject to minimum standards established by the federal government. Although unemployment benefits vary widely among states, they average about a third of what an average worker makes while employed, and in most cases the benefits are terminated after twenty-six weeks.

The unemployment program does not have the high level of public support that social security enjoys because of the widespread belief that many individuals receiving unemployment payments make no effort to look for a new job until their benefits are about to expire. Nevertheless, because the program is based on the insurance principle, it is less controversial than some other programs.

[18]See Paul Light, *Artful Work: The Politics of Social Security Reform* (New York: Random House, 1985), ch. 9.

The unemployment-benefits program is based on the insurance principle: workers pay into the fund while they are employed and receive payments from it if they lose their jobs. (David S. Strickler/The Picture Cube)

## Medicare

When Roosevelt was preparing the 1935 Social Security Act, he rejected the idea of providing medical assistance to people who cannot afford to pay for it. He feared that the idea was too great a departure from America's individualistic tradition and might jeopardize passage of the retirement program. After World War II, however, most European democracies instituted systems of government-paid health care, and President Harry Truman proposed a similar program for Americans. The American Medical Association (AMA) called Truman's plan

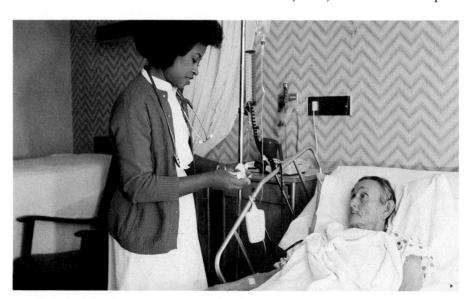

Medicare pays part of the hospitalization and other medical expenses of millions of Americans over age sixty-five. (David Kennedy/TexaStock)

**Health Care and Health Costs**

The United States is the only advanced industrial democracy that does not have a government-paid health-care system for all persons. Although such a system has been proposed in Congress from time to time during the past fifty years, it has never come close to enactment. Major objections are that it will expand government, will result in poorer health care, and will lead to rising health-care costs. Only the first of these objections appears to be completely valid. The quality of the health care that Western Europeans get through their government-run systems is apparently as good as or better than the care Americans get from their private health-care systems. The infant mortality rate is higher in the United States than in every Western European country except Italy. In addition, health-care costs—private and public combined—are higher in the United States than in European democracies, despite the fact that an estimated one in six Americans do not have access to essential health care because they cannot afford it.

| Country | Total Health Expenditure (Percent of GNP) | Infant Mortality Rate (Deaths per 1,000 Live Births) |
|---|---|---|
| Canada | 8.4% | 7.9 |
| Denmark | 6.1 | 7.9 |
| France | 8.4 | 8.2 |
| Great Britain | 6.1 | 9.4 |
| Italy | 6.7 | 10.9 |
| Japan | 6.6 | 5.5 |
| Netherlands | 8.3 | 8.0 |
| Norway | 6.4 | 8.5 |
| United States | 10.7 | 10.5 |
| Sweden | 9.4 | 6.8 |
| West Germany | 8.2 | 8.9 |

SOURCE: Health expenditures, OECD data, 1988; infant mortality rate, United Nations data, 1986.

"socialized medicine" and "un-American," lobbied hard against it, and threatened to mobilize local physicians to campaign against members of Congress who supported it. Truman's proposal never came to a vote in Congress. In 1961 President John F. Kennedy proposed a health-care program restricted to social security recipients, but the AMA, the insurance industry, and conservative members of Congress succeeded in blocking the plan.

However, the 1964 elections swept a tide of liberal Democrats into Congress, and the result was Medicare. Enacted in 1965, the program provides medical assistance to retirees and is funded primarily through payroll taxes.[19] Spending on Medicare patients reached $73 billion in 1988. Medicare, too, is based on the insurance principle, so it has gained nearly the same high level of public support as social security. A 1984 ABC/*Washington Post* survey indicated that 90 percent of Americans prefer that Medicare spending be either kept at current levels or increased.

Medicare does not pay all health-care costs for the elderly. It provides for care

[19]For a general overview of disputes over social-welfare policy in the 1950s and 1960s, see James Sundquist, *Politics and Policy* (Washington, D.C.: Brookings Institution, 1968).

in a hospital or nursing home, but the recipient must pay part of the initial cost and after 100 days must pay most of the rest. Medicare does not cover all physicians' fees, but enrollees in the program have the option of paying an insurance premium for fuller coverage of these fees. Enrollees who cannot afford the additional premium can apply to have the government pay it.

## PUBLIC ASSISTANCE PROGRAMS

Unlike social insurance programs, **public assistance** programs are funded through general tax revenues and are available only to the financially needy. Eligibility for such entitlement programs is established by a **means test,** a demonstration that the applicant has a genuine economic need for the benefit. In short, applicants for public assistance must prove that they are poor. Public assistance programs are commonly referred to as "welfare" and the recipients as "welfare cases." Public assistance programs have less public support than do social insurance programs. Fewer than 70 percent of respondents in a 1985 *Los Angeles Times* poll favored current or higher levels of spending on welfare programs for the poor (compared with the 90 percent who favor current or higher levels of spending on social security).

About 25 million Americans receive public assistance, typically through programs established by the federal government, administered mainly by the states, and funded jointly by the state and federal governments. Some Americans have the mistaken impression that public assistance programs account for the lion's share of federal welfare spending. In fact, the federal government spends roughly $75 billion on its major public assistance programs (described below), as against roughly $300 billion on its two major social insurance programs, social security and Medicare.

### Supplemental Security Income (SSI)

A major public assistance program is Supplemental Security Income (SSI), which originated as federal assistance to the blind and elderly poor as part of the Social Security Act of 1935. By the 1930s most states had begun or were considering such programs. Although the federal legislation was designed to replace their efforts, the states have retained a measure of control over benefits and eligibility and are required to provide some of the funding. In 1974 programs for poor people who are elderly, blind, or disabled were combined in the SSI program.* Because SSI recipients have obvious reasons for their inability to provide for themselves, this public assistance program is not widely criticized. About 4 million Americans receive SSI at an annual cost of $12 billion.

### Aid to Families with Dependent Children (AFDC)

A more controversial public assistance program is Aid to Families with Dependent Children (AFDC). Partly funded by the federal government but administered by the states, the AFDC program was created in the 1930s as survivors' insurance to assist children whose fathers had died. Almost no one

---

*Disability assistance was solely a state responsibility until the 1950s, when the federal government also became involved.

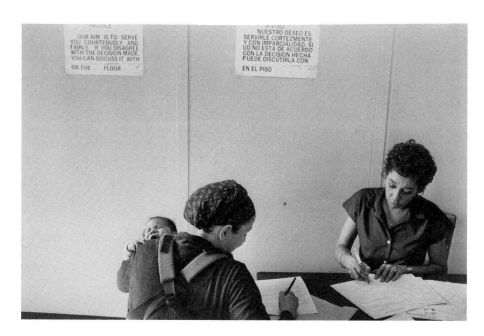

OUR AIM IS TO SERVE YOU COURTEOUSLY AND FAIRLY. IF YOU DISAGREE WITH THE DECISION MADE, YOU CAN DISCUSS IT WITH ON THE FLOOR

AVISO NUESTRO DESEO ES SERVIRLE CORTEZMENTE Y CON IMPARCIALIDAD. SI UD NO ESTA DE ACUERDO CON LA DECISION HECHA PUEDE DISCUTIRLA CON EN EL PISO

Aid to Families with Dependent Children is the public assistance program that many people have in mind when they think of "welfare." (George Cohen/Impact Visuals)

objected to AFDC until it increasingly became a program of assistance to families whose male head was absent from the home because of divorce or abandonment. By 1970 about 75 percent of AFDC cases fell into this category, and AFDC had become an object of criticism. Some of the attacks were rooted in social prejudice because many AFDC recipients were unwed minority mothers. But the program's skyrocketing costs were also an issue. During the 1960s alone the number of AFDC recipients more than tripled and the costs rose fivefold, to $5 billion. In 1988 the nationwide cost of AFDC was $10 billion, which was used to assist 3.8 million families.

The amounts of monthly AFDC payments are set by each state's government. As a result, AFDC benefits vary widely throughout the nation, depending on the wealth, welfare attitudes, and other characteristics of a state's population (see Figure 27-3). Payments are usually much smaller in areas where voters tend to be antagonistic to government "handouts" than in areas where the public is more tolerant of public welfare. In 1986 Mississippi gave the least to AFDC families, an average of $115 a month; Alaska was the most generous state, providing an average of $564 a month per family. By federal law, eligibility for AFDC is restricted to families with net assets below $1,000, and states are permitted to include subsidies for food and housing in calculating whether a family's income is too high to qualify it for AFDC benefits.

## Food Stamps

The food-stamp program, which took its present form in 1961, is fully funded by the federal government. Food stamps are available only to people who qualify on the basis of low income. The program is intended to improve the nutrition of poor families by enabling them to purchase qualified items, mainly foodstuffs, with food stamps. Critics say that food stamps stigmatize their users by making it obvious to onlookers in the checkout line that they are "welfare cases." More prevalent criticisms are that the program is too costly and that too many undeserving people receive food stamps. In the 1980s, by tightening

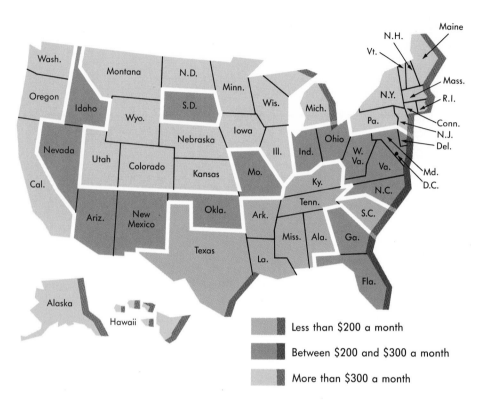

**FIGURE 27-3 Average AFDC Payment per Family in the Fifty States, 1986**
America's federal system allows the fifty states to establish their own social-welfare policies. A state's policies reflect in part its political traditions, population, and level of economic development. As an example, the states vary greatly in their average monthly payments to families under the Aid to Families with Dependent Children (AFDC) program. *Source: Adapted from data compiled by the Social Security Administration.*

Less than $200 a month

Between $200 and $300 a month

More than $300 a month

eligibility rules (for example, excluding striking workers and self-supporting students), the Reagan administration cut more than a million recipients from the food-stamp program. In 1988, 19 million Americans received food stamps at a cost of $12.5 billion.

### Subsidized Housing

Low-income persons are also eligible for subsidized housing. The federal government spent $13 billion on subsidized housing in 1988, most of which went for housing vouchers rather than the construction of low-income housing units. Under the voucher system, the individual receives a monthly rent-payment voucher, which is given in lieu of cash to the landlord, who then hands the voucher over to the government in exchange for cash. The welfare recipient is given a voucher rather than cash in order to ensure that the funds are actually used to obtain housing. The voucher system is generally preferred to the construction of low-income housing projects because it offers tenants more freedom of choice about where to live. Roughly 6.5 million households received a federal housing subsidy in 1988.

### Medicaid

When it enacted Medicare in 1965, Congress also established Medicaid, which provides health care for poor people who are already on welfare. It is considered a public assistance program, rather than a social insurance program like Medicare, because it is based on need and funded by general tax revenues. Half of Medicaid funding is provided by the federal government and half by the

Fueling the debate over federal housing policy is the growing number of homeless people in cities across the United States. These homeless men in San Antonio are enjoying a free Christmas dinner provided by a charitable organization. (Bob Daemmrich/The Image Works)

states. More than 20 million Americans received Medicaid assistance in 1988, at a cost to the federal government of $28 billion.

Before Medicaid, 20 percent of all Americans with incomes below the poverty level had *never* been to a physician. Within a decade of Medicaid's passage, that figure had dropped to 8 percent.[20] Nevertheless, like other public assistance programs, Medicaid has been criticized for supposedly serving too many people who could take care of themselves if they tried harder. Medicaid is also attacked because of its cost. As health-care costs have spiraled rapidly upward (by 17 percent in 1987 alone), so have the costs of Medicaid. It absorbs more than a third of all public assistance dollars spent by the U.S. government.

## OPPORTUNITY PROGRAMS

Americans' belief in individualism and self-reliance includes a recognition of the importance of equality of opportunity (see Chapter 6). If individuals are expected to provide for themselves, logic demands that they be given the chance to do so. In terms of public policy, this concept is best reflected in the U.S. system of education. Unlike European educational systems, which have a distinct class bias, U.S. primary and secondary schools are relatively egalitarian, and U.S. colleges and universities are open to nearly any high school graduate who wants to attend.

Yet many American children have no hope of obtaining a high-quality education. Many children receive almost no encouragement at home and attend public schools that provide poor instruction, no discipline, and inadequate facilities. These children start out at a disadvantage and cannot reasonably be expected to achieve academic success and a decent life on their own. Their world is unknown and almost unimaginable to the more fortunate Americans who live comfortably, but they number in the millions. From urban slums to rural backwaters, theirs is a different America, one marked by squalor, hunger, and ignorance. Michael Harrington called it "the other America."[21]

★ ANALYZE THE ISSUE

**Cultural Differences in Welfare Policy**
The United States has a greater number of welfare programs and more welfare restrictions than the European democracies. Whereas European democracies provide government-paid health care for all citizens, for example, the United States provides it through separate programs for only some elderly people and some poor people, all of whom must prove they are eligible in order to receive benefits. What are the advantages and disadvantages of the American approach to welfare? Of the European approach?

[20]John E. Schwarz, *America's Hidden Success*, rev. ed. (New York: Norton, 1988), 38.
[21]Michael Harrington, *The Other America: Poverty in the United States* (New York: Macmillan, 1962).

Head Start can help disadvantaged preschool children develop their learning skills, but the program is so underfunded that only 10 percent of eligible children are able to participate. (Alan Carey/The Image Works)

*The other America, the America of poverty, is hidden today in a way that it never was before. Its millions are socially invisible to the rest of us. . . . They are not simply neglected . . . they are not seen.*

Michael Harrington

*If a free society cannot help the many who are poor, it cannot save the few who are rich.*

John F. Kennedy

"The other America" has not consistently received special help from government, but two substantial education and training programs—the War on Poverty and CETA—have recently been tried.

### The War on Poverty

While campaigning for the presidency in 1960, John F. Kennedy was shocked by the poverty and illiteracy he saw in the Appalachian region of West Virginia. Three years later, as president, Kennedy proposed a set of programs to assist the nation's poor and educationally disadvantaged people, saying that the time had come for "a basic attack on the problems of poverty and waste of human resources."[22] After Kennedy's assassination, his successor as president, Lyndon Johnson, pushed hard for the measures, confiding, "This is my kind of program."[23] A march on Washington by 200,000 civil rights activists helped persuade Congress to pass the Economic Opportunity Act of 1964, whose provisions collectively came to be called "the War on Poverty."

The War on Poverty consisted of a variety of programs designed to educate and train the poor and disadvantaged. Among these programs were occupational training for young people (the Job Corps), local initiative opportunities (Community Action programs), on-the-job training for welfare recipients (the Work Experience Program), and preschool education for children (Head Start).

Although these programs conformed with the American tradition of helping people to help themselves, they failed to gain broad support. A major problem was that better-off Americans had little interest in an effort that did not immediately either threaten or benefit themselves. As a result, congressional appropriations for the War on Poverty programs never totaled as much as $2

[22]Quoted in Daniel Patrick Moynihan, *Maximum Feasible Misunderstanding* (New York: Free Press, 1969), xiii.
[23]Quoted in Robert D. Plotnick and Felicity Skidmore, *Progress against Poverty* (New York: Academic Press, 1975), 3.

billion in a given year. In addition, many War on Poverty programs were poorly conceived and administered. A substantial percentage of program funds never reached the intended beneficiaries but instead went to pay administrators' salaries. The War on Poverty also consistently fell short of targeted training and employment goals. The problems of poverty and ignorance were more severe than program advocates had foreseen. An evaluation of Head Start, for example, revealed that because the program could do nothing to change the children's impoverished home environments, many of them soon lost their new learning skills.[24]

## Employment and Training

Employment policy and welfare policy have been loosely linked since the Great Depression, when Roosevelt combined public jobs programs with social security legislation. In 1973 an ambitious jobs program began under the Comprehensive Employment and Training Act (CETA). Designed to provide employment and job training for poor, disadvantaged, and undertrained individuals, the CETA program conformed to Nixon's philosophy of "a new federalism," which, as we noted earlier, called for a shifting of responsibility to state and local governments. Elected city officials were given responsibility for administering CETA's programs. By 1979 CETA was providing jobs for almost 4 million people on a budget of $9.4 billion. Local officials favored the program, but federal officials complained that local governments were using CETA funds for routine administrative expenses and were using CETA workers in place of regular public employees rather than training them for jobs in the private sector. Only about 20 percent of the funds were being spent to train unemployed and underemployed people for future jobs. Also, most local officials did not sufficiently encourage private businesses to hire CETA trainees.[25] Performance improved after national officials developed more stringent regulations to force local officials to administer the program properly, but CETA was terminated in 1983 because of federal budgetary pressures. The program that replaced it, the 1982 Job Training and Partnership Act (JTPA), was funded at a relatively low level.

## EDUCATION AND WORK REQUIREMENTS FOR THOSE ON WELFARE

In late 1988 Congress enacted legislation that its sponsors hailed as the most significant reform of the U.S. welfare system since the New Deal. Like the War on Poverty and CETA, the legislation emphasized education, training, and work as the solutions to welfare problems. The legislation was different, however, in its mandatory basis: those on welfare who refuse to accept education, training, or work would lose their welfare eligibility.

The 1988 law directs the states to establish education, training, and work programs that are designed to help those on welfare obtain gainful employment. The legislation also contains a requirement that welfare mothers be provided the child support necessary to enable them to participate in these

---

[24]Henry M. Levin, "A Decade of Policy Developments," in Robert Haveman, ed., *A Decade of Federal Antipoverty Programs* (New York: Academic Press, 1977), 44.
[25]Robert A. Milne, "Welfare Policy in Texas," mimeo, 1980.

programs. The federal government would provide money (nearly $3 billion in the first year) to fund the programs and the child-care requirement. Individuals who are receiving welfare and meet the eligibility requirements have no choice but to participate in the programs if they want to continue to receive welfare benefits.

The legislation was passed by overwhelming majorities in the Senate and House. Conservative members of Congress were persuaded by the legislation's emphasis on training and work in place of income maintenance. Liberal members were attracted by provisions of the legislation, such as the child-support requirement, that would lend encouragement and assistance to those who otherwise would be punished by a requirement that they either get out of the home or lose their welfare support. Most observers believe that the impact of the 1988 welfare reform legislation will not be clear until the early 1990s.

## DO FEDERAL WELFARE PROGRAMS HELP THE POOR?

Do public assistance programs really help the poor? In his book *Losing Ground,* Charles Murray contends that welfare programs are likely to produce welfare dependency.[26] Once people discover that they can get by on welfare benefits, Murray claims, they are disinclined to seek gainful employment. Murray further contends that some welfare recipients, such as teenage unwed mothers, actually do better financially by staying on welfare than by working. According to Murray, such people form the basis of a permanent underclass of unproductive Americans. They have children who receive no educational encouragement at home and grow up in environments where crime, delinquency, drug abuse, and illegitimacy are a way of life. When these children reach their teens, they behave like the adults around them, so the destructive pattern is perpetuated.

In his book *America's Hidden Success,* John Schwarz presents an argument in opposition to Murray's. Schwarz argues that the welfare system works. Between 1960 and 1980, when welfare spending rose substantially, there was a sharp reduction in malnutrition among low-income Americans, a decline in infant mortality rates among the poor and minorities, a 50 percent decrease in the number of Americans living in overcrowded and substandard housing, an increase in employment and job skills among poor Americans, and a steep drop in the proportion of Americans living in poverty.[27] Of course, welfare programs are not the sole influence on such trends, but financial assistance, food stamps, and rent subsidies have an obvious and direct impact on poor people's standard of living.

One aspect of poverty in America is beyond dispute: it is a large and persistent problem. The government defines the **poverty line** as the annual cost of a thrifty food budget for an urban family of four, multiplied by three to allow for the cost of housing, clothing, and other expenses. In 1987 the poverty line was set at an annual income of about $11,500. According to U.S. Census Bureau figures, the proportion of Americans living below the poverty line has been 12 percent or higher throughout recent decades (see Figure 27-4). Poverty declined sharply in the 1960s and early 1970s, and a few analysts spoke optimistically about the prospect of its elimination. When the proportion of Americans living

**Welfare Dependency**
Charles Murray in *Losing Ground* presents statistics indicating that welfare programs often lead to the chronic dependency of their recipients. John Schwarz in *America's Hidden Success* presents data showing that welfare programs meet people's needs without creating dependency. Which view do you agree with? Is your view based on personal experience, study of the issue, or ''educated guessing''?

[26]Charles Murray, *Losing Ground: American Social Policy, 1950–1980* (New York: Basic Books, 1984).
[27]Schwarz, *America's Hidden Success,* 68; and John E. Schwarz, ''The War We Won,'' *New Republic,* June 18, 1984, 19.

A high proportion of newly created jobs are in fast-food restaurants and other service businesses, many of which do not pay well enough to provide individuals with long-term economic security. (Hazel Hankin)

in poverty then rose in the 1980s, no analyst was willing to say that the problem could be solved.

## A Welfare Bias: Helping the Middle Class

Social welfare is the arena in which many of the conflicts of the American political system come together: individualism vs. equality, Congress vs. the president, national authority vs. local authority, public sector vs. private sector, Republicans vs. Democrats, poorer vs. richer. At best, the politics of social welfare is the politics of hope—the expectation that a touch of compassion blended with the provision of opportunity will result in economic security for all. But, of course, not everyone can attain economic security in a system that makes no guarantee that everyone's basic needs will be provided for. Instead, a

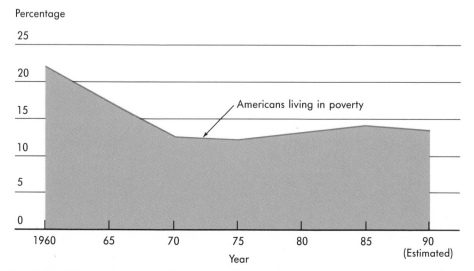

**FIGURE 27-4 Percentage of Americans Living in Poverty, 1960–1990**
The War on Poverty during the 1960s helped to bring about a significant reduction in the percentage of Americans living in poverty, but the figure leveled off as funding for antipoverty programs was cut back beginning in the 1970s. *Source: U.S. Bureau of the Census, Statistical Abstract of the United States, 1988 (Washington, D.C.: U.S. Government Printing Office, 1987), 454. Estimate for 1990 based on projections from 1987 data and economic trends.*

politics of hope is a trade-off of contradictory values, which ensures that social-welfare policy will be untidy and controversial and, most significant, will not fully satisfy anyone.

## INEFFICIENCY: THE WELFARE WEB

The United States has by far the most intricate system of social welfare in the world. Scores of separate programs have been established to address different, often overlapping needs. A single individual in need of public assistance may qualify for many, none, or one of these programs, and the eligibility criteria are often perplexing. Consider the case of Gary Myers of Springfield, Missouri, who declared bankruptcy in 1988 because he could not afford to pay $1,400 in hospital bills that his family had incurred. Had Myers made exactly $4 less than his $509 monthly wage as a security guard, he would have qualified for government payment of his medical expenses. Because of the extra $4, however, Myers received nothing.[28]

Beyond the question of the equity of such rules is the question of their efficiency. The unwritten principle that the individual must somehow earn or deserve a particular benefit makes the U.S. welfare system highly labor-intensive. Consider, for example, the AFDC program, which limits eligibility to families with incomes below a certain level and, in most states, to families with a single parent living in the home. Because of these requirements, the eligibility of each AFDC applicant must be periodically checked by a caseworker (see Figure 27-5). Such procedures make such programs as AFDC doubly expensive: in addition to payments to the recipients, there are the costs of paying caseworkers, supervisors, and support staffs and of processing the extensive paperwork involved.

Leaders as diverse as George McGovern, Jimmy Carter, Richard Nixon, and the conservative economist Milton Friedman have argued the need to reduce the enormous administrative costs of social welfare. Their ideas have all been variations on the idea of a guaranteed annual income for every American family. Families with little or no income would get regular government payments up to a maximum level. These payments would be sent directly to recipients, just as social security checks are mailed monthly to beneficiaries. Recipients would establish their eligibility by filing an annual tax return documenting their low income. The enormous size and complexity of the welfare bureaucracy could thus be reduced considerably.

Of the various proposals, Nixon's Family Assistance Plan came the closest to becoming law. Nixon's plan, developed in 1969, would have replaced other

[28]Matt Clark, "Forgotten Patients," *Newsweek*, August 22, 1988, 52.

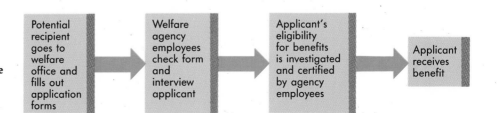

**FIGURE 27-5 The Cumbersome Administrative Process by Which Welfare Recipients Get Their Benefits**

Potential recipient goes to welfare office and fills out application forms → Welfare agency employees check form and interview applicant → Applicant's eligibility for benefits is investigated and certified by agency employees → Applicant receives benefit

forms of federal aid by providing each family in America with a minimum annual income. Recognizing that the concept of a guaranteed income was contrary to the American ideal of individualism, Nixon stressed that the payments of his Family Assistance Plan would "be scaled in such a way that it would always pay to work."[29] Nixon described welfare as "a failure that grows worse every day," and his bill made it through the House of Representatives before being defeated in the Senate by an unlikely coalition of conservatives, who attacked the plan as too costly and likely to produce welfare dependency, and liberals, who feared the program would provide insufficient support for the truly needy.[30]

## INEQUITY: MAJORITY VS. MINORITY WELFARE

Most Americans hold to the traditional belief in individualism and self-reliance, which they generalize to other people. Although they recognize a need for programs for the poor and disadvantaged, they tend to minimize both the number of such individuals and the extent of their need. Surveys have repeatedly indicated that a majority of Americans are convinced that *most* people on welfare could get along without it if they tried. Such opinions do not conform with the facts of being poor or jobless in America.[31] Most unemployed Americans have been laid off from jobs because of economic slowdowns; are disadvantaged in finding work because of mental, physical, or educational deficiencies; are too old or ill to work at a regular job; do not qualify for particular jobs because of inexperience (a major problem for young workers); or cannot work profitably because of other factors, such as being a single parent of young children. An economic slowdown alone puts massive numbers of Americans in need of assistance. At the depths of the 1981–1983 recession, 12 million people were unemployed. Between 1978 and 1982—a time of two recessions—9.9 million Americans dropped below the poverty line.[32]

Another persistent problem in America is the single-parent family. More than 12 million children live in households in which the father is absent. These families are at a disadvantage because women generally earn less than men for comparable work, especially in nonprofessional fields. Often they cannot find jobs that pay enough to cover the child-care expenses they incur when they work. Nearly half of all Americans living below the poverty line are members of families headed by divorced or unmarried mothers. Poverty in America has increasingly become a women's problem, a situation referred to as "the feminization of poverty."

However, the facts about poverty in America are sometimes less important to the fate of public assistance programs than the popular belief that many if not most of the people on welfare do not really deserve help. Because assistance programs have limited public support, there are constant political pressures to reduce welfare expenditures and to weed out undeserving recipients.[33]

[29]Cited in Gilbert Steiner, *The State of Welfare* (Washington, D.C.: Brookings Institution, 1971), 10.
[30]Daniel Patrick Moynihan, *The Politics of a Guaranteed Income* (New York: Random House, 1973), 446.
[31]See Harrell R. Rogers, Jr., *Crisis in Democracy* (Reading, Mass.: Addison-Wesley, 1978), 164–173.
[32]U.S. House of Representatives, Ways and Means Committee, Subcommittee on Oversight and Subcommittee on Public Assistance, *Background Material on Poverty, October 17, 1983* (Washington, D.C.: U.S. Government Printing Office, 1983), ix, 47.
[33]Joseph A. Califano, Jr., *Governing America* (New York: Simon & Schuster, 1981), 327–328.

Of the 33 million Americans who live below the poverty line, 10 million are female heads of households and their children. (Bettye Lane/Photo Researchers)

*It's no disgrace t' be poor, but it might as well be.*

Abe Martin

America's poor and disadvantaged citizens are in a weak position to fight back politically. Their numbers are large—one in seven Americans lives below the poverty line—but they have a low rate of voting and do not vote as a bloc. This situation reflects the historical lack of class consciousness among poorer Americans and the absence of strong political organizations (such as a major socialist party) to mobilize them. They are also hampered by traditional American attitudes toward welfare, which diminish the legitimacy of their claim to help and even lead many of them to feel ashamed to ask for it. In view of all the obstacles to political action by the poor and disadvantaged, it is perhaps no surprise that the United States ranks *last* among industrialized Western democracies in relative level of spending for public assistance.

Social security and Medicare are another story entirely. These two social insurance programs have broad public support even though together they cost the federal government roughly $300 billion annually, nearly four times what is spent on the major public assistance programs (see Table 27-4). One major reason for the difference in public funding and approval for social security is that it benefits the majority. Most Americans are either actual or potential social security recipients. It is good politics for elected officials to appeal to the 40 million retired Americans who get a monthly social security check.[34] In 1972 the Republican president Nixon and a Democratic-controlled Congress conducted a virtual auction on social security until they agreed to a 20 percent increase in benefits, which took effect a month before the November election.

Social security recipients do not hesitate to assert their right to benefits; they feel entitled to them by virtue of their payroll-tax contributions. In fact,

---

[34]See William Mitchell, *The Popularity of Social Security: A Political Paradox* (Washington, D.C.: American Enterprise Institute, 1977).

**TABLE 27-4  Federal Outlays for Major Social Insurance and Public Assistance Programs, 1988**

| Program | Millions of Recipients | Outlay (Billions of Dollars) |
|---|---|---|
| Social insurance | | |
| Social security | 40.0 | $219.4 |
| Medicare | 32.0 | 73.0 |
| Total | | $292.4 |
| Public assistance | | |
| SSI | 4.0 | $12.3 |
| AFDC | 3.8* | 9.8 |
| Food stamps | 19.3 | 12.5 |
| Housing subsidies | 6.5* | 13.4 |
| Medicaid | 24.0 | 28.1 |
| Total | | $76.1 |

*Families.

SOURCE: Data are based on estimates provided in *The United States Budget in Brief, Fiscal Year 1988* (Washington, D.C.: Office of Management and Budget, 1988), 72–78.

however, social security is *not* a pure insurance program. As we indicated earlier, recipients receive far greater benefits than they have "earned" through their payroll taxes. So they are, in a sense, getting public assistance: federal dollars beyond what they themselves contributed during their working years. Of course, the existence of social security substantially lessens the demand for other forms of public assistance. Monthly social security checks keep millions of Americans, mostly widows, out of poverty. About a fourth of social security recipients have no other significant source of income. Without social security, they would be completely dependent on public assistance programs.

However, many social security recipients, while legally entitled to the benefits they receive, have no actual financial need for them. Only a third of social security recipients are in the lowest fifth of the population in income. Many recipients are high-income Americans for whom social security is simply additional retirement income. In 1985 families in the top fifth of the income population received about $35 billion in federal social insurance benefits, which is more money than is spent on AFDC, food stamps, and housing subsidies combined.

The contradictions and difficulties of social welfare in America come together in the contrasting cases of social insurance and public assistance. Although the latter is targeted toward the truly needy, it is less acceptable politically and culturally and receives much less funding. The situation testifies to the strength of traditional American values of individualism and self-reliance and to the power of money and votes.

★ ANALYZE THE ISSUE

**Social Security's Impact on Poverty**
According to 1986 U.S. Census Bureau statistics, social security payments had the effect of keeping the proportion of Americans living below the poverty line from increasing to 21.2 percent from its actual level of 14.9 percent. Should social security therefore be properly regarded as an antipoverty program? Why, or why not?

## Summary

The United States has a complex social-welfare system of multiple programs addressing specific welfare needs. Each program applies only to those individuals who qualify for benefits by meeting the specific eligibility criteria. In general, these criteria are designed to reward and promote self-reliance or, when help is necessary, to ensure that laziness is not rewarded or fostered—in short, to limit benefits to those individuals who truly cannot help themselves. This approach to social welfare reflects Americans' traditional belief in individualism.

Welfare benefits fall into two broad categories: social insurance and public assistance. The former includes such programs as social security for retired workers and Medicare for the elderly. Social insurance programs are funded by payroll taxes on potential recipients, who thus, in a sense, earn the benefits they later receive. Because of this arrangement, social insurance programs have broad public support. Public assistance programs, in contrast, are funded by general tax revenues and are targeted toward needy individuals and families. These programs are not controversial in principle: most Americans believe that government should assist the truly needy. However, because of a widespread belief that most welfare recipients could get along without assistance if they tried, these programs do not have universal public support, are only modestly funded, and are politically vulnerable.

The social-welfare system in the United States is criticized in all quarters, but reform efforts have been largely unsuccessful. A major reason is that opposing sides disagree fundamentally on the nature of the problem. In one view, social welfare is too costly and assists too many people who could help themselves; another view holds that social welfare is not broad enough and that too many poor and disadvantaged Americans live in poverty. In light of these irreconcilable differences, in combination with federalism and the widely shared view that welfare programs should target specific problems, the existing system of multiple programs, despite its administrative complexity and inefficiency, has been the only politically feasible alternative. Yet it results in social spending that is not fully targeted toward the people most in need of help.

## Major Concepts

| | |
|---|---|
| block grants | means test |
| categorical grants | poverty line |
| entitlement program | public assistance |
| general revenue sharing | social insurance |
| in-kind benefits | |

## Suggested Readings

Blumberg, Paul. *Inequality in an Age of Decline.* New York: Oxford University Press, 1980. An analysis of the perplexing issue of national equality in a period of nonexpanding governmental resources.

Derthick, Martha. *Policy Making for Social Security.* Washington, D.C.: Brookings Institution, 1979. An overview of the development of social security.

James, Dorothy B. *Poverty, Politics, and Change.* Englewood Cliffs, N.J.: Prentice-Hall, 1972. An analysis of factors affecting poverty policy.

Light, Paul. *Artful Work: The Politics of Social Security Reform.* New York: Random House, 1985. An analysis of the issues and politics of the recent reforms of the social security system.

Murray, Charles. *Losing Ground: American Social Policy, 1950–1980.* New York: Basic Books, 1984. An unfavorable assessment of the U.S. welfare system.

O'Toole, Laurence J., ed. *American Intergovernmental Relations.* Washington, D.C.: Congressional Quarterly Press, 1985. An excellent series of articles on the changing relationships among local, state, and federal governments.

Piven, Frances Fox, and Richard A. Cloward. *The New Class War: Reagan's Attack on the Welfare State and Its Consequences.* New York: Pantheon, 1982. A critical evaluation of the social welfare philosophy of the Reagan administration.

Schwarz, John E. *America's Hidden Success,* rev. ed. New York: Norton, 1988. A favorable assessment of the U.S. welfare system.

Steiner, Gilbert Y. *The State of Welfare.* Washington, D.C.: Brookings Institution, 1971. An overview of the U.S. social-welfare system.

# Chapter 28

## NATIONAL SECURITY POLICY: PROTECTING THE AMERICAN WAY

*We the people of the United States, in order to . . . provide for the common defense . . .*
*—Preamble, U.S. Constitution*

In late spring of 1989, the West German government announced its interest in a rapid and sharp reduction in the number of battlefield nuclear weapons in Europe. The policy had been proposed by Soviet leader Mikhail Gorbachev, and opinion polls indicated that the idea was very popular among West Germans. However, the Bush administration held a different view. President George Bush had personally said that a cautious approach to European arms reductions was the only prudent course, and his secretary of state, James Baker, warned West German officials that they were playing into Gorbachev's hand by rushing to accept his idea. The Soviets' long-range plans, Baker argued, included an effort to undermine the will of Western European peoples and thereby to drive a wedge into the unity that had prevailed between the United States and its European allies. The national security of the U.S. and its allies, Baker claimed, was inseparable and could be properly maintained only by a unified alliance led by the United States.

National security is unlike other areas of government policy because it rests on relations with powers outside rather than within a country. There is no governmental authority to settle disputes between nations, unlike the case when disputes occur within a country. As a result, the chief instruments of national security policy—diplomacy, economic exchange, and military force—differ from those of domestic policy. President Bush had no choice but to hope that persuasion would convince the West Germans to change their position. He had no authority to order them to do so.

The national security policy of the United States embraces an extraordinary array of activities—so many, in fact, that they could not possibly be addressed adequately in an entire book, much less a single chapter of one. There are some 160 countries in the world, and the United States has relations of one kind or another—military, diplomatic, and economic—with all of them. This chapter narrows the subject of national security policy by focusing on a variety of general issues, including U.S. defense doctrine, nuclear strategy, Third World insurgencies, the military-industrial complex, international markets, and the threat that world insecurity poses to American values.

The primary goal of U.S. national security policy is preservation of the American state. This objective requires military preparedness in order to protect the territorial integrity of the United States. But the American state is more than a physical entity; it is also an economic way of life and a political idea. As a consequence, national security is an issue of economics and ideals as well as an issue of defense forces. The main ideas discussed in this chapter are the following:

★ *Since World War II, the United States has pursued a policy of containment toward the Soviet Union.* This policy is based on the presumption that the USSR is an aggressor country committed to a strategy of global domination. Containment policy has taken different forms at different times and was modified substantially in the 1970s by a period of détente.

★ *The United States maintains a high degree of defense preparedness.* Such preparedness mandates a substantial level of defense spending and a worldwide deployment of U.S. conventional and strategic forces. A consequence of these requirements is a military-industrial complex that benefits from and is a cause of high levels of military spending.

★ *Changes in the international marketplace have led to increased economic interdependence among nations, which has had a marked influence on the United States' economy and on its security planning.* Economic conditions are also a root cause of Third World insurgencies, which pose a "no-win" problem for U.S. interests abroad.

## Superpower Conflict: Contending with the Soviet Union

U.S. national security policy since World War II has focused on a concern with the power and intentions of the Soviet Union. At the Yalta Conference in 1945, U.S. President Franklin Roosevelt and Soviet leader Josef Stalin had agreed that Eastern European nations were entitled to self-determination within a Soviet zone of influence, which Stalin took to mean governments aligned closely with the Soviet Untion. After the war, Soviet occupation forces assisted the Communist parties of Eastern European nations to capture state power, usually by coercive means. Poland, East Germany, Hungary, Bulgaria, Albania, the Baltic states, and Yugoslavia came under communist control. In 1948 the Soviet Union completed its domination of Eastern Europe by engineering an internal coup in Czechoslovakia which ousted its democratically elected leadership. In the words of Britain's wartime prime minister, Winston Churchill, an "iron curtain" had fallen across Europe.

Great Britain's Winston Churchill, America's Franklin D. Roosevelt, and the Soviet Union's Josef Stalin meet at Yalta in 1945 to discuss the order of the postwar world.

The United States had understood the Yalta agreement on self-determination to mean that Eastern Europeans would have an opportunity through free elections to decide their own forms of government. When instead the Communists used force and deception to gain control and eliminate opposition, U.S. policymakers began to reassess Soviet aims.[1] Particularly noteworthy was the evaluation made by George Kennan, a U.S. diplomat and expert on Soviet affairs. Kennan concluded that invasions from the west in World Wars I and II had made the Soviet Union almost paranoid in its concern for regional security. Although Kennan believed that the USSR would someday mature into a responsible world power, he contended that it was an immediate threat to neighboring countries and that the United States, although not directly endangered, would have to take the lead in discouraging Soviet aggression. He counseled a policy of "long-term, patient but firm, and vigilant containment."[2]

Kennan's analysis contributed to the formulation of the postwar U.S. security doctrine: containment. The doctrine of **containment** is based on the idea that the Soviet Union is an aggressor nation and that only a determined United States can block its territorial ambitions. Although Kennan's assessment of the Soviet Union was influential, it was not accepted in its entirety by Harry S Truman, who had become president after Roosevelt's death in 1945. Truman rejected Kennan's view that the USSR was motivated by a concern for regional security. Truman saw the Soviet Union as an ideological foe that was bent on *global* domination and that could be stopped only by the aggressive use of U.S.

*From Stettin in the Baltic to Trieste in the Adriatic an iron curtain has descended across the Continent.*

Winston Churchill, address at Westminster College, Fulton, Missouri, 1946

[1] See John Lewis Gaddis, *Strategies of Containment* (New York: Oxford University Press, 1982).
[2] Mr. X. (George Kennan), "The Sources of Soviet Conduct," *Foreign Affairs* 25 (July 1947): 566–582.

power. Like other U.S. policymakers of the postwar period, Truman accepted the notion that "appeasement" would only encourage Soviet aggression. This lesson was derived from territorial concessions made by Britain and France in 1938 to Germany's Adolf Hitler; rather than appeasing Hitler, these concessions convinced him that Germany could bully its way to further gains. Thus efforts at appeasement propelled Europe toward World War II.

Truman's view became the basis of the thinking of most U.S. policymakers during the ensuing four decades. U.S. national security policy cannot be understood apart from a fear of the Soviet Union.

## THE HISTORICAL ROOTS OF U.S.–SOVIET CONFLICT

The origins of the U.S.–Soviet conflict lie deep in history. Each country's development set it on a course that was almost certain to lead eventually to a clash with the other.

During the nineteenth century, the United States played a relatively small role in world affairs because of its geographical separation from Europe and its preoccupation with internal development. The major U.S. foreign policy declaration during that century, the Monroe Doctrine (1823), warned the European powers to stay out of the Americas: "We should consider any attempt on their part to extend their system to any portion of this hemisphere as dangerous to our peace and safety."[3] Ironically, at the same time that the United States was telling the European powers to forgo their territorial ambitions, it was systematically expanding into the lands of Mexico to the south and of Indian tribes to the west. Once this expansion was complete, the United States looked toward the Caribbean and Asia for additional territories, annexing Cuba, Puerto Rico, Hawaii, and the Philippine Islands.

Tsarist Russia also pursued a path of expansion in the nineteenth century. Blocked to the west by stronger European powers, Russia looked eastward, toward Asia. By 1900 Russia had extended its territory to the Pacific Ocean. Russia was also shedding its feudal past: Russia's rate of industrial growth during the late nineteenth century was proportionally the fastest in the world.

Russia and the United States possessed huge areas of land and were rich in natural resources and thus had the capacity to overshadow the Western European powers, which were geographically much smaller. Their decline was hastened by World War I, which was waged almost entirely on the European continent.

Another consequence of World War I was the collapse of tsarist Russia. The superior strength of German armies on the eastern front was a large factor in the ability of Vladimir Ilich Lenin's Bolshevik party to seize power in Russia. Lenin called for revolution in Europe and proposed communism as the model of a new international order. With its emphases on state ownership of economic production, material equality, armed revolution, and dictatorial leadership, Soviet communism was directly at odds with traditional American values. Americans had much earlier come to see their country as the vanguard of a new political order based on liberty, equality, and self-government. Consistent with this historical view of American exceptionalism, and in opposition to Lenin's claim,

[3]Message of President James Monroe to Congress, December 1823.

President Woodrow Wilson in 1918 announced his Fourteen Points for world peace based on self-determination for all peoples.[4]

Wilson's and Lenin's conflicting visions presaged the future tension between their two countries, but the United States and the Soviet Union virtually went their separate ways in the 1920s and 1930s. When Lenin's international communist revolution failed to materialize, Soviet leaders concentrated on internal development, including national consolidation (the USSR includes peoples of more than a hundred European and Asian nationalities). The United States, for its part, returned to isolationism, refusing even to join the League of Nations. By the time World War II broke out, the United States was far more concerned with Nazi Germany than with the Soviet Union.[5] In fact, before entering the war as a cobelligerent (not quite an ally) of the USSR, the United States gave the Soviets material support for their war effort through the Lend-Lease Act of 1941.

## THE DOCTRINE OF CONTAINMENT

Although World War II was a global conflict, none of the fighting took place on the American mainland. With no war damage to recover from the United States emerged as the world's strongest military and economic power and the only nation with nuclear weapons. By comparison, the Soviet Union suffered extensive damage during the war. Between 20 million and 30 million Soviet citizens died (compared with 500,000 Americans), and the country's western agricultural lands and cities were ravaged. The Soviet Union concluded that its security against future attacks from Europe depended on the creation of an Eastern European buffer zone between itself and Germany.

America's response was to put the doctrine of containment into action. In 1947 President Truman pursued containment through the so-called Truman Doctrine, which held that "the policy of the United States [is] to support free peoples who are resisting attempted subjugation by armed minorities or outside pressure." A first step was to provide military and economic assistance to the government of Greece, which was engaged in a civil war with communist insurgents.

Truman followed with the European Recovery Plan, better known as the Marshall Plan. Proposed in 1947 and named after one of its chief architects, the widely respected general George Marshall, who had become Truman's secretary of state after the war, the plan was perhaps the most successful U.S. foreign policy initiative of the twentieth century. It called for $3 billion in immediate aid for the postwar rebuilding of Europe with an additional $10 billion or so to follow. The Marshall Plan was unprecedented both in its scope (in today's dollars, the cost was roughly $100 billion) and in its implications—for the first time, the United States was committed to an ongoing major role in European affairs. The program worked as expected: U.S. assistance through the Marshall Plan enabled the countries of Western Europe to regain economic and political stability in a relatively short time.

*Our policy [that is, the Marshall Plan] is directed not against any country or doctrine but against hunger, poverty, desperation and chaos. Its purpose should be the revival of a working economy in the world so as to permit the emergence of political and social conditions in which free institutions can exist.*

George Marshall

[4]See Norman Levin, *Woodrow Wilson and World Politics* (New York: Oxford University Press, 1968).
[5]See George Kolko, *The Politics of War: The World and U.S. Foreign Policy, 1943–1945* (New York: Random House, 1969).

**Short-Term Analysis of Policy Costs**
When the Marshall Plan was proposed, opponents labeled it a giveaway. Why, they asked, should America give billions to help devastated European nations get back on their feet? Why was this view shortsighted? Can you think of problems today, foreign or domestic, in which an obsessive concern for short-term costs has led policymakers to oppose programs that would provide significant long-term benefits? What are some plausible reasons for officials to fail to take the long view?

**The Effectiveness of the Containment Doctrine**
The dominant view among Western leaders after World War II was that aggression should never be rewarded because it only encourages the aggressor nation to seek further gains. As a result of this view, Western nations concluded that containment was the best strategy to adopt toward the Soviet Union. Do you think this view was the correct one? Can you think of postwar developments that support your position? Do you think this view is still applicable today? Are there recent examples to support your position?

Containment policy also dictated that the United States maintain a military presence on the Soviet Union's flanks. After World War II, instead of demobilizing its military forces as it had done at the end of World War I, the United States ordered its troops to occupy Japan and a section of West Germany.

Today the United States has more than 2 million military personnel, about 500,000 of whom are stationed overseas (see Table 28-1). There are 65,000 U.S. troops in Japan and 40,000 in South Korea. Since World War II, Asia has twice been a battleground for U.S. forces, in the Korean and Vietnam wars.

Europe has the largest contingent of U.S. military personnel, with approximately 250,000 in West Germany alone. These troops are linked with the military forces of America's allies in the North Atlantic Treaty Organization (NATO). NATO countries conduct joint military exercises and engage in joint strategic and tactical military planning that centers on the defense of Western Europe. The NATO forces are under an integrated command except for France, which since the mid-1960s has maintained full command of its own forces. NATO is countered by the Warsaw Pact, which consists of the Soviet Union and its Eastern European allies. The Warsaw Pact has a numerical edge in equipment (see Table 28-2), while NATO has more technically advanced weaponry.

## THE COLD WAR

Developments in the late 1940s embroiled the United States in a **cold war** with the Soviet Union. The term refers to the fact that the two countries were not directly engaged in actual combat (a "hot war"), but were locked in deep-seated hostility. From the United States' perspective, the cold war was an extension of containment policy and included support for governments threatened by communist takeovers. In China the Nationalist government had the support of

**TABLE 28-1   Number of U.S. Military Personnel around the World, 1988**

| Area | Military Personnel |
|---|---|
| U.S. territory | 1,677,040 |
| Western Europe | |
| West Germany | 245,700 |
| United Kingdom | 29,800 |
| Italy | 9,750 |
| Other | 42,960 |
| All Western Europe | 328,210 |
| East Asia and Pacific | |
| Japan | 64,700 |
| South Korea | 40,200 |
| Philippines | 16,400 |
| Other | 11,650 |
| All East Asia and Pacific | 132,950 |
| Other overseas (estimated) | 25,000 |
| All areas | 2,163,200 |

SOURCE: Calculated from *The Military Balance 1988–1989* (London: International Institute for Strategic Studies, 1988), 18, 25–28.

**TABLE 28-2 NATO and Warsaw Pact Conventional Forces in Europe**

| | U.S. and Other NATO Countries | USSR and Other Warsaw Pact Countries |
|---|---|---|
| Troops (active duty) | 2,340,000 | 2,143,000 |
| Battle tanks | 22,200 | 53,000 |
| Artillery/mortar | 13,500 | 44,300 |
| Antitank weapons | 11,000 | 13,700 |
| Infantry combat vehicles (MICV) | 6,200 | 23,600 |
| Armed helicopters | 864 | 1,220 |

SOURCE: *The Military Balance 1988–1989* (London: International Institute for Strategic Studies, 1988), 237.

the United States, but it was defeated in 1949 by the Soviet-supplied Communist forces of Mao Zedong. In June 1950 the Soviet-backed North Koreans invaded South Korea, and President Truman immediately committed U.S. troops to the conflict, which ended in stalemate at a loss of 35,000 American lives.

One of the staunchest "cold warriors" of the postwar era was John Foster Dulles, President Dwight D. Eisenhower's secretary of state. Dulles pledged that the United States would block Soviet expansionism by all possible means, including the use of nuclear weapons (a policy known as "brinkmanship"). Dulles's warning was probably not an empty threat; the United States at the time had a 10-to-1 advantage in nuclear warheads over the Soviet Union. Dulles also wanted to roll back Soviet gains in Eastern Europe, and he appeared to promise U.S. support should Eastern Europeans rise up against their Commu-

Cold War propaganda, like this poster warning Americans of the danger of Soviet-backed communist encroachment in the Philippines in the late 1940s, contributed to an atmosphere of distrust and fear in the United States. (Library of Congress)

At the climax of the Cuban missile crisis in October 1962, an American patrol plane and destroyer supervise the departure from Cuban waters of a Soviet freighter (*foreground*). The canvas-covered objects on its deck were identified as missiles. (AP/Wide World)

*You have to take chances for peace, just as you must take chances in war. . . . The ability to get to the verge without getting into the war is the necessary art. If you try to run away from it, if you are scared to go to the brink, you are lost.*

John Foster Dulles

nist governments. When the Hungarians revolted in 1956, however, the United States did not intervene and Soviet tanks crushed the rebellion.

In 1963 President John F. Kennedy took the country close to a war with the Soviet Union. U.S. intelligence sources had discovered that the Soviet Union was constructing nuclear missile sites in Cuba, which lies only 90 miles from Key West, Florida. Kennedy responded with a naval blockade of Cuba and informed the Soviet Union that the United States would attack any Soviet ship that tried to pass through the blockade. At the last moment, Soviet ships heading for Cuba turned around, and Premier Nikita Khrushchev ordered the dismantling of the missile sites. Kennedy himself estimated the odds that the Soviet Union would choose war rather than capitulation at about "1 out of 3."[6] The Cuban missile crisis was a personal triumph for Kennedy but provoked an arms race. The Soviets backed down over Cuba in part because they had an inconsequential navy and an inferior nuclear force. Pledging not to be humiliated again, they began a twenty-year buildup of their naval and nuclear forces.

## NUCLEAR DETERRENCE: FROM MAD TO "STAR WARS"

The main threat to the physical security of the United States today is not invasion but nuclear attack. The United States has followed a policy of **deterrence,** the idea that the Soviet Union can be deterred from launching a nuclear attack by the knowledge that the United States has the capacity to retaliate in kind.

[6]Quoted in Graham Allison, "Conceptual Models and the Cuban Missile Crisis," *American Political Science Review* 63 (September 1969): 689.

## Mutually Assured Destruction (MAD)

The cornerstone of deterrence is a theory called "mutually assured destruction" (MAD).[7] Each side develops, builds, and deploys nuclear weapons in the knowledge that the other side is doing the same. Each side has enough warheads to destroy the other several times over and is inhibited from initiating a nuclear war by the knowledge that it too would be sure to be destroyed.

America's nuclear weapons are deployed in what is called the "nuclear triad," which refers to the three ways in which nuclear weapons can be launched: by air (bombers), land (missile launchers), and sea (submarines). Each part of the triad by itself is theoretically capable of destroying the Soviet Union, and together they provide a "second-strike capability"—the ability to absorb a nuclear attack (first strike) and survive with enough nuclear weaponry for massive retaliation (second strike). Submarine-launched missiles are particularly important to the second-strike capability because the Soviets do not yet have the capacity to locate and destroy the U.S. submarine fleet at sea. The United States has also developed cruise missiles, which are subsonic missiles that can be launched from the air, land, or sea and fly so low that they can evade detection by radar.

The Soviet nuclear arsenal is less versatile than that of the United States. The Soviets depend primarily on land-based missiles. As of 1985, the United States reportedly had 11,494 long-range nuclear warheads, of which 2,120 were on land-based missiles, 5,760 were submarine-based, and 3,614 were bomber-based. By comparison, the Soviet Union had 9,468 long-range warheads, of which 6,250 were land-based, 2,178 were submarine-based, and 1,040 were bomber-based.

MAD is essentially a defensive strategy. If the United States or the Soviet Union were intent on destroying the other with a first strike, nuclear overkill would not be necessary. The justification for huge nuclear arsenals is that each side must have enough warheads to respond to a first strike with a totally destructive second strike. This is why the superpowers agreed in the early 1970s that they would *not* develop antiballistic missile (ABM) defense systems. If either side were to perfect an ABM system, it might be tempted to launch a first strike because its ABM system would prevent the other side from retaliating effectively.

Although MAD has been a governing principle, not all U.S. leaders have fully accepted the thinking behind it.[8] A major shortcoming of MAD is that it would probably be a credible deterrent only in an extreme situation—if, for example, the United States were about to be conquered. The United States would not be likely to risk its own destruction by launching an all-out nuclear attack on the Soviet Union in order to prevent a Soviet victory in a war confined to Europe. Thus the United States during the Kennedy and Johnson administrations formulated a "flexible-response" strategy, which holds that the United States should use only the level of force that is appropriate to the level of the military

---

[7]See Jerome H. Kahan, *Security in the Nuclear Age* (Washington, D.C.: Brookings Institution, 1975); Robert Jervis, "Why Nuclear Superiority Doesn't Matter," *Political Science Quarterly* 94 (Winter 1979/1980); Glenn Snyder, *Deterrence and Defense* (Princeton, N.J.: Princeton University Press, 1961); Spurgeon M. Keeny, Jr., and Wolfgang K. H. Panofsky, "MAD vs. NUTS: The Mutual Hostage Relationship of the Superpowers," *Foreign Affairs* 60 (Winter 1981/1982): 287–304.
[8]See Ian Clark, *Limited Nuclear War* (Princeton, N.J.: Princeton University Press, 1982).

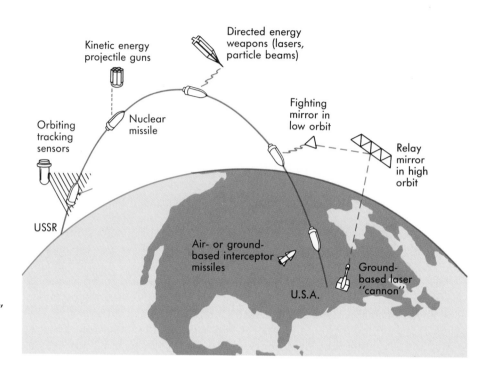

**FIGURE 28-1 How "Star Wars" Is Intended to Work**
*Source:* New York Times, *November 18, 1985, A7.*

threat against it. If the Soviet Union invaded Western Europe with conventional (nonnuclear) forces, flexible response dictates that the attack would be met first with NATO's conventional forces and then, if the NATO forces began to lose, with the first-strike use of battlefield nuclear weapons. The result would be a "limited" nuclear war, as contrasted with the threat of "unlimited" war that underlies MAD.

### "Star Wars"

President Reagan departed from the MAD concept in 1983 when he proposed a space-based defense system, the Strategic Defense Initiative (SDI)—or "Star Wars," as it is popularly known. SDI would consist of weapons deployed in outer space which could destroy incoming Soviet missiles (see Figure 28-1). SDI's proponents have argued that it would bring an end to the threat of nuclear destruction.[9] Research has begun on SDI's components, and the estimated cost of the completed project exceeds $1 trillion. Many people object to the militarization of space, and scientists are still debating the feasibility of the project (new technology will have to be developed to meet SDI's requirements).

The Soviet Union has contested the United States' claim that SDI is a defensive system. Even U.S. analysts acknowledge that SDI probably could not be made 100 percent effective, and the Soviets have therefore reasoned that SDI would guard the United States only against a greatly weakened Soviet Union's second-strike response to an American first strike. At a 1986 summit meeting in Iceland, Reagan tried to assure Gorbachev that the United States would never

[9]See Keith B. Payne and Colin S. Gray, "Nuclear Policy and the Defensive Transition," *Foreign Affairs* 62 (Spring 1984): 820–842; but see also Richard Garwin, "Star Wars: Shield or Threat?" *Journal of International Affairs* (Summer 1985): 31–44.

launch an unprovoked first strike at the Soviet Union. It was reported that Reagan said, "Trust me," to which Gorbachev replied, "Would you entrust your nation's security to a promise?"

## THE LIMITS OF AMERICAN POWER: THE LESSON OF VIETNAM

The major turning point of late-twentieth-century U.S. foreign policy was the Vietnam war. It was the most costly application of the containment doctrine: 58,000 American soldiers lost their lives. America's defeat in Vietnam forced U.S. policymakers to reconsider the country's international role.

### "The Making of a Quagmire"

In 1954 Vietnamese guerrilla forces, led by Ho Chi Minh, a nationalist with communist sympathies, defeated the French forces occupying their country. The Geneva conference that ended the war resulted in a partitioning of Vietnam: the northern region was placed under Ho Chi Minh's leadership and the southern region under anticommunist leaders. The United States provided economic assistance to South Vietnam, anticipating that its government would quickly develop the public support that would enable it to prevail in a Vietnam unification election that was scheduled for 1956. When it became apparent that Ho Chi Minh would easily win the election, the United States helped to get it canceled and began to increase its military assistance to the South Vietnamese army. By the time of President Kennedy's assassination in 1963, the United States had about 17,000 military advisers in South Vietnam. Lyndon Johnson sharply escalated the war in 1965 by committing U.S. combat units to the conflict. By the late 1960s, 550,000 Americans were fighting in South Vietnam. Underlying the U.S. involvement was the so-called domino theory, which holds that a communist takeover in one country encourages revolution in neighboring countries. America's intervention in South Vietnam was justified by an interest not only in keeping it from falling to the Communists but also in preventing the downfall of other countries of Southeast Asia, including Cambodia, Laos, Thailand, Malaysia, and Singapore.

U.S. forces were technically superior in combat to the communist guerrillas, but they were at a fatal disadvantage: they were fighting an enemy they could not easily identify in a society they did not fully understand.[10] The communists' promises of land reform and their long and ultimately victorious struggle against the French had won them broad popular support. Vietnam was a guerrilla war with no front lines and few set battles. The United States controlled the air, the sea, and the cities, but the war was to be won in the countryside by an enemy that was determined to outlast its stronger foe.

As the war dragged on, American public opinion, most visibly among the young, turned against continued U.S. involvement. The war's unpopularity was the main reason President Johnson decided not to run for reelection in 1968. Richard Nixon, who became president in 1969, continued the war effort, but public opinion forced him to aim not for victory, but for what he called "peace

---

[10]See David Halberstam, *The Making of a Quagmire: America and Vietnam during the Kennedy Era*, 2d ed. (New York: Random House, 1988); Stanley Karnow, *Vietnam: A History* (New York: Penguin, 1983).

In the jungle warfare of Vietnam, American soldiers had difficulty finding the enemy and adapting to guerrilla tactics. (UPI/ Bettmann Newsphotos)

with honor." Nixon pursued a policy of gradual withdrawal, punctuated by B-52 bombing raids on the major North Vietnamese cities of Hanoi and Haiphong—raids that represented futile attempts to persuade North Vietnam to end its pursuit of the war in the south.

## Détente

America's frustrations in Vietnam led to a reassessment of the containment policy. Nixon concluded that the United States could no longer act as the "Lone Ranger" for the Free World and sought to reduce tensions with communist countries. If armed confrontation was unproductive, then perhaps diplomacy and trade would be more effective. Nixon was convinced that the Soviet Union had achieved permanent status as a world power and that the United States had no practical alternative but to work with the USSR to preserve the status quo.[11] This new philosophy was highlighted by the Helsinki Accords of 1971, in which the United States accepted the territorial boundaries of Eastern Europe—a tacit recognition of Soviet domination of the region. Then Nixon took a historic journey to the People's Republic of China in 1972, the first official contact with that country since the communists took power in 1949.

These diplomatic efforts were accompanied by the Strategic Arms Limitation Talks (SALT), which began in 1969. The SALT talks presumed that the United States and the Soviet Union each had an interest in retaining enough nuclear weapons to deter the other from an attack but that neither side had an interest in mutual destruction. Under the doctrine known as "nuclear parity," the two sides would work to stabilize the arms race by agreeing to maintain nuclear arsenals of approximately equal destructive power. After two and a half years of negotiations, Nixon and Leonid Brezhnev, Khrushchev's successor as leader of

[11]Charles Kegley and Eugene Wittkopf, *American Foreign Policy* (New York: St. Martin's Press, 1979), 48.

the Soviet Union, signed an agreement known as SALT I in May 1972. Each country would limit itself to its existing number of intercontinental ballistic missiles (ICBMs) and would sharply limit its subsequent production of antiballistic missiles (ABMs). Nixon and Brezhnev signed additional, less sweeping arms-limitation accords in 1973 and 1974.

These agreements, along with the recognition of China and the lowering of East–West trade barriers, marked the start of a new era of communication and cooperation, or **détente** (a French word meaning "a relaxing"), between the United States and the Soviet Union.[12] Détente assumed that the free and communist worlds have contradictory goals and ideals but that neither side can benefit in the long run from continuing instability and conflict. Under détente, the two sides would work together to reduce tensions and promote mutual gain.

Détente continued through the administration of President Gerald Ford. In 1974 Ford signed an interim agreement with Brezhnev to cap the number of strategic missiles, multiple-warhead delivery systems, and heavy bombers that each superpower could possess. Ford also negotiated new trade agreements with the Soviet Union.

## INSURGENCIES: A CHANGING U.S. RESPONSE

The United States was ill prepared for a war of the type that was fought in Vietnam. U.S. military forces and planning had been designed for four other types of military conflict:

*Unlimited conventional warfare*, of which the two world wars were examples.

*Limited conventional warfare*, of which Korea was an example.

*Unlimited nuclear warfare*, for which MAD was a strategy.

*Limited nuclear warfare*, for which flexible response was a strategy.

Vietnam was a different kind of war: an **insurgency.** Uprisings by irregular soldiers against established regimes are an old form of conflict, but they have taken on new importance in the twentieth century as they have become more widespread and more lethal.

Insurgencies do not easily yield to military force. As Vietnam made clear, it is difficult to defeat an irregular army, even one that is outmanned and outgunned. Conventional combat units are not very effective against an enemy that can simply run and hide. Even with troops trained in counterinsurgency, a capacity that the U.S. military acquired during the Vietnam war, victory is not assured.

In most Third World countries, insurgencies originate in the grievances of people who are at the bottom of the economic heap. Insurgent forces emerge from the mass of ordinary citizens who are struggling against the monopoly of economic and political power by a tiny elite. Typically this elite controls the military and has the backing of international corporations. Most insurgencies accordingly pose a threat to U.S. business interests. In addition, the willingness of insurgents to accept military supplies from any source, which usually turns out to be the Soviet Union or its allies, further increases the likelihood that their interests will be perceived as antagonistic to those of the United States.

[12]See Paul Y. Hammond, *Cold War and Détente* (New York: Harcourt Brace Jovanovich, 1975).

A democratic impulse known as "people power," coupled with the belated backing of the United States, helped Corazón Aquino unseat Philippine dictator Ferdinand Marcos in 1986. (Greg Smith/Picture Group)

Consequently, the United States has in fact treated many Third World insurgencies as threats to its security. Vietnam was a case in point, and so are the more recent uprisings in Central America. When in 1987 the governments of Central America developed a joint peace plan for the region, the Reagan administration reacted with ambivalence because the plan would have left in place the Sandinista government of Nicaragua, which has declared itself to be outside the sphere of American influence.

U.S. attempts to quell Third World insurgencies have declined somewhat since the Vietnam war, which reduced public support for U.S. military involvement in the internal affairs of other countries. Throughout the 1980s, polls showed that a large majority of Americans were steadfastly opposed to sending American troops into Central America. During most of this period, there was even public opposition to providing military assistance on a small scale. An April 1984 Gallup poll, for example, indicated that only 39 percent of those interviewed favored supplying military equipment to friendly governments in Central America.

U.S. policymakers have become increasingly aware that military power is not likely to stop insurgencies. Abject poverty is a deep-seated condition in Third World countries, and there are always desperate people willing to fill the ranks of the insurgents. Rather than automatically siding with the ruling elite, the United States has increasingly pressured friendly governments to improve the economic and political situation of the underclass as a condition for continued U.S. support. In the Philippines in 1986, for example, the United States withdrew its longtime support from President Ferdinand Marcos and backed reform-minded Corazón Aquino, urging her to carry through on her promises of economic reform, including redistribution of land. President Jimmy Carter had earlier made respect for human rights a condition of foreign aid to pro–United States military dictatorships. Although Reagan criticized the idea of basing foreign policy on progress in human rights, he did apply the concept in selected cases.

★ ANALYZE THE ISSUE

**Insurgencies as Threats to U.S. Interests**
Most revolutions in Third World countries have been opposed by the U.S. government. Do most such insurgencies really represent a substantial threat to the interests of the United States? What criteria could be used in judging which Third World revolutions are likely to jeopardize U.S. interests and which are not?

## RECENT DEVELOPMENTS IN SUPERPOWER RELATIONS

Although the period of détente during the 1970s marked a major shift in U.S.–Soviet relations, it was not a lasting one.[13] The Soviet invasion of Afghanistan in 1979 convinced U.S. leaders that the USSR was still bent on expansion and threatened Western interests in the oil-rich Middle East. Ronald Reagan, elected president in 1980, called for a renewed emphasis on U.S. military power as a way of dealing with the Soviet Union, which he labeled an "evil empire."[14]

Reagan's proposal for a doubling of defense expenditures during the next five years marked the beginning of the largest peacetime military buildup in the

[13]Robert G. Kaiser, "U.S.–Soviet Relations: Goodbye to Détente," *Foreign Affairs* 59 (Winter 1979/1980): 500–521.
[14]See Russell J. Ling, "Reagan and the Russians," *American Political Science Review* 78 (June 1984): 338–355; Seweryn Bialer and Joan Afferica, "Reagan and Russia," *Foreign Affairs* 61 (Winter 1982/1983): 249–271.

**FIGURE 28-2 National Security Organization within the Executive Branch (Simplified)**

**President**

As commander in chief, head of state, chief diplomat, and chief executive, the president has executive leadership on national security policy.

**National Security Council (NSC)**

The NSC advises the president on issues of national security. The NSC includes the president, the vice-president, and the secretaries of state and defense as full members, and the CIA director and the chairman of the Joint Chiefs of Staff as advisory members. State, Defense, and the CIA often have conflicting and self-centered ideas about the conduct of security policy, and the NSC acts to keep the president in charge by providing a broader perspective. The NSC's work is directed by the president's national security adviser, who, with an office in the White House and access to defense, diplomatic, and intelligence sources, has become influential in the setting of U.S. policy.

**Department of Defense (DOD)**

The DOD includes the three armed services—the Army, the Navy, and the Air Force. Although each service is separate from the others, the secretary of defense represents all of them in relations with Congress and the president. An effective secretary must have strong managerial skills because of DOD's enormous size, weapons-development programs, and rivalries among the services for resources. The stature of recent secretaries has varied widely, depending on the secretary's personality and the president's emphasis on military power.

**Central Intelligence Agency (CIA)**

The CIA gathers and assesses information on foreign affairs. Much of this effort consists of routine monitoring of international developments, but the CIA also engages in covert operations. The CIA is prohibited by law from conducting surveillance on domestic targets, but has not always respected this limitation on its activities and has also at times flouted other restrictions. In order to prevent the CIA from getting further out of hand, Congress in the mid-1970s established House and Senate committees to oversee CIA activities.

**Department of State**

The State Department conducts most of the country's day-to-day business with foreign countries through its embassies, headed by U.S. ambassadors. State's traditional duties include negotiating political agreements with other nations, protecting U.S. citizens and interests abroad, promoting U.S. economic interests, gathering foreign intelligence, and representing the United States abroad. The secretary of state is usually second in importance only to the president within the executive branch in the determination of national security policy.

nation's history. Reagan pushed for deployment of new nuclear weapons systems, including MX missiles, cruise missiles, and Pershing missiles. During his presidency 4,500 tanks and 300 attack helicopters were added to the Army, 80 ships were added to the Navy, and 1,300 fighter jets were added to the Air Force. The Soviet Union, for its part, had been building up its conventional and nuclear forces since the Cuban missile crisis of 1962.[15]

After the Afghanistan invasion, strategic arms talks between the two superpowers came to a virtual standstill.* Although the two sides continued to meet in Geneva, Switzerland, the United States refused to make any concessions to the Soviet Union. In late 1983, when the United States decided to deploy Pershing and cruise missiles in Western Europe, the Soviet delegation in Geneva walked out of the talks. Reagan was unconcerned. "Only if the Soviets recognize the West's determination to modernize its own military forces will they see an incentive to negotiate a verifiable agreement establishing equal, lower levels [of nuclear arms]," he said.[16]

In 1987 the Reagan administration achieved a major breakthrough with the signing of the U.S.–Soviet agreement to limit intermediate-range nuclear forces (INF). The signing of the INF treaty came during the third meeting in as many years between Reagan and Gorbachev and appeared to vindicate Reagan's decision to negotiate from strength. It had cost the United States nearly $10 billion to build and deploy new missile systems in Europe, and the INF treaty calls for their phased destruction in the 1990s. But the INF treaty marked the first time that the superpowers had agreed to cutbacks in their existing nuclear arsenals, and it is doubtful that the Soviet Union would have agreed to remove its medium-range missiles from Europe if the United States had not deployed new medium-range missiles there.

When he took office, George Bush pledged that he would work with Gorbachev toward further arms reductions, conventional as well as nuclear. Such reductions would diminish the possibility of war between the superpowers, but they also have an economic rationale. The cost of being a superpower is wearing on both the United States and the Soviet Union. Since World War II the Soviet Union has diverted so many of its resources to military purposes that it is far behind the West economically. The United States has also felt the economic burden of military spending, a topic that will now be discussed.

## The Economics of National Security Policy

Economic considerations are a vital component of national security policy. In the simplest sense, economic strength is a prerequisite of military strength: a powerful defense establishment can be maintained only by a country of substantial economic means. But economic well-being is a core component of national security in a broader and more important sense: economic prosperity enables a people to "secure" their way of life. The Soviet Union's recent efforts

*In 1981, strategic arms talks were labeled START (Strategic Arms Reduction Talks) to distinguish them from the earlier series of SALT talks.

[15]See William Zimmerman and Glenn Palmer, "Words and Deeds in Soviet Foreign Policy: The Case of Soviet Military Expenditures," *American Political Science Review* 77 (June 1983): 358–367.

[16]Quoted in Congressional Quarterly, *U.S. Defense Policy*, 3d ed. (Washington, D.C.: Congressional Quarterly Press, 1983), 41.

to cut back on military spending reflect a belated recognition by its leadership that in the long run economic stagnation may be a greater threat to its communist system than is military conflict with the West.

## THE UNITED STATES' DECLINING INFLUENCE ON WORLD TRADE

A major goal of U.S. security policy is the maintenance of an international economic order that can serve America's interests. The United States depends on other countries for raw materials, finished goods, and capital to meet Americans' production and consumption demands. Meeting this objective requires the United States to have influence on world markets.

The peak era of U.S. influence on the international marketplace came after World War II. Industrialized Europe was devastated, but U.S. factories and farmlands had been untouched by the war and were producing nearly half of the world's goods. While European nations were rebuilding, U.S. businesses were in an ideal position to expand. Investment opportunities were open throughout the world, and U.S. business interests had the necessary capital. The Middle East is an illustration. Before World War II began, U.S. oil companies controlled one-tenth of Middle Eastern oil reserves; just twenty years later, they controlled six-tenths.[17]

The big oil companies, such as Shell and Mobil, are examples of **multinational corporations**—firms that have major operations in more than one country.[18]

[17]Harry Magdoff, *The Age of Imperialism: The Economics of U.S. Foreign Policy* (New York: Monthly Review Press, 1969), 43.
[18]See Raymond Vernon, *Storm over the Multinationals* (Cambridge, Mass.: Harvard University Press, 1977); Richard J. Barnet and Ronald E. Muller, *Global Reach: The Power of the Multinational Corporations* (New York: Simon & Schuster, 1975).

This American bank building in Buenos Aires, Argentina, represents one of thousands of multinational corporations with foreign investments. (Stuart Cohen/Stock, Boston)

These corporate giants have spread their operations, and their financial and political power, across the globe since the end of World War II. By some estimates, multinationals now account for more than a fourth of the total world economy. Many multinationals are headquartered in the United States: more than 500 U.S. firms have an ownership interest of 50 percent or more in foreign affiliates. Some U.S.-based multinationals have pursued policies that are contrary to U.S. security policy. For example, while the U.S. government was providing assistance to insurgents in Angola during the 1980s, U.S. oil firms were managing the oilfields that were the major source of revenue for Angola's Marxist government.

By and large, however, foreign investment works to America's advantage in several ways. First, it sends a flow of overseas profits back to the United States, which strengthens the country's financial structure. Second, it assures the United States of the raw materials it needs. American corporations have direct control of certain resources, as in the case of a portion of Middle Eastern oil. Third, it makes other nations dependent on the prosperity of the United States; their economies are linked to the condition of U.S. business.

The net effect is substantial. Because of their country's economic power, the American people enjoy levels of employment and productivity and a standard of living that are among the highest in the world. International economic power also enables the United States to make diplomatic and military demands on its trading partners.

However, America's position in the world marketplace has weakened substantially in the past two decades.[19] West Germany and Japan, which were once America's junior trading partners, have become powerful economic rivals of the United States. In addition, Western Europe as a whole has become a less receptive market for U.S. goods; European countries are now one another's best customers, trading among themselves through their trading alliance, the European Economic Community, which was organized in its present form in 1967.

The indicators of the decline in America's economic leverage are many.[20] Today Japan, not the United States, is the world's leading exporting nation, and trade between the two countries results in a huge surplus for Japan. In fact, the United States in the early 1980s become a "debtor" nation; its trade deficit (the amount of imports in excess of exports) reached $170 billion in 1987. Japan's yen and West Germany's Deutschemark have become stronger currencies than the American dollar, which once was the monetary standard against which all other currencies were compared. In early 1988 the United States was humbled when Japan and West Germany had to intervene to halt the dollar's drop in value on world financial markets.

For the United States, economic difficulty has obviously not brought economic deprivation. America remains one of the world's strongest nations economically, and its people continue to have an enviable standard of living. But whereas the United States at one time could almost define international economic conditions, it is now also defined by them.[21]

[19]William Diebold, Jr., "The United States in the World Economy: A Fifty-Year Perspective," *Foreign Affairs* 62 (Fall 1983): 81–104.
[20]See Walter Russell Mead, *Mortal Splendor: The American Empire in Transition* (Boston: Houghton Mifflin, 1987).
[21]See Robert W. Tucker, "America in Decline: The Foreign Policy Maturity," *Foreign Affairs* 58 (Winter 1979/1980): 449–484.

★ ANALYZE THE ISSUE

**The United States in a Global Economy**
All countries are now closely linked in a global economy. How does this situation limit America's foreign policy options? Why might this situation make it even more important for the United States to get its budget deficit under control in order to reduce the amount of money it borrows from other countries?

## A WEAKENING CONNECTION BETWEEN ECONOMIC POWER AND MILITARY POWER

When the Marshall Plan was established in 1947, its stated purpose was to strengthen the countries of Western Europe so that they could better confront the perceived Soviet military and political threat. However, the Marshall Plan was also designed to provide for the economic needs of the United States. Wartime production had lifted the country out of the Great Depression, but the end of the war in 1945 brought a recession and renewed fears of hard times. A rejuvenated Western Europe would furnish a market for U.S. goods. In effect, Western Europe would become a junior partner within a system of international trade dominated by the United States.

America's military power buttressed this international economic system. The worldwide umbrella of U.S. naval and nuclear forces assured the United States

---

### ★ HOW THE UNITED STATES COMPARES

**The Burdens of Military Spending and Foreign Assistance**

The United States bears a disproportionate share of the defense costs of the world's democracies. The U.S. military establishment is huge and is deployed all over the world, and the United States spends about $300 billion annually to maintain it. These military expenditures directly account for more than 6 percent of the U.S. gross national product (total output of goods and services). By comparison, defense spending accounts for only 1 percent of Japan's GNP. Japan's small defense force is confined to the country's islands and adjoining waters. The United States has pressured its allies to carry a larger share of the free world's defense burden, but they have resisted, contending that the cost would be too high and that their security would not be substantially improved. Some of these countries have cited their foreign aid programs as an area in which their contribution to world security is greater than that of the United States. France, for example, allocated 3.3 percent of its national budget to economic and other assistance to developing nations in 1986, compared to 1.1 percent for the United States.

| Country | Military Expenditures (Percent of GNP) | Aid to Developing Countries (Percent of National Budget) |
| --- | --- | --- |
| Canada | 2.2% | 2.1% |
| France | 4.1 | 3.3 |
| Great Britain | 5.3 | 1.2 |
| Israel | 27.1 | NA |
| Italy | 2.7 | 1.0 |
| Japan | 1.0 | 1.2 |
| Mexico | 0.7 | NA |
| Soviet Union | 12.6 | NA |
| Sweden | 3.1 | 2.5 |
| United States | 6.3 | 1.1 |
| West Germany | 3.3 | 2.6 |

SOURCES: *Statistical Abstract of the United States, 1988* (Washington, D.C.: U.S. Government Printing Office, 1987), 827 (military data); OECD, 1988 (aid data). Data are for 1986. No data on aid are available for Israel, Mexico, and the Soviet Union.

and its friends of open markets. The Soviet Union was more or less frozen out of trade with the free world.

U.S. military power was also used to support governments that could be expected to promote America's security and economic goals. In the Middle East, for example, the new state of Israel provided the United States with an opportunity to form a secure friendship in a region that was sometimes hostile to Western interests. By helping Israel both militarily and economically, the United States acquired an ally that could be counted on to counter threats from either Arab nationalism or Soviet intervention in the Middle East. Today Israel gets more U.S. foreign aid ($3 billion annually) than any other country.

Economic and military concerns were also behind U.S. participation in a coup that changed the government of Iran in 1953. Iran had nationalized its oil production in 1951, thus taking control away from foreign oil companies. The United States sent CIA agents to undermine the regime and provided arms that enabled the shah of Iran to seize power in 1953. The shah responded by giving U.S. interests more control of oil production and by building Iran into a pro-Western regional military power. However, in order to maintain his control within Iran, the shah resorted to repressive measures against this Islamic fundamentalist opponents. In 1979 they overthrew the shah, seized the oilfields, and established an anti-American government.

America's helplessness during the Iranian revolution demonstrated a fact that had become increasingly apparent in the preceding decade: U.S. military power was becoming a less and less effective means of preserving U.S. economic leverage.[22] If military strength was a key to the emergence of a U.S.-centered world market after World War II, the very creation of that market reduced the efficacy of military force. The economies of most of the world's countries are now so interconnected that military intervention is almost certain to be counterproductive. War with an anti-American government in the Middle East, for example, could be ruinous to all because it would disrupt the flow of the oil that fuels Western economies.

Japan exemplifies the changing relationship between economic power and military power. Japan's small military force is designed for homeland defense rather than global deployment. Japan's leverage in world markets is based strictly on economic factors, such as the quality and pricing of its products. Not only is Japan the world's leading trade country, but its economy benefits significantly from not having to carry a heavy burden of military spending. In contrast, the financial weight of playing the role of superpower has taken its toll on the American economy. The cost of the Vietnam war, estimated at $150 billion (roughly $450 billion in 1989 dollars), fueled the spiraling inflation that weakened the U.S. economy in the late 1970s. Then came the huge peacetime military buildup of the 1980s (see Figure 28-3), which, for domestic political reasons, U.S. policymakers funded through deficit spending rather than through tax increases. As a result, the national debt nearly tripled between 1980 and 1988, to more than $2.5 trillion, and is a threat to the country's future prosperity.

[22]See Robert O. Keohane and Joseph S. Nye, *Power and Interdependence: World Politics in Transition* (Boston: Little, Brown, 1977).

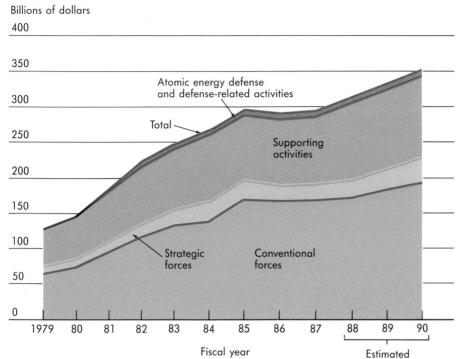

Billions of dollars

**FIGURE 28-3 Defense Spending in the 1980s**
Spending on national defense, which more than doubled during the 1980s, contributed to a sharp increase in the national debt. *Source: Office of Management and Budget, The United States Budget in Brief, Fiscal Year 1988 (Washington, D.C.: U.S. Government Printing Office, 1988), 52.*

## THE ROLE OF THE MILITARY-INDUSTRIAL COMPLEX IN DEFENSE SPENDING

Since World War II, the costs of maintaining global nuclear and conventional forces have kept U.S. defense spending at high levels.[23] In fiscal year 1988, the U.S. defense budget was $300 billion, or 7 percent of the gross national product. These enormous expenditures have been justified by reference to the nation's security needs. However, an alternative explanation for high defense spending has been offered: the insatiable demands of the U.S. armed services and defense firms. In his 1961 farewell address, President Dwight D. Eisenhower warned against the "unwarranted influence" and "misplaced power" of what he called a military-industrial complex.[24]

The **military-industrial complex** has three components: the military establishment, the industries that manufacture weapons, and the members of Congress from states and districts that depend heavily on the arms industry. The military-industrial complex is not, as is sometimes suggested, a well-coordinated, unified network of interests engaged in a conspiracy to keep the United States on a wartime footing. Rather it is an aggregation of interests that benefit from a high level of defense spending, regardless of the demonstrable necessity of these expenditures for national security.

Many corporations could not survive without military contracts. Among U.S.

*The conjunction of an immense military establishment and a large arms industry is new in the American experience. . . . In the councils of government, we must guard against the acquisition of unwarranted influence, whether sought or unsought, by the military-industrial complex. The potential for the disastrous rise of misplaced power exists and will persist.*

Dwight D. Eisenhower

[23]Murray L. Weidenbaum, *The Economics of Peacetime Defense* (New York: Praeger, 1974), 25.
[24]See Steve Rosen, *Testing Theories of the Military-Industrial Complex* (Lexington, Mass.: Lexington Books, 1973), 1.

aircraft manufacturers, for example, only Boeing and McDonnell-Douglas make passenger planes. Others, such as Northrop and Rockwell, make only military aircraft. Defense firms obviously do not act purely out of nationalistic motives; they are profit-making businesses.[25] Many weapons designs are aggressively sold by industry to the Department of Defense.[26]

The U.S. military does not need much persuading. New weapons systems are naturally attractive to the military establishment; it wants the latest-model tanks, planes, guns, and ships.[27] The cost of modern weaponry is staggering: as of 1987, the Army's M-1 tanks cost $2.2 million each; the Air Force's B-1 bombers, more than $300 million apiece; the Navy's Trident II submarines, more than $1 billion each.

Many members of Congress are eager to approve arms contracts (or at least reluctant to oppose them) because of their economic impact on constituents. The B-1 bomber, for example, has 5,200 subcontractors located in forty-eight states and in all but a handful of congressional districts. "This geographic spread gives all sections of the country an important stake in the airplane," one assessment of the B-1 concluded.[28] Each $1 billion spent on defense is estimated to create more than 30,000 jobs. A sharp reduction in defense spending would cause havoc in many local economies; about one in ten American jobs is directly or indirectly related to military spending.

Without doubt, some proportion of defense spending reflects the workings of the military-industrial complex rather than the requirements of national security.[29] The problem is that no one knows exactly what this proportion is, and the

[25]John Perry Miller, "Procurement Policies and Renegotiation," in J. Fred Weston, ed., *Procurement and Profit Renegotiation* (San Francisco: Wadsworth, 1966), 95.
[26]Quoted in David Sims, "Spoon Feeding the Military: How New Weapons Systems Come to Be," in L. S. Rodberg and Dereck Seyr, eds., *The Pentagon Watchers* (Garden City, N.Y.: Doubleday/Anchor, 1970), 249–250.
[27]See James Fallows, *National Defense* (New York: Random House, 1981).
[28]"The B-1: A Flight through Adversity," *Los Angeles Times,* reprinted in *Syracuse Post-Standard,* July 29, 1983, A7.
[29]Seymour Melman, *Pentagon Capitalism* (New York: McGraw-Hill, 1970), 175.

The Stealth bomber is unveiled in California in 1988—one of the newest and most expensive weapons in America's arsenal. (AP/Wide World)

estimates vary widely. There is also a larger question: How many ships, planes, tanks, nuclear missiles, and troops are necessary to protect the United States and its worldwide interests? No one knows exactly how much the United States must spend each year to maintain its security. U.S. policymakers have preferred to err on the side of caution; between 1980 and 1985, for example, military spending doubled even though the country was not at war.

The Soviet Union has its own version of a military-industrial complex.[30] Critics say that a buildup of military forces in one country convinces the other country that it too must modernize and expand its defense capability.

## The Tension between American Ideals and National Security

As the American colonies prepared in 1776 for their war with England, the task of writing the Declaration of Independence was assigned to the high-minded Thomas Jefferson. The job of checking his work was given to the tough-minded Benjamin Franklin and John Adams, who would ensure that Jefferson's themes of universal liberty and equality were balanced by fighting words that could inspire ordinary citizens to enlist in a war to create a powerful American state.

The tension between democratic idealism and national power which was evident during the drafting of the Declaration of Independence has persisted throughout the country's history. Even as the freedom that Americans enjoy is protected by a powerful American state, such a state can also threaten that freedom.

### SECURITY NEEDS AS A THREAT TO AMERICAN IDEALS

In the late 1940s, the domestic political scene in the United States was dominated by anticommunist hysteria and fear. In the House of Representatives, the Committee on Un-American Activities conducted investigations aimed at uncovering subversive elements that had allegedly infiltrated various areas of American life. The State Department was accused of having "lost" China to the communists and of being a haven for communist sympathizers; many prominent diplomats lost their jobs because of their supposed communist learnings. Trade unionists with any hint of a communist past were eliminated from union bureaucracies. Actors and playwrights believed to have communist loyalties were blacklisted—no major movie studio or theater company would hire them. In some American universities, professors suspected of having communist sympathies were fired. Arthur Miller's play *The Crucible* compared these purges with the Salem "witch hunts" of the 1690s.

The leading figure in the modern-day communist witch hunt was Senator Joseph McCarthy (R-Wis.), who equated liberty not with individual rights but with preservation of the American state. McCarthy used innuendo, intimidation, and outright lies to whip up an anticommunist frenzy and to suppress protests against his sweeping allegations of subversion. McCarthy's rampage ended with his censure by the U.S. Senate in late 1954, but only after his accusations had become so outrageous that only right-wing fringe elements

★ ANALYZE THE ISSUE

**The Revolving Door**
In March 1989 the U.S. Senate narrowly rejected John Tower's nomination to become secretary of defense. One objection raised by Tower's opponents was that after having served as a U.S. senator and a U.S. arms-control negotiator, he had stepped almost immediately through the "revolving door" into well-paid work as a consultant to defense contractors. Do you agree that by doing so, Tower created a serious conflict of interest? Should former members of Congress be required to wait several years before being permitted to work for special interests?

*When public excitement runs high as to alien ideologies, is the time when we must be particularly alert not to impair the ancient landmarks set up in the Bill of Rights.*

Luther W. Youngdahl,
*United States* v.
*Lattimore,* 1953

[30]See Paul A. Koistinen, *The Military-Industrial Complex* (New York: Praeger, 1980), 5; David Holloway, *The Soviet Union and the Arms Race* (New Haven, Conn.: Yale University Press, 1982).

Actor Humphrey Bogart attends the hearings of the House Un-American Activities Committee in the late 1940s, during which many Hollywood personalities were interrogated about their suspected communist sympathies. (Martha Holmes/Life Magazine-Time Inc.)

★ ANALYZE THE ISSUE

**Accountability in Foreign Policy**
During the summer of 1987, congressional hearings revealed that some staffers on the National Security Council had been involved in illegal arms deals with Iran and covert operations to supply the Nicaraguan Contras. These activities constituted a systematic attempt to avoid the political accountability that is at the core of American democracy. Two of the principal operatives, Lt. Col. Oliver North and NSC head John Poindexter, said that their actions were justified by national security concerns—specifically, by the threat of communism in Central America. Do you believe that in this case the end justified the means? In general, how far should the U.S. government be allowed to go in keeping its foreign policy secret from the American people? Explain your position in terms of both democratic accountability and the likely effectiveness of extreme secrecy in foreign policy.

continued to support him. The McCarthy era stands as a reminder that in the face of world insecurity, Americans' political ideals can be threatened by events at home as well as abroad.[31]

## AMERICAN IDEALS AS A THREAT TO NATIONAL SECURITY

Although misguided patriotism can threaten democratic practices, it is also true that open debate and majority rule cannot be completely reconciled with the country's defense needs, which at times include secrecy, deception, and decisive action. The perennial question is whether the rules governing a democracy's national security policy should differ from those that guide its domestic policy. In fact, of course, different rules *are* applied. Certain types of national security information are officially "classified"—the information cannot lawfully be made public. In addition, as we saw in Chapter 21, the president has considerable freedom to act without congressional approval in the national security realm. For instance, the War Powers Act of 1973 allows the president to send U.S. troops into combat abroad for short periods without the approval of Congress.

Some people advocate more radical departures from democratic practices in the conduct of national security policy, such as granting the president and the various intelligence agencies broad freedom to operate on their own authority. Such proposals overlook the fact that the true strength of a democracy rests with its people. When they are left out of the policy process, and when policy then goes awry (as it did during the Vietnam war), their trust in government is shaken and their unity is disrupted. The American people still have not recovered the high level of public trust and unity that they had before Vietnam, which, as President Bush acknowledged in his first State of the Union address, has made it nearly impossible for the United States to conduct a coherent and effective foreign policy.

[31]See Fred J. Cook, *The Nightmare Decade* (New York: Random House, 1971).

# Summary

Since World War II, U.S. foreign and defense policies have been dominated by a concern with the Soviet Union. During most of this period the United States has pursued a policy of containment based on the premise that the Soviet Union is an aggressor nation bent on global conquest. Containment policy has led the United States, for example, into wars in Korea and Vietnam and into maintaining a large defense establishment. U.S. governmental forces are deployed around the globe and the nation has a large nuclear arsenal designed to deter a Soviet nuclear attack through the threat of mutual destruction. The dangers and costs of U.S.–USSR hostilities have encouraged the two nations to negotiate strategic arms reductions and seek peaceful means of settling their differences. Except for a period of détente in the 1970s, however, the two superpowers have generally been unable to avoid an arms race.

Military preparedness is a main goal of national security policy; economic prosperity is another. In the post-1945 era, the United States helped establish and became the center of a global trading system. The nation's international economic position, however, has gradually weakened, owing to the emergence of strong competitors, particularly Japan and West Germany, and to the growing demands of smaller nations for a larger share of the world's wealth. Nations' increasing economic interdependence has made all of them more vulnerable to international disturbances and has made military force a less appropriate means of settling their disputes.

# Major Concepts

| | |
|---|---|
| cold war | insurgency |
| containment | military-industrial complex |
| détente | multinational corporations |
| deterrence | |

# Suggested Readings

Block, Fred L. *The Origins of International Economic Disorder.* Berkeley: University of California Press, 1977. An analysis of developments that have shaped international economics.

Congressional Quarterly. *U.S. Defense Policy,* 3d ed. Washington, D.C.: Congressional Quarterly Press, 1983. A basic survey of U.S. defense policy and military preparedness.

Fallows, James. *National Defense.* New York: Random House, 1981. A critical assessment of U.S. security policy.

Jervis, Robert. *The Illogic of American Nuclear Strategy.* Ithaca, N.Y.: Cornell University Press, 1984. A critical view of U.S. nuclear policy.

Karnow, Stanley. *Vietnam: A History.* New York: Penguin, 1983. A thorough history of American involvement in Vietnam.

Kegley, Charles, and Eugene Wittkopf. *American Foreign Policy,* 2d ed. New York: St. Martin's Press, 1982. A basic textbook on American foreign policy and the process by which it is made.

Keohane, Robert O., and Joseph S. Nye. *Power and Interdependence: World Politics in Transition.* Boston: Little, Brown, 1977. A penetrating analysis of the effects of global interdependence on U.S. power.

Koistinen, Paul A. *The Military-Industrial Complex.* New York: Praeger, 1980. An analysis of the military-industrial complex and its effect on defense spending and policy.

Quester, George H. *The Future of Nuclear Deterrence.* Lexington, Mass.: Lexington Books, 1986. A forward look at nuclear strategy.

Vernon, Raymond. *Storm over the Multinationals.* Cambridge, Mass.: Harvard University Press, 1977. An analysis of the international political influence of global corporations.

Weidenbaum, Murray L. *The Economics of Peacetime Defense.* New York: Praeger, 1974. An economist's analysis of the impact of defense spending on the nation's economy.

Yergin, Daniel. *Shattered Peace: The Origins of the Cold War and the National Security State.* Boston: Houghton Mifflin, 1977. A study of the origins, policies, and effects of the cold war between the United States and the USSR.

# Is the United States Past Its Peak as an Economic and Military Power?

### STEPHEN D. KRASNER

*The United States has not yet adjusted to its new, more vulnerable international position.*

At the end of World War II the United States was the most powerful country in the world. In fact, it was the most powerful state that had ever existed in the 300-year history of the modern international system. It was the only country that possessed nuclear weapons. Its gross national product was three times that of the Soviet Union and six times that of the United Kingdom, the next most economically productive nation in the noncommunist world. American industries held the commanding heights in high-technology industries. The United States was a net exporter of petroleum.

These extraordinary resources made it possible for American leaders to adopt very ambitious foreign policies. The United States created a system of alliances designed to contain the Soviet Union's expansionism. America fought bloody wars in Korea and Vietnam, countries that had few economic resources and were of little strategic importance. Large numbers of American troops were more or less permanently garrisoned in Western Europe and Japan. Defeats, especially the communist victory in China, were attributed to internal betrayal, not to any limitations of American power.

In the past two decades, however, American power has declined, in some areas dramatically. The gross national product of the United States is now only about 40 percent larger than that of Japan, which has half our population and few natural resources. Germany and Japan export more manufactured products than does the United States. The Soviet Union has achieved parity in nuclear weapons. Japan has challenged America's supremacy in high-technology industries. The United States has been a net importer of petroleum since 1970. Even though the United States remains very powerful, it can no longer consider itself able either to control the international environment or to extricate itself from it.

The United States has not yet adjusted to its new, more vulnerable international position. Even crushing setbacks, most notably the loss of the Vietnam war and the quadrupling of oil prices in the 1970s (which could have been prevented if the United States had had surplus productive capacity), have not prompted a fundamental reassessment of American policies. Commitments that were made forty years ago have not been radically changed. Half the American army is still dedicated to the defense of Western Europe, even though Western Europe's gross national product is now higher than that of the United States. American leaders continue to treat trade and financial relations with Japan as purely an economic issue, rather than a matter of national power, except in some rare instances where American defense capabilities are directly affected by Japanese control of specific technologies. The stability of the American economy is now hostage to the public and private foreign-investment decisions made in Japan, because neither the American people nor American leaders have been willing to adopt fiscal policies that would close the budget and trade deficits. Hard choices are ahead for Americans, but our attitudes, our history, and our institutions are not particularly well suited to make them.

*Stephen D. Krasner is Chair of the Department of Political Science at Stanford University. He is the author of* Structural Conflicts: The Third World Against Global Liberalism.

**BRUCE M. RUSSETT**

*The basic interests of the United States, and the values that Americans cherish, are more secure than ever.*

As an individual nation-state, the United States probably has passed its peak of power. But the Western alliance, which the United States leads and has nurtured, is still rising in power and influence. As a result, the basic interests of the United States, and the values that Americans cherish, are more secure than ever. In November 1988 British Prime Minister Margaret Thatcher declared, "The cold war is over." And the West has won.

Immediately after World War II the United States was the world's dominant military and economic power. Europe and Japan were devastated and economically exhausted; Germany and Japan were also defeated and occupied; the Soviet Union was victorious and had vast new territories under its control, but it too was devastated by the war and remained technologically backward. Against this low point, subsequent American power would necessarily look diminished as the war-torn economies recovered. Just as important, the United States *chose* to help many of its wartime allies and enemies rebuild, thereby hastening its own relative decline from its temporary solitary splendor.

In so choosing, American leaders acted in the true long-term interests of the country. The United States needed strong allies to help contain the perceived threat from Soviet communism. It also needed a prosperous world economy that could serve as both a market for American goods and a source of competitors to supply American markets and keep American producers on their toes. American policy sought these ends, and achieved them.

Communism, by contrast, has been a political and economic failure—in the Third World, China, Eastern Europe, and the Soviet Union itself. Communist countries of the Third World have stagnated, and some have turned to the West for capital and technology. China's economy has prospered only since it became more open to the West and began to abandon socialist ownership and central planning. Mikhail Gorbachev and many East European leaders have begun to realize that their own stagnant economies cannot prosper unless they adopt many features of capitalism. They also know that in order to grow, their economies need political liberalization and a greater degree of democracy. Even noncommunist Third World countries have moved away from state control of the economy as well as from authoritarian political rule. After decades of military dictatorship, many Asian and Latin American countries have returned to democratic government.

Democracy and free-market capitalism are central American values; they are what the cold war was all about. As these values have become entrenched around the world, American security has increased. American military power is no longer superior to the Soviet Union's, as it was just after World War II, but it has not become inferior, either. The Soviet–American military balance has in fact helped maintain peace between the two countries. Neither that balance nor the military superiority of either superpower over any other state is really now in question.

True, both the United States and the Soviet Union risk losing economic competitiveness if they continue to devote so much of their resources to the military. The United States must raise its rate of saving and investment if it is to maintain its technological edge. In the decades ahead, Japan and other countries may surpass it in important respects. But if that happens, it will do so in a world that is basically the one that the leaders of postwar America hoped would come into being.

*Bruce M. Russett is Dean Acheson Professor of International Relations and Political Science at Yale University. He is the author of* Controlling the Sword: The Democratic Governance of National Security.

# Chapter 29

## CONCLUSION: RENEWING AMERICAN IDEALS

*Out of the experiences and ideas of many people in many places in the course of centuries, there has come a great deal of agreement about what democracy is, but nobody has a monopoly of it and the last word has not been spoken.*

*E. E. Schattschneider[1]*

After he was sworn in as president in January 1989, George Bush called a halt to arms negotiations with the Soviet Union in order to give his new administration time to study the issue thoroughly. Despite his previous experience as vice president, director of the CIA, envoy to China, and member of Congress, Bush admitted that he did not have a clear sense of the direction that the United States should take on arms-control policy. Not until four months later, on May 29, 1989, did Bush take a stand, proposing a reduction in conventional armed forces in Europe.

Ironically, Bush's arms-reduction proposal was not based on the comprehensive interagency foreign policy review that he had ordered. A Bush administration official said that "the quality and scope of ideas [produced by the review] were poor to mediocre." Bush's proposal was hatched in haste for presentation at a NATO summit meeting. Bush feared an irretrievable loss of prestige if he arrived emptyhanded at his first meeting of the leaders of the Western democracies.[2] Bush's plan called for major cuts in NATO and Warsaw Pact armies, a proposal that admiring observers called bold and farsighted and that critics said was ill-conceived and dangerous.

This episode illustrates a basic feature of modern government: its complexity. Public policy issues today can be so complex as to defy resolution. Despite months of close study by some of the country's most knowledgeable defense

[1]E. E. Schattschneider, *Two Hundred Million Americans in Search of a Government* (New York: Holt, Rinehart and Winston, 1969), 42.
[2]*Washington Post* wire story, May 30, 1989.

analysts, the Bush administration was unable to come up with a comprehensive arms-reduction policy. Bush was compelled to make a quick decision on a vital issue of national security.

A second characteristic of modern government is its bigness. The scope of public policy is almost beyond imagination. Washington has its hand to one degree or another in nearly every aspect of Americans' lives. Arms control is one of hundreds of national policies, many of which are so interconnected that a change in one affects all the others. Bush's arms-reduction plan, for example, was acknowledged to have implications for the national debt, the balance of trade, the domestic economy, and other policy areas.

Complexity and bigness have made the work of government exceedingly difficult. Complexity increases both the cost of the search for policy solutions and the probability that policy actions will not work as expected. Bigness dilutes the resources of society, forcing trade-offs among goals that all agree are worthwhile. Hard choices are everywhere. For example, although everyone would like to stop acid rain and the greenhouse effect, which are creating environmental havoc, no one wants to shut down the industries and scrap the automobiles that are the main causes.

In a word, the problem of modern government is "overload." As more and more is expected of government, it becomes less and less capable of effective action. This situation poses extraordinary challenges for America's leaders, citizens, and political ideals.

## The Challenge of Leadership

Modern leaders need help, lots of it, if they are to govern effectively. Help is available, particularly from the bureaucrats who staff executive agencies and the groups that lobby government. They are storehouses of the information and expertise that are essential components of effective policymaking in the modern age. Government simply could not do its work properly without the specialized contributions of groups and bureaucratic agencies. Yet their help comes at a stiff price: their overriding goal is to further their own narrow interests, not the broad public interest (see Chapters 13–14, 22–23).

Of course, special interests and the general interest have always been somewhat at odds. The U.S. Constitution's elaborate system of checks and balances was designed to prevent a factional interest from gaining all power and using it to the detriment of other interests and the community as a whole. In *Federalist* No. 51, James Madison explained the necessity of constitutional safeguards against the selfish and potentially tyrannical tendencies of special interests: "In framing a government to be administered by men over men, the great difficulty lies in this: you must first enable the government to control the governed; and in the next place oblige it to control itself." The Framers' system has served its purpose well (see Chapters 2, 3, 5, and 7). In fact, for a long period in U.S. history, constitutional checks and balances were nearly an unqualified benefit. They kept government at bay, which, under conditions that prevailed during the nation's early years, had the effect of simultaneously preserving individual liberty and promoting social and economic progress and stability (see Chapter 6).

However, private forces cannot be granted free play in today's world. Their power is enormous, and at the very least they must be kept from doing great harm to the individual and the community. Government can go wrong by overreaching its authority in a particular instance, but government does not have the choice of a hands-off policy. Social and economic complexity and interdependence dictate that government act energetically (see Chapters 26–28).

Constitutional checks and balances are an obstacle to energetic government and, in combination with the conflicting demands of special interests, cause policy delays and deadlocks. A case in point is the comprehensive welfare reform bill that Congress enacted in 1988. Although policymakers had come to realize by the late 1960s that the welfare system was in need of a thorough revamping, two decades went by without any basic change because of conflicts among various groups and among governing institutions. In one instance, welfare reform had the firm backing of the White House and the House of Representatives but was blocked by an irresolvable dispute between Senate liberals and conservatives. The 1988 reform effort almost met a similar fate. At one point in the legislative process it appeared as if the proposed law was dead; several weeks of intense negotiation and compromise were necessary in order to save it.

In the United States, policy is typically reactive. Rarely are problems addressed in their early stages. Separate interests and institutions are not inclined to give up their individual agendas until a sense of urgency develops. Even then, there is no guarantee that decisive action will be taken. The prime example in recent years has been the national debt, which tripled in the 1980s to nearly $3 trillion. At no time during the decade did officials try to reverse the flow of red ink. Neither the executive nor the legislative branch was willing to scale down its spending demands significantly, and neither side was willing to accept responsibility for a tax increase. The best that policymakers could do was the Graham-Rudman-Hollings bill, which commits the federal government to a balanced annual budget in the early 1990s. By the time Graham-Rudman-Hollings takes full effect, $1 trillion will have been added to the national debt.

The shape of America's future will depend substantially on the ability of its leaders to confront the national debt and other difficult policy issues. Of all the marks of genuine leadership, none is more crucial than the courage to build public support for burdensome policies—those that require people to sacrifice their short-term and special interests to the long-term and general interest. Such leadership is typically in short supply, and recent years have been no exception to this pattern. As an example, during the 1980s Washington officials were not compelled by the force of a national emergency, such as a catastrophic war or depression, to overspend federal revenues by hundreds of billions of dollars. They did so willfully, bending to the public's immediate wants and needs and passing on to future generations the burdens of the debt.

Such actions are fostered by an ascendant form of candidate-centered politics that serves the personal power and reelection needs of public officials at the expense of their collective accountability and the effectiveness of the institutions within which they operate (see Chapters 12, 16, 17, and 20). The writers of the Constitution warned that leadership wrenched from an institutional context cannot serve the public's true interest, and the axiom is as valid today as it was

200 years ago. A truer measure of the quality of American leadership than the 95 percent of officeholders who win reelection time after time is the condition of the institutions that, over the long run, give reason and force to public policy.

The checks and balances introduced into the political system by the Constitution have protected Americans from heavyhanded rule by a single leader or faction. At the same time, however, Americans cannot afford the situation where no one is in charge. There must be effective instruments of collective action and purpose. Historically, political parties have served this critical need best. So momentous was the development of grass-roots parties during the 1830s that James MacGregor Burns has referred to them collectively as "the people's constitution."[3] Parties give majorities the only realistic means on a continuing basis of overcoming the fragmentation within the American political system without threatening the liberty that this fragmentation reflects and preserves (see Chapters 4, 10, 11, 12, 14, 18, and 21). Parties are institutions that do not center on a single faction or leader. It remains to be seen for how long and at what price the United States, alone among Western democracies, will persist in the illusion that a leadership system based on political entrepreneurs is preferable to one based on political parties.

## The Challenge of Citizenship

The scope and complexity of modern government are as much a challenge to citizenship as they are to leadership. Since the time of Aristotle, the principal objection to democracy has been that the people are prone to rash judgments, that self-government devolves inexorably into majority tyranny. The more appropriate objection today may be that the people are not capable of any public judgment at all—that democracy devolves into formlessness. The complex nature of contemporary issues and their great number combine with the sheer size of the public and the relative insignificance of any one of its members to discourage civic involvement. The problem is not that Americans are indifferent to how they are governed. The problem is that they are too diverse in their lives and too pressed for time to recognize easily their common interests and act upon them (see Chapters 8 and 9).

A great deal of misplaced romanticism surrounds the concept of citizenship. It is not realistic to think that citizenship requires individuals to take an active role in all decisions that affect them. Any society of substantial size requires the delegation of broad power and responsibility to a small set of leaders. Yet true citizenship requires that individuals be something more than subjects of government and followers of leaders. True citizenship involves an active role in public affairs.

Political participation is at a relatively low ebb. Barely half of all adults bother to vote in a presidential election, and even fewer show up for other elections; furthermore, those who vote do so as much for reasons of personal habit as out of concern for public policy (see Chapter 9). As for public debate that engages a significant proportion of the citizenry in an active and ongoing way, there is

### ★ ANALYZE THE ISSUE

**The Power of Personalized Leadership**

In late spring of 1989, millions of students and workers in China began to demand democratic reforms. The country's hard-line leaders used the army and the courts in a brutal suppression of the democracy movement. The goal of the student protesters was summarized in one of their sayings, that it was better to be ruled by ten devils who had to operate within a system of democratic checks and balances than to be ruled by one mandarin, however enlightened he might be in a particular instance. Does the Chinese episode have a lesson to teach Americans? In particular, are there inherent dangers posed by the recent shift in the United States from an institutionalized system of leadership to a more personalized form of leadership?

---

[3]James MacGregor Burns, *The Vineyard of Liberty* (New York, Knopf, 1982), 372.

none. The closest that most people come to taking part in debate over public policy is watching or reading the news in the privacy of their homes.

True citizenship is "public" rather than "private" in nature. The community and not the individual is the realm of citizenry. Although individualism can heighten self-esteem and personal security, and in this way strengthen the basis of community, individualism can also, as de Tocqueville recognized as early as the 1830s, undermine people's sense of community by degenerating into downright selfishness (see Chapter 6). In addition to its ability to drive people ever deeper into their private affairs, individualism can foster a form of politics in which the chief goal is narrow gain, the public is seen merely in terms of the special interests within it, and public policy is believed to be justly determined by the relative strength of the contending interests (see Chapters 9 and 14).

Thus, the sharp rise in interest-group activity since the 1960s is not necessarily an indication of deepening citizenship. Although many lobbying groups seek policies that can serve the general interest and actively engage their members in the pursuit of these goals, most of them do not. Group membership today is often of the mail-order variety: participation consists of sending money in response to a letter prepared by computer. Moreover, most groups are self-seeking: they aim to promote the narrow interests of their member individuals or firms. Participation in lobbying groups is an essential part of the representational process, but it is not the same thing as citizenship. There is no genuine sense of "the public" in political participation that is dedicated to the furthering of special interests (see Chapter 14).

Lobbying groups also highlight the gap in the participation rates of rich and poor. Interest-group activity has traditionally been dominated by persons of higher economic status. In recent years there has been a relative decline in the number of groups, such as labor unions, that enroll significant numbers of working-class people, and a relative as well as absolute increase in the number of groups with a middle-class membership (see Chapter 13). Increasingly, the vote is also dominated by persons with higher levels of income and education; the decline in turnout in recent decades is attributable largely to a sharp drop in the participation of Americans who are in the lowest categories of income and education (see Chapter 9).

Participation differences are part of a widening gap between the poor and the rest of America. Although critics of American society with a Marxist or elite perspective have usually concentrated their attention on the richest 1 or 2 percent of the U.S. population, Karl Marx's collaborator, Friedrich Engels, chose to focus on those at the low end. A century ago, Engels claimed that the most remarkable feature of American society was the optimism and progress of its working class; unlike their counterparts in other industrialized societies, they were not mired in poverty or trapped in their position. As a result, he concluded, they had no reason for a high degree of class antagonism. However, in recent years, for the first time in the country's history, the position of poorer Americans has deteriorated in relation to the position of those who are better off. Technological and scientific change threaten to make a permanent underclass of those who cannot meet its educational, social, and economic demands. There can be no effective citizenship, much less equal citizenship, for individuals who have lost the ability to direct their own lives and futures.

The impersonal nature of modern life is another obstacle to effective citizenship. For more than a century, Americans have been moving from self-contained towns and neighborhoods, where face-to-face interaction and civic involvement are highest, to diffuse metropolitan areas and neighborhoods, where this interaction and involvement are lowest. Without a clear sense of a physical community, people are less likely to acquire a clear sense of a political community.

The challenge of citizenship is today, as it has always been, a matter, not of a spontaneous outpouring of civic energy by the masses, but of conditions conducive to civic interest and involvement (see Chapters 4, 5, and 7–15). When politics takes on the appearance of a game played among entrepreneurial leaders and the policy process seems designed for the benefit of special interests, citizenship will not flourish at any level of society. Indeed, citizenship will take on a false character: it will appear to be an issue of what is good for me, the individual, rather than what is good for us, the public. A strengthening of citizenship can come through attention to those things that, 200 years ago, Thomas Jefferson identified as the proper foundation of public life: sound education, a general prosperity, meaningful work, personal liberty, exemplary leadership, a free and vigorous press, strong face-to-face institutions, a broad sharing of political power, and social tolerance. These are demanding requirements, but citizenship is not a trivial pursuit. As the ancient Greeks first recognized, citizenship is nothing less than a way of life.

## The Challenge of Ideals

For 200 years, Americans have been guided by the same set of ideals: liberty, equality, self-government, individualism, diversity, and unity (see Chapter 1). These ideals have challenged each generation, but today, as a result of the complexity and scale of modern government, the challenge has new dimensions.

A crucial difference is that the action necessary for a fuller realization of America's traditional ideals is now less evident. In the past, the question in many cases was not so much what could be done as when and at what cost it would be accomplished. For example, the ink was barely dry on the Constitution before advocates of popular government began their efforts to extend suffrage and to broaden the range of offices filled by popular election (see Chapters 4, 9, and 19). This pursuit lasted 175 years; not until 1965, with the passage of the Voting Rights Act, was it truthful to say that the vote belonged to all Americans (see Chapter 7). Like other developments, such as judicial protection of civil liberties from infringement by the state governments (see Chapter 5), the struggle to extend suffrage met strong resistance, but always could claim the morally superior position. How could it truly be proclaimed that Americans were a self-governing people when whole groups of them were not allowed to participate in the election of their leaders?

Today it is less clear what might be done to advance America's principles. As an example, consider further the question of self-government. At present the United States holds more public elections than any other country, is the only

> ★ ANALYZE THE ISSUE
>
> **The Expansion of Citizenship Responsibility** Benjamin Barber argues in *Strong Democracy* that Americans will never truly control their government as long as most of them confine their political participation to voting. Barber argues that citizens must be given added responsibility, including the right to make mistakes. Do you agree with Barber? At the national level, what responsibilities, other than voting, should citizens be given? Can they exercise these responsibilities effectively? Are they likely to exercise them at all, if given the opportunity?

country in which the voters regularly choose party nominees through primary elections, and has laws and procedures that safeguard the right to vote of those who want to exercise it. In view of all this, the question of self-government in America might be thought to be more or less settled. The reality, however, is that the challenge of self-government grows increasingly difficult.[4] Modern America is more than a representative democracy: it is also a bureaucratic society, a corporate society, a mass communication society, a scientific-technological society, and more (see Chapters 13, 15, and 22–26). Each of these dimensions of contemporary America poses special problems for the practice of self-government. More elections and more voters are not the answer, for example, to the problem of popular control of bureaucratic agencies. What, then, is the answer? The fact is, no one is quite sure. There is agreement on the need to make the bureaucracy more accountable to the people it serves, but there is no agreement on how this might best be accomplished (see Chapter 23).

In addition, the complexity and large scale of modern government have challenged America's ideals by intensifying the conflicts between them. America's principles have never been fully reconcilable with one another. There are, for example, inherent tensions between the ideal of self-government, which implies that the view of the many should prevail over the opinion of the few, and the ideal of liberty, which implies that individuals have rights and interests that must be preserved. Such tensions were formerly eased by the simplicity of society and government. During the whole of the nineteenth century, for example, there was no reason to abridge personal liberty because of the threat of foreign powers (see Chapter 5). However, as society has become increasingly interdependent and government increasingly intrusive, conflicts among America's ideals have grown exponentially. For example, each of the many extensions of individual rights in recent years has narrowed the realm of self-government. It is impossible today to set aside an area of individual discretion—that is, to grant or extend a right—without taking substantial power away from the majority. This fact does not necessary diminish a claim to a particular right, but it does put the claim in perspective: no right is granted without cost to other values. The axiom applies generally to each and all of America's traditional values.

Modern challenges to the fuller realization of America's ideals will have to be met under conditions that, in historical perspective, are unfavorable. The advancement of principles such as liberty, equality, and self-government requires that people be able to look beyond their selfish and immediate concerns to the universal and enduring benefits of a society in which power and opportunity are shared by all, not hoarded by those who already possess most of it (see Chapters 1, 4, 6, and 7). This outlook is fostered when people believe that their progress will not be retarded by the progress of others.

In the past, Americans had special advantages that made it easier for them to believe that collective progress was possible. The first of these advantages was the country's open frontier—what the nineteenth-century historian Frederick Jackson Turner called the "Great West."[5] As long as there was abundant cheap land in America, there was unbridled opportunity. The second advantage was a

---

[4]David Mathews, "We, the People . . .," *National Forum* 50 (Fall, 1983): 65.
[5]Cited in Ralph Volney Harlow, *The Growth of the United States*, Vol. 2 (New York: Holt, 1943), 134.

result of the timing of America's Industrial Revolution. The industrial age began in the late 1700s in England and spread to Western Europe before its major impact was felt in the United States. The delay did not substantially affect prosperity in the United States, because the country was still in the process of westward expansion. However, because of its later start and abundant natural resources, the United States, once industrialization did take firm hold, quickly had the most modern and productive industrial sector in the world. The final advantage was provided by the Second World War, which left the industrial capacity of Western Europe and Japan in ruins. In 1946 the United States, which had emerged from the war with its industrial base intact, was producing half of all goods and services in the world. The result was a level of affluence that no previous society in history had enjoyed.

Since the 1970s, the United States has had to compete on a more nearly equal basis with other highly developed countries. It no longer enjoys an extraordinary advantage and has had to struggle economically as it has attempted to adjust to the change (see Chapters 26 and 28). The change is permanent, so the issue is not choice but challenge. Confronting such a situation 200 years ago, the writers of the Constitution found in America's ideals the basis for a lasting union. Today's Americans can do nothing less than work to maintain the tradition that the Framers began.

# THE DECLARATION OF INDEPENDENCE

*In Congress, July 4, 1776,*

THE UNANIMOUS DECLARATION
OF THE THIRTEEN UNITED
STATES OF AMERICA

When, in the course of human events, it becomes necessary for one people to dissolve the political bands which have connected them with another, and to assume, among the powers of the earth, the separate and equal station to which the laws of nature and of nature's God entitle them, a decent respect to the opinions of mankind requires that they should declare the causes which impel them to the separation.

We hold these truths to be self-evident, that all men are created equal; that they are endowed by their Creator with certain unalienable rights; that among these, are life, liberty, and the pursuit of happiness. That, to secure these rights, governments are instituted among men, deriving their just powers from the consent of the governed; that, whenever any form of government becomes destructive of these ends, it is the right of the people to alter or to abolish it, and to institute a new government, laying its foundation on such principles, and organizing its powers in such form, as to them shall seem most likely to effect their safety and happiness. Prudence, indeed, will dictate that governments long established, should not be changed for light and transient causes; and, accordingly, all experience hath shown, that mankind are more disposed to suffer, while evils are sufferable, than to right themselves by abolishing the forms to which they are accustomed. But, when a long train of abuses and usurpations, pursuing invariably the same object, evinces a design to reduce them under absolute despotism, it is their right, it is their duty, to throw off such government and to provide new guards for their future security. Such has been the patient sufferance of these colonies, and such is now the necessity which constrains them to alter their former systems of government. The history of the present King of Great Britain is a history of repeated injuries and usurpations, all having, in direct object, the establishment of an absolute tyranny over these States. To prove this, let facts be submitted to a candid world:

He has refused his assent to laws the most wholesome and necessary for the public good.

He has forbidden his governors to pass laws of immediate and pressing importance, unless suspended in their operation till his assent should be obtained; and, when so suspended, he has utterly neglected to attend to them.

He has refused to pass other laws for the accommodation of large districts of people, unless those people would relinquish the right of representation in the legislature; a right inestimable to them, and formidable to tyrants only.

He has called together legislative bodies at places unusual, uncomfortable, and distant from the depository of their public records, for the sole purpose of fatiguing them into compliance with his measures.

He has dissolved representative houses repeatedly for opposing, with manly firmness, his invasions on the rights of the people.

He has refused, for a long time after such dissolutions, to cause others to be elected; whereby the legislative powers, incapable of annihilation, have returned to the people at large for their exercise; the state remaining, in the meantime, exposed to all the danger of invasion from without, and convulsions within.

He has endeavored to prevent the population of these States; for that purpose, obstructing the laws for naturalization of foreigners, refusing to pass others to encourage

694

their migration hither, and raising the conditions of new appropriations of lands.

He has obstructed the administration of justice, by refusing his assent to laws for establishing judiciary powers.

He has made judges dependent on his will alone, for the tenure of their officers, and the amount and payment of their salaries.

He has erected a multitude of new offices, and sent hither swarms of officers to harass our poeple, and eat out their substance.

He has kept among us, in time of peace, standing armies, without the consent of our legislatures.

He has affected to render the military independent of, and superior to, the civil power.

He has combined, with others, to subject us to a jurisdiction foreign to our Constitution, and unacknowledged by our laws; giving his assent to their acts of pretended legislation:

For quartering large bodies of armed troops among us:

For protecting them by a mock trial, from punishment, for any murders which they should commit on the inhabitants of these States:

For cutting off our trade with all parts of the world:

For imposing taxes on us without our consent:

For depriving us, in many cases, of the benefit of trial by jury:

For transporting us beyond seas to be tried for pretended offences:

For abolishing the free system of English laws in a neighboring province, establishing therein an arbitrary government, and enlarging its boundaries, so as to render it at once an example and fit instrument for introducing the same absolute rule into these colonies:

For taking away our charters, abolishing our most valuable laws, and altering, fundamentally, the powers of our governments:

For suspending our own legislatures, and declaring themselves invested with power to legislate for us in all cases whatsoever.

He has abdicated government here, by declaring us out of his protection, and waging war against us.

He has plundered our seas, ravaged our coasts, burnt our towns, and destroyed the lives of our people.

He is, at this time, transporting large armies of foreign mercenaries to complete the works of death, desolation, and tyranny, already begun, with circumstances of cruelty and perfidy scarcely paralleled in the most barbarous ages, and totally unworthy the head of a civilized nation.

He has constrained our fellow citizens, taken captive on the high seas, to bear arms against their country, to become the executioners of their friends, and brethren, or to fall themselves by their hands.

He has excited domestic insurrections amongst us, and has endeavored to bring on the inhabitants of our frontiers, the merciless Indian savages, whose known rule of warfare is an undistinguished destruction of all ages, sexes, and conditions.

In every stage of these oppressions, we have petitioned for redress, in the most humble terms; our repeated petitions have been answered only by repeated injury. A prince, whose character is thus marked by every act which may define a tyrant, is unfit to be the ruler of a free people.

Nor have we been wanting in attention to our British brethren. We have warned them, from time to time, of attempts made by their legislature to extend an unwarrantable jurisdiction over us. We have reminded them of the circumstances of our emigration and settlement here. We have appealed to their native justice and magnanimity, and we have conjured them, by the ties of our common kindred, to disavow these usurpations, which would inevitably interrupt our connections and correspondence. They, too, have been deaf to the voice of justice and consanguinity. We must, therefore, acquiesce in the necessity which denounces our separation, and hold them as we hold the rest of mankind, enemies in war, in peace, friends.

We, therefore, the representatives of the United States of America, in general Congress assembled, appealing to the Supreme Judge of the world for the rectitude of our intentions, do, in the name, and by the authority of the good people of these colonies, solemnly publish and declare, that these united colonies are, and of right ought to be, free and independent states: that they are absolved from all allegiance to the British Crown, and that all political connection between them and the state of Great Britain is, and ought to be, totally dissolved; and that, as free and independent states, they have full power to levy war, conclude peace, contract alliances, establish commerce, and to do all other acts and things which independent states may of right do. And, for the support of this declaration, with a firm reliance on the protection of Divine Providence, we mutually pledge to each other our lives, our fortunes, and our sacred honor.

The foregoing Declaration was, by order of Congress, engrossed, and signed by the following members:

## JOHN HANCOCK

*New Hampshire*
Josiah Bartlett
William Whipple
Matthew Thornton

*Massachusetts Bay*
Samuel Adams
John Adams
Robert Treat Paine
Elbridge Gerry

*Rhode Island*
Stephen Hopkins
William Ellery

*Connecticut*
Roger Sherman
Samuel Huntington
William Williams
Oliver Wolcott

*New York*
William Floyd
Philip Livingston
Francis Lewis
Lewis Morris

*New Jersey*
Richard Stockton
John Witherspoon
Francis Hopkinson
John Hart
Abraham Clark

*Pennsylvania*
Robert Morris
Benjamin Rush
Benjamin Franklin
John Morton
George Clymer
James Smith
George Taylor
James Wilson
George Ross

*Delaware*
Caesar Rodney
George Reed
Thomas M'Kean

*Maryland*
Samuel Chase
William Paca
Thomas Stone
Charles Carroll,
  of Carrollton

*Virginia*
George Wythe
Richard Henry Lee
Thomas Jefferson
Benjamin Harrison
Thomas Nelson, Jr.
Francis Lightfoot Lee
Carter Braxton

*North Carolina*
William Hooper
Joseph Hewes
John Penn

*South Carolina*
Edward Rutledge
Thomas Heyward, Jr.
Thomas Lynch, Jr.
Arthur Middleton

*Georgia*
Button Gwinnett
Lyman Hall
George Walton

*Resolved,* That copies of the Declaration be sent to the several assemblies, conventions, and committees, or councils of safety, and to the several commanding officers of the continental troops; that it be proclaimed in each of the United States, at the head of the army.

# THE CONSTITUTION OF THE UNITED STATES OF AMERICA[1]

We the People of the United States, in Order to form a more perfect Union, establish Justice, insure domestic Tranquility, provide for the common defence, promote the general Welfare, and secure the Blessings of Liberty to ourselves and our Posterity, do ordain and establish this CONSTITUTION for the United States of America.

## Article 1

### SECTION 1

All legislative Powers herein granted shall be vested in a Congress of the United States, which shall consist of a Senate and House of Representatives.

### SECTION 2

The House of Representatives shall be composed of Members chosen every second Year by the People of the several States, and the Electors in each State shall have the Qualifications requisite for Electors of the most numerous Branch of the State Legislature.

No Person shall be a Representative who shall not have attained to the Age of twenty-five Years, and been seven Years a Citizen of the United States, and who shall not, when elected, be an Inhabitant of that State in which he shall be chosen.

[Representatives and direct Taxes[2] shall be apportioned among the several States which may be included within this Union, according to their respective Numbers, which shall be determined by adding to the whole Number of free Persons, including those bound to Service for a Term of Years, and excluding Indians not taxed, three fifths of all other Persons.][3] The actual Enumeration shall be made within three Years after the first Meeting of the Congress of the United States, and within every subsequent Term of ten Years, in such Manner as they shall by Law direct. The Number of Representatives shall not exceed one for every thirty Thousand, but each State shall have at Least one Representative; and until such enumeration shall be made, the State of New Hampshire shall be entitled to chuse three, Massachusetts eight, Rhode-Island and Providence Plantations one, Connecticut five, New York six, New Jersey four, Pennsylvania eight, Delaware one, Maryland six, Virginia ten, North Carolina five, South Carolina five, and Georgia three.

When vacancies happen in the Representation from any State, the Executive Authority thereof shall issue Writs of Election to fill such Vacancies.

The House of Representatives shall chuse their Speaker and other Officers; and shall have the sole Power of Impeachment.

### SECTION 3

The Senate of the United States shall be composed of two Senators from each State, chosen by the Legislature thereof, for six Years; and each Senator shall have one Vote.

Immediately after they shall be assembled in Consequence of the first Election, they shall be divided as equally as may be into three Classes. The Seats of the Senators of the first Class shall be vacated at the Expiration of the second Year, of the second Class at the Expiration of the fourth Year, and of the third Class at the Expiration of the sixth Year, so that one-third may be chosen every second Year; and if Vacancies happen by Resignation, or otherwise, during the Recess of the Legis-

---

[1]This version, which follows the original Constitution in capitalization and spelling, was published by the United States Department of the Interior, Office of Education, in 1935.

[2]Altered by the Sixteenth Amendment.

[3]Negated by the Fourteenth Amendment.

lature of any State, the Executive thereof may make temporary Appointments until the next Meeting of the Legislature, which shall then fill such Vacancies.

No Person shall be a Senator who shall not have attained to the Age of thirty Years, and been nine Years a Citizen of the United States, and who shall not, when elected, be an Inhabitant of that State for which he shall be chosen.

The Vice President of the United States shall be President of the Senate, but shall have no vote, unless they be equally divided.

The Senate shall chuse their other Officers, and also a President pro tempore, in the absence of the Vice President, or when he shall exercise the Office of President of the United States.

The Senate shall have the sole Power to try all Impeachments. When sitting for that purpose they shall be on Oath or Affirmation. When the President of the United States is tried, the Chief Justice shall preside: And no person shall be convicted without the Concurrence of two thirds of the Members present.

Judgment in Cases of Impeachment shall not extend further than to removal from Office, and disqualification to hold and enjoy any Office of honor, Trust, or Profit under the United States: but the Party convicted shall nevertheless be liable and subject to Indictment, Trial, Judgment and Punishment, according to Law.

## SECTION 4

The Times, Places and Manner of holding Elections for Senators and Representatives, shall be prescribed in each State by the Legislature thereof; but the Congress may at any time by Law make or alter such Regulations, except as to the Places of Chusing Senators.

The Congress shall assemble at least once in every Year, and such Meeting shall be on the first Monday in December, unless they shall by Law appoint a different Day.

## SECTION 5

Each House shall be the Judge of the Elections, Returns and Qualifications of its own Members, and a Majority of each shall constitute a Quorum to do Business; but a smaller number may adjourn from day to day, and may be authorized to compel the Attendance of absent Members, in such Manner, and under such Penalties, as each House may provide.

Each House may determine the Rules of its Proceedings, punish its Members for disorderly Behaviour, and, with the Concurrence of two thirds, expel a Member.

Each House shall keep a Journal of its Proceedings, and from time to time publish the same, excepting such Parts as may in their Judgment require Secrecy; and the Yeas and Nays of the Members of either House on any question shall, at the Desire of one fifth of those Present, be entered on the Journal.

Neither House, during the Session of Congress, shall, without the Consent of the other, adjourn for more than three days, nor to any other Place than that in which the two Houses shall be sitting.

## SECTION 6

The Senators and Representatives shall receive a Compensation for their Services, to be ascertained by Law, and paid out of the Treasury of the United States. They shall in all Cases, except Treason, Felony, and Breach of the Peace, be privileged from Arrest during their Attendance at the Session of their respective Houses, and in going to and returning from the same; and for any Speech or Debate in either House, they shall not be questioned in any other Place.

No Senator or Representative shall, during the Time for which he was elected, be appointed to any civil Office under the Authority of the United States, which shall have been created, or the Emoluments whereof shall have been increased, during such time; and no Person holding any Office under the United States shall be a Member of either House during his continuance in Office.

## SECTION 7

All Bills for raising Revenue shall originate in the House of Representatives; but the Senate may propose or concur with Amendments as on other bills.

Every Bill which shall have passed the House of Representatives and the Senate, shall, before it becomes a Law, be presented to the President of the United States; If he approve he shall sign it, but if not he shall return it, with his Objections, to that House in which it shall have originated, who shall enter the Objections at large on their Journal, and proceed to reconsider it. If after such Reconsideration two thirds of that House shall agree to pass the bill, it shall be sent, together with the objections, to the other House, by which it shall likewise be reconsidered, and if approved by two thirds of that House, it shall become a Law. But in all such Cases the Votes of both Houses shall be determined by Yeas and Nays, and the Names of the Persons voting for and against the Bill shall be entered on the Journal of each House respectively. If any Bill shall not be returned by the President within ten Days (Sundays excepted) after it shall have been presented to him, the Same shall be a Law, in like Manner as if he had signed it, unless the Congress by their Adjournment prevent its Return, in which Case it shall not be a Law.

Every Order, Resolution, or Vote to which the Concurrence of the Senate and House of Representatives may be necessary (except on a question of Adjournment) shall be presented to the President of the United States; and before the Same shall take Effect, shall be approved by him, or being disapproved by him, shall be repassed by two thirds of the Senate and House of Representatives, according to the Rules and Limitations prescribed in the Case of a Bill.

## SECTION 8

The Congress shall have Power To lay and collect Taxes, Duties, Imposts and Excises, to pay the Debts and provide for the common Defence and general Welfare of the United States; but all Duties, Imposts and Excises shall be uniform throughout the United States;

To borrow money on the credit of the United States;

To regulate Commerce with foreign Nations, and among the several States, and with the Indian Tribes;

To establish a uniform rule of Naturalization, and uniform Laws on the subject of Bankruptcies throughout the United States;

To coin Money, regulate the Value thereof, and of foreign Coin, and fix the Standard of Weights and Measures;

To provide for the Punishment of counterfeiting the Securities and current Coin of the United States;

To establish Post Offices and post Roads;

To promote the Progress of Science and useful Arts, by securing for limited Times to Authors and Inventors the exclusive Right to their respective Writings and Discoveries;

To constitute Tribunals inferior to the Supreme Court;

To define and punish Piracies and Felonies committed on the high Seas, and Offenses against the Law of Nations;

To declare War, grant Letters of Marque and Reprisal, and make Rules concerning Captures on Land and Water;

To raise and support Armies, but no Appropriation of Money to that Use shall be for a longer Term than two Years;

To provide and maintain a Navy;

To make Rules for the Government and Regulation of the land and naval forces;

To provide for calling forth the Militia to execute the Laws of the Union, suppress Insurrections and repel Invasions;

To provide for organizing, arming, and disciplining the Militia, and for governing such Part of them as may be employed in the Service of the United States, reserving to the States respectively, the Appointment of the Officers, and the Authority of training the Militia according to the discipline prescribed by Congress;

To exercise exclusive Legislation in all Cases whatsoever, over such District (not exceeding ten Miles square) as may, by Cession of particular States, and the acceptance of Congress, become the Seat of the Government of the United States, and to exercise like Authority over all Places purchased by the Consent of the Legislature of the State in which the Same shall be, for the Erection of Forts, Magazines, Arsenals, Dock-yards, and other needful Buildings;—And

To make all Laws which shall be necessary and proper for carrying into Execution the foregoing Powers, and all other Powers vested by this Constitution in the Government of the United States, or in any Department or Officer thereof.

## SECTION 9

The Migration or Importation of such Persons as any of the States now existing shall think proper to admit, shall not be prohibited by the Congress prior to the Year one thousand eight hundred and eight, but a tax or duty may be imposed on such Importation, not exceeding ten dollars for each Person.

The privilege of the Writ of Habeas Corpus shall not be suspended, unless when in Cases of Rebellion or Invasion the public Safety may require it.

No bill of Attainder or ex post facto Law shall be passed.

No capitation, or other direct, Tax shall be laid unless in Proportion to the Census or Enumeration herein before directed to be taken.

No Tax or Duty shall be laid on Articles exported from any State.

No Preference shall be given by any Regulation of Commerce or Revenue to the Ports of one State over those of another: nor shall Vessels bound to, or from, one State, be obliged to enter, clear, or pay Duties in another.

No Money shall be drawn from the Treasury, but in Consequence of Appropriations made by Law; and a regular Statement and Account of the Receipts and Expenditures of all public Money shall be published from time to time.

No Title of Nobility shall be granted by the United States: And no Person holding any Office of Profit or Trust under them, shall, without the Consent of the Congress, accept of any present, Emolument, Office, or Title, of any kind whatever, from any King, Prince, or foreign State.

## SECTION 10

No State shall enter into any Treaty, Alliance, or Confederation; grant Letters of Marque and Reprisal; coin Money; emit Bills of Credit; make any Thing but gold and silver Coin a Tender in Payment of Debts; pass any Bill of Attainder, ex post facto Law, or Law impairing the Obligation of Contracts, or grant any Title of Nobility.

No State shall, without the Consent of the Congress, lay any Imposts or Duties on Imports or Exports, except what may be absolutely necessary for executing its inspection Laws; and the net Produce of all Duties and Imposts, laid by any State on Imports or Exports, shall be for the use of the Treasury of the United States; and all such Laws shall be subject to the Revision and Control of the Congress.

No state shall, without the Consent of Congress, lay any duty of Tonnage, keep Troops, or Ships of War in time of Peace, enter into any Agreement or Compact with another State, or with a foreign Power, or engage in War, unless actually invaded, or in such imminent Danger as will not admit of delay.

# Article II

## SECTION 1

The executive Power shall be vested in a President of the United States of America. He shall hold his Office during the Term of four years, and, together with the Vice President, chosen for the same Term, be elected, as follows:

Each State shall appoint, in such Manner as the Legislature thereof may direct, a Number of Electors, equal to the whole Number of Senators and Representatives to which the State may be entitled in the Congress: but no Senator or Representative, or Person holding an Office of Trust or Profit under the United States, shall be appointed an Elector.

[The Electors shall meet in their respective States, and vote by Ballot for two persons, of whom one at least shall not be an Inhabitant of the same State with themselves. And they shall make a List of all the Persons voted for, and of the Number of Votes for each; which List they shall sign and certify, and transmit sealed to the Seat of the Government of the United States, directed to the President of the Senate. The President of the Senate shall, in the Presence of the Senate and House of Representatives, open all the Certificates, and the Votes shall then be counted. The Person having the greatest Number of Votes shall be the President, if such Number be a Majority of the whole Number of Electors appointed; and if there be more than one who have such Majority, and have an equal Number of Votes, then the House of Representatives shall immediately chuse by Ballot one of them for President; and if no Person have a Majority, then from the five

highest on the List the said House shall in like Manner chuse the President. But in chusing the President, the Votes shall be taken by States, the Representation from each State having one Vote; a quorum for this Purpose shall consist of a Member or Members from two-thirds of the States, and a Majority of all the States shall be necessary to a Choice. In every Case, after the Choice of the President, the Person having the greatest Number of Votes of the Electors shall be the Vice President. But if there should remain two or more who have equal votes, the Senate shall chuse from them by Ballot the Vice President.][4]

The Congress may determine the Time of chusing the Electors, and the Day on which they shall give their Votes; which Day shall be the same throughout the United States.

No person except a natural-born Citizen, or a Citizen of the United States, at the time of the Adoption of this Constitution, shall be eligible to the Office of President; neither shall any Person be eligible to that Office who shall not have attained to the Age of thirty-five years, and been fourteen Years a Resident within the United States.

In Case of the Removal of the President from Office, or of his Death, Resignation, or Inability to discharge the Powers and Duties of the said Office, the same shall devolve on the Vice President, and the Congress may by Law provide for the Case of Removal, Death, Resignation, or Inability, both of the President and Vice President, declaring what Officer shall then act as President, and such Officer shall act accordingly, until the disability be removed, or a President shall be elected.

The President shall, at stated Times, receive for his Services a Compensation, which shall neither be increased nor diminished during the Period for which he shall have been elected, and he shall not receive within that Period any other Emolument from the United States, or any of them.

Before he enter on the execution of his Office, he shall take the following Oath or Affirmation:—"I do solemnly swear (or affirm) that I will faithfully execute the Office of President of the United States, and will, to the best of my Ability, preserve, protect, and defend the Constitution of the United States."

## SECTION 2

The President shall be Commander in Chief of the Army and Navy of the United States, and of the Militia of the several States, when called into the actual Service of the

[4]Revised by the Twelfth Amendment.

United States; he may require the Opinion, in writing, of the principal Officer in each of the executive Departments, upon any subject relating to the Duties of their respective Offices, and he shall have Power to Grant Reprieves and Pardons for Offenses against the United States, except in Cases of Impeachment.

He shall have Power, by and with the Advice and Consent of the Senate, to make Treaties, provided two-thirds of the Senators present concur; and he shall nominate, and by and with the Advice and Consent of the Senate, shall appoint Ambassadors, other public Ministers and Consuls, Judges of the supreme Court, and all other Officers of the United States, whose Appointments are not herein otherwise provided for, and which shall be established by Law: but the Congress may by Law vest the Appointment of such inferior Officers, as they think proper, in the President alone, in the Courts of Law, or in the Heads of Departments.

The President shall have Power to fill up all Vacancies that may happen during the Recess of the Senate, by granting Commissions which shall expire at the End of their next Session.

## SECTION 3

He shall from time to time give to the Congress Information of the State of the Union, and recommend to their Consideration such Measures as he shall judge necessary and expedient; he may, on extraordinary occasions, convene both Houses, or either of them, and in Case of Disagreement between them, with respect to the Time of Adjournment, he may adjourn them to such Time as he shall think proper; he shall receive Ambassadors and other public Ministers; he shall take care that the Laws be faithfully executed, and shall Commission all the Officers of the United States.

## SECTION 4

The President, Vice President and all civil Officers of the United States, shall be removed from Office on Impeachment for, and Conviction of, Treason, Bribery, or other high Crimes and Misdemeanors.

## *Article III*

## SECTION 1

The judicial Power of the United States, shall be vested in one supreme Court, and in such inferior Courts as the Congress may from time to time ordain and establish. The Judges, both of the supreme and inferior Courts, shall hold their Offices during good Behaviour, and shall, at stated Times, receive for their Services, a Compensation, which shall not be diminished during their Continuance in Office.

## SECTION 2

The judicial Power shall extend to all Cases, in Law and Equity, arising under this Constitution, the Laws of the United States, and Treaties made, or which shall be made, under their Authority;—to all Cases affecting ambassadors, other public ministers and consuls;—to all cases of admiralty and maritime Jurisdiction;—to Controversies to which the United States shall be a Party;—to Controversies between two or more States;—between a State and Citizens of another State;[5]—between Citizens of different States—between Citizens of the same State claiming Lands under Grants of different States, and between a State, or the Citizens thereof, and foreign States, Citizens, or Subjects.

In all Cases affecting Ambassadors, other public Ministers and Consuls, and those in which a State shall be Party, the supreme Court shall have original Jurisdiction. In all the other Cases before mentioned, the supreme Court shall have appellate Jurisdiction, both as to Law and Fact, with such Exceptions, and under such Regulations as the Congress shall make.

The trial of all Crimes, except in Cases of Impeachment, shall be by Jury; and such Trial shall be held in the State where the said Crimes shall have been committed; but when not committed within any State, the Trial shall be at such Place or Places as the Congress may by Law have directed.

## SECTION 3

Treason against the United States, shall consist only in levying War against them, or in adhering to their Enemies, giving them Aid and Comfort. No Person shall be convicted of Treason unless on the Testimony of two Witnesses to the same overt Act, or on Confession in open Court.

The Congress shall have power to declare the Punishment of Treason, but no Attainder of Treason shall work Corruption of Blood, or Forfeiture except during the Life of the Person attainted.

[5]Qualified by the Eleventh Amendment.

## Article IV

### SECTION 1

Full Faith and Credit shall be given in each State to the public Acts, Records, and judicial Proceedings of every other State. And the Congress may by general Laws prescribe the Manner in which such Acts, Records and Proceedings shall be proved, and the Effect thereof.

### SECTION 2

The Citizens of each State shall be entitled to all Privileges and Immunities of Citizens in the several States.

A Person charged in any State with Treason, Felony, or other Crime, who shall flee from Justice, and be found in another State, shall on demand of the executive Authority of the State from which he fled, be delivered up, to be removed to the State having Jurisdiction of the crime.

No Person held to Service or Labour in one State, under the Laws thereof, escaping into another, shall, in Consequence of any Law or Regulation therein, be discharged from such Service or Labour, but shall be delivered up on Claim of the Party to whom such Service or Labour may be due.

### SECTION 3

New States may be admitted by the Congress into this Union; but no new State shall be formed or erected within the Jurisdiction of any other State; nor any State be formed by the Junction of two or more States, or parts of States, without the Consent of the Legislatures of the States concerned as well as of the Congress.

The Congress shall have Power to dispose of and make all needful Rules and Regulations respecting the Territory or other Property belonging to the United States; and nothing in this Constitution shall be so construed as to Prejudice any Claims of the United States, or of any particular State.

### SECTION 4

The United States shall guarantee to every State in this Union a Republican Form of Government, and shall protect each of them against Invasion; and on Application of the Legislature, or of the Executive (when the Legislature cannot be convened) against domestic Violence.

## Article V

The Congress, whenever two-thirds of both Houses shall deem it necessary, shall propose Amendments to this Constitution, or, on the Application of the Legislatures of two-thirds of the several States, shall call a Convention for proposing Amendments, which, in either Case, shall be valid to all Intents and Purposes, as part of this Constitution, when ratified by the Legislatures of three-fourths of the several States, or by Conventions in three-fourths thereof, as the one or the other Mode of Ratification may be proposed by the Congress; Provided that no Amendment which may be made prior to the Year One thousand eight hundred and eight shall in any Manner affect the first and fourth Clauses in the Ninth Section of the first Article; and that no State, without its Consent, shall be deprived of its equal Suffrage in the Senate.

## Article VI

All Debts contracted and Engagements entered into, before the Adoption of this Constitution, shall be as valid against the United States under this Constitution, as under the Confederation.

This Constitution, and the Laws of the United States which shall be made in Pursuance thereof; and all Treaties made, or which shall be made, under the Authority of the United States, shall be the supreme Law of the Land; and the Judges in every State shall be bound thereby, any Thing in the Constitution or Laws of any State to the Contrary notwithstanding.

The Senators and Representatives before mentioned, and the Members of the several State Legislatures, and all executive and judicial Officers, both of the United States and of the several States, shall be bound by Oath or Affirmation to support this Constitution; but no religious Tests shall ever be required as a qualification to any Office or public Trust under the United States.

## Article VII

The Ratification of the Conventions of nine States shall be sufficient for the Establishment of this Constitution between the States so ratifying the same.

Done in Convention by the Unanimous Consent of the States present the Seventeenth Day of September in the Year of our Lord one thousand seven hundred and Eighty seven, and of the Independence of the United States of America the Twelfth. In Witness whereof We have hereunto subscribed our Names.[6]

[6]These are the full names of the signers, which in some cases are not the signatures on the document.

George Washington
*President and deputy from Virginia*

| *New Hampshire* | *New Jersey* | *Delaware* | *North Carolina* |
|---|---|---|---|
| John Langdon | William Livingston | George Read | William Blount |
| Nicholas Gilman | David Brearley | Gunning Bedford, Jr. | Richard Dobbs |
| | William Paterson | John Dickinson | Spaight |
| | Jonathan Dayton | Richard Bassett | Hugh Williamson |
| | | Jacob Broom | |

| *Massachusetts* | *Pennsylvania* | *Maryland* | *South Carolina* |
|---|---|---|---|
| Nathaniel Gorham | Benjamin Franklin | James McHenry | John Rutledge |
| Rufus King | Thomas Mifflin | Daniel of | Charles Cotesworth |
| | Robert Morris | St. Thomas Jenifer | Pinckney |
| | George Clymer | Daniel Carroll | Charles Pinckney |
| *Connecticut* | Thomas FitzSimons | | Pierce Butler |
| William Samuel | Jared Ingersoll | | |
| Johnson | James Wilson | | |
| Roger Sherman | Gouverneur Morris | | |

| *New York* | | *Virginia* | *Georgia* |
|---|---|---|---|
| Alexander Hamilton | | John Blair | William Few |
| | | James Madison, Jr. | Abraham Baldwin |

*Articles in Addition to, and Amendment of, the Constitution of the United States of America, Proposed by Congress, and Ratified by the Legislatures of the Several States, Pursuant to the Fifth Article of the Original Constitution*[7]

## Amendment I

Congress shall make no law respecting an establishment of religion, or prohibiting the free exercise thereof; or abridging the freedom of speech, or of the press; or the right of the people peaceably to assemble, and to petition the Government for a redress of grievances.

## Amendment II

A well regulated Militia, being necessary to the security of a free State, the right of the people to keep and bear Arms shall not be infringed.

[7]This heading appears only in the joint resolution submitting the first ten amendments, which are collectively known as the Bill of Rights. They were ratified on December 15, 1791.

## Amendment III

No Soldier shall, in time of peace, be quartered in any house, without the consent of the Owner, nor in time of war, but in a manner to be prescribed by law.

## Amendment IV

The right of the people to be secure in their persons, houses, papers, and effects, against unreasonable searches and seizures, shall not be violated, and no Warrants shall issue, but upon probable cause, supported by Oath or affirmation, and particularly describing the place to be searched, and the persons or things to be seized.

## Amendment V

No person shall be held to answer for a capital or otherwise infamous crime, unless on a presentment or indictment of a Grand Jury, except in cases arising in the land or naval forces, or in the Militia, when in actual service in time of War or public danger; nor shall any person be subject for the same offence to be twice put in jeopardy of life or limb; nor shall be compelled in any criminal case to be a witness against himself, nor be deprived of life, liberty, or property, without due process of law; nor shall private property be taken for public use, without just compensation.

## Amendment VI

In all criminal prosecutions, the accused shall enjoy the right to a speedy and public trial, by an impartial jury of the State and district wherein the crime shall have been committed, which district shall have been previously ascertained by law, and to be informed of the nature and cause of the accusation; to be confronted with the witnesses against him; to have compulsory process for obtaining witnesses in his favour, and to have the Assistance of Counsel for his defence.

## Amendment VII

In suits at common law, where the value in controversy shall exceed twenty dollars, the right of trial by jury shall be preserved, and no fact tried by a jury, shall be otherwise reexamined in any Court of the United States, than according to the rules of the common law.

## Amendment VIII

Excessive bail shall not be required, nor excessive fines imposed, nor cruel and unusual punishments inflicted.

## Amendment IX

The enumeration of the Constitution, of certain rights, shall not be construed to deny or disparage others retained by the people.

## Amendment X

The powers not delegated to the United States by the Constitution, nor prohibited by it to the States, are reserved to the States respectively, or to the people.

## Amendment XI [1798]

The Judicial power of the United States shall not be construed to extend to any suit in law or equity, commenced or prosecuted against one of the United States by Citizens of another State, or by Citizens or Subjects of any Foreign State.

## Amendment XII [1804]

The Electors shall meet in their respective States and vote by ballot for President and Vice-President, one of whom, at least, shall not be an inhabitant of the same State with themselves; they shall name in their ballots the person voted for as President, and in distinct ballots the person voted for as Vice-President, and they shall make distinct lists of all persons voted for as President, and of all persons voted for as Vice-President, and of the number of votes for each, which lists they shall sign and certify, and transmit sealed to the seal of the government of the United States, directed to the President of the Senate;— The President of the Senate shall, in the presence of the Senate and House of Representatives, open all the certificates and the votes shall then be counted;—The person having the greatest number of votes for President, shall be the President, if such number be a majority of the whole number of Electors appointed; and if no person have such majority, then from the persons having the highest numbers not exceeding three on the list of those voted for as President, the House of Representatives shall choose immediately, by ballot, the President. But in choosing the President, the votes shall be taken by states, the representation from each state having one vote; a quorum for this purpose shall consist of a member or members from two-thirds of the states, and a majority of all the states shall be necessary to a choice. And if the House of Representatives shall not choose a President whenever the right of choice shall devolve upon them, before the fourth day of March next following, then the Vice-President shall act as President, as in the case of the death or other constitutional disability of the President.—The person having the greatest number of votes as Vice-President, shall be the Vice-President, if such number be a majority of the whole number of Electors appointed, and if no person have a majority, then from the two highest numbers on the list, the Senate shall choose the Vice-President; a quorum for the purpose shall consist of two-thirds of the whole number of Senators, and majority of the whole number shall be necessary to a choice. But no person constitutionally ineligible to the office of President shall be eligible to that of Vice-President of the United States.

# Amendment XIII [1865]

## SECTION 1

Neither slavery nor involuntary servitude, except as a punishment for crime whereof the party shall have been duly convicted, shall exist within the United States, or any place subject to their jurisdiction.

## SECTION 2

Congress shall have power to enforce this article by appropriate legislation.

# Amendment XIV [1868]

## SECTION 1

All persons born or naturalized in the United States, and subject to the jurisdiction thereof, are citizens of the United States and of the State wherein they reside. No State shall abridge the privileges or immunities of citizens of the United States; nor shall any State deprive any person of life, liberty, or property, without due process of law; nor deny to any person within its jurisdiction the equal protection of the laws.

## SECTION 2

Representatives shall be apportioned among the several States according to their respective numbers, counting the whole number of persons in each State, excluding Indians not taxed. But when the right to vote at any election for the choice of electors for President and Vice-President of the United States, Representatives in Congress, the Executive and Judicial officers of a State, or the members of the Legislature thereof, is denied to any of the male inhabitants of such State, being twenty-one years of age, and citizens of the United States, or in any way abridged, except for participation in rebellion, or other crime, the basis of representation therein shall be reduced in the proportion which the number of such male citizens shall bear to the whole number of male citizens twenty-one years of age in such State.

## SECTION 3

No person shall be a Senator or Representative in Congress, or elector of President and Vice-President, or hold any office, civil or military, under the United States, or under any State, who, having previously taken an oath, as a member of Congress, or as an officer of the United States, or as a member of any State legislature, or as an executive or judicial officer of any State, to support the Constitution of the United States, shall have engaged in insurrection or rebellion against the same, or given aid or comfort to the enemies thereof. But Congress may by a vote of two-thirds of each House, remove such disability.

## SECTION 4

The validity of the public debt of the United States, authorized by law, including debts incurred for payment of pensions and bounties for services in suppressing insurrection or rebellion, shall not be questioned. But neither the United States nor any State shall assume or pay any debts or obligation incurred in aid of insurrection or rebellion against the United States, or any claim for the loss or emancipation of any slave; but all such debts, obligations, and claims shall be held illegal and void.

## SECTION 5

The Congress shall have the power to enforce, by appropriate legislation, the provisions of this article.

# Amendment XV [1870]

## SECTION 1

The right of citizens of the United States to vote shall not be denied or abridged by the United States or by any State on account of race, color, or previous condition of servitude—

## SECTION 2

The Congress shall have power to enforce this article by appropriate legislation.

# Amendment XVI [1913]

The Congress shall have power to lay and collect taxes on incomes, from whatever source derived, without apportionment among the several States, and without regard to any census or enumeration.

## Amendment XVII [1913]

The Senate of the United States shall be composed of two Senators from each State, elected by the people thereof, for six years; and each Senator shall have one vote. The electors in each State shall have the qualifications requisite for electors of the most numerous branch of the State legislatures.

When vacancies happen in the representation of any State in the Senate, the executive authority of such State shall issue writs of election to fill such vacancies: *Provided,* That the legislature of any State may empower the executive thereof to make temporary appointments until the people fill the vacancies by election as the legislature may direct.

This amendment shall not be so construed as to affect the election or term of any Senator chosen before it becomes valid as part of the Constitution.

## Amendment XVIII [1919]

### SECTION 1

After one year from the ratification of this article the manufacture, sale, or transportation of intoxicating liquors within, the importation thereof into, or the exportation thereof from the United States and all territory subject to the jurisdiction thereof for beverage purposes is hereby prohibited.

### SECTION 2

The Congress and the several States shall have concurrent power to enforce this article by appropriate legislation.

### SECTION 3

This article shall be inoperative unless it shall have been ratified as an amendment to the Constitution by the legislatures of the several States, as provided in the Constitution, within seven years from the date of the submission hereof to the States by the Congress.

## Amendment XIX [1920]

The right of citizens of the United States to vote shall not be denied or abridged by the United States or by any State on account of sex.

Congress shall have power to enforce this article by appropriate legislation.

## Amendment XX [1933]

### SECTION 1

The terms of the President and Vice-President shall end at noon on the 20th day of January, and the terms of Senators and Representatives at noon on the 3d day of January, of the years in which such terms would have ended if this article had not been ratified; and the terms of their successors shall then begin.

### SECTION 2

The Congress shall assemble at least once in every year, and such meeting shall begin at noon on the 3d day of January, unless they shall by law appoint a different day.

### SECTION 3

If, at the time fixed for the beginning of the term of the President, the President elect shall have died, the Vice-President elect shall become President. If a President shall not have been chosen before the time fixed for the beginning of his term or if the President elect shall have failed to qualify, then the Vice-President elect shall act as President until a President shall have qualified; and the Congress may by law provide for the case wherein neither a President elect nor a Vice-President elect shall have qualified, declaring who shall then act as President, or the manner in which one who is to act shall be selected, and such person shall act accordingly until a President or Vice-President shall have qualified.

### SECTION 4

The Congress may by law provide for the case of the death of any of the persons from whom the House of Representatives may choose a President whenever the right of choice shall have devolved upon them, and for the case of the death of any of the persons from whom the Senate may choose a Vice-President whenever the right of choice shall have devolved upon them.

### SECTION 5

Sections 1 and 2 shall take effect on the 15th day of October following the ratification of this article.

## SECTION 6

This article shall be inoperative unless it shall have been ratified as an amendment to the Constitution by the legislatures of three-fourths of the several States within seven years from the date of its submission.

## Amendment XXI [1933]

### SECTION 1

The eighteenth article of amendment to the Constitution of the United States is hereby repealed.

### SECTION 2

The transportation or importation into any State, Territory, or possession of the United States for delivery or use therein of intoxicating liquors, in violation of the laws thereof, is hereby prohibited.

### SECTION 3

This article shall be inoperative unless it shall have been ratified as an amendment to the Constitution by conventions in the several States, as provided in the Constitution, within seven years from the date of the submission hereof to the States by the Congress.

## Amendment XXII [1951]

No person shall be elected to the office of the President more than twice, and no person who has held the office of President, or acted as President, for more than two years of a term to which some other person was elected President shall be elected to the office of the President more than once.

But this Article shall not apply to any person holding the office of President when this Article was proposed by the Congress, and shall not prevent any person who may be holding the office of President, or acting as President, during the term within which this Article becomes operative from holding the office of President or acting as President during the remainder of such term.

This article shall be inoperative unless it shall have been ratified as an amendment to the Constitution by the legislatures of three-fourths of the several states within seven years from the date of its submission to the states by the Congress.

## Amendment XXIII [1961]

### SECTION 1

The District constituting the seat of Government of the United States shall appoint in such manner as the Congress may direct:

A number of electors of President and Vice-President equal to the whole number of Senators and Representatives in Congress to which the District would be entitled if it were a State, but in no event more than the least populous State; they shall be in addition to those appointed by the States, but they shall be considered, for the purposes of the election of President and Vice-President, to be electors appointed by a State; and they shall meet in the District and perform such duties as provided by the twelfth article of amendment.

### SECTION 2

The Congress shall have power to enforce this article by appropriate legislation.

## Amendment XXIV [1964]

### SECTION 1

The right of citizens of the United States to vote in any primary or other election for President or Vice President, for electors for President or Vice President, or for Senator or Representative in Congress, shall not be denied or abridged by the United States or any state by reason of failure to pay any poll tax or other tax.

### SECTION 2

The Congress shall have the power to enforce this article by appropriate legislation.

## Amendment XXV [1967]

### SECTION 1

In case of the removal of the President from office or of his death or resignation, the Vice President shall become President.

## SECTION 2

Whenever there is a vacancy in the office of the Vice President, the President shall nominate a Vice President who shall take office upon confirmation by a majority vote of both Houses of Congress.

## SECTION 3

Whenever the President transmits to the President Pro Tempore of the Senate and the Speaker of the House of Representatives his written declaration that he is unable to discharge the powers and duties of his office, and until he transmits to them a written declaration to the contrary, such powers and duties shall be discharged by the Vice President as Acting President.

## SECTION 4

Whenever the Vice President and a majority of either the principal officers of the executive departments or of such other body as Congress may by law provide, transmit to the President Pro Tempore of the Senate and the Speaker of the House of Representatives their written declaration that the President is unable to discharge the powers and duties of his office, the Vice President shall immediately assume the powers and duties of the office as Acting President.

Thereafter, when the President transmits to the President Pro Tempore of the Senate and the Speaker of the House of Representatives his written declaration that no inability exists, he shall resume the powers and duties of his office unless the Vice President and a majority of either the principal officers of the executive departments or of such other body as Congress may by law provide, transmit within four days to the President Pro Tempore of the Senate and the Speaker of the House of Representatives their written declaration that the President is unable to discharge the powers and duties of his office. Thereupon Congress shall decide the issue, assembling within forty-eight hours for that purpose if not in session. If the Congress, within twenty-one days after receipt of the latter written declaration, or, if Congress is not in session, within twenty-one days after Congress is required to assemble, determines by two-thirds vote of both Houses that the President is unable to discharge the powers and duties of his office, the Vice President shall continue to discharge the same as Acting President; otherwise, the President shall resume the powers and duties of his office.

## *Amendment XXVI [1971]*

### SECTION 1

The right of citizens of the United States, who are eighteen years of age or older, to vote shall not be denied or abridged by the United States or by any State on account of age.

### SECTION 2

The Congress shall have power to enforce this article by appropriate legislation.

# FEDERALIST NO. 10
# (JAMES MADISON)

Among the numerous advantages promised by a well-constructed Union, none deserves to be more accurately developed than its tendency to break and control the violence of faction. The friend of popular governments never finds himself so much alarmed for their character and fate as when he contemplates their propensity to this dangerous vice. He will not fail, therefore, to set a due value on any plan which, without violating the principles to which he is attached, provides a proper cure for it. The instability, injustice, and confusion introduced into the public councils have, in truth, been the mortal diseases under which popular governments have everywhere perished, as they continue to be the favorite and fruitful topics from which the adversaries to liberty derive their most specious declamations. The valuable improvements made by the American constitutions on the popular models, both ancient and modern, cannot certainly be too much admired; but it would be an unwarrantable partiality to contend that they have as effectually obviated the danger on this side, as was wished and expected. Complaints are everywhere heard from our most considerate and virtuous citizens, equally the friends of public and private faith and of public and personal liberty, that our governments are too unstable, that the public good is disregarded in the conflicts of rival parties, and that measures are too often decided, not according to the rules of justice and the rights of the minor party, but by the superior force of an interested and overbearing majority. However anxiously we may wish that these complaints had no foundation, the evidence of known facts will not permit us to deny that they are in some degree true. It will be found, indeed, on a candid review of our situation, that some of the distresses under which we labor have been erroneously charged on the operation of our governments; but it will be found, at the same time, that other causes will not alone account for many of our heaviest misfortunes; and, particularly, for that prevailing and increasing distrust of public engagements and alarm for private rights which are echoed from one end of the continent to the other. These must be chiefly, if not wholly, effects of the unsteadiness and injustice with which a factious spirit has tainted our public administration.

By a faction I understand a number of citizens, whether amounting to a majority or minority of the whole, who are united and actuated by some common impulse of passion, or of interest, adverse to the rights of other citizens, or to the permanent and aggregate interests of the community.

There are two methods of curing the mischiefs of faction: the one, by removing its causes; the other, by controlling its effects.

There are again two methods of removing the causes of faction: the one, by destroying the liberty which is essential to its existence; the other, by giving to every citizen the same opinions, the same passions, and the same interests.

It could never be more truly said than of the first remedy that it was worse than the disease. Liberty is to faction what air is to fire, and aliment without which it instantly expires. But it could not be a less folly to abolish liberty, which is essential to political life, because it nourishes faction than it would be to wish the annihilation of air, which is essential to animal life, because it imparts to fire its destructive agency.

The second expedient is as impracticable as the first would be unwise. As long as the reason of man continues fallible, and he is at liberty to exercise it, different opinions will be formed. As long as the connection subsists between his reason and his self-love, his opinions and his passions will have a reciprocal influence on each other; and the former will be objects to which the latter will attach themselves. The diversity in the faculties of men, from which the rights of property originate, is not less an insuperable obstacle to a uniformity of interest. The protection of these faculties is the first object of government. From the protection of different and unequal faculties of acquiring property, the possession of different degrees and kinds of property immediately results; and from the influence of these on the sentiments and views of the respective proprietors ensues a division of the society into different interests and parties.

The latent causes of faction are thus sown in the nature of man; and we see them everywhere brought into different degrees of activity, acccording to the different circumstances of civil society. A zeal for different opinions concerning religion, concerning government, and many other points, as well of speculation as of practice; an attachment to different leaders ambitiously contending for pre-eminence and power; or to persons of other descriptions whose fortunes have been interesting to the human passions, have, in turn, divided mankind into parties, inflamed them with mutual animosity, and rendered them much more disposed to vex and oppress each other than to co-operate for their common good. So strong is this propensity of mankind to fall into mutual animosities that where no substantial occasion presents itself the most frivolous and fanciful distinctions have been sufficient to kindle their unfriendly passions and excite their most violent conflicts. But the most common and durable source of factions has been the various and unequal distribution of property. Those who hold and those who are without property have ever formed distinct interests in society. Those who are creditors, and those who are debtors, fall under a like discrimination. A landed interest, a manufacturing interest, a mercantile interest, a moneyed interest, with many lesser interests, grow up of necessity in civilized nations, and divide them into different classes, actuated by different sentiments and views. The regulation of these various and interfering interests forms the principal task of modern legislation and involves the spirit of party and faction in the necessary and ordinary operations of government.

No man is allowed to be a judge in his own cause, because his interest would certainly bias his judgment, and, not improbably, corrupt his integrity. With equal, nay with greater reason, a body of men are unfit to be both judges and parties at the same time; yet what are many of the most important acts of legislation but so many judicial determinations, not indeed concerning the rights of single persons, but concerning the rights of large bodies of citizens? And what are the different classes of legislators but advocates and parties to the causes which they determine? Is a law proposed concerning private debts? It is a question to which the creditors are parties on one side and the debtors on the other. Justice ought to hold the balance between them. Yet the parties are, and must be, themselves the judges; and the most numerous party, or in other words, the most powerful faction must be expected to prevail. Shall domestic manufacturers be encouraged, and in what degree, by restrictions on foreign manufacturers? are questions which would be differently decided by the landed and the manufacturing classes, and

probably by neither with a sole regard to justice and the public good. The apportionment of taxes on the various descriptions of property is an act which seems to require the most exact impartiality; yet there is, perhaps, no legislative act in which greater opportunity and temptation are given to a predominant party to trample on the rules of justice. Every shilling with which they overburden the inferior number is a shilling saved to their own pockets.

It is in vain to say that enlightened statesmen will be able to adjust these clashsng interests and render them all subservient to the public good. Enlightened statesmen will not always be at the helm. Nor, in many cases, can such an adjustment be made at all without taking into view indirect and remote considerations, which will rarely prevail over the immediate interest which one party may find in disregarding the rights of another or the good of the whole

The inference to which we are brought is that the *causes* of faction cannot be removed and that relief is only to be sought in the means of controlling its *effects*.

If a faction consists of less than a majority, relief is supplied by the republican principle, which enables the majority to defeat its sinister views by regular vote. It may clog the administration, it may convulse the society; but it will be unable to execute and mask its violence under the forms of the Constitution. When a majority is included in a faction, the form of popular government, on the other hand, enables it to sacrifice to its ruling passion or interest both the public good and the rights of other citizens. To secure the public good and private rights against the danger of such a faction, and at the same time to preserve the spirit and the form of popular government, is then the great object to which our inquiries are directed. Let me add that it is the great desideratum by which alone this form of government can be rescued from the opprobrium under which it has so long labored and be recommended to the esteem and adoption of mankind.

By what means is this object attainable? Evidently by one of two only. Either the existence of the same passion or interest in a majority at the same time must be prevented, or the majority, having such coexistent passion or interest, must be rendered, by their number and local situation, unable to concert and carry into effect schemes of oppression. If the impulse and the opportunity be suffered to coincide, we well know that neither moral nor religious motives can be relied on as an adequate control. They are not found to be such on the injustice and violence of individuals, and lose their efficacy in proportion to the number combined together, that is, in proportion as their efficacy becomes needful.

From this view of the subject it may be concluded that a pure democracy, by which I mean a society consisting of a small number of citizens, who assemble and administer the government in person, can admit of no cure for the mischiefs of faction. A common passion or interest will, in almost every case, be felt by a majority of the whole, a communication and concert results from the form of government itself; and there is nothing to check the inducements to sacrifice the weaker party or an obnoxious individual. Hence it is that such democracies have ever been spectacles of turbulence and contention; have ever been found incompatible with personal security or the rights of property; and have in general been as short in their lives as they have been violent in their deaths. Theoretic politicians, who have patronized this species of government, have erroneously supposed that by reducing mankind to a perfect equality in their political rights, they would at the same time be perfectly equalized and assimilated in their possessions, their opinions, and their passions.

A republic, by which I mean a government in which the scheme of representation takes place, opens a different prospect and promises the cure for which we are seeking. Let us examine the points in which it varies from pure democracy, and we shall comprehend both the nature of the cure and the efficacy which it must derive from the Union.

The two great points of difference between a democracy and a republic are: first, the delegation of the government, in the latter, to a small number of citizens elected by the rest; secondly, the greater number of citizens and greater sphere of country over which the latter may be extended.

The effect of the first difference is, on the one hand, to refine and enlarge the public views by passing them through the medium of a chosen body of citizens, whose wisdom may best discern the true interest of their country and whose patriotism and love of justice will be least likely to sacrifice it to temporary or partial considerations. Under such a regulation it may well happen that the public voice, pronounced by the representatives of the people, will be more consonant to the public good than if pronounced by the people themselves, convened for the purpose. On the other hand, the effect may be inverted. Men of factious tempers, of local prejudices, or of sinister designs, may, by intrigue, by corruption, or by other means, first obtain the suffrages, and then betray the interests of the people. The question resulting is, whether small or extensive republics are most favorable to the election of proper guardians of the public weal; and it is clearly decided in favor of the latter by two obvious considerations.

In the first place it is to be remarked that however small the republic may be the representatives must be raised to a certain number in order to guard against the cabals of a few; and that however large it may be they must be limited to a certain number in order to guard against the confusion of a multitude. Hence, the number of representatives in the two cases not being in proportion to that of the constituents, and being proportionally greatest in the small republic, it follows that if the proportion of fit characters be not less in the large than in the small republic, the former will present a greater option, and consequently a greater probablility of a fit choice.

In the next place, as each representative will be chosen by a greater number of citizens in the large than in the small republic, it will be more difficult for unworthy candidates to practice with success the vicious arts by which elections are too often carried; and the suffrages of the people being more free, will be more likely to center on men who possess the most attractive merit and the most diffusive and established characters.

It must be confessed that in this, as in most other cases, there is a mean, on both sides of which inconveniencies will be found to lie. By enlarging too much the number of electors, you render the representative too little acquainted with all their local circumstances and lesser interests; as by reducing it too much, you render him unduly attached to these, and too little fit to comprehend and pursue great and national objects. The federal Constitution forms a happy combination in this respect; the great and aggregate interests being referred to the national, the local and particular to the State legislatures.

The other point of difference is the greater number of citizens and extent of territory which may be brought within the compass of republican than of democratic government; and it is this circumstance principally which renders factious combinations less to be dreaded in the former than in the latter. The smaller the society, the fewer probably will be the distinct parties and interests composing it; the fewer the distinct parties and interests, the more frequently will a majority be found of the same party; and the smaller the number of individuals composing a majority, and the smaller the compass within which they are placed, the more easily will they concert and execute their plans of oppression. Extend the sphere and you take in a greater variety of parties and interests; you make it less probable that a majority of the whole will have a common motive to invade the rights of other citizens; or if such a common motive exists, it will be more difficult for all who feel it to discover their own strength and to act in unison with each other. Besides other impediments, it may be remarked that, where there is a consciousness of unjust or dishonorable purposes, communication is always checked by distrust in proportion to the number whose concurrence is necessary.

Hence, it clearly appears that the same advantage which a republic has over a democracy in controlling the effects of faction is enjoyed by a large over a small republic—is enjoyed by the Union over the States composing it. Does this advantage consist in the substitution of representatives whose enlightened views and virtuous sentiments render them superior to local prejudices and to schemes of injustice? It will not be denied that the representation of the Union will be most likely to possess these requisite endowments. Does it consist in the greater security afforded by a greater variety of parties, against the event of any one party being able to outnumber and oppress the rest? In an equal degree does the increased variety of parties comprised within the Union increase this security. Does it, in fine, consist in the greater obstacles opposed to the concert and accomplishment of the secret wishes of an unjust and interested majority? Here again the extent of the Union gives it the most palpable advantage.

The influence of factious leaders may kindle a flame within their particular States but will be unable to spread a general conflagration through the other States. A religious sect may degenerate into a political faction in a part of the Confederacy; but the variety of sects dispersed over the entire face of it must secure the national councils against any danger from that source. A rage for paper money, for an abolition of debts, for an equal division of property, or for any other improper of wicked project, will be less apt to pervade the whole body of the Union than a particular member of it, in the same proportion as such a malady is more likely to taint a particular county or district than an entire State.

In the extent and proper structure of the Union, therefore, we behold a republican remedy for the diseases most incident to republican government. And according to the degree of pleasure and pride we feel in being republicans ought to be our zeal in cherishing the spirit and supporting the character of federalists.

# FEDERALIST NO. 51 (JAMES MADISON)

To what expedient, then, shall we finally resort, for maintaining in practice the necessary partition of power among the several departments as laid down in the Constitution? The only answer that can be given is that as all these exterior provisions are found to be inadequate, the defect must be supplied, by so contriving the interior structure of the government as that its several constuent parts may, by their mutual relations, be the means of keeping each other in their proper places. Without presuming to undertake a full development of this important idea I will hazard few general observations which may perhaps place it in a clearer light, and enable us to form a more correct judgment of the principles and structure of the government planned by the convention.

In order to lay a due foundation for that separate and distinct exercise of the different powers of government, which to a certain extent is admitted on all hands to be essential to the preservation of liberty, it is evident that each department should have a will of its own; and consequently should be so constituted that the members of each should have as little agency as possible in the appointment of the members of the others. Were this principle rigorously adhered to, it would require that all the appointments for the supreme executive, legislative, and judiciary magistracies should be drawn from the same fountain of authority, the people, through channels having no communication whatever with one another. Perhaps such a plan of constructing the several departments would be less difficult in practice than it may in contemplation appear. Some difficulties, however, and some additional expense would attend the execution of it. Some deviations, therefore, from the principle must be admitted. In the constitution of the judiciary department in particular, it might be inexpedient to insist rigorously on the principle: first, because peculiar qualifications being essential in the members, the primary consideration ought to be to select that mode of choice which best secures these qualifications; second, because the permanent tenure by which the appointments are held in that department must soon destroy all sense of dependence on the authority conferring them.

It is equally evident that the members of each department should be as little dependent as possible on those of the others for the emoluments annexed to their offices. Were the executive magistrate, or the judges, not independent of the legislature in this particular, their independence in every other would be merely nominal.

But the great security against a gradual concentration of the several powers in the same department consists in giving to those who administer each department the necessary constitutional means and personal motives to resist encroachments of the others. The provision for defense must in this, as in all other cases, be made commensurate to the danger of attack. Ambition must be made to counteract ambition. The interest of the man must be connected with the constitutional rights of the place. It may be a reflection on human nature that such devices should be necessary to control the abuses of government. But what is government itself but the greatest of all reflections on human nature? If men were angels no government would be necessary. If angels were to govern men, neither external nor internal controls on government would be necessary. In framing a government which is to be administered by men over men, the great difficulty lies in this: you must first enable the government to control the governed; and in the next place oblige it to control itself. A dependence on the people is, no doubt, the primary control on the government; but experience has taught mankind the necessity of auxiliary precautions.

This policy of supplying, by opposite and rival interests, the defect of better motives, might be traced through the whole system of human affairs, private as well as public. We see it particularly displayed in all the subordinate distributions of power, where the constant aim is to divide and arrange the several offices in such a manner as that each may be a check on the other—that the private interest of every individual may be a sentinel over the public rights. These inventions of prudence cannot be less requisite in the distribution of the supreme powers of the State.

But it is not possible to give to each department an equal power of self-defense. In republican government, the legislative authority necessarily predominates. The remedy for this inconveniency is to divide the legislature into different branches; and to render them, by different modes of election and different principles of action, as little connected with each other as the nature of their common functions and their common dependence on the society will admit. It may even be necessary to guard against dangerous encroachments by still further precautions. As the weight of the legislative authority requires that it should be thus divided, the weakness of the executive may require, on the other hand, that it should be fortified. An absolute negative on the legislature appears, at first view, to be the natural defense with which the executive magistrate should be armed. But perhaps it would be neither altogether safe nor alone sufficient. On ordinary occasions it might not be exerted with the requisite firmness, and on extraordinary occasions it might be perfidiously abused. May not this defect of an absolute negative be supplied by some qualified connection between this weaker department and the weaker branch of the stronger department, by which the latter may be led to support the constitutional rights of the former, without being too much detached from the rights of its own department?

If the principles on which these observations are founded be just, as I persuade myself they are, and they be applied as a criterion to the several State constitutions, and to the federal Constitution, it will be found that if the latter does not perfectly correspond with them, the former are infinitely less able to bear such a test.

There are, moreover, two considerations particularly applicable to the federal system of America, which place that system in a very interesting point of view.

*First.* In a single republic, all the power surrendered by the people is submitted to the administration of a single government; and the usurpations are guarded against by a division of the government into distinct and separate departments. In the compound republic of America, the power surrendered by the people is first divided between two distinct governments, and then the portion allotted to each subdivided among distinct and separate departments. Hence a double security arises to the rights of the people. The different governments will control each other, at the same time that each will be controlled by itself.

*Second.* It is of great importance in a republic not only to guard the society against the oppression of its rulers, but to guard one part of the society against the injustice of the other part. Different interests necessarily exist in different classes of citizens. If a majority be united by a common interest, the rights of the minority will be insecure. There are but two methods of providing against this evil: the one by creating a will in the community independent of the majority—that is, of the society itself; the other, by comprehending in the society so many separate descriptions of citizens as will render an unjust combination of a majority of the whole very improbable, if not impracticable. The first method prevails in all governments possessing an hereditary or self-appointed authority. This, at best, is but a precarious security; because a power independent of the society may as well espouse the unjust views of the major as the righful interests of the minor party, and may possibly be turned against both parties. The second method will be exemplified in the federal republic of the United States. Whilst all authority in it will be derived from and dependent on the society, the society itself will be broken into so many parts, interests and classes of citizens, that the rights of individuals, or of the minority, will be in little danger from interested combinations of the majority. In a free government the security for civil rights must be the same as that for religious rights. It consists in the one case in the multiplicity of interests, and in the other in the multiplicity of sects. The degree of security in both cases will depend on the number of interests and sects; and this may be presumed to depend on the extent of country and number of people comprehended under the same government. This view of the subject must particularly recommend a proper federal system to all the sincere and considerate friends of republican government, since it shows that in exact proportion as the territory of the Union may be formed into more circumscribed Confederacies, or States, oppressive combinations of a majority will be facilitated; the best security, under the republican forms, for the rights of every class of citizen, will be diminished; and consequently the stability and independence of some member of the government, the only other security, must be proportionally increased. Justice is the end of government. It is the end of civil society. It ever has been and ever will be pursued until it be obtained, or until liberty be lost in the pursuit. In a society under the forms of which the stronger faction can readily unite and oppress the weaker, anarchy may as truly be said to reign as in a state of nature, where the weaker individual is not secured against the violence of the stronger; and as, in the latter state, even the stronger individuals are prompted, by the uncertainty of their condition, to submit to a government which may protect the weak as well as themselves; so, in the former state, will the more powerful factions or parties be gradually induced, by a like motive, to wish for a government which will protect all parties, the weaker as well as the more powerful. It can be little doubted that if the State of Rhode Island was separated from the Confederacy and left to itself, the insecurity of rights under the popular form of government within such narrow limits would be displayed by such reiterated oppressions of factious majorities that some power altogether independent of the people would soon be called for by the voice of the very factions whose misrule had proved the necessity of it. In the extended republic of the United States, and among the great variety of interests, parties, and sects which it embraces, a coalition of a majority of the whole society could seldom take place on any other principles than those of justice and the general good; whilst there being thus less danger to a minor from the will of a major party, there must be less pretext, also, to provide for the security of the former, by introducing into the government a will not dependent on the latter, or, in other words, a will independent of the society itself. It is no less certain than it is important, notwithstanding the contrary opinions which have been entertained, that the larger the society, provided it lie within a practicable sphere, the more duly capable it will be of self-government. And happily for the *republican cause*, the practicable sphere may be carried to a very great extent by a judicious modification and mixture of the federal principle.

# GLOSSARY

**accountability**  The ability of the public to hold government officials responsible for their actions.

**affirmative action**  A term that refers to programs designed to ensure that women, minorities, and other traditionally disadvantaged groups have full and equal opportunities in employment, education, and other areas of life.

**agency point of view**  The tendency of bureaucrats to place the interests of their agency ahead of other interests and ahead of the priorities sought by the president or Congress.

**appellate jurisdiction**  The authority of a given court to review cases that have already been tried in lower courts and are appealed to it by the losing party; such a court is called an appeals court or appellate court. (See **original jurisdiction.**)

**authority**  The recognized right of an official or institution to exercise power. (See **power.**)

**bill**  A proposed law (legislative act) within Congress or other legislature. (See **law.**)

**Bill of Rights**  The first ten amendments to the Constitution, which set forth basic protections for individual rights to free expression, fair trial, and property.

**block grants**  Federal grants-in-aid that permit state and local officials to decide how the money will be spent within a general area, such as education or health. (See **categorical grants.**)

**bureaucracy**  A system of organization and control based on the principles of hierarchical authority, job specialization, and formalized rules. (See **formalized rules; hierarchical authority; job specialization.**)

**cabinet**  A group consisting of the heads of the fourteen executive departments, who are appointed by the president, subject to confirmation by the Senate. (See **cabinet departments.**)

**cabinet (executive) departments**  The fourteen major organizations within the federal executive bureaucracy, each of which has responsibility for a major function of the federal government, such as defense, agriculture, or justice. (See **cabinet.**)

**candidate-centered politics**  Election campaigns and other political processes in which candidates, not political parties, have most of the initiative and influence. (See **party-centered politics.**)

**categorical grants**  Federal grants-in-aid to states and localities that can be used only for designated projects. (See **block grants.**)

**caucus**  An informal group of legislators with a shared interest who meet to exchange information and coordinate a legislative strategy designed to foster that interest.

**checks and balances**  The elaborate system of divided spheres of authority provided by the U.S. Constitution as a means of controlling the power of government. The separation of powers among the branches of the national government, federalism, and the different methods of selecting national officers are all part of this system.

**civic duty**  The belief of an individual that civic and political participation is a responsibility of citizenship.

**civil liberties**  The fundamental individual rights of a free society, such as freedom of speech and the right to a jury trial, which in the United States are protected by the Bill of Rights.

**civil (equal) rights**  The right of every person to equal protection under the laws and equal access to society's opportunities and public facilities.

**civil service system**  See **merit system.**

**clear and present danger test**  A test devised by the Supreme Court in 1919 in order to define the limits of free speech in the context of national security. According to the test, government cannot abridge political expression unless it presents a clear and present danger to the nation's security.

**clientele groups**  Special-interest groups that benefit directly from the activities of a particular bureaucratic agency and are therefore strong advocates of the agency.

**cloture**  A parliamentary maneuver which, if a three-fifths majority votes for it, limits Senate debate to 100 hours and has the effect of defeating a filibuster. (See **filibuster.**)

**cold war**  The period after World War II when the United States and the USSR were not engaged in actual combat (a "hot war") but were nonetheless locked in a state of deep-seated hostility.

**collective (public) goods** Benefits that are offered by groups (usually noneconomic groups) as an incentive for membership, but that can be obtained by nonmembers as well as members of the particular group. (See **private goods; free-rider problem.**)

**comity** The legal principle that, when court jurisdictions overlap in a given case, the laws of the relevant governing authority (such as a state) will be respected even though the dispute is being settled by a court of a different authority (such as another state or the national government). (See **jurisdiction.**)

**commerce clause** A clause of the Constitution (Article I, Section 8) that empowers the federal government to regulate commerce among the states and with other nations.

**common-carrier role** The media's function as an open channel through which political leaders and the public can communicate.

**comparable worth** The idea that men and women should get equal pay for work that requires similar levels of training and responsibility.

**compelling governmental interest** The theoretical standard against which claims of constitutional rights are upheld or rejected.

**compliance** The issue of whether a court's decisions will be respected and obeyed.

**concurring opinion** A separate opinion written by a Supreme Court justice who votes with the majority in the decision on a case but who disagrees with their reasoning. (See **majority opinion.**)

**conference committee** A temporary committee that is formed to bargain over the differences in the House and Senate versions of a bill. The committee's members are usually appointed from the House and Senate standing committees that originally worked on the bill.

**conservatism** An ideology that in contemporary U.S. politics includes beliefs in economic individualism, traditional social values, and a strong defense establishment. (See **liberalism.**)

**constituency** The individuals who live within the geographical area represented by an elected official. More narrowly, the body of citizens eligible to vote for a particular representative.

**containment** A doctrine developed after World War II, based on the assumptions that the Soviet Union is an aggressor nation and that only a determined United States can block Soviet territorial ambitions.

**contract clause** The clause of the U.S. Constitution (Article I, section 10) that forbids a state to pass laws that impair "the obligation of contracts" or that allow payment of debts by means other than legal tender.

**dealignment** A situation in which voters' partisan loyalties have been substantially weakened. (See **party identification; realigning election.**)

**decision** A vote of the Supreme Court in a particular case that indicates which party the justices side with and by how large a margin.

*de facto* **discrimination** Discrimination on the basis of race, sex, religion, ethnicity, and the like that results from social, economic, and cultural biases and conditions. (See *de jure* **discrimination.**)

*de jure* **discrimination** discrimination on the basis of race, sex, religion, ethnicity, and the like that results from a law. (See *de facto* **discrimination.**)

**delegates** The idea of elected representatives as obligated to carry out the expressed wishes of the electorate. The delegate model of representation assumes that the people themselves are the best judge of the public interest. (See **trustees.**)

**demand-side economics** A form of fiscal policy that emphasizes "demand" (consumer spending). Government can use increased spending or tax cuts to place more money in consumers' hands and thereby increase demand. (See **fiscal policy; supply-side economics.**)

**democracy** A form of government in which the people rule, either directly or through elected representatives.

**denials of power** A constitutional means of limiting governmental action by listing those powers that government is expressly prohibited from using. For example, the U.S. Constitution prohibits *ex post facto* laws.

**deregulation** The rescinding of government regulations for the purpose of promoting economic activity.

**détente** A French word meaning "a relaxing" and used to refer to an era of improved relations between the United States and the Soviet Union that began in the early 1970s.

**deterrence** The idea that nuclear war can be discouraged if each side in a conflict has the capacity to destroy the other with nuclear weapons.

**dissenting opinion** The opinion of a justice in a Supreme Court case that explains the reasons for disagreeing with the majority position. (See **majority opinion.**)

**economic groups** Interest groups that are organized primarily for economic reasons, but which engage in political activity in order to seek favorable policies from government. (See **interest group; noneconomic groups.**)

**economy** A system of production and consumption of goods and services, which are allocated through exchange among sellers and buyers.

**efficiency** An economic principle which holds that firms should fulfill as many of society's needs as possible while using as few of its resources as possible.

**electoral mastery** A strong base of popular support that frees a congressional incumbent from constant worry over reelection.

**elite theory** The view that the United States is essentially run by a tiny economic elite (composed of wealthy individuals and corporate managers) who control public policy through both direct and indirect means.

**entitlement program** Any of a number of individual benefit programs, such as social security, that require government to provide a designated benefit to any person who meets the established criteria for eligibility.

**enumerated powers** The seventeen powers granted to the national government under Article I, section 8 of the Constitution. These powers include taxation and the regulation of commerce as well as the authority to provide for the national defense.

**equal-protection clause** A clause of the Fourteenth Amendment that forbids any state to deny equal protection of the laws to any individual within its jurisdiction.

**equal rights** See **civil rights.**

**equality of opportunity** The idea that all individuals should be given an equal chance to succeed on their own.

**equality of result** The objective of policies intended to reduce or eliminate the effects of discrimination so that members of traditionally disadvantaged groups will have the same benefits of society as do members of advantaged groups.

**equity** (in relation to economic policy) The principle that economic transactions ought to be fair to each party involved. A transaction can be considered equitable if each party enters into it freely and is not unknowingly at a disadvantage.

**equity** (in relation to court cases) The idea that the courts should resort to general principles of fairness in cases where existing law is inadequate.

**establishment clause** The First Amendment provision that government may not favor one religion over another, or religion over no religion and that prohibits Congress from passing laws respecting the establishment of religion.

**exclusionary rule** The legal principle that government is prohibited from using in trials evidence that was obtained by unconstitutional means (for example, illegal search and seizure).

**executive leadership system** An approach to managing the bureaucracy that is based on presidential leadership and presidential management tools, such as the president's annual budget proposal. (See **merit system; patronage system.**)

**externalities** Burdens that society incurs when firms fail to pay the full cost of resources used in production. An example of an externality is the pollution that results when corporations dump industrial wastes into lakes and rivers.

**facts** (of a court case) The relevant circumstances of a legal dispute or offense as determined by a trial court. The facts of a case are crucial because they help to determine which law or laws are applicable in the case.

**federalism (federal system)** A governmental system in which authority is divided between two sovereign levels of government: national and regional.

**filibuster** A procedural tactic in the U.S. Senate whereby a minority of legislators prevent a bill from coming to a vote by holding the floor and talking until the majority gives in and the bill is withdrawn from consideration. (See **cloture.**)

**fiscal policy** A tool of economic management by which government attempts to maintain a stable economy through its taxing and spending decisions. (See **demand-side economics; monetary policy; supply-side economics.**)

**formalized rules** A basic principle of bureaucracy that refers to the standardized procedures and established regulations by which a bureaucracy conducts its operations. (See **bureaucracy.**)

**free-exercise clause** A First Amendment provision that prohibits the government from interfering with the practice of religion or enacting any law prohibiting the free exercise of religion.

**free-rider problem** The situation in which the incentives offered by a group to its members are also available to nonmembers. The incentive to join the group and to promote its cause is reduced because nonmembers (free riders) receive the benefits without having to pay any of the group's costs. (See **collective goods.**)

**freedom of expression** A First Amendment right which guarantees individuals freedom of conscience, speech, press, assembly, and petition.

**general revenue sharing** Federal grants-in-aid that can be spent as state and local officials see fit.

**gerrymandering** The deliberate redrawing of an election district's boundaries to give a particular party or candidate an advantage.

**government corporations** Bodies, such as the U.S. Postal Service and Amtrak, that are similar to private corporations in that they charge for their services, but different in that they receive federal funding to help defray expenses and their directors are appointed by the president with Senate approval.

**grants of power** The method of limiting the U.S. government by confining its scope of authority to those powers expressly granted in the Constitution.

**grass-roots lobbying**  A form of lobbying designed to persuade officials that a group's policy position has strong public support.

**hierarchical authority**  A basic principle of bureaucracy that refers to the chain of command within an organization, whereby officials and units have control over those below them. (See **bureaucracy.**)

**ideology**  A consistent pattern of opinion on political issues that stems from a basic underlying belief or set of beliefs.

**implied powers**  The constitutional principle (Article I, section 8) that Congress shall have the power to enact all laws deemed "necessary and proper" for the carrying out of the powers granted it by the Constitution. (See **necessary and proper clause.**)

**inalienable (natural) rights**  Those rights which persons theoretically possessed in the state of nature, prior to the formation of governments. These rights, including those of life, liberty, and property, are considered inherent, and as such are inalienable. Since government is established by people, government has the responsibility to preserve these rights.

**independent agencies**  Bureaucratic agencies that are similar to cabinet departments but usually have a narrower area of responsibility. Each such agency is headed by a presidential appointee who is not a cabinet member. An example is the National Aeronautics and Space Administration (NASA). (See **cabinet departments.**)

**individual goods**  See **private goods.**

**individualism**  A philosophical belief that stresses the values of hard work and self-reliance and holds that the individual should be left to succeed or fail on his or her own.

**in-kind benefits**  Government benefits that are cash equivalents, such as food stamps or rent vouchers. This form of benefit ensures that recipients will use public assistance in a specified way.

**inside lobbying**  Direct communication between organized interests and policymakers, which is based on the assumed value of close ("inside") contacts with policymakers.

**insurgency**  A type of military conflict in which irregular soldiers rise up against an established regime.

**interest group**  A set of individuals who are organized to promote a shared political interest. (See **economic groups; noneconomic groups.**)

**interest-group liberalism**  The tendency of public officials to support the policy demands of self-interested groups (as opposed to judging policy demands according to whether or not they serve "the public interest").

**iron triangle**  A small and informal but relatively stable group of legislators, executives, and lobbyists who are determined to promote policies beneficial to a particular interest. (See **issue network.**)

**issue network**  An informal network of public officials and lobbyists who have a common interest and expertise in a given area and who are brought together by a proposed policy in that area. (See **iron triangle.**)

**job specialization**  A basic principle of bureaucracy which holds that the responsibilities of each job position should be explicitly defined and that a precise division of labor within the organization should be maintained. (See **bureaucracy.**)

**judicial activism**  The doctrine that the courts should develop new legal principles when judges see a compelling need, even if this action places them in conflict with the policy decisions of elected officials. (See **judicial restraint.**)

**judicial conference**  A closed meeting of the justices of the U.S. Supreme Court to discuss the points of the cases before them; the justices are not supposed to discuss conference proceedings with outsiders.

**judicial restraint**  The doctrine that the judiciary should be highly deferential to the judgment of legislatures. The doctrine claims that the job of judges is to work within the confines of laws set down by the lawmaking majorities. (See **judicial activism.**)

**judicial review**  The power of courts to decide whether a governmental institution has acted within its constitutional powers and, if not, to declare its action void.

**jurisdiction** (of a court)  A given court's authority to hear cases of a particular kind. Jurisdiction may be original or appellate. **(See comity.)**

**jurisdictions** (of congressional committees)  The policy areas in which particular congressional committees are authorized to act.

**laissez-faire doctrine**  A classic economic philosophy which holds that owners of business should be allowed to make their own production and distribution decisions without government regulation or control.

**law** (as enacted by Congress)  A legislative proposal, or bill, that is passed by both the House and Senate and is either signed or not vetoed by the president. (See **bill.**)

**lawmaking function**  The responsibility of a legislature to make the laws deemed necessary to meet society's needs. (See **representation function.**)

**laws** (of a court case)  The constitutional provisions, legislative statutes, or judicial precedents that apply to a court case.

**legitimacy** (in relation to courts)  The issue of the proper limits of judicial authority in a political system based on the principle of majority rule.

**legitimacy** (of election)  The idea that the voters must choose the party nominees for public office as well as the final winner if the outcome is truly to reflect the people's will. (See **primary election.**)

**liberalism**  An ideology that in contemporary U.S. politics includes beliefs in social-welfare programs (activist government), tolerance for social change and diversity, and opposition to "excessive" military spending and involvement. (See **conservatism.**)

**limited government**  A government that is subject to strict limits on its lawful uses of powers, and hence on its ability to deprive people of their liberty.

**lobbying**  The process by which interest-group representatives (lobbyists) attempt to influence public policy through contacts with public officials.

**logrolling**  The trading of votes between legislators so that each gets what he or she most wants.

**majority opinion**  A Supreme Court opinion that reflects the agreement of a majority of the justices on the legal basis of their decision. (See **concurring opinion; dissenting opinion; plurality opinion.**)

**means test**  The criteria for economic need that an applicant for public assistance must meet in order to be eligible for the assistance. (See **public assistance.**)

**merit system**  An approach to managing the bureaucracy whereby people are appointed to government positions on the basis of either competitive examinations or special qualifications, such as professional training. (See **executive leadership system; patronage system.**)

**military-industrial complex**  The three components (the military establishment, the industries that manufacture weapons, and the members of Congress from states and districts that depend heavily on the arms industry) that mutually benefit from a high level of defense spending.

**momentum**  A strong showing by a candidate in early presidential nominating contests, which leads to a buildup of public support for the candidate.

**monetary policy**  A tool of economic management, available to government, based on manipulation of the amount of money in circulation. (See **fiscal policy.**)

**multinational corporations**  Firms that have major business operations in more than one country.

**multiparty system**  A system in which three or more political parties have the capacity to gain control of government separately or in coalition.

**natural rights**  See **inalienable rights.**

**necessary and proper clause (elastic clause)**  The authority granted Congress in Article I, section 8 of the Constitution "to make all laws which shall be necessary and proper" for the implementation of its enumerated powers. (See **implied powers.**)

**negative government**  A philosophical belief that government governs best by staying out of people's lives, thus giving individuals as much freedom as possible to determine their own pursuits. (See **positive government.**)

**neutral competence**  The administrative objective of a merit-based bureaucracy. Such a bureaucracy should be "competent" in the sense that its employees are hired and retained on the basis of their expertise and "neutral" in the sense that it operates by objective standards rather than partisan ones.

**nomination**  The designation of a particular individual to run as a political party's candidate (its "nominee") in a given election.

**noneconomic groups**  Organized interests formed by individuals drawn together by opportunities to promote a cause in which they believe but which does not provide them significant individual economic benefits. (See **interest group; economic groups).**

**objective journalism**  A model of news reporting based on the communication of "facts" rather than opinions and which is "fair" in that it presents all sides of partisan debate. (See **partisan press.**)

**open party caucuses**  Meetings at which a party's candidates for nomination are voted upon and which are open to all of the party's rank-and-file voters who want to attend.

**open-seat election**  An election race in which the incumbent is not seeking reelection.

**opinions** (of a court)  A court's written explanations of its decision which serves to inform others of the court's interpretations of laws. (See **concurring opinion; dissenting opinion; majority opinion; plurality opinion.**)

**original jurisdiction**  The authority of a given court to be the first court to hear a case. (See **appellate jurisdiction.**)

**outside lobbying**  A form of lobbying in which an interest group seeks to mobilize public support as a means of influencing officials.

**oversight function**  A supervisory activity of Congress that centers on its constitutional responsibility to see that the executive carries out the laws faithfully and spends appropriations properly.

**partisan press**  Newspapers and other communication media that openly support a political party and whose news in significant part follows the party line. (See **objective journalism.**)

**party-centered politics**  Election campaigns and other political processes in which political parties and political leaders hold most of the initiative and influence. (See **candidate-centered politics.**)

**party coalition** The groups and interests that support a political party.

**party competition** A process in which conflict over society's goals is transformed by political parties into electoral competition in which the losers accept the winners' right to make policy decisions.

**party identification** The personal sense of loyalty that an individual may feel toward a particular political party. (See **dealignment; realigning election.**)

**party leaders** Members of the House and Senate who are chosen by the Democratic or Republican caucus in each chamber to represent the party's interests in that chamber and who give some central direction to the chamber's deliberations.

**party organizations** The party organizational units at national, state, and local levels; their influence has decreased over time due to many factors. (See **candidate-centered politics; party-centered politics; primary election.**)

**patronage system** An approach to managing the bureaucracy whereby people are appointed to important government positions as a reward for political services they have rendered and because of their partisan loyalty. (See **executive leadership system; merit system; spoils system.**)

**pluralism** A leading theory of American politics which holds that society's interests are substantially represented through the activities of groups. (See **interest group.**)

**plurality opinion** A court opinion that results when a majority of justices hearing a case agree on a decision in the case but do not agree on the legal basis for the decision. In this instance, the opinion held by most of the justices on the winning side is called a plurality opinion. (See **concurring opinion; majority opinion; opinions.**)

**policy implementation** The primary function of the bureaucracy is policy implementation, which refers to the process of carrying out of the authoritative decisions of Congress, the president, and the courts.

**political action committees (PACs)** The organizations through which interest groups raise and distribute funds for election purposes. By law, the funds must be raised through voluntary contributions.

**political culture** The characteristic and deep-seated beliefs of a particular people.

**political participation** A sharing in activities designed to influence public policy and leadership, such as voting, joining political parties and interest groups, writing to elected officials, demonstrating for political causes, and giving money to political candidates.

**political party** An ongoing coalition of interests joined together to try to get their candidates for public office elected under a common label.

**political socialization** The learning process by which people acquire their enduring political beliefs and values.

**politics** The process by which it is determined whose values will prevail in the making of public policy.

**population** In a public opinion poll, the term *population* refers to the people (for example, the citizens of a nation) whose opinions are being estimated through interviews with a sample of these people.

**pork-barrel legislation** A law whose tangible benefits are targeted at a particular legislator's constituency.

**positive government** A philosophical belief that government intervention is necessary in order to enhance personal liberty when individuals are buffeted by economic and social forces beyond their control. (See **negative government.**)

**poverty line** As defined by the federal government, the poverty line is the annual cost of a thrifty food budget for an urban family of four, multiplied by three to allow also for the cost of housing, clothes, and other expenses.

**power** The ability of persons or institutions to control policy. (See **authority.**)

**precedent** A judicial decision in a given case that serves as a rule for settling subsequent cases of a similar nature; courts are generally expected to follow precedent.

**preferred position** The doctrine that First Amendment rights of free expression, because they are fundamental to a free society, are deserving of utmost protection against infringement by government.

**presidential commissions** These organizations within the bureaucracy are headed by commissioners appointed by the president. An example of such a commission is the Commission on Civil Rights.

**primary election (direct primary)** A form of election in which voters choose a party's nominees for public office. Most primaries are closed (only those voters who are registered as members of the party are eligible to participate), with less than a fifth of the states utilizing open primaries (all voters may participate, but they are prohibited from participating in both parties' primaries simultaneously). (See **legitimacy.**)

**prior restraint** The idea that the government is prohibited from censoring printed materials before publication unless the restriction can be justified by overwhelming national security needs.

**private (individual) goods** Benefits that a group (most often an economic group) can grant directly and exclusively to the individual member of the group. (See **collective goods.**)

**privilege** An individual claim that does not have clearly defined legal status and protection. (See **right.**)

**probability sample** A sample for a poll in which each individual in the population has a known probability of being selected randomly for inclusion in the sample. (See **public opinion poll.**)

**procedural due process** The constitutional requirement that government must follow proper legal procedures before a person can be legitimately punished for an alleged offense.

**property rights** Rights of ownership, use, and contract, which are defined mainly through common law.

**proportional representation** A form of representation in which seats in the legislature are allocated proportionally according to each political party's share of the popular vote. (See **single-member districts.**)

**prospective voting** A form of electoral judgment in which voters choose the candidate whose policy stands most closely match their own preferences. (See **retrospective voting.**)

**public assistance** A term that refers to social-welfare programs funded through general tax revenues and available only to the financially needy. Eligibility for such a program is established by a means test. (See **means test; social insurance.**)

**public goods** See **collective goods.**

**public opinion** Those opinions held by ordinary citizens that officials take into account when choosing to act or not to act.

**public opinion poll** A device for measuring public opinion whereby a relatively small number of individuals (the sample) are interviewed for the purpose of estimating the opinions of a whole community (the population). (See **probability sample.**)

**public representative role** A role whereby the media act as the public's chosen representative.

**purposive incentives** Reasons for joining a noneconomic group. Purposive incentives are opportunities to promite a cause in which an individual believes.

**realigning (critical) election** An election or set of elections in which the electorate responds strongly to an extraordinarily powerful issue that has disrupted the established political order. A realigning election has a lasting impact on public policy, popular support for the parties, and the composition of the party coalitions. (See **dealignment; party identification.**)

**reasonable-basis test** A test applied by courts to laws that treat individuals unequally. Such a law may be deemed constitutional if its purpose is held to be "reasonably" related to a legitimate government interest.

**redistricting** The process of rearranging election districts in order to make them as nearly equal in population as possible. Redistricting takes place every ten years, after each population census.

**registration** The practice of requiring citizens to put their names on an official list of eligible voters before they can exercise their right to vote.

**regulation** A term that refers to government restrictions on the economic practices of private firms.

**regulatory agencies** The bureaucratic executive bodies, such as the Interstate Commerce Commission and the Environmental Protection Agency, that have responsibility for the ongoing economic activities.

**representation function** The responsibility of a legislature to represent various interests in society. (See **lawmaking function.**)

**representative democracy** A system in which the people participate in the decision-making process of government not directly but indirectly, through the election of officials to represent their interests. In this way, decisions are reached through the combined workings of deliberative procedures and popular influence.

**republic** Historically, the form of government in which representative officials met to decide on policy issues. These representatives were expected to serve the public interest but were not subject to the people's immediate control. Today, the term *republic* is used interchangeably with *democracy.*

**reserved powers** The powers granted to the states under the Tenth Amendment to the Constitution.

**retrospective voting** A form of electoral judgment in which voters support the incumbent party when its policies are judged to have succeeded and oppose it when its policies are judged to have failed. (See **prospective voting.**)

**right** An individual claim that has unquestioned legal status and protection. (See **privilege.**)

**sample** In a public opinion poll, the relatively small number of individuals who are interviewed for the purpose of estimating the opinions of an entire population. (See **public opinion poll.**)

**sampling error** A measure of the accuracy of a public opinion poll. The sampling error is mainly a function of sample size and is usually expressed in percentage terms. (See **probability sample.**)

**select committee** A temporary legislative committee that is created to perform specific tasks and is disbanded after it has done so. Unlike a standing committee, a select committee generally does not have authority to draft legislation. (See **standing committee.**)

**selective incorporation** The absorption of certain provisions of the Bill of Rights (for example, freedom of speech) into the Fourteenth Amendment so that these rights are protected from infringement by the states.

**seniority** A member of Congress's consecutive years of service on a particular committee.

**separated institutions sharing power** The principle that, as a way to limit government, its powers should be divided among separate branches, each of which also shares in the power of others as a means of checking and balancing them. The result is that no one branch can exercise power decisively without the support or acquiescence of the others.

**service strategy**   Use of personal staff by members of Congress to perform services in order to build support among their constituents.

**signaler role**   The perceived responsibility of the media to alert the public to important developments as soon as possible after they happen or are discovered.

**single-issue politics**   The situation in which separate groups are organized around nearly every conceivable policy issue and press their demands and influence to the utmost.

**single-member districts**   A form of representation in which only a single candidate is elected to a particular office by the voters of that district. This system favors major parties because only candidates who can gain a large proportion of votes in an election district have a realistic chance of winning. (See **proportional representation.**)

**social insurance**   Social-welfare programs based on the "insurance" concept, so that individuals must pay into the program in order to be eligible to receive funds from it. An example is social security for retired people. (See **public assistance.**)

**sovereignty**   The ultimate authority to govern within a certain geographical area.

**split-ticket voting**   The pattern of voting in which the individual voter in a given election casts a ballot for one or more candidates of each major party. This pattern is the opposite of straight-ticket voting, in which the voter supports only candidates of one party in a particular election.

**spoils system**   The practice of granting public office to individuals in return for political favors they have rendered. (See **patronage system.**)

**standing committee**   A permanent congressional committee with responsibility for a particular area of public policy. An example is the Senate Foreign Relations Committee. (See **select committee.**)

**stewardship theory**   A theory that argues for a strong, assertive presidential role, with presidential authority limited only at points specifically prohibited by law. (See **Whig theory.**)

**strict-scrutiny test**   A test applied by courts to laws that attempt a racial or ethnic classification. In effect, the strict-scrutiny test eliminates race or ethnicity as a basis for discrimination in law. (See **suspect classifications.**)

**substantive due process**   The form of constitutional due process that is based on the questions of whether government has acted reasonably and whether the substance of a law is reasonable.

**suffrage**   The right to vote.

**supply-side economics**   A form of fiscal policy that emphasizes "supply" (production). An example of supply-side economics would be a tax cut for business. (See **demand-side economics; fiscal policy.**)

**supremacy clause**   Article VI of the Constitution, which makes national law supreme over state law when the national government is acting within its constitutional limits.

**suspect classifications**   Legal classifications, such as race and national origin, that have invidious discrimination as their purpose and are therefore unconstitutional. (See **strict-scrutiny test.**)

**trustees**   The idea of elected representatives as obligated to act in accordance with their own consciences as to what policies are in the best interests of the public. (See **delegates.**)

**two-party system**   A system in which two political parties compete for the chance of acquiring control of the government, thus compelling candidates and voters with diverse opinions to find common ground.

**tyranny of the majority**   The potential of a majority to monopolize power for their own gain and to the detriment of minority rights and interests. In order to avoid this risk, the Framers tempered the power of the majority by dividing power among branches of government and by establishing staggered terms of office and indirect election of the president and U.S. senators.

**unitary system**   A governmental system in which the national government alone has sovereign (ultimate) authority.

**voter turnout**   The proportion of persons of voting age who actually vote in a given election.

**watchdog role**   The accepted responsibility of the media to protect the public from deceitful, careless, incompetent, and corrupt officials by standing ready to expose any official who violates accepted legal, ethical, or performance standards.

**Whig theory**   A theory that prevailed in the nineteenth century and held that the presidency was a limited or restrained office whose occupant was confined to expressly granted constitutional authority. (See **stewardship theory.**)

**whistle blowing**   An internal check on the bureaucracy whereby individual bureaucrats report instances of mismanagement that they observe.

**writ of *certiorari***   Permission granted by a higher court to allow a losing party in a legal case to bring the case before it for a ruling; when such a writ is requested of the U.S. Supreme Court, four of the Court's nine justices must agree to accept the case before it is granted *certiorari*.

# NAME INDEX

# SUBJECT INDEX